# Changing the Global Political Economy:

## BRICS Countries and Alternative Relations Strategies

Ayfer Gedikli
*Düzce University, Turkey*

Seyfettin Erdogan
*Istanbul Medeniyet University, Turkey*

Hande Çalışkan Terzioğlu
*Düzce University, Turkey*

IGI Global
Scientific Publishing
Publishing Tomorrow's Research Today

| | |
|---|---|
| Vice President of Editorial | Melissa Wagner |
| Managing Editor of Acquisitions | Mikaela Felty |
| Managing Editor of Book Development | Jocelynn Hessler |
| Production Manager | Mike Brehm |
| Cover Design | Phillip Shickler |

Published in the United States of America by
IGI Global Scientific Publishing
701 East Chocolate Avenue
Hershey, PA, 17033, USA
Tel: 717-533-8845
Fax: 717-533-8661
Website: https://www.igi-global.com E-mail: cust@igi-global.com




Library of Congress Cataloging-in-Publication Data

Names: Gedikli, Ayfer, 1970- editor. | Erdoğan, Seyfettin, 1969- editor. | Çalışkan Terzioğlu, Hande, 1992- editor.
Title: Changing the global political economy : BRICS countries and alternative relations strategies / edited by: Ayfer Gedikli, Seyfettin Erdogan, Hande Çalışkan Terzioğlu.
Description: Hershey, PA : IGI Global Scientific Publishing, [2025] | Includes bibliographical references. | Summary: "This book will analyze and evaluate these negotiations and economic/political cooperation among these countries. The authors will also put forth some comments about the future of the BRICS. Our book offers a different perspective in analyzing the economic and political relations of the BRICS members and the Global South countries. We will also analyze if these countries can be a center of gravity in the global economic and political order"-- Provided by publisher.
Identifiers: LCCN 2024047681 (print) | LCCN 2024047682 (ebook) | ISBN 9798369373934 (hardcover) | ISBN 9798369373941 (paperback) | ISBN 9798369373958 (ebook)
Subjects: LCSH: BRIC countries--Foreign relations. | BRIC countries--Foreign economic relations.
Classification: LCC D887 .C48 2025 (print) | LCC D887 (ebook) | DDC 327--dc23/eng/20250201
LC record available at https://lccn.loc.gov/2024047681
LC ebook record available at https://lccn.loc.gov/2024047682

British Cataloguing in Publication Data
A Cataloguing in Publication record for this book is available from the British Library.

# Table of Contents

# Detailed Table of Contents



The aim of this chapter is to analyze the economic importance of the BRICS in the world economy. The BRICS was established in 2010 to bring together the world's five most important developing countries and to create a more advanced and competitive economic power against developed Western economies. This study will analyze whether BRICS has fulfilled its founding purpose and the economic role it plays in the world economy. For this aim, by using the main macroeconomic indicators obtained from the World Bank WDI database for the years 2000-2023 (World Bank, 2024), the economic development processes of the BRICS countries both within themselves and in the world economy will be analyzed comparatively in terms of the pre-2010 (2000-2009) and post-2010 periods (2010-2023). Although China dominates the BRICS as the leading country, the findings reveal that the BRICS has increased its economic power and influence in the world economy.



The BRICS's countries are not equally committed to the alliance. As the alliance works to influence global norms and dynamics, it has become evident that the original members have diverse goals and interests, resulting in differing levels of commitment to BRICS. The chapter seeks to analyze the level of commitment of the BRICS' countries by measuring four critical variables in each country – socioeconomic well-being, soft power, external vulnerabilities, and capacity to preserve the environment. Once measured, each of these variables are compared across the five original member countries to determine the level of commitment of each country to BRICS. The results indicate that Brazil has a significant level of commitment, followed by China with a moderate-high level. Next in line are India,

Russia, and South Africa, all exhibiting a moderate-low level of commitment. These findings demonstrate how the structural and institutional backdrop of each country influences their strategies and dynamics of a budding alliance.



The chapter attempts to explain the origin and growth of "BRICS Plus" countries and their economic, productive and developmental position in the present scenario by analyzing the available data from various international organization. This grouping's fifteen years history is explored for understanding in what direction it is moving forward. The chapter critically evaluates the developmental policies and measures that are so far undertaken by this intergovernmental organization. The conflict of interests that are prevalent among some of the member-states are critically analyzed and evaluated. Benefits of widening the horizon of its "circle of friends" are explored for analyzing its influence among the developing countries. The chapter also explores the possibilities for its emergence as an eminent body in global governance by critically evaluating its plan of action. Furthermore, it discusses the prospective role of this grouping in global governance for ensuring a sustainable future to the emerging economies.



Southeast Asia (SEA) has emerged as a critical battleground for global powers . China, US and BRIC are playing a central role in shaping the geopolitical dynamics of region. As the largest economy within BRICS (Brazil, Russia, India, China, South Africa), China leverages its economic statecraft through initiatives like the Belt and Road Initiative (BRI) and the Regional Comprehensive Economic Partnerships to solidify its influence in SEA region. Framed by its strategic competition with the United States, India and the Quadrilateral Security Dialogue (QUAD), the role of China presence in Southeast Asia as mutipolars. This paper explores China's geopolitical strategy to highlight its use of economic diplomacy, infrastructure development and bilatral agreements to foster regional dominance. The responses of Southeast Asian nations have adopted hedging strategies to balance economic ties with China while maintaining security relationships with the U.S. and other powers.

In armed conflicts, bias significantly influences mediation procedures, yet its specific role still needs to be explored. This chapter examines bias in mediation within the Ukraine conflict, focusing on the Organization for Security and Co-operation in Europe's (OSCE) Special Monitoring Mission (SMM). Content analysis of OSCE member states' interpretations reveals biases favoring Ukraine and disfavoring Russia. Such predispositions, evident in member states' declarations, have implications for international mediation scholars and practitioners. The study underscores the challenges of maintaining impartiality in mediation amidst armed conflicts, emphasizing the urgent need for nuanced understanding to foster more effective mediation processes.



The study explores the strategic affairs of BRICS member states with a special reference to India's geopolitical and economic stature with neighboring countries and regional blocs. The chapter examines the existing research and practical policy implications where India leverages BRICS for its advancing regional cooperation and interest. In this way regional ambitions, maritime security concerns, trade disputes, and diplomatic relations will be explored in the chapter. The study aims to evaluate how BRICS impacts India's geopolitical relations with South Asia, with a special reference to the maritime strategies in the Indian Ocean in view of China's increased assertiveness. The chapter would follow a qualitative methodology, aided by primary sources like BRICS communiqués and official statements of the Indian government, aided by scholarly articles and expert analyses.

BRICS alliance: Brazil, Russia, India, China, and South Africa unite as major emerging economies with global influence and economic strength. They advocate for inclusive growth, sustainable development, and reforms in global financial institutions. Annual summits promote economic collaboration and social development. India and China, prominent BRICS members, feature distinct economic models—China state-driven, India market-oriented—impacting global markets and policies. ARIMA models analyze GDP, GDP per capita, and Gross National Income trends in both countries. India uses simpler ARIMA(0,2,1) models for stable trends, while China employs more complex ARIMA(2,2,2) for volatile data. Comparable accuracy underscores ARIMA's utility in economic forecasting, aiding policymaking, investment strategies, and academic research.



This study examines the multifaceted impacts of the U.S.-China trade war on global trade dynamics, with a particular focus on the role of BRICS. Initiated in 2018, the trade war marked a significant disruption in 21st-century global trade, leading to increased tariffs and strained economic relations between the world's two largest economies. The research explores how this conflict has reshaped global trade patterns, disrupted international supply chains, and influenced the strategies of multinational enterprises (MNEs). Additionally, it investigates the strategic responses of BRICS nations, highlighting their efforts to strengthen intra-group cooperation, reduce dependency on Western countries, and enhance their global influence. By analyzing mutual FDI flows, trade deficits, and GDP growth, this study provides a comprehensive understanding of the broader implications of the U.S.-China trade war, particularly in the context of BRICs and the evolving global economic order.

The BRICS members have been working on an alternative currency to the reserve currencies such as US dollar and euro, for international trades and foreign currency reserves to diversify investments, enhance fund security, preserve value, strengthen country relations, improve trade efficiency, and rebalance global financial power. By reducing dependence on the US dollar, they aim to enhance their economic resilience, promote a more multipolar global financial system, and protect against geopolitical and financial risks. The stunning improvements in IT technologies let both sovereign governments and nongovernment entities to initiate their own digital currencies. Between 2017-2024, the number of people using cryptocurrencies increased by more than 70 folds. With these revolutionary improvements and advantages of cyrptocurrencies, there has been a rising question of whether cryptocurrencies can be used as common BRICS money, and whether the proposed BRICS currency dethrone the dollar.



A digital, nature-based currency (NBDC) is backed by real value and forms the basis of a genuinely sustainable, nature-based economy. The NBDC and the underlying technologies offer a new perspective on how digital resilience can be built in ecological contexts. It shows how an NBDC can function as a model. As natural capital accounting becomes the fundamental asset for new monetary systems, blockchain's inherent trust and sequential accounting capabilities are essential for monitoring and verifying the state of nature and its corresponding financial value. In addition, the legal anchoring of rights of nature and nature-based solutions are essential conditions for establishing an NBDC. Given the reservoir of natural resources in the BRICS countries, the project seems predestined for them. BRICS countries could be pioneers in establishing NBDCs. The chapter presents an innovative approach to the design of an NBDC.

# Preface

In recent years, the improvements in the BRICS group have been a hot topic in the world media. The roots of BRICS go back to June 19, 2009. Brazil, Russia, India, and China declared BRIC to enhance economic and trade cooperation. In 2011, the BRICS core group was formed with the inclusion of the Republic of South Africa. In the first years after the formation of BRICS, no significant economic or political developments were recorded. The recent surge of interest in the BRICS was in fact nothing more than emerging markets, particularly China and Russia, seeking alternatives to the existing global financial and economic system. In 2024, the UAE, Saudi Arabia, Egypt, Ethiopia, and Iran have joined the BRICS group. All of the new members are very important countries in terms of oil, natural gas, and other natural resources. The Suez Canal, a very strategic canal for maritime transportation, rich natural resources such as oil, manganese, zinc, copper, lead, phosphate, chromium, and gold show the importance of Egypt as a new member of BRICS+. Ethiopia's geographical location and minerals such as gold, titanium, platinum, nickel, and potassium have significantly increased the power of the union against the Western bloc. Iran, which has been subjected to sanctions imposed by the US and the Western bloc for many years, is a country with natural resource abundance such as oil and natural gas reserves as well as valuable minerals, zinc, copper, iron, uranium, lead, chromium, manganese, coal, sulfur and gold. Iran, whose economic and social life has been severely affected by the sanctions, supports a number of economic policies, in particular the establishment of trade between member states in local currencies. The inclusion of these countries in the group alongside Russia has made BRICS an important center of gravity with their natural resource endowment and their global energy supply. BRICS+ also accounts for 40% of the global population and 25% of global economic transactions.

It is not accidental that BRICS has become such a powerful center of gravity. With the end of the Cold War and the disintegration of the Union of Soviet Socialist Republics, the world transitioned from a bipolar world order to a unipolar world order led by the United States. While the political and economic power of the US was tremendous all over the world, the Western bloc also strongly supported the US. In the 2000s, China initiated a quiet economic growth, with its unique model of state capitalism leading to remarkable improvements in its economic performance. Using its huge population of 1.5 billion as a cheap labor force, China has managed to become the biggest player in global trade through imitation products and price competition with its unique state capitalism model. With these policies, China has managed to become the most important link in the world's supply chain, especially in intermediate goods. Many international companies found the opportunity to reduce their production costs by using cheap intermediate goods supplied from China. The sales prices of products with lower production costs were also reduced, and the products were delivered to buyers at competitive prices without any loss of profit. Unfortunately, with the shutdown of economies during the pandemic period, the supply chain was broken and the production cost advantage provided by China's cheap intermediate goods was largely eliminated. Aside from cheap intermediate goods, Chinese government also invested in the production of high-value-added goods before and after the pandemic. Thus, the country started to gain a larger share in its international trade by creating its own brands especially in the communication, renewable energy, and automotive sectors. China's economic relations have also spread to many European countries, especially Italy and Serbia. It has continued to make significant investments in many countries in Africa and Asia. China's quiet but incredible development would annoy the US as the global economic and political leader since 1990's.

China's investments, especially in high-tech fields, have led it to produce cheaper and higher quality brands than the dominant Western countries and the US. Trade barriers and high tariffs have been imposed against Chinese goods in the US and EU countries. These trade barriers and tariffs caused a shift in the balance of global trade and this tension exacerbated the east-west tensions. During the post-pandemic economic recovery period, countries started to diverge sharply. The trade barriers were initiated during Donald Trump's first presidential term, led to increased tensions between the US and China and trade wars with negative consequences for both countries. In 2023, the GDP of the US was announced as 27.36 trillion dollars, while China's GDP reached 17.79 trillion dollars as the second largest economy. This performance has made China one of the pioneer countries in BRICS together with Russia.

The other important state of BRICS, the Russian Federation went through a painful period after the dissolution of the Union of Soviet Socialist Republics. Russia began to recover after former president Boris Yeltsin was replaced by Vladimir Putin in 2000. Although the Russian economy is far behind China with a GDP of 2.021 trillion dollars in 2023, and an economy based on energy exports, the country has a very important center of gravity in its hinterland. The consistent growth of the

Chinese economy and Russia's economic and political reemergence as a center of gravity seem to impact the long-standing US-led unipolar world order.

The pandemic period caused the global economy and global politics to enter a two-year deep hibernation. In the post-pandemic period, a rapid recovery process started in international economic relations in order to alleviate the devastating effects of the pandemic on developed and developing countries. However, at a time when hopes were rising all over the world to get rid of the negative impacts of the pandemic, the world met a different crisis with the news that Russia annexed Ukraine on the morning of February 24, 2022. In the early days of the military operation, the world was unaware that the Ukraine crisis would have such global consequences. For many Western countries, the United States, and even countries in the Middle East and Far Asia, it seemed like a border dispute between two neighboring countries. In the following months, however, the Russia-Ukraine crises turned into a global and intricate problem involving not only the two countries but also all countries near and far, especially Europe.

In fact, the Ukrainian conflict has been a source of tension between the US and NATO countries, and Russia for many years. Russia wanted Ukraine to remain as a buffer country between Russia and NATO, while the US and NATO were preparing to become neighbors with Russia by including Ukraine in NATO. The Ukrainian government, headed by Volodymyr Zelensky, was also pursuing a policy of joining NATO against Russia by establishing close relations with Europe. With the outbreak of the war, the EU countries and the US quickly organized and imposed a large number of sanctions on Russia, including trade and individual restrictions, especially on finance, energy, and transportation. The number of embargoes imposed on Russia was 5,530, surpassing Iran (3,616), Syria (2,608), and North Korea (2,077). The US and Western countries seized the assets of Russian businessmen and froze Russian accounts in various Swiss banks. Most challenging of all was Russia's exclusion from the US-controlled SWIFT payment system, headquartered in Brussels. This was initially a critical problem for Russia. It was a hard problem for Russia to be able to settle its receivables and payments arising from international trade once it is excluded from the SWIFT system. The aim of the sanctions was to cut Russia's foreign trade and bring Russia to its knees financially. As soon as the sanctions were initiated Western international companies operating in Russia quickly closed their investments and left the country.

However the sanctions did not have the expected impact. In response to the EU and US sanctions, Russia maintained its ability to supply the goods it needs through China, the UAE, Kazakhstan, and other partner countries with which it has good economic relations. A significant relief was provided in international transportation through Türkiye. Payment transfers were provided through accounts opened in

Chinese banks or through cryptocurrencies and blockchain systems. Russia's own payment system, MIR, was put into use in the following months.

Russia used its energy in response to the sanctions against it. It cut off the energy that it had been supplying to Europe at very low prices for many years. This was unexpected for industrialized European countries and led to a severe energy crisis in all European countries, especially in Germany since at least 40% of their energy supply had been provided by Russia. Until then the EU countries did not intend to diversify their energy supply since the Russian gas and oil are cooperatively much cheaper than its competitors. Natural gas, which until then had always been cheap and plentiful for industry and households, was now scarce and very expensive. Moreover, industrial production was hit in many countries, especially in Germany due to the gas supply interruptions. The scarcity of energy and rising prices pushed up the cost of production and therefore the price of goods, while the uncertainty of the process led to the closure of many factories. Germany lost its automotive sector and technological superiority and competitiveness in the post-World War II period to China. Especially in the EV sector, China has become a major competitor to the US-based Tesla by producing cheap and high-quality cars.

These economic and political problems that the two leading countries of BRICS have recently experienced with Western countries and the US have paved the way for increased efforts for the BRICS bloc to gain a stronger place in the global economy.

The trade barriers China often faces under US leadership and the embargoes Russia faces have increased the BRICS group's efforts to become an economic and political center of gravity. China and Russia, as well as the rest of the world, were forced to submit to the US-led global financial system by the necessity of using the US dollar as a reserve currency in global trade. From the post-World War II period to the present day, the US dollar has been the global reserve currency and the US has enjoyed the advantage of being the center of global trade. From World War II until today, the US dollar has been used as a reserve currency in international trade. This has necessitated all countries to hold and accumulate US dollars at both import and export levels. Although the collapse of the Bretton Wood system, in which 1 ounce of gold was tied to 32 dollars, has been abolished, the US dollar is still the reserve currency. In every trade transaction, the process of converting the local currency into dollars and converting the payment received in dollars by the other country back into its own currency results in significant cost increases.

While excluding Russia from global trade, the US also aimed to render it unable to conduct foreign trade by leaving it lack of dollars. This compulsion led to the search for new methods that would bypass the obligation to use the dollar in global trade.

Just like Russia, countries such as Iran and Venezuela, which have been subjected to sanctions by Western countries and the United States for many years, have announced that they support initiatives for trade parties to trade in their local currencies instead of using the dollar in international trade. India, with a GDP of 3.55 trillion dollars, is the world leader, especially in the IT sector. Brazil is a country of global importance in the production of agricultural products. Brazil has been one of the greatest exporters of tropical agricultural products such as coffee, sugar, and cacao as well as soybeans, corn, cotton, sugar, coffee, orange juice, meat, and ethanol. Brazil is the second largest global iron ore exporter and one of the 5 biggest world producers of aluminum (bauxite-), manganese, tin, and niobium (98% of the known niobium reserves in the world). The country also has copper, gold, and nickel mines. Besides, Brazil is the world's largest producer of amethyst, topaz, and agate and is a big producer of tourmaline, emerald, aquamarine, garnet, and opal. Aside from its geopolitical location, South Africa is another important country in mining precious resources. The country is the world's largest producer of platinum, chromium, and manganese. South Africa is also one of the greatest producers of titanium, gold, cobalt, phosphate, and uranium.

Many countries, uncomfortable with the hegemonic power of the US and Western countries over the global economy and politics, have been sending their requests to the BRICS countries to be included in the BRICS group. However, considering the core countries and the countries that joined the group later on, it is not possible to say that there is a strong cohesion among the members. The long-lasting border tensions and political conflicts between the two core countries China and India have not yet been resolved. India also has strong trade relations with Israel while Israel supports Ukraine during the Russia-Ukraine war. Furthermore, although BRICS+ announced the support to Palestinians, India continued to export rockets and explosives to Israel during the Gaza attacks.

There are some structural problems of BRICS, as well. Just as Germany and France are the driving forces in the European Union, China and Russia seem to have a dominant position in the BRICS group. Considering its weight in global trade and GDP, it is clear that China has the potential to economically dominate all other BRICS members. In this case, the countries of the global south, which complain about the hegemonic power of the US, will have to accept China's dominant leadership. In recent months, Saudi Arabia has proposed that oil, which has been sold in dollars until now, be sold in yuan. If this proposal is accepted, the global hegemony of the US dollar will be replaced by the Chinese yuan. The sale of oil in yuan instead of dollar is unlikely to be accepted by either the BRICS+ member states or other partner countries. In this case, only the yuan will replace the dollar and the yuan will be the new reserve currency. Therefore, in the very short term, the conditions are not yet suitable for the BRICS coin to be produced and the policy of trading in a common currency among the members of the union to be implemented. Despite all problematic and bottleneck situations, important steps are being taken to trade in local currencies instead of dollars between member countries.

The BRICS coin (BRICS currency), which has been frequently mentioned in recent months, seems to be a theoretical application for the time being. Proposals to be pegged to gold or to a basket to be created by weighing the currencies of member countries are still at the project stage. There are also different opinions among member countries on the common currency. South Africa, in particular, argues that it is too early to have a common currency. The fact is that the problems of the transition to a common currency in the European Union continued for many years. In particular, peripheral countries experienced significant economic problems during the transition to the euro. Currently, the central monetary policy and the discrete fiscal policy are among the most important problems of the EU. In this vein, the transition to a common currency in the BRICS bloc among the countries with different levels of economic development seems quite challenging for now.

Despite all these unsolved problems, the mere possibility to trade in their own currencies and thus reduce the dependence on the dollar in international trade can be considered one of the greatest changes in the global financial system since World War II.

It will be possible to see how successful BRICS will be and what kind of initiatives it will take as an alternative to the global financial system in the coming periods and make more concrete assessments. What is certain, however, is that economic and political relations between the Western countries and the global south will no longer be the same.

These developments on a global scale in recent years have attracted the attention of not only the world of politics and economics but also academia. The changing balance of power in the global system and the rapidly changing structure of BRICS have been important motivations for this book. Especially in the aftermath of the Ukraine crisis, the global south countries, which have started to rally around Russia and China against the Western bloc clustered around the US and the EU, signal that the world has begun to move out of the unipolar world order led by the US.

The BRICS nations and partner countries that have commercial and diplomatic relations with these countries prefer to use local currencies in their internal trade, indicating that the role of the dollar as a reserve currency will be significantly eroded in the future.

This interdisciplinary editorial book focuses on the economic and political relations of the BRICS within the bloc and with partner countries, the US and EU countries, as well as the reflections on the recent global events on the member countries. In this context, our editorial book consists of 12 chapters. Brief explanations about the chapters are presented below.

The aim of the first chapter is to analyze the economic importance of the BRICS in the world economy. The BRICS was established in 2010 to bring together the world's five most important developing countries and to create a more advanced and competitive economic power against developed Western economies. This chapter analyzes whether BRICS has fulfilled its founding purpose and the economic role it plays in the world economy. For this aim, by using the main macroeconomic indicators obtained from the World Bank WDI database for the years 2000-2023 (World Bank, 2024), the economic development processes of the BRICS countries both within themselves and in the world economy are investigated comparatively in terms of the pre-2010 (2000-2009) and post-2010 periods (2010-2023). The macroeconomic indicators used in the study are GDP, GDP per capita, GDP growth rate, FDI net inflows, manufacturing value added (MVA), and exports of goods and services (nominal and as % of GDP).

The second chaper searches the level of commitment to BRICS since all BRICS member countries are not equally committed to the alliance. As the alliance works to influence global norms and dynamics, it has become evident that the original members have diverse goals and interests, resulting in differing levels of commitment to BRICS. The chapter seeks to analyze the level of commitment of the BRICS countries by measuring four critical variables in each country—socioeconomic well-being, soft power, external vulnerabilities, and capacity to preserve the environment through selected indicators of how specific factors of the BRICS' member countries determine their level of commitment to the alliance. Thus, the chapter aims to provide an understanding of the transforming global order in the following decades.

In the third chapter, the prospective Role of "BRICS Plus" countries in global governance is investigated. The chapter attempts to explain the origin and growth of "BRICS Plus" countries and their economic, productive, and developmental position in the present scenario by analyzing the available data from various international organizations. Fifteen years of history are explored to understand in what direction it is moving forward. The chapter critically evaluates the developmental policies and measures that are so far undertaken by this intergovernmental organization. The conflicts of interest that are prevalent among some of the member-states are critically analyzed and evaluated. The benefits of widening the horizon of its "circle of friends" are explored for analyzing its influence among developing countries. The chapter also explores the prospective role of this grouping in global governance for ensuring a sustainable future for emerging economies.

In the fourth chapter, China's strategic influence and rivalries in Southeast Asia are investigated. As the largest economy within the BRICS bloc, China leverages its economic statecraft through initiatives like the Belt and Road Initiative (BRI) and the Regional Comprehensive Economic Partnerships to solidify its influence in the SEA region. Thus, this chapter explores the role of China's presence in Southeast Asia as multipolar, China's geopolitical strategy to highlight its use of economic diplomacy, infrastructure development, and bilateral agreements to foster regional dominance. The responses of Southeast Asian nations have adopted hedging strategies to balance economic ties with China while maintaining security relationships with the U.S. and other powers.

In the fifth chapter, the authors tried to find an answer to the question of 'Biasness' in the Russia-Ukraine Conflict. This chapter examines bias in mediation within the Ukraine conflict, focusing on the Organization for Security and Co-operation in Europe's (OSCE) Special Monitoring Mission (SMM). Content analysis of OSCE member states' interpretations reveals biases favoring Ukraine and disfavoring Russia. Such predispositions, evident in member states' declarations, have implications for international mediation scholars and practitioners. The study underscores the challenges of maintaining impartiality in mediation amidst armed conflicts, emphasizing the urgent need for nuanced understanding to foster more effective mediation processes.

In the sixth chapter, the authors investigate how BRICS impacts India's geopolitical relations with South Asia, with a special reference to the maritime strategies in the Indian Ocean in view of China's increased assertiveness. The study explores the strategic affairs of BRICS member states with a special reference to India's geopolitical and economic stature with neighboring countries and regional blocs. The chapter also examines the existing research and practical policy implications where India leverages BRICS for its advancing regional cooperation and interest. In this way, regional ambitions, maritime security concerns, trade disputes, and diplomatic relations are explored.

The seventh chapter explores India and China's economic trends by using ARIMA Model Accuracy. As the two prominent BRICS members India and China feature distinct economic models—China state-driven, India market-oriented—impacting global markets and policies. By employing ARIMA models, the authors aim to investigate GDP, GDP per capita, and Gross National Income trends in both countries. India uses simpler ARIMA(0,2,1) models for stable trends, while China employs more complex ARIMA(2,2,2) for volatile data.

In the eighth chapter, the US-China Trade War and the role of BRICS in this conflict are discussed. The author examines the multifaceted impacts of the U.S.-China trade war on global trade dynamics, with a particular focus on the role of BRICS. The chapter explores how this conflict has reshaped global trade patterns, disrupted international supply chains, and influenced the strategies of multinational enterprises. Additionally, it investigates the strategic responses of BRICS nations, highlighting their efforts to strengthen intra-group cooperation, reduce dependency on Western countries, and enhance their global influence. By analyzing mutual FDI flows, trade deficits, and GDP growth, this study provides a comprehensive understanding of the broader implications of the U.S.-China trade war, particularly in the context of BRICs and the evolving global economic order.

The ninth chapter investigates the future of the US dollar and the applicability of the expected BRICS currency. One of the basic aims of the BRICS bloc is to reduce dependence on the US dollar in order to bring economic resilience, promote a more multipolar global financial system, and protection against geopolitical and financial risks. With these revolutionary improvements and advantages of cryptocurrencies, there has been a rising question of whether cryptocurrencies can be used as common BRICS money, and whether the proposed BRICS currency can dethrone the dollar. Accordingly, the expected BRICS currency will be analyzed for whether it can be an alternative currency to traditional fiat money. Considering the population and GDP of BRICS+ countries, there may be advantages as well as challenges to using common BRICS currency.

In the tenth chapter, the author explored the opportunities of digital nature-based currencies for the BRICS Countries. A digital, nature-based currency (NBDC) and the underlying technologies offer a new perspective on how digital resilience can be built in ecological contexts. As natural capital accounting becomes the fundamental asset for new monetary systems, blockchain's inherent trust and sequential accounting capabilities are essential for monitoring and verifying the state of nature and its corresponding financial value. In addition, the legal anchoring of rights of nature and nature-based solutions are essential conditions for establishing an NBDC. Given the reservoir of natural resources in the BRICS countries, the project seems predestined for them. BRICS countries could be pioneers in establishing NBDCs. An NBDC offers the BRICS states a powerful tool to counter the constraints of the global monetary hierarchy, empowering them to shape their own financial future and simultaneously be victims of the greatest victims of climate change.

The eleventh chapter explores the role of BRICS+ countries in global energy policy and examines the potential impact of these evolving power dynamics on energy markets. Notably, it highlights BRICS+ leadership in renewable energy investments and the global energy transition. BRICS+ is positioned to become a decisive force in the supply of energy resources such as oil and natural gas, particularly with the inclusion of energy-rich countries. With Russia and Saudi Arabia—two of the world's largest energy producers—as well as major energy consumers like China and India, BRICS+ is poised to drive a new equilibrium in energy markets. While BRICS+ countries are focused on developing existing energy infrastructures and advancing sustainable energy investments, they are also adopting a more autonomous approach regarding energy pricing and supply security. The twelfth chapter provides an analysis of the agricultural policies of BRICS+ countries. The study, prepared with a focus on the cooperation among these nations in the field of agriculture, underscores the significance of rural development, sustainability, and food security. As a growing bloc, BRICS+ holds substantial influence in the global agricultural and food sectors. Facilitating the exchange of agricultural knowledge, promoting the dissemination of innovative technologies, and advancing sustainable agricultural practices within BRICS+ will enhance the effectiveness and efficiency of agricultural policies. Furthermore, the study examines the role of BRICS+ countries in shaping global agricultural and food policies and analyzes the potential implications of these shifting power dynamics on agricultural markets.

This book is expected to be read by scholars working in different fields of social sciences such as international relations, political economy, energy economics, monetary banking, and financial systems. It can be used as a textbook or a reference book by undergraduate and postgraduate students in various sub-disciplines of international relations and economics. It is also an important reference source for policymakers working in BRICS+ countries, partner countries that have economic and political ties with these countries, EU countries, and countries belonging to the Western bloc such as the USA.

As editors, we would like to express our gratitude to the scholars from different countries who contributed to our editorial book and to the IGI Global editorial team and valuable employees who provided all kinds of support in the completion of the work.

**Ayfer Gedikli**
*Düzce University, Turkey*

**Seyfettin Erdogan**
*Istanbul Medeniyet University, Turkey*

**Hande Caliskan Terzioglu**
*Düzce University, Turkey*

# Chapter 1
# Importance of BRICS Countries in the World Economy

**Alper Sönmez**
https://orcid.org/0000-0001-5476-7627
*Selçuk University, Turkey*

**Doğan Uysal**
https://orcid.org/0000-0001-9406-0757
*Manisa Celal Bayar University, Turkey*

**Fazal Rahman Amirzai**
https://orcid.org/0000-0002-5389-2378
*Selçuk University, Turkey*

## ABSTRACT

*The aim of this chapter is to analyze the economic importance of the BRICS in the world economy. The BRICS was established in 2010 to bring together the world's five most important developing countries and to create a more advanced and competitive economic power against developed Western economies. This study will analyze whether BRICS has fulfilled its founding purpose and the economic role it plays in the world economy. For this aim, by using the main macroeconomic indicators obtained from the World Bank WDI database for the years 2000-2023 (World Bank, 2024), the economic development processes of the BRICS countries both within themselves and in the world economy will be analyzed comparatively in terms of the pre-2010 (2000-2009) and post-2010 periods (2010-2023). Although China dominates the BRICS as the leading country, the findings reveal that the BRICS has increased its economic power and influence in the world economy.*

DOI: 10.4018/979-8-3693-7393-4.ch001

## INTRODUCTION

The BRICS countries, consisting of Brazil, Russia, India, China, and South Africa, emerged as a coalition in the global economic landscape. Initially formed as BRIC in 2009, the addition of South Africa in 2010 expanded the group to BRICS. These countries are recognized as some of the most developed among emerging markets (Nistor, 2015). The concept of BRICS dates back to the early 2000s when the term "BRIC" was coined to describe the rapidly growing economies of Brazil, Russia, India, and China. In 2009, these four countries officially formed the BRIC group, marking the beginning of a formal alliance aimed at fostering economic cooperation, development, and political coordination. The group's expansion in 2010, with the inclusion of South Africa, transformed it into BRICS, enhancing its representation and influence (Cooper, 2016).

However, as the initial expectations surrounding BRIC countries have waned, it is crucial to assess BRICS' current role in the global economy. The last decade, marked by economic turbulence, has challenged the perception of BRICS countries as primary drivers of global growth. Despite this, these countries collectively account for a significant portion of global economic activities. In the current global economic context, BRICS countries are not viewed as the sole solution to the economic challenges faced by the USA and Europe. They must navigate various economic challenges to sustain growth over the coming decades, addressing structural issues and positioning themselves beyond being merely alternative investment options or providers of low-cost solutions (Atale, 2012).

The period leading up to 2010 and the years following have witnessed notable developments within BRICS, both in terms of economic performance and trade. Before 2010, the original BRIC countries were recognized for their rapid economic growth, large populations, and increasing influence in global affairs. Each member brought distinct strengths to the group. Brazil's vast natural resources, Russia's energy exports, India's growing technology and service sectors, and China's manufacturing capabilities. The inclusion of South Africa in 2010 marked a pivotal moment for the group, extending BRICS' reach to the African continent and enhancing its geopolitical diversity. South Africa's entry symbolized the broader inclusion of emerging economies in global economy (Roberts et al., 2018).

The post-2010 era has seen BRICS evolve into alliance, with a growing focus on enhancing intra-BRICS trade, investment, and economic integration. Several key institutions have been established, reflecting the group's evolving priorities and strategies:

- **New Development Bank (NDB):** Created in mid-2014, it aims to support infrastructure and sustainable development projects in BRICS and other emerging economies. Its purpose is to provide financial resources, such as loans and grants, to projects that promote economic growth and development, particularly in areas like infrastructure, energy, and sustainable development (Roberts et al., 2018). The NDB's creation was intended to offer an alternative financing mechanism for development projects, particularly in the member countries and other emerging economies (Abdenur & Folly, 2015).

- **Contingent Reserve Arrangement (CRA):** Also established in 2014, it was conceived as a $100 billion pooled reserve fund during the fifth BRICS Summit in Durban, aimed at helping emerging nations address liquidity shortages and strengthen financial systems during crises. An analysis of the CRA highlights its potential role in stabilizing economies that experience high economic volatility, particularly those that have rapidly liberalized their capital accounts, which often leads to increased economic uncertainty and challenges in implementing stabilization policies (Biziwick et al., 2015).
- **BRICSCESS:** It was first conceived during the 18th International Scientific Congress held in Kazakhstan in 2014. It was established to tackle health and wellness issues in BRICS countries through the promotion of exercise, physical activity, and sports science. It focuses on fostering communication and collaboration among research institutes, universities and scientists. The council addresses the educational needs of young professionals in these fields, aiming to enhance their contributions to scientific literature and professional organizations. It also seeks to develop mentoring programs for junior scientists, graduate, and undergraduate students to better prepare them for success in their careers (Uvinha et al., 2018).
- **BRICS Think Tanks Council (BTTC):** It was initially proposed during a meeting of the think tanks from the BRICS countries in March 2013 and was subsequently ratified by the BRICS leaders at the eThekwini Summit. This council is designed to unite research institutions and think tanks from BRICS countries to facilitate academic collaboration and policy research. It aims to enhance policy-making and promote joint research on global issues through activities such as conducting research, organizing conferences, and producing policy papers. According to the Declaration on the Establishment of the BTTC, the council's key objectives are to create a platform for exchanging ideas among researchers, academia, and think tanks; to organize the BRICS Academic Forum; and to provide policy recommendations and advice to BRICS Leaders (BTTC, 2024).
- **BRICS Digital Economy Working Group:** It is dedicated to advancing digital cooperation and innovation among BRICS countries. Its mission is to tackle the challenges and seize the opportunities presented by the digital economy by crafting strategies for digital transformation, fostering

technology-driven growth, and enabling cross-border digital collaborations. Key activities include developing digital infrastructure and promoting innovation in the digital sector. The task force recognizes the transformative potential of the digital economy for emerging countries, facilitating accelerated development and economic diversification through the adaptation of digital technologies. It emphasizes enhancing digital capabilities and infrastructure, driving innovation, and improving connectivity within the BRICS countries. This approach aims to strengthen the digital ecosystem and bolster economic integration both within the BRICS bloc and on a global scale (BTTC, 2024).

This chapter analyzes the economic and trade of the BRICS group, focusing on how they evolved over time. It examines the economic performance of BRICS countries by evaluating key macroeconomic indicators GDP, GDP growth, GDP per capita, FDI, manufacturing production, and foreign trade across for two periods: (i) 2000-2009 period before BRICS formed and (ii) 2010-2023 period after BRICS formed. The analysis aims to assess how the formal establishment of BRICS has influenced economic trends, global integration, and the group's role in the contemporary global economy, providing insights into their challenges, opportunities, and future trajectory.

## 1. ECONOMIC GROWTH TRAJECTORIES OF BRICS

The BRICS represent some of the world's most significant emerging economies. Understanding their economic growth trajectories provides insights into the dynamics of global economic power. The economic rise of these countries has reshaped global trade and investment flows (Li, 2019). Analyzing their growth patterns is crucial for assessing their impact on the world economy and understanding how these countries navigate challenges such as income inequality, technological advancements, and resource management.

### 1.1. Pre-2010 Economic Landscape

The pre-2010 economic landscape of BRICS countries offers a foundational understanding of their development paths before they became prominent players on the global economy. By examining GDP, annual GDP growth rates, and GDP per capita, we can gauge the initial conditions and economic structures that influenced their later successes and challenges. This period was marked by varying levels of industrialization, investment, and policy reforms, which set the stage for the subsequent decade of economic evolution (Naudé et al., 2013). Understanding this era is essential for contextualizing the later economic developments in these countries.

## GDP (current US$)

Before the formal establishment of BRICS in 2010, the economic landscapes of its member countries exhibited diverse growth trends. China, for instance, showcased rapid economic expansion, significantly increasing its GDP and solidifying its position as a global economic power. Meanwhile, India also experienced considerable growth, reflecting its burgeoning market potential and economic reforms. In contrast, Brazil, Russia, and South Africa faced more fluctuating economic conditions due to varying internal and external factors.

Table 1 shows the GDP of BRICS countries in current US$ over the 2000 and 2009 period. For this period, the GDP growth of BRICS countries demonstrated a notable upward trend. The average share of BRICS countries in total world GDP increased from 8.12% in 2000 to 15.91% in 2009. This data reveals that the share of the BRICS countries in the world GDP increased by almost two times in this period. Brazil's GDP grew from $655 billion in 2000 to $1.667 trillion in 2009, showing resilience despite a slight dip during the global financial crisis. Russia also experienced significant growth, from $260 billion to $1.223 trillion over the same period, though its GDP dropped in 2009 due to the global financial crisis. India's GDP increased steadily from $468 billion to $1.342 trillion, reflecting consistent economic expansion. China's economy showed the most remarkable growth, with its GDP rising from $1.211 trillion to $5.102 trillion, making it the largest economy among the BRICS countries by 2009 by reflecting an exceptional growth trajectory. South Africa's growth was more modest, increasing from $152 billion to $330 billion. The combined GDP of five BRICS countries surged from $2.747 trillion in 2000 to $9.663 trillion in 2009 (correspond to 252% increase), indicating their rising economic influence compared to the world economy. In comparison, the world's GDP also grew in this period but at a slower rate, increasing by 79% from $33.839 trillion to $60.718 trillion, with a peak in 2008 before declining in 2009 due to the global financial crisis. This data highlights the rapid economic advancement of BRICS countries relative to the world economy during this period.

*Table 1. GDP of BRICS, 2000-2009 (in billions of current US$)*

| Countries/ Years | World | BRA | RUS | IND | CHN | ZAF | BRICS | Share of BRICS in World GDP (%) |
|---|---|---|---|---|---|---|---|---|
| **2000** | 33839 | 655 | 260 | 468 | 1211 | 152 | 2747 | 8 |
| **2001** | 33627 | 560 | 307 | 485 | 1339 | 135 | 2827 | 8 |
| **2002** | 34918 | 510 | 345 | 515 | 1471 | 129 | 2970 | 9 |
| **2003** | 39152 | 558 | 430 | 608 | 1660 | 197 | 3454 | 9 |
| **2004** | 44116 | 669 | 591 | 709 | 1955 | 256 | 4181 | 9 |
| **2005** | 47760 | 892 | 764 | 820 | 2286 | 289 | 5051 | 11 |
| **2006** | 51750 | 1108 | 990 | 940 | 2752 | 304 | 6094 | 12 |
| **2007** | 58315 | 1397 | 1300 | 1217 | 3550 | 333 | 7797 | 13 |
| **2008** | 64072 | 1696 | 1661 | 1199 | 4594 | 316 | 9466 | 15 |
| **2009** | 60718 | 1667 | 1223 | 1342 | 5102 | 330 | 9663 | 16 |
| **Ave.** | **46827** | **971** | **787** | **830** | **2592** | **244** | **5425** | **11** |

Source: Authors' compilation based on World Bank (2024), World Development Indicators (WDI).

The figure 1 displays notable growth trends for each BRICS country. China's GDP rises sharply, particularly from 2005 onwards, reflecting its rapid economic expansion. India shows steady growth, while Brazil and Russia indicate significant increases, with slight dips around 2009 due to the global financial crisis. South Africa's line is flatter, indicating more modest growth. The combined BRICS red line shows a steep increase, highlighting the group's faster economic growth compared to the world GDP. This figure underscores the growing economic influence of the BRICS countries in the world GDP during this period.

*Figure 1. GDP of BRICS, 2000-2009 (in billions of current US$)*

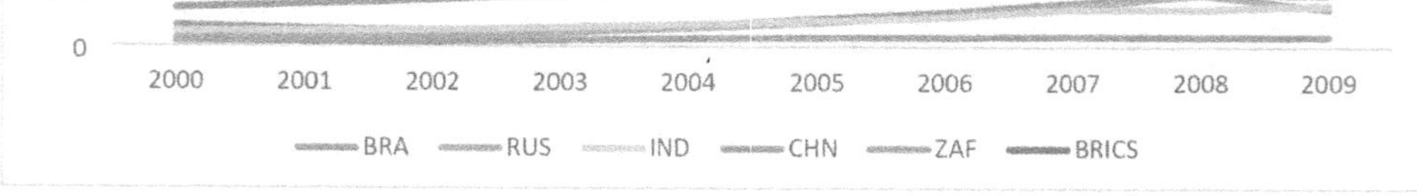


*(Authors' compilation based on World Bank (2024), WDI)*

## GDP Growth (annual %)

Table 2 shows the GDP growth rates of BRICS countries for the period 2000-2009. The annual GDP growth rates for BRICS countries in this period reveal a period of dynamic economic change. China and India consistently achieved high growth rates, driven by robust industrialization and expanding domestic markets. On the other hand, Brazil, Russia, and South Africa encountered periods of stagnation and economic contraction, influenced by global economic fluctuations and domestic challenges.

As seen from the table 2, the GDP growth rates of BRICS countries from 2000 to 2009 reveal a range of economic performances, with China consistently leading the group with the average growth rate of 10.35% over this period. China's growth peaked at 14.23% in 2007 and remained strong at 9.40% in 2009. China's average GDP growth rate (10.35%) is more than 3 times the world average (3%), demonstrating its robust economic expansion despite the global financial crisis. India also showed notable resilience with steady high growth rates, reaching 8.06% in 2006 and recovering to 7.86% by 2009. India's average GDP growth rate (6.28%) is also more than twice the world's average (3%), reflecting its solid economic progress throughout the decade. In contrast, Russia experienced significant volatility, with a high growth rate of 10% in 2000 but a severe drop to negative 7.80% in 2009 due to the global crisis, illustrating its susceptibility to global economic shocks. Brazil's growth fluctuated between moderate and high, peaking at 6.07% in 2007 and ending with a slight contraction of negative 0.13% in 2009, indicating both potential and vulnerability. South Africa exhibited the slowest but stable growth among the BRICS, with rates ranging from 4.20% in 2000 to 5.60% in 2006 before dropping to negative 1.54% in 2009. While the world GDP growth rate peaked at 4.53% in 2000 and fell to negative 1.36% in 2009, the BRICS countries, particularly China and India, demonstrated faster and more varied growth, highlighting their increasing economic influence and resilience relative to the world average during this period.

*Table 2. Growth rates of GDP for BRICS, 2000-2009 (annual %)*

| Countries/ Years | World | BRA | RUS | IND | CHN | ZAF | BRICS |
|---|---|---|---|---|---|---|---|
| **2000** | 4.53 | 4.39 | 10.00 | 3.84 | 8.49 | 4.20 | 6.18 |
| **2001** | 2.03 | 1.39 | 5.10 | 4.82 | 8.34 | 2.70 | 4.47 |
| **2002** | 2.30 | 3.05 | 4.70 | 3.80 | 9.13 | 3.70 | 4.88 |
| **2003** | 3.10 | 1.14 | 7.30 | 7.86 | 10.04 | 2.95 | 5.86 |
| **2004** | 4.47 | 5.76 | 7.20 | 7.92 | 10.11 | 4.55 | 7.11 |
| **2005** | 4.01 | 3.20 | 6.40 | 7.92 | 11.39 | 5.28 | 6.84 |

continued on following page

*Table 2. Continued*

| Countries/ Years | World | BRA | RUS | IND | CHN | ZAF | BRICS |
|---|---|---|---|---|---|---|---|
| **2006** | 4.44 | 3.96 | 8.20 | 8.06 | 12.72 | 5.60 | 7.71 |
| **2007** | 4.37 | 6.07 | 8.50 | 7.66 | 14.23 | 5.36 | 8.36 |
| **2008** | 2.06 | 5.09 | 5.20 | 3.09 | 9.65 | 3.19 | 5.24 |
| **2009** | -1.36 | -0.13 | -7.80 | 7.86 | 9.40 | -1.54 | 1.56 |
| **Ave.** | **3** | **3.39** | **5.48** | **6.28** | **10.35** | **3.60** | **5.82** |

Source: Authors' compilation based on World Bank (2024), WDI.

The figure 2 also displays the GDP growth rates for BRICS countries and the world from 2000 to 2009. This figure shows diverse trends for BRICS countries compared to the world. However, during this period, the average growth rate of the BRICS countries (5.82%) was well above the world average (3%). Globally, growth rates of world GDP fluctuated, peaking at 4.53% in 2000 and dipping to -1.36% in 2009, correspond to a GDP growth rate of 3% in this period. Brazil experienced an average growth rate of 3.39% in this period, peaking at 6.07% in 2007 before a slight contraction in 2009. Russia had strong growth early on but faced a significant drop to -7.80% in 2009. During this period, Russia's average GDP growth rate was 5.4%. India maintained stable growth, recovering to 7.86% in 2009. China consistently posted high growth, peaking at 14.23% in 2007, and remained robust at 9.40% in 2009. South Africa had moderate growth, with a decline to -1.54% in 2009. For this period, the average growth rate of BRICS countries (5.82%) was more than twice the world average (3%). In sum, BRICS countries showed higher and more varied growth rates compared to the world average, underscoring their dynamic and increasingly influential role in the global economy, especially during periods of global downturn.

*Figure 2. Growth rates of GDP for BRICS, 2000-2009 (annual %)*

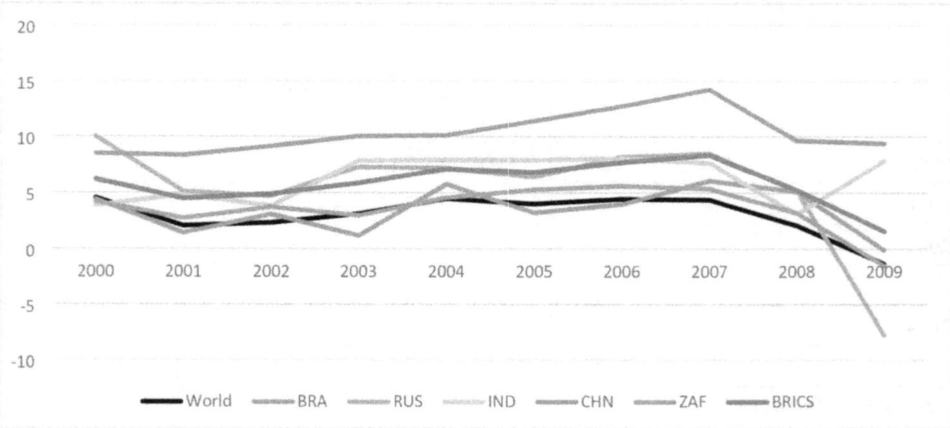


*(Authors' compilation based on World Bank (2024), WDI)*

## GDP Per Capita (current US$)

GDP per capita provides a lens into the average economic output per individual, reflecting living standards and economic prosperity (Smeeding & Rainwater, 2004). India and China are the most populous countries in the world with 1.43 billion and 1.41 billion people in 2023, respectively (World Bank, 2024). For China and India, significant increases in GDP per capita during this period indicate notable improvements in living standards. Conversely, Brazil, Russia, and South Africa saw more moderate increases, with fluctuations indicative of varying economic stability and growth rates.

The table 3 indicates GDP per capita for BRICS countries and the world from 2000 to 2009 in current US$, highlighting distinct growth trends and economic disparities. During this period China experienced the most significant rise with GDP per capita increasing from $959 in 2000 to $3,832 in 2009. This data corresponds to 300% increase and reflecting rapid economic growth and improved living standards of China. India also saw substantial growth, moving from $442 to $1,097 over the same period (correspond to 148% increase), though its per capita income remains lower compared to China. Russia showed a remarkable increase, with GDP per capita climbing from $1,772 to $8,563, indicating substantial economic development and high per capita income by the end of the decade. Brazil's GDP per capita grew from $3,727 to $8,570, reflecting strong economic progress, though it still lags behind Russia. South Africa had a more moderate increase, with GDP per capita rising from $3,242 to $6,444, suggesting steady but slower growth relative to other BRICS countries.

*Table 3. GDP per capita of BRICS, 2000-2009 (in thousands of current US$)*

| Countries/ Years | World | BRA | RUS | IND | CHN | ZAF | BRICS | Ratio of BRICS to World (%) |
|---|---|---|---|---|---|---|---|---|
| **2000** | 5507 | 3727 | 1772 | 442 | 959 | 3242 | 2028 | 37 |
| **2001** | 5401 | 3142 | 2100 | 450 | 1053 | 2867 | 1923 | 36 |
| **2002** | 5535 | 2825 | 2378 | 469 | 1149 | 2708 | 1906 | 34 |
| **2003** | 6127 | 3057 | 2975 | 544 | 1289 | 4096 | 2392 | 39 |
| **2004** | 6817 | 3623 | 4102 | 624 | 1509 | 5268 | 3025 | 44 |
| **2005** | 7289 | 4773 | 5323 | 711 | 1753 | 5893 | 3691 | 51 |
| **2006** | 7799 | 5866 | 6920 | 802 | 2099 | 6140 | 4365 | 56 |
| **2007** | 8681 | 7323 | 9101 | 1023 | 2694 | 6662 | 5361 | 62 |
| **2008** | 9420 | 8802 | 11635 | 994 | 3468 | 6252 | 6230 | 66 |
| **2009** | 8818 | 8570 | 8563 | 1097 | 3832 | 6444 | 5701 | 65 |
| **Ave.** | **7140** | **5171** | **5487** | **715** | **1981** | **4957** | **3662** | **49** |

Source: Authors' compilation based on World Bank (2024), WDI.

Globally, GDP per capita in world increased from $5,507 in 2000 to $8,818 in 2009 and this corresponds to 60% increase, with the BRICS countries showing varying degrees of improvement in living standards compared to the world average. For this period, the average per capita income in the world was $7,140, while the average per capita income of the BRICS countries was $3662. Last column of the table 3 shows the ratio of BRICS countries per capita GDP to the world, and this ratio increased from 37% in 2000 to 65% in 2009, and this corresponds to 75% increase when compared to the world average. Moreover, for this period, the average ratio of the per capita GDP of the BRICS countries to the world average was 49%. Although all of the BRICS countries remained below the world average in per capita GDP, they managed to increase the ratio of their per capita GDP to the world from 37% in 2000 to 65% in 2009, an improvement of approximately 75%.

The figure 3 showing GDP per capita from 2000 to 2009 reveals distinct economic trends for each BRICS country and the world. China shows a steep and consistent upward trajectory, starting at $959 in 2000 and rising sharply to $3,832 by 2009, highlighting its rapid economic expansion and significant improvement in living standards. India illustrates a steady, gradual increase from $442 to $1,097, reflecting stable economic growth but at a slower pace compared to China. The figure for Russia features a dramatic rise from $1,772 to $8,563, with a steep increase in the earlier years followed by a notable decline towards the end, indicating the severe impact of the global financial crisis. Among the BRICS countries, only Russia managed to exceed the world average per capita GDP in 2007 and 2008. Brazil demonstrates a steady climb from $3,727 to $8,570, showing robust economic progress, though the growth is not as rapid as Russia's. South Africa displays a more gradual rise from $3,242 to $6,444, indicating slower but consistent economic growth. In contrast, the world GDP per capita shows a moderate and steady increase, beginning at $5,507 in 2000 and rising to $8,818 by 2009. This gradual upward trend reflects overall improvements in global living standards with less pronounced fluctuations compared to the more variable growth in the BRICS countries.

*Figure 3. GDP per capita of BRICS, 2000-2009 (in thousands of current US$)*

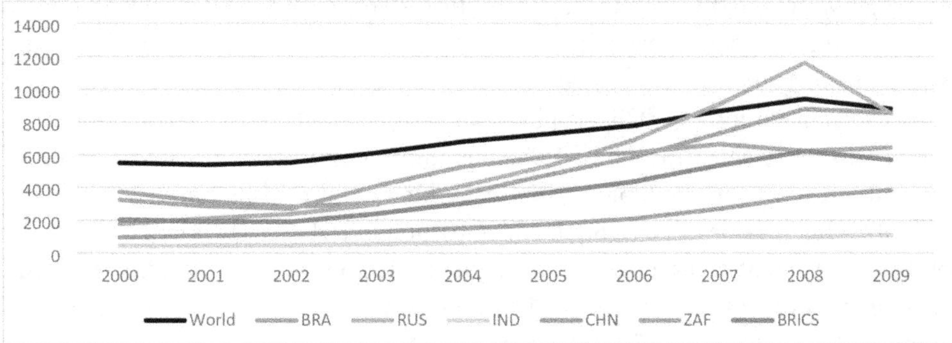


*(Authors' compilation based on World Bank (2024), WDI)*

## 1.2. Post-2010 Economic Developments

The post-2010 period marks a critical phase in the economic evolution of BRICS countries, characterized by increased global integration, rapid technological change, and evolving domestic policies. During this period, the BRICS countries experienced diverse growth patterns, influenced by global economic trends, commodity price fluctuations, and domestic challenges such as political instability and structural reforms (Naudé et al., 2015). Analyzing GDP, GDP growth rates, and GDP per capita in this period provides valuable insights into how these countries adapted to new economic realities and their roles in the global world economy.

### GDP (current US$)

In the period following the official establishment of BRICS in 2010, economic developments continued in the member countries. GDP growth of China remained robust, further consolidating its status as the world's second-largest economy. India also continued its upward trajectory, benefiting from ongoing economic reforms and expanding domestic markets. Brazil and Russia, however, faced significant economic challenges, including commodity price fluctuations and geopolitical tensions, which impacted their GDP growth.

As illustrated by the table 4, the world's GDP increased by 58% from $66.5 trillion in 2010 to $105 trillion in 2023, with a notable decline in 2020 to $85.5 trillion, likely due to the global impact of the COVID-19 pandemic, followed by a strong recovery in subsequent years. During this period, the average world GDP was approximately $84 trillion. Brazil's economy showed significant volatility. GDP of Brazil peaked at $2.6 trillion in 2011 but experienced a sharp decline to $1.4 trillion in 2020, before recovering to $2.1 trillion in 2023. The table reveals that GDP of Russia grew until 2013, then faced a downturn starting in 2014, with notable lows in 2015 and 2016, before partially recovering to $2 trillion by 2023. GDP of India exhibited steady growth throughout the period, starting at $1.6 trillion in 2010 and rising to $3.55 trillion by 2023, despite a slight dip in 2020. This data demonstrated continued robust performance of India economy despite a pandemic-related dip. The data presented in the table shows that China continued its rapid growth. The GDP of China was almost tripling from $6 trillion in 2010 to $17.8 trillion in 2023, solidifying its position as a major global economic power. South Africa's economy remained relatively stable but did not exhibit significant growth, concluding at $378 billion in 2023, close to its 2010 level of $417 billion.

*Table 4. GDP of BRICS, 2010-2023 (in billions of current US$)*

| Countries/ Years | World | BRA | RUS | IND | CHN | ZAF | BRICS | Share of BRICS in World GDP (%) |
|---|---|---|---|---|---|---|---|---|
| **2010** | 66514 | 2209 | 1525 | 1676 | 6087 | 417 | 11914 | 18 |
| **2011** | 73958 | 2616 | 2046 | 1823 | 7552 | 458 | 14495 | 20 |
| **2012** | 75604 | 2465 | 2208 | 1828 | 8532 | 434 | 15468 | 20 |
| **2013** | 77751 | 2473 | 2292 | 1857 | 9570 | 401 | 16593 | 21 |
| **2014** | 79894 | 2456 | 2059 | 2039 | 10476 | 381 | 17411 | 22 |
| **2015** | 75360 | 1802 | 1363 | 2104 | 11062 | 347 | 16678 | 22 |
| **2016** | 76588 | 1796 | 1277 | 2295 | 11233 | 324 | 16924 | 22 |
| **2017** | 81551 | 2064 | 1574 | 2651 | 12310 | 381 | 18981 | 23 |
| **2018** | 86687 | 1917 | 1657 | 2703 | 13895 | 405 | 20577 | 24 |
| **2019** | 87946 | 1873 | 1693 | 2836 | 14280 | 389 | 21071 | 24 |
| **2020** | 85578 | 1476 | 1493 | 2675 | 14688 | 338 | 20670 | 24 |
| **2021** | 97527 | 1671 | 1843 | 3167 | 17820 | 420 | 24922 | 26 |
| **2022** | 101225 | 1952 | 2266 | 3353 | 17882 | 405 | 25858 | 26 |
| **2023** | 105435 | 2174 | 2021 | 3550 | 17795 | 378 | 25918 | 25 |
| **Ave.** | **83687** | **2067** | **1809** | **2468** | **12370** | **391** | **19106** | **23** |

Source: Authors' compilation based on World Bank (2024), WDI.

The table 4 also highlights that the collective GDP of the BRICS countries increased by 118% from $12 trillion in 2010 to $26 trillion in 2023 with China's substantial contribution being a major driver of this growth. Last column of the table displays the share of BRICS countries in the world GDP. Thanks to China and India, the share of the BRICS countries in the world GDP increased from 18% in 2010 to 25% in 2023. The data underscores the varied economic trajectories of these countries, with some like China and India demonstrating sustained robust growth, while others, Brazil, Russia and South Africa experienced more volatile and challenging economic conditions.

World GDP follows a generally steady upward trend from 2010 to 2023, with a notable dip around 2020, likely attributed to the COVID-19 pandemic's impact. This dip is followed by a recovery, demonstrating the resilience and adaptability of the global world economy in the face of challenges. The GDP of the BRICS countries, as portrayed in the figure 4, reveals a more significant upward trend compared to the world GDP. During this period, the share of BRICS countries in the world GDP has managed to increase from 18% in 2010 to 25% in 2023. This is important in terms of showing that a quarter of the world's GDP is generated by the BRICS countries. Also, this increase underscores the growing economic importance of the BRICS on the world economy. The figure 4 highlights particularly sharp rises during periods of strong GDP growth in China, illustrating China's pivotal role in driving the overall economic performance of the BRICS. On an individual level, the graph shows China's GDP growth as robust and consistent, with its economy more than doubling over the period. India's GDP also shows steady growth, reflecting its increasing economic strength. In contrast, the figure shows GDP of Brazil peaking around 2011, then declining, especially around 2015, before starting to recover by 2023. Similarly, GDP of Russia experiences growth until 2013, followed by a downturn and a partial recovery, indicating economic fluctuations. GDP of South Africa remains relatively flat, suggesting limited economic growth over the years. This figure 4 effectively captures the diverse economic paths and challenges faced by the BRICS countries.

*Figure 4. GDP of BRICS, 2010-2023 (in billions of current US$)*

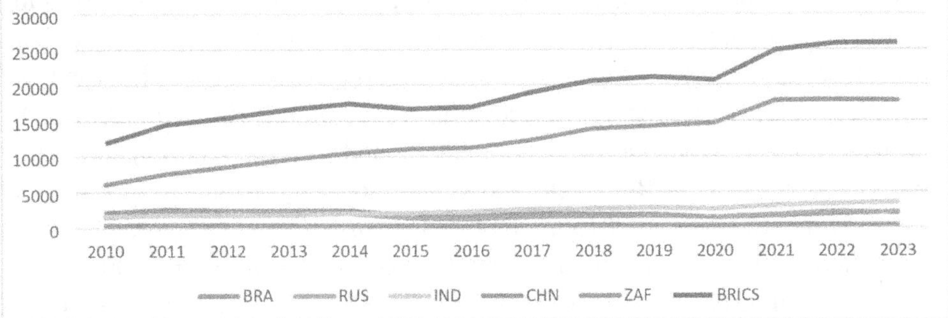


*(Authors' compilation based on World Bank (2024), WDI)*

Overall, while BRICS countries have demonstrated impressive growth, the period post-2010 underscores divergent recovery patterns and economic trajectories within the BRICS, reflecting both resilience and volatility in the face of global economic challenges.

## GDP Growth (annual %)

From 2010 to 2023, GDP growth rates in BRICS displayed notable variations. China and India maintained relatively high growth rates when compared to the world average, reflecting their economic resilience and expansion. In contrast, Brazil, Russia, and South Africa experienced periods of slower growth or economic contraction, affected by global economic uncertainties and internal structural issues.

The table 5 outlines the GDP growth rates for the BRICS and the world from 2010 to 2023, revealing distinct economic patterns across BRICS countries. During this period, the world GDP growth rate was 2.93% on average, while the average growth rate of BRICS countries was 3.51%, above the world average GDP. China (6.83%) and India (6.06%) achieved growth rates more than twice the world's average, while Russia (1.78%), Brazil (1.56%) and South Africa (1.34%) remained at half the world average. The growth rate of world GDP started at 4.5% in 2010 but showed a gradual decline, reaching 2.6% by 2019. The COVID-19 pandemic caused a sharp contraction to -2.9% in 2020, followed by a significant rebound to 6.3% in 2021. The world GDP growth then stabilized at 3.1% in 2022 before slightly declining to 2.7% in 2023, reflecting a resilient global economy amid various challenges. Among the BRICS countries, GDP growth rate of India remained robust, starting at 8.5% in 2010 and recovering strongly to 9.7% in 2021, despite a notable dip to -5.8% in 2020 due to the pandemic. China also demonstrated high growth rates initially, peaking at 10.6% in 2010, but experienced a slowdown to 6.0% by 2019, with a pandemic-related dip to 2.2% in 2020 and a subsequent recovery to 5.2% by 2023. The GDP growth rate of Brazil was more volatile, with a peak of 7.5% in 2010 followed by significant downturns, including -3.5% in 2015, and a partial recovery to 2.9% in 2023. The growth rate of Russia showed similar volatility, with a peak at 4.5% in 2010, a decline to -2.0% in 2015, and a recovery to 3.6% in 2023. South Africa's growth was relatively low and inconsistent, marked by a severe contraction to -6.0% in 2020 and a modest recovery to 0.6% by 2023. This data highlights the diverse economic trajectories and recovery patterns within the BRICS countries and the broader global world economy context.

*Table 5. GDP growth rates for BRICS, 2010-2023 (annual %)*

| Countries/Years | World | BRA | RUS | IND | CHN | ZAF | BRICS |
|---|---|---|---|---|---|---|---|
| **2010** | 4.53 | 7.53 | 4.50 | 8.50 | 10.64 | 3.04 | 6.84 |
| **2011** | 3.33 | 3.97 | 4.30 | 5.24 | 9.55 | 3.17 | 5.25 |
| **2012** | 2.71 | 1.92 | 4.02 | 5.46 | 7.86 | 2.40 | 4.33 |
| **2013** | 2.87 | 3.00 | 1.76 | 6.39 | 7.77 | 2.49 | 4.28 |
| **2014** | 3.12 | 0.50 | 0.74 | 7.41 | 7.43 | 1.41 | 3.50 |
| **2015** | 3.13 | -3.55 | -1.97 | 8.00 | 7.04 | 1.32 | 2.17 |
| **2016** | 2.82 | -3.28 | 0.19 | 8.26 | 6.85 | 0.66 | 2.54 |
| **2017** | 3.46 | 1.32 | 1.83 | 6.80 | 6.95 | 1.16 | 3.61 |
| **2018** | 3.29 | 1.78 | 2.81 | 6.45 | 6.75 | 1.56 | 3.87 |
| **2019** | 2.64 | 1.22 | 2.20 | 3.87 | 5.95 | 0.26 | 2.70 |
| **2020** | -2.93 | -3.28 | -2.65 | -5.78 | 2.24 | -5.96 | -3.09 |
| **2021** | 6.26 | 4.76 | 5.61 | 9.69 | 8.45 | 4.70 | 6.64 |
| **2022** | 3.09 | 3.02 | -2.07 | 6.99 | 2.99 | 1.91 | 2.57 |
| **2023** | 2.72 | 2.91 | 3.60 | 7.58 | 5.20 | 0.60 | 3.98 |
| Ave. | **2.93** | **1.56** | **1.78** | **6.06** | **6.83** | **1.34** | **3.51** |

Source: Authors' compilation based on World Bank (2024), WDI.

Figure 5 based on the GDP growth rates from 2010 to 2023 reveals distinct economic patterns across the world and the BRICS. The GDP growth trend of the BRICS countries (red line) is similar to the world. While the GDP growth rates of China and India were above the world growth rates, the growth rates of Russia, Brazil and South Africa were below the world GDP. The world GDP growth rate shows a general decline from 2010 to 2019, with a significant drop in 2020 due to the COVID-19 pandemic, followed by a sharp recovery in 2021. The BRICS members display diverse economic growth trajectories. India stands out with consistently high growth, notably rebounding in 2021 after a significant decline in 2020. China initially experienced rapid growth, peaking in 2010, but then gradually slowed down, with a pandemic-related dip in 2020 and a recovery by 2023. Brazil's economy has been marked by significant volatility, with strong growth in 2010, followed by sharp declines and a partial recovery by 2023. Russia shows a similar pattern of volatility, with growth fluctuations and a recovery by 2023. In contrast, South Africa has had a relatively flat and low growth trajectory, suffering a severe contraction in 2020 and achieving only modest recovery by 2023. The figure 5 highlights the varied economic experiences and recovery patterns of BRICS countries, reflecting both resilience and volatility in the face of global challenges.

*Figure 5. GDP growth rates for BRICS and World, 2010-2023 (annual %)*

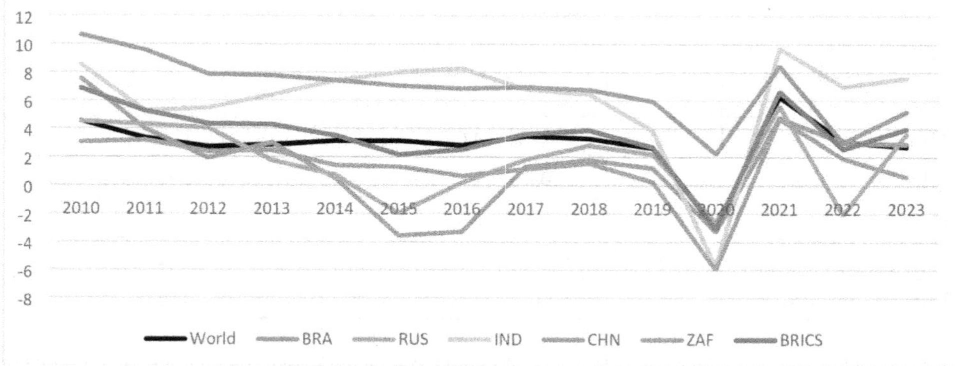


*(Authors' compilation based on World Bank (2024), WDI)*

## GDP Per Capita (current US$)

The trends in GDP per capita from 2010 to 2023 highlight continued improvements in living standards especially in China and India. These increases reflect their sustained economic growth and development efforts. For Brazil, Russia, and South Africa, the growth in GDP per capita was more uneven, influenced by economic volatility and varying rates of economic advancement.

*Table 6. GDP per capita of BRICS, 2010-2023 (in thousands of current US$)*

| Countries/ Years | World | BRA | RUS | IND | CHN | ZAF | BRICS | Ratio of BRICS to World (%) |
|---|---|---|---|---|---|---|---|---|
| **2010** | 9543 | 11249 | 10675 | 1351 | 4550 | 8060 | 7177 | 75 |
| **2011** | 10485 | 13201 | 14305 | 1450 | 5614 | 8737 | 8661 | 83 |
| **2012** | 10587 | 12328 | 15402 | 1434 | 6301 | 8174 | 8728 | 82 |
| **2013** | 10755 | 12259 | 15941 | 1438 | 7020 | 7441 | 8820 | 82 |
| **2014** | 10919 | 12071 | 14055 | 1560 | 7636 | 6965 | 8457 | 77 |
| **2015** | 10178 | 8783 | 9278 | 1590 | 8016 | 6205 | 6774 | 67 |
| **2016** | 10224 | 8681 | 8663 | 1714 | 8094 | 5735 | 6577 | 64 |
| **2017** | 10763 | 9897 | 10659 | 1958 | 8817 | 6734 | 7613 | 71 |
| **2018** | 11315 | 9121 | 11212 | 1974 | 9905 | 7068 | 7856 | 69 |
| **2019** | 11358 | 8845 | 11448 | 2050 | 10144 | 6703 | 7838 | 69 |
| **2020** | 10942 | 6924 | 10108 | 1916 | 10409 | 5753 | 7022 | 64 |
| **2021** | 12362 | 7795 | 12522 | 2250 | 12618 | 7074 | 8452 | 68 |
| **2022** | 12730 | 9066 | 15445 | 2366 | 12663 | 6766 | 9261 | 73 |

continued on following page

*Table 6. Continued*

| Countries/ Years | World | BRA | RUS | IND | CHN | ZAF | BRICS | Ratio of BRICS to World (%) |
|---|---|---|---|---|---|---|---|---|
| **2023** | 13138 | 10044 | 13817 | 2485 | 12614 | 6253 | 9043 | 69 |
| **Ave.** | **11093** | **10019** | **12395** | **1824** | **8886** | **6976** | **8020** | **72** |

Source: Authors' compilation based on World Bank (2024), WDI.

The table 6 shows GDP per capita trends from 2010 to 2023 for the BRICS countries and the world. The world GDP per capita increased steadily from $9,543 in 2010 to $13,138 in 2023, with a notable dip in 2020 due to the COVID-19 pandemic and a strong recovery afterward. The world's per capita GDP increased by approximately 38% during this period and amounted to an average of $11,093. Among the BRICS countries, only Russia has achieved a rate above the world average with an average per capita GDP of $12,395. On the contrary, Brazil and South Africa's per capita GDP has decreased in 2023 compared to 2010. GDP per capita of Brazil peaked at $13,201 in 2011 but declined significantly, reaching $6,924 in 2020, and it has since recovered to $10,044 by 2023. GDP per capita of South Africa declined from $8,060 in 2010 to $6,253 in 2023, with a significant drop in 2020 and slow recovery thereafter. GDP per capita of Russia rose from $10,675 in 2010 to $15,445 in 2022 before slightly falling to $13,817 in 2023. GDP per capita of India grew consistently from $1,351 in 2010 to $2,485 in 2023, with a brief dip in 2020 but a strong recovery. China saw a substantial GDP growth from $4,550 in 2010 to $12,614 in 2023, reflecting rapid economic growth despite some recent slowdown. The GDP per capita of BRICS countries increased by 26% from $7,177 in 2010 to $9,043 in 2023, with an average of $8,020.

The figure 6 displays GDP per capita of BRICS countries and the world from 2010 to 2023. The figure reveals significant economic trends and disparities among the BRICS countries and the world economy. The world GDP per capita shows a steady increase from 2010 to 2023, with a notable dip in 2020 due to the COVID-19 pandemic. The figure highlights a strong recovery, with GDP per capita rising in 2021 and continuing its upward trajectory thereafter. Among the BRICS countries, China exhibits the most substantial growth, despite recent deceleration. China's per capita GDP has been on a steady rise between 2010 and 2020, and is catching up with the world in 2020. India's GDP per capita shows steady growth from 2010 to 2023, with a brief dip during the pandemic but a robust recovery. Brazil's line is marked by significant volatility, peaking in 2011 before falling sharply in 2020, and recovering slowly by 2023. Russia shows a general upward trend with some fluctuations. South Africa illustrates a steady downward trend from 2010 to 2023, with a steep drop in 2020, reflecting persistent economic challenges.

*Figure 6. GDP per capita of BRICS and World, 2010-2023 (in thousands of current US$)*

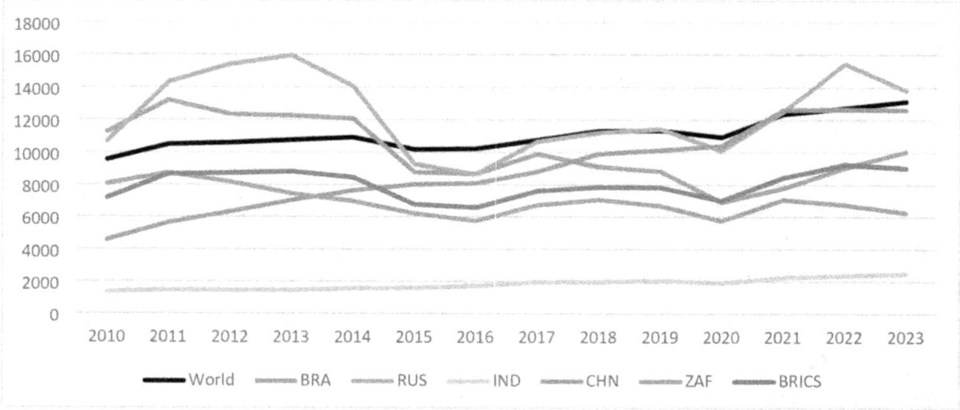


*(Authors' compilation based on World Bank (2024), WDI)*

The GDP per capita data illustrates varied economic growth and recovery patterns among the BRICS countries, with China and India showing robust economic performance, on the other hand Brazil and Russia experiencing significant fluctuations, and South Africa facing persistent economic challenges. Although the per capita GDP of China and India increased significantly during this period, the ratio of the per capita GDP of the BRICS countries to the world per capita GDP decreased from 75% in 2010 to 69% in 2023 as a result of the weak economic performance of Russia, Brazil and South Africa.

## 1.3. Comparative Analysis

A comparative analysis of GDP, GDP growth, and GDP per capita data before and after the establishment of the BRICS in 2010 highlights significant shifts in economic performance and growth patterns. Also, it is essential to understand the relative economic strengths and weaknesses of BRICS countries. This analysis reveals the disparities and commonalities in their economic performances, helping to identify the factors driving growth in each member of BRICS and how they compare on a global scale. By comparing these key economic indicators, one can assess the effectiveness of different economic policies and strategies, and understand the broader implications of the BRICS countries' rise for global economic competition and cooperation. For this purpose, a comparative analysis of the data is conducted for two periods: (i) the 10-year period before the establishment of the BRICS (2000-2009) and (ii) the 14-year period after the establishment of the BRICS (2010-2023).

## Comparative GDP Analysis

Figure 7 displays the average GDP of BRICS Countries for two periods: (i) 2000-2009 and (ii) 2010-2023. As can be seen from the figure, the average GDP of the BRICS increased almost four times in the second period ($19,106 billion) compared to the first period ($5,425 billion). In these two periods, the average world GDP increased by only 79%, from $46,827 billion to $83,687 billion (see Tables 1 and 4). Globally, the average World GDP almost doubled in the later period, highlighting substantial worldwide economic growth. The average GDP for each member of BRICS, and the BRICS group as a whole was higher in the second period compared to the first period. Within the BRICS countries, China saw the highest increase, with its average GDP nearly five times higher in the second period ($12,370 billion) than in the first period ($2,592 billion). India also experienced significant growth, with its average GDP nearly tripling (from $830 billion to $2,468 billion). Brazil and Russia more than doubled their average GDPs in the second period. South Africa, while experiencing a more modest increase, also saw a higher average GDP in the second period ($391 billion). Furthermore, the average GDP share of BRICS in the world GDP is increased from 11% in the first period to 23% in the second period (see Tables 1 and 4). These data show that the BRICS countries have increased their GDP more than twice compared to the world. This situation reveals the institutional success of BRICS.

*Figure 7. Average of GDP for BRICS countries, (in billions of current US$)*

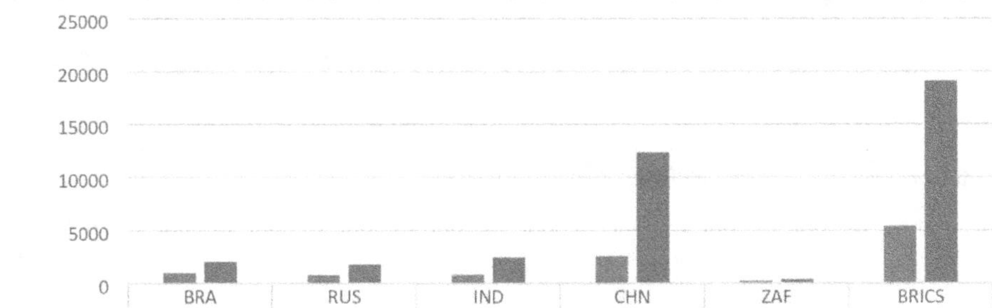


| | BRA | RUS | IND | CHN | ZAF | BRICS |
|---|---|---|---|---|---|---|
| 2000-2009 | 971 | 787 | 830 | 2592 | 244 | 5425 |
| 2010-2023 | 2067 | 1808 | 2468 | 12370 | 391 | 19106 |

2000-2009 2010-2023

*(Authors' compilation based on World Bank (2024), WDI)*

## Comparative GDP Growth Analysis

Figure 8 indicates the average GDP Growth rates for BRICS countries and the world for 2000-2009 and 2010-2023. As can be seen from the figure, the average GDP growth rates declined globally and across the BRICS countries in the second period. The world's growth slightly decreased from 3% in the first period to 2.93% in the second period. Within BRICS, Brazil, Russia, and South Africa experienced sharper declines, with Brazil dropping from 3.39% in the first period to 1.56% in the second period, Russia from 5.48% to 1.76%, and South Africa from 3.6% to 1.34%. China's growth slowed from average 10.35% to average 6.82%, while India remained relatively stable, with a minor slope from 6.28% to 6.07%. In addition, the BRICS group's average GDP growth rate fell from 5.82% to 3.51%. Compared to the first period, only China and India managed to achieve GDP growth rates more than twice as high as the world average.

*Figure 8. Average of GDP growth for BRICS countries and world, (annual %)*

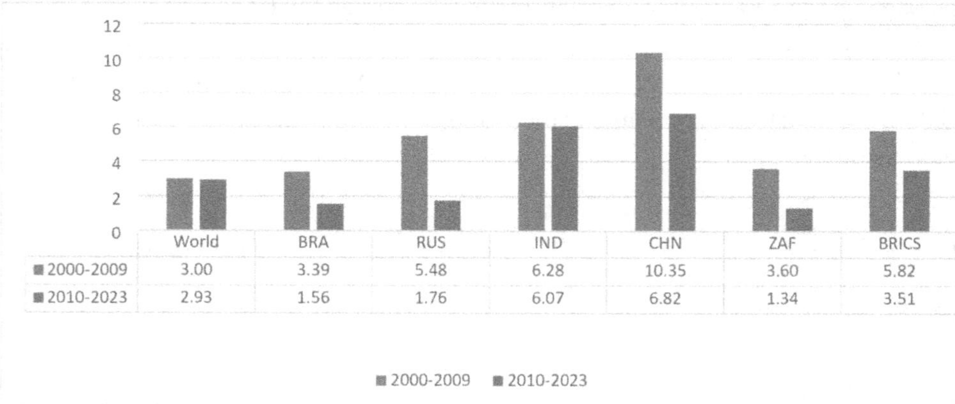


| | World | BRA | RUS | IND | CHN | ZAF | BRICS |
|---|---|---|---|---|---|---|---|
| 2000-2009 | 3.00 | 3.39 | 5.48 | 6.28 | 10.35 | 3.60 | 5.82 |
| 2010-2023 | 2.93 | 1.56 | 1.76 | 6.07 | 6.82 | 1.34 | 3.51 |

*(Authors' compilation based on World Bank (2024), WDI)*

## Comparative GDP per capita Analysis

Average GDP per capita for BRICS countries and the world are illustrated in Figure 9 for the periods 2000-2009 and 2010-2023. The average GDP per capita was higher in the second period (2010-2023) compared to the first period (2000-2009) for all BRICS countries and the world. Average world GDP per capita increased by 55%, from $7,139 in the first period to $11,093 in the second period. All the BRICS countries saw higher GDP per capita in the second period. China's GDP per capital increased by 350% from $1,981 to $8,886, India's by 155% from $716 to $1,824,

Russia's by 125% from $5,487 to $12,395, Brazil's increased by 94% from $5,171 to $10,019, and South Africa's by 41% from $4,957 to $6,976. Also, the average GDP per capita of BRICS countries increased by 120% from $3,662 to $8,020. In sum, in the second period (2010-2023), after the establishment of BRICS, the average GDP per capita for BRICS countries and the group as a whole increased more significantly compared to the world average. While the world's average GDP per capita increased only 55%, BRICS countries average GDP per capital increased by 120% saw larger proportional increases, narrowing the gap with the world average.

*Figure 9. Average of GDP per capita for BRICS and World, (in thousands of current US$)*

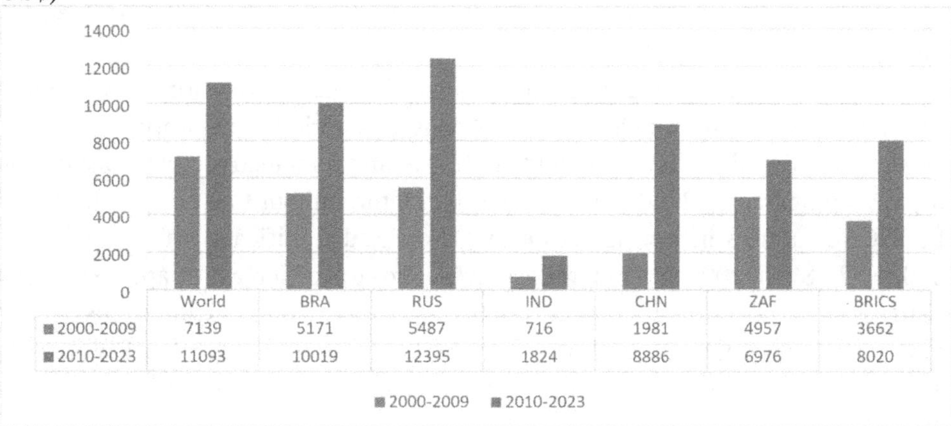


*(Authors' compilation based on World Bank (2024), WDI)*

## 2. FOREIGN DIRECT INVESTMENT (FDI) INFLOWS

FDI is seen as one of the most important tools that promote economic growth, employment, technology transfer and currencies' inflows in a country (Gandou & Sönmez, 2022). FDI plays a pivotal role in the economic development of emerging markets, providing capital, technology, and management expertise that can spur growth. In emerging economies, technology spillovers from foreign to domestic firms are widely recognized as the principal channel through which FDI exerts its influence on the host economy (Sönmez & Pamukçu, 2013; Sönmez & Çetin, 2018; Sönmez, 2018). For the BRICS countries, FDI has also been a critical factor in their integration into the global economy, influencing sectors ranging from manufacturing to services. Understanding FDI trends is essential for gauging how these countries attract foreign capital, manage economic reforms, and navigate global market dynamics. It also helps in assessing the impact of FDI on domestic industries, employment, and technological advancement.

## 2.1. Trends for FDI Inflows Before 2010

Before 2010, the BRICS countries experienced varying levels of FDI inflows, reflecting their unique economic conditions, policy environments, and stages of development. Analyzing FDI net inflows in this period reveals how these countries positioned themselves as attractive destinations for foreign investors, despite challenges such as political instability, infrastructure gaps, and regulatory hurdles. Understanding these trends is crucial for comprehending the foundation upon which later FDI strategies and growth were built, and how early investments influenced long-term economic trajectories.

Table 7 and figure 10 highlight the trends in FDI net inflows for BRICS countries and the world from 2000 to 2009. During this period, total world FDI flows averaged $1,567 billion between 2000 and 2009 and remained almost constant for 10 years compared to 2000. On the other hand, throughout this period, the share of BRICS countries in world FDI inflows increased significantly, from 5.25% in 2000 to 17.18% in 2009. This increase corresponds to an increase of approximately 3.3 times. The most important shares in this increase belong to China, Russia and India, respectively. China's FDI inflows were the highest among the BRICS, with an average of $96 billion. Russia showed notable growth, particularly in the second half of the decade. India's FDI inflows saw a significant increase, especially after 2005 from $7 billion to $36 billion. Unlike other BRICS countries, Brazil has shown a decline in FDI flows from 2000 to 2007. And, South Africa's FDI inflows remained relatively slow, with an average of $4 billion. Moreover, the table indicates that there was a significant decrease in FDI flows across BRICS in 2009 as a result of the global financial crisis.

*Table 7. FDI net inflows, 2000-2009 (in billions of current US$, BoP)*

| Countries / Years | World | BRA | RUS | IND | CHN | ZAF | BRICS | Share of BRICS in World (%) |
|---|---|---|---|---|---|---|---|---|
| **2000** | 1569 | 33 | 3 | 4 | 42 | 1 | 82 | 5.25 |
| **2001** | 896 | 23 | 3 | 5 | 47 | 7 | 86 | 9.55 |
| **2002** | 752 | 17 | 3 | 5 | 53 | 1 | 80 | 10.62 |
| **2003** | 737 | 10 | 8 | 4 | 58 | 1 | 80 | 10.92 |
| **2004** | 1009 | 18 | 15 | 5 | 68 | 1 | 108 | 10.69 |
| **2005** | 1553 | 15 | 16 | 7 | 104 | 7 | 149 | 9.58 |
| **2006** | 2189 | 19 | 38 | 20 | 124 | 1 | 202 | 9.22 |

continued on following page

*Table 7. Continued*

| Countries / Years | World | BRA | RUS | IND | CHN | ZAF | BRICS | Share of BRICS in World (%) |
|---|---|---|---|---|---|---|---|---|
| **2007** | 3113 | 45 | 56 | 25 | 156 | 7 | 289 | 9.27 |
| **2008** | 2442 | 51 | 75 | 43 | 172 | 10 | 350 | 14.35 |
| **2009** | 1410 | 31 | 37 | 36 | 131 | 8 | 242 | 17.18 |
| **Ave.** | **1567** | **26** | **25** | **15** | **96** | **4** | **167** | **11** |

Source: Authors' compilation based on World Bank (2024), WDI.

*Figure 10. FDI net inflows for BRICS, 2000-2009 (in billions of current US$, BoP)*

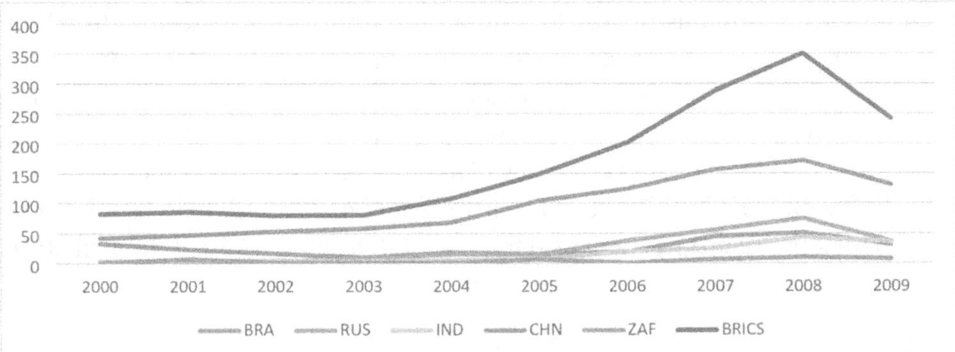


*(Authors' compilation based on World Bank (2024), WDI)*

In sum, while there were significant fluctuations in some BRICS countries, the data reveals a significant increase in FDI inflows to BRICS countries. FDI is a key indicator of economic attractiveness and development. Prior to the formal establishment of BRICS in 2010, China attracted substantial FDI, reflecting its large market and favourable investment climate. In contrast, other BRICS countries experienced more variable FDI inflows, influenced by economic and political factors.

## 2.2. FDI Trends After 2010

The period after 2010 witnessed significant changes in FDI patterns among the BRICS countries, driven by factors like economic reforms, globalization, and shifts in investor sentiment. Examining FDI net inflows during this period provides insights into how BRICS countries responded to global economic shifts, adjusted their policies to attract or retain FDI, and leveraged FDI for economic diversification and growth. This analysis is important for understanding the evolving role of FDI inflows to BRICS countries and how it has impacted their global economic standing.

Table 8 and Figure 11 show net FDI inflows for BRICS countries and the world between 2010 and 2022. In this thirteen-year period, FDI flows worldwide averaged $2 trillion annually. The world FDI inflows increased from $1.9 trillion in 2000 and reached a peak of $2.75 trillion in 2015. During this period, total FDI net inflows of the BRICS countries varied between a minimum of $274 billion in 2002 and a maximum of $516 billion in 2021, amounting to an average of $388 billion. BRICS countries maintained a strong share of world FDI inflows, averaging 21% over this period. In 2018, the share of BRICS in world FDI inflows reached a high of 41% in 2018. China's FDI inflows remained the largest among the BRICS, contributing significantly to the group's overall figures, particularly with a peak in 2021 at $344 billion. During this period, FDI inflows to China amounted to $239 billion per year on average. The country that attracted the most FDI inflows after China was Brazil, with an average of $73 billion annually. For this period, FDI inflows to India showed a stable growth with an annual average of $41 billion, reaching a peak of $64 billion in 2020. By the way, FDI inflows to Russia were more unstable, especially with a sharp decline into negative figures in 2022 due to Russia-Ukraine war. South Africa's inflows remained low overall but spiked to $41 billion in 2021.

*Table 8. FDI net inflows, 2010-2022 (in billions of current US$, BoP)*

| Countries/ Years | World | BRA | RUS | IND | CHN | ZAF | BRICS | Share of BRICS in World (%) |
|---|---|---|---|---|---|---|---|---|
| **2010** | 1903 | 82 | 43 | 27 | 244 | 4 | 400 | 21 |
| **2011** | 2363 | 102 | 55 | 36 | 280 | 4 | 478 | 20 |
| **2012** | 2053 | 93 | 51 | 24 | 241 | 5 | 413 | 20 |
| **2013** | 2171 | 75 | 69 | 28 | 291 | 8 | 472 | 22 |
| **2014** | 1931 | 88 | 22 | 35 | 268 | 6 | 418 | 22 |
| **2015** | 2758 | 65 | 7 | 44 | 242 | 2 | 360 | 13 |
| **2016** | 2740 | 74 | 33 | 44 | 175 | 2 | 328 | 12 |
| **2017** | 2195 | 69 | 29 | 40 | 166 | 2 | 306 | 14 |
| **2018** | 895 | 78 | 9 | 42 | 235 | 6 | 370 | 41 |
| **2019** | 1850 | 69 | 32 | 51 | 187 | 5 | 344 | 19 |
| **2020** | 1230 | 38 | 9 | 64 | 253 | 3 | 368 | 30 |
| **2021** | 2287 | 46 | 40 | 45 | 344 | 41 | 516 | 23 |
| **2022** | 1790 | 75 | -40 | 50 | 180 | 9 | 274 | 15 |
| Ave. | **2013** | **73** | **28** | **41** | **239** | **7** | **388** | **21** |

Source: Authors' compilation based on World Bank (2024), WDI.

Figure 11 displays FDI net inflows from 2010 to 2022 and reveals distinct trends for each BRICS member. Since China has a large weight in FDI inflows, it shows a similar trend with the red line chart of all the BRICS countries. Other members of the BRICS show a stable trend, remaining below $100 billion throughout the period, indicating ongoing challenges in attracting FDI.

*Figure 11. FDI net inflows for BRICS (2010-2022) (in billions of current US$, BoP)*

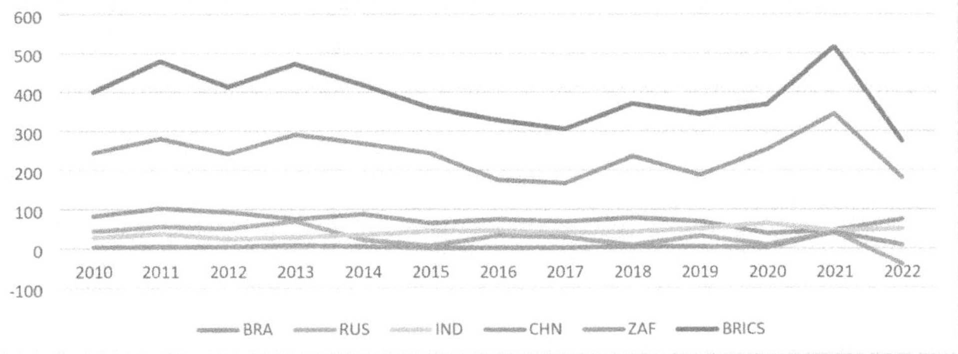


*(Authors' compilation based on World Bank (2024), WDI)*

## 2.3. Comparative Analysis of FDI Inflows

Figure 12 displays the average FDI inflows in BRICS countries for 2000-2009 and 2010-2023 periods. Average world FDI inflows increased by 28% from $1,567 billion in the first period to $2,013 billion in the second period (see tables 7 and 8). For the same period, average FDI inflows to BRICS increased from $167 billion to $388 billion, correspondence to an increase of 132%. While the average world FDI inflows increased by only 28% in these two periods, the 132% increase in the FDI inflows of the BRICS is a remarkable achievement of the BRICS. Figure 12 also reveals a significant increase in average FDI inflows for each BRICS countries from 2000-2009 to 2010-2022 period. Brazil's average FDI net inflows grew from $26 billion to $73 billion, showing a significant rise in FDI inflows. India's average FDI inflows more than doubled, increasing from $15 billion to $41 billion. Russia's average FDI inflows indicates lower increase from $25 billion to $28 billion. By the way, China's average FDI inflows experienced a dramatic surge, rising from $96 billion to $239 billion, correspond to 150% increase. South Africa's average FDI inflows increased from $4 billion to $7 billion, showing a smaller positive trend.

*Figure 12. Average FDI inflows in BRICS (2000-2022), (in billions of current US$, BoP)*

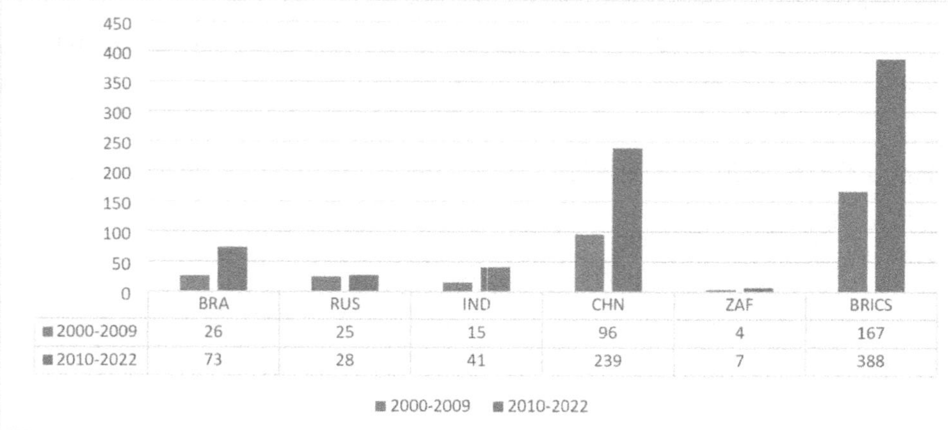


*(Authors' compilation based on World Bank (2024), WDI)*

Overall, average FDI inflows to China have seen a dramatic increase in the second period (2010-2022) after the establishment of BRICS in 2010. The country achieved very high FDI inflows of $344 billion in 2021. Russia shows a mix of positive and negative trends, with notable peaks in 2011 and 2013 but experiencing downturns in other years. South Africa's FDI inflows are relatively modest. In sum, the data highlights significant fluctuations in FDI inflows, with China attracts more FDI inflows strongly, while other members of BRICS continue to face challenges in attracting FDI inflows. After 2010, the FDI landscape for BRICS countries continued to evolve. China remained major recipient of FDI, driven by its expanding economy and continued reforms. Russia, India and Brazil saw fluctuations in FDI inflows due to global economic conditions and domestic policy changes. South Africa's FDI inflows remained relatively modest, reflecting both opportunities and challenges in its investment climate.

## 3. MANUFACTURING PRODUCTION

Manufacturing production is a key indicator of industrial development and economic health, particularly for emerging economies like the BRICS countries. The manufacturing industry not only contributes significantly to GDP but also provides employment, drives innovation, and facilitates export growth. Understanding the trends in manufacturing production helps gauge the industrial capabilities of the BRICS countries, their progress in moving up the value chain, and their ability to compete in the global market. It also highlights the role of manufacturing industry in their broader economic strategies.

### 3.1. Pre-2010 Manufacturing Landscape

The manufacturing landscape of the BRICS countries before 2010 reflects their early efforts at industrialization and economic modernization. By examining manufacturing value added (MVA) in current US$, one can assess the contributions of this industry to overall economic growth and the challenges these countries faced in building robust industrial bases. This pre-2010 period is crucial for understanding the foundational industrial policies, investment patterns, and infrastructural developments that set the stage for later manufacturing advancements.

The manufacturing industry is crucial for economic development and industrialization. Before 2010, China significantly expanded its manufacturing base. India also made strides in manufacturing, though not at the scale of China. Brazil, Russia, and South Africa had smaller manufacturing sectors, with varying degrees of focus on industrial development.

*Table 9. Manufacturing value added, 2000-2009 (in billions of current US$)*

| Countries/ Years | World | BRA | RUS | IND | CHN | ZAF | BRICS | Share of BRICS in World (%) |
|---|---|---|---|---|---|---|---|---|
| **2000** | 6187 | 86 | - | 75 | - | 29 | 189 | 3.06 |
| **2001** | 5786 | 73 | - | 74 | - | 26 | 173 | 3.00 |
| **2002** | 5855 | 63 | 52 | 80 | - | 25 | 220 | 3.76 |
| **2003** | 6500 | 81 | 62 | 95 | - | 36 | 274 | 4.21 |
| **2004** | 7264 | 101 | 90 | 112 | 625 | 46 | 974 | 13.42 |
| **2005** | 7766 | 131 | 120 | 131 | 734 | 50 | 1166 | 15.01 |
| **2006** | 8397 | 156 | 151 | 163 | 893 | 47 | 1411 | 16.80 |
| **2007** | 9443 | 198 | 196 | 205 | 1150 | 51 | 1801 | 19.07 |
| **2008** | 10212 | 237 | 248 | 205 | 1476 | 49 | 2215 | 21.69 |
| **2009** | 9339 | 218 | 158 | 230 | 1612 | 48 | 2265 | 24.25 |
| Ave. | **7675** | **134** | **135** | **137** | **1082** | **41** | **1069** | **12** |

Source: Authors' compilation based on World Bank (2024), WDI.

Table 9 shows the MVA for the BRICS and the world from 2000 to 2009. For this period, the world MVA increased significantly by 51%, from $6187 billion in 2000 to $9339 billion in 2009, reflecting broad industrial expansion. During this period, the average world MVA was $7675 billion. According to average values, the BRICS countries with the largest share are China, India, Russia, Brazil and South Africa, respectively. Especially China emerged as a dominant force in world manufacturing after 2004, highlighting its rapid industrial growth. India also saw steady growth, reaching $230 billion by 2009. Brazil and Russia experienced modest increases in MVA, with Brazil growing from $86 billion to $218 billion and Russia from $52 billion to $158 billion. South Africa's manufacturing industry remained the smallest, increasing from $29 billion to $48 billion. Collectively, BRICS countries saw substantial growth, with their combined MVA rising from $974 billion in 2004 to $2265 billion in 2009. Moreover, the share of the BRICS countries in the world's MVA increased from 13% to over 24% with the accession of China in 2004. For the year 2009, approximately one-quarter of the world's MVA was produced by the BRICS. These figures highlight BRICS' growing industrial capabilities, though China's rapid expansion was a major driver of this trend.

*Figure 13. Manufacturing value added, 2000-2009 (in billions of current US$)*

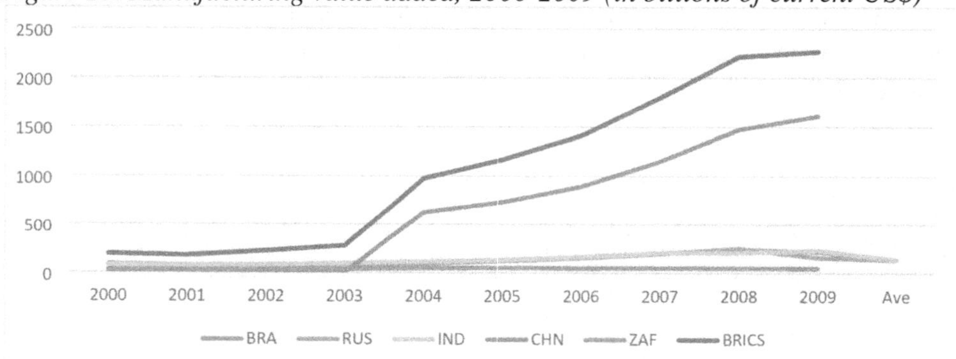


*(Authors' compilation based on World Bank (2024), WDI)*

Figure 13 displays the MVA trends of the BRICS countries for 2000-2009. From 2000 to 2009, MVA showed distinct trends across countries. China experienced explosive growth especially after 2004, significantly outpacing other BRICS countries. India saw steady, consistent growth, while Brazil had a more modest upward trend. Russia's MVA increased sharply from 2002 onwards, and South Africa displayed the smallest and slowest growth, reflecting its relatively smaller manufacturing sector. Globally, MVA grew by 29%, from $7264 billion in 2004 to $9339 billion in 2009, with BRICS countries collectively growing by approximately 133%, from $974 billion in 2004 to $2265 billion in 2009. China's dramatic rise was the key driver of this global industrial expansion, far surpassing the growth rates of other BRICS countries.

## 3.2. Post-2010 Manufacturing Developments

Post-2010, the BRICS countries have seen varied trajectories in their manufacturing industries, influenced by global economic shifts, technological advancements, and domestic policy changes. Analysing MVA during this period sheds light on how these countries have adapted to new economic realities, such as increased competition, supply chain disruptions, and the demand for higher-value products. This analysis is key to understanding the ongoing transformation of the BRICS economies and their efforts to enhance industrial competitiveness in the global market.

The period after 2010 saw continued growth and transformation in the manufacturing industries of BRICS countries. China's dominance in manufacturing continued, while India made further progress in expanding its industrial base. Brazil, Russia, and South Africa sought to enhance their manufacturing capabilities as part of broader economic strategies.

*Table 10. Manufacturing value added, 2010-2023, (in billions of current US$)*

| Countries/ Years | World | BRA | RUS | IND | CHN | ZAF | BRICS | Share of BRICS in World (%) |
|---|---|---|---|---|---|---|---|---|
| **2010** | 10570 | 281 | 195 | 285 | 1924 | 58 | 2744 | 25.96 |
| **2011** | 11802 | 308 | 235 | 294 | 2421 | 59 | 3318 | 28.11 |
| **2012** | 12051 | 263 | 252 | 289 | 2690 | 54 | 3549 | 29.45 |
| **2013** | 12276 | 259 | 253 | 283 | 2935 | 50 | 3781 | 30.80 |
| **2014** | 12721 | 254 | 233 | 307 | 3184 | 48 | 4026 | 31.65 |
| **2015** | 12352 | 190 | 169 | 328 | 3203 | 43 | 3932 | 31.84 |
| **2016** | 12412 | 194 | 149 | 348 | 3153 | 40 | 3885 | 31.30 |
| **2017** | 13264 | 221 | 194 | 398 | 3460 | 48 | 4321 | 32.58 |
| **2018** | 14194 | 202 | 212 | 402 | 3868 | 50 | 4735 | 33.36 |
| **2019** | 14043 | 194 | 220 | 382 | 3823 | 48 | 4666 | 33.23 |
| **2020** | 13652 | 158 | 200 | 378 | 3861 | 40 | 4636 | 33.96 |
| **2021** | 16077 | 199 | 233 | 455 | 4909 | 50 | 5846 | 36.36 |
| **2022** | 16028 | 255 | 286 | 440 | 4840 | 50 | 5871 | 36.63 |
| **2023** | 16182 | 290 | 252 | 456 | 4659 | 49 | 5705 | 35.25 |
| Ave | **13402** | **233** | **220** | **360** | **3495** | **49** | **4358** | **32.18** |

Source: Authors' compilation based on World Bank (2024), WDI.

Table 10 reveals notable trends in MVA for the BRICS countries and the world for 2010 and 2023. The world's MVA experienced robust growth and increased by 53% from $10570 billion in 2010 to $16182 billion in 2023, an average of $13402 billion for the fourteen (14) years. China's dominance in manufacturing continues to grow, with its value-added increasing by 142%, from $1924 billion in 2010 to $4659 billion in 2023. In 2023, China's share in world MVA alone was 29%. This substantial growth underscores China's sustained role as a global manufacturing leader. India's manufacturing sector also shows significant progress, with MVA rising from $285 billion to $456 billion, indicating ongoing expansion and development in its industrial base. In contrast, Brazil, Russia, and South Africa experienced more modest growth. Brazil's MVA increased from $281 billion in 2010 to $290 billion in 2023, reflecting a gradual upward trend despite fluctuations. Russia grew from $195 billion to $252 billion, showing a consistent increase over the period. South Africa's MVA remains the smallest among the BRICS, rising slightly from $58 billion to $49 billion, suggesting limited growth in its manufacturing sector. The BRICS countries collectively saw significant growth, reaching $5705 billion by 2023, driven primarily by China's dominant expansion. The share of the BRICS countries in the world MVA has also increased from 26% in 2010 to over 35% in 2023. This growth highlights the continuing transformation and development of manufacturing capabilities within the BRICS countries and the broader global context.

*Figure 14. Manufacturing value added, 2010-2023 (in billions of current US$)*

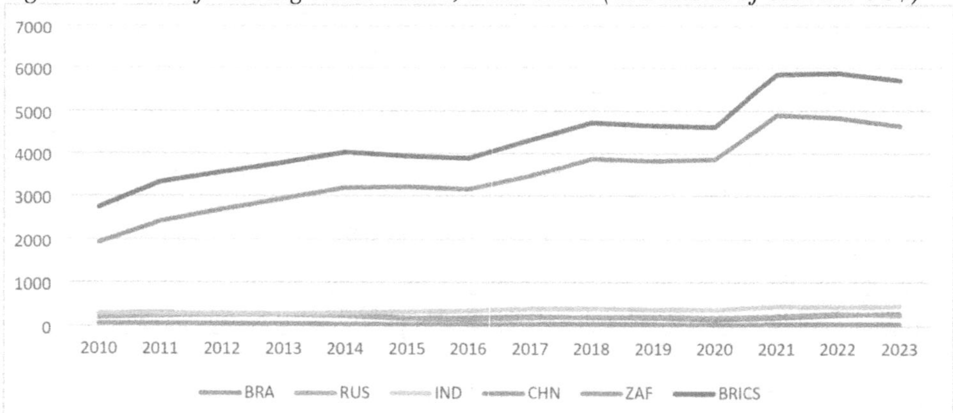


*(Authors' compilation based on World Bank (2024), WDI)*

Figure 14 indicates the trend of MVA for the BRICS countries. As can be seen from the figure, China alone dominates the BRICS and the world MVA. China's manufacturing industry saw a dramatic 142% increase, rising from $1924 billion to $4659 billion, reinforcing its global manufacturing dominance. India achieved a 60% growth, with its MVA increasing from $285 billion to $456 billion, reflecting steady industrial progress. Brazil experienced modest growth, with a 3% increase from $281 billion to $290 billion, while Russia saw a 29% rise from $195 billion to $252 billion, indicating steady but less pronounced growth. In contrast, South Africa's manufacturing sector declined by about 16%, from $58 billion to $49 billion, highlighting limited expansion. Globally, MVA grew by 53%, with the BRICS countries collectively seeing a 108% increase from $2744 billion to $5705 billion. This increase was led alone by China, but BRICS countries' combined growth was higher than the world trend reflecting a faster overall expansion in manufacturing.

Figure 15 displays the average MVA in BRICS countries for 2000-2009 and 2010-2023 periods. Average world MVA increased by 75% from $7675 billion in the first period to $13402 billion in the second period (see tables 9 and 10). For the same period, the MVA in BRICS increased from $1069 billion to $4358 billion, correspondence to an increase of 308%. While the average world MVA increased by only 75%, the 308% increase of MVA in the BRICS is a significant achievement. Although almost all BRICS countries increased their average MVA, this 308% increase was significantly led by China alone, which increased by 223%, from $1082 billion in the first period to $3495 billion in the second period.

*Figure 15. Average manufacturing value added, 2000-2023 (in billions of current US$)*

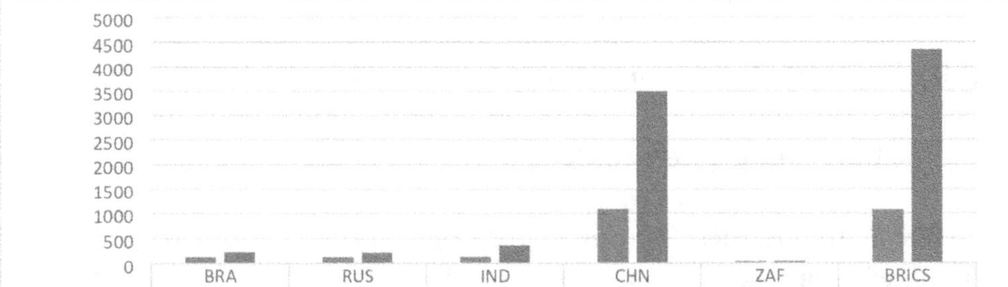


| | BRA | RUS | IND | CHN | ZAF | BRICS |
|---|---|---|---|---|---|---|
| ■ 2000-2009 | 134 | 135 | 137 | 1082 | 41 | 1069 |
| ■ 2010-2023 | 233 | 220 | 360 | 3495 | 49 | 4358 |

■ 2000-2009 ■ 2010-2023

*(Authors' compilation based on World Bank (2024), WDI)*

Figure 15 also indicates a significant increase in average MVA for each BRICS countries. Brazil's average increased by 74% from $134 billion to $233 billion, and Russia's average increased by 63% from $135 billion to $220 billion. India's average MVA increased by 163% from $137 billion to $360 billion, showing a significant rise in MVA. By the way, China's average MVA experienced a dramatic surge, rising from $1082 billion to $3495 billion, correspond to 223% increase. South Africa's average increased by 19% from $41 billion to $49 billion, showing a smaller positive trend. Overall, average MVA in China have seen a dramatic increase in the second period (2010-2023). The country achieved very high MVA of $4.6 trillion in 2023.

As of 2023, almost one-third of the world's MVA was conducted by China. This is important as it shows that China has become the world's production base.

## 4. FOREIGN TRADE

Effective trade and investment cooperation of the countries is a fundamental factor of their stable economic development and competitiveness in the world economy (Gusarova, 2019). Foreign trade is also a vital component of economic growth for the BRICS countries, providing access to global markets, fostering competitiveness, and generating foreign exchange earnings. By examining trends in exports of goods and services, one can gauge the effectiveness of trade policies, the degree of integration into the global economy, and the role of trade in driving overall economic performance. Understanding foreign trade patterns is essential for assessing how these countries navigate global trade dynamics and leverage their comparative advantages. For this aim, export trends of the BRICS countries are analysed by two ways: (I) exports of goods and services in current US$ and (ii) exports of goods and services as % of GDP.

### 4.1. Exports of Goods and Services in Current US$

#### 4.1.1. Export Trends Before 2010

Before 2010, the BRICS countries developed their export sectors to varying degrees, reflecting their diverse economic structures and strategic priorities. By analysing exports of goods and services in current US$, one can understand the early stages of their integration into global trade networks, the impact of export-oriented policies, and the challenges they faced in expanding their market reach. This period is crucial for understanding the groundwork laid for later export growth and the role of trade in their economic strategies.

Exports play a critical role in the economic development of BRICS countries. Prior to 2010, China led in export volumes, with a diversified range of goods and services. India also increased its export capacity, particularly in services. Brazil and Russia's exports were largely commodity-driven, while South Africa focused on minerals and manufactured goods.

Table 11 indicates the data on exports of goods and services for the BRICS countries and the world from 2000 to 2009. The figures reveal important trends and comparisons between BRICS countries and the world. China emerges as a dominant player, with exports growing from $253 billion in 2000 to $1263 billion in 2009, correspondence to an increase by 400%. India's exports also show significant growth, increased by 350% from $61 billion to $274 billion, reflecting its expanding role in global services and manufactured goods. Brazil and Russia experience notable increases in exports, with Brazil growing from $67 billion to $181 billion (170%) and Russia from $114 billion to $342 billion (200%). Both countries' export growth is heavily commodity-driven, highlighting their focus on natural resources and energy. South Africa's exports increased modestly by 122% from $37 billion to $82 billion, showing steady growth in minerals and manufactured goods.

*Table 11. Exports of goods and services, 2000-2009 (in billions of current US$)*

| Countries/ Years | World | BRA | RUS | IND | CHN | ZAF | BRICS | Share of BRICS in World (%) |
|---|---|---|---|---|---|---|---|---|
| **2000** | 7961 | 67 | 114 | 61 | 253 | 37 | 532 | 6.69 |
| **2001** | 7714 | 69 | 113 | 61 | 272 | 36 | 551 | 7.14 |
| **2002** | 8100 | 73 | 122 | 73 | 333 | 37 | 637 | 7.87 |
| **2003** | 9381 | 85 | 152 | 91 | 448 | 47 | 822 | 8.77 |
| **2004** | 11398 | 111 | 203 | 127 | 607 | 58 | 1106 | 9.71 |
| **2005** | 12952 | 136 | 269 | 161 | 773 | 68 | 1407 | 10.86 |
| **2006** | 14905 | 159 | 334 | 200 | 992 | 79 | 1764 | 11.84 |
| **2007** | 17352 | 186 | 392 | 253 | 1258 | 93 | 2183 | 12.58 |
| **2008** | 19823 | 230 | 520 | 289 | 1498 | 102 | 2638 | 13.31 |
| **2009** | 16004 | 181 | 342 | 274 | 1263 | 82 | 2141 | 13.38 |
| **Ave.** | **12559** | **130** | **256** | **159** | **770** | **64** | **1378** | **10.21** |

Source: Authors' compilation based on World Bank (2024), WDI.

During this ten-year period, the average share of the BRICS countries in the world exports was 10%. Compared to the world, which saw a rise in export volumes from $7961 billion in 2000 to $16004 billion in 2009, the BRICS countries also experienced significant growth, with their combined exports increasing from $532 billion to $2141 billion. The world's exports grew by about 101% during this period, while BRICS' exports grew by 302%, indicating a substantial increase in their global trade presence, though still a smaller proportion compared to the world exports. This growth reflects the expanding role of BRICS in global trade, although the other four members' share of global exports remained smaller relative to China's dominant position.

Figure 16 displaying the exports of goods and services for the BRICS countries from 2000 to 2009 reveals several key trends. China shows a dramatic and continuous upward trajectory, with exports growing steadily after 2000, highlighting its rise as a major global exporter. India demonstrates substantial growth, reflecting its expanding export capacity, especially in services. Brazil shows a more gradual increase, with steady but less pronounced growth compared to China and India. Russia illustrates a significant upward trend, driven primarily by commodities. South Africa shows a modest increase in exports, indicating a smaller but consistent rise in its export volumes. Overall, while the BRICS countries collectively saw impressive growth, China's dominance stands out prominently against the backdrop of the world's expanding export volumes.

*Figure 16. Exports of goods and services, 2000-2009 (in billions of current US$)*

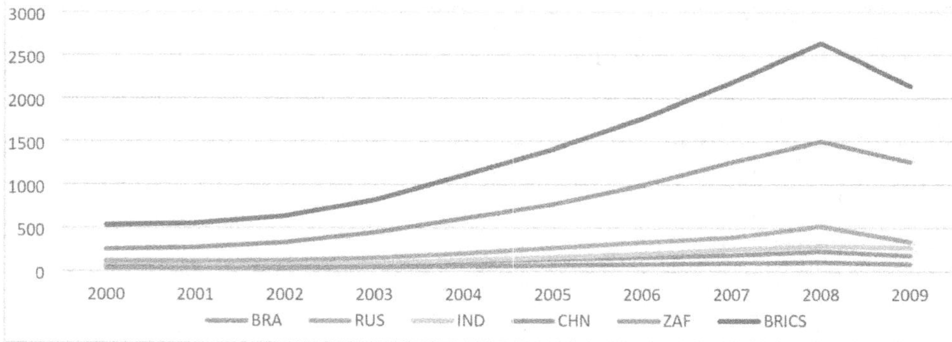


*(Authors' compilation based on World Bank (2024), WDI)*

## 4.1.2. Export Trends After 2010

The period after 2010 has seen significant shifts in the export patterns of the BRICS countries, influenced by global economic trends, trade agreements, and shifts in demand. Examining exports of goods and services during this period reveals how the BRICS countries have adapted to changes in the global trade environment, diversified their export bases, and enhanced their competitiveness. Understanding these trends is vital for assessing the ongoing evolution of the BRICS economies and their roles as key players in international trade.

After the official formation of BRICS in 2010, export trends continued to evolve. China maintained its lead in exports, with ongoing diversification and expansion into new markets. India increased its export of services, while Brazil, Russia, and South Africa adapted their export strategies in response to changing global demand and economic conditions.

Table 12 shows the exports of goods and services for the BRICS countries and the world over the 2010-2023 period. For this period, the world's exports grew by 62%, from $19073 billion in 2010 to $30857 billion in 2023, reflecting a robust expansion across global markets. The BRICS countries saw substantial growth in their exports, with their combined exports increased by 87%, from $2823 billion to $5275 billion. This represents a significant increase; their growth was somewhat high pronounced compared to the overall global trend. In the same period, the share of the BRICS countries in total world exports increased from 14.80% in 2010 to 17.10% in 2023. In sum, while BRICS countries increased their share of global exports, their growth rates were above the world average. This shows that while the global export market as a whole grew during this period, BRICS countries also grew faster and increased their global trade footprint.

*Table 12. Exports of goods and services, 2010-2023 (in billions of current US$)*

| Countries/ Years | World | BRA | RUS | IND | CHN | ZAF | BRICS | Share of BRICS in World (%) |
|---|---|---|---|---|---|---|---|---|
| **2010** | 19073 | 240 | 446 | 375 | 1655 | 108 | 2823 | 14.80 |
| **2011** | 22544 | 303 | 574 | 447 | 2006 | 127 | 3458 | 15.34 |
| **2012** | 22878 | 293 | 594 | 448 | 2175 | 118 | 3628 | 15.86 |
| **2013** | 23516 | 290 | 592 | 472 | 2354 | 114 | 3823 | 16.26 |
| **2014** | 23895 | 270 | 558 | 468 | 2463 | 111 | 3870 | 16.20 |
| **2015** | 21315 | 232 | 391 | 417 | 2362 | 96 | 3499 | 16.41 |
| **2016** | 20927 | 224 | 330 | 440 | 2200 | 91 | 3285 | 15.70 |
| **2017** | 23060 | 258 | 411 | 498 | 2424 | 104 | 3696 | 16.03 |
| **2018** | 25264 | 281 | 510 | 539 | 2656 | 111 | 4097 | 16.21 |
| **2019** | 24865 | 265 | 481 | 529 | 2629 | 106 | 4010 | 16.13 |
| **2020** | 22529 | 243 | 381 | 500 | 2730 | 93 | 3947 | 17.52 |
| **2021** | 28197 | 319 | 549 | 678 | 3554 | 131 | 5231 | 18.55 |
| **2022** | 31401 | 383 | 635 | 778 | 3718 | 136 | 5650 | 17.99 |
| **2023** | 30857 | 394 | 467 | 777 | 3513 | 125 | 5275 | 17.10 |
| **Ave.** | **24309** | **285** | **494** | **526** | **2603** | **112** | **4021** | **16** |

Source: Authors' compilation based on World Bank (2024), WDI.

The figure 17 displaying the exports from 2010 to 2023 for the BRICS countries highlights several key trends. China shows a strong and consistent upward trajectory, with exports increased by 112% from $1655 billion in 2010 to $3513 billion in 2023. This reflects China's sustained dominance and expansion in global trade. India reveals steady growth in exports, increased by 107% from $375 billion to $777 billion, indicating significant progress, particularly in the services sector. Brazil's exports show a gradual increase by 64% from $240 billion to $394 billion, with some fluctuations, suggesting a steady adaptation to changing global conditions. Russia shows initial growth, peaking at $635 billion in 2022, but then a decline, ending at $467 billion in 2023. This indicates a period of adjustment in response to global economic shifts. South Africa exhibits modest and steady growth, from $108 billion to $125 billion, reflecting slower but consistent expansion.

*Figure 17. Exports of goods and services, 2010-2023 (in billions of current US$)*

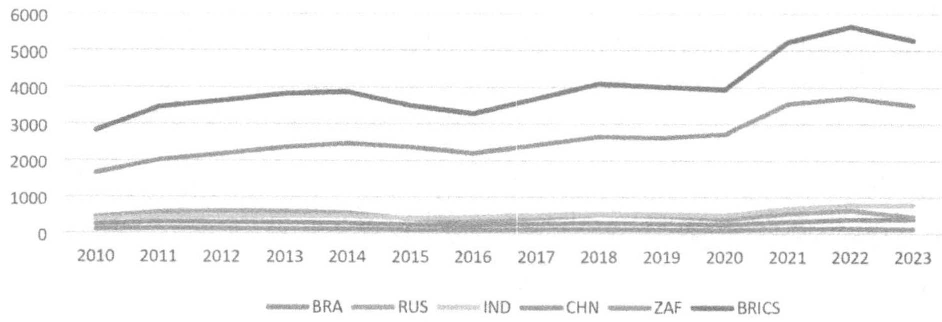


*(Authors' compilation based on World Bank (2024), WDI)*

Figure 18 displays the average exports in BRICS countries for the two periods (i) 2000-2009; (ii) 2010-2023 periods. The average exports of world increased by 94% from $12559 billion in the first period to $24309 billion in the second period (see tables 11 and 12). For the same period, the average exports of BRICS increased from $1378 billion to $4021 billion, correspondence to an increase of 192%. While the average world exports increased by only 94%, the 192% increase of exports in the BRICS is a significant achievement. Although almost all the BRICS countries increased their average exports, this 192% increase was significantly led by China alone, which increased by 238%, from $770 billion in the first period to $2603 billion in the second period.

*Figure 18. Average exports of goods and services, 2000-2023 (in billions of current US$)*

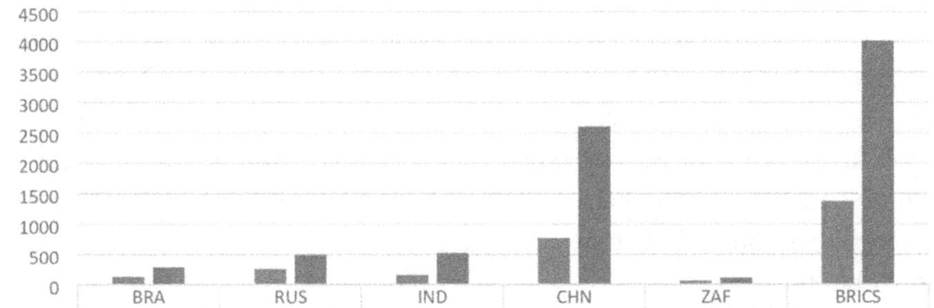


| | BRA | RUS | IND | CHN | ZAF | BRICS |
|---|---|---|---|---|---|---|
| 2000-2009 | 130 | 256 | 159 | 770 | 64 | 1378 |
| 2010-2023 | 285 | 494 | 526 | 2603 | 112 | 4021 |

■ 2000-2009 ■ 2010-2023

*(Authors' compilation based on World Bank (2024), WDI)*

Figure 15 also indicates a significant increase in average exports for each BRICS country. Brazil's average increased by 119% from $130 billion to $285 billion, and Russia's average increased by 93% from $256 billion to $494 billion. India's average increased by 231% from $159 billion to $526 billion, showing a significant rise in exports. By the way, China's average experienced a dramatic surge and increased by 238%. South Africa's average increased by 75% from $64 billion to $112 billion, showing a positive trend. Overall, average exports in China have seen a dramatic increase in the second period (2010-2023). The country achieved very high exports value of $3.5 trillion in 2023, and this correspondence to 11% of the world's exports. This is an important indicator since it shows that China has become the world's export hub. It also highlights China's dominant role in exports as well as being a manufacturing hub, and as the BRICS countries expand their trade footprint.

## 4.2. Exports of Goods and Services as % of GDP

The share of BRICS countries in world trade reflects their growing influence in the global economy and their success in leveraging trade for economic development. By examining their share of exports of goods and services as a percentage of GDP, we can gauge their relative position in global trade, the effectiveness of their trade policies, and their impact on global markets. Understanding their share in world trade is crucial for assessing their contribution to global economic growth and their potential to shape future trade dynamics.

### 4.2.1. Foreign Trade Position Before 2010

Before 2010, the global trade position of the BRICS countries varied significantly, reflecting their different stages of economic development, trade policies, and global integration. Analysing their share in world trade (as % of GDP) during this period provides insights into their early efforts to expand their global market presence and the challenges they faced in doing so. This period is important for understanding the initial conditions that influenced their later trade performance and their roles in the global economy. The share of exports in GDP reflects a country's integration into global trade.

The table 13 presents the share of exports in GDP for the BRICS countries and the world from 2000 to 2009. The table illustrates the varying degrees of global trade integration among BRICS countries and compares them to the world average. During this period, the average export as % of GDP for the world was 26%. Before 2010, Russia (34%), China (28%) and South Africa (26%) had high export-to-GDP ratios, demonstrating significant global economic integration. India (18%) and Brazil (13%) had lower ratios, reflecting a more domestically oriented economic structure. Only Russia and China have achieved a success above the world average with 34% and 28% respectively. Russia consistently had a high export-to-GDP ratio, peaking at 44% in 2000 and falling to 28% in 2009, demonstrates significant dependency on commodity exports, though its global trade share decreased over the period. China also had a high ratio, peaking at 36% in 2006 and ending at 25% in 2009, underscoring its prominent role in world trade. India also showed notable growth, with its ratio increasing from 13% to 20%, reflecting its expanding global trade presence, especially in services. Brazil's ratio was more modest and variable, ranging from 10% to 16%, indicating a relatively lower and less consistent integration into global trade. South Africa's ratio ranged from 24% to 32%, reflecting a stable but moderate level of global trade integration.

*Table 13. Exports of goods and services, 2000-2009 (% of GDP)*

| Countries/ Years | World | BRA | RUS | IND | CHN | ZAF | BRICS |
|---|---|---|---|---|---|---|---|
| **2000** | 23.53 | 10.19 | 44.06 | 13.00 | 20.89 | 24.40 | 22.51 |
| **2001** | 22.94 | 12.37 | 36.89 | 12.56 | 20.31 | 26.36 | 21.70 |
| **2002** | 23.20 | 14.23 | 35.21 | 14.26 | 22.64 | 28.43 | 22.96 |
| **2003** | 23.96 | 15.18 | 35.25 | 14.95 | 26.98 | 23.92 | 23.25 |
| **2004** | 25.84 | 16.55 | 34.42 | 17.86 | 31.06 | 22.76 | 24.53 |
| **2005** | 27.12 | 15.24 | 35.20 | 19.61 | 33.83 | 23.60 | 25.50 |
| **2006** | 28.80 | 14.37 | 33.73 | 21.27 | 36.04 | 26.10 | 26.30 |

continued on following page

*Table 13. Continued*

| Countries/ Years | World | BRA | RUS | IND | CHN | ZAF | BRICS |
|---|---|---|---|---|---|---|---|
| **2007** | 29.76 | 13.33 | 30.16 | 20.80 | 35.43 | 27.96 | 25.54 |
| **2008** | 30.94 | 13.53 | 31.31 | 24.10 | 32.60 | 32.25 | 26.76 |
| **2009** | 26.36 | 10.85 | 27.94 | 20.40 | 24.75 | 24.98 | 21.78 |
| **Ave.** | **26.24** | **13.58** | **34.42** | **17.88** | **28.45** | **26.08** | **24.08** |

Source: Authors' compilation based on World Bank (2024), WDI.

Compared to the world, which saw an increase in the export-to-GDP ratio from 23.53% in 2000 to 26.36% in 2009, the BRICS countries showed a mixed picture. During this period, the average ratio of exports as % of GDP for the BRICS countries was 24%, below the world average. China's high ratio and its decline highlight its dominant yet volatile role in global trade. India's growing ratio indicates increasing integration, while Brazil, Russia, and South Africa exhibited lower and more stable ratios. This comparison shows that while BRICS countries, particularly China and India, contributed significantly to global trade, their integration levels varied, with BRICS as a group having a more complex and diverse trade profile relative to the overall global trend.

Figure 19 displays the export-to-GDP trends for the BRICS countries and the world from 2000 to 2009. The figure reveals distinct export-to-GDP trends among BRICS countries compared to the world. China's ratio shows a sharp increase especially from 2001 to 2006, reflecting its expanding global trade role. India's ratio steadily rises from 2000 to 2008, indicating growing global trade integration, especially in services. Brazil's ratio fluctuates, suggesting a less consistent and more domestically oriented trade profile. Russia's ratio peaks in 2000 and falls until 2009. South Africa's ratio remains relatively stable, showing steady but moderate trade integration. In comparison, the world's export-to-GDP ratio increases from 2000 to 2008, indicating a general rise in global trade integration. While BRICS countries, particularly China and India, demonstrate significant growth in their export ratios, Brazil, Russia, and South Africa show varied and more stable patterns. This highlights the diverse roles of BRICS countries in world trade relative to the overall global trend.

*Figure 19. Exports of goods and services, 2000-2009 (% of GDP)*

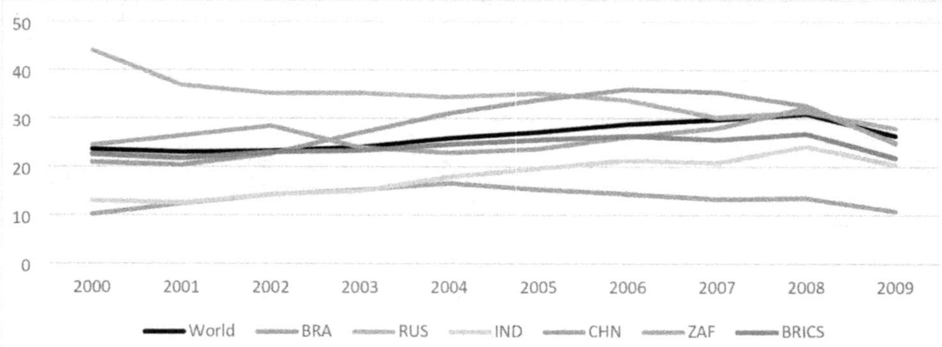


*(Authors' compilation based on World Bank (2024), WDI)*

## 4.2.2. Foreign Trade Position After 2010

After 2010, the BRICS countries have increasingly asserted their presence in global trade, driven by rapid economic growth, diversification of export bases, and strategic trade partnerships. By examining their exports share in GDP during this time, we can assess how these countries have enhanced their global competitiveness, adapted to shifts in global demand, and influenced international trade dynamics. Understanding this period is crucial for appreciating the BRICS countries' growing role in shaping the future of global trade. Following the formal establishment of BRICS in 2010, the global trade positions of its member countries evolved. China and India continued to have high export-to-GDP ratios, indicating strong global trade integration. Brazil, Russia, and South Africa showed changes in their trade positions, influenced by both global economic shifts and domestic economic policies.

*Table 14. Exports of goods and services, 2010-2023 (% of GDP)*

| Countries/ Years | World | BRA | RUS | IND | CHN | ZAF | BRICS |
|---|---|---|---|---|---|---|---|
| **2010** | 28.68 | 10.87 | 29.22 | 22.40 | 27.19 | 25.78 | 24.02 |
| **2011** | 30.48 | 11.58 | 28.06 | 24.54 | 26.57 | 27.70 | 24.82 |
| **2012** | 30.26 | 11.88 | 26.91 | 24.53 | 25.49 | 27.14 | 24.37 |
| **2013** | 30.25 | 11.74 | 25.85 | 25.43 | 24.60 | 28.38 | 24.37 |
| **2014** | 29.91 | 11.01 | 27.11 | 22.97 | 23.51 | 29.00 | 23.92 |
| **2015** | 28.28 | 12.90 | 28.70 | 19.81 | 21.35 | 27.71 | 23.13 |
| **2016** | 27.32 | 12.47 | 25.85 | 19.16 | 19.58 | 28.16 | 22.09 |
| **2017** | 28.28 | 12.52 | 26.09 | 18.79 | 19.69 | 27.34 | 22.12 |

continued on following page

*Table 14. Continued*

| Countries/ Years | World | BRA | RUS | IND | CHN | ZAF | BRICS |
|---|---|---|---|---|---|---|---|
| **2018** | 29.14 | 14.63 | 30.79 | 19.93 | 19.11 | 27.50 | 23.52 |
| **2019** | 28.27 | 14.12 | 28.43 | 18.66 | 18.41 | 27.20 | 22.52 |
| **2020** | 26.33 | 16.45 | 25.52 | 18.68 | 18.59 | 27.53 | 22.18 |
| **2021** | 28.91 | 19.11 | 29.77 | 21.40 | 19.94 | 31.11 | 25.04 |
| **2022** | 31.02 | 19.63 | 28.03 | 23.20 | 20.79 | 33.54 | 26.03 |
| **2023** | 29.27 | 18.11 | 23.08 | 21.89 | 19.74 | 33.02 | 24.19 |
| Ave | **29.03** | **14.07** | **27.39** | **21.53** | **21.76** | **28.65** | **23.74** |

Source: Authors' compilation based on World Bank (2024), WDI.

Table 14 demonstrates the exports of goods and services as % of GDP for the BRICS countries and the world from 2010 to 2023. The export-to-GDP ratios for the BRICS countries reflect varying global trade positions. China's ratio decreased from 27% to 20%, indicating a shift towards more domestic consumption while maintaining a major global trade role. India's ratio remained stable around 22%, showing consistent global trade integration. Brazil's ratio increased from 11% to 18%, highlighting gradual growth in trade integration. Russia's ratio fell from 29% to 23%, reflecting reduced export dependency due to economic and geopolitical factors. South Africa's ratio rose from 26% to 33%, demonstrating improved trade performance and integration. Compared to the world average, which stayed around 29%, BRICS countries showed different trends. China and India continued to play major roles in global trade, though China's share decreased and India's remained stable. Brazil's share grew slowly, indicating more involvement in global trade. Russia's share dropped, partly due to economic challenges, while South Africa's share increased, showing better trade performance. In fact, BRICS countries had varied changes in their global trade positions, reflecting different approaches to global trade and economic conditions.

*Figure 20. Exports of goods and services, 2010-2023 (% of GDP)*

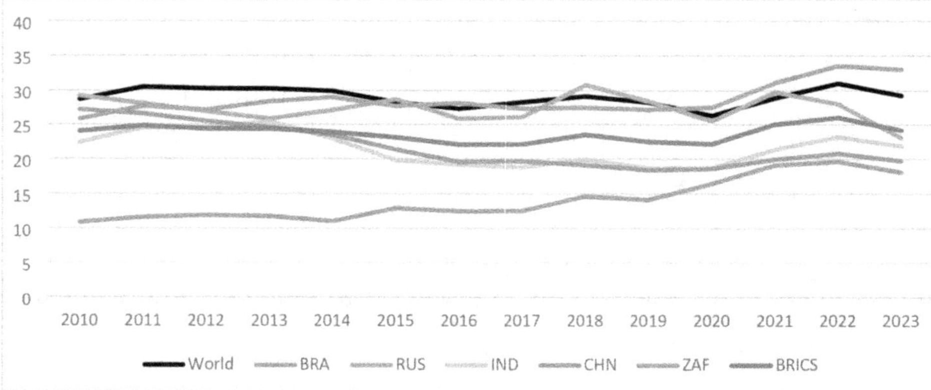


*(Authors' compilation based on World Bank (2024), WDI)*

The figure 20 displays the exports trends as % of GDP for the BRICS countries and the world from 2010 to 2023. China's ratio declines steadily from 2000 to 2020, reflecting a shift from export-focused growth to increased domestic consumption. India's ratio remains relatively stable, showing consistent global trade integration. Brazil's share gradually rises from 2010 to 2022, indicating a growing role in global trade. Russia's ratio decreases, highlighting reduced export dependency due to economic and geopolitical factors. South Africa's ratio increases from 2000 to 2022, demonstrating improved trade performance and greater global integration. Compared to the world average, which stayed relatively stable around 29%, BRICS countries exhibit a range of changes. While some BRICS countries such as China and India show steady integration, Brazil, Russia, and South Africa display varied trends, reflecting differing national responses to global trade dynamics.

Figure 21 displays the average exports ratios as % of GDP for the BRICS countries and the world for two periods (i) 2000-2009 and (ii) 2010-2023. The average exports rates for the world increased slightly from 26% in the first period to 29% in the second period. On the other hand, the average exports rates for the BRICS countries as a whole remained relatively stable, decreased from 24% to 23.74% during this period. Within BRICS, Russia and China experienced sharper declines, with Russia dropping from 34% to 27%, China from 28% to 22%. Brazil average exports ratio increased from 13.58% to 14.07%, India's ratio increased from 17.88% to 21.53%, South Africa's ratio growth from average 26% to average 28.65%. Compared to the first period, only India, South Africa and Brazil have managed to increase their exports to GDP ratios.

*Figure 21. Average exports of goods and services, 2000-2023 (% of GDP)*

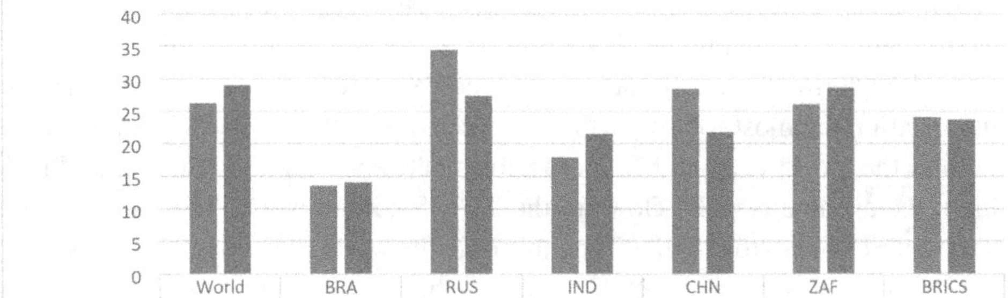


| | World | BRA | RUS | IND | CHN | ZAF | BRICS |
|---|---|---|---|---|---|---|---|
| 2000-2009 | 26.24 | 13.58 | 34.42 | 17.88 | 28.45 | 26.08 | 24.08 |
| 2010-2023 | 29.03 | 14.07 | 27.39 | 21.53 | 21.76 | 28.65 | 23.74 |

■ 2000-2009 ■ 2010-2023

*(Authors' compilation based on World Bank (2024), WDI)*

## CONCLUSION

From 2000 to 2009, the BRICS countries saw significant GDP growth, especially Russia (370%) and China (321%), with BRICS as a whole growing by 252%. This was much faster than the world growth of 79% in the same period. However, in the 2010-2023 period, BRICS growth slowed to 118%, with a particularly marked slowdown in Brazil and South Africa, while the world economy grew by 58%. Thus, BRICS countries expanded more rapidly in the first period compared to the second, though the growth momentum slowed in the latter years. However, despite these developments, with the high GDP figures of China and India, the average share of the BRICS countries in the world GDP increased from 11% in the first period to 23% in the second period.

Between 2000 and 2009, the world's GDP per capita growth was 60%. During this period, GDP per capita growth was much higher and significant across BRICS countries, with China leading at a remarkable 300% increase. Russia also saw substantial growth of 383%, followed by India with a 148% rise, Brazil with 130%, and South Africa with a more modest 99% increase. In contrast, growth rates slowed down between 2010 and 2023. The world GDP per capita growth being only 38% during this period, while the per capita GDP growth rate of the BRICS countries was 26%, well below the world average. China's GDP per capita grew by 177%, maintaining strong performance, while India's increased by 84%, and Russia's by 29%. In the second period, Brazil and South Africa experienced negative GDP per capita growth ratios, by 11% and 22%, respectively. Thanks to China and India, the average ratio of the per capita income of the BRICS countries to the world average per capita income increased from 49% in the first period to 72% in the second period. This data highlights that while all BRICS countries saw growth in GDP per capita over the long term, the rate of increase has slowed in recent years, with China still demonstrating the most robust performance relative to the other BRICS countries.

While the world average FDI net inflows between 2000 and 2009 was $1.56 trillion, the average net FDI flows to the BRICS countries was $167 billion. The ratio of net FDI flows to the BRICS countries in the world FDI net inflows was 11%. During this first period, the BRICS countries showed varied FDI net inflows, with China experiencing significant inflows peaking at $172 billion in 2008 but ending at $131 billion in 2009. China was followed by Brazil, Russia, India and South Africa respectively. In the first period, net FDI flows to the BRICS countries increased by 195% from $82 billion in 2000 to $242 billion in 2009. In the second period from 2010 to 2023, the world average FDI net inflows was $2 trillion, and the average net FDI flows to the BRICS countries was $388 billion. During the second period, the ratio of net FDI flows to the BRICS countries in the world FDI net inflows was 21%. Moreover, average net FDI flows to the BRICS countries increased by 132%, from $167 billion in the first period to $388 billion in the second period. For comparison, average world FDI inflows increased by 28% in these two periods. These figures reveal that FDI inflows to the BRICS countries have increased more than four times the world average and show the incredible success of the BRICS countries in attracting FDI. China has the largest share in this success, followed by Brazil and India, respectively.

Between 2000 and 2009, the MVA showed robust growth across the BRICS countries, with China experiencing a remarkable increase by 158% from 2004 to 2009, while India's MVA grew by 207%, Russia's by 204%, and Brazil's by 153%. South Africa saw a more modest increase of 66%. While the world average MVA was $7.7 trillion, the BRICS' average was $1 trillion. In the subsequent period from 2010 to 2023, the growth rate of MVA slowed significantly. The world's MVA increased by 53% from 2010 to 2023, while BRICS' MVA increased by 108%, above the world average. During this period, China's MVA increased by 142%, India's by 60%, Russia's by 29%, and Brazil's almost stagnated at 3%. South Africa's MVA growth was negative at 16%. The average share of MVA of BRICS countries in the world MVA increased from 12% in the first period to 32% in the second period. The overall trend indicates a deceleration in MVA growth across BRICS countries, reflecting shifts in economic dynamics and varying impacts on their manufacturing sectors. By the way, China continues to be the leading country with the highest share among BRICS countries in MVA, with 80%. Also, China alone will realize almost one-third of the world's MVA, with 4.6 trillion in 2023. This figure reveals that China has become the world's production base.

From 2000 to 2009, most BRICS countries, particularly China and India, experienced significant growth in exports as a % of GDP, aligning with global trends of increasing trade integration. In contrast, Russia saw a marked decline in export dependence. During 2010 to 2023, Brazil and South Africa showed improved export performance, while China and Russia reduced their reliance on exports, with China focusing more on domestic consumption. Overall, global export levels stabilized in the second period, with varied trends across the BRICS countries.

The BRICS countries made significant economic gains from 2000 to 2009, particularly in GDP growth, GDP per capita, and MVA. However, the pace of these gains slowed considerably between 2010 and 2023, especially in Brazil, Russia, and South Africa, reflecting challenges in sustaining high growth rates. China and India continued to drive the economic performance of the BRICS, although even they experienced a deceleration in some areas, particularly in FDI and exports. Despite these slowdowns, the BRICS countries have collectively increased their engagement in global economic activity, although the rate of their global economic integration has moderated in the in subsequent years.

## Implications and Future Directions

The findings from the comparative analysis of the BRICS countries' economic performance have several important implications and suggest future directions for policy and research. The divergent economic trajectories within the BRICS group highlight the need for tailored economic strategies that address each country's unique challenges and opportunities.

For China and India, sustaining high growth rates and economic stability will require continued focus on innovation, infrastructure development, and expanding access to education and skills. These countries must also navigate the challenges of transitioning from export-led growth to more balanced, consumption-driven economies. Additionally, China's significant role in global manufacturing and trade underscores the importance of maintaining strong international trade relationships and managing geopolitical tensions.

Brazil, Russia, and South Africa face different sets of challenges. Brazil's economic volatility suggests a need for structural reforms to diversify its economy beyond commodities and enhance its industrial base. Russia's economy, heavily reliant on energy exports, must also diversify and build resilience against global commodity price fluctuations and geopolitical risks. For South Africa, addressing structural issues such as unemployment, inequality, and infrastructure deficits will be crucial for achieving sustainable economic growth.

The varying trends in FDI inflows among the BRICS countries point to the need for more robust and attractive investment climates. This includes improving regulatory frameworks, ensuring political and economic stability, and investing in human capital to attract and retain foreign investors. China's success in turning around its FDI inflows can serve as a model for other BRICS countries aiming to enhance their investment appeal.

In terms of future directions, there is a clear need for these countries to continue deepening their economic cooperation, both within the BRICS and with other global partners. This could involve expanding trade agreements, increasing joint investments in R&D, technology and infrastructure, and collaborating on sustainable development initiatives.

Research into the specific economic policies and practices that have enabled or hindered growth in these countries could provide valuable insights for policymakers. Further study is also needed on the impact of global trends such as digitalization, climate change, and demographic shifts on the BRICS economies. Understanding these factors will be crucial for developing strategies that ensure sustainable and inclusive growth in the future. While the BRICS countries have made significant strides in economic development, their varied experiences highlight the need for tailored strategies that address specific national contexts. Continued economic cooperation, diversification, and structural reforms will be key to their future growth and stability. As these countries navigate the complex global landscape, they have the potential to significantly influence the future direction of the global economy.

## Final Thoughts

In reflecting on the economic journeys of the BRICS countries over the past two decades, it is evident that each nation has navigated its unique path of growth, challenges, and opportunities. While China and India have emerged as major global economic players with sustained growth and increasing global influence, Brazil, Russia, and South Africa have faced more complex challenges, marked by economic volatility and slower growth trajectories.

The analysis underscores the importance of tailored economic strategies that consider each country's specific circumstances, strengths, and vulnerabilities. For the BRICS as a collective, fostering deeper economic cooperation and addressing structural issues such as diversification, investment attraction, and sustainable development will be crucial in maintaining their growth momentum and global relevance. As these countries continue to evolve and adapt to global economic shifts, their experiences provide valuable lessons for other emerging economies. The future of the BRICS countries will likely hinge on their ability to innovate, reform, and collaborate, both within the group and with the wider world, shaping not only their destinies but also the broader global economic landscape.

## REFERENCES


Abdenur, A. E., & Folly, M. (2015). The New Development Bank and the Institutionalization of the BRICS. *BRICS-Studies and Documents*, 77-111.

Atale, N. (2012). (Forthcoming). A Decade of BRICS: Prospects and Challenges for Next Decade. *Indian Journal of Management.*

Biziwick, M., Cattaneo, N., & Fryer, D. (2015). The Rationale for and Potential Role of the BRICS Contingent Reserve Arrangement. *South African Journal of International Affairs*, 22(3), 307–324. DOI: 10.1080/10220461.2015.1069208

BTTC. (2024). *BRICS Think Tanks Council.* https://bricsthinktankscouncil.org/, Access date: 15/08/2024.

Cooper, A. F. (2016). *The BRICS: A Very Short Introduction* (Vol. 471). Oxford University Press. DOI: 10.1093/actrade/9780198723394.001.0001

Council, B. B. (2024). https://sabricsbusinesscouncil.co.za/working-groups/digital-economy-working-group/#

Gandou, A. S., & Sönmez, A. (2022). The Role of Human Capital in FDI Inflows: A Panel Study on ECOWAS Countries. *Fiscaoeconomia*, 6(3), 1350–1366. DOI: 10.25295/fsecon.1126129

Gusarova, S. (2019). Role of China in the Development of Trade and FDI Cooperation with BRICS Countries. *China Economic Review*, 57, 101271. DOI: 10.1016/j.chieco.2019.01.010

Li, L. (2019). BRICS: A Limited Role in Transforming the World. *Strategic Analysis*, 43(6), 499–508. DOI: 10.1080/09700161.2019.1677017

Naudé, W., Szirmai, A., & Lavopa, A. (2013). Industrialization Lessons from BRICS: A Comparative Analysis.

Naudé, W., Szirmai, A., & Lavopa, A. (2015). Industrialization and Technological Change in the BRICS. *Structural Change and Industrial Development in the BRICS*, 324.

Nistor, P. (2015). FDI Implications on BRICS Economy Growth. *Procedia Economics and Finance*, 32, 981–985. DOI: 10.1016/S2212-5671(15)01557-9

Roberts, C. A., Armijo, L. E., & Katada, S. N. (2018). *The BRICS and Collective Financial Statecraft.* Oxford University Press.

Smeeding, T. M., & Rainwater, L. (2004). Comparing Living Standards across Nations: Real Incomes at the Top, the Bottom, and the Middle. *What Has Happened to the Quality of Life in the Advanced Industrialized Nations*, 153-183.

Sönmez, A. (2018). Foreign Direct Investment Inflows to EME. In Sönmez, A., & Çetin, D. (Eds.), *Issues in Emerging Market Economies* (pp. 259–288). Peter Lang., DOI: 10.3726/b14784

Sönmez, A., & Çetin, D. (2018). Issues in Emerging Market Economies. (eds.) Sönmez, A. & Çetin, D., ISBN 978-3-631-76614-9, Berlin, Peter Lang.

Sönmez, A., & Pamukçu, M. T. (2013). Foreign Direct Investment and Technology Spillovers in the Turkish Manufacturing Industry. In *Industrial Dynamics, Innovation Policy, and Economic Growth through Technological Advancements* (pp. 30–51). IGI Global. DOI: 10.4018/978-1-4666-1978-4.ch003

Uvinha, R. R., de Oliveira, N. R., de Ridder, J. H., Chin, M.-K., & Durstine, J. L. (2018). The BRICS Council for Exercise and Sport Science (BRICSCESS) - A new era has dawned. *Journal of Sport and Health Science*, 7(4), 425–428. DOI: 10.1016/j.jshs.2018.06.004 PMID: 30450250

World Bank. (2024). World Development Indicators (WDI). Accessed date: 18.08.2024. https://databank.worldbank.org/source/world-development-indicators

# Chapter 2
# Member Countries' Level of Commitment to BRICS: Measurements and Propositions

**Helder Ferreira do Vale**
https://orcid.org/0000-0002-4993-7932
*Federal University of Bahia, Brazil*

**Laurisabel Maria de Ana da Silva**
*Federal University of Bahia, Brazil*

**Raianna Morais Soto**
https://orcid.org/0000-0003-3203-6203
*Federal University of Bahia, Brazil*

## ABSTRACT

*The BRICS's countries are not equally committed to the alliance. As the alliance works to influence global norms and dynamics, it has become evident that the original members have diverse goals and interests, resulting in differing levels of commitment to BRICS. The chapter seeks to analyze the level of commitment of the BRICS' countries by measuring four critical variables in each country – socioeconomic well-being, soft power, external vulnerabilities, and capacity to preserve the environment. Once measured, each of these variables are compared across the five original member countries to determine the level of commitment of each country to BRICS. The results indicate that Brazil has a significant level of commitment, followed by China with a moderate-high level. Next in line are India, Russia, and South Africa, all exhibiting a moderate-low level of commitment. These findings demonstrate how the structural and institutional backdrop of each country influences their strategies and dynamics of a budding alliance.*

DOI: 10.4018/979-8-3693-7393-4.ch002

## 1. INTRODUCTION

Several speculations and predictions followed the emergence of Brazil, Russia, India, China, and South Africa (BRICS) as an alliance in the first decade of the 21st century. Its consolidation as a grouping that is shaping the future of the global order is still being questioned (Pant, 2013; Thakur, 2014; Li, 2019). Despite the promises and the economic as well as political relevance of the alliance for the new emerging global order (Iqbal, 2022), significant questions still surround these countries' capacity to collaborate under the BRICS banner.

As an alliance of increasingly influential countries, BRICS is enduring despite the differences among its members. These differences stem from factors including economic wealth, security strategies, domestic political regime type, state capacity and scope of global influence. Trying to understand the way these differences impact the ongoing consolidation of BRICS, this chapter analyzes how asymmetries among the BRICS' members influence the level of commitment of each of its members to the future development of the alliance.[1]

The chapter argues that the BRICS' members have different levels of commitment to the alliance, and that their individual level of commitment is determined to a great extent by domestic structural and institutional factors. Here we measure through selected indicators how specific factors of the BRICS' member countries determine their level of commitment to the alliance. By identifying their level of commitment, we hope to contribute to the scholarship regarding the emerging patterns of international alliances in the 21st century.

Specifically, this analysis is important to understanding the transforming global order for the following reasons. First, the level of commitment to a political group must be better dissected to comprehend what conditions impact the commitment to a political project (e.g., political will, structural capabilities) and the possibility of an effective alignment among participants of such project. Second, the different levels of commitment might determine the political capital each member country invests on the alliance, indicating which members might be more influential in determining the future development of BRICS. Third, understanding the different levels of commitment among members can provide insight into their willingness to overcome disagreements in order to keep alive a promising project. And fourth, in a changing global order, finding patterns of behavior among crucial stakeholders of a nascent alliance is critical for understanding global dynamics.

This research should be interpreted in the context of world order transformations in which there is an absence of a structure in an international system whose interactions historically favored inequality (Donnelly, 2017). Against this background, there are favorable push conditions (e.g., relative accolated growth of emerging economies, economic crisis in advanced economies, new sustainable perspective on development, emergence of new international regimes) for the formation of BRICS as a group that attempts to incorporate new norms in the international system. Although countries within BRICS show little convergence of interest overtime, the internal dynamics of alliances are complex because they develop in multiple dimensions.

Furthermore, BRICS is innovative in an international context marked by an important diffusion of power (Donnelly, 2017). The members of the alliance already took the first initial steps to overcome collective action problems and create a platform to build norms in a multipolar world. This innovation can be interpreted from different perspectives: as being a type of new regionalism (Donnelly, 2006), as part of strategies and trajectories of global status seeking (Do Vale & Costa, 2024), and as being more accommodating to the majority of countries (Larson, 2018).

Considering BRICS as an innovative global alliance that propels changes, this chapter advances a measurement of commitment of BRICS' countries to the alliance under certain assumptions. First, BRICS lacks a set of common concrete goals, and the future orientation is unknown, hence the commitment of member countries varies depending on the issue-areas and country contexts. Second, there is leeway for negotiation among BRICS to determine the shape, extent, and depth of institutionalization of the alliance depending on individual preferences of member countries. And third, the aspirations, choices and obligations of any member country engaging in the BRICS' institutionalization are greatly shaped by their own institutions.

The chapter proceeds as follows. In the next section, the chapter provides an overview of the analysis' framework and delves into the concept of "level of commitment" and its measurement. In the third section, we assess the rationale behind the measures used to determine the level of commitment exhibited by different countries. Also in this section, the propositions that establish the relationship between structural/institutional factors and commitment are explained. In the upcoming section, the chapter turns to the future of the alliance with the analysis of the international context and global issues that affect the alliance. In the concluding section, we provide an overview of the key trends in the evolution of BRICS as a burgeoning coalition of nations, as well as highlight potential areas for future investigation.

## 2. DEFINING LEVEL OF COMMITMENT

Countries might disagree in terms of goals and actions, and the disagreements under certain contexts might lead to rivalry and eventually conflict. The reverse might hold true: agreed goals and actions can lead to an alliance. However, even if countries are part of an alliance, the commitment to it might differ among countries despite shared general objectives. BRICS is a case in point. The alliance over the years has shown a growing heterogeneity of interests among its members (Liu,

2016) and it lacks a coherent strategy being deemed as an "imagined community" (Brütsch & Papa, 2013). Determining the level of commitment of countries in an alliance such as BRICS, which lacks a clear agenda, is pressing particularly knowing that the alliance relies on the willingness and ability of a country to commit to this global initiative.

One of the first attempts to conceptualize commitment in international relations was made by Weinstein (1969) who distinguished between situational and non-situational commitments. Whereas the former is transitory and inherently determined by a specific situation to defend national interest, the latter regards a prolonged position to defend a principle that is not contextual. Also, attempts have been made to correlate democratic regimes and their commitment to an alliance, suggesting that democracies tend to commit to alliances much longer than other countries that embrace other types of political regimes (Gaubatz, 1996).

Commitment is defined here as a country's willingness to engage in a new alliance by adopting strategies that are both contextual and principled based. Due to variations in nations' strategies, motives and preferences in joining an alliance, and the level of commitment to it differs among countries and across time. For a commitment to be enduring, convergence among member countries must increase as the alliance deepens and enlarges. That being applied to BRICS, it is important to understand the level of commitment of member countries to the alliance.

## 2.1 Propositions

It is worth mentioning that in this chapter we understand that the level of commitment (high or low) of a country to BRICS is related to structural and institutional pre-conditions that determine strategies, motives, and preferences of countries. Based on this understanding, this chapter identified four variables —socioeconomic well-being, soft power, external vulnerabilities, capacity to preserve the environment— that indicate a predisposition of a country to commit to BRICS.

It is possible to advance that there is a connection between the variables and the level of commitment, particularly under certain institutional incentives. The institutional linkages identified in the chapter are related to the welfare system, military self-reliance, plurality and veto points in the decision-making process, ability to sustainably mobilize resources, and promotion of global influence.

Theoretically, the connection between domestic institutions and level of commitment lies on the idea of universalization of local norms that is theorized by Amitav Acharya (2011). He ascertains that under the notion of "norm subsidiarity" certain non-Western countries can challenge the dominance of great powers in global norm-making through a "bottom-up" process of norm creation to maintain their autonomy.[2] It is possible to interpret BRICS considering this process of norm subsidiarity and, as such, the alliance is at least creating parallel global structures (Duggan et al., 2022) and even challenging the global power distribution (Chakraborty, 2018).

In this context, the question becomes how a group of heterogenous countries that want to be international norm-makers might influence the development of BRICS. Under the view that each country has a different level of commitment, a more committed member has higher aspirations to use BRICS as a platform for international normative resistance potentializing the possibility to become a rule-maker. Below we present the four propositions.

While BRICS has strong unifying objectives, its members' levels of commitment vary. We present four propositions that provide an explanation about the pathways for member countries' commitment to BRICS. We will elucidate the connection between the variable and the dedication to BRICS.

1. Socioeconomic wellbeing proposition: *A country with a higher level of wellbeing among its inhabitants is more inclined to actively participate in international affairs to sustain and advocate for its welfare model.* This proposition focuses on the linkage between socioeconomic wellbeing and the emergence of a new developmental agenda that the BRICS' members are interested in influencing.

The idea that governments should prioritize wellness is growing and giving salience to objectives of increasing happiness, longevity, trust, and inclusivity. Such idea has reshaped policy priorities to improve welfare systems to guarantee the wellbeing of the population. Countries that prioritize wellbeing are likely to use BRICS to foster an economic agenda that favors economic growth based on a wellbeing economy. This proposition maintains that countries with better wellbeing are more committed to BRICS. The indicators used to measure countries' wellbeing are the Gross Domestic Product (GDP) per capita and the Human Development Index (HDI).

2. Global status proposition: *A country with a stronger soft power status has more opportunities to use BRICS as a platform to promote its desired image and hence increase its commitment to the alliance.* The critical element linking the search for global status and commitment to BRICS is the ability of countries to turn BRICS into a platform for influencing the world through their soft power.

The search for an international status can be partly achieved through the creation of an image of a country that is shaped by its ideas, visions, and culture. This process of creating a country's ideal image to influence the world is about socialization and building a worldwide reputation. BRICS offers the opportunity for countries that accumulated soft power to increase their global status and influence. The way we measure soft power of countries is through the number of times they appear on the top of soft power rankings.

3. External vulnerability proposition: *A country with inferior defensive and offensive capabilities will rely more on BRICS in security cooperation and demonstrate a greater commitment to it.* The central element in this proposition is a country's external vulnerability which determines its military strength and autonomy from international alliances.

Depending on the degree of threats countries face, governments develop stronger military capabilities. As the likelihood of encountering conflicting events remains high or even increases, so does the country's need to be self-reliant in reacting to these occurrences. As countries grow self-reliant in their military defense, they reduce their commitment to an international alliance. External vulnerability in this research is measured by the number of conflictive events countries faced after WWII.

4. Capacity to preserve the environment proposition: *The more capable a country is in preserving its environmental resources, the more likely it is to utilize BRICS as a platform for constructing a global environment regime.* This proposition holds that the relationship between commitment to BRICS derives from a country's ability to manage resources responsibly, providing it a competitive advantage in the evolving global environmental regime.

In a burgeoning global environmental regime, understanding environmental problems and its solutions improves the abilities of countries to protect the environment. Leadership under this regime plays an important role in mitigating global environmental issues (Do Vale, 2020). A country's capacity to contribute to environmental preservation leverages its leadership in the development of the global environmental regime, and BRICS serve as a platform for such a country. The indicators that are selected to measure the capacity of countries to preserve are the percentage of renewable energy over primary energy sources and the percentage of environmentally protected land.

## 2.2 Temporal Frame

The development of BRICS as an alliance started in the first BRICS' summit in 2009. Ever since the summits have become the most important events paving the evolution of the alliance. It is possible to distinguish three phases of BRICS' development considering the three different summits: the 2009 summit, the 2011 summit including South Africa for the first time, and the 2022 summit with Russia already at war with Ukraine. Considering these critical events, it is possible to identify three distinct phases of BRICS' evolution.

The first phase marks the creation of the alliance, which shows the attempt of the four initial members to create a permanent forum for alignment of interests. The second phase starts with the entry of South Africa in BRICS showing that the founding members have a strategic goal of representing the interests of the developing parts of the world. In this phase, the alliance becomes strategic to further approximate interests of the member countries. During the third phase, BRICS countries are under increased pressure to adopt specific positions, particularly considering that one of its members, Russia, is currently engaged in a war and facing international sanctions. Figure 1 summarizes the evolution of BRICS.

Our interpretation of critical events concerning the BRICS' formation has served as a basis for this phasing of the alliance's evolution. Despite the absence of a theoretical foundation concerning the periodization of the evolution of BRICS, this interpretation bears similarities to the methodology employed in Korolev's (2019) framework for examining the Sino-Russian military relationship. He argues that this relationship aims to achieve a "functioning alignment" through a three-stage process. The early stage is characterized as a period of confidence building, which is then followed by the cooperative phase that falls under the moderate stage. At the advanced stage, the partnership between countries allow them to develop common policies.

This framework contributes to our analysis by identifying a step-by-step alignment process that considers varying stages of functionality in nascent alliances. This approach helps us comprehend the evolution of BRICS, which exhibits the following characteristics: an initial stage focused on building trust among its members, a gradual transition towards a moderate stage in which cooperative dynamics are expected to arise, and the eventual attainment of a more advanced stage of common policy in the long term. In other words, the timeline represented in Figure 1 reflects some of the elements of Korolev's framework.

*Figure 1. BRICS' temporal evolution*

| | Initial context | Phase 1 | Phase 2 |
|---|---|---|---|
| Critical Events | ● *2009 First Summit* | ● *2011 Summit of Five Members* (with S.A.) | ● *2022 Summit in China* (with Russia at war) |
| Result | Alignment of interests | Confidence building | Pursuit of common interests |

*(Author's own elaboration)*

## 2.3 Level of Commitment: Results

Table 1 summarizes the findings obtained from measuring the four variables discussed in the next sections. Each variable is assessed on a scale from 1 to 5, representing the following levels of commitment: 1 represents "low", 2 indicates "medium-low", 3 denotes "medium", 4 signifies "medium-high", and 5 corresponds to "high". The overall commitment level of each country presented in Table 1 represents the average of the country's commitment received across the four variables.

Brazil (4.6 average) demonstrates a significant level of commitment to BRICS, with China (3.6 average) closely following suit. Brazil's strong commitment is driven by three factors: its pursuit of global status, its ability to preserve environmental resources, and its low external security vulnerability. Brazil's commitment to BRICS is hindered by its performance in the socioeconomic indicators. China, ranked second, has strong commitment to the alliance primarily due to its ability to demonstrate significant soft power. China's remaining variables are measured as moderate.

Russia (3.1 average) ranks third and demonstrates a high performance in the socioeconomic variable, positioning the country favorably in its commitment to BRICS regarding wellbeing. Furthermore, Russia's global status seeking is notably high, while its commitment in the military-security dimension is very low, given the country's high level of external vulnerability. India (1.6 average) and South Africa (1.7 average) exhibit a comparable level of commitment. Both countries reveal similarities in their performance across various indicators: on one hand, a moderate level of socioeconomic wellbeing, external vulnerability, as well as capacity to preserve resources, and, on the other hand, a low level of global status seeking.

*Table 1. Overall level of commitment of member countries*

| Variable | Indicator | Brazil | China | India | Russia | South Africa |
|---|---|---|---|---|---|---|
| Socioeconomic Wellbeing | GDP per capita, HDI | Medium (3) | Medium (3) | Medium low (2) | High (5) | Medium low (2) |
| External Vulnerability | No. of conflictive events | High (5) | Medium (3) | Low (1) | Low (1) | Medium low (2) |
| Capacity to Preserve Resources | Renewable energy, Land protection | High (5) | Medium (3) | Medium low (1,5) | Medium (2,5) | Medium (2) |

continued on following page

*Table 1. Continued*

| Variable | Indicator | Brazil | China | India | Russia | South Africa |
|---|---|---|---|---|---|---|
| Global Status | Soft power | High (5) | High (5) | Low (2) | Medium high (4) | Low (1) |
| **OVERALL LEVEL OF COMMITMENT (based on average of four variables)** | | **High (4.6)** | **Medium-High (3.6)** | **Medium-Low (1.6)** | **Medium-High (3.1)** | **Medium-Low (1.7)** |

Source: Own elaboration

## 3. MEASUREMENT OF VARIABLES

As explained above, the level of commitment of the BRICS members depends on domestic institutional and structural conditions. To determine the specific level of commitment of each country, we measure here four variables which are associated with specific indicators. The period of measurement follows the temporal evolution of BRICS mentioned above.

### 3.1 Economic Wellbeing

Countries that successfully attain significant economic growth over time often witness corresponding social transformations if the benefits of this growth are distributed among the general population through welfare institutions (Hassell & Palier, 2023). These changes have permanent effects and create a sense of urgency for governments to uphold or enhance the economic welfare of the population (Dostal, 2010). Countries that undergo this transformative socioeconomic process attempt to be more influential in international economic governance (Kutlay & Karaoğuz 2023). As such, the commitment to BRICS depends on the level of influence the alliance offers in terms of impacting the international economy and maintaining their socioeconomic wellbeing.

The notion that countries should focus on wellbeing even to the sacrifice of economic growth has been gaining force and adapts. This notion has become known as "wellbeing economy", which values policies that favor happiness, longevity, trust, inclusiveness, among others (Hayden & Dasilva, 2022). Wellbeing as an indicator for international development is not new. It has been used to redefine policy priorities (Copestake, 2008) and to reassess the basic requirements for a fair and secure place for human development (Custodio et al., 2023).

The increasing importance of wellbeing in societies has brought issues like health to the forefront on an international scale. This presents an opportunity to reshape power dynamics through the development of health policies and health sciences giving rise to the "global health diplomacy" (Kickbusch & Liu, 2022). Wellbeing has indeed become an important asset of countries to engage and transform international governance and politics. Hence, it is possible to suggest that *a country with a higher level of wellbeing among its inhabitants is more inclined to actively participate in international affairs to sustain and advocate for its welfare model.*

To assess the level of commitment based on socioeconomic indicators, we have chosen two fundamental measures of economic development that serve as the foundation for the overall wellbeing of a country's population: wealth, health, and education. Ideally, we would use indicators "beyond GDP" (e.g., happiness) to follow the conceptualization of wellbeing mentioned above (Kubiszewski et al., 2013). However, due to unavailability of information on such indicators across time and countries, we chose more basic indicators related to income and human development, both of which are correlated to happiness (OECD, 2015).

According to the data presented in Table 2, Russia stands out as the most committed member of BRICS due to its comparatively high GDP per capita and HDI. When comparing Russia's average GDP per capita based on 2011 and 2020, it becomes evident that it is nearly twice that of Brazil's and more than doubles the value of other countries. The Russian HDI is significantly higher than that of other countries. Brazil and China demonstrate a considerable level of commitment to BRICS, as evidenced by their respectable performance in terms of GDP per capita and the HDI. India and South Africa exhibit the lowest commitment to the alliance in the wellbeing dimension. This can be attributed to their comparatively lower average GDP per capita and HDI. It is important to highlight that, over time, all countries have made progress in their HDI and GDP per capita, except for Brazil, which experienced a slight decline in per capita income from 2011 to 2020.

*Table 2. Socioeconomic wellbeing*

| | GDP per capita (thousands of USD) | | | Human Development Index | | | |
|---|---|---|---|---|---|---|---|
| | **2011** | **2020** | **Average** | **2011** | **2020** | **Average** | **Level of commitment** |
| **Brazil** | 15,3 | 14 | 14,6 Medium low | 0,72 | 0,76 | 0,74 Medium high | **3,5 Medium** |
| **China** | 9,7 | 16,3 | 13 Medium low | 0,69 | 0,76 | 0,72 Medium high | **3,5 Medium** |
| **India** | 8,6 | 11,5 | 10,0 Medium low | 0,57 | 0,64 | 0,6 Medium | **2,5 Medium Low** |
| **Russia** | 25 | 26,6 | 25,8 High | 0,79 | 0,83 | 0,81 High | **5 High** |
| **South Africa** | 13,7 | 12,8 | 13,2 Medium low | 0,67 | 0,72 | 0,69 Medium | **2,5 Medium Low** |

Source: Own elaboration based on Nguyen & Khominich (2023)

Scale: GDP per capita: High (above 20,000 USD), Medium high (15,000-20,000 USD), Medium (15,000-19,999 USD), Medium low (10,000-14,999 USD), Low (below 10,000 USD). HDI: High (above 0,8), Medium high (0,7-0,79), Medium (0,6-0,69), Medium low (0,5-0,59), Low (below 0,5)

## 3.2 Global Status

The quest for global influence depends on the power of a country to influence others without the employment of coercion (Nye, 1990). And influence without coercive power has been built on the ability to develop an image of a country through the promotion of culture and values (Rabêlo Neto et al., 2020). The image of a country is a category of power that, although it often draws on pre-existing conditions and factors (e.g., military, economic capabilities), relies on soft power.

Soft power reflects a conscientious attempt to build an image based on ideals and visions of the world. This process of carefully building a country's "ideal" image often accrues in a global status. As a process of socialization in which the perception of other countries matter, building alliances contributes to the augmentation of the international status of a country (Gallarotti, 2017), to the point where there is a possibility of creating a "compound soft power" (Gallarotti, 2016).[3] As such, *a country with a stronger soft power status has a larger opportunity to use BRICS as a platform to promote its desired image and hence increase its commitment to the alliance.*

There are problems in interpreting the use of soft power in the current global context. Some of these problems come from the different sources of soft power development, and the execution of soft power in practice (Chatin & Gallarotti 2016).

In addition to these problems, which impact measurement of soft power, there is the issue of benchmarking soft power through ranking of countries based on indexes.

Although it is useful to measure the capacity to be influential in the world, the indexes of soft power have considerable bias given their heavily reliance on western sources (Zhang & Ruiqin, 2019). Notwithstanding the issues regarding sources, standards, and approaches in developing soft power ranks, they provide a general picture of nations in the global scene to assess their "soft" influence. With this goal, four different indexes, namely the Brand Finance's Global Soft Power, Monocle's Soft Power Survey, and the Portland's Soft Power 30 were used to assist us.

Given that the BRICS countries, except for China, do not appear systematically in the yearly soft power indexes, we decided to disregard the ranking of the countries in the indexes. Instead, we consider the appearance of the country in the index, if the country is in the top 30 positions of a rank. Provided that the different indexes were created and ended in different years, it is difficult to systematize the appearance of countries synchronically across all the indexes, and as such we considered the appearance of the country in their first and last publicly available index on Table 3, the appearance of countries in the indexes is identified with a "1" and their non-appearance with a "0".

Table 3 shows that Brazil and China appeared five times in these indexes, followed by Russia, with four appearances. India and South Africa have respectively two and one appearances. According to this reasoning, Brazil and China have a greater potential to exercise soft power than the rest of the countries. Translating this result into the level of commitment to BRICS, it is likely that Brazil's and China's engagement in the alliance might be aimed at using it as a platform for further augmentation of soft power, whereas the laggards, namely, South Africa and India, are least likely to use BRICS for such purpose.

*Table 3. Country's presence in a soft power index*

| | Brand Index | | Monocle Index | | Portland Index | | Total Score | Level of Commitment |
|---|---|---|---|---|---|---|---|---|
| | 2019 | 2024 | 2011 | 2023 | 2015 | 2019 | | |
| Brazil | 1 | 0 | 1 | 1 | 1 | 1 | 5 | **5 High** |
| China | 1 | 1 | 1 | 1 | 1 | 1 | 5 | **5 High** |
| India | 1 | 1 | 0 | 0 | 0 | 0 | 2 | **2 Low** |

continued on following page

*Table 3. Continued*

| | Brand Index | | Monocle Index | | Portland Index | | Total Score | Level of Commitment |
|---|---|---|---|---|---|---|---|---|
| | 2019 | 2024 | 2011 | 2023 | 2015 | 2019 | | |
| Russia | 1 | 1 | 1 | 0 | 0 | 1 | 4 | **4**<br>**Medium High** |
| South Africa | 0 | 0 | 1 | 0 | 0 | 0 | 1 | **1**<br>**Low** |

Source: Brand Finance's Global Soft Power, Monocle's Soft Power Survey, and the Portland's Soft Power 30.

Scale: High soft power (score 5); Intermediate soft power (score 2-4); Low soft power (score 0-1).

## 3.3 External Vulnerabilities

Geopolitics, international order challenges as well as economic and environmental crises matter for security strategies. Often countries that are in complex geopolitical contexts find greater incentives to develop military, intelligence, and institutional capacity (Gennaioli & Voth, 2015). In effect, countries face different levels of security risks requiring different capability to manage external challenges.

We identified four main categories of events that represent geopolitical risks for countries: wars, international territorial conflict, domestic territorial conflict, and protection of commons.[4] Depending on the level of risk countries face, they develop more defensive and offensive capacities. With higher possibility of facing conflictive events, the greater the desire of the country to be self-reliant in responding to these events.[5] As such, a country with inferior defensive and offensive capabilities will depend more on BRICS and demonstrate a greater commitment to it. Put differently, *the higher the defensive and offensive capacity of a country, the less reliant it will be on BRICS.*

This mechanism of self-reliance is consistent with the notion that military-strong countries do not necessarily desire to be entangled in conflicts with allied weaker countries.[6] In other words, asymmetry of capability might prevent strong countries militarily to commit to alliances. However, BRICS is not a military alliance, which in principle does not represent an impediment to develop collective security priorities and interests as a group (Ramos et al., 2021).

Another particularity of BRICS is the existence of conflict between members of the alliance. An example of this is the border conflict between China and India, which has escalated since India joined the Quadrilateral Security Dialogue, also known as the Quad, a group that includes the United States and was established in 2007 prior to the BRICS' inaugural meeting (Brethouwer et al., 2022). Despite the

Sino-Indian conflict, both countries seem to be inclined to reach a political solution instead of a military one (Brethouwer et al., 2022, p. 16).

Military cooperation is not in the agenda of the BRICS. However, despite the lack of interest from China, India, and Russia to partake in any military cooperation within the alliance, Brazil and South Africa have shown interest in greater cooperation (Han & Papa, 2022; Williams & Papa, 2020). China, Russia, and India seem to have deeper concerns regarding the involvement of the West in conflicts that they have a stake. Particularly, the United States' meddling in Asia with its military superiority together with its discourse of universalization of human rights and its capacity to create political play are of concern to certain BRICS countries (Troitskiy, 2015, p. 78).

Coordination among BRICS for joint political actions exists since its first meeting, in 2008 (Apolinário Júnior & Branco, 2022). Although there are no joint declarations on security issues, BRICS countries have shown signs of coordination in the area. One example is the statements that highlight the significance of state sovereignty and territorial integrity of countries. In this regard, 2011, the year in which all members were in the UN Security Council, they embraced similar positions in the Council's resolutions regarding interventions, imposition of economic sanctions and the containment of the United States (Apolinário Júnior & Branco, 2022, pp. 9-10).

In terms of security partnership formed within BRICS, they have been more noticeable between Brazil and South Africa. South Africa's position has important ambiguities provided that the country does not have a consolidated position among the African regional alliances and is vulnerable to transnational networks of crime and violence (Shaw, 2014). Furthermore, South Africa's position is perceived as uncertain, among other reasons because the implementation of the security agenda is unstable and there are domestic calls for revision (Esterhuyse, 2021). Brazil's position, previously viewed as a middle-power with no international security ambitions, has shifted toward embracing a security agenda through a strategy known as "development-security alliance formation," under which Brazil eventually expands cooperation in security matters while deepening a developmental agenda (Ham & Papa, 2022). This has happened precisely with South Africa, with which Brazil has a maritime and an anti-terrorism cooperation agreement. Yet, under their respective right-wing governments, Brazil and India became closer as the USA granted Brazil in 2019 the status of "major non-NATO" ally (Do Vale, 2019).

The relationship among BRICS nuclear powers, namely, China, India and Russia, is complex considering the strategically multilayered security dynamics of the three most important military powers outside the West. For this very reason, security cooperation among these three countries is weak and present considerable challenges (Hsiung, 2019). Since 1998 Russia has attempted to create an active strategic triangular dynamic between the three powers (Pant, 2004), however it was not very successful due to important asymmetries and persistent geopolitical tensions among them. A prosperous bilateral relation between China and Russia has been viable above all because it is a partnership of convenience (Mishra & Louis, 2024). Also, this same partnership can be interpreted as a gradual alliance based on confidence building with potential for advancements and reversals (Korolev, 2019). It is evident that any actions taken by one of these three countries, both within and outside of BRICS, have an impact on the security agenda of each other and the remaining BRICS members.

To assess the level of commitment from a security perspective, we developed our own notion of external vulnerability based on four criteria. The first criterion is involvement of a country in a full-blown war in the current and past century (after WWII), which is interpreted as an event that requires the extensive use of military capacity against another country. The second criterion is the existence of an international border dispute, which indicates that a country has a contention with neighbors over territorial control that can lead to an armed conflict. Another type of territorial conflict considered is the one confined to domestic borders in which a country is facing a systematic threat of separatism from groups claiming territorial self-determination. The last criterion is the protection of commons, which relates to the challenge to protect an international common good such as forests, rivers, oceans, and other natural goods, that are within national borders. Given the unique nature of common goods such as their exhaustibility and non-excludability, there is an international pressure for the country to preserve such good, which culminate in discursive threats of its internationalization.[7]

Based on these criteria, we determined the external vulnerability score of each country. The result is presented in Table 4, where it is possible to observe that Brazil has low levels of external vulnerability, while India and South Africa have intermediate levels of vulnerability. China and Russia present high levels of external vulnerability, given their particularly high number of events related to international border disputes and to domestic territorial conflict. That said, high levels of external vulnerability generate a high capacity of self-reliance of countries in security matters, thus a low dependence on international alliances. As such, China and Russia have low levels of commitment to the BRICS in the security realm, while Brazil has high levels of commitment to the BRICS, followed by South Africa and India with lower levels of commitment.

*Table 4. External vulnerabilities*

| | **Full-Blown War** | | **International border dispute** | | **Domestic Territorial Conflict** | | **Protection of Commons** | | **Total average score** |
|---|---|---|---|---|---|---|---|---|---|
| | *Events* | *Score* | *Events* | *Score* | *Events* | *Score* | *Events* | *Score* | |
| **Brazil** | No record | 0 | No record | 0 | No record | 0 | The Amazon | 1 | *Low (1)* |
| **China** | No record | 0 | India: a conflict dating back to the mid-20th century with the following events in the last two decades:<br><br>2013: Border Defense Agreement to establish peace and tranquility after the deadlock in Depsang. | 1 | Hong Kong (since 2016) Taiwan (intensification since 2019) | 2 | Cooperation efforts in cybersecurity and conservation technologies | 0 | *Medium (3)* |
| **India** | No record | 0 | China<br><br>2007: India's entry into the Quad<br><br>2012: establishment of a working group for consultation and coordination on border issues between India and China along the Current Line of Control. (LAC)<br><br>2014: Chinese incursion in Chumur<br><br>2017: stalemate in Doklam<br><br>2020: deadlock in the Galwan River Valley | 5 | Pakistan (since the mid-20th century, with more intense border events between 2011 and 2021)<br><br>Bangladesh (permanent tensions since 2001)<br><br>Nepal (dispute over the Kalapani territory since 1950) | 3 | Cooperation efforts in cybersecurity and conservation technologies | 0 | *High (5)* |

continued on following page

*Table 4. Continued*

| | Full-Blown War | | International border dispute | | Domestic Territorial Conflict | | Protection of Commons | | Total average score |
|---|---|---|---|---|---|---|---|---|---|
| | *Events* | *Score* | *Events* | *Score* | *Events* | *Score* | *Events* | *Score* | |
| **Russia** | Ukraine 2022 (intensification of bombings across Ukrainian territory). | 1 | Ukraine (since 2014)<br><br>Georgia (2008, with occasional tensions)<br><br>Poland (intensification of tensions following the invasion of Ukraine in 2022) | 3 | Caucasus (territorial claims by Russia since the late 1990s, with intensifications during the 2000s)<br><br>Chechnya (recognition of Russia's "temporary occupation" of the Chechen Republic of Ichkeria by Ukraine in 2022) | 2 | Siberia | 0 | *High (5)* |
| **South Africa** | No active conflict, however, the invasion of Rhodesia (now Zimbabwe) and Angola was considered between 1964 and 1979. | 2 | No record | 0 | No record | 0 | Cooperation efforts in cybersecurity and conservation technologies | 0 | *Medium (2)* |

Source: Own elaboration

Scale: From 0 to 1 event: Low (1 score), From 2 to 4 events: Medium (2-4 score), 5 and above: High (5 score)

Full blown war: Number of wars in the past 50 years. Categorize war: offensive, defensive, proxy-war. International border dispute: Number of border disputes in the past 50 years that lead to "frozen conflicts" (associate with deterrence). Domestic territorial conflict: Number of active self-determination (search for international sovereignty) movements in the past 50 years. Protection of commons: Number of commons that are of interest of the international community to preserve the global environment.

## 3.4 Capacity to Preserve Resources

The capacity of states to efficiently mobilize and allocate human as well as natural resources was once associated with high potential for economic growth and development. This transformative capacity was linked to positive changes in social and economic contexts. This parameter has changed with the rise of a global environmental regime, which demands greater state capacity to responsibly use natural resources in the move towards sustainability transformations (Patterson, 2017). In a rising global environmental regime, knowledge of environmental problems enhances the ability of countries to preserve the environment (Breitmeier et al., 2011).

The ability to influence and lead the international environmental regime has become an important issue in global politics. There are many roads to influence a complex regime such as the environmental one (Bernstein & Cashore, 2012), including the development of domestic capacities (e.g., policy making, development of networks, fostering civil society organization) for environmental preservation. The exercise of leadership in this regime will be influential in solving problems such as the reduction of carbon monoxide and the adoption of other sustainable recourses and measures. That said, a country's ability to contribute to environmental preservation provides leverage for a leadership in building the global environmental regime. As such, *the greater the capacity to preserve, the higher the probability of a country's commitment to BRICS as a platform for global environment regime building*.

While BRICS has not acted collectively in the global environmental regime (Davenport, 2012), it comprises relevant countries in the shaping of such regime. To achieve this objective, challenges such as Russia's obstinate position in not accommodating environmental concerns to its development model and is not addressing environmental preservation (Rinaldi & Martuscelli, 2016). It is also important to highlight differences among the BRICS countries regarding gas emission targets, for example. There are common incentives for BRICS to adopt a common position provided that they have an untapped potential to develop renewable energy sources, which can be enhanced through green financing (Udeagha & Ngepah, 2023).

Nonetheless, it is worth highlighting that the exercise of leadership in the global environmental regime is difficult to attain. The leadership in this regime has been irregular as potential leaders depending on the moment and the issue might be a pusher or a laggard (Andresen & Agrawala, 2002). Brazil serves as a prime example of how political shifts in the country significantly impacted its domestic and international policies in several aspects of environmental conservation (Viola & Korber, 2019).

Brazil is an example of a leading performance, as shown in Table 5, in the protection of the environment followed by China. Based on the share of renewable energy over the total primary energy (e.g., nuclear energy, fossil energy), and the area of protected land, Brazil demonstrates a remarkable ability to preserve resources, particularly in its advancements in renewable energy sources. This commitment positions the country as a strong advocate within and with BRICS platform, with a great possibility to influence the global environmental regime. China ranks second in terms of land protection indicators, demonstrating a strong performance. Russia shows a moderate level of land protection, however, its contribution to renewable energy remains significantly low. South Africa and India have demonstrated a lack of commitment to BRICS, as they lag in their capacity to protect natural resources.

*Table 5. Capacity to preserve*

| | Share of renewable energy (%) | | | Land protection (%) | | | |
|---|---|---|---|---|---|---|---|
| | **2011** | **2020** | **Average** | **2011** | **2020** | **Average** | **Level of commitment** |
| Brazil | 43,9 | 49,5 | 46,7<br>High | 28,9 | 30,3 | 29,6<br>High | **5**<br>**High** |
| China | 7,08 | 14,2 | 10,64<br>Medium low | 17,1 | 15,6 | 16,35<br>Medium high | **3**<br>**Medium** |
| India | 7,5 | 9,7 | 8,6<br>Low | 6 | 7,5 | 6,75<br>Medium low | **1,5**<br>**Medium**<br>**Low** |
| Russia | 5,58 | 7,1 | 6,34<br>Low | 9,7 | 11,5 | 10,6<br>Medium high | **2,5**<br>**Medium** |
| South Africa | 0,69 | 3,2 | 1,94<br>Low | 14,1 | 8,7 | 11,4<br>Medium | **2**<br>**Medium**<br>**Low** |

Source: Nguyen & Khominich (2023)

Land protection: High (above 20%), Medium high (15-19%), Medium (10-14%), Medium low (5-9%), Low (below 5%).

Share of renewable energy: High (above 40%), Medium high (30-39%), Medium (20-29%), Medium low (10-19%), Low (below 10%).

## 4. DISCUSSIONS

The analysis is guided by critical observations about BRICS. The first observation is that the alliance has little decision rules, which could potentially increase friction between its members. Second, the alliance had a limited number of member countries prior to the 2023 expansion. This suggests that the transaction costs involved in decision making were relatively low. And third, there is a preference heterogeneity within the alliance provided that member countries have different agenda concerning topics relevant for global governance.

Given the limited decision rules within BRICS, it can be inferred that the alliance has minimal impact on the behavior and actions of member countries. As a default, the dynamics among the members of BRICS are of great importance, as they have the potential to shape the formation of the alliance and influence the actions of individual members even beyond the alliance. The contrary also holds true: there is a possibility that individual members have a great influence over the alliance.

Concerning preference heterogeneity, whenever it is high, there is a likelihood that members of the alliance employ soft mechanisms to resolve frictions (Zhelyazkova et al.,2023). These reflections provide an opportunity to discuss, based on the level of commitment, how heterogeneity of preferences and absence of decision rules within BRICS allow member countries to exert influence over the alliance.

Figure 2 shows that three countries —Brazil, China and Russia— lead at least one dimension established here as determinant for the level of commitment. In principle, while Brazil shows a high commitment to BRICS, a behavior pushed by its low external vulnerability and high capacity to preserve, Russia leads the socioeconomic wellbeing dimension. China does not exhibit isolated leadership in any dimension, as it consistently shares its position of having moderate levels of commitment with another member country. The high commitment of these countries allows us to assess the validity of the propositions and make further conclusions by examining these three countries and their potential to influence BRICS.

*Figure 2. Overall level of commitment of countries to BRICS in four dimensions*

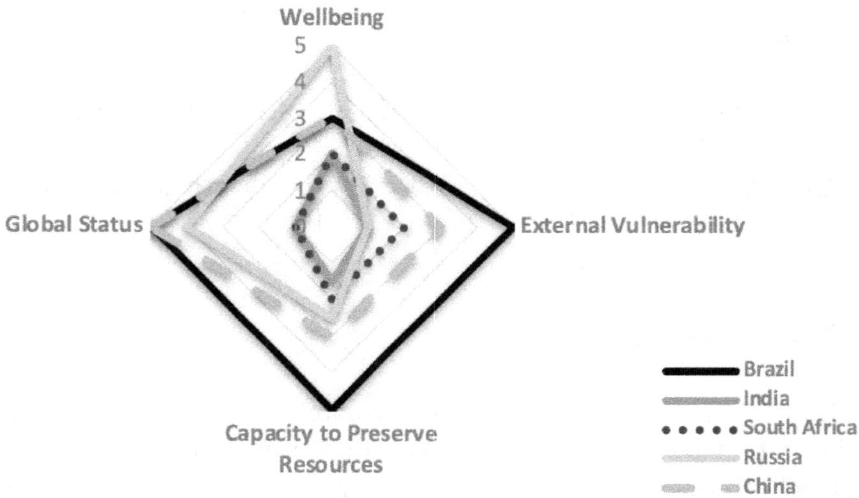


*(Author's own elaboration)*

Our first proposition on socioeconomic wellbeing puts Russia in the limelight. The country has a relatively high GDP per capita and HDI for two main reasons. Russia's abundant natural resources, especially in gas and crude oil, allows the country to maintain high exports (Yang et al., 2021). While the reliance on natural resources for GDP growth does not mean that the GDP distribution is equitable, it also suggests that the premise of wellbeing economy might not hold true in Russia as the country frequently prioritizes economic expansion over environmental sustainability. Also, it is possible to suggest that Russia's high HDI comes in part from the cumulative high investment in human development inherited from its Soviet past (Pichon & Russell, 2022). In other words, these indicators don't reflect in an active Russian promotion of any particular welfare model based on new approaches to economic growth and wellbeing. As such, Russia's commitment to BRICS based on social economic wellbeing is weak in practice. Differently, socioeconomic well-being in Brazil and China has significantly increased over the past decades. These countries have shown to be more willing to accept redistributive welfare models even in their context of high inequality (Ravallion, 2011).

In India, while socioeconomic wellbeing has enhanced over the past decade, poverty, inequality, and infrastructure deficiencies persist revealing a rural-urban divide and the influence of the caste system (Kulkarni et al., 2023). The standard of public health and nutrition is deficient due to difficult access to public health services and facilities (Antony & Laxmaiah, 2008). South Africa confronts substantial socioeconomic problems such as deep economic inequalities, which reduced in the post-apartheid governments, but new spheres of inequality emerged, specifically, intra-race (McKeever, 2024) and territorial inequalities (Do Vale & Cameron, 2018). The high unemployment rates, particularly among teenagers, constitute an important socioeconomic issue that hinders progress in socioeconomic indicators. Access to education and healthcare is inequitable and contributes substantially to the unemployment issue.

In the second proposition Brazil and China are ahead of the other countries regarding the use of BRICS to promote peaceful coexistence based on the selected indicators of external vulnerability. However, China has a far greater potential than Brazil, provided that the country systematically appears in all rankings measuring soft power, while Brazil doesn't. China's soft power is growing; nonetheless, it is constrained by geopolitical conflicts and human rights concerns. In fact, one of China's aims in the promotion of its soft power is to dilute the idea of "China threat" (Chen & Chang, 2013, 18). The country takes strategic actions to increase its soft powers by adopting a diplomatic strategy of investing in multilateralism and increasing economic cooperation (Liu & Tsai, 2014). Furthermore, the proliferation of Confucius Institutes internationally might be viewed as an endeavor to enhance China's cultural ties globally (Sun, 2023). Brazil's soft power is not just weaker but also lacks a sustainable plan of expansion and promotion. Brazil's diplomatic approach of enhancing soft power is primarily centered on fostering a discourse of consensus about the nation's ambitions (e.g., to enter the UN Security Council) (Valença & Carvalho, 2014). However, certain aspirations cannot be simply realized through discourse (Amorin, 2013). Given Brazil's and China's aspirations, diplomatic initiatives, and actions, it is conceivable that both countries might push BRICS to evolve into an effective platform for the dissemination of soft power.

Russia's soft power is significant in some places (e.g., former Soviet states), however constrained by its fragile relations with Western countries and in its near abroad with the rise of anti-Russian sentiment. Russia has several potential sources of soft power – literature, music, ballet, cinema, and education. However, since Vladmir Putin said in 2012 that Russian foreign policy will be led by soft power, it has only remained so in the discourse, as Russia has not hesitated to use its hard power. Russia's approach to soft power has been deemed pragmatic since it has been predicated on the spread of its influence in "Russia World" (Sergunin & Karabeshkin, 2015), which may be defined as the former Soviet states where Russians account for a large proportion of the population. In addition to pragmatism, other limitations for Russian exercise of soft power are the legacies of the Soviet Union that develops pre-existing negative image, a lack of strategic vision in foreign policy in the transition to a market economy and the preponderance of hard power in its conflicts (Rutland & Kazantsev, 2016). In short, Russia is not committed to BRICS under the premises of peaceful coexistence with its persistent use of military power.

India and South Africa despite their more limited capacity to use soft power clearly abide to the doctrine of peaceful coexistence. India's soft power is anchored in its rich cultural heritage, diaspora, and democratic principles, conferring the country considerable global influence. The Indian film industry is undoubtedly a primary promoter of the country. Indian persistent democratic tradition since the 1940s bolster the images of the country as the largest democracy in the world. However, these traits have not been translated into practical gains from India, which fell short in creating a positive image regionally and in the West (Mukherjee, 2014).

South Africa's soft power mostly stems from its cultural heritage, being home of eleven official languages. The country's struggle to dismantle the apartheid regime and transit to democracy under Nelson Mandela has endowed it with considerable worldwide soft power. This potential to use soft power has been considered as a mechanism for the consolidation of South Africa's contested leadership in Africa (Ogunnubi & Okeke-Uzodike, 2015). Nonetheless, South Africa faces challenges in practice to exercise this soft power potential mainly due to South African regional leadership ambivalence (Ogunnubi & Amao, 2016), although the country has great potential for soft balancing within BRICS (Tella, 2017).

The third proposition suggests that a country that experience low external vulnerability is more committed to BRICS. Brazil ranks high in terms of commitment based on its low external vulnerability, followed by China. This means that Brazil has a commitment to rely on BRICS as a diplomatic bloc that would be enough to meet its military ambitions, which is reliant on cooperation with members of the alliance. As a diplomatic alliance with no security agenda, BRICS as a forum for security cooperation is coherent with Brazil's security vision as a promoter of global peace favoring diplomatic solutions over military conflict. Resonating this Brazilian historical position in diplomatic conflicts, Brazil has been seen as a peace mediator with some potential to be more influential in high-stake conflicts (Buarque & Ribeiro, 2023). Furthermore, in contrast to other BRICS' countries, notably Russia, Brazil has been a country that defends innovative solutions and ideas in a changing world based upholding the principles of multilateralism and non-intervention (Kotyashko et al., 2018).

Although China's external vulnerability is minimal it has the biggest standing army in the world. Its foreign policy based on transformation of the current world order aimed at greater autonomy makes the country potentially more susceptible to conflicts, especially in the Asia-Pacific area. However, it is possible to interpret, despite its military mighty, China's foreign policy as that of building a harmonious world order, yet with pragmatism (Chih-yu & Jiwu, 2013). Just like Brazil, China is a defender of "non-interference", this has been one of the cornerstones of Chinese promotion of peace and stability abroad (Campbell et al, 2012, p. 10). Yet China's growing confidence and assertiveness has been raising suspicion among Southeast Asian countries as the country shows signs of employing its coercive military power (Baviera, 2016). Given this scenario in which China has not used its offensive capacity and has been a history of foreign aggression, it is possible to interpret Chinese military power as that associated with deterrence as means to achieve its goals (Cheng, 2021). All considered, both Brazil and China with low external security vulnerability have embraced an approach to their international role as promoters of peace, which is compatible with a commitment to transform BRICS as a diplomatic bloc that can enhance their approach.

The remaining countries, particularly Russia, which is the least likely to use BRICS as a diplomatic bloc for security purposes, is the least committed to the bloc considering this dimension. In effect, unlike other BRICS' members, Russia external security vulnerability significantly escalated during the past decade. Its invasion of Ukraine in 2022, following its the annexation of Crimea in 2014, created the biggest military conflict in Europe since WWII. In stark contrast with the position of non-intervention of the other BRICS' countries, Russia has been demonstrating readiness to employ force to preserve influence and safeguard national interests. Its direct involvement in Syria is also a case in point.

India's military external vulnerability has been greatly influenced by its intricate relationships with China and Pakistan. Despite being a nuclear power for deterrence, India embraces a conciliatory approach to its multiple levels of security (Singh, 2004). Alongside these defining conflicts for India, the country faces internal insurgencies in the northeastern states and Maoist insurgencies, as well as internationally sponsored terrorism (Simon, 2022). In terms of military capability, South Africa possesses one of the most sophisticated armed forces on the African continent, mostly oriented to peacekeeping operations (Garcia, 2018), but also to domestic security issues, such as crime and violence (Montesh & Basdeo, 2012).

As for the last proposition on the preservation of environmental resources, Brazil presents a high level of commitment to BRICS through its capacity to preserve natural resources. Brazil's safeguard of environmental resources becomes evident through its efforts to promote alternative renewable energy and land protection. By strengthening policies that are essential for sustaining and improving environmental worldwide, Brazil is a natural candidate to play a leadership role in the evolving global environmental governance. But this leadership could encounter major hurdles considering the resistance of certain elite groups and sectors of the population in implementing more ambitious policies on environmental preservations (Pereira & Viola, 2022). One could contend that Brazil seeks to take a leadership role in the global food regime, which, while not necessarily at odds with the environmental regime, emphasizes the production and consumption of food driven by market objectives (Do Vale, 2018). In effect, Brazil despite being ahead of its peers in conservation, it has adopted a moderately conservative position in the international climate governance (Basso, 2019). That said, Brazil is in a privileged position to be among the leaders of an international environmental regime and utilize BRICS as another platform to play such a role, however it is not clear how this role will be played within BRICS.

China's conversation capacity does not equal that of Brazil. However, China's willingness to influence the international environmental regime seems to be far greater. China shows willingness to take more responsibility in this regime as part of its transforming identity of being at the center of a world stage portraying the country as an "ecological civilization" (Yang, 2022). For China, the conservation of natural resources is a significant concern as the country grapples with pollution, water scarcity, and climate change. By embracing a prominent position in renewable energy, China's global leadership can come in the form of facilitator of building an international climate governance system through climate financing, technology transfers, alternative renewable energy, and transformation of infrastructure (Qi & Dauvergne, 2022).

As for the remaining countries, despite Russia's important potential to participate in the international regime with its hydropower and nuclear energy, its government has been slow in adaptating to renewable energy sources. Part of Russia's neglect of environmental problems comes from the political utilization of environmental issues in Vladmir Putin's environmental politics (Martus, 2021) and the weak environmental governance in Russia among different stakeholders (Crotty & Ljubownikow, 2022). Clearly, Russia is in a weak position to participate in the global environmental regime together with Brazil and China.

South Africa and India, as vulnerable countries to climate change, have interest in the effective creation of global environmental regime. South Africa is significantly susceptible to the effects of climate change, and its substantial dependence on coal hinders the shift to cleaner energy alternatives (Smarte Anekwe et al., 20224). The South African government has invested in renewable energy initiatives; nonetheless, the magnitude of expenditure is insufficient to alleviate climate problems (WWF, 2012). Furthermore, the country faces water scarcity and climate change has intensified drought conditions. India's status as a global leader in renewable energy programs is mainly exercised through the important role of public-private partnership (Kurmar & Majid, 2020). However, access to potable water continues to be a significant concern for the country, requiring considerable investment efforts from the public sector. Yet, initiatives such as the Jal Jeevan Mission seek to ensure access to potable water to rural inhabitants.

In conclusion, Brazil, China, and Russia are positioned as the most capable countries of transforming the BRICS having as a parameter their level of commitment to the alliance. However, these countries reveal uncontroversial heterogeneity in their preferences regarding various dimensions of the issues at hand. Despite the differences, Brazil and China's high level of commitment seems to favor the emergence of critical synergies within BRICS. Russia's menu of preferences doesn't coincide with Brazil and China, and as such, there are indications that the nature of its commitment to BRICS is different. India and South Africa, although signaling low performance in some indicators, show a credible commitment to peaceful coexistence, use of soft power to solve conflict and create initiatives to improve the wellbeing of their population.

## 5. BEYOND BRICS'S LEVEL OF COMMITMENT

The level of commitment is crucial for the future of BRICS; however, other factors, such as the international context, the alliance's new initiatives, and global issues, are also essential to consider as they influence the future of the alliance. We provide below an overview of these various factors and their potential impact on the commitment levels and collaboration among the alliance's members.

### 5.1 BRICS's Collaboration and Expansion

The COVID pandemic has exposed the need for a new global power dynamics in which collaboration is essential in high-risk circumstances. The BRICS' countries might utilize their combined influence to promote mechanisms for new forms of collaboration and expansion of global innovation in areas that proved to be critical during the pandemic, namely, health, infrastructure, and global technology.

By prioritizing infrastructure investment, public-private health partnership, and global technology, BRICS is positioning itself as a leader in the recovery process. The efficacy of these measures will hinge on their capacity to manage internal disparities and portray a cohesive stance in promoting their collective interests internationally.

Weaknesses in the international supply chains were expensed during the pandemic, and as such BRICS is expected to foster intra-group trade and investment to bolster economic stability and diminish dependence on Western markets. In this direction, the BRICS' members acknowledge the necessity of significant investment in infrastructure to promote economic growth. The New Development Bank (NDB) is crucial in funding initiatives that generate employment and bolster economic resilience provided that NDB's fundings are focused on "infrastructure sustainability" (Costa Vazquez, 2020).

The BRICS' countries are striving for self-sufficiency in healthcare through the production and distribution of vaccines and pharmaceuticals. Prior to the COVID pandemic, initiatives aimed at this objective had already been implemented. However, the pandemic prompted BRICS to establish mechanisms for enhanced collaboration in vaccine and pharmaceutical technology, notably through the establishment of the BRICS Vaccine Research and Development (R&D) Center (Zhang et al., 2023). The BRICS' countries are undergoing significant transformations in their health systems, primarily influenced by increasing health expenditures attributed to private sector initiatives (Sahoo et al., 2023). Investment in healthcare infrastructure and systems is essential for reinforcing BRICS in the post-pandemic context; however, the capacity for public investment remains constrained (Sahoo et al., 2023).

As the post-pandemic context for collaboration among the BRICS' members becomes increasingly desirable, it may offer a foundation for joint responses. Despite the desire for increasing collaboration, BRICS is undergoing new changes such the acceptance of new members in 2023 that could also jeopardize the level of commitment of countries to the expanded alliance, BRICS+. Although BRICS+ has been viewed with some optimism (Kamin & Langhammer, 2024), the level of commitment of member countries in the expanded version of BRICS might change because of the increase of heterogeneity of interests and fragmentation within the alliance. This change could possibly reduce the ability of any single member to influence the alliance. This affects particularly Brazil and India, which may have difficulties in reconciling their interests with those of the new members.

India's geopolitical rivalry with China may hinder Indian engagement within BRICS+, especially as China's influence expands with the inclusion of new members (Do Vale, 2023). As for Brazil, the BRICS+, which mainly includes autocratic countries, might hinder the engagement of the country in the expanded alliance, after all the Brazilian foreign policy is influenced by democratic, multilateral, and human rights values in international politics. It is worth mentioning that before its expansion, BRICS seemed to have a potential to shape global democratic politics through the coordinated influence of Brazil, India and South Africa (Öniş & Gençer, 2018).

An alternative for Brazil and India is to deepen collaboration with the alliance in order to explore new opportunities within BRICS+ and take joint actions to counterbalance China's influence within the alliance. By presenting a cohesive stance, they may champion improvements within BRICS+ as representatives of the interests of weaker developing nations. Another alternative for Brazil and India is to manage their influence in conjunction with larger economies such as China, which might potentially diminish their voices in decision-making processes.

## 5.2 BRICS's Global Challenges

BRICS as a progressively important coalition must confront global concerns. The most urgent challenges are climate change, food security, and global information technology (IT). The capacity of BRICS to influence the global landscape hinges on the alliance's readiness to cooperate and address these challenges.

BRICS plays a crucial role in tackling climate change, considering its emissions profile and developmental requirements. Through collaboration, knowledge sharing, and the promotion of equitable climate policy, the BRICS countries may facilitate significant advancements in global climate action. BRICS crafted a joint initiative to advance sustainable practices such as the BRICS Action Plan for Green Economy.

The varied experiences of the BRICS' countries present potential for information exchange, especially in domains such as sustainable agriculture, urban planning, and catastrophe resilience. Each BRICS country has presented its respective Nationally Determined Contributions under the Paris Agreement, detailing commitments to mitigate emissions. These contributions differ greatly in aim and methodology, reflecting the economic environment and goals of each BRICS country.

Food insecurity remains a global challenge as it is a multifaceted problem that several issues including agricultural output, distribution networks, alleviation of poverty, and environmental concern. The BRICS' countries are significant producers of essential crops, including rice, wheat, and soybeans. Undoubtedly, their agriculture policies and practices significantly influence the world food supply through innovation and effective land management (Magazzino et al., 2024). Among BRICS, Brazil and Russia present an outstanding performance compared to the remaining countries in terms of food security (Tantri & Shaurav, 2018). Each of the BRICS' countries work to realize food security even if self-sufficiency is highly volatile in some of them (e.g., Russia, South Africa) (Ren et al., 2020).

To enhance agricultural productivity these countries have been progressively investing in agricultural technology and infrastructure. Although the performance in agricultural innovation and technology is high among BRICS, in terms of infrastructure for trade of agricultural commodities the members of the alliance present important deficiencies which negatively affect export and import of agricultural products (Xin et al., 2024). Also, climate change presents substantial threats to agricultural output, and as such the BRICS' countries are collaborating to establish methods for climate resilience in agriculture by exchanging knowledge and resources. In the specific area of food security, the greatest partnership to guarantee food security is between Brazil and China, followed by Russia-China and India-South Africa partnership (Ren et al., 2020).

As far as IT is concerned, BRICS possesses the capacity to profoundly impact the global IT landscape by utilizing its varied assets and promoting collaborative initiatives (Franco & de Oliveira, 2017). By tackling regulatory obstacles, and improving collaboration in technological advancement, BRICS can become a significant influence in defining the future of worldwide information technology. Divergent regulatory frameworks among the BRICS' countries may impede collaboration. Aligning legislation concerning data protection, cybersecurity, and digital trade is essential for cultivating a more cohesive IT environment (Kumar & Sharma, 2015).

All BRICS's members present important potential to influence global IT. China and India are the most prominent IT members of the group. India is a preeminent global authority in IT services, exhibiting a highly capable human resource, a robust industry of software development, IT consulting, and business process outsourcing, all of which is the result of a long-term policy that combined state incentives to business entrepreneurship and computer science education (Sharma, 2013). China has achieved considerable advancements in technological innovation, especially in sectors such as telecommunications, artificial intelligence, and e-commerce (Franco & de Oliveira, 2017).

BRICS can promote global IT governance advocating for equitable access to technology and tackling digital disparities (Lavrikova et al., 2023). Furthermore, as cyber threats escalate, BRICS states started to collaborate among themselves to strengthen cybersecurity cooperation (Belli, 2021). The increase in IT trade of services has been noticeable among BRICS, yet the export of IT services has been unstable (Biryukova & Matiukhina, 2019).

Although the BRICS' countries show low levels of technological cooperation among themselves (Kubota, 2020), the alliance can cultivate scientific and technological collaborations for innovation. Potential for collaborative initiatives in domains including artificial intelligence, and e-governance may augment their combined IT competencies. Furthermore, cooperating on digital trade policies can enhance the efficiency of cross-border e-commerce. Every BRICS country possesses a rapidly developing startup ecosystem that promotes innovation. Examples of collaboration in science, technology and innovation include the Research Infrastructure Platform and the BRICS STI Framework Program (Kubota, 2020). By fostering startup exchanges and funding efforts, these countries may stimulate innovation and entrepreneurship.

## 6. FINAL REMARKS

Based on the historical patterns of effective coalition formation on a global scale, it would be improbable that BRICS would establish itself as a credible alliance. Indeed, the BRICS countries do not necessarily respond to patterns of coalition building that, as Modelski and Thompson (1999) predicted, would be based on re-alignment of new influential countries with traditional global leaders as part of the evolution of the international system in the 20$^{th}$ century. Differently, the incentives for BRICS were that of pursuit of global status with reform of global governance seizing the windows of opportunities (e.g., Great Recession, political instability in Western political systems) for world order change.

Attempting to unveil the factors that influence the BRICS type of alliance, the chapter turned to domestic structural and institutional factors of the original member countries from the alliance provided that the BRICS's current decision rules are vague, preferences heterogeneous and membership size small. The connection between domestic factors and formation of an international alliance is interpreted considering the level of commitment of countries. The chapter holds that domestic conditions of a member country feed into the process of building commitment, which varies across member countries.

The level of commitment was classified as high, medium-high, medium, medium-low, and low. As qualitative measurements, the level of commitment was established through objectifiable indicators that allow to assess propositions that identify institutions and mechanism conducive to country's commitment to BRICS.

Brazil presents the strongest commitment to the alliance because of its high global soft influence, capacity to preserve natural resource, and low external vulnerability. China is the second-most committed BRICS member mainly due to its soft power influence. The country scores well on remaining criteria. Russia comes next with a strong performance in the socioeconomic wellbeing indicators. Its low commitment to BRICS stems from its external vulnerability and low capacity to preserver natural resources. India and South Africa exhibit a limited commitment to the alliance, as evidenced by deficiencies in soft power, environmental preservation, and relatively high external vulnerability.

One of the main limitations of the argument presented here is that it has not demonstrated the existence of causal mechanisms linking variables and commitment to BRICS. For a full understanding of the connection between institutional and structural variables and level of commitment to BRICS, it would be important to show causality. This would mean to understand the influence of these mechanisms in different dimensions —security, soft power, environment, and wellbeing— that influence the compromising behavior and actions of countries to BRICS.

The chapter has treated BRICS considering each individual membership overlooking the potential for informal socialization among member countries during ministerial meetings (Guerrero, 2022). The networks established within BRICS enable member states to utilize them beyond the confines of the alliance. This process of "functional non-differentiation" creates an opportunity for BRICS to function as an effective "diplomatic bloc" (Gallarotti, 2017). Furthermore, this process, if enduring, may establish self-enforcing mechanisms that in fact consolidates the alliance as a diplomatic player that might be very influential. This implies that the level of commitment may be socialized in the process of alliance consolidation. All said, the analysis should have incorporated socialization among countries within BRICS as the very process of socializing impacts the level of commitment.

Despite its limitations, the chapter offers insights into the further development of the theme of survival and the expansion of a new alliance. The structure of decision-making in international affairs requires further analysis within the context of BRICS. It is essential to comprehend the factors contributing to success, as well as the inherent weaknesses in the political leadership of any country joining a new alliance. This chapter serves as an initial step in this direction by providing a comparative analysis of the fundamental structures and institutions that influence the foreign policy of the BRICS countries. Further exploration is necessary to understand the role of BRICS in the collective decision-making process considering its actual dynamics.

This research can also serve as a steppingstone to identify the role of each BRICS's member more precisely in the redefinition of the international order in the 21st century, contingent upon their level of commitment to the alliance. One may utilize Bloomfield's (2016) spectrum of actors in the dynamics of norms. This research may facilitate the correlation between countries' commitments and Bloomfield's objectives regarding the actions of international actors to either challenge or uphold the status quo.

Investigating the relationship between leadership and commitment would be another avenue for further research. Does increased commitment to BRICS lead to enhanced regional and global leadership for a country? Existing analyses suggest that the membership of certain countries in BRICS has enhanced their regional leadership. Indeed, BRICS has the potential to augment the regional authority of countries and establish a "multi-alignment foreign policy" due to a redefining effect on international leadership (Brosig, 2024). In terms of leadership within BRICS, the alliance appears to have established a unique leadership pattern known as "follow-up leadership," which is defined as state activity that begins after negotiations on a specific failed topics (Han & Papa, 2024). These leadership patterns and issues warrant additional examination.

The employment of a comparative approach is important for further dissecting the idea of compromise among alliance members. In this regard, additional research comparing BRICS to other alliances such as the United Nations (UN), the EU, the defunct League of Nations, the North Atlantic Treaty Organization (NATO), among others, could improve our understanding of the various determinants of commitment and how they differ depending on the nature of the alliance. There is already critical knowledge on the subject that can be used to draw conclusions about individual and collective behavior in an evolving alliance like the BRICS. For example, alliances fail because they are unable to provide protection to their members at times of heightened military tensions, as it was the case of the League of Nations. In specific military alliances, such as NATO, we already know that regime norms and standards increase the compliance of member's compliance to the alliance. Furthermore, the more cooperative security networks are formed, the lower the financial expenses that individual countries incur in security (Kinne, 2023). Also, important lessons can be drawn from the EU, which appears to have built its high level of compromise among member countries to the supranational organization through a process of compromise building ("inclusive compromise"), inclusion of member-specific characteristics ("procedural accommodation"), and the development of vertical intergovernmental networks between the EU and each state ("constitutional compatibility") (Reh, 2012). Simply put, future studies should comparatively analyze BRICS and other alliances.

As an emerging alliance that is currently in the process of enlargement, the different levels of commitment might help us to further elucidate critical aspects that the alliance is currently facing, namely, its institutionalization. Internal institutionalization, which is slowly progressing, is connected to external institutionalization of the alliance (Hooijmaaijers, 2022). As such, new research should be undertaken based on the following proposition: A country that is highly committed to BRICS demonstrates principled actions and shows compromise to the institutionalization of the alliance, and a country with lower commitment is less grounded in principles, and less inclined to institutionalization.

## REFERENCES


Acharya, A. (2004). How Ideas Spread: Whose Norms Matter? Norm Localization and Institutional Change in Asian Regionalism. *International Organization*, 58(2), 239–275. DOI: 10.1017/S0020818304582024

Acharya, A. (2011). Norm Subsidiarity and Regional Orders: Sovereignty, Regionalism, and Rule-Making in the Third World. *International Studies Quarterly*, 55(1), 95–123. DOI: 10.1111/j.1468-2478.2010.00637.x

Amorin, C. (2013, July 16). Hardening Brazil's Soft Power. *Project Syndicate*. https://www.project-syndicate.org/commentary/a-more-robust-defense-policy-for-brazil-by-celso-amorim

Andresen, S., & Agrawala, S. (2002). Leaders, pushers and laggards in the making of the climate regime. *Global Environmental Change*, 12(1), 41–51. DOI: 10.1016/S0959-3780(01)00023-1

Antony, G. M., & Laxmaiah, A. (2008). Human development, poverty, health & nutrition situation in India. *The Indian Journal of Medical Research*, 128(2), 198–205. PMID: 19001685

Apolinário Júnior, L., & Branco, G. D. (2022). The BRICS Countries and the Russia-Ukraine Conflict. *Carta Internacional*, 17(3), e1286. DOI: 10.21530/ci.v17n3.2022.1286

Basso, L. (2019). Brazilian energy-related climate (in)action and the challenge of deep decarbonization. *Revista Brasileira de Política Internacional*, 69(1), e002. DOI: 10.1590/0034-7329201900202

Baviera, A. S. P. (2016). China's Strategic Foreign Initiatives Under Xi Jinping: An ASEAN Perspective. *China Quarterly of International Strategic Studies*, 2(1), 57–79. DOI: 10.1142/S2377740016500032

Beckley, M. (2015). The Myth of Entangling Alliances: Reassessing the Security Risks of U.S. Defense Pacts. *International Security*, 39(4), 7–48. DOI: 10.1162/ISEC_a_00197

Belli, L. (2021). Cybersecurity Policymaking in the BRICS Countries: From Addressing National Priorities to Seeking International Cooperation. *The African Journal of Information and Communication*, 28, 1–14. DOI: 10.23962/10539/32208

Bernstein, S., & Cashore, B. (2012). Complex global governance and domestic policies: Four pathways of influence. *International Affairs*, 88(3), 585–604. DOI: 10.1111/j.1468-2346.2012.01090.x

Biryukova, O. V., & Matiukhina, A. I. (2019). ICT Services Trade in the BRICS Countries: Special and Common Features. *Journal of the Knowledge Economy*, 10(3), 1080–1097. DOI: 10.1007/s13132-017-0517-6

Bloomfield, A. (2016). Norm antipreneurs and theorising resistance to normative change. *Review of International Studies*, 42(2), 310–333. DOI: 10.1017/S026021051500025X

Breitmeier, H., Underdal, A., & Young, O. R. (2011). The Effectiveness of International Environmental Regimes: Comparing and Contrasting Findings from Quantitative Research. *International Studies Review*, 13(4), 579–605. DOI: 10.1111/j.1468-2486.2011.01045.x

Brethouwer, J. T., Fokkink, R., Greene, K., Lindelauf, R., Tornquist, C., & Subrahmanian, V. S. (2022). Rising tension in the Himalayas: A geospatial analysis of Chinese border incursions into India. *PLoS One*, 17(11), e0274999. DOI: 10.1371/journal.pone.0274999 PMID: 36355678

Brosig, M. (2024). Has BRICS lost its appeal? The foreign policy value added of the group. *International Politics*, 61(1), 106–124. DOI: 10.1057/s41311-021-00327-y

Brütsch, C., & Papa, M. (2013). Deconstructing the BRICS: Bargaining Coalition, Imagined Community, or Geopolitical Fad? *The Chinese Journal of International Politics*, 6(3), 299–327. DOI: 10.1093/cjip/pot009

Buarque, D., & Ribeiro, M. M. (2023). Status and Brazil's role as a peace mediator: Lessons of the foreign perceptions of the failed Tehran deal. *Revista Brasileira de Política Internacional*, 66(1), e014. DOI: 10.1590/0034-7329202300114

Campbell, I., Wheeler, T., Attree, L., Butler, D. M., & Mariani, B. (2012). *China and conflict-affected states: Between principle and pragmatism*. SaferWorld. Available at: https://assets.publishing.service.gov.uk/media/57a08aad40f0b649740006f2/China-and-conflict-affected-states.pdf

Casarões, G. (2022). Amazon and the International Order: From Promise to Peril. *Journal of International Affairs*, 75(1).

Chakraborty, S. (2018). Significance of BRICS: Regional Powers, Global Governance, and the Roadmap for Multipolar World. *Emerging Economy Studies*, 4(2), 182–191. DOI: 10.1177/2394901518795070

Chatin, M., & Gallarotti, G. M. (2016). The BRICS and soft power: An introduction. *Journal of Political Power*, 9(3), 1–18. DOI: 10.1080/2158379X.2016.1232284

Chen, Z., & Chang, L. (2013). *The Power Strategy of Chinese Foreign Policy: Bringing Theoretical and Comparative Studies Together*. NFG Working Paper Series, No. 03. Available at: https://refubium.fu-berlin.de/bitstream/handle/fub188/19101/wp313-power-strategy-chinese-foreign-policy.pdf

Cheng, D. (2021). An Overview of Chinese Thinking About Deterrence. In F. Osing & T. Sweijs (Eds), *NL ARMS Netherlands Annual Review of Military Studies 2020. Deterrence in the 21st Century: Insights from Theory and Practice* (pp. 171-200). T.M.C. Asser Press. DOI: 10.1007/978-94-6265-419-8_10

Chih-yu, S., & Jiwu, Y. (2013). Between Core National Interest and a Harmonious World: Reconciling Self-role Conceptions in Chinese Foreign Policy. *The Chinese Journal of International Politics*, 6(1), 59–84. DOI: 10.1093/cjip/pos023

Copestake, J. (2008). Wellbeing in international development: What's new? *Journal of International Development*, 20(5), 577–597. DOI: 10.1002/jid.1431

Costa Vazquez, K. (2020). Development impact, public-private partnerships and regional integration: Possible way-forward for the BRICS-led new development bank. *Revista Tempo do Mundo*, 22, 175–187.

Cowshish, A. (2022). India's Defence Industry: From Dependence Towards Self Reliance: International Ramifications. *Indian Foreign Affairs Journal*, 17(1/2), 118–131.

Crotty, J., & Ljubownikow, S. (2022). Environmental governance in the Russian federation: Firms and regulator perception of environmental NGOs. *East European Politics*, 39(1), 39–56. DOI: 10.1080/21599165.2022.2138352

Custodio, H. M., Hadjikakou, M., & Bryan, B. A. (2023). A review of socioeconomic indicators of sustainability and wellbeing building on the social foundations framework. *Ecological Economics*, 203, 107608. DOI: 10.1016/j.ecolecon.2022.107608

Davenport, D. (2012). BRICs in the Global Climate Regime: Rapidly Industrializing Countries and International Climate Negotiations. In Bailey, I., & Compston, H. (Eds.), *Feeling the Heat* (pp. 38–56). Palgrave Macmillan. DOI: 10.1057/9780230374973_3

Do Vale, H. F. (2018). Local-global linkages in the food regime: Global history and the internationalization of Brazilian agribusiness. *Revista Brasileira de Política Internacional*, 61(1).

Do Vale, H. F. (2019, September 8). From global leader to U.S. follower. *Korean JoongAng Daily*. https://koreajoongangdaily.joins.com/2019/09/08/columns/From-global-leader-to-US-follower/3067724.html

Do Vale, H. F. (2020). Global Environmental Governance in a Changing World Order. *International Studies Review*, 22(1), 173–175. DOI: 10.1093/isr/viz063

Do Vale, H. F. (2023, September 7). Brazil and India in the 'New' Brics. *Korean JoongAng Daily*. https://koreajoongangdaily.joins.com/news/2023-09-07/opinion/columns/Brazil-and-India-in-the-New-Brics/1864645

Do Vale, H. F., & Cameron, R. (2017). The Mosaic of Local Governments in Post-Apartheid South Africa: Municipal Asymmetries and Spatial Inequality. In Sellers, J., Arretche, M., Kübler, D., & Razin, E. (Eds.), *Inequality and Governance in the Metropolis: Comparative Territorial Politics* (pp. 165–182). Palgrave Macmillan. DOI: 10.1057/978-1-137-57378-0_8

Do Vale, H. F., & Costa, L. (2024). *State capitalism in a changing global order: Brazil and China's strategies for greater global influence*. Research in Globalization., DOI: 10.1016/j.resglo.2024.100265

Donnelly, J. (2006). Sovereign Inequalities and Hierarchy in Anarchy: American Power and International Society. *European Journal of International Relations*, 12(2), 139–170. DOI: 10.1177/1354066106064505

Donnelly, J. (2017). Beyond Hierarchy. In Zarakol, I. (Ed.), *Hierarchies in World Politics* (pp. 243–265). Cambridge University Press. DOI: 10.1017/9781108241588.013

Dostal, J. M. (2010). The Developmental Welfare State and Social Policy: Shifting from Basic to Universal Social Protection. *Korean Journal of Policy Studies*, 25(3), 147–172. DOI: 10.52372/kjps25308

Duffield, J. S. (1992). International regimes and alliance behavior: Explaining NATO conventional force levels. *International Organization*, 46(4), 819–855. DOI: 10.1017/S0020818300033269

Duggan, N., & Azalia, J. C. L. (2020). From Yekaterinburg to Brasilia: BRICS and the G20, road to nowhere? *Revista Brasileira de Política Internacional*, 63(1), e009. DOI: 10.1590/0034-7329202000109

Duggan, N., Hooijmaaijers, B., Rewizorski, M., & Arapova, E. (2022). Introduction: 'The BRICS, Global Governance, and Challenges for South–South Cooperation in a Post-Western World'. *International Political Science Review*, 43(4), 469–480. DOI: 10.1177/01925121211052211

Eloranta, J. (2011). Why did the League of Nations fail? *Cliometrica*, 5(1), 27–52. DOI: 10.1007/s11698-010-0049-9

Esterhuyse, A. (2021). The South African security predicament: Making sense of the objective realities. *Scientia Militaria. South African Journal of Military Studies*, 49(1).

Franco, C., & de Oliveira, R. H. (2017). Inputs and outputs of innovation: Analysis of the BRICS. *RAI Revista de Administração e Inovação*, 14(1), 79–89. DOI: 10.1016/j.rai.2016.10.001

Gallarotti, G. (2017). The practical paradox: The BRICS as a venue for soft power. *Hermès. Law Review*, 79(3), 183–191.

Gallarotti, G. M. (2016). Compound soft power: The BRICS and the multilateralization of soft power. *Journal of Political Power*, 9(3), 467–490. DOI: 10.1080/2158379X.2016.1232292

Garcia, A. (2018). *South Africa and United Nations Peacekeeping Offensive Operations: Conceptual Models*. Mwanaka Media and Publishing. DOI: 10.2307/j.ctvh9vz8k

Gaubatz, K. T. (1996). Democratic states and commitment in international relations. *International Organization*, 50(1), 109–139. DOI: 10.1017/S0020818300001685

Gennaioli, N., & Voth, H.-J. (2015). State Capacity and Military Conflict. *The Review of Economic Studies*, 82(4), 1409–1448. DOI: 10.1093/restud/rdv019

Guerrero, M. G. (2022). A Neoinstitutionalist Proposal to Study the BRICS. *Contexto Internacional*, 44(2), e20200120. DOI: 10.1590/s0102-8529.20224402e20200120

Han, Z., & Papa, M. (2022). Brazilian Alliance Perspectives: Towards a BRICS Development–Security Alliance? *Third World Quarterly*, 43(5), 1115–1136. DOI: 10.1080/01436597.2022.2055539

Han, Z., & Papa, M. (2024). Leadership and performance in informal institutions: The internal dynamics of BRICS. *Contemporary Politics*, 30(1), 87–107. DOI: 10.1080/13569775.2023.2264065

Hassel, A., & Palier, B. (2023). Same Trend, Different Paths: Growth and Welfare Regimes Across Time and Space. *Annual Review of Political Science*, 26(1), 347–368. DOI: 10.1146/annurev-polisci-051921-103030

Hayden, A., & Dasilva, C. (2022). The wellbeing economy: Possibilities and limits in bringing sufficiency from the margins into the mainstream. *Frontiers in Sustainability, 3*.

Hooijmaaijers, B. (2022). The internal and external institutionalization of the BRICS countries: The case of the New Development Bank. *International Political Science Review*, 43(4), 481–494. DOI: 10.1177/01925121211024159

Hsiung, C. W. (2019). A tenuous trilateral? Russia-India-China relations in a changing world order. *UI Brief 1/2019*. The Swedish Institute of International Affairs. https://www.ui.se/globalassets/ui.se-eng/publications/ui-publications/2019/ui-brief-no.-1-2019.pdf

Iqbal, B. A. (2022). BRICS as a Driver of Global Economic Growth and Development. *Global Journal of Emerging Market Economies*, 14(1), 7–8. DOI: 10.1177/09749101211067096

Kamin, K., & Langhammer, R. (2024). BRICS+: A Wake-Up Call for the G7? *Cuadernos Económicos de ICE*, 107(107), 133–145. DOI: 10.32796/cice.2024.107.7802

Kickbusch, I., & Liu, A. (2022). Global health diplomacy: Reconstructing power and governance. *Lancet*, 399(10341), 2156–2166. DOI: 10.1016/S0140-6736(22)00583-9 PMID: 35594877

Kinne, B. J., & Kang, S. N. (2023). Free Riding, Network Effects, and Burden Sharing in Defense Cooperation Networks. *International Organization*, 77(2), 405–439. DOI: 10.1017/S0020818322000315

Korolev, A. (2019). How Closely Aligned Are China and Russia? Measuring Strategic Cooperation in IR. *International Politics*, 57(5), 760–789. DOI: 10.1057/s41311-019-00178-8

Kotyashko, A., Ferreira-Pereira, L. C., & Guedes Vieira, A. V. (2018). Normative resistance to responsibility to protect in times of emerging multipolarity: The cases of Brazil and Russia. *Revista Brasileira de Política Internacional*, 61(1). Advance online publication. DOI: 10.1590/0034-7329201800101

Kubiszewski, I., Costanza, R., Franco, C., Lawn, P., Talberth, J., Jackson, T., & Aylmer, C. (2013). Beyond GDP: Measuring and achieving global genuine progress. *Ecological Economics*, 93, 57–68. DOI: 10.1016/j.ecolecon.2013.04.019

Kubota, L. C. (2020). BRICS cooperation in science, technology and innovation: Progress to be shown. *Revista Tempo do Mundo*, 22, 95–110.

Kulkarni, V. S., Kulkarni, V. S., Gaiha, R., & Imai, K. S. (2023). Changes in Subjective Well-Being in India. *Social Indicators Research*, 168(1-3), 607–644. DOI: 10.1007/s11205-023-03115-8

Kumar, C. R., & Majid, M. A. (2020). Renewable energy for sustainable development in India: Current status, future prospects, challenges, employment, and investment opportunities. *Energy, Sustainability and Society*, 10(2). Advance online publication. DOI: 10.1186/s13705-019-0232-1

Kumar, S., & Sharma, D. (2015). Factors Influencing ICT Development in BRICS Countries. [IJSODIT]. *International Journal of Social and Organizational Dynamics in IT*, 4(2), 73–91. DOI: 10.4018/IJSODIT.2015070103

Kutlay, M., & Karaoğuz, H. E. (2023). Development and Foreign Policy: State of the Art. In Kutlay, M., & Karaoğuz, H. E. (Eds.), *Development and Foreign Policy in Turkey*. Palgrave Macmillan. DOI: 10.1007/978-3-031-12116-6_3

Larson, D. W. (2018). New Perspectives on Rising Powers and Global Governance: Status and Clubs. *International Studies Review*, 20(2), 247–254. DOI: 10.1093/isr/viy039

Lavrikova, N. I., Magomaeva, L. R., Kochyan, G., Ponomarevm, S. V., & Borshchevskaya, E. P. (2023). Assessing the digital divide in OECD and BRICS countries: Implications for public policy. *International Journal of Technology. Policy and Management*, 24(3), 285–302.

Li, L. (2019). BRICS: A Limited Role in Transforming the World. *Strategic Analysis*, 43(6), 499–508. DOI: 10.1080/09700161.2019.1677017

Liu, M. (2016). BRICS development: A long way to a powerful economic club and new international organization. *The Pacific Review*, 29(3), 443–453. DOI: 10.1080/09512748.2016.1154688

Liu, T., & Tsai, T.-C. (2014). Swords into ploughshares? China's Soft Power strategy in Southeast Asia and its challenges. *Revista Brasileira de Política Internacional*, •••, 57.

Magazzino, C., Gattone, T., Usman, M., & Valente, D. (2024). Unleashing the power of innovation and sustainability: Transforming cereal production in the BRICS countries. *Ecological Indicators*, 167, 112618. DOI: 10.1016/j.ecolind.2024.112618

Martus, E. (2021). Policymaking and Policy Framing: Russian Environmental Politics under Putin. *Europe-Asia Studies*, 73(5), 869–889. DOI: 10.1080/09668136.2020.1865275

McKeever, M. (2024). Social stratification and inequality in South Africa. *Sociology Compass*, 18(2), 13173. DOI: 10.1111/soc4.13173

Mishra, R., & Louis, Y. M. (2024, June 29). The China-Russia 'Axis' Is Overhyped. *The Diplomat*. https://thediplomat.com/2024/06/the-china-russia-axis-is-overhyped/

Modelski, G., & Thompson, W. R. (1999). The Long and the Short of Global Politics in the Twenty-First Century: An Evolutionary Approach. *International Studies Review*, 1(2), 109–140. DOI: 10.1111/1521-9488.00157

Montesh, M., & Basdeo, V. (2012). The Role of the South African National Defence Force in Policing. *Scientia Militaria South African Journal of Military Studies, 40*(1).

Mukherjee, R. (2014). The False Promise of India's Soft Power. *Geopolitics, History, and International Relations*, 6(1), 46–62.

Nguyen, D. H., & Khominich, I. P. (2023). The measurement of green economic quality in the BRICS countries: Should they prioritize financing for environmental protection, economic growth, or social goals? *Russian Journal of Economics*, 9(2), 183–200. DOI: 10.32609/j.ruje.9.101612

Nye, J. S. (1990). *Bound to lead: The changing nature of American power* (1st ed.). Basic Books.

OECD. (2015). *How's Life? 2015: Measuring Well-being*. OECD Publishing.

Ogunnubi, O., & Amao, O. B. (2016). South Africa's Emerging "Soft Power" Influence in Africa and Its Impending Limitations: Will the Giant Be Able to Weather the Storm? *African Security*, 9(4), 299–319. DOI: 10.1080/19392206.2016.1242978

Ogunnubi, O., & Okeke-Uzodike, U. (2015). South Africa's foreign policy and the strategy of soft power. *South African Journal of International Affairs*, 22(1), 23–41. DOI: 10.1080/10220461.2015.1007078

Öniş, Z., & Gençer, A. Ş. (2018). Democratic BRICS as role models in a shifting global order: Inherent dilemmas and the challenges ahead. *Third World Quarterly*, 39(9), 1791–1811. DOI: 10.1080/01436597.2018.1438185

Pant, H. V. (2004). The Moscow–Beijing–Delhi "Strategic Triangle": An Idea Whose Time May Never Come. *Security Dialogue*, 35(3), 311–328. DOI: 10.1177/0967010604047529

Pant, H. V. (2013). The BRICS Fallacy. *The Washington Quarterly*, 36(3), 91–105. DOI: 10.1080/0163660X.2013.825552

Patterson, J., Schulz, K., Vervoort, J., van der Hel, S., Widerberg, O., Adler, C., Hurlbert, M., Anderton, K., Sethi, M., & Barau, A. (2017). Exploring the governance and politics of transformations towards sustainability. *Environmental Innovation and Societal Transitions*, 24, 1–16. DOI: 10.1016/j.eist.2016.09.001

Pereira, J. C., & Viola, E. (2021). Brazilian climate policy (1992–2019): An exercise in strategic diplomatic failure. *Contemporary Politics*, 28(1), 55–78. DOI: 10.1080/13569775.2021.1961394

Pichon, E., & Russell, M. (2022). *Human development in Putin's Russia What the data tell us?* European Parliamentary Research Service (EPRS). Available at: https://www.europarl.europa.eu/RegData/etudes/BRIE/2022/729375/EPRS_BRI(2022)729375_EN.pdf

Qi, J. J., & Dauvergne, P. (2022). China's rising influence on climate governance: Forging a path for the global South. *Global Environmental Change*, 73, 102484. DOI: 10.1016/j.gloenvcha.2022.102484

Rabêlo Neto, A., de Sousa-Filho, J. M., Leocádio, Á. L., & do Nascimento, J. C. H. B. (2020). Internationalization of cultural products: The influence of soft power. *International Journal of Market Research*, 62(3), 335–349. DOI: 10.1177/1470785319871473

Ramos, L., Rocha, P. D., & Zahreddine, D. (2021). A Agenda de Segurança Internacional no BRICS (2009-2019). *Dados*, 64(3), e20190244. DOI: 10.1590/dados.2021.64.3.245

Ravallion, M. (2011). A Comparative Perspective on Poverty Reduction in Brazil, China, and India. *The World Bank Research Observer*, 26(1), 71–104. DOI: 10.1093/wbro/lkp031

Reh, C. (2012). European Integration as Compromise: Recognition, Concessions and the Limits of Cooperation. *Government and Opposition*, 47(3), 414–440. DOI: 10.1111/j.1477-7053.2012.01369.x

Rinaldi, A. L., & Martuscelli, P. N. (2016). The BRICS on climate change global Governance. *Meridiano*, 47(17), e17020. DOI: 10.20889/M47e17020

Rutland, P., & Kazantsev, A. (2016). The limits of Russia's 'soft power.'. *Journal of Political Power*, 9(3), 395–413. DOI: 10.1080/2158379X.2016.1232287

Sahoo, P. M., Rout, H. S., & Jakovljevic, M. (2023). Dynamics of Health Financing among the BRICS: A Literature Review. *Sustainability (Basel)*, 15(16), 12385. DOI: 10.3390/su151612385

Sergunin, A., & Karabeshkin, L. (2015). Understanding Russia's Soft Power Strategy. *Politics*, 35(3-4), 347–363. DOI: 10.1111/1467-9256.12109

Sharma, D. C. (2013). Nehru: The Unlikely Hero of India's Information Technology Revolution. NMML Occasional Papers, Perspectives in Indian Development New Series 8. Nehru Memorial Museum and Library.

Shaw, M. (2014). Transnational organized crime in Africa. In Albanese, J., & Reichel, P. (Eds.), *Transnational organized crime: an overview from six continents* (pp. 93–115). Sage. DOI: 10.4135/9781483349091.n6

Simon, M. S. (2022). India's Internal Security: Issues, Challenges and Options. In Behera, A., & Mishra, S. (Eds.), *Varying Dimensions of India's National Security* (pp. 107–120). Springer. DOI: 10.1007/978-981-16-7593-5_8

Singh, B. (2004). India's Security Concerns: National, Regional and Global. *Indian Journal of Poultry Science*, 65(3), 345–364.

Smarte Anekwe, I. M., Akpasi, S. O., Mkhize, M. M., Zhou, H., Moyo, R. T., & Gaza, L. (2024). Renewable energy investments in South Africa: Potentials and challenges for a sustainable transition: A review. *Science Progress*, 107(2), 00368504241237347. DOI: 10.1177/00368504241237347 PMID: 38614460

Sun, S.-C. (2023). Confucius Institutes: China's Cultural Soft Power Strategy. *Journal of Culture and Values in Education*, 6(1), 52–68. DOI: 10.46303/jcve.2023.4

Tantri, M. L., & Shaurav, K. (2018). Food security in BRICS: Current status and issues. Working Papers No 419. Institute for Social and Economic Change.

Tella, O. (2017). South Africa in BRICS: The Regional Power's Soft Power and Soft Balancing. *Politikon: South African Journal of Political Studies*, 44(3), 387–403. DOI: 10.1080/02589346.2017.1295620

Thakur, R. (2014). How representative are BRICS? *Third World Quarterly*, 35(10), 1791–1808. DOI: 10.1080/01436597.2014.971594

Troitskiy, M. (2015). BRICS Approaches to Security Multilateralism. *Air & Space Power Journal*, 6(2), 76–88.

Udeagha, M. C., & Ngepah, N. (2023). The drivers of environmental sustainability in BRICS economies: Do green finance and fintech matter? *World Development Sustainability*, 3, 100096. DOI: 10.1016/j.wds.2023.100096

Valença, M. M., & Carvalho, G. (2014). Soft Power, Hard Aspirations: The Shifting Role of Power in Brazilian Foreign Policy. *Brazilian Political Science Review*, 8(3), 66–94. DOI: 10.1590/1981-38212014000100021

Viola, E., & Korber, V. (2019). Brazil ups and downs in global environmental governance in the 21st century. *Revista Brasileira de Política Internacional*, 62(2), e010. DOI: 10.1590/0034-7329201900210

Weinstein, F. B. (1969). The concept of a commitment in international relations. *The Journal of Conflict Resolution*, 13(1), 39–56. DOI: 10.1177/002200276901300103

Williams, C., & Papa, M. (2020). Rethinking 'Alliances': The Case of South Africa as a Rising Power. *African Security*, 13(4), 325–352. DOI: 10.1080/19392206.2020.1871796

World Wildlife Fund (WWF). (2012). Responsible investing for climate change and water in South Africa. Technical Report 2012. http://awsassets.wwf.org.za/downloads/responsible_investing_for_climate_change_and_water_wwf_nov_2012.pdf

Xin, G., Khan, H., & Ling, X. (2024). The impact of BRICS trade facilitation on China's import and export trade in agricultural products. *Frontiers in Sustainable Food Systems*, 8, 1397350. DOI: 10.3389/fsufs.2024.1397350

Yang, J. (2022). Understanding China's changing engagement in global climate governance: A struggle for identity. *Asia Europe Journal*, 20(4), 357–376. DOI: 10.1007/s10308-021-00643-1 PMID: 35035337

Yang, J., Rizvi, S. K. A., Tan, Z., Umar, M., & Koondhar, M. A. (2021). The competing role of natural gas and oil as fossil fuel and the non-linear dynamics of resource curse in Russia. *Resources Policy*, 72, 102100. DOI: 10.1016/j.resourpol.2021.102100

Zhang, C., & Wu, R. (2019). Battlefield of global ranking: How do power rivalries shape soft power index building? *Global Media and China*, 4(2), 179–202. DOI: 10.1177/2059436419855876

Zhang, Y., Li, H., Xu, X., & Antwi, H. A. (2023). On the momentum toward vaccine self-sufficiency in the BRICS: An integrative review of the role of pharmaceutical entrepreneurship and innovation. *Frontiers in Public Health*, 11, 1116092. DOI: 10.3389/fpubh.2023.1116092 PMID: 37876712

Zhelyazkova, A., Haverland, M., & Joosen, R. (2023). Legislating softly: The effect of preference heterogeneity on the share of EU soft-law instruments over time. *European Union Politics*, 24(3), 447–469. DOI: 10.1177/14651165231162510

## ENDNOTES

1 The chapter considers the BRICS' configuration before its expansion in 2023, when the alliance admitted as new members Argentina, Egypt, Ethiopia, Iran, Saudi Arabia, and the United Arabic Emirates.

2 Actors in the international arena adapt norms in different ways, including a top-down process of congruence of local and international norms. Acharya (2004) also developed the concept of "norms localization" which entail the method of actively developing new norms by local actors with the intention to empower existing local institutions and the preservation of local custom and beliefs. From this perspective, international norms should be changed in line with domestic institutions.

3 This concept aids ours understanding about the soft power incentives that countries have in joining alliances. This is particularly important because, as Gallarotti (2017) observes, the notion of soft power has been mainly analyzed considering individual countries.

4 Cybersecurity is an important realm of the security dimension, however, due to the intersectionality of the issues regarding cybersecurity, the number of variables necessary to measure this realm would be large, extrapolating the boundaries of external vulnerabilities. As such, it was excluded from the analysis.

5 Self-reliance means the ability of a state to meet its security interest with their own capabilities. This understanding is based on the following definition which suggests that "self-reliance would mean being able to indigenously design, develop, and manufacture major equipment, platforms, and weapon" (Cowshish, 2022).

6 The "theory of entanglement" predicts that a superpower is involved in conflict due to obligations to a defend an ally. However, this prediction has not been confirmed in the case of the US (Beckley, 2015).

7 For example, the claims for internationalization of the Amazon rainforest come from the argument that there is a responsibility of preserving this common good whose depletion has transborder externalities raising claims to consider this good as "global". This situation creates a paradox provided that the international community often is inclined to treat the Amazon as a global common good while recognizing the national sovereignty of countries whose territory encompasses the rainforest (Casarões, 2022).

# Chapter 3
# Prospective Role of "BRICS Plus" Countries in Global Governance: An Exploratory Study

**Jipson Joseph**
https://orcid.org/0009-0005-1795-5051
*Christ University, India*

**Ananya Pandey**
https://orcid.org/0000-0002-2419-6314
*Christ University, India*

## ABSTRACT

*The chapter attempts to explain the origin and growth of "BRICS Plus" countries and their economic, productive and developmental position in the present scenario by analyzing the available data from various international organization. This grouping's fifteen years history is explored for understanding in what direction it is moving forward. The chapter critically evaluates the developmental policies and measures that are so far undertaken by this intergovernmental organization. The conflict of interests that are prevalent among some of the member-states are critically analyzed and evaluated. Benefits of widening the horizon of its "circle of friends" are explored for analyzing its influence among the developing countries. The chapter also explores the possibilities for its emergence as an eminent body in global governance by critically evaluating its plan of action. Furthermore, it discusses the prospective role of this grouping in global governance for ensuring a sustainable future to the emerging economies.*

DOI: 10.4018/979-8-3693-7393-4.ch003

## 1. INTRODUCTION

Global political order is being redefined in the 21st century. This shift started with the end of the Cold War. Instead of the two power blocs that ruled global economic, social, and political relationships, there emerged new regional and non-Western partnerships particularly attentive to the development of Global South. It focused on pluralism and diversity instead of Western universalism (Lagutina, 2019). Against hegemonism, it puts forward regionalism (Acharya, 2012). Regionalism is not an "institutional phenomenon" but a "socially constructed process" that is "shaped by political, social and cultural discourses" (Fioramonti, 2012, p. 157). The "BRICS Plus" (BRICS+) countries adhere to the affirmation of this regional identity. However, it does not specify any geographic proximity. It belongs to the special category of 'global regions' that promotes a cross-cutting nature permeating to local, bilateral, regional, and global levels (Sergunin & Gao, 2018). This grouping is also identified as "the best example of the hybrid form of the interregional interaction" (Naik, 2018, p. 106). It affirms the beauty of diversity and universality of life claims (UNDP, 1994).

Almost fifteen years back when the BRIC countries were officially gathered together in Russia on 16 June 2009, no one thought that it will have such a long-lasting and broadened role in international affairs. Many studies have undertaken on the role and general perspectives of BRICS in the global scenario (Armijo, 2007; Käkönen, 2014; Thakur, 2014; Mansfield, 2014; Naik, 2018; Arapova, 2019; Lissovolik, 2023a). Many studies have also focused on various specific aspects like its active role in global trade and economic interaction (Mathur & Dasgupta, 2013; Rolland, 2013; Lowe, 2016; Hopewell, 2017; Maryam & Mittal, 2020; Mohammed, 2024), significance for economic growth and international security (Abdenur, 2017), energy resources and global impacts (Pathak & Shah, 2019; Kazelko & Semeghini, 2024), role in international relations (Sergunin & Gao, 2018), scientific and technological cooperation (Sokolov et al., 2021), and evaluation of its status seeking efforts (Røren & Beaumont, 2019). All these studies attest to the growing significance of this grouping in the academic circle. Though there are differences of opinion, many authors find it as an advocate of inter-regionalism against Western hegemony. Many others also find it as a means to establish key roles for the emerging economies in global scenario.

In light of above, this chapter explores the emergence and prospective role of BRICS+ countries in global governance for ensuring an egalitarian global order where there is no unjust and unfair differentiation between Global North and Global South in terms of mere financial and technological developments. This chapter shall also explore the possibilities of the BRICS+ countries to make more responsible and collaborative interventions in the member-states and other countries of Global South for guaranteeing sustainable development paradigm. Besides, a critical evaluation is attempted with regard to its action plan for exploring its logically extractable visionary mission and perspectives for the upcoming decades.

## 2. BRICS+ COUNTRIES: A HISTORICAL SKETCH

Global governance cannot be equated only with the formal institutions that sustain the management of international affairs. It consists of "systems of rule at all levels of human activity—from the family to the international organization—in which the pursuit of goals through the exercise of control has transnational repercussions" (Rosenau, 1995, p. 13). The globe has shifted towards a "polycentric world order" (Lagutina, 2019, p. 443) accompanied by the inputs of the power transition theory (Arapova, 2019) affirming the significance of a regional global order. More than being specifically confined to a particular region, the new partnerships focus on transregional or interregional perspectives. This has energized the growth of BRICS+ countries as well. The BRICS+ countries had an insignificant origin (Beeson & Zeng, 2018). The term BRIC was first used by Jim O'Neill to refer to an evolving relationship between Brazil, Russia, India, and China (2001). In the beginning, there was no proper economic and political coordination and interaction among these nations. But later on, they realized the need for an alliance to make a strong geopolitical influence at the global level (Lagutina, 2019). Though a preliminary discussion was done by the foreign ministers of these countries in 2006, this geopolitical bloc was officially formed at the first BRIC summit in Russia in 2009. South Africa became a member of this bloc in 2011 and thereafter, it came to be known as BRICS (BRICS India, 2021).

The idea of BRICS Plus started with the 2016 summit, but it became the core element of its trans-regional agenda at the 2017 summit (Arapova, 2019). It was the Chinese Foreign Minister Wang Yi who first proposed the BRICS Plus concept as a mechanism to widen the circle of friends (Sokolov et al., 2021). The Xiamen declaration of 2017 giving invitation to many countries affirmed that this grouping is inclusive and open to beneficial cooperation and friendship with other developing countries (Basile, 2017). But Russia, Brazil, and India did not readily support this move. Russia suggested for the 'integration of integrations' in which BRICS countries are part of, arguing that such kind of integrations may be more helpful in widening the influence of the group (Lissovolik 2023b). Based on the summit discussions, it formulated the guidelines for membership expansion (BRICS South Africa, 2023), and in its 15$^{th}$ summit in 2023 they admitted five other countries—Egypt, Ethiopia, Iran, Saudi Arabia, and United Arab Emirates (UAE)—into the organization and thus came to be known as BRICS+ countries. Though Argentina was also given the formal invitation, it finally refused to join (Joint Statement of the 15th Summit, 2023). All these 10 countries together cover a good portion of the globe, which is expanded into four continents like Africa, Asia, Europe, and South America. The leadership role is for one year and on rotation basis. Besides, no member country has any veto power on its decisions. It shows that even the conflicting interests can be settled in open and amicable discussions leading to an enduring impact.

The formation of this bloc is an epitome of global diversity and its diverse interests (Lagutina, 2019). BRICS+ can be called as a 'quasi-organization' as it does not have a clear organizational structure and a permanent secretariat. From 2015 onwards it has a virtual secretariat to coordinate the exchange of information. The group takes the major decisions in its annual summit. These summits work as a platform for making important agreements and documents and to announce its official standpoints. This grouping is focused on bilateral, regional, and global level engagements and cooperation (Naik, 2018). It is designed as a platform for dialogue and cooperation among the growing economies that consist of almost 50% of world population. They intend to promote peace, security, and development through collective efforts (Bijarnia, 2013). Since it ultimately focuses on sustainable future of the developing world, it is an appropriate partnership as per the directive of sustainable development goal (SDG) no. 17.

The total population of BRICS+ countries is approximately 3.65 billion covering almost 46% of the world population. The first two largest populous countries, India and China, are members of this organization. As per the Forbes 2024 ranking, three of the BRICS+ countries (China #2, India #5, and Brazil #8) are in the list of world's top largest economies. The world's 6th richest country (UAE) is also its member (Forbes India, 2024). The member countries also occupy top positions in the largest economies based on the Gross Domestic Product (GDP) calculus in their respective continents like China #1, India #3, Saudi Arabia #7, UAE #11, and Iran #18 in Asia; South Africa #1, Egypt #2, and Ethiopia #5 in Africa; Russia #5 in Europe; and Brazil #1 in South America. Except in Europe, one of the BRICS+ members is the leading economy in all other three continents. According to BBC reports the economic worth of all these countries, if put together, come around $28.5tn, which constitutes about 28% of the world economy (BBC, 01 February 2024). In 2020, the BRICS countries' total GDP in Purchasing Power Parity (PPP) crossed that of the G7 countries and thereafter it shows a steady growth by making a difference of 2.22% with the latter in 2023 as well (Statista Research Department, 2024). All these above-mentioned statistics affirms that BRICS+ countries is a group of regional leaders that are having a decisive role in their particular region (Lagutina, 2019). The significance of BRICS should be analyzed on the basis of this unique perspective of growth and interface.

## 3. BRICS+: EMERGING ECONOMIES AND KEY ROLES IN INTERNATIONAL LEVEL

Since the 2008 global financial crisis, the world economy has shifted from the traditional market centers of the West to the emerging economies (Käkönen, 2014). The 2013 *Human Development Report* (HDR) used the term "rise of the South" for referring to the rapid economic growth made by Brazil, China, India, Indonesia, South Africa, and Turkey. The report claims that this growth has been in an unprecedented speed and scale (UNDP, 2013). Except Indonesia and Turkey, all other four countries in the list are members of BRICS. In comparison to UK and USA who took 150 and 50 years respectively for substantial economic growth, China and India took just 20 years to reach in a higher position (Thakur, 2014). For the first industrialists it was not an easy process as they had to start from point-zero in terms of scientific and technological advancements. But for the emerging economies, the framework was already well-established. However, the first industrialists got the benefit of the natural resources and cheap labor of their colonies, which are mostly the present-day emerging economies. They benefitted from the scientific growth but denied its share to the colonies making them vulnerable to all sorts of insecurities (Kniivilä, 2007; Mohajan, 2021; Eckersley, 2023). The BRICS+ bloc was formulated neither to retaliate nor to confront the Global North, but instead, they aim at empowering the emerging economies with collaborative efforts. They "encourage creating more balanced global architecture based on the principles of non-discrimination, equal access to resources, and their fair distribution" (Arapova, 2019, p. 42). Emergence and active participation of BRICS+ countries in international trade promotes a multipolar global economy (Gouvea & Gutierrez, 2023). In the beginning, many academicians considered it as an "assortment of countries" with similar economic features and motives rather than a "legitimate grouping," but now it has almost become like a "political club" that has wider geopolitical significance (Lowe, 2016, p. 50). The central principle for the growing significance of BRICS+ countries in the geopolitical space is its economic size (Armijo, 2007).

All the members of BRICS+ countries are part of the United Nations Organizations (UNO/UN) with Russia and China as the permanent members of the UN Security Council. All of them are also members of the World Bank. Except Iran and Ethiopia, all others are members of World Trade Organization (WTO). None of them is currently a member of the Organization for Economic Cooperation and Development (OECD) but in 2022 discussions were started about the possible membership of Brazil. Though none of them is a member of G7, most of them are part of G20. Except Russia all of them are members of G77, and Russia, China, and India are members of Shanghai Cooperation Organization (Jütten & Falkenberg, 2024). Besides, the list of world's powerful countries on the basis of military strength shows that Russia #2, China #3, and India #4 rank just behind the USA (Gupta, 2024). It affirms the prominence of BRICS+ countries in global security and peace operations. In terms of agricultural production, China #1, Brazil #3, India #4, and Russia #5 (Das, 2024), and in terms of oil production Saudi Arabia #2, Russia #3, China #4, Iran #7, UAE #8, and Brazil #9 are in the list of top 10 countries in the world (Worldometer, 2024). All these above-mentioned data show that BRICS+ countries have a deciding role with their collaborative efforts in the contemporary global order in terms of production, military strength, and key roles in international organizations (Käkönen, 2014). Although the inclusion of new members added just 4% of their total GDP, its significance lies in their increasing influence in international organizations and financial institutions (Jütten & Falkenberg, 2024). It underlines the group's opportunity and responsibility to ensure economic development of Asia, Africa, and Latin America (Thakur, 2014).

Some authors criticize that these States desire to acquire higher social and economic status in the world (Røren & Beaumont, 2019). It is not merely a desire but they really deserve it through their active involvement and collective efforts in capacity building projects. They are the leading economies in their own continents or sub-regions. They are also part of many regional integration activities like Brazil in Southern Common Market (Mercosur), Russia in the Eurasian Economic Union (EEU), India in South Asian Association for Regional Cooperation (SAARC), China in Shanghai Cooperation Organization (SCO), and South Africa in South African Development Community (SADC). Through bilateral and regional interaction and integration, this grouping empowers the emerging economies and tries to ensure key roles for them in global economic and political order.

## 3.1 Roles in International Bodies

Globalization has reshaped the global order promoting more interdependence and interaction among the States. It also advanced the emergence of new actors into the global dynamics of decision-making. The UN and other international institutions were the creations of the West in the Post-Second World War context and they always exhibited the Western dominance. International financial institutions also affirm this Western hegemony (Hopewell, 2017). Even in the changed political and economic scenario, the developing countries lack equitable share in decision-making processes. Western countries and their MNCs and TNCs prioritize their concerns and interests without showing much interest towards the needs of Global South (Käkönen, 2014). BRICS+ countries severely criticize the international organizations for their outdated rules and regulations, inequitable representations, and favoritism towards certain countries (Jütten & Falkenberg, 2024). They thus demand for more inclusive approach. It should reflect in the expansion of the UN security council and the increased voting rights for them in the Bretton Woods Institutions (Joint Statement by the 4th Summit, 2012). The functioning of the Security Council sticking on with its five permanent members system and the veto power is outdated. It has to be reformed and redefined taking into account the new perspectives of the globalized world. The UN must promote multilateralism and universality, which should be echoed in giving appropriate roles for the developing countries in its decision-making bodies (Joint Statement by the 5th Summit, 2013). The first three joint statements clearly argued for the reform of the international financial institutions claiming that in its absence the legitimacy of these institutions will be at risk (Käkönen, 2014).

## 3.2 Economic Strength and Interrelations

The emergence of BRICS in the global political order was in the context of the financial crisis in 2008. China was the first country that recovered from this crisis. The restructuring of the global order started from this period, and the economic strength is transferred from the North to the South (Lagutina, 2019). BRICS got its momentum in this background. This new transregional grouping is oriented towards "enhancing the stability and transparency of the world trading system and strengthening positions of developing countries in the global economy" (Arapova, 2019, p. 33). Both transparency and accountability are essential for a stable economic order and it can be ensured only when more actors are involved in key positions. Except Russia, all other members were predominantly having specific national and regional economic interests while taking part in this grouping. Russians try to restructure the international financial system with the help of this bloc (Käkönen, 2014). They try to realize their economic and political aspirations by an increased participation in global trade, increased production and exports, enhanced voting capacity in WTO, and reduced dependency on the developed world. They also demand flexible foreign trade agreements for promoting and safeguarding the interests of their own investors (Rolland, 2013). In the past, most of them were yielding to the Western hegemony in trade agreements due to their insecure and unstable economic situations. The trade agreements were one-sided and another form of colonization. But with the efforts of BRICS+, they start to collectively raise their voice against such injustice.

Their exports range from minerals and agricultural goods to manufactured products and software. These countries together constitute the largest exporters of many essential products (Gouvea & Gutierrez, 2023). Brazil and Russia are the largest exporters of raw materials, India has a leading role among the global service providers, China is the world's largest exporter of manufactured goods, South Africa's economy is recognized for its diversity and low-risk nature (Lowe, 2016), and the newly included members Iran, Saudi Arabia, UAE, Egypt and Ethiopia are rich energy sources (Kazelko & Semeghini, 2024). As already noted, the PPP GDP of the BRICS countries were higher than the G7 in 2022 and it affirms their substantial economic growth (Jütten & Falkenberg, 2024). Their strength in global economic transactions also enhances their bargaining power that can help to ensure transparency and accountability in global financial system (Drysdale, 2011).

Economic interactions between these countries are vital for the growth of this grouping and their economies. Since these countries account the major share of global population, its demands are high. The trade relations between these countries help them to boost their production and export possibilities. For instance, Russia's export of crude oil to China and India increased from 20% to 40% in the last decades (Gouvea & Gutierrez, 2023). There is great diversity among the BRICS+ economies. However, this diversity is the greatest advantage of this grouping as they can complement each other. It can help them to develop like a trading bloc against the Western path of modernization and liberalization (Käkönen, 2014). This grouping can also function as a platform to resolve the trade disputes between the members and thus try for a sustainable future (Lissovolik, 2023b). What they need is an efficient and effective coordination.

The BRICS Contingent Reserve Arrangement (CRA) was established in 2014. It is formulated for supporting the member-States with precautionary financial resources to confront short-term balance of payment-related challenges. It was active in the early times of its creation, but became inactive in later periods (Lissovolik, 2024). It can reduce the dependency of the member countries on western dominated financial institutions. In 2015, BRICS countries established the New Development Bank (NDB) for infrastructural and sustainable development projects in emerging economies and developing countries with special focus on its member countries. It concentrates on six specific areas like clean energy and energy efficiency, transport infrastructure, water and sanitation, environmental protection, social infrastructure and digital infrastructure. In 2021, Bangladesh, UAE, and Egypt became members of the NDB, but they have less percentage of share compared to the founding members. The NDB's intention is to secure positive and long-lasting impact on its member economies and to ensure them sustainable future (NDB, n.d.; Chin, 2024). However, both NDB and CRA transactions are in US dollars, which is a biggest drawback of the policy framework of BRICS+ (Gray & Gills, 2016).

## 3.3 Political Interactions

Drysdale argues that the BRICS countries may become strong actors of global economy but they will not be so capable in establishing a strategic cooperation in the global political scenario (2011). But the consortium of these emerging economies grows into such a position to seek respect towards the positive and progressive values of the Westphalian political order like unity, sovereignty, territorial integrity, and independence of all nations. They oppose any sorts of interference in these Westphalian principles (Käkönen, 2014). In that sense, it is a protective bloc as it focuses on safeguarding the Rule of Law and the principles of international relations (Laidi, 2011). One of the main aspirations of this group's formation was to promote an inclusive vision instead of unipolarity in global governance (Lagutina, 2019). It advances traditional values and inclusive growth without subsiding to foreign values and expansion tactics (Arapova, 2019). They should take a common stand in global political issues as they stood unanimously against the encroachment of the NATO in Libya arguing that it was a violation of the 1973 resolution (Käkönen, 2014). Just like their role in supporting other emerging economies, the BRICS+ should function as an active advocate of the developing world in confronting various political issues.

## 3.4 Collective Efforts

Emergence of BRICS+ countries as an intergovernmental organization of the developing economies affirmed that their collaborative efforts can make meaningful changes. They collaborate with each other to confront emerging challenges, ensure peace and security, promote sustainable development, and address various complex issues like poverty, unemployment, and inequality for the benefit of their people and the global community (Joint Statement of the 7$^{th}$ Summit, 2015). They showed enthusiasm to strengthen their voting rights in international financial institutions for empowering the objectives of the emerging economies (Arapova, 2019). They assert that in the absence of reformation of the international financial institutions, the globe will not be in a position to achieve financial stability and sustainable future (Bijarnia, 2013). Since majority of world population and resources belong to Global South, there is an urgent need for their voices to be heard and respected in international platforms. Irrespective of the difference in GDP or GNP, all the countries in the world should have equal role in global governance and this organization can make some meaningful steps in that direction. However, mostly they remained as a political grouping that occasionally voiced together for the rights of the developing countries rather than supporting and collaborating with each other for political and economic sustainability (Mathur & Dasgupta, 2013).

## 4. BRICS+ AND CONFLICT OF INTERESTS: A CRITICAL ANALYSIS

BRICS+ group is often criticized for its incapacity to develop a collective position due to the diverse interests of its members (Bremmer, 2012; Rolland, 2013). Absence of a common strategy and internal tensions among the members are serious drawbacks for its effectiveness. They advance neither a joint standpoint in international level nor an alternate model of global political order (Glosny, 2010). India, Brazil, and South Africa define themselves as non-aligned countries, Russia always positioned itself as a strong opponent of western dominance but China sometimes shows its alliance and sometimes does not. Their economic character also differs from each other. Many members complain against China's undervaluation of their currency. They are also competitors of each other albeit being their main trade partners (Rolland, 2013). Besides, there are severe conflicting issues between its members like China-India and China-Russia border issues, Egypt-Ethiopia dispute on Nile River water sources, and Saudi Arbia and Iran longstanding rivalry issues (Jütten & Falkenberg, 2024). Russia's invasion in Ukraine is also a serios global issue in which many of the BRICS+ countries are forced to take a stand against the war politics of Russia. China's unparalleled economic growth, communist ideology and unnecessary interference in the internal affairs of other countries in the zone also cause apprehension. All these show that there is lack of unity among its members (Hopewell, 2017). They lack a coherent vision, which is essential for global governance (Beeson & Zeng, 2018). The members are so diverse in nature, which also hinders its cooperative functioning (Roberts, 2010). Mansfield thus uses the term heterogenous club to identify this grouping (2014). Their divergent interests and mutual mistrust may hinder or delay their efforts to challenge the Western dominance (Downie, 2015).

Even in the midst of all these issues and complexities, they all have a common interest, that is, to establish a sustainable future for the developing countries. But unlike the developed countries, most of the BRICS+ members have their own particular strategies of economic development and the majority of their markets is in the developing world. This creates confusion and competition among themselves. Besides, when there are global political issues like Russia-Ukraine War, Israel-Palestine and Iran-Israel issues, they fail to raise a common standpoint because of their economic insecurity. They are in the stage of economic growth and any kind of trade embargo (Shambaugh, 2024) or economic blockade will restrict their economic aspirations. In order to confront such dilemma, they should expand the circle of friends with more members (Sokolov et al., 2021) and ensure perfect cooperation and coordination among themselves. For this, it is better to formulate a permanent secretariat either in South Africa or UAE (the first to give a respectful stand to the

African continent, the second for its strong liberal and non-aligned stand) with a secretary general for a term of three years on rotation basis and secretaries representing each member States working under the guidance of the BRICS leaders' summit. The secretariat should effectively contribute to promote respect for human dignity and common values among the members (Benjamin, 2024), and to become a reliable bloc in global geopolitics. Besides, as the BRICS+ grouping tries to arrive at decisions by consensus in its annual summits, it also will contribute to resolve the conflicting interests.

## 5. BRICS+ AND OTHER INTERNATIONAL ORGANIZATIONS: A COMPARATIVE STUDY

Regionalism was mostly considered antithetical to globalization. But they are complementary as regional integrations can make a powerful voice for their real needs and demands in the global framework. Adaptation of global policies and guidelines in regional levels also will be more efficient through such an integration (Lagutina, 2019). The origin of BRICS+ grouping was a substantial leap towards the redefinition of international systems. It can stand as a renewing mechanism against the Bretton Woods Institutions and the UN. They can collectively strive for redistribution of power in global architecture. The loss of faith in the Bretton Woods and the UN institutions exponentiated the demand for this grouping (Arapova & Lissovolik, 2021). Majority of the countries lost their faith in these institutions due to their favoritism towards certain countries. It is a fact that the advanced economies with a minority of population retain higher voting rights in the UN and other international institutions. Developing countries lack decisive roles in collective decision-makings and are burdened with many trade barriers (Thakur, 2014). They thus demand increased voting powers in the financial institutions like World Bank and IMF in order to protect their specific demands (Rolland, 2013). In this section, a comparison is made between BRICS+ and UN, EU, G7 & G20, and Bretton Woods Institutions.

### 5.1 UN and BRICS+ Countries

Four of the BRICS Countries (Russia, China, India and South Africa) were the original signatories of the UN and Brazil was a subsequent signatory (UN, n.d.). But except Russia and China, who were part of the Allied powers, no other members had a decisive role in the UN. Both India and South Africa were under the British rule and they were not given respectful positions. Western dominance was explicit throughout the evolution of the UN institutions (Luard, 1982). It continued during the Cold War period that distanced the communist countries like Russia and China (Berkes, 1959). But due to their dignified position in the security council, they survived. However, it led to the unification of the Western world. Whereas, the developing countries on account of their insecure social and economic situations had to depend on these rich countries instead of demanding their deserved positions (Medhat, 2020). But now, a paradigm shift has taken place due to the scientific and technological advancements, liberal policies and the like in the developing world. They are in a position to demand their rights. BRICS+ grouping insists the developing countries to stand united for the rights of the South. The 2023 Johannesburg declaration also underlined the intention to enhance cooperation in the UN General Assembly for empowering the needs of the emerging economies. However, analyzing the voting cohesion of BRICS+ countries during 2006-2014 Hooijmaaijers and Keukeleire argue that there is no such a notable increase (2016). But in 2011, when all of the then BRICS members were part of the UN security council, they exhibited a unanimous stance in its resolutions (Jütten & Falkenberg, 2024).

## 5.2 BRICS+ and European Union

The European Union (EU) has no direct relationship with the BRICS+ grouping but it has bilateral and interregional financial and trade agreements. From 1985 onwards it has various trade and other cooperation agreements with the individual members of this grouping. The first of this kind was signed with China and the last one was with South Africa. The agreements with Russia are subject to annual extensions. But it has no free trade or investment agreements with any of the members of this bloc. It has started free trade agreements with India and Brazil but not yet finalized. It does not actively involve in economic interactions with BRICS+ considering it as a political grouping (Jütten & Falkenberg, 2024).

## 5.3 BRICS+, G7, and G20

G7 is the grouping of the world's richest countries, whereas G20 stands for the collaborative functioning of both developed and developing countries. G20 affirms that both these economies should not stand in confrontation with each other but work together for global sustainable future. Compared to G7, the rise of G20 affirms the democratization of global governance as it gives a platform of discussion and collaboration for the emerging economies (UNDP, 2013). G20 was founded in 1999 comprising of 19 countries and the European Union. It represents almost 85% of global GDP, 75% of global trade and 2/3 of world population (G20 Brazil, 2024). All the five founding members and Saudi Arabia of BRICS+ are also G20 members. BRICS+ brings together the largest emerging markets that are spread in four continents with diverse political systems, economic orders, and values (Thakur, 2014). BRICS+ grouping from the very beginning of its formation upheld the central role of G20 for systematically addressing the global financial issues (Joint Statement of the 1st Summit, 2009). The growing participation of BRICS+ countries in G20 has challenged the legitimacy of G7 (Rolland, 2013). At the same time, it also has contributed for mutual empowerment and collaboration. Both developed and developing countries are able to reap the fruits of this inclusive grouping in terms of economic benefits, political standpoints, and transnational perspectives.

### 5.4 BRICS+ and Bretton Woods Institutions

Though BRICS+ countries are the largest exporters of many products and contribute a good percentage of total exports accounting to a substantial GDP, they are underrepresented in the Bretton Woods Institutions. They have only less than 15% of the voting rights in these institutions (Gouvea & Gutierrez, 2023). The Bretton Woods Institutions are largely dominated by the Global North. BRICS+ thus demands "democratic and transparent decision-making and implementation process" at these institutions (Joint Statement of the 1st Summit, 2009, no. 4). They call for more voting rights, open and merit-based selection of the heads of these institutions irrespective of nationality, and the selection of staff that reflects its diversity of membership (Joint Statement of the 2nd Summit, 2010). The WTO that supervises trade interactions takes its decisions on the basis of consensus. Many believe that the WTO unnecessarily interferes into the economic activities of developing countries showing its favoritism towards the West (Wade, 2003). But from 2008 Doha round meeting, there is a considerable shift in this approach as Brazil, India, and China came to the forefront (Hopewell, 2017). Except Iran and Ethiopia (observers), all other BRICS+ countries are also members of WTO. All of them are also members of both World Bank and IMF. This shows that through their collective efforts, regional integration strategies, and effective coordination, they can make changes in the functioning of these financial institutions.

## 6. BRICS+ AND GLOBAL SOUTH: AN EMERGING LEADERSHIP

The IMF groups all BRICS+ countries in the category of emerging and developing economies, and Brazil, Russia, India, and China lead this group. All these countries also come under 'Global South' in its wider definition. This intergovernmental organization of the prominent countries of the developing world can make their voice heard in international forums by their collective efforts. BRICS+ lead the emerging economies against the unjust and unfair global structures. Global economic order has reached a turning point in which it realized the role of developing economies in international trade, industrial and technological growth, and capital flow. They have realized the advantages of industrialization, technological advancements, open market, and liberalization of economic policies for their financial growth and well-being. This progressive vision has led these countries to establish a firm position in global scenario (Kniivilä, 2007; Joint Statement of the 1st Summit, 2009). This has resulted in a conflict with the Western-led policies and decisions. In such a context, this grouping stands as an advocate for the rights of the emerging economies. It acts as a tool for promoting the interests of the developing world (Arapova & Lissovolik, 2021). They also target the de-dollarization process by mutual cooperative efforts for strengthening their national currencies (Arapova, 2019). Russia and China have already started this move announcing that they will no more use dollar for their bilateral trade transactions (Mohammed, 2024). In spite of that, global economic order is unipolar as both US dollar (42%) and Euro (35%) are the preferred first two SWIFT transaction modes (Gouvea & Gutierrez, 2023). The BRICS+ should energize its attempts to empower the national currencies for enhancing their economic growth and protecting the interests of the developing world.

From the very beginning, this grouping has been analyzed as a resistance to the unipolar global order emphasizing the South-South cooperation for sustainable growth (Kipgen & Chakrabarti, 2022). It has the potential to stand for the interests of the developing countries in the international level. It can collectively stand against the environmental, labor, and human rights standards that are prioritizing the interests of the Western people. With regard to intellectual property in the areas of life-saving medicines, agricultural seeds and traditional medicine, they face severe injustice from the lobbying powers of the big Western MNCs and TNCs. In such a context they should unanimously stand together for the protection of the rights of poor people, farmers, and indigenous people (Thakur, 2014). Besides, its NDB provides financial support to the member countries for infrastructure and sustainable development projects affirming that this intergovernmental organization is ultimately oriented towards the development of its member-states and global south. They always desire to represent and protect the interests of the emerging powers (Kipgen & Chakrabarti, 2022).

## 7. BRICS+ AND GLOBAL NORTH: MUTUAL RESPECT AND COLLABORATIVE EFFORTS

Global North countries are those that have developed and mature economies, stable political system, strong technological advancements, and low population. They have roughly 25% of global population but owns 80% of global wealth (World Population

Review, 2024). Global North was controlling the international institutions and global policy-making throughout, without seriously considering the developing world's needs and apprehensions. Some authors argue that though BRICS+ countries still have contradicting opinions with the Western policies, they should adhere to peaceful coexistence aspirations for a sustainable future (Sergunin & Gao, 2018). It should not be a program of action just for the South but the North also should adhere to it. First of all, it requires restructuring of the hierarchical system of global governance where the developed world dominated all the international bodies with their wealth (Tripathi, 2021). Instead of the hierarchical system, the globe requires a circular model where each State is equally represented and heard. Unequal distribution of the natural resources and global assets have done enough damage to universality of life claims (UNDP, 1994). The UN's 2030 agenda of sustainable future will not be achievable without positive and progressive coordination between the North and South. Universal brotherhood, which is the spirit of the UN and all the world religions, should not remain merely a slogan but a sincere practice across the globe without any differentiation on the basis of culture, region, race, and economic status. Both the North and South should become ambassadors of mutual respect and collective action. The divisive walls should be bridged together by humanitarian perspectives.

## 8. BRICS+: PROSPECTIVE ROLES IN GLOBAL GOVERNANCE

Basing on the constructivist theory's mapping BRICS+ countries develop a collective identity and cooperation in international arena (Arapova, 2019). The biggest common interest of BRICS+ countries is to acquire a substantial position in global economic governance (Thakur, 2014). But until now, BRICS+ grouping has not been faithful to its true potential. The vested interests of the member-States confuse and complicate its functioning. Conflict of interests among the members outweigh their common interests and make the bloc insignificant in international framework. Whenever they stood united, their position was respected. But such things were rarely happened due to their peculiar national and economic interests. It gives advantage to the Global North as they could shape the decisions of international organizations in their favor. However, in its fifteen years of history BRICS+ has grown from just initial four members in 2009 to five members in 2011 and now to ten members. Many countries have also applied for its membership. This shows that the developing countries see this bloc as a suitable framework of collaboration for economic growth, sustainable future, and global governance (Joint Statement of the 3rd Summit, 2011). While G20 functions as a mechanism to bridge both developed and developing worlds, BRICS+ can function as a platform to unite together all the emerging economies and collaborate with each other for greater benefits.

## 8.1 Sustainable Development Paradigm

BRICS+ bloc gives great weightage to sustainable development paradigm and considers it as an important vehicle for the economic growth and sustainable future of the emerging economies (Joint Statement of the 3rd Summit, 2011). Sustainable development attempts to bridge both developmental and environmental aspirations of the globe. It captured the global attention with the Brundtland report, which argued that the present generation's developmental needs should not obstruct the environmental aspirations of the future generation (WCED, 1987). The Global South cannot compensate its developmental concerns for environmental aspirations and vice versa. Unbalanced ecological burdens should not be placed on the emerging economies that may hinder their growth. Economic development is an essential prerequisite for them to ensure a sustainable future. BRICS+ countries should mutually cooperate besides collaborating with the developed world in order to ensure an ecofriendly developmental model for the realization of SDGs (Caglar et al., 2022). For the developing countries, innovation is a key area of sustainable development (Joint Statement of the 8th Summit, 2016). All the BRICS summits have underlined the importance of research and innovation for an equitable, open, all-round, and inclusive development (Joint Statement of the 9th Summit, 2017). Developed world also should support the green industrialization procedures of the South for advancing global welfare.

## 8.2 Poverty Eradication Strategies

BRICS+ has called for international cooperation to give special attention to the most vulnerable people of the society. Global community's fight against poverty, social exclusion, and inequality should particularly focus on the special needs of the developing world (Joint Statement of the 2nd Summit, 2010). Poverty is a moral, social, economic, and political exclusion and it cannot be eradicated without growth and development (Joint Statement of the 3rd Summit, 2011). Majority of world's poor lives in the South. The rich-poor gap is also enormously huge leading to the cry that "we belong to the 99%." Concentration of the global wealth on a minority and the denial of basic standard of life for the majority demand that there should be equitable distribution of the benefits of economic growth. BRICS+ should energize the poverty eradication strategies of the South advocating mutual cooperation and positivity. Attempts should be made to enhance employment opportunities, small-scale industries, infrastructure development, and bilateral trade. Proper attention should be given to the development of agricultural sector as it is where most of the poor people work. Since the member States are the leading producers of many products, their collaborative efforts can contribute to the realization of SDG#1.

## 8.3 Effective Coordination for Positive Results in Essential Sectors

For empowering the agricultural sector, BRICS+ planned for mutual cooperation focused on family farming that can increase food production and ensure food security (Joint Statement of the 2nd Summit, 2010). Sharing of experience and expertise of the agricultural sector especially the irrigation techniques would be advantages for the whole group (Joint Statement of the 8th Summit, 2016). Cooperation in agricultural sector is centered around five key areas like food security and nutrition, adaptation of agriculture to climate change, technological cooperation and innovation in agriculture, agricultural trade, and ICT application in agriculture (Joint Statement of the 9th Summit, 2017). Further, they focus on ensuring the basic standard of healthcare for their people (Joint Statement of the 7th Summit, 2015). During the time of Covid-19, this grouping supported each other in view of vaccine and other essential medical equipment. They also support each other in cases of medical emergencies. Besides, they need to focus on investing in basic healthcare infrastructure development of the developing countries. Energy sector is an essential area for economic development and environmental protection (Erdoğan et al., 2020). Cleaner and more affordable energy and the increased use of renewable energy sources are prerequisites for the efficient use of energy (Joint Statement of the 2nd Summit, 2010). They also suggested the expansion of civil nuclear energy capacity in order to meet the commitments of the 2015 Paris Climate Change Conference (Joint Statement of the 8th Summit, 2016). Popularization of energy efficient life style is an effective method of sustainable energy use (Joint Statement of the 10th Summit, 2018). They demand strong international actions against terrorism, drug trafficking, and corruption as these are greatest hurdles for the economic growth of the developing world (Joint Statement of the 3rd Summit, 2011). Such an investment and cooperation in the essential sectors will help them to ensure a respectful position in international dynamics.

## 8.4 Giving Voice to the Voiceless

The joint statement of the first summit demanded for greater voice and representation of the emerging economies in global forums (2009). BRICS+ countries emphasize the need for giving voice to the historically silenced and marginalized countries on account of their poverty and economic dependency. The voice of the Global South needs to be respected as it is a miniature of global diversity (Bijarnia, 2013). In 2013, in view of its empowering strategies, it offered substantial help to the African continent for sustainable infrastructure development and showed moral and social concern towards the issues of Iran, Afghanistan, and Congo (Joint Statement of the 5th Summit). To strengthen global economic landscape, it demanded to increase the voice and representation of the emerging economies (Joint Statement of the 9th Summit, 2017). Developed world is urged to increase their Official Development Assistance (ODA) commitments so that the developing countries can make extensive progress in their economy (Joint Statement of the 14th Summit, 2022). BRICS+ should continue as an advocate for the rights and needs of the developing world. The globe cannot rely on unequal distribution of natural resources and the benefits of economic growth. It should promote universalism of life claims basing on the demands of universal brotherhood and that can be ensured only when there is a suitable mechanism to stand for the rights and sufferings of the marginalized.

## 8.5 Mutual Support and Coordination in International Trade

BRICS+ has realized the great potential of the emerging economies to actively lead and energize economic growth and prosperity. They can reduce imbalances in economic development and foster social inclusion by working together with other countries (Joint Statement of the 2nd Summit, 2010). In order to establish an open economy and to promote consensus building, it supports the initiatives of the United Nations Conference on Trade and Development (UNCTAD) (Joint Statement of the 6th Summit, 2014). Their economic relationship focused on core areas like trade and investment, production and minerals processing, financial integration, infrastructure connectivity, scientific and technological innovation and advancements, and information and communication technology (Joint Statement of the 9th Summit, 2017). They strengthened their initiatives and mutual collaboration in various fields like E-commerce, railways, roadways, seaports, and airports by increasing their investment possibilities (Joint Statement of the 7th Summit, 2015).

Economic integration is one of the trademarks of this grouping (Arapova, 2019). It is fast-growing in international economic architecture by its world trade share, GDP, foreign currency reserve, and investment (Rolland, 2013). They can become a dependent alternative to the existing economic order by giving more concentration to economic cooperation and integration (Lissovolik, 2023). Arapova (2019) suggests to choose their own national currencies for bilateral trade, so that they can strengthen their currency value. In the 2023 summit they started discussions on having a common currency that can be used as a reserve currency, accounting unit, and digital currency for settlements. The Brazilian President even suggested R5 as the name of the proposed common currency in reference to the first alphabet of their national currencies (Lissovolik, 2023a). This can function as a reserve currency for BRICS+ countries in addition to their national currencies for building and expanding a secure international finance system (Lissovolik, 2023b). Without active involvement in bilateral and international trade, this grouping cannot establish itself as a trustworthy agent of the emerging economies.

### 8.6 Mutual Support in International Leadership Roles

In the beginning BRICS countries had a likeminded leadership and that resulted in its growth (Lagutina, 2019). Their ultimate aim was to create a multipolar world order based on values like rule of law, equality, mutual respect, cooperation, and collective action (Joint Statement of the 1st Summit, 2009). Both Russia and China are in the UN Security Council. India and Brazil strongly desire and strive to become its members. But many times, they lack support from China. Regional and political interests of China should not become a barrier for the other members to gain their respective position in the international bodies. India is the most populous country of the globe and it is one of the leading emerging economies. Brazil is the leading economy of the Latin America. South Africa is the leading democracy and economy of Africa. Both South America and Africa are not represented in the UN Security Council. Besides, if these countries are given representation in the Security Council as permanent members, it will increase the strength of BRICS+ as well. They should also support each other in getting the leadership roles in the Bretton Woods institutions and collectively demand for more voting rights. Mutual support and collaborative efforts in the international level will enhance the growth of the developing world. This is not to substitute the Northern dominance with the Southern, but to establish an equitable global vision and approach.

## 9. CONCLUSION

BRICS+ grouping, a 21st century initiative, attempts to promote intergovernmental cooperation and collaboration for the sustainable future of emerging economies. Since its horizon is growing with the inclusion of new countries and many others are waiting for their turn to be included, a serious reconsideration is needed on its acronym. It was BRIC in the beginning, BRICS from 2011 with the inclusion of South Africa, BRICS+ from 2023 with the incorporation of five other countries, and sometimes BRICS++ after the inclusion of other countries in the future. The acronym was a perfect match till 2023 when there were only five countries. Now, five more countries are added and they also plan to widen its circle of friends with more members. The 2023 summit affirmed that almost 40 countries showed their willingness to join the group and 22 have formally applied for the membership (Jütten & Falkenberg, 2024). The authors therefore suggest the name Emerging Economies' Intergovernmental Cooperative Organization (EEICO) for making the name of the group more inclusive. This new name sums up the whole idea of this bloc as it is an intergovernmental cooperative organization of the emerging economies. This name also sums up the whole analysis that we have undertaken in this chapter. Bilateral, regional, and global cooperation of the emerging economies is the core of this group. The acronym, BRICS, can be retained with respect to the five founding members but it will not do justice to the inclusive and universal vision that this group puts forward.

The problem with BRICS+ grouping is that they fail to propose an alternate political order in its real depth (Käkönen, 2014). However, it should be taken into account that this bloc has only a history of fifteen years and unlike the Global North, all its member States are growing economies with multitude of needs. It would not be feasible for them to make a ready-made alternate political order instantly. Their foremost objective is to ensure sustainable future for their countries and other emerging economies. Though the process is slow, it will have a lasting impact in the forthcoming decades. It is because of this realization that many other countries want to become members of this circle of friends.

The prospective role of this grouping is highly depended on the various measures that it undertakes to resolve the conflicting interest of its members. A global vision that goes beyond the nation and the region is an essential prerequisite. They also need to support each other for coming into the leadership roles of the international institutions. Continuous dialogue and collaboration with each other to increase their voting rights and international trade possibilities will also enhance their growth. Such collaborative efforts only can strengthen their attempts against the polarization of the South in the global space.

## REFERENCES


G20 Brazil. (2024). About the G20. https://www.g20.org/pt-br/sobre-o-g20

Abdenur, A. E. (2017). Can the BRICS Cooperate in International Security? *International Organizations Research Journal*, 12(3), 73–93. DOI: 10.17323/1996-7845-2017-03-73

Acharya, A. (2012). Comparative Regionalism: A Field whose Time has come? *The International Spectator*, 47(1), 3–15. DOI: 10.1080/03932729.2012.655004

Arapova, E. Y. (2019). The "BRICS Plus" as the First International Platform Connecting Regional Trade Agreements. *Asia-Pacific Social Science Review*, 19(2), 30–46. DOI: 10.59588/2350-8329.1220

Arapova, E. Y., & Lissovolik, Y. D. (2021). The BRICS Plus Cooperation in International Organizations: Prospects for Reshaping the Global Agenda. *Asia-Pacific Social Sciences Review*, 21(4), 192–205.

Armijo, L. E. (2007). The BRICS Countries as Analytical Category: Mirage or Insight? *Asian Perspective*, 31(4), 7–42. DOI: 10.1353/apr.2007.0001

Basile, E. (2017). BRICS Leaders Xiamen Declaration 4th September 2017. *Revista di Studi Politici Internazionali*, 84(3), 465–469.

BBC. (01 February 2024). BRICS: What is the Group and Which Countries have Joined? https://www.bbc.com/news/world-66525474

Beeson, M., & Zeng, J. (2018). The BRICS and Global Governance: China's Contradictory Role. *Third World Quarterly*, 39(10), 1962–1978. DOI: 10.1080/01436597.2018.1438186

Benjamin, R. (2024). BRICS Needs Common Values, Respect for Human Dignity. https://infobrics.org/post/41912

Berkes, R. N. (1959). The United Nations and the Cold War Conflict. *Current History (New York, N.Y.)*, 37(218), 228–232. DOI: 10.1525/curh.1959.37.218.228

Bijarnia, B. S. (2013). Whither Global Economic Governance? The Emerging Role of BRICS: An Alternative. *Indian Journal of Asian Affairs*, 26(1/2), 75–92.

Bremmer, I. (2012). *Every Nation for Itself: Winners and Losers in a G-Zero World*. Portfolio.

Caglar, A. E., Guloglu, B., & Gedikli, A. (2022). Moving Towards Sustainable Environmental Development for BRICS: Investigating the Asymmetric Effect of Natural Resources on $CO_2$. *Sustainable Development (Bradford)*, 30(5), 1313–1325. DOI: 10.1002/sd.2318

Chin, G. T. (2024). The Evolution of New Development Bank (NDB): A Decade Plus in the Making. *Global Policy*, 15(2), 368–382. DOI: 10.1111/1758-5899.13399

Das, K. (2024). [Agricultural Producing Countries in the World. *GeeksforGeeks*. https://www.geeksforgeeks.org/agricultural-producing-countries-in-the-world/.]. *Top (Madrid)*, 10, •••.

Downie, C. (2015). Global Energy Governance: Do the BRICs have the Energy to Drive Reform? *International Affairs*, 91(4), 799–812. DOI: 10.1111/1468-2346.12338

Drysdale, P. (2011). The BRICS, the G-7 and Developing New Global Economic Power. *European View*, 10(2), 159–164. DOI: 10.1007/s12290-011-0187-x

Eckersley, R. (2023). (Dis)order and (In)justice in a Heating World. *International Affairs*, 99(1), 101–119. DOI: 10.1093/ia/iiac259

Erdoğan, S., Kirca, M., & Gedikli, A. (2020). Is there a Relationship between CO2 Emissions and Health Expenditures? Evidence from BRICS-T Countries. *Business and Economic Research Journal*, 11(2), 293–305. DOI: 10.20409/berj.2019.231

Fioramonti, L. (2012). Conclusion — Building Regions from Below: Has the Time Come for Regionalism 2.0? *The International Spectator*, 47(1), 151–160. DOI: 10.1080/03932729.2012.655015

Forbes India. (2024). The Top 10 Largest Economies in the World in 2024. https://www.forbesindia.com/article/explainers/top-10-largest-economies-in-the-world/86159/1

Glosny, M. A. (2010). China and the BRICS: A Real (but limited) Partnership in a Unipolar World. *Polity*, 42(1), 100–129. DOI: 10.1057/pol.2009.14

Gouvea, R., & Gutierrez, M. (2023). "BRICS Plus": A New Global Economic Paradigm in the Making? *Modern Economy*, 14(5), 539–550. DOI: 10.4236/me.2023.145029

Gray, K., & Gills, B. K. (2016). South-South Cooperation and the Rise of the Global South. *Third World Quarterly*, 37(4), 557–574. DOI: 10.1080/01436597.2015.1128817

Gupta, C. (2024). Top 10 Most Powerful Countries in the World by Military Strength in 2024: Where does India Rank? *The Indian Express*. https://indianexpress.com/article/trending/top-10-listing/top-10-most-powerful-countries-in-the-world-by-military-strength-in-2024-9382565/

Hooijmaaijers, B., & Keukeleire, S. (2016). Voting Cohesion of the BRICS Countries in the UN General Assembly, 2006-2014: A BRICS Too Far? *Global Governance*, 22(3), 389–407. DOI: 10.1163/19426720-02203006

Hopewell, K. (2017). The BRICS — Merely a Fable? Emerging Power Alliances in Global Trade Governance. *International Affairs*, 93(6), 1377–1396. DOI: 10.1093/ia/iix192

India, B. R. I. C. S. (2021). Evolution of BRICS. https://brics2021.gov.in/about-brics

Joint Statement of the 10th Summit. (2018). Johannesburg Declaration. South Africa.

Joint Statement of the 14th Summit. (2022). Beijing Declaration. China.

Joint Statement of the 15th Summit. (2023). Johannesburg II Declaration. South Africa.

Joint Statement of the 1st Summit. (2009). Joint Statement of the BRIC Countries' Leaders. Russia.

Joint Statement of the 2nd Summit. (2010). 2nd BRIC Summit of Heads of State and Government: Joint Statement. Brazil.

Joint Statement of the 3rd Summit. (2011). Sanya Declaration. China.

Joint Statement of the 5th Summit. (2013). eThekwini Declaration. South Africa.

Joint Statement of the 6th Summit. (2014). Fortaleza Declaration. Brazil.

Joint Statement of the 7th Summit. (2015). Ufa Declaration. Russia.

Joint Statement of the 8th Summit. (2016). Goa Declaration. India.

Joint Statement of the 9th Summit. (2017). Xiamen Declaration. China.

Jütten, M., & Falkenberg, D. (2024). Expansion of BRICS: A Quest for Greater Global Influence. European Parliamentary Research Service. https://www.europarl.europa.eu/RegData/etudes/BRIE/2024/760368/EPRS_BRI(2024)760368_EN.pdf

Käkönen, J. (2014). BRICS as a New Power in International Relations? *Geopolitics, History, and International Relations*, 6(2), 85–104.

Kazelko, A., & Semeghini, U. S. (2024). Expansion of BRICS: Implications for Global Energy Markets. *BRICS Journal of Economics*, 5(1), 53–67. DOI: 10.3897/brics-econ.5.e117048

Kipgen, K. T., & Chakrabarti, S. (2022). The Politics Underpinning the BRICS Expansion. *Journal of Liberty and International Affairs*, 8(3), 445–458.

Kniivilä, M. (2007). Industrial Development and Economic Growth: Implications for Poverty Reduction and Income Inequality. In *Industrial Development for the 21st Century: Sustainable Development Perspectives* (pp. 295-332). United Nations Department of Social and Economic Affairs.

Lagutina, M. L. (2019). BRICS in a World of Regions. *Third World Thematics*, 4(6), 442–458. DOI: 10.1080/23802014.2019.1643781

Laidi, Z. (2011). The BRICS against the West? *CERI Strategi Papers*, 11, 1–12.

Lissovolik, Y. (2023a). BRICS+ after the 2023 "Expansion Summit.". *Pathways to Peace and Security*, 65(2), 42–52. DOI: 10.20542/2307-1494-2023-2-42-52

Lissovolik, Y. (2023b). BRICS Plus: The New Force in Global Governance. *Journal of International Analytics*, 134(1), 138–148. DOI: 10.46272/2587-8476-2023-14-1-138-148

Lissovolik, Y. (2024). BRICS Expansion: New Geographies and Spheres of Cooperation. *BRICS Journal of Economics*, 5(1), 1–12. DOI: 10.3897/brics-econ.5.e120071

Lowe, P. (2016). The Rise of the BRICS in the Global Economy. *Teaching Geography*, 41(2), 50–53.

Luard, E. (1982). *A History of the United Nations: Volume 1: The Years of Western Domination, 1945-1955*. Springer.

Mansfield, E. (2014). Rising Power in the Global Economy: Issues and Questions. *International Studies Review*, 16(3), 437–442. DOI: 10.1111/misr.12148

Maryam, J., & Mittal, A. (2020). Foreign Direct Investment into BRICS: An Empirical Analysis. *Transnational Corporations Review*, 12(1), 1–9. DOI: 10.1080/19186444.2019.1709400

Mathur, S., & Dasgupta, M. (Eds.). (2013). *BRICS: Trade Policies, Institutions and Areas of Deepening Cooperation*. Centre for WTO Studies.

Medhat, A. (2020). A Critical Analysis to the United Nations' Performance in the Light of Contemporary Global Challenges. *SSRN*. http://dx.doi.org/DOI: 10.2139/ssrn.3564486

Mohajan, H. K. (2021). Third Industrial Revolution Brings Global Development. *Journal of Social Sciences and Humanities*, 7(1), 239–251.

Mohammed, S. (2024). BRICS Plus: De-Dollarization and Global Power Shifts in New Economic Landscape. *BRICS Journal of Economics*, 5(1), 13–32. DOI: 10.3897/brics-econ.5.e117828

Naik, S. (2018). Rising BRICS: A Path to Multipolar World Reality? *Comparative Politics Russia*, 1, 100–108.

NDB (National Development Bank). (n.d.). https://www.ndb.int/

O'Neil, J. (2001). Building better Global Economic BRICs. *Global Economics Paper*, 66, 1–16.

Pathak, L., & Shah, K. (2019). Renewable Energy Resources, Policies and Gaps in BRICS Countries and the Global Impact. *Frontiers in Energy*, 13(3), 506–521. DOI: 10.1007/s11708-018-0601-z

Robets, C. (2010). Challengers or Stakeholders? BRICs and the Liberal World Order. *Polity*, 42(1), 1–13.

Rolland, S. (2013). The BRICS' Contribution to the Architecture and Norms of International Economic Law. *Proceedings of the ASIL Annual Meeting* 107, 164-170. DOI: 10.5305/procannmeetasil.107.0164

Røren, P., & Beaumont, P. (2019). Grading Greatness: Evaluating the Status Performance of the BRICS. *Third World Quarterly*, 40(3), 429–450. DOI: 10.1080/01436597.2018.1535892

Rosenau, J. N. (1995). Governance in the Twenty-First Century. *Global Governance*, 1(1), 13–43. DOI: 10.1163/19426720-001-01-90000004

Sergunin, A., & Gao, F. (2018). BRICS as the Subject of Study of International Relations Theory. *International Organizations Research Journal*, 13(4), 55–73. DOI: 10.17323/1996-7845-2018-04-03

Shambaugh, G. (2024). Embargo. https://www.britannica.com/money/embargo-international-law

Sokolov, A., Shashnov, S., & Kotsemir, M. (2021). From BRICS to BRICS Plus: Selecting Promising Areas of S & T Cooperation with Developing Countries. *Scientometrics*, 126(11), 8815–8859. DOI: 10.1007/s11192-021-04142-3

South Africa, B. R. I. C. S. (2023). BRICS Membership Expansion Guiding Principles, Standards, Criteria and Procedures. https://brics2023.gov.za/wp-content/uploads/2023/11/BRICS-Membership-expansion-guiding-principles-criteria-and-standards-2023.pdf

Statista Research Department. (2024). GDP in PPP of BRICS and G7 Countries 2000-2024. https://www.statista.com/statistics/1412418/gdp-development-g7-brics/

Thakur, R. (2014). How Representative are BRICS? *Third World Quarterly*, 35(10), 1791–1808. DOI: 10.1080/01436597.2014.971594

Tripathi, S. (2021). International Relations and the 'Global South': From Epistemic Hierarchies to Dialogic Encounters. *Third World Quarterly*, 42(9), 2039–2054. DOI: 10.1080/01436597.2021.1924666

UN. (n.d.). Preparatory Years: UN Charter History. https://www.un.org/en/about-us/history-of-the-un/preparatory-years#:~:text=The%20UN%20Charter%20was%20signed,UN's%20original%2051%20Member%20States

UNDP. (2013). *Human Development Report*. UNDP.

UNDP (United Nations Development Program). (1994). *Human Development Report*. UNDP.

Wade, R. (2003). What Strategies are Viable for Developing Countries Today? The World Trade Organization and the Shrinking of 'Development Space'. *Review of International Political Economy*, 10(4), 621–644. DOI: 10.1080/0969229031000l601902

WCED (World Commission on Environment and Development). (1987). *Our Common Future*. UN.

World Population Review. (2024). Global North Countries 2024. https://worldpopulationreview.com/country-rankings/global-north-countries

Worldometer. (2024). Oil Production by Country. https://www.worldometers.info/oil/oil-production-by-country/

# Chapter 4
# China's Strategic Influence and Rivalries in Southeast Asia: BRIC and China's Geopolitical Strategy

**Tin Maung Htwe**
https://orcid.org/0009-0002-3002-169X
*Chiang Mai University, Thailand*

## ABSTRACT

*Southeast Asia (SEA) has emerged as a critical battleground for global powers . China, US and BRIC are playing a central role in shaping the geopolitical dynamics of region. As the largest economy within BRICS (Brazil, Russia, India, China, South Africa), China leverages its economic statecraft through initiatives like the Belt and Road Initiative (BRI) and the Regional Comprehensive Economic Partnerships to solidify its influence in SEA region. Framed by its strategic competition with the United States, India and the Quadrilateral Security Dialogue (QUAD), the role of China presence in Southeast Asia as mutipolars. This paper explores China's geopolitical strategy to highlight its use of economic diplomacy, infrastructure development and bilatral agreements to foster regional dominance. The responses of Southeast Asian nations have adopted hedging strategies to balance economic ties with China while maintaining security relationships with the U.S. and other powers.*

DOI: 10.4018/979-8-3693-7393-4.ch004

## INTRODUCTION

Geopolitical strategies of China toward Southeast Asia reflects a broader pattern of influence exerted through both economic and security mechanisms. Initiatives such as the Belt and Road Initiative (BRI) have facilitated significant infrastructure investments across the region (Sihaloho, Prabowo, & Pamungkas, 2024). They are emblematic of China's economic statecraft. These investments serve not only to integrate Southeast Asia into broader trades and infrastructure networks with China and nourborings each other but also to exert soft power influence in long term. By deepening economic dependencies shift regional alignments in its favor. However, alongside economic diplomacy, China engages in military posturing in the South China Sea. The Maritime Silk Road Initiative is a significant component of China's global strategy, with extensive geopolitical implications (Blanchard & Flint, 2017). China have faced territorial dispute with several Southeast Asian nations and intensified regional tensions. Morevoer, Taiwan issue of one China Policy, border conflict with India and current interventions of China role in Myanmar and vitien make tensions of anti China sentitments. However, China is positioning itself as the preeminent power in Southeast Asia and regions as both hard and soft powers. The US Taiwan policy has transitioned significantly, reflecting a shift from strategic ambiguity to a more assertive stance (Ye, 2022). Through a mix of diplomatic engagement, strategic partnerships within BRICS, and military assertiveness, It become the challenging the influence of rival powers like the U.S, India, Japan and their regional allies.

Since 2009, Through leadership of Xi president, Beijing's strategies increasingly have focused on Southeast Asia as a focal point for asserting its regional dominance and global ambitions (Goldstein, 2020). As a member of BRICS, China tries to utilize this coalition not only to foster South-South cooperation but also as a mechanism to challenge Western hegemony. China gradually assert its leadership in the Global South and espicially, South East Asia region (Sheng & do Nascimento, 2021). The region's strategic location, thriving economies and pivotal maritime routes have made it central to China's efforts to reshape the global political economy.

As this chapter explores about regional influence, geopolitical maneuvers in Southeast Asia are deeply intertwined with the broader context of BRICS influence. Those rivalries stem from competing global visions. Since World War II, the United States has largely dominated Southeast Asia, with countries like the Philippines, Thailand, Indonesia, Cambodia, Malaysia, Singapore, and even Vietnam traditionally aligning with and engaging the U.S. However, China's rise began to take shape after the 1978 reforms. Through expanding economic and military power, China shifted its policies from a focus on domestic foreign direct investment and production to a broader international investment sphere. This strategic rivalry between the United

States and China now plays a crucial role in shaping the geopolitical landscape of Southeast Asia (Shambaugh, 2020). As a dominant power within the BRICS framework, China amplifies its capacity to build alliances. It become challenges toward the unipolarity traditionally dominated by the United States. Moreover, Another BRICS member closely to region in Asia, India presents a distinct challenge for China in influencing Southeast Asia. Both nations of BRICS compete for influence through economic projects and diplomatic ties. China's leadership in the BRICS+ expansion is aimed at establishing legitimacy through diversity for global balance (Lee & Sims, 2024). Therefore, the BRICS platform itself offers China a unique avenue to counterbalance U.S.-led initiatives like the QUAD and foster a multipolar world order. This chapter highlights about China leverages and its role within BRICS. Chapter also discuss China strategic economic and security policies and advocacy to redefine power dynamics in Southeast Asia.

## LITERATURE REVIEW

Geopolitical theory explores the impact of geographic factors on political power and international relations. It discusses about the geography influences and state behavior in terms of military strategy, economic development and diplomatic relations. The interplay between geopolitics and international trade shapes global economic relations (Barbieri, 2024). Geographical factors play a significant role in shaping the political strategies of states. Southeast Asia become a prime example due to its strategic location and resources sharing with China (Koga, 2022). China has strengthened its land links with Myanmar, Laos, and Vietnam, extending its influence in Southeast Asia. Additionally, it connects to Thailand and Cambodia via the Mekong River. In the maritime realm, China's claims in the South China Sea overlap with the territorial waters of the Philippines, Indonesia, Brunei, Malaysia, and Vietnam. Moreover, its strategic presence in the Andaman Sea and near the Malacca Strait creates competitive pressures for India in critical trading routes (Rising, 2024).

The rise of China as a global power and need of trading places Southeast Asian nations in a precarious strategic position and and become challenges the established balance of power in the region. The post-9/11 period has seen significant changes in South Asia's security landscape, driven by evolving regional dynamics (Jamil, Ahmad, Rizvi, & Gwadabe, 2020). Egberink and Van der Putten (2010) illustrate the balancing act performed by ASEAN nations. As they manage China's influence amid other great powers like India and the US, ASEAN countries often employ strategic hedging to ensure that no single power dominates the region. ASEAN's strategy in the South China Sea aims to navigate the complex dynamics of great power politics (Koga, 2022). Hedging serves as a key element in Southeast Asian countries' grand strategies to manage relations with competing global powers (Jones & Jenne, 2022). The hierarchical order and security strategies define foreign policy approaches. While China BRI influence into Middle East. US focus toward South China Sea and Taiwan issue in the context of the US-China rivalry (Singh, 2021). The natural consequences of China's growing regional influence. It forces Southeast Asian countries to carefully navigate their relationships with major powers like the US and China and perceptive of Taiwan issues and one China policy. As these nations seek to benefit from Chinese economic investments, they must also mitigate the risks associated with Beijing's expanding geopolitical reach. The geopolitical rivalry in Southeast Asia between major powers like the United States and China has profound implications for regional stability (Stromseth, 2021; Shambaugh, 2020).

China's Belt and Road Initiative (BRI) plays a central role in its geopolitical strategy in Southeast Asia. Gong (2019) explors that the BRI enhances China's influence through infrastructure investments and economic ties (Li, 2020). Southeast Asian countries leverage their strategic positions to secure economic benefits while safeguarding their sovereignty. The growing role of regional powers significantly impacts contemporary US-China relations and the broader dynamics of great power rivalry (Roberts & Bano, 2023). The BRI's challenges that the initiative faces financial and geopolitical resistance. China's geopolitical strategy success in regional power. Particularly its competition with the US, China stregitally uses inter govermental economic diplomacy, public private initiatives and soft power to reshape regional dynamics while the US employs strategic alliances and multilateral agreements to counterbalance Beijing's influence. Despite significant spending, China's investment in soft power has yet to yield substantial returns (Albert, 2018).

Southeast Asian nations have responded to China's rise. By engaging in multilateral diplomacy and leveraging external powers, they try to avoid becoming overly dependent on Beijing. ASEAN's policy of "hedging" is a prime example of regional states to navigate between competing powers by ensuring no single actor dominates the geopolitical landscape. These nations maintain strategic autonomy by engaging in diplomatic initiatives and fostering relations with multiple global powers ASEAN's centrality faces complex challenges that necessitate strategic reconstruction (Yunqi, 2023). Strangio (2020) explores the influence of China on Southeast Asia. He argue that the pushback from Southeast Asian nations against China's assertive stance. Regarding territorial claims in the South China Sea through anti China sitiment in vietnam eventhough historically and ideological being political partners in the past. Despite China's aggressive posturing, countries like Vietnam, the Philippines, Thailand, Singapore and Malaysia continue to resist Chinese encroachment on their territorial sovereignty and often seek the support from external powers like the US and Japan (Scott, 2021).

The rivalry between the United States and China in Southeast Asia is multifaceted. Gur and Dilek (2023) discuss the impact of the U.S.-China economic rivalry on global supply chains. The trade war between the two superpowers in region has disrupted supply chains and trade flows. It impact the region's economies. The pressures of Southeast Asian countries in choosing between US and Chinese technologies. Southeast Asian countries hedge their bets amid US-China tech competition. The trade-offs between economic opportunities from Chinese investments and security risks by Chinese technology, particularly in the 5G sector. Southeast Asian countries employ technological hedging to navigate US-China competition in AI and new modern techonology. The strategic competition in the 5G market through companies like Huawei, with US pressure on Southeast Asian countries to avoid Chinese technology and degital assistances. The implications for supply chains and security in Southeast Asia (Zhao, 2024). The strategic dynamics of U.S.-China relations have significant implications for Indo-Pacific security and policy-making (Pacific Forum, 2019). The intensifying strategic competition between the US and China significantly impacts Southeast Asia. Roberts and Bano (2023) argued both countries try to influence regional security dynamics and economic policies. Southeast Asian states are not passive players. They possess agency and leverage to navigate this rivalry to their advantage. They mainly depend on demestic power and resource. The strategic aproach become importance of the region. Despite limitations in US initiatives compared to China's economic incentives, SEA countries highlights the role of ASEAN in maintaining regional security and economic prosperity.

## BACKGROUND

China's strategic alliances within the BRICS framework and its competition with the United States and India is complex reltionship. China's geographic position and its extensive borders with several countries impact its foreign policy and security strategies. China's initiatives of the Belt and Road Initiative (BRI) and the China-Pakistan Economic Corridor (CPEC) are not merely economic but also geopolitical tools to expand its influence. It can counterbalance the US presence in Asia. The strategic importance of regions like the South China Sea is crucial for China's maritime dominance and resource acquisition. The BRI and CPEC play a significant role in reshaping China's soft power in South Asia and the Middle East (Siddique & Shafqat, 2021).

The influences of both the United States and China shape the geopolitical landscape of Southeast Asia significantly. During the Cold War, the US aimed to contain the spread of communism. Thereofre, it lead to substantial military, economic and political involvement in the region. Countries such as Vietnam, Laos, Myanmar and

Cambodia were key battlegrounds for US efforts to counter communist insurgencies Southeast Asia's strategic relations with the U.S. and China involve a nuanced balance of influence and alignment (Goh et al., 2005). The establishment of alliances like the Southeast Asia Treaty Organization (SEATO) and military bases in the Philippines exemplified US strategic interests in maintaining a foothold in Southeast Asia. The concept of a "Pacific NATO" raises questions about its viability and practicality in the context of Asian security (Bartnick, 2020).

On the other hand, China's influence in Southeast Asia has deep historical roots but became more pronounced post-Cold War. The soft power competition between Japan, China, and Korea in promoting language learning in Thailand and South East Asia seem broader regional dynamics (Han, 2022). Through rasie of economic power, China has utilized both soft and hard power strategies to expand its influence. Through economic investments, trade partnerships and infrastructure projects under the BRI, China has fostered strong bilateral relationships with Southeast Asian countries. deLisle (2020) discusses China's shift to political warfare as a tool of foreign policy, combining hard and soft power strategies to influence the United States. The interplay between US and Chinese influence in Southeast Asia continues to evolve. Since beginning of 21 century, the US enforce on maintaining its strategic alliances in promoting democratic and civic development while China leverage its economic clout to draw countries into its orbit (Denmark, 2020).

China approach seem inline with most of South East Asia dream of development. Southeast Asia's relationship with China and the strategic ambitions of the Belt and Road Initiative illustrate China's growing influence in global affairs (Emmerson, 2020; Pröpper, 2020). However, China's territorial claims and strategic interests in Southeast Asia are centered around its desire to secure resources, enhance its maritime dominance and expand its geopolitical influence. One of the most contentious areas is the South China Sea. China claims vast swathes of territory delineated by the "nine-dash line". This claim overlaps with those of several Southeast Asian nations, including Vietnam, the Philippines, Malaysia and Brunei The sovereignty issues in the South China Sea carry significant legal and geopolitical implications (Bukhari et al., 2024). The South China Sea is strategically vital for several reasons. Macaraig and Fenton (2021) examine the underlying causes and significant effects of the South China Sea dispute on regional stability. It is one of the world's busiest maritime corridors and a significant portion of global trade passing through its waters. The region is believed to be rich in oil and natural gas reserves and crucial for China's energy security and transporation in long term. Control over the South China Sea enhances China's ability to project power and secure its southern coastline. To assert its claims, China has undertaken extensive land reclamation and constructed military installations on various islands and reefs. This militarization has raised tensions with other claimant states. Therefore, by supporting of the US and alliance, South East Asia nations try to conduct freedom of navigation operations to challenge China's assertions. The territorial disputes in the South China Sea involve multiple nations and have significant implications for regional stability (Center for Preventive Action, 2024).

Beyond the South China Sea, China's strategic interests in Southeast Asia include securing vital trade routes, establishing economic corridors (such as the China-Indochina Peninsula Economic Corridor) and fostering regional stability favorable to its development goals of overall SEA nations. China's diplomatic engagements, infrastructure investments and participation in regional organizations like ASEAN are part of its broader strategy to build a stable and prosperous neighborhood that aligns with both China and SEA interests The Indo-Pacific region is experiencing enhanced connectivity and new supply-chain linkages as part of regional integration efforts (Herrero et al., 2023). SEA nations and ASEAN notice that without China facilitation and investments, the dream of One South East Community is impossible. The Belt and Road Initiative promotes China's concept of a **"Community of Destiny"** and **"One Vision, One Identity, One Community" of The motto of ASEAN** in Southeast Asia (Du Rocher, 2020). Therefore, China investment throught BRI link SEA region in overall integration. For example, the Kunming-Singapore railway is a promising project for both trade and the energy sector across China, Laos, Thailand, Malaysia, and Singapore. Even Myanmar, Cambodia, and Vietnam could benefit through additional trade linkages (Wu, 2016; Railway Technology, n.d.; Kuik & Rosli, 2023). Therefore, understanding the geopolitical context through the lens of Geopolitical Theory provides a comprehensive framework to analyze China's strategic behavior in Southeast Asia. The historical context of US-China competition and China's territorial claims underscore the complexity and significance of the region in global geopolitics.

## China's Strategic Mechanisms in Southeast Asia

The arrival of Chinese power in Southeast Asia bases on its economic, military, and cultural influence. China's economic reforms initiated by Deng Xiaoping in 1978 have led to unprecedented economic growth and has intensified interdependence between China and Southeast Asia. This interdependence, howeverv is asymmetrical. China exertes significant influence over the region. China-ASEAN relations have evolved significantly since their formalization in the early 1990s. The foundation for these relations started with the establishment of the China-ASEAN dialogue in 1991 and attached the creation of a full dialogue partnership in 1996. This partnership saw substantial development with China's accession to the Treaty of Amity and Cooperation in Southeast Asia in 2003 to ensure marking the commitment to peace and stability in the region (Khoo, 2023). Several key agreements and initiatives have been pivotal in shaping China-ASEAN relations. Established in 2010, the China-ASEAN Free Trade Area (CAFTA) is one of the largest free trade areas in the world. It encompass over 1.8 billion people of overall region population. This partnership had strengthened and significantly boosted economic ties between the two entities (Chinvanno, 2015). This agreement has facilitated increased trade and investment flows between China and ASEAN member states by reducing tariffs and other trade barriers.

China has been ASEAN's largest trading partner since 2009, with trade nearly quadrupling since the 2005 ASEAN-China Trade in Goods Agreement. Between 2010 and 2019, trade doubled from USD 235.5 billion to USD 507.9 billion, resulting in an increased trade deficit for ASEAN, rising from USD 10.4 billion to USD 102.9 billion. Exports from ASEAN to China grew at an average of 10.4% annually, while imports grew by 12.5%. In terms of investment, Chinese FDI in ASEAN reached USD 9.1 billion in 2019, making China ASEAN's fourth largest FDI source among Dialogue Partners. Notably, during the first half of 2020, ASEAN overtook other regions to become China's top trading partner, with trade rising 2.2% despite the pandemic, underscoring strong economic ties (ASEAN 2024). Launched by China in 2013, the Belt and Road Initiative (BRI) aims to enhance regional connectivity through overall infrastructure development, trade and investment. Many ASEAN countries are key participants in the BRI. They can foreseem benefits from Chinese investments in infrastructure projects such as railways, ports and highways through linking toward China and one another. Signed in 2020, the Regional Comprehensive Economic Partnership (RCEP) liberalize trade and investment in the region and promote deeper economic integration of China, ASEAN member states and other Asia-Pacific countries. Adopted in 2018, the China-ASEAN Strategic Partnership Vision 2030 outlines the long-term goals for the strategic partnership. Enhancing cooperation in various sectors, trade, investment, digital economy, and people-to-people exchanges among ASEAN nations and China could growth together (Huy, 2023).

China has become ASEAN's largest trading partner after 2010. Trade volumes have been increasing significantly after globel economic crisis in 2008. Bilateral trade driven by CAFTA and RCEP, China exports to ASEAN including machinery, electronics and textiles while ASEAN exports agricultural products, minerals and electronics to China (Shen & Li, 2023). Chinese investments in ASEAN countries have surged as direct foregin investment particularly in the infrastructure, manufacturing, agriculture and real estate sectors (Xu & Lim, 2024). The BRI plays a crucial role in those investment. Tourism of China become a vital component of economic ties in South East Asia. Millions of Chinese tourists visite ASEAN countries annually and contribute significantly to their economies (Tan & Chin, 2020). Major projects such as the China-Laos railway, the development of deep-sea ports like Kyauk Phyu in Myanmar, and investments in Cambodia's Sihanoukville Special Economic Zone demonstrate China's ambition to integrate the region into its broader economic ecosystem. These projects facilitate trade flows and offer China significant geopolitical leverage (Sun, 2017), (Banerjee, 2024). China has been ASEAN's largest trading partner, with trade relations underpinned by mechanisms such as the ASEAN-China Free Trade Area (ACFTA) and, more recently, the Regional Comprehensive Economic Partnership (RCEP). The RCEP is the world's largest trade agreement and includes ASEAN member states alongside China, Japan, South Korea, Australia and New Zealand. This agreement not only enhances China's economic footprint in Southeast Asia but also solidifies its role as the primary economic driver in the region, making it a preferred partner over the U.S. and India (Huld, 2024).

The State of Southeast Asia (2024) Survey reveals a significant increase in China's influence within the region. 50.5% of respondents favored alignment with China over the U.S. This notable rise from the previous year 2023 (Seah et al., 2024). This shift shows to understand China's extensive economic engagement through the Belt and Road Initiative (BRI) and its role in regional trade agreements. Malaysia, Indonesia, and Laos are major benefiting from China's investments and survey show increased positive China sentiment in those countries (Lin, 2024). However, concerns persist regarding China's assertive policies and domestic actions, such as the Counter-Espionage Law and its behavior in the South China Sea (Hung et al., 2023). Khoo (2023) highlights the complexity of this relationship, noting both the economic benefits and the political tensions that have emerged (Hu, 2023).

Cultural exchanges have strengthened mutual understanding and people-to-people ties between China and ASEAN. Scholarships and student exchange programs have increased overall. China allows students from ASEAN countries to study in China and vice versa. Various cultural festivals and events, such as the China-ASEAN Expo and China-ASEAN Education Cooperation Week, promote cultural understanding and collaboration (Chirathivat, 2022). Confucius Institutes, oversea chinese associations and other cultural centers in ASEAN countries help promote Chinese language and culture and foster closer ties. Politically, China-ASEAN relations based on economical cooperation and strategic dialogue after the cold world. Despite some underlying tensions, China and ASEAN engage in regular dialogues on regional security issues (Rachana & Sreynich, 2021). While there are challenges, mechanisms like the Declaration on the Conduct of Parties in the South China Sea (DOC) and ongoing negotiations for a Code of Conduct (COC) aim to manage and resolve conflicts peacefully (Nguyen & Pham, 2021). China and ASEAN collaborate in various multilateral forums such as the ASEAN Regional Forum (ARF), East Asia Summit (EAS) and the Asia-Pacific Economic Cooperation (APEC). Those collaborations address regional and global issues collectively. Bilateral and multilateral dialogues help address common challenges and build trust. High-level visits and summits, such as the annual China-ASEAN Summit, underscore the importance of the relationship (Budiana, 2024). Therefore, generally, China-ASEAN relations encompass a multifaceted partnership of robust economic ties, dynamic cultural exchanges and strategic political cooperation.

## US-China Rivalry in Southeast Asia

Both China and the USA face significant constraints in establishing leadership in Southeast Asia. China's internal constraints include fragmented authority, the need of coordinating economic resources and foreign policy, involvement of numerous government departments and the autonomy of state-owned enterprises (SOEs) make china relationship in chaos. Taylor (2015) argued that China's fragmented authoritarianism hampers the coordination of economic resources and foreign policy. The role of intermediaries and institutions shape China's influence in Southeast Asia (Fung, Han, Quek, & Strange, 2023). China's internal structure and governance stracture make challenges in combinatination of clear pathway. These complexities impact China's ability to implement foreign policy and economic strategies effectively. Enze Han (2019) characterizes China as an unconventional great power. Its' fragmented, decentralized, and internationalized, affect foreign policy implementation. The complex operations of SOEs undermine China's economic statecraft in the region. For example, the intrest upon Myanmar based on Yunan government and sometime out of connect to Beijing policy. On the other hand, Southeast Asian countries' domestic politics also influence their foreign policies. Those domestic intrests drive to contribute to bilateral frictions and anti-Chinese sentiment. The strategic dilemmas of Southeast Asian countries in the South China Sea dispute, development projects and unresolved territorial disputes shape perceptions of China as a threat (Rubiolo, 2020). In this cases, US can take advantage of taking role of protection of democracy and human rights.

The USA's strategy in Southeast Asia often oscillates between systemic neglect and over-militarization present. Actualy, it make weakening its position in long term. On the economic front, the U.S. has engaged Southeast Asia through the Indo-Pacific Economic Framework for Prosperity (IPEF), which aims to offer an economic alternative to China's BRI. Diplomatically, the U.S. has increased engagement with ASEAN through forums like the East Asia Summit and ASEAN-U.S. summits. However, these efforts have often been overshadowed by China's large-scale investments and trade agreements, making it difficult for the U.S. to compete on an economic level. Boone, Nkamwa, & Cao (2023) discuss about the lack of sustained attention and economic engagement that contributes to regional dissatisfaction. As a global power, the USA prioritized other regions over Southeast Asia and further alienated regional countries during the time of Trump administration.

Mäkinen (2018) provides insights into the domestic political and economic issues of US attention from Southeast Asia. He argue that Domestic turmoil and internal political and economic issues of US politics and party priority make unconstistance international relationship. In the Trump administration's withdrawal from the Trans-Pacific Partnership impact the weakness of foreign policy and strategic engagements of USA in the region. President Joe Biden's efforts to re-engage with Southeast Asia and counterbalance China's growing dominance face challenges due to the absence of effective economic statecraft (The Economist 2023). Therefore, without effective supports and economic collaboration, the role of USA seem disadvantage in real political affiliation. In the time of Covid pandamic and after recovery, investments and assistance of China toward South East Asia boost the economy of individual nations. Therefore, in reality South East Asia countries and their governments prefer China over US in general. However, due to US still influence on European and regional alliance such as Japan, Korea and Australia, South East Asia engages USA as main partner in dialogue. In response to these dynamics, Southeast Asian states adopt hedging strategies. They try to balance economic, political and security policies to maximize returns while minimizing risks. Hedging involves continuous adjustment between cooperation and counterbalancing based on changing geopolitical realities. Stromseth (2020) emphasizes the role of state elites' perceptions and public opinion in shaping strategic behavior. This complex interplay shapes the region's strategic behavior and the sustainability of hedging strategies of domestic intrests in international relationship.

Security dynamics in the region are also complex. The rivalry between China and the United States in Southeast Asia is one of the most significant geopolitical contests in the region. Since the end of the Cold War, the U.S. has maintained a dominant security presence in the region through alliances with countries like the Philippines and Thailand, as well as partnerships with Singapore, Vietnam, and Malaysia. However, China's rise has increasingly challenged this status quo. Through the BRI, China has strategically invested in critical infrastructure projects in Southeast Asia, offering an alternative to U.S. influence, particularly in countries that seek to balance their relations between the two powers. Southeast Asian countries balance their relationships to maximize strategic autonomy in competing rivalry. Singh (2020) discusses how this rivalry creates a challenging security environment. Roy (2021) discusses the strategic impact of China's artificial islands in the South China Sea and the resulting diplomatic confrontations. The US has responded by strengthening its alliances and promoting a free and open Indo-Pacific strategy. The rivalry between the US and China in Southeast Asia extends beyond economic interests to include political, diplomatic and security concerns. Stromseth (2019) highlights that China's rise has influenced US policy adjustments in the region. Vo, Nguyen, Tran, & Bui (2023) mention the US response as conducting freedom of navigation operations and enhancing defense cooperation. This strategic competition is increasingly complex and could lead to geopolitical conflicts in the coming years. Yet, despite U.S. efforts to maintain its influence, many Southeast Asian countries have chosen to deepen economic ties with China to prioritize economic growth over security concerns.

## India-China Rivalry in Southeast Asia

The India-China border disputes, particularly over Aksai Chin and Arunachal Pradesh have been a longstanding source of tension. The 1962 Sino-Indian War and recent incidents like the 2020 Galwan Valley clash underscore this ongoing rivalry (Seagroatt, 2019). These disputed regions are critical to both countries' national security interests. It shape their military and diplomatic strategies (Das, 2020). China's infrastructure development in Tibet is a strategic effort to consolidate control over these areas. India has responded by modernizing its military along the border by enhancing surveillance and fortification to counter China's assertiveness (Goetz, 2019).

This rivalry extends to Southeast Asia. Impacting maritime security and regional influence, both nations seek to expand their naval capabilities in the Indian Ocean and South China Sea to influence regional maritime security and the balance of power (Panda, 2020). India's Act East policy and China's Belt and Road Initiative (BRI) intersect in Southeast Asia, leading to competing infrastructure and development projects, presenting both opportunities and challenges for Southeast Asian nations (Mohan, 2018). China's BRI plays a central role in expanding its influence across Southeast Asia, with key projects like the China-Myanmar Economic Corridor (CMEC) and significant investments in the South China Sea. These efforts aim to establish China as a dominant regional power. In contrast, India's Act East Policy represents a strategic counterbalance, focusing on strengthening ties with Southeast Asian countries through trade, strategic partnerships, and capacity-building initiatives. India's involvement in the Quadrilateral Security Dialogue (Quad) with the United States, Japan, and Australia further underscores its efforts to maintain a regional balance of power (Srivithaya, 2021).

India's strategic alliances are pivotal in countering China's influence in Southeast Asia. The partnership with the United States, characterized by defense cooperation, joint military exercises, and strategic dialogues, is central to India's regional strategy. This collaboration enhances India's military capabilities and supports its role in countering China's expanding influence. The U.S. views India as a key ally in preserving regional stability and maintaining a balance of power (Shahzad & Khan, 2022).

India's strategic partnership with Japan also has significant implications for regional dynamics. This alliance focuses on economic cooperation, technological exchange, and infrastructure development, reflecting a shared interest in countering China's dominance. Japan's investments in Indian infrastructure and support for maritime security are crucial aspects of this partnership. Strengthening these ties bolsters India's strategic capabilities and reinforces its position against China's expansive reach. Regionally, India's engagement with ASEAN nations highlights its commitment to enhancing influence and supporting stability through trade agreements, security dialogues, and collaborative projects. Participation in ASEAN-led frameworks such as the East Asia Summit (EAS) and the ASEAN Regional Forum (ARF) underscores India's dedication to regional cooperation. Strategic projects like the India-Myanmar-Thailand Trilateral Highway further emphasize India's active role in the region, aiming to enhance integration and provide a counterweight to China's initiatives (Mishra, 2021).

Despite the competition, there are opportunities for India and China to collaborate in areas like trade liberalization, investment in key sectors, and regional economic integration. Enhancing economic cooperation between India, China, and ASEAN could lead to a more prosperous and stable regional environment (Sahbzada, 2021).

The rivalry between China and India has deep roots, stemming from border disputes in the Himalayas and competition for influence across Asia. In Southeast Asia, this rivalry has taken on a more subtle form, with both countries vying for economic and strategic influence. India's Act East Policy, which seeks to deepen ties with ASEAN, is a direct response to China's growing presence in the region. India has promoted economic cooperation through initiatives like the Mekong-Ganga Cooperation and the India-ASEAN Free Trade Area, yet its economic engagement in the region pales in comparison to China's.

## The QUAD's Role in the Indo-Pacific

Initially established in 2007 and revitalized in 2017, the Quadrilateral Security Dialogue (QUAD) is a strategic partnership between the United States, Japan, India, and Australia. This alliance aims to promote a free, open, and inclusive Indo-Pacific region by addressing various multifaceted challenges through enhanced cooperation among its member nations. The QUAD's primary objectives include countering China's growing influence in the region, particularly through its assertive policies in the South China Sea and its expansive Belt and Road Initiative (BRI) (Wei, 2024).

Despite its focus on military and security cooperation, critics argue that the QUAD's effectiveness is limited by its neglect of underlying political and economic issues. They advocate for a more comprehensive approach that includes economic development and diplomatic engagement to address the root causes of regional instability. The QUAD champions a rules-based maritime order, emphasizing adherence to international laws such as the United Nations Convention on the Law of the Sea (UNCLOS) to counter China's efforts to assert control over contested waters (Heiduk & Wirth, 2023). Strategically, the QUAD provides a counterbalance to China's economic and strategic initiatives by promoting alternative regional development models aligned with international standards. The alliance also engages in joint military exercises and intelligence sharing to bolster collective defense capabilities, enhance interoperability, and ensure a cohesive response to regional security threats.

Beyond security, the QUAD focuses on economic cooperation by supporting infrastructure projects, digital connectivity, and economic resilience in the Indo-Pacific, aiming to create a stable and prosperous economic environment. Diplomatically, the QUAD addresses common challenges such as climate change and disaster response through collaborative initiatives, contributing to a stable and predictable regional governance framework. Jaffery and Pervez (2023) argue that while China views the QUAD as a threat to its regional ambitions, it also seeks to engage with QUAD members through economic and diplomatic channels. This dual approach aims to mitigate the QUAD's impact while advancing China's strategic interests.

While China's influence is pervasive, it is not uncontested by other BRIC countries. Schmidt (2011) highlights the growing rivalry between India and China in Southeast Asia, particularly regarding security and economic influence. India's Act East policy aims to counterbalance China's influence by fostering closer ties with ASEAN nations. By promoting regional security and enhancing trade relations between India and South East Asia through bilatrally and QUAD alliance. Meanwhile, Russia's involvement seem less pronounced. Facilitated through platforms like the Shanghai Cooperation Organization (SCO) and direct military ties for example Myanmar, Russia role in south East asia seem less influence comparing with rest of BRIC memebrs China and India.. Skalamera (2023) argues that Russia and China maintain a delicate balance in their regional interests and often cooperate through multilateral forums. Therefore, Southeast Asian nations strategically positioned at the crossroads of global power competition. They continue to perform a delicate balancing act to protect their interests while benefiting from the economic opportunities offered by external powers.

The Quadrilateral Security Dialogue (QUAD), which includes India, the U.S., Japan, and Australia, has emerged as a strategic counterbalance to China's influence in Southeast Asia. Although not explicitly framed as an anti-China alliance, the QUAD aims to promote a free and open Indo-Pacific, challenging China's assertiveness in the region. For Southeast Asian nations, the QUAD offers an alternative security framework that can help balance China's economic dominance. However, the QUAD's success in curbing China's influence remains limited, as most Southeast Asian countries are reluctant to fully align with either the QUAD or China, preferring instead to maintain strategic autonomy.

Japan, driven by historical grievances and ongoing territorial disputes with China, particularly over the East China Sea, has significantly ramped up its military capabilities and defense budget (Eisentraut & Gaens, 2018). Japan's strategic vision focuses on infrastructure investment, economic partnerships, and security cooperation, reinforcing its role as a key regional player (Harris & Hahn, 2023). Japan has actively opposed China's maritime claims in the East China Sea and has strengthened its military capabilities and alliances, especially with the United States. Smith (2019) discusses how Japan's strategic response to China's rise includes military modernization and diplomatic initiatives aimed at building a network of regional partners to counterbalance China's influence (Irsadanar, 2023). Japan's "soft balancing" tactics encompass economic engagement, diplomatic initiatives, security cooperation, and multilateralism. Through investments, development aid, and trade agreements, Japan seeks to enhance its economic ties with Southeast Asian countries. Diplomatically, Japan strengthens its presence in regional forums and promotes the Free and Open Indo-Pacific Strategy. Security cooperation involves joint military exercises and defense capacity-building programs. Multilateral efforts emphasize a rules-based international order and peaceful dispute resolution. Key areas of focus include Japan's investment in regional infrastructure, participation in multilateral forums, and collaboration with key allies like the United States and Australia. These strategies collectively aim to counterbalance China's influence and maintain regional stability (Choudhury, 2023).

India's competition with China in Southeast Asia extends beyond economic and military spheres. Both countries have engaged in soft power diplomacy, promoting cultural ties and people-to-people exchanges to win hearts and minds in the region. While India emphasizes its historical and civilizational links to Southeast Asia, China's cultural diplomacy is heavily tied to its Confucius Institutes and economic investments, offering scholarships, educational exchanges, and business opportunities. However, China's economic advantage has allowed it to maintain the upper hand in the region, despite India's attempts to expand its influence.

By upholding international norms and strengthening partnerships with other countries and regional organizations, the QUAD plays a crucial role in shaping regional security dynamics and ensuring the stability and openness of the Indo-Pacific region. The QUAD emphasizes maintaining freedom of navigation, promoting democratic values, and countering Chinese influence (Wallace, 2022). This strategic focus directly impacts Southeast Asia's security policies and alliances. While the QUAD is important for promoting a free and open Indo-Pacific, enhancing maritime security, and fostering regional cooperation, Shahzad and Khan (2022) note that China's counterbalance strategies, such as strengthening bilateral ties with other regional actors and expanding its Belt and Road Initiative, present significant challenges to the QUAD's objectives. Continuous engagement and coordination among QUAD members are essential to address these challenges effectively. Additionally, the joint military exercises and coordinated policies among QUAD members aim to provide a counterbalance to China's assertiveness in the region.

## Geopolitics Among China, South East Asia and BRICS

China's role within the BRICS framework and its economic diplomacy in Southeast Asia can be analyzed through the lens of Geopolitical Theory, which emphasizes how geography, economics, and strategy shape power dynamics. As a leading member of BRICS (Brazil, Russia, India, China, and South Africa), China aims to expand its influence globally, positioning itself as a key player in the formation of a new global order that challenges Western, especially U.S., dominance. China's strategic leadership within BRICS signals its intent to reshape international governance by creating a multipolar world where emerging economies, like itself, can exert greater influence (Stuenkel, 2023). In Southeast Asia, China's economic diplomacy is showcased through initiatives like the Belt and Road Initiative (BRI) and the Regional Comprehensive Economic Partnership (RCEP). These initiatives leverage economic tools to advance geopolitical goals, using investments in infrastructure, such as ports, railways, and energy grids, to strengthen its control over vital trade corridors (Lew & Roughead, 2021). China's actions as part of a broader strategy to enhance its maritime power and dominate critical chokepoints, ensuring its preeminence in the region.

Southeast Asian nations view BRICS with a mixture of optimism and caution. While many see BRICS as a counterbalance to U.S.-led financial dominance and an opportunity to foster regional cooperation, concerns about China's growing influence within the bloc remain (Özekin & Sune, 2023). Countries like Indonesia and Malaysia, in particular, are wary of China using BRICS to advance its own geopolitical and economic objectives, potentially at the expense of smaller member states. Nonetheless, countries such as Malaysia and Thailand have expressed interest in joining BRICS+, recognizing the economic opportunities the bloc could provide (Hutt, 2024). By fostering institutions like the New Development Bank (NDB) and the Contingent Reserve Arrangement (CRA), BRICS offers financial alternatives (Aleksia & Bakhtiar, 2023). This can enable South East Asia countries to bypass Western-controlled financial mechanisms such as the IMF and World Bank (Moyo, 2024). By help of BRICS, China's geopolitical strategy extend its economic influence while reducing reliance on Western financial institution and further integrate Southeast Asia into its sphere of influence.

China strengthens its geopolitical position in sectors like energy and trade deepen its influence in Southeast Asia and the broader Global South (Delina, 2021). China's economic diplomacy in Southeast Asia, seen through its BRI and RCEP engagements, can also be understood through Geoeconomics. The use of economic power enchance for strategic purposes. By creating long-term dependencies through infrastructure investments and fostering economic interdependence, China strengthens its influence in Southeast Asia. As Southeast Asian nations increasingly rely on Chinese investments, they become more economically tied to China's growth and stability. This become a vital component of China's broader geopolitical strategy. China's influence in Southeast Asia is not confined to its economic heft. It extends deeply into security and diplomatic spheres. Through the Belt and Road Initiative (BRI), China has invested in infrastructure development across the region, creating extensive trade routes and enhancing connectivity with Southeast Asia. China's strategic alliances extend beyond economic partnerships. In the South China Sea, China's assertiveness in its territorial claims has led to tensions with several ASEAN countries, including the Philippines, Vietnam, and Malaysia. Yet, China's strategy of combining economic carrots, such as investment and infrastructure projects, with diplomatic engagement has allowed it to mitigate some of the political fallout from these disputes. By offering economic incentives through the BRI and RCEP, China has maintained relatively stable relations with key ASEAN nations despite ongoing territorial disputes.The BRICS coalition provides China with a platform to counter the U.S.-dominated global financial system. Despite a generally favorable view, Most of Southeast Asian countries are cautious. They try to balance their approaches and seek a constructive relationship with China while emphasizing the need for respect for sovereignty and adherence to international laws. Evethough China Kumming- Singapore rail way project seem overall regional development, Thailand, malaysia and Singapore still resit to cooperate with China (Singh, 2024). Therefore, this prject seems as a failure. The internal tensions within BRICS, such as the Sino-Indian border disputes, also raise concerns about the long-term cohesion and effectiveness of the bloc. Southeast Asian nations are carefully navigating these dynamics to engage with BRICS in ways that align with their national interests while maintaining strong ties with Western institutions. Therefore, While China's economic and cultural diplomacy has strengthened its regional influence, China political and strategic behavior highlight the need for careful management of Sino-Southeast Asian relations.

China's policy of non-interference, in contrast to the interventionist strategies often employed by the U.S., is another aspect of its geopolitical strategy in Southeast Asia. By presenting itself as a partner that respects the sovereignty of its neighbors, China enhances its image as a reliable ally, further deepening its influence in the region. This approach reflects China's broader geopolitical ambitions to undermine

U.S. influence without direct confrontation, leveraging soft power to advance its strategic goals. Finally, China's vision of a multipolar world, where global power is distributed across several centers, resonates strongly with many Southeast Asian countries. This vision aligns with the desire of these nations to see a more balanced global order, one that provides them with alternatives to the U.S.-led liberal order. Through its leadership in BRICS, China advocates for a global governance model that empowers the Global South, positioning itself as a leader of emerging economies. In doing so, China seeks to create a geopolitical bloc capable of challenging traditional Western alliances such as the QUAD and the G7. Therefore, China's economic diplomacy through the BRICS framework and its strategic initiatives in Southeast Asia are deeply rooted in Geopolitical Theory. By leveraging economic tools, forging alliances, and employing soft power, China is reshaping the geopolitical landscape of Southeast Asia, positioning itself as the dominant regional power. Through its leadership in BRICS, China extends its influence across the region, challenging the global power structures traditionally dominated by the West and advancing its vision of a multipolar world order.

## CONCLUSION

China's expanding influence in Southeast Asia, underpinned by its leadership within BRICS, strategic partnerships, and economic diplomacy, is profoundly altering the geopolitical landscape of the region. Initiatives such as the Belt and Road Initiative (BRI), the Regional Comprehensive Economic Partnership (RCEP), and the China-ASEAN Free Trade Area (CAFTA) have significantly bolstered China's presence in Southeast Asia. Through these mechanisms of economic integration and extensive infrastructure development, China has successfully positioned itself as a key partner for many Southeast Asian countries, offering substantial economic advantages and long-term development prospects.

Southeast Asia's response to China's ascendancy has been characterized by strategic hedging. ASEAN member states have been carefully managing their relationships with China, the United States, and India, seeking to maximize the economic benefits from Chinese investment while simultaneously preserving their sovereignty and ensuring national security. China's consistent diplomatic engagement and strategic coherence have reinforced its status as a dependable and influential actor in the region, particularly when contrasted with the unpredictability of U.S. foreign policy and India's comparatively smaller economic presence. Nevertheless, the attractiveness of China's economic model, coupled with its advocacy for a multipolar world order through BRICS, has rendered it a compelling partner for many Southeast Asian states. China's leadership within BRICS not only enhances its influence across Southeast Asia but also resonates with the region's aspirations for greater autonomy from Western powers and its support for South-South cooperation. Therefore, China's geopolitical strategy in Southeast Asia is a reflection of its broader global objectives of challenging Western dominance and asserting itself as a leading regional power. As Southeast Asian countries navigate the complexities of great power competition, China's capacity to sustain its economic and strategic influence will be crucial in shaping the future balance of power in the region. The rise of China's influence in Southeast Asia underscores its adept use of economic, diplomatic, and military instruments, which will continue to shape the region's geopolitical realities in the foreseeable future.

## REFERENCES


Abadi, F. A., & Al-Fadhat, F. (2023). *The influence of Indo-Pacific Economic Framework on peace and stability in the ASEAN region.* Global Strategis. DOI: 10.20473/jgs.17.1.2023.33-50

Acharya, A. (2012). *The End of the American World Order.* Polity Press.

Afzaal, M., & Naqvi, S. B. (2024). *How strategic representations together with geo-political and economic dynamics are mediating the global image of China's Belt Road Initiative.* Taylor & Francis.

Agnew, J. A. (2000). Global political geography beyond geopolitics. *International Studies Review*, 2(1), 91–99. DOI: 10.1111/1521-9488.00185

Albert, E. (2018, February 9). China's big bet on soft power. Council on Foreign Relations. https://www.cfr.org/backgrounder/chinas-big-bet-soft-power

Aleksia, C., & Bakhtiar, A. R. (2023). BRICS as New Alternatives in Reforming International Financial Institutions and Economic Partnerships. Insignia. *Journal of International Relations*, 10(2), 128–143.

Amin, H., & Rafique, A. (2021). *The Maritime Rise of China in Indo-Pacific and Indo-US Counter Balancing Approach.* ResearchGate. DOI: 10.11648/j.jpsir.20210401.13

Arif, M. S., Shah, S. L., & Talha, M. (2023). Strategic competition between USA and China in Asia Pacific Region. *South Asian Studies.*

ASEAN. (2024). ASEAN-China economic relation. ASEAN Main Portal. Retrieved from https://asean.org/our-communities/economic-community/integration-with-global-economy/asean-china-economic-relation/

Asian Development Bank. (2020). *Reports on the Greater Mekong Subregion (GMS) Economic Corridors.* Asian Development Bank.

Banerjee, S. (2024). India and China's competing infrastructural engagements in Southeast Asia: Case studies of Myanmar, Cambodia, and Vietnam. In Ranjan, A., Chattoraj, D., & Ullah, A. A. (Eds.), *India and China in Southeast Asia. South Asia's Geopolitical & Strategic Engagement* (pp. xx–xx). Palgrave Macmillan., DOI: 10.1007/978-981-97-6903-2_6

Barbieri, K. (2024). Geopolitics and International Trade. In *The Palgrave Handbook of Contemporary Geopolitics* (pp. 1–23). Springer Nature Switzerland.

Bartnick, A. (2020). *Asia Whole and Free?: Assessing the Viability and Practicality of a Pacific NATO*. Belfer Center for Science and International Affairs.

Blanchard, J. M. F., & Flint, C. (2017). The geopolitics of China's maritime silk road initiative. *Geopolitics*, 22(2), 223–245. DOI: 10.1080/14650045.2017.1291503

Boone, M., Nkamwa, M., & Cao, S. (2023). International Perspectives on China. In Order, Counter-Order, Disorder.

Budiana, M. (2024). Regional Organizations and Global Governance: The Case of ASEAN. *Journal of Student Collaboration Research*, 1(2), 1–15.

Bukhari, S. R. H., Khan, A. U., Noreen, S., Bashir, F., Rafi, G., & Haq, I. U. (2024). Navigating Sovereignty: Legal and Geopolitical Implications of Territorial Disputes in South China Sea. Remittances Review, 9(1).

Center for Preventive Action. (2024, September 17). Territorial disputes in the South China Sea. Council on Foreign Relations. Retrieved from https://www.cfr.org/global-conflict-tracker/conflict/territorial-disputes-south-china-sea

Chirathivat, S. (2022). China's Belt and Road Initiative and ASEAN connectivity in development: Can both bring synergy and opportunities together? In *China's Belt and Road Initiative in ASEAN* (pp. 153–182). Growing Presence, Recent Progress and Future Challenges. DOI: 10.1142/9789811241314_0006

Choudhury, S. R. (2023). Japan and Its Partners in the Indo-Pacific: Engagements and Alignment. Taylor & Francis. Retrieved from https://books.google.co.th/books?id=VF20EAAAQBAJ

Das, P. (2020). Evolution of Quadrilateral Security Dialogue (Quad) In Changing The Dynamics of India-China Relations. Semantic Scholar. Retrieved from https://www.semanticscholar.org/paper/Evolution-of-Quadrilateral-Security-Dialogue-(Quad)-Das/

Delina, L. L. (2021). Promises and pitfalls of China-Southeast Asia energy connectivity. *Energy Strategy Reviews*, 33, 100574. DOI: 10.1016/j.esr.2020.100574

deLisle, J. (2020). Foreign policy through other means: Hard power, soft power, and China's turn to political warfare to influence the United States. PMCID: PMC7102532, PMID: 32292215.

Denmark, A. M. (2020). *US strategy in the Asian century: Empowering allies and partners*. Columbia University Press. DOI: 10.7312/denm19764

Du Rocher, S. B. (2020). The Belt and Road: China's "Community of Destiny" for Southeast Asia? Asie. *Visions : the Journal of BC's Mental Health*, •••, 113.

Eisentraut, S., & Gaens, B. (2018). The US-Japan, India, Australia Quadrilateral Security Dialogue. Finnish Institute of International Affairs. Retrieved from https://www.fiia.fi/wp-content/uploads/2018/05/bp239_quad.pdf

Emmerson, D. K. (Ed.). (2020). *The deer and the dragon: Southeast Asia and China in the 21st century*. Rowman & Littlefield.

Fung, C. J., Han, E., Quek, K., & Strange, A. (2023). Conditioning China's Influence: Intentionality, Intermediaries, and Institutions. *Journal of Contemporary China*, 32(139), 1–16. DOI: 10.1080/10670564.2022.2052436

Goetz, W. W. (2019). INDIA: The Counterbalance to China's Grand Strategy in the Indo-Asia Pacific. Defense Technical Information Center (DTIC). Retrieved from https://apps.dtic.mil/sti/pdfs/AD1177993.pdf

Goh, E., Kraft, H. J. S., Lanti, I. G., Beng, T. K., Ahmad, Z. H., Chinwanno, C., Lan, L. L., Chanto, S. D., Ba, A. D., & Capie, D. (Eds.). (2005). Betwixt and between: Southeast Asian strategic relations with the U.S. and China. Institute of Defence and Strategic Studies, Nanyang Technological University. Retrieved from https://www.rsis.edu.sg/wp-content/uploads/2000/01/MN07-Betwixt-and-Between-Southeast-Asian-Strategic-Relations-with-the-U.S.-and-China.pdf

Gokmen, A. (2021). An Investigation of Future Educational Leaders' Metaphoric Perceptions Regarding Sustainability According to Their Knowledge Levels. *International Online Journal of Education & Teaching*, 8(2), 1151–1171.

Gur, N., & Dilek, S. (2023). US–China economic rivalry and the reshoring of global supply chains. *The Chinese Journal of International Politics*, 16(1), 61–83. DOI: 10.1093/cjip/poac022

Han, E. (2019). Asymmetrical Neighbors: Borderland State Building Between China and Southeast Asia.

Han, N. (2022). East Asia's soft power competition in Southeast Asia: A case study of public diplomacy efforts in promoting Japanese, Chinese, and Korean language learning in Thailand since the 2000s [Master's thesis, Chulalongkorn University]. Chula Digital Collections. Retrieved from https://digital.car.chula.ac.th/cgi/viewcontent.cgi?article=7041&context=chulaetd

Harris, P., & Hahn, M. (2023). The Japan-US Relationship: Imagining Its Future in the Indo-Pacific Era. In Japan and its Partners in the Indo-Pacific (pp. 77-94). Routledge India. Retrieved from https://www.taylorfrancis.com/chapters/edit/10.4324/9781003393634-5

Heiduk, F., & Wirth, C. (2023). The Quadrilateral Security Dialogue between Australia, India, Japan and the United States: More symptom than solution to the problem of growing instability in the Indo-Pacific. SSOAR. Retrieved from https://www.ssoar.info/ssoar/handle/document/89350

Herrero, A. G., Czapnik, B., Chen, L., Shrestha, R., Verico, K., Dash, P., & Hawke, G. (2023). *Regional Integration in Indo-Pacific: Connectivity, Cooperation, and New Supply-Chain Linkages* (Prakash, A., Ed.). Economic Research Institute for ASEAN and East Asia.

Huld, A. (2024, August 9). China-ASEAN trade and investment relations. China Briefing. Retrieved from https://www.china-briefing.com/news/china-asean-trade-and-investment-relations/

Hutt, D. (2024, July 26). Who cares if Malaysia and Thailand join BRICS? The Diplomat. Retrieved from https://thediplomat.com/2024/07/who-cares-if-malaysia-and-thailand-join-brics/

Irsadanar, R. J. P. (2023). Japan's Security Policy Expansion in Southeast Asia During the Shinzo Abe Administration: Case of Japan–Indonesia Security Cooperation. *Journal of Asian Security and International Affairs*, 10(2), 190–222. https://journals.sagepub.com/doi/abs/10.1177/23477970231173538. DOI: 10.1177/23477970231173538

Jaffery, T., & Shoaib Pervez, M. (2023). China's Response Towards QUAD in the Indo-Pacific: A Paradoxical Strategy? Strategic Analysis, 47(4), 363-375. Retrieved from https://www.tandfonline.com/doi/full/10.1080/09700161.2023.2263702

Jamil, S., Ahmad, A. A., Rizvi, S. Z. A., & Gwadabe, N. L. M. (2020). An Analysis of Regional Security Dynamics of South Asia in Post 9/11 Period. Internatioanl Journal of Scientific and Technology Research, 9(01).

Jones, D. M., & Jenne, N. (2022). Hedging and grand strategy in Southeast Asian foreign policy. *International Relations of the Asia-Pacific*, 22(2), 205–235. DOI: 10.1093/irap/lcab003

Khoo, N. (2023). Great power rivalry and Southeast Asian agency: Southeast Asia in an era of US-China strategic competition. *Political Science (Wellington, N.Z.)*, 74(2-3), 141–154. DOI: 10.1080/00323187.2023.2186251

Koga, K. (2022). *Managing great power politics: ASEAN, institutional strategy, and the South China Sea.* Springer Nature. DOI: 10.1007/978-981-19-2611-2

Koga, K. (2022). *Managing great power politics: ASEAN, institutional strategy, and the South China Sea.* Springer Nature. DOI: 10.1007/978-981-19-2611-2

Kuik, C.-C., & Rosli, Z. (2023). Laos-China infrastructure cooperation: Legitimation and the limits of host-country agency. *Journal of Contemporary East Asia Studies*, 12(1), 32–58. DOI: 10.1080/24761028.2023.2274236

Lee, B. T. F., & Sims, J. P. (2024). Legitimacy through Diversity: China's Leadership in the BRICS+ Expansion for Global Balance. *Fudan Journal of the Humanities and Social Sciences*, •••, 1–38. DOI: 10.1007/s40647-024-00411-6

Lew, J. J., & Roughead, G. (2021, March). China's Belt and Road: Implications for the United States. Council on Foreign Relations. Retrieved from https://www.cfr.org/task-force-report/chinas-belt-and-road-implications-for-the-united-states/findings

Li, M. (2020). The Belt and Road Initiative: Geo-economics and Indo-Pacific security competition. *International Affairs*, 96(1), 169–187. DOI: 10.1093/ia/iiz240

Macaraig, C. E., & Fenton, A. J. (2021). Analyzing the causes and effects of the south china sea dispute. *The Journal of Territorial and Maritime Studies*, 8(2), 42–58.

Mäkinen, T. (2018). Debating Transatlantic Security in the United States Congress. Retrieved from https://trepo.tuni.fi/handle/10024/102838

Mishra, R. (2021). Vietnam's Regional Security Perceptions and Priorities: Role of India. India Quarterly. *Journal of International Affairs*, 77(2), 123–140. DOI: 10.1177/09749284211009433

Mohan, C. R. (2018). The Impact of India's Act East Policy on Southeast Asia. ResearchGate. Retrieved from https://www.researchgate.net/publication/325284243_The_Impact_of_India's_Act_East_Policy_on_Southeast_Asia

Moyo, G. (2024). World Bank, IMF, and WTO as Agents of Financial Imperialism. In *Africa in the Global Economy: Capital Flight, Enablers, and Decolonial Responses* (pp. 41–59). Springer Nature Switzerland. DOI: 10.1007/978-3-031-51000-7_3

Nguyen, V. H., & Pham, N. T. (2021). ASEAN's position in training peace in the South China Sea. *International Journal of Social Science and Human Research*, 4(3), 264–269. DOI: 10.47191/ijsshr/v4-i3-07

Özekin, M. K., & Sune, E. (2023). Contesting Hegemony: The Rise of BRICS and the Crisis of US-led Western Hegemony in the MENA Region. *The Korean Journal of International Studies*, 21(3), 409–446. DOI: 10.14731/kjis.2023.12.21.3.409

Pacific Forum. (2019). Issues & insights: U.S.-China strategic competition and implications for the Indo-Pacific (Vol. 19, Working Paper 8). Pacific Forum. https://pacforum.org/wp-content/uploads/2019/08/issuesinsights_Vol19-WP8FINAL.pdf

Panda, J. P. (2020). India's Strategic Hedging Policy in The South China Sea. ResearchGate. Retrieved from https://www.researchgate.net/publication/372365839_India's_Strategic_Hedging_Policy_in_The_South_China_Sea

Pröpper, H. (2020). The" Chinese Dream": An Analysis of the Belt and Road Initiative. International Social Science Review (Online), 96(1), 0_1-24.

Rachana, V., & Sreynich, C. (2021). The Belt and Road Initiative and ASEAN Community Development. Final Report, Royal University of Law and Economics, International Program, Bachelor's Degree in International Relations.

Rising, D. (2024, January 30). Myanmar, South China Sea Conflicts Top Agenda as ASEAN Foreign Ministers Meet. The Diplomat. https://thediplomat.com/2024/01/myanmar-south-china-sea-conflicts-top-agenda-as-asean-foreign-ministers-meet/

Roberts, K., & Bano, S. (Eds.). (2023). *The Ascendancy of Regional Powers in Contemporary US-China Relations: Rethinking the Great Power Rivalry*. Springer Nature. DOI: 10.1007/978-3-031-37612-2

Roberts, K., & Bano, S. (Eds.). (2023). *The ascendancy of regional powers in contemporary US-China relations: Rethinking the great power rivalry*. Springer Nature. DOI: 10.1007/978-3-031-37612-2

Rubiolo, M. F. (2020). *The South China Sea Dispute: A Reflection of Southeast Asia's Economic and Strategic Dilemmas*. Revista de Relaciones Internacionales, Estrategia y Seguridad.

Sahbzada, M. U. (2021). India and China's Trade Ties with ASEAN Nations. *Journal of Indian Studies*, 7(2), 77–92. https://pu.edu.pk/images/journal/indianStudies/PDF/7_v7_2_21.pdf

Schmidt, J. D. (2011). India-China rivalry and competition in Southeast Asia. In India in International Relations: European and Indian Perspectives. Retrieved from https://vbn.aau.dk/files/61143145/India_China_Rivalry_and_Competition_in_Southeast_Asia_pres_in_Delhi.vbn_version.docx

Scott, C. P. (2021). A Proposal to Cease Chinese Expansion in the South China Sea and Encroachment into the Sovereign Waters of Regional US Allies.

Seagroatt, M. T. (2019). US-China Competition: India's Role as a Counterbalance. Defense Technical Information Center (DTIC). Retrieved from https://apps.dtic.mil/sti/pdfs/AD1178202.pdf

Seah, S., Lin, J., Martinus, M., Fong, K., Aridati, I., Pham, T. P. T., & Chee, D. (2024). The State of Southeast Asia: 2024 Survey Report. ISEAS - Yusof Ishak Institute. Retrieved from https://www.iseas.edu.sg/wp-content/uploads/2024/03/The-State-of-SEA-2024.pdf

Shahzad, S. M., & Khan, M. R. (2022). Quad: The US Strategic Alliance for the Indo-Pacific Region and the Chinese Counterbalance. *Pakistan Journal of Multi-disciplinary Research*, 3(2), 55–67. http://pjmr.org/pjmr/article/view/329/72

Shahzad, S. M., & Khan, M. R. (2022). Quad: The US Strategic Alliance for the Indo-Pacific Region and the Chinese Counterbalance. *Pakistan Journal of Multi-disciplinary Research*, 3(2), 55–67. http://pjmr.org/pjmr/article/view/329/72

Shambaugh, D. (2020). Where Great Powers Meet: America & China in Southeast Asia. Oxford University Press.

Shambaugh, D. (2020). Where Great Powers Meet: America & China in Southeast Asia. Oxford University Press.

Shen, M., & Li, H. (2023). Insight into China–Cambodia Economic and Trade Cooperation: The Value Chain Perspective. In *Cambodia-China Comprehensive Strategic Partnership Towards a Community with a Shared Future* (pp. 99–112). Springer Nature Singapore. DOI: 10.1007/978-981-19-9155-4_14

Sheng, L., & do Nascimento, D. F. (2021). *The Belt and Road Initiative in South–South cooperation: The impact on world trade and geopolitics*. Springer Nature. DOI: 10.1007/978-981-16-6357-4

Siddique, A., & Shafqat, S. (2021). How Belt and Road Initiative (BRI) and the China-Pakistan Economic Corridor (CPEC) are Reshaping China's Soft Power? *Journal of South Asian and Middle Eastern Studies*, 44(3), 61–94. DOI: 10.1353/jsa.2021.0007

Sihaloho, R. A. H., Prabowo, T. B., & Pamungkas, C. (2024). China's Belt and Road Initiative Implementation Maneuvers in the South Pacific Region. *Nation State: Journal of International Studies*, 7(1), 53–70. DOI: 10.24076/nsjis.v7i1.1185

Singh, D. (2020). *American Foreign Policy and Southeast Asia*. De Gruyter. DOI: 10.1355/aa20-1d

Singh, M. K. (2021). China and the United States in the Middle East: between dependency and rivalry. In The Great Power Competition Volume 1: Regional Perspectives on Peace and Security (pp. 369-395). Cham: Springer International Publishing DOI: 10.1007/978-3-030-64473-4_18

Singh, R. (2024, July 6). Why China plans to run trains from Kunming all the way to Singapore. The Indian Express.Retrieved from https://indianexpress.com/article/explained/explained-global/china-pan-asian-trains-network-bri-9421068/

Skalamera, M. (2023). Russia's lasting influence in Central Asia. In *Central Asia's Strategic Importance* (pp. 123–145). Taylor & Francis., Retrieved from https://www.taylorfrancis.com/chapters/edit/10.4324/9781003422228-9

Smith, R. (2019). Japan's strategic response to China's rise: Soft balancing and military modernization. *Journal of Japanese Studies*, 45(1), 34–56. DOI: 10.1353/jjs.2019.0002

Srivithaya, S. (2021). The QUAD Diplomacy and the New Regional Order in Southeast Asia. Business and Interdisciplinary Studies ICEBIS2020, 6(4), 112-120. Retrieved from https://ibba.siamnet.asia/wp-content/uploads/2021/07/2020-16-The-QUAD-Diplomacy-and-the-New-Regional-Order-by-Suraphol-Srivithaya.pdf

Strangio, S. (2020). *In the Dragon's Shadow: Southeast Asia in the Chinese Century*. Yale University Press.

Stromseth, J. (2019). *Don't make us choose: Southeast Asia in the throes of US-China rivalry*. Brookings Institution.

Stromseth, J. R. (Ed.). (2021). *Rivalry and response: Assessing great power dynamics in Southeast Asia*. Brookings Institution Press.

Sun, Y. (2017, November 3). Winning projects and hearts? Three cases of Chinese mega-infrastructure projects in Southeast Asia. The Asan Forum. Retrieved from https://theasanforum.org/winning-projects-and-hearts-three-cases-of-chinese-mega-infrastructure-projects-in-southeast-asia/

Tan, W. Y., & Chin, C. F. (2020). High-level visits and the Belt and Road Initiative: The case of Southeast Asia. *Contemporary Chinese Political Economy and Strategic Relations*, 6(1), 217–XI.

Taylor, M. (2015). *The Chinese State, Oil and Energy Security*. HeinOnline.

Technology, R. (n.d.). Singapore-Kunming Rail Link (SKRL). Retrieved from https://www.railway-technology.com/projects/singapore-kunming-rail-link-skrl/

The Economist. (2023). Joe Biden's China strategy is not working. The Economist. tuenkel, O. (2023, August 18). BRICS expansion would be a sign of China's growing influence. The Economist. Retrieved from https://www.economist.com/by-invitation/2023/08/18/brics-expansion-would-be-a-sign-of-chinas-growing-influence-says-oliver-stuenkel

Vo, Nguyen, Tran, & Bui (2023). US response as conducting freedom of navigation operations and enhancing defense cooperation.

Wallace, J. B. (2022). *Establishing a first island chain balance of power: Cooperative development of the quadrilateral security dialogue. Doctoral dissertation.* US Army Command and General Staff College., Retrieved from https://scholar.google.com/scholar?hl=en&as_sdt=0%2C5&q=Scott%2C+2020+The+QUAD+emphasizes+maintaining+freedom+of+navigation%2C+promoting+democratic+values%2C+and+countering+Chinese+influence.+&btnG=

Wei, Z. (2024). The Evolution of the 'QUAD'. Horizons: Journal of International Relations and Sustainable Development, (25), 82-99. Retrieved from https://www.jstor.org/stable/48761182

Wu, S. (2016, June 17). Singapore-Kunming Rail Link: A 'Belt and Road' case study. The Diplomat. Retrieved from https://thediplomat.com/2016/06/singapore-kunming-rail-link-a-belt-and-road-case-study/

Xu, C., & Lim, G. (2024). Chinese investment in Southeast Asia:(how) does it matter? *Eurasian Geography and Economics*, •••, 1–18. DOI: 10.1080/15387216.2024.2394555

Ye, X. (2022). From Strategic Ambiguity to Maximum Pressure? Explaining the Logic of the US Taiwan Policy in the Post–Cold War Era. *Journal of Asian and African Studies*, 57(8), 1511–1543. DOI: 10.1177/00219096211058887

Yunqi, W. (2023). The dilemma and reconstruction of ASEAN's centrality: A neoclassical realist perspective. [JKoB]. *Jurnal Komunikasi Borneo*, 11, 174–201.

Zhao, X. (2024). Technological hedging and differentiated responses of Southeast Asian countries to US–China technological competition: A case study on artificial intelligence (AI). *The Pacific Review*, •••, 1–32. DOI: 10.1080/09512748.2024.2408010

# Chapter 5
# The Question of 'Biasness' in the Middle of the Conflict:
## Geopolitical Impact of the Mediation Process by Parties on the Russia–Ukraine Conflict

**Bhavya Tandon**
https://orcid.org/0009-0001-2882-9473
*O.P. Jindal Global University, India*

**Pratiti Nayak**
*KIIT University, India*

**Ipsita Das**
https://orcid.org/0000-0002-1745-8638
*KIIT Law School, KIIT University, India*

**Zeenat Taher**
https://orcid.org/0000-0001-8576-9086
*KIIT Law School, KIIT University, India*

## ABSTRACT

*In armed conflicts, bias significantly influences mediation procedures, yet its specific role still needs to be explored. This chapter examines bias in mediation within the Ukraine conflict, focusing on the Organization for Security and Co-operation in Europe's (OSCE) Special Monitoring Mission (SMM). Content analysis of OSCE member states' interpretations reveals biases favoring Ukraine and disfavoring*

DOI: 10.4018/979-8-3693-7393-4.ch005

*Russia. Such predispositions, evident in member states' declarations, have implications for international mediation scholars and practitioners. The study underscores the challenges of maintaining impartiality in mediation amidst armed conflicts, emphasizing the urgent need for nuanced understanding to foster more effective mediation processes.*

## INTRODUCTION

The invasion of Ukraine by Russia in February 2022, despite prior mediation attempts dating back to 2014, has resulted in significant loss of life, with over 13,000 casualties within the first five years of conflict, including a substantial civilian toll (Oberson, 2021, p. 49). The failure of international mediation efforts in the Ukrainian conflict and the subsequent escalation of violence may be attributed to various factors, including contextual, behavioral, and mediator-related variables (Vuković, 2011, p. 114). This chapter scrutinizes the role of mediators, mainly focusing on their interests, influence, and impartiality. The Organization for Security and Co-operation in Europe (OSCE), an international organization committed to promoting democracy, stability, and peace, is one of the key mediators in the Ukrainian conflict, employing a monitoring mission on the ground to support its efforts. By examining the Special Monitoring Mission to Ukraine (SMM) of the OSCE between 2014 and 2021, this study assesses mediator qualities, with a particular emphasis on impartiality as a guiding principle. The chapter highlights concern regarding impartiality when participating states are biased toward or against conflict parties, particularly when conveying information with a blame-oriented approach (Oberson, 2021, p. 47). Bias is delineated as the mediator favoring one side over the other, while favoritism denotes freedom from bias (Arad & Carnevale, 1994, p. 426; Stenner, 2016, p. 268). The OSCE's "*participating states*" terminology is adopted herein to refer to all nations involved in the organization, reflecting a broader engagement beyond mere observation roles in the SMM.

## BACKGROUND

The start of the Conflict and the annexation of Crimea in 2014 are described to put this chapter into context. Following is a timeline of the military war in Donbas from 2014 through 2021, along with explanations of its terminology. The OSCE's participation through the SMM is highlighted in the second section's discussion of international mediation attempts in Ukraine.

## Armed Conflict in Ukraine

In November 2013, protests broke out all around Ukraine due to the previous president, Yanukovych, 's refusal to sign an EU association agreement (Biersack & O'Lear, 2014, p. 248). The name "*Euromaidan*" refers to the square in Kyiv where the pro-European demonstrations took place. The Ukrainian authorities forcefully put down the large-scale protests (UCDP, 2022). A pro-European Union administration took over when President Yanukovych fled Ukraine as the protests turned violent and he faced impeachment. As "puppets of an EU/US-backed coup," this new government was denounced by Russia (Biersack & O'Lear 2014, p. 248). Russia asserts that it has a strong bond with Ukraine. The new Ukrainian government was portrayed as "threaten[ing] to Russian speakers and ethnic Russians in Ukraine, such as in Crimea," as a result of the revocation of a language law that would have allowed for Russian and other minority languages to be regional languages (Biersack & O'Lear, 2014, p. 249). Consequently, Ukraine became a "ground of geopolitical conflict between Russia and the West" (Biersack & O'Lear, 2014, p. 248). Russian soldiers in masks, known as "little green men," encircled and captured the Crimean Peninsula in February 2014 (Biersack & O'Lear, 2014, p. 249). In March 2014, a referendum was held to validate the occupation of Crimea. The illegal takeover of Crimea and subsequent fighting were met with international censure and penalties (Biersack & O'Lear, 2014, p. 251; Tsybulenko & Francis, 2018, p. 124). An armed war broke out in the Donbas region of Eastern Ukraine in the spring of 2014. Aggressions increased. Henceforth, the short-version Donbas describes the Donbas Basin region ("Donetskyi Basin") in Eastern Ukraine. (Figure 1) depicts the Crimean Peninsula in the south, the Donbas (the hatching area), and the contact line between them. Referendums were held in May 2014 in the two proclaimed "People's republics," Donetsk and Luhansk (The 'People's Republics' Luhansk and Donetsk are self-declared and their "independence" from Ukraine are internationally not recognized)(Fischer, 2019, p. 9). The Ukrainian state does not have jurisdiction over the territory (Twickel et al., 2018, p. 2).

*Figure 1. Ukraine and the Donbas*

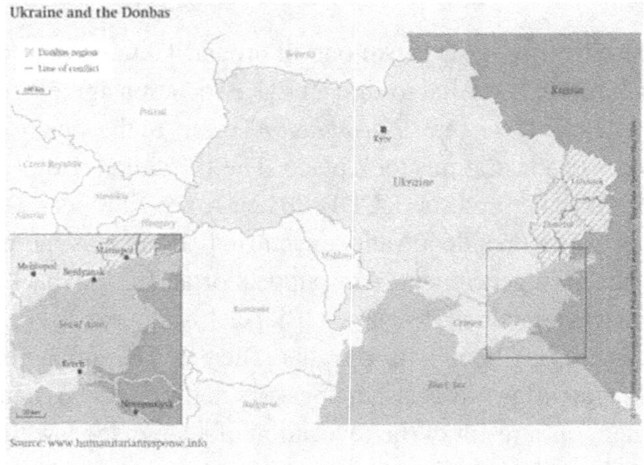


*(Fischer 2019: 8)*

## Terminology

While discussing Russia's participation in Eastern Ukraine, scholars emphasize domestic reasons more than external ones (Hauter, 2019, p. 96). Some support referring to it as a civil war, signifying a domestic battle in which "separatists" fight for independence from Ukraine, while others argue that it is a Russian invasion disguised as "separatists" backed by Russia (ibid.: 100). Direct Russian involvement has been seen from the start, despite Russia's repeated denials that it is involved in the war by supporting "separatists" (Twickel et al., 2018, p. 2). But because the collaborators are still part of Russia, calling them 'separatists' or 'rebels' would suggest an internal war (Tsybulenko & Francis, 2018, p. 128). Tsybulenko and Francis contend that non-state armed groups and local allies have played a significant part in the Conflict between the Russian and Ukrainian militaries in Donbas before February 2022 (Tsybulenko & Francis, 2018, p. 128). Although naming the actors in the Conflict may appear insignificant, the terminology greatly impacts the legislation governing the Conflict. Thus, it is essential to distinguish between internal civil war and armed combat on a global scale. Due to the limited scope of this chapter, conflicting classifications of the armed Conflict in Ukraine are not extensively discussed (Hauter, 2019; Tsybulenko & Francis, 2018). Russian aggression and regular and irregular Russian forces prove Ukraine is an international armed conflict. That is why quotation marks are used throughout the chapter when referring to 'separatists.' (Tsybulenko & Francis 2018, p. 140). Russian engagement and its relationship with the collaborators is crucial for understanding conflicts and informing conflict resolution strategies like mediation.

## International Mediation in Ukraine

The OSCE settles disputes on a global scale and locally in Ukraine. The OSCE plays a significant role in international mediation through the Trilateral Contact Group (TCG). The TCG was created by the Normandy Format and is made up of delegates from Ukraine, Russia, and the OSCE. The Normandy Format consists of representatives of France, Germany, Ukraine, and Russia and has performed international mediation to settle the dispute in Ukraine since June 2014. The TCG framework was used to negotiate the Minsk agreements, which were supported by the Normandy Format (Fischer, 2019, p. 11). The Minsk Protocol established an OSCE-monitored cease-fire in September 2014 (Fischer, 2019, p. 12). However, the Conflict in Eastern Ukraine did not stop, and in February 2015, the Minsk document was released with detailed implementation plans (Fischer, 2019, p. 12). The measures cover a new cease-fire, withdrawal of heavy weapons and foreign armed formations, etc. (Trilateral Contact Group (2015) shows the Normandy Format on the left and the TCG on the right as the participants in the Minsk accord. The lack of elections in the territories controlled by "separatists," the situation in Donbas, and the evacuation of Russian-backed soldiers are among the issues that the Minsk agreements do not address (Bentzen, 2020). The Minsk agreements state that Russia is not considered a party to the Conflict. Hence Russia has no duties under them (Fischer, 2019, p. 12). The Minsk agreements guide the OSCE's engagement despite great problems.

## OSCE's Special Monitoring Mission to Ukraine

The OSCE is the largest regional security organization in the world, with 57 participating states (Smit & Tidblad-Lundholm, 2018). The OSCE is an extension of the Conference on Security and Co-operation in Europe, created for negotiations between East and West in the 1970s (Smit & Tidblad-Lundholm, 2018). Through political discussion and practical effort, they achieve their goals of stability, peace, and democracy. Relevant actors from "the West," including the EU, the US, and the former Soviet Union, are represented in the OSCE. The fact that Russia and Ukraine are members of the OSCE is significant for this chapter. The OSCE sent the SMM to be present on the ground and contribute to mediation at the local level to carry out the Minsk agreements. The SMM began in March 2014 in response to a request from Ukraine. The PC made a choice and carried out the deployment and extensions of the SMM.

The PC also governed the decision to deploy an "Observer Mission at the Russian Checkpoints Gukovo and Donetsk" between July 2014 and September 2021, but it is not explained in detail here. For more information, see OSCE (OSCE, 2022b). Consensus-based decision-making is used in the PC, which implies that all member states must agree to any decisions. The mission was abandoned in March 2022 due to Russia's obstruction of consensus-based decision-making (OSCE, 2022a). The SMM was the largest OSCE mission, with 1.291 mission personnel and 477 national employees (OSCE, 2022a). The "principles of impartiality and transparency" are highlighted in the SMM mandate (OSCE, 2014b). These guidelines apply to all SMM tasks, such as providing unbiased information on the security environment and cease-fire violations. Mediation components are also present in other tasks, such as facilitating conversations. The latter tries to promote peace and reduce conflicts. The SMM mission, however, lacks specific guidelines on how conversation facilitation should be carried out. The OSCE strengthens appropriate tools such as dialogue facilitation, mediation, and confidence-building initiatives (OSCE, 2021, p. 17-21). This chapter concentrates on the OSCE's SMM intervention for the above reasons.

## RESEARCH PROBLEM

The discourse surrounding international mediation, particularly in the context of the armed Conflict in Ukraine, has attracted significant scholarly attention. The OSCE, with its member states often involved as belligerent parties, plays a crucial role in these mediations (Remler, 2021; Umland, 2021). While scholars highlight the importance of political commitment from involved governments for the effectiveness of the OSCE (Oberson, 2021; Stenner, 2016), existing inquiries often overlook state perspectives and potential biases, leaving significant gaps for conjecture and theoretical debates. While OSCE's emphasis on impartiality in mediating conflicts, notably through the Special Monitoring Mission (SMM), is frequently highlighted in the literature, empirical examinations of this aspect remain scarce compared to other international organizations like the European Union (EU) and the United Nations (UN). Bias, a critical determinant impacting mediation outcomes, warrants closer investigation due to its potential to undermine the process. This chapter addresses this research lacuna by systematically evaluating biases favoring or disfavoring conflict parties in the Ukrainian conflict, utilizing a text analysis of statements made before the OSCE's primary decision-making body, the Permanent Council (PC). By delving into state perspectives and their alignment with conflicting parties, the study sheds light on potential biases among participating states. Understanding these biases is essential for enhancing future OSCE mediation efforts and fostering peacebuilding processes.

## Research Aim and Research Questions

This chapter aims to scrutinize the Special Monitoring Mission (SMM) conducted by the Organization for Security and Co-operation in Europe (OSCE), which claimed impartiality. The analysis, conducted with utmost objectivity, focuses on assessing bias in interpretive remarks made before the OSCE's Permanent Council (PC), specifically those addressing the mandate and extensions of the mission in Ukraine. Interpretative comments, elucidating states' reactions, and perspectives on previous PC decisions form the basis of this study.

The primary objective of this analysis is not to undermine the OSCE's mission or mediation endeavors, but to provide a fresh perspective by identifying potential biases in interpretive remarks. This approach aims to enhance understanding of the OSCE's mediation efforts by shedding light on a critical aspect of mediator characteristics: bias. The central research question guiding this inquiry is:

*"How do the biases of the OSCE nations manifest in the interpretations of the extended Special Monitoring Mission to Ukraine?"*

To facilitate a structured analysis, the chapter employs sub-questions as follows:

1. How do interpretive statements imply bias? For instance, a statement that emphasizes the Ukrainian government's efforts in maintaining peace while downplaying the role of the separatists could be seen as biased towards the Ukrainian government.
2. Is bias observed in favour of or against conflict parties (pro-Ukraine, pro-collaborator, con-Ukraine, con-Russia, or collaborators)?
3. In what context does bias occur?

The first sub-question establishes the presence of bias in interpretive comments, guiding subsequent analyses. The second sub-question identifies the bias direction, distinguishing between support for or opposition against involved parties. Specific terms such as "*pro-conflict party*" (favouring one of the conflicting parties), "*con-conflict party*" (opposing one of the conflicting parties), "*pro-collaborator*" (favouring a party collaborating with the OSCE), "*pro-Ukraine*" (favouring Ukraine), "*con-Ukraine*" (opposing Ukraine), "*con-collaborator*" (opposing a party collaborating with the OSCE), and "*con-Russian*" (opposing Russia) are utilized to categorize biases accordingly. The third sub-question delves into the contextual dimensions of bias, facilitating a nuanced understanding of its manifestations. Content analysis addresses these sub-questions and elucidates the contextual nuances of bias.

## The Need for the Chapter

International mediation is crucial in resolving enduring conflicts, constituting a significant domain within the broader peace and conflict studies framework. The protracted conflict in Ukraine since 2014, characterized by the Russian annexation of Crimea and escalating violence in Eastern Ukraine, underscores the salience of international mediation efforts. Recent scholarship has emphasized the growing importance of such endeavours (Wallensteen & Svensson, 2014). Research indicates that biased mediators can either facilitate or hinder the mediation process. Examining state perspectives, particularly through the lens of interpretative statements, offers valuable insights into the manifestation of bias. Of particular relevance is scrutinizing states' self-interests, especially when they are simultaneously engaged in mediating conflicts while actively contributing to their perpetuation. Against the backdrop of heightened tensions between Russia and Ukraine, this chapter contributes to the academic discourse on objectivity and bias in mediation. It holds practical significance for forthcoming mediation endeavours led by the OSCE and other stakeholders.

## LITERATURE REVIEW

An overview of the research on OSCE's SMM-related mediation is provided in this part. Finally, investigations on bias in international mediation in Ukraine are provided. First, scholarly conclusions about the mandate and interpretative claims are reviewed. Reviewing the literature on the subject helps to identify what is already known about it and reveals unanswered questions or the research gap, which this chapter fills. However, this should be interpreted as a portion of the most pertinent material to embed the analysis in rather than a comprehensive evaluation of the research on bias in international mediation and the SMM.

## Mediation and the SMM

While scholarly attention to the Organization for Security and Co-operation in Europe (OSCE) as an international entity has been substantial, comparatively little effort has been directed towards comprehending its role as a mediator. Academics highlight the OSCE's mediation activities as characterized by innovative capacities for facilitating discourse and conflict resolution (Stenner, 2016, p. 256). These novel mediation capacities, as elucidated by Stenner, emphasize the distinctive features of the mediation system in Ukraine, particularly the operational capacities developed by the Special Monitoring Mission (SMM) present in the region (Schläpfer,

2016, p. 340). While acknowledging the SMM's influence on international mediation, Schläpfer underscores the need for further research into the SMM from an international mediation perspective. Scholars have primarily examined the SMM by scrutinizing its mandate and extensions and analyzing the mission's objectives and constraints (Härtel et al., 2021). Despite claims that the mandate underwent minimal annual changes, access to Crimea, a region encompassed by the mandate but de facto inaccessible, remains a persistent issue (Härtel et al., 2021). This restriction is compounded by Russia's annexation of Crimea, leading to stringent entry limitations (Umland, 2021, p. 7). However, while mandate restrictions have been acknowledged, the root causes underlying these limitations have not received adequate scholarly attention. The focus on mandate constraints has eclipsed the thorough exploration of interpretative assertions attached to the mandate. Scholars have predominantly fixated on the mandate's requirements rather than delving into the broader contextual implications of these limitations.

## OSCE'S Impartiality

Many researchers have discussed the OSCE's impartiality, mainly about the consensus principle. Scholars argue for and against the consensus principle by analyzing the OSCE's decision-making process. On the one hand, because every state must approve choices, consensus-building promotes credibility, legitimacy, and neutrality. Schläpfer argues for the benefit of objectivity in his article, noting that Russia and Ukraine saw the OSCE as an "impartial facilitator for dialogue" (Schläpfer, 2016, p. 328). However, as consensus depends on the will of participating nations, Remler contends that it undermines OSCE mediation and poses a challenge (Remler, 2021, p. 1). The dual involvement of Russia and Ukraine, who serve as mediators while both taking part in the fight, has an even greater impact on the degradation (Schläpfer, 2016, p. 328). Russian involvement in the mission is put into context by (Härtel et al., 2021), who claims that despite Moscow's "*official approving of its creation, Moscow was, from the beginning, unsupportive of the OSCE SMM*" (Härtel et al., 2021: 26). Russia reluctantly accepted the mission and also tried to stall the deployment. (Härtel et al., 2021) Explain the cause of Russia's response by claiming that the SMM prevents Russia from carrying out its plans for the Donbas (Härtel et al., 2021). The author's justification is consistent with Kropatcheva's claim that Russia had obstructive and disinterested behavior toward the OSCE before the military crisis in Ukraine (Kropatcheva, 2012, p. 370). As a result of Russia's propensity for cooperation, but only when it serves its interests, Kropatcheva links Russia's position to its more "pragmatic, selective, and instrumentalist" approach to the OSCE (Kropatcheva, 2012, p. 375).

## Interpretative Statements

In their research, a few academics have referred to interpretative remarks, but these comments are rarely given in-depth analysis. This disregard contradicts the use of interpretive comments that participating governments frequently employ. The exception is Müller's analysis, which covers interpretative comments from 1994 to 2001. The OSCE's founding text is a reference for interpreting statements (Müller, 2002, p. 347). In the sense that delegates might "have the last word on the matter" concerning PC decisions, the remarks relate to the decisions that have already been made (Müller, 2002, p. 350). "Reflecting a rising difficulty to reach an official or accurate understanding of the meaning of PC Decisions," according to Müller, an increase in declarations in 2001 (Müller, 2002, p. 350). Umland supports Müller's perspective on the challenges surrounding the statements to the degree that a statement by Russia violates fundamental OSCE standards in their disclosure of the SMM's accomplishments and shortcomings (Umland, 2021, p. 7). These transgressions concern "participating states' political sovereignty and territorial integrity" (Umland, 2021, p. 7). Ukraine is the country Umland refers to, and the territory in question includes sections of Crimea and Eastern Ukraine. Following this declaration about territory, various states—including Ukraine—immediately responded with interpretative comments. Contrarily, an OSCE reflection document on the first five years of the SMM highlights the benefits of interpretative remarks. According to former PC Chairperson Greminger, such interpretative remarks allowed nations to convey their "views and perspectives after the decision [to deploy the SMM] was adopted" (OSCE, 2021, p. 10). Greminger concludes that despite opposing views on geography, the mandate talks were successful since a consensus was reached. Collectively, the (OSCE (2021) sees the comments as a chance, whereas Müller, (2002) and Umland, (2021) acknowledge that the statements undermine the OSCE acquis, but neither of them makes the connection between the erosion and mediator traits like prejudice. Thus, it becomes clear that bias in interpretative claims needs to be addressed.

## Biased Mediators in Ukraine

Examining two studies linking prejudice to international mediation in Ukraine sheds light on pertinent issues. Landwehr's study scrutinizes the prejudice of mediators in the Normandy Format, mainly focusing on mediation in the Donbas region. The contention is that the EU and the US exhibit marginal bias in support of Ukraine. At the same time, Russia displays pronounced bias toward Eastern Ukraine collaborators, underscoring the complexities of international mediation dynamics (Landwehr, 2019, p. 303). Landwehr also delves into the impact of sanctions imposed by the EU, US, and Canada on Russia, positing that the provision of information to "their" dispute party influences the preferences for biased mediators among the disputing parties in Ukraine (Landwehr, 2019, p. 304). While historically, scholars have advocated for complete impartiality in mediation endeavors, Landwehr's argument aligns with academics who recognize the potential benefits of bias in mediation, citing leverage and negotiation possibilities (Arad & Carnevale, 1994; Kydd, 2003; Svensson, 2009). Furthermore, Elgström et al.'s investigation into the perception of the EU as a biased arbitrator sheds additional light on the issue. Through interviews with local commercial, political, and civil society figures, the study reveals a perception of EU bias in favor of Ukraine, rooted in the perception of close relations with one or more conflict parties (Elgström et al., 2018, p. 301). While prejudice is acknowledged, it is not deemed the primary cause of the EU's unsuccessful mediation efforts, challenging conventional beliefs from mediation theory (Elgström et al., 2018, p. 300). This chapter's focus on examining bias in OSCE state statements provides a valuable complement to existing research, offering insights into the role of bias in international mediation from a different perspective.

## BRICS and International Mediation

Together with BRICS (Brazil, Russia, India, China, and South Africa), such an aspiration is taken up by a significant player in the global geopolitical landscape, which calls for the establishment of the multipolar world order and to challenge Western dominance in the international mediation (Stephen, 2014). BRICS is known mainly for its economic cooperation which has recently been increasingly present in diplomatic initiatives that form the basis of many processes of global mediation. Research has demonstrated that BRICS often align against interventionist policies espoused by Western countries by seeking diplomatic solutions of sovereignty and non-interference (Qobo & Soko, 2015). However, both the United States and the European Union take a more interventionist approach than this approach which has set them up with a diverse set of principles on international conflict resolution (Roberts, 2017). BRICS has by promoting multilateralism sought to reform international institutions to better reflect the views of developing countries (Singh, 2016). The Ukraine crisis has shown strains in the cohesion of BRICS, driven to a degree by the involvement of Russia, BRICS' key, wealthiest member. Secondly, other BRICS members like China and India have been placing themselves in a rather uncomfortable position because they have chosen to be neutral in the Ukraine war, endorsing the peace talks without combatting Russia's actions (Krönig, 2022).

According to studies, China's response stems from its prioritization of strategic partnership with Russia and a wish to avoid being in confrontation with the West, whereas India's neutrality is derived from its non-aligned foreign policy (Stuenkel,

2020). These are also supported by Brazil and South Africa who have also maintained a neutral stance given the importance of diplomacy and multilateral dialogue, congruent with the BRICS Ministry of (non)interference (de Carvalho & Nel, 2019). The complexity of BRICS in solving conflicts in which member states have vested interest is reflected in this internal divergence. BRICS is gaining importance in international mediation, especially in the reformation of the international governance framework, such as the United Nations Security Council and International Monetary Fund, at a fast pace. They argue that BRICS institutions are too heavily skewed toward Western interests and do not adequately capture the world south (Stephen, 2017). BRICS states propagate a posture in conflict resolution that is more equitable focuses on sovereignty and opposes external military interventions, as per Lundgren and Svensson (2014). The BRICS Development Bank is also considered as a possible 'peace engineering' tool - for instance, it could contribute to the recovery of war-ravaged nations (Cooper & Farooq 2015). Yet, while Roberts (2017) argues that the bloc's ability to moderate conflict, like Ukraine, is hamstrung by the diverse political and strategic interests of its members, most especially between Russia and the rest of the group, the bloc has perhaps proven more of a mixed record on achieving these aims.

## THEORETICAL UNDERPINNINGS

In this section, the focus is on integrating the central question and its sub-questions into the broader literature on mediator bias. To facilitate this integration, a comprehensive review of international mediation and dialogue facilitation is presented. The terms bias, impartiality, and neutrality are elucidated based on scholarly definitions, as this chapter does not seek to test a specific theory of international mediation. Rather, it employs the concept of bias as a general framework to inform the analysis and discourse. The sub-questions outlined in the chapter are utilized to structure the subsequent section. By organizing the discussion around these sub-questions, the chapter aims to provide a systematic exploration of mediator bias within the context of international mediation and dialogue facilitation.

### International Mediation

International conflict mediation seeks to transform adversarial disputes into constructive engagements (Wallensteen & Svensson, 2014, p. 315). Vuković (2011, p. 114) underscores that environmental, behavioral, and mediator-specific factors intricately influence the mediation process, an assertion echoed across various scholarly perspectives. Extensive peace mediation research has scrutinized factors such as the frequency of mediation, tactics employed, mediator bias, coordination efforts, and the perceived success of mediation endeavors (Wallensteen & Svensson, 2014). However, this chapter delves specifically into the realm of bias, following Bercovitch's delineation of mediation as a component of conflict management aimed at altering perceptions or behavior without resorting to force or legal enforcement (Bercovitch & Gartner, 2008, p. 6). Ukraine, as a party to the conflict, solicited assistance from the OSCE through its monitoring mission. It's noteworthy that the OSCE's rulings lack legal enforceability, and the unarmed nature of the Special Monitoring Mission (SMM) precludes the use of physical coercion. Consequently, the SMM operates within Bercovitch's framework of global mediation, encompassing both monitoring and mediation functions, including facilitating communication between conflicting parties (Kyselova, 2017, p. 125). While the OSCE's definition of mediation emphasizes structured communication and impartiality, it distinguishes dialogue facilitation as a complementary yet distinct process aimed at fostering trust and comprehension between parties (OSCE, 2014a, p. 10). Unlike mediation, dialogue facilitation prioritizes understanding opposing viewpoints over achieving specific resolutions and hinges on the voluntary participation of conflict parties (OSCE, 2014a, p. 45). Given the pivotal role of impartiality and the potential impact of bias on mediators, the subsequent section scrutinizes these concepts in greater detail, underscoring their significance within the mediation framework.

## Bias

### Defining Bias, Neutrality, and Impartiality

*A definition of bias as it is employed in theories* on international mediation is necessary to answer the first sub-question, which asks how bias is conveyed in the interpretative assertions (Conceptualising bias functions also as the basis for the codebook, which is explained in the methodology chapter and applied in the analysis). When "the mediator is closer to one side than the other," bias is generally evident (Arad & Carnevale, 1994, p. 426). Although some minor differences exist among definitions of bias, they always involve ideas that favor one side. For instance, Kydd states that "[i]f the mediator's preferences are aligned with one party or the other, she is said to be biased in favor of that party" (Kydd, 2003, p. 601). When defining bias, other definitions refer to the disputants' "closeness" or "the mediator's closer ties with one party" (Arad & Carnevale, 1994, p. 44; Elgström et al., 2018, p. 302). The mediator is considered impartial or unbiased if they have no preference for any party (Arad & Carnevale, 1994, p. 44; Elgström et al., 2018, p. 302). Bias in mediation can be classified as either "*bias of source*" or "*bias of content*," according to Carnevale and Arad. The bias of source results from the mediator's intimate ties to one party, as opposed to the bias of content, which refers to the settlement plan, or the content of the negotiation outcome (Arad & Carnevale, 1994, p. 45). This chapter focuses on the source's bias (Henceforth only referred to as bias). Because dialogue facilitation does not seek a particular resolution. The acceptance and efficiency of the mediator are impacted by the source's bias (Gent & Shannon, 2011, p. 129). This implies that prejudice can undermine the SMM's usability and potency. The approach relies on a chapter that looks at 'neutrality' at the UN to identify bias in interpretative remarks. The authors contend that "condemning" or "calling upon" conflict sides is against neutrality (Benson & Satana, 2008, p. 141). "Denying or curbing one's self-interest and suspension of judgment" are two definitions of *Neutrality* (Stenner, 2016, p. 269). The OSCE cannot be impartial since it upholds international law (IL). Given the OSCE's claim of impartiality, this may initially seem paradoxical, but neutrality would also entail acting impartially against IL violations (Scholars have traditionally advocated for neutral mediators, but the OSCE's argumentation is in line with research arguing that neutrality is not a necessary characteristic for successful mediators (Kydd, 2003, p. 608). Even though the term "neutrality" is not utilized in the analysis, it was thought necessary to provide a quick overview. However, it makes it possible to identify biased from neutral phrases. When prejudice is found in sentences, the OSCE's claimed impartiality might be called into question. The OSCE "principles of impartiality and transparency" that govern the mission are mentioned in the initial paragraph of the SMM mandate (OSCE, 2014b). "freedom from favoritism and bias in either word or action" is *Impartiality* (Stenner, 2016, p. 268). The OSCE defines impartiality as "even-handed conduct by the mediator towards the conflict parties," which does not exactly match Stenner's definition (OSCE, 2014a, p. 45). This implies that objectivity and behavior are related. The OSCE clarifies that to uphold the impartiality principle; facts must be published without placing the responsibility on one of the sides (OSCE, 2021, p. 47). Interpretative statements that appeal to conflict parties exhibit bias, according to that argument and the provided conceptualization of bias. Finding bias in speech or deeds could undermine the SMM's claim that they uphold impartiality. The OSCE combines monitoring and mediation, making the issue of bias pertinent. On the one hand, objective factual reporting is essential for monitoring the truce (Clayton & Sticher, 2021, p. 3). The benefits of biased mediators over impartial mediators are becoming more widely acknowledged in theories of international mediation.

## Addressees of Bias

We draw on earlier research to conceptualize bias for the material chapter. The following information should not be viewed as a review of the chapter area. Instead, several scholarly viewpoints are described to arrive at the conceptualization used in the chapter. To better explain the bias, scholars distinguish between conflict parties that the biased mediator favors or disfavors. Benson and Satana distinguish between "criticism of any kind 'against state A'" and "clear support for 'state B'" (Benson & Satana, 2008, p. 141). The recipient, in this case, is just divided by state. According to research on bias in such resolutions, most resolutions pass the UN Security Council (UNSC) to express a statement against a state (Benson & Satana, 2008, p. 143). However, non-state actors are not included in their chapter. Others distinguish between mediator bias in favor of conflict parties in a more nuanced way. The next two paragraphs describe investigations to demonstrate additional actors to state actors. (Svensson, 2009) examines how biased mediators affect the nature of peace agreements compared to neutral mediators in their empirical chapter on civil wars. They distinguish between impartial, rebel-biased, and government-biased arbitrators for this reason. The findings, which span civil wars from 1989 to 2004, demonstrate that neutral mediators can negotiate settlements more quickly but with worse quality (Svensson, 2009, p. 464). Therefore, Svensson supports using biased mediators in the mediation process. Because of their ability to influence the preferred side, such as through financial backing, biased mediators have an edge (Svensson, 2009, p. 448). Because it fits the nature of the combatants in the Conflict in Ukraine, the idea of "rebel-biased" mediators is added to the chapter (Following the argumentation about terminology, the term collaborator is used instead of 'rebels').

Government bias is also included because it shows prejudice in Ukraine's favor. Most current work on bias in international mediation has concentrated on state mediators rather than the bias of states that are members of an umbrella IO like the OSCE. However, (Lundgren & Svensson, 2014, p. 318) turns to this gap, suggesting that studies on the mediation of IOs ought to incorporate bias and leverage since the political interests of states are present and "these interests appear to affect mediation outcomes." They add "balanced biasedness" to the pro-government and pro-rebel bias. When the preferences, or perceived bias, among the participating states are equal, the authors speak of balanced IOs. The 1975–2004 data set focuses on civil war mediation as well. They "find that IOs, where member states provide support to both sides in a conflict, outperform IOs whose member states remain disinterested" (Lundgren & Svensson, 2014, p. 316). Because they can benefit from this tight interaction, balanced IOs with states supporting either side of the dispute are more successful (Lundgren & Svensson, 2014, p. 318).

Given that the OSCE is an IO, the discussion will also touch on the issue of balanced bias. This refers to whether bias toward various disputing parties is dispersed fairly among participating governments. This feature, which derives from the OSCE's assumption of impartiality, is particularly interesting because a balanced IO might perform better than an OSCE that upholds impartiality. While the two other studies solely cover civil wars, the chapter (Benson & Satana, 2008) does not focus on non-state players, leaving out the element of numerous state actors. Combining these biased addressees, the current analysis encompasses the cooperating non-state players in Eastern Ukraine and the operational state actors, namely Ukraine and Russia. Additionally, the OSCE will be addressed as a potential balanced IO.

### Content of Bias

The third question is a sub-question about biased sentences. Bias in this chapter refers to having stronger ties to one of the parties, which may be personal, political, or both (Arad & Carnevale, 1994, p. 45). Other researchers looked at datasets on outside support for armed Conflict and bias based on economic and military sanctions (Benson & Satana, 2008, p. 140; Lundgren & Svensson, 2014). By doing this, they operationalize bias depending on many types of support, such as troop supply, delivery of weapons, and training, to name a few. Only the years 1975 through 2009 are covered in the database on external support. Therefore, this chapter could not follow the same pattern because there was a lack of data on the Ukraine crisis. The secret tie between Russian supplies to the collaborators, as explained in the background chapter, hinders this even further. This sub-question takes the biased sentences detected in the first sub-question and analyzes their content rather than investigating bias using the database on external support. However, it is outside the purview of this research to determine if bias results from linkages to the economy, politics, or personal relationships; biased phrases can nevertheless be closely examined. This makes it possible to identify bias at a lower level than when sending troops or weapons. The literature review's descriptions of general SMM-related topics are utilized to compare the results. The content analysis aims to investigate the various themes that appear in prejudiced utterances.

## METHODOLOGY

The burgeoning recognition of the pivotal role of language and meaning in political analysis has spurred scholarly interest in text analysis (Halperin & Heath, 2020, p. 364). Text analysis is a potent tool for delving into political phenomena, particularly concerning the intricate interplay between bias and mediation examined in this chapter (Halperin & Heath, 2020, p. 386). Proximity to textual data empowers researchers to immerse themselves in the words and experiences of the subjects under scrutiny, in this case, the OSCE states (Wutich & Gravlee, 2010). Notably, contested concepts like bias lend themselves well to examination through text analysis due to their adaptability (Wutich & Gravlee, 2010). Embracing an inclusive approach advocated by Wutich and Gravlee, which seamlessly integrates textual analysis with quantitative and qualitative dimensions, the employed text analysis strikes a delicate balance between numerical data and interpretive insights (Wutich & Gravlee, 2010, p. 188). The emphasis on written interpretative statements aligns perfectly with the focus of this analysis, as it revolves around scrutinizing written texts. The primary sources for this investigation comprise decisions made by the Permanent Council (PC) regarding the OSCE's Special Monitoring Mission (SMM).

The deployment of the SMM elicited interpretative responses from OSCE states, as did each of the eight mandate extensions spanning from 2014 to 2021. Consequently, the analysis draws upon a comprehensive dataset encompassing all 45 interpretative statements appended to these documents, totaling 77 pages of text emanating from eight OSCE states. Content analysis emerges as the predominant method for conducting text analysis, emphasizing an inward examination of the text rather than its broader contextual backdrop. Nevertheless, adopting a qualitative content analysis (QlCA) approach injects a heightened sensitivity to contextual nuances, a dimension often overlooked in traditional quantitative content analyses (Halperin & Heath, 2020, p. 365). Drawing upon Hsieh and Shannon's characterization, a QlCA serves as a research method that facilitates the subjective interpretation of textual content through a systematic classification process involving coding and identifying emergent themes or patterns (Hsieh & Shannon, 2005, p. 1278). This nuanced approach ensures a comprehensive exploration of the text's intricacies while remaining attuned to the broader contextual framework underpinning the analysis.

## Analysis

The examination of 45 interpretative statements initiates with a broad overview, subsequently delineating analyses by three sub-questions.

*Figure 2. Interpretative statements by states*

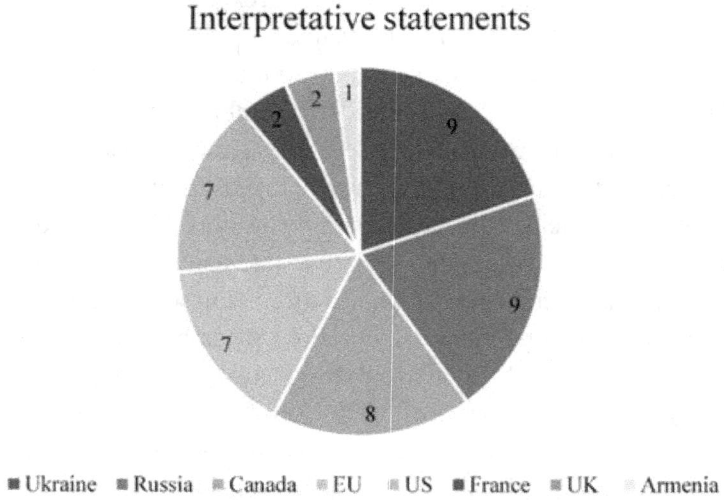


Figure 2 illustrates the dispersion of interpretative statements attributed to OSCE states, with the number of statements from each state denoted on the outer circumference of the circle. Predominantly, Ukraine and Russia emerged as the most prolific contributors, trailed by Canada and statements emanating from EU representatives and the US. Notably, France and the United Kingdom (UK) each contributed a single statement, while Armenia provided one. Remarkably, eight out of 57 participating states expressed explicit positions regarding the mandate. This phenomenon partially stems from states aligning themselves with particular statements, thereby signaling support for their content. The literature review underscores the challenge posed by states occupying dual roles as belligerents and mediators in the Conflict, a dynamic that can potentially undermine OSCE mediation endeavors (Remler, 2021). Leveraging this perspective, this chapter contends that Russia and Ukraine's pronounced involvement in both belligerent and mediator capacities accounts for their heightened engagement in statement issuance. Their intricate entanglement in the Conflict underscores their substantial stakes in the mediation process, motivating their active participation.

## Detecting Bias

A comprehensive scrutiny of 111 sentences reveals a notable disparity, with 31 sentences deemed neutral and 80 exhibiting bias (Neutral sentences either abstain from addressing any conflict party or encompass all conflict parties). The graphical representation in Figure 4 vividly underscores this disproportion, vividly illustrating the prevalence of biased expressions in comparison to their neutral counterparts. Focusing exclusively on the 80 biased sentences, this analysis excludes neutral findings from further scrutiny, as delineated in Figure 3.

*Figure 3. Biased versus neutral sentences*

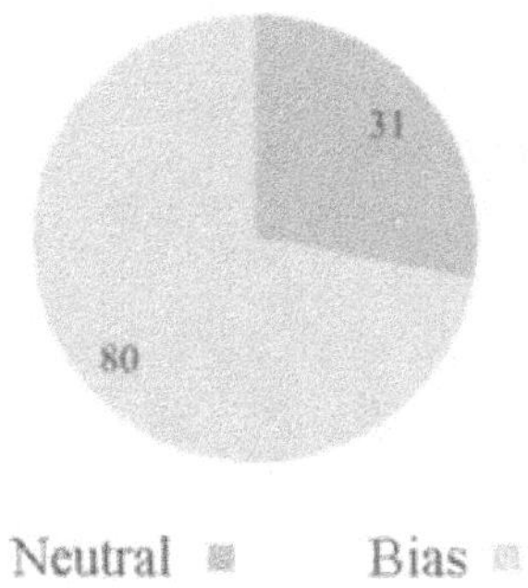


*Figure 4. Frequency of indicator words*

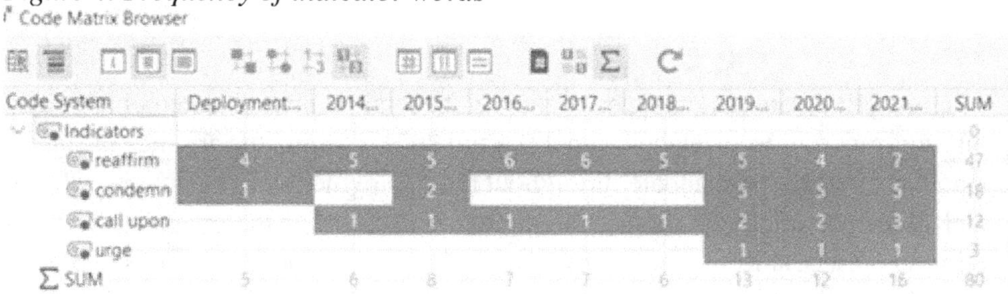


| Code System | Deployment... | 2014... | 2015... | 2016... | 2017... | 2018... | 2019... | 2020... | 2021... | SUM |
|---|---|---|---|---|---|---|---|---|---|---|
| Indicators | | | | | | | | | | 0 |
| reaffirm | 4 | 5 | 5 | 6 | 6 | 5 | 5 | 4 | 7 | 47 |
| condemn | 1 | | 2 | | | | 5 | 5 | 5 | 18 |
| call upon | | 1 | 1 | 1 | 1 | 1 | 2 | 2 | 3 | 12 |
| urge | | | | | | | 1 | 1 | 1 | 3 |
| Σ SUM | 5 | 6 | 8 | 7 | 7 | 6 | 13 | 12 | 16 | 80 |

Delving into the mechanisms through which bias permeates interpretative statements unveils a prevalent employment of standardized language, which mirrors findings regarding the UN's utilization of "standard language depending on the severity of the situation at hand" (Benson & Satana, 2008, p. 139), akin to the observed trend within the OSCE. This trend is evidenced by many expressions replicating each other, as illustrated in Figure 4, featuring indicator codes denoting various biases. Notably, the frequency distribution of these indicator codes reveals a predominance of 'reaffirm' (47 sentences), followed by 'condemn' (18 sentences), 'call upon' (12 sentences), and 'urge' (three sentences) directives towards the conflict parties. The color-coded visualization delineates a discernible escalation in biased expressions over time, with a noteworthy surge from five biased sentences in 2014 to 16 in the final extension of 2021. Concomitant with the proliferation of biased sentences is a discernible augmentation in interpretative statements throughout the SMM deployment, as depicted in Figure 5. This graphical representation succinctly captures the concurrent increase in interpretative statements and biased expressions embedded within these statements. The alignment of the y-axis with the total number of statements each year and the x-axis with the total number of biased sentences offers a comprehensive snapshot of the escalating trend over the years.

*Figure 5. Increase of statements and bias*

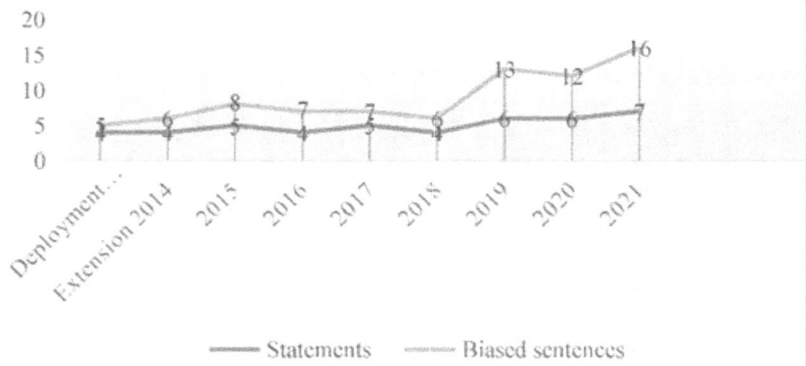


Figure 5 illustrates a notable escalation in the total number of statements, nearly doubling from four to seven between 2014 and 2021. Despite the absence of significant alterations to the mandate throughout the deployment years (Umland, 2021), which could potentially rationalize the surge in interpretative statements, this proliferation suggests a shift in attitude towards the OSCE mission or the armed Conflict in Ukraine. This observation resonates with Müller's contention that heightened difficulties prompt an increased pursuit of an "*authoritative or authentic interpretation*" of PC decisions (Müller, 2002, p. 350), aiming for a consensus regarding the mandate and its extensions. The augmented frequency of biased remarks can partially be ascribed to the surge in total statements, indicative of the mounting challenges in achieving unanimity. However, the notable peaks observed between 2019 and 2021 signify a substantial surge in biased expressions. This implies a potential alteration in either the on-ground situation or the disposition of OSCE states towards the conflict parties.

*Table 1. Indicators by states*

| Code System | EU | Ukraine | US | Canada | Russia | UK | France | Armenia |
|---|---|---|---|---|---|---|---|---|
| Indicators\reaffirm | 13 | 4 | 8 | 19 | 9 | 3 | 0 | 0 |
| Indicators\condemn | 6 | 8 | 0 | 0 | 2 | 2 | | |
| Indicators\call upon | 0 | 1 | 7 | 2 | | | | |
| Indicators\urge | 0 | 3 | | | | | | |

Table 1 reveals a notable concentration of biased sentences within statements issued by various entities. Specifically, the EU leads with 19 biased sentences, followed closely by Ukraine with 16 and the US with 15. Canadian statements exhibit 12 instances of bias, while Russian statements show 11. UK statements, however, contain only seven biased sentences. France and Armenia's statements lack identified biased expressions, reflected in a sum zero in the far-right columns. The prevalence of bias in interpretative statements is striking, with 80 sentences identified as biased. Furthermore, a discernible trend of escalating biased remarks from 2014 to 2021, coinciding with the rise in total statements. Bias manifests through expressions that either reaffirm, condemn, call upon, or urge conflict parties, aligning with Lundgren and Svensson's assertion that states' interests and positions are evident in international organizations (Lundgren & Svensson, 2014). However, this analysis is confined to the positions of only eight participating states that issued interpretative statements, and of these, only six exhibit bias. Thus, while shedding light on biased OSCE states concerning the SMM, this examination does not encompass all states' positions within the OSCE.

## Addressees of Bias

*Figure 6. Addressees of bias*

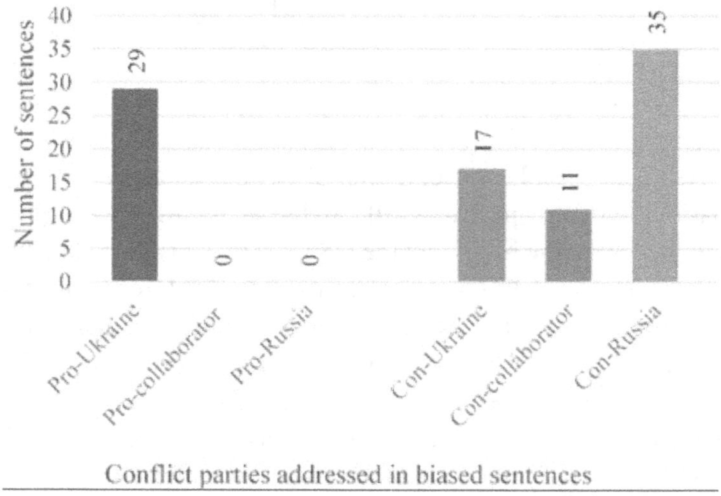


Bias is evident in expressions favoring and disfavoring conflict parties, as depicted in Figure 7. Analyzing all 80 biased sentences, it becomes clear that bias towards conflict parties is not evenly distributed. Pro-Ukraine sentiments dominate with 29 instances, while bias against parties varies: 17 sentences oppose Ukraine, 35 target Russia, and 11 target collaborators in Eastern Ukraine. It is worth noting that six sentences express bias against multiple parties, and thus, they are counted towards each respective party for clarity in visualization. Around 36 percent of biased sentences favor Ukraine, with the highest proportion stemming from EU representatives, accounting for nine instances. The EU provides an illustrative example of this pro-Ukraine stance: "*We reiterate our unwavering support to Ukraine's independence, sovereignty, unity, and territorial integrity within its internationally recognized borders*" (OSCE, 2016). This aligns with the findings by Elgström et al. (2018), who observed a perceived bias in favor of Ukraine attributed to the EU's support for the SMM. In seven instances, the US exhibits pro-Ukraine bias, lending partial support to Landwehr's contention that the US is heavily biased towards Ukraine (Landwehr, 2019 p. 304). However, while Landwehr posits the EU as slightly biased compared to the US, the present analysis suggests otherwise, with the EU displaying more bias in statements. Additionally, Canada demonstrates pro-Ukraine bias in eight instances, a facet not extensively discussed in scholarly discourse. Nonetheless, Canada's sanctions on Russia may elucidate its position (Landwehr, 2019 p. 299). Interestingly, despite Russia's support for collaborators in Eastern Ukraine, no statements emerge in their favor. This deviates from Landwehr's assertion that Russia is unequivocally biased toward these collaborators (Landwehr, 2019 p. 304).

The absence of explicit support for collaborators aligns with existing research, underscoring Russia's covert backing of Ukrainian collaborators (Hauter, 2019; Twickel et al., 2018). Given Russia's official backing of the SMM, openly endorsing collaborators could undermine its stance. Analyzing mediators categorized as government-biased, rebel-biased, and neutral by Svensson (2009), coding revealed sentences expressing disfavor towards Ukraine, predominantly from Russia. For instance, a Russian statement condemns Ukraine for alleged human rights violations and calls for increased scrutiny of domestic political affairs and manifestations of nationalism (OSCE, 2019).

While identifying Russian bias against Ukraine might appear trivial, it bolsters the validity of the applied qualitative content analysis (QlCA). Instances of bias against Ukraine remained relatively consistent throughout the SMM's deployment, comprising one or two sentences annually. Conversely, approximately 44 percent of biased remarks target Russia, with Ukraine leading the charge. The EU's bias against Russia, evidenced by seven instances, correlates with its sanction policies enacted since 2014 (Landwehr, 2019, p. 305). Both the US and Canada issued singular demands on Russia, with the US urging Russia to cease support for separatists, exemplifying a unified stance (OSCE, 2014c). Despite limited scholarly discourse on the UK's bias, the analysis reveals four instances of blame directed at Russia for SMM restrictions. Notably, expressions disfavoring Russia nearly tripled from deployment inception to 2021, paralleling the increase in pro-Ukraine sentiments. The juxtaposition of pro-Ukraine expressions from Western countries with Russian sentiments against Ukraine underscores Ukraine's status as a "*geopolitical battleground between Russia and the West*" (Biersack & O'Lear, 2014, p. 248). In contrast, blame attributed to collaborators remains relatively minor, accounting for approximately 14 percent. Notably, collaborators are variably referred to as "*Russian-backed forces*" or "*Russia-backed separatists*," highlighting differing perspectives within interpretative statements (OSCE, 2015, 2021b).

The data presented indicates that collaborators in the conflict are not perceived as an independent party, but their connection with Russia is recognized. Consequently, assigning blame for collaborators' actions could be construed as bias against Russia. Notably, despite the OSCE's official stance of not recognizing Russia as a party to the Donbas conflict (Härtel et al., 2021, p. 33), participating states circumvent this position by implicating Russia in their statements regarding the conflict. Although typically, a sentence addresses one conflict party, six US statements between 2015 and 2021 targeted "*Ukraine, Russia, and Russian-backed forces*." The notable bias exhibited by the US against Ukraine contradicts Landwehr's assertion that the US is a "*mediator fully biased towards Ukraine*" (Landwehr, 2019, p. 304). While

Landwehr focuses on the US's potential role in the Normandy Format, the findings reveal bias against Ukraine within the OSCE context. This suggests that the US may have different roles in the OSCE concerning Ukraine compared to its hypothetical role in the Normandy Format. However, the detection of pro-Ukraine bias by the US suggests that states can address Ukraine's responsibility despite potential bias. In summary, biases are observed in favor and against warring parties, with most articulations directed against Russia and the collaborators, followed by bias in favor of the Ukrainian government.

## Content of Bias

The analysis delves into the themes present within biased sentences, shedding light on the contextual usage of these themes. The identified themes encompass international law, geography, threat, access, Russian action, and mandate (refer to Figure 8). To facilitate a more nuanced examination, these categories were subdivided, enabling a detailed exploration of the years in which these themes were prevalent and distinguishing between OSCE states expressing bias and the targeted recipients of such bias.

*Figure 7. Occurring themes*

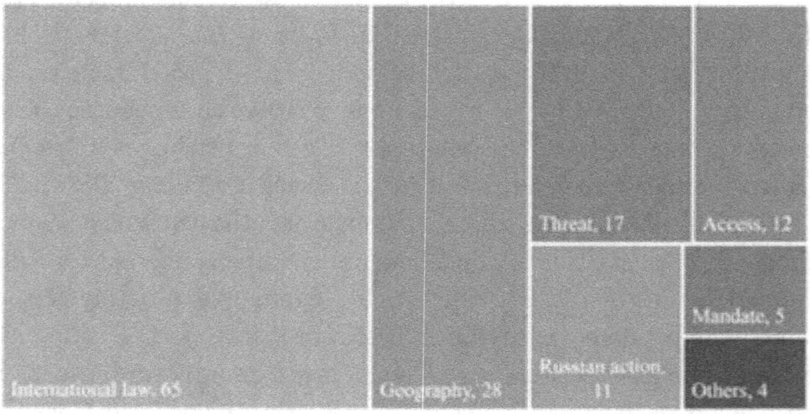


## International Law

The analysis reveals that the most prominent category within the interpretative statements is international law, comprising 65 biased sentences. Within this category, expressions concerning Ukraine's political sovereignty and territorial integrity dominate, accounting for 36 instances. These expressions favoring Ukraine are predominantly articulated by the EU representative, followed by Ukraine itself, Canada, and the US, and acknowledged by the UK. Furthermore, a cluster of states emphasizes Ukraine's internationally recognized borders, including references to international waters, on 20 occasions. Conversely, seven sentences by Russia evoke "*political and legal realities*" to limit the deployment area of monitors. These references to political and legal realities, occurring annually from deployment until 2019, are exclusively attributed to Russia. As noted by Umland (2021), such expressions contravene OSCE principles concerning the political sovereignty and territorial integrity of each OSCE state. Lastly, two distinct references to human rights were identified.

*Figure 8. Bias, IL*

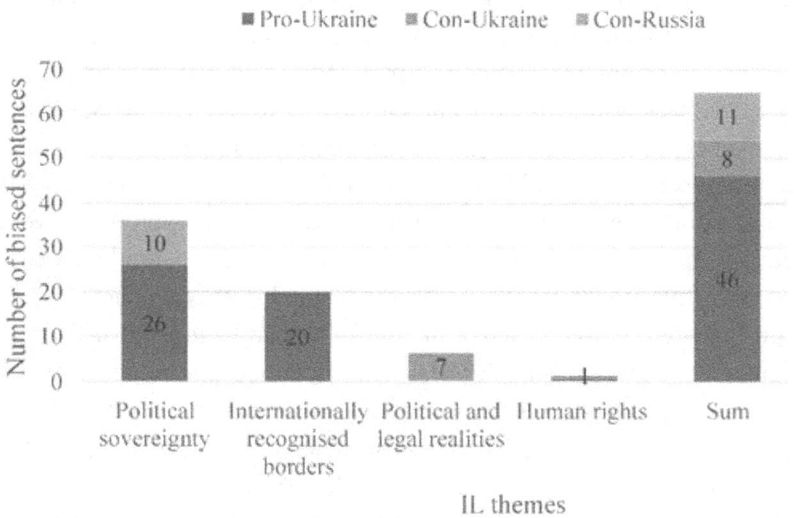


The figure highlights two significant accusations exchanged between Ukraine and Russia. Firstly, Russia condemns Ukraine for allegedly violating its human rights commitments under international law, including OSCE commitments. This condemnation extends to instances of what Russia perceives as flagrant violations of human rights in Ukraine, including discriminatory legislative measures adopted by the Ukrainian authorities, which Russia claims infringe upon the linguistic, religious, cultural, educational, and other rights of Ukrainian citizens (OSCE, 2019). Secondly, Ukraine urges Russia to provide Crimea access to the Special Monitoring Mission (SMM). Ukraine argues that the dire human rights situation in Crimea, coupled with Russia's ongoing illegal activities aimed at further militarizing the peninsula, necessitate special international attention (OSCE, 2021b). These examples underscore the intense accusations levied by both Ukraine and Russia, with each side accusing the other of human rights violations. The distribution of sentences regarding the four subcategories of international law (IL) reveals the extent of bias attributed to each party in the conflict. Most remarks, totaling 46, favor Ukraine, followed by 11 expressions of bias against Russia and eight against Ukraine. This distribution sheds light on the contentious accusations between the conflicting parties.

## Geography

The geography category in the analyzed sentences predominantly revolves around the contentious issue of the annexation of Crimea. Most of these sentences, nine in total, address the illegal annexation of Crimea. Additionally, seven confirmations assert that the OSCE Special Monitoring Mission (SMM) mandate covers Crimea. However, opposing these assertions, Russia contends nine times that Crimea is an integral part of its territory. Russia's stance is exemplified by its statement that Crimea and Sevastopol are an integral part of the Russian Federation, reflecting what it perceives as political and legal realities (OSCE, 2018). Essentially, Russia views Crimea as part of its sovereign territory, contrary to the viewpoint that Crimea is illegally annexed and should fall under the OSCE mandate. This disagreement underscores a fundamental divide, with Russia asserting its sovereignty over Crimea. At the same time, other parties view its annexation as illegal and advocate for the inclusion of Crimea under the OSCE mandate. Notably, this conflict of perspectives is most pronounced between Russia and the European Union (EU). The EU, acting as a prominent voice opposing Russia, takes a stance that aligns with Ukraine's interests. This opposition to Russia's position reflects the EU's broader stance of favoring Ukraine, as highlighted in previous research (Elgström et al., 2018). Despite not explicitly addressing the EU's role within the OSCE, this perceived bias towards Ukraine is evident in the current findings. It is important to note that Ukrainian statements also significantly shape the narrative around the conflict in Donbas. They refer to Donbas twice as being occupied by Russia and once as 'temporarily occupied parts of Donbas' (OSCE, 2021b). These references underscore Ukraine's perspective on the situation in Donbas, emphasizing Russia's role in the conflict and its control over certain territories.

*Figure 9. Bias, geography*

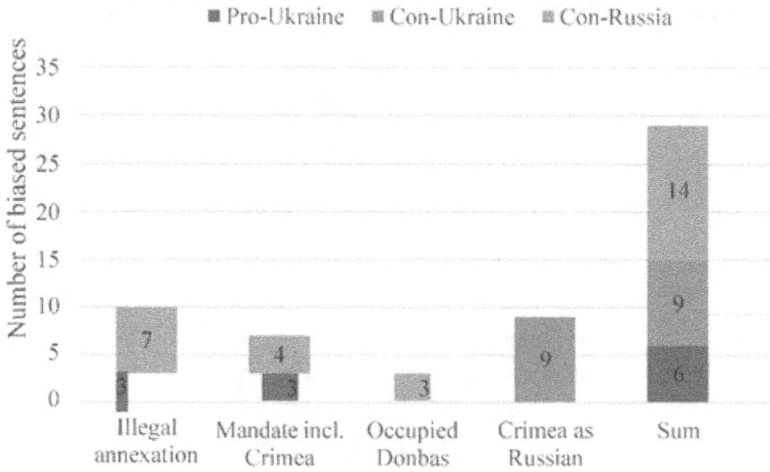


Figure 10 shows the distribution of sentences about the four subcategories of geography according to the conflict party attributed to the bias. The bar on the right displays the sum of biased sentences with the previously attributed colors to warring parties. In total, most comments oppose Russia, namely 14, followed by nine articulations of disfavor of Ukraine and six expressions in favor of Ukraine. Notably, Russia is the only state arguing that Crimea belongs to Russia. Also, no state aligns with their statements. States condemning the illegal annexation and advocating that the mandate covers Crimea is more prominent.

## Threat

The United States, Ukraine, and Canada statements emphasize the importance of ensuring the safety and security of the monitors involved in the conflict. Specifically, they strongly urge the Russian Federation to cease threats, attacks, and intimidations directed towards these monitors. This call for action has been reiterated 12 times across various statements (OSCE, 2015, 2021b). Interestingly, during the initial year of the monitoring mission's deployment, the biased comments did not mention threats. However, starting from 2015, there has been a noticeable increase in references to threats, with further escalation observed in 2019 and 2021. It is noteworthy that the discussions surrounding threats tend to either cast a negative light on Russia and its affiliated troops or express collective disapproval towards Ukraine, Russia, and the Russian-backed troops. This pattern suggests a growing concern among certain parties regarding the safety of the monitors, particularly about perceived threats posed by Russian forces or those aligned with them. The increasing frequency of these references over time underscores the evolving dynamics and challenges faced by the monitoring mission in the regions.

*Figure 10. Distribution of blame for security threats*

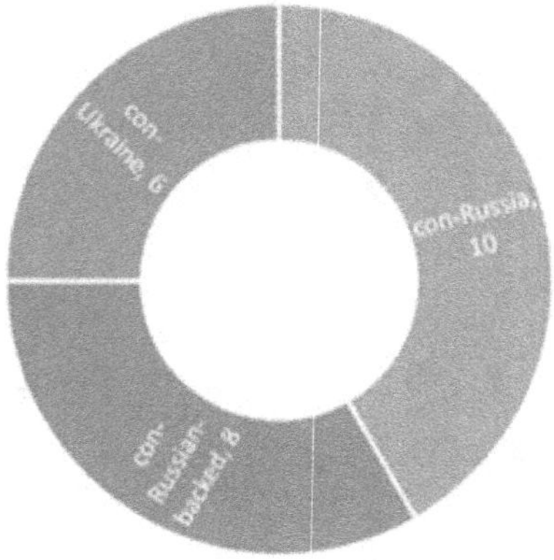


The data presented in Figure 11 elucidates the attribution of bias in sentences concerning security issues related to monitors, highlighting a discernible pattern of blame towards Russia, Russian-backed troops, and Ukraine to a lesser extent. The delineation of blame across these actors underscores the perceived roles in exacerbating threats to the safety of Special Monitoring Mission (SMM) personnel and reflects broader geopolitical tensions. Oberson's analysis separates the discussion of security threats the SMM faces from the specific conflict actors involved, potentially abstracting the complex interplay of local and external influences on these security challenges. In contrast, Umland explicitly connects these threats to pro-Russian elements and separatist factions, offering a more pointed critique of the sources of instability. Further scrutiny of the Special Monitoring Mission's operational constraints reveals a parity in criticisms from Ukraine and the UK regarding restrictions, with all such limitations ultimately ascribed to Russian influence. The call by OSCE member states for Russia to alleviate the SMM's operational hurdles in non-government-controlled territories encapsulates Russia's perceived significant sway over these areas. Additionally, the specific mention of a new tier of constraints imposed by Russia in 2020 under the guise of pandemic-related safety measures highlights the opportunistic use of global health crises to justify stringent controls, thereby intensifying pre-existing operational barriers for the SMM. This analysis brings to the fore the intricate dynamics of blame, influence, and operational challenges within conflict zones, shedding light on the multifaceted roles that different actors play in shaping the security landscape confronting international monitoring missions.

*Figure 11. Bias, threat*

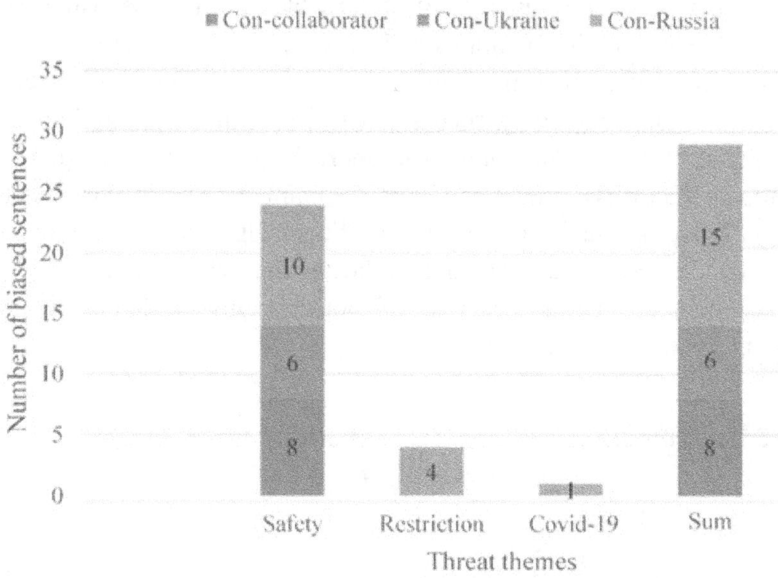


Figure 12 provides a clear visual representation of the distribution of accusations regarding safety infringements, with the majority directed towards Russia, followed by its collaborators, and, to a lesser extent, Ukraine. This pattern of attributions not only highlights the perceived primary role of Russia in these safety violations but also underscores the involvement of associated actors, thereby painting a comprehensive picture of the blame hierarchy within the context of these accusations. The narrative of impeded and exacerbated restrictions attributed solely to Russia, particularly under the guise of COVID-19 pandemic measures, merits critical examination. This portrayal suggests a strategic manipulation of global health crises to justify or intensify restrictions, a tactic that raises significant concerns about the exploitation of emergency measures for non-health-related agenda.

## Access

The demands for enhanced access for monitors in Ukraine predominantly call for unimpeded entry across the entire territory, with specific grievances expressed about denied access to crucial conflict areas like Donetsk and Luhansk. The explicit demand for access to "*temporarily occupied Crimea*" (OSCE, 2021b) underscores the critical geopolitical sensitivities and operational challenges monitoring missions face. The focus on access infringements aligns with the findings of Härtel et al. (2021) and Umland (2021), who elucidate that, despite the official mandate permitting full territorial access, the mission has consistently been barred from Crimea and encountered frequent access denials in parts of Eastern Ukraine. This persistent restriction complicates the mission's operations and raises questions about the efficacy and enforcement of international mandates in conflict zones. Figure 15 elucidates the distribution of blame regarding access restrictions, uniquely highlighting that in the category of 'Access,' collaborators are more frequently implicated in impeding infringements than Russia, with collaborators blamed 11 times compared to Russia's seven. This suggests local proxies' significant, albeit often overlooked, role in conflict-related access issues. The data indicates that while Ukraine is mentioned in joint statements concerning access, it is not explicitly singled out as a primary impediment to monitoring access.

*Figure 12. Bias, access*

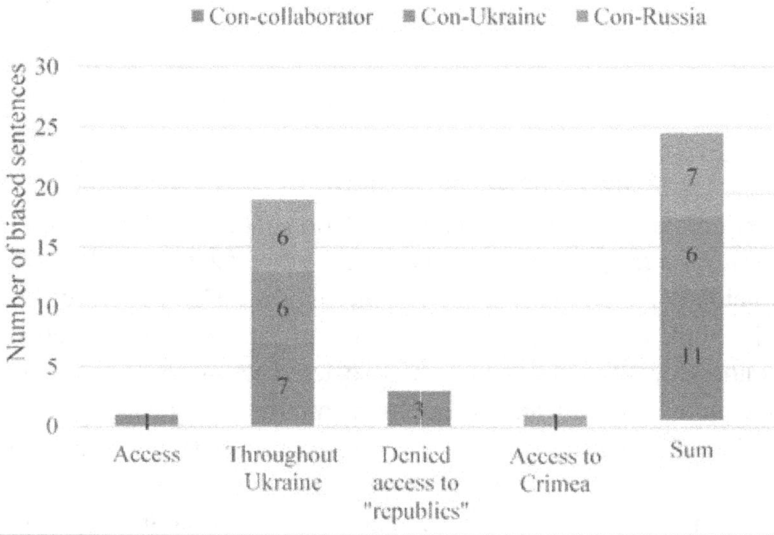


Ukraine is the sole state explicitly demanding access to Crimea, despite broader geopolitical discourse surrounding the peninsula. The United States and Canada, while not singling out Crimea, assert the necessity of access "throughout the entire territory of Ukraine," implicitly including Crimea as articulated at different points in their statements (OSCE, 2017).

## Russian Action

The condemnation of Russian aggression is prominent, cited nine times, including specific references to "*Russia's ongoing illegal activities*" (OSCE, 2021b). This criticism predominantly emanates from Ukraine, followed by the European Union and the United Kingdom, with notable support from the OSCE for Ukraine in "countering the severe consequences of the aggression pursued by the Russian Federation against Ukraine" (OSCE, 2017). The recent years of the deployment have marked an uptick in denunciations of Russian aggression, which could be attributable either to an escalation of hostilities by Russia or a shift in the diplomatic postures of OSCE member states. Interestingly, Russian actions were not explicitly mentioned during the initial extension period from 2014 to 2016, a phenomenon that warrants further examination. Contrasting with the frequent use of "*aggression*" by member states to describe Russian actions, the OSCE itself refrains from using the term when discussing the armed conflict in Eastern Ukraine, suggesting a discrepancy between the organization's official language and the terminology favored by politicians (Oberson, 2021, p. 61). This divergence highlights a significant tension within the OSCE between the diplomatic language employed by the organization and the more pointed terms used by its member states. Moreover, the consistent focus on Russian-induced violence, to the exclusion of actions by collaborators or Ukraine, underscores a selective attribution of blame that shapes the narrative of the conflict.

## Mandate and Others

References to the Special Monitoring Mission (SMM) mandate have predominantly emerged in the last three years, with Ukraine explicitly emphasizing the necessity for its full implementation. Russia is attributed as a hindrance to this implementation, with a specific call for Russia "*to put an end to them and to allow the SMM to implement its mandate*" (PC.DEC/1366). This positions Russia as a central impediment to the fulfillment of the SMM's objectives. The European Union and the UK assert that the SMM's mandate extends across all of Ukraine, explicitly including "*illegally annexed Crimea and the Ukraine-Russia State border*" (OSCE, 2019). This assertion underscores the strategic importance of monitoring the Ukrainian-Russian border to trace the influx of weapons and other supplies into the conflict zones of Donbas, a critical issue highlighted by Härtel et al. (2021, p. 25). In 2020, Ukraine specifically condemned the impediment to the acquisition of additional drones, which would enhance technical monitoring capabilities, attributing the obstruction to Russia. This incident aligns with Umland's findings (2021), further suggesting that Russia's actions were deliberate attempts to curtail the mission's capabilities (Härtel et al., 2021).

The frustration of adopting specific Permanent Council (PC) declarations in 2015 and 2019 was also noted, with Russia accused of obstructing these declarations twice, compared to Ukraine's single instance of condemnation. This mutual blame game extends to Russia accusing the US of frustrating a PC decision that would have supported a segment of the Minsk agreements, denouncing Russia's "*unconstructive position*" (OSCE, 2015). These dynamics are consistent with Kropatcheva's analysis of Russia's historically disinterested and obstructive policies towards the OSCE before the armed conflict in Ukraine (Kropatcheva, 2012, p. 370). The overarching narrative reveals a clear bias in favor of Ukraine across themes of international law, geography, and mandate, reflecting states' selective use of these themes to frame their accusations. Despite this, the predominant blame across most themes is directed at Russia, except a joint call by the US for Ukraine, Russia, and Russian-backed forces to grant access to monitors, indicating a complex interplay of blame and diplomacy within the OSCE framework.

## DISCUSSION

The chapter effectively challenges the Special Monitoring Mission's (SMM) declared neutrality by illustrating that blame is apportioned among all significant parties to the Ukraine conflict from 2014 to 2021, which contradicts the OSCE's principle of impartiality. According to Stenner (2016, p. 268), impartiality is "*freedom from favoritism and prejudice in either word or action.*" The findings suggest biased commentary undermines the OSCE's proclaimed objectivity, signaling a deviation from this scholarly definition. However, it is essential to note that the chapter restricts its scrutiny to the statements made by OSCE nations, not their actions. Therefore, the OSCE's operational definition of impartiality, which is "*even-handed conduct of the mediator towards the conflict parties*" (OSCE, 2014a, p. 45), remains unchallenged in this context. This nuanced approach differentiates between potential bias in statements versus actions, allowing for a more focused analysis of rhetorical bias without disputing the overall conduct of the OSCE. The analysis also addresses the broader academic discourse on bias, which traditionally emphasizes favoritism rather than antagonism (Kydd, 2003). This focus might overlook the implications of bias against certain parties, as those negatively portrayed could be adversely affected by biased mediation, a possibility not fully encompassed in the definitions by Arad & Carnevale (1994, p. 41). This oversight is critical as it misses out on the negative ramifications for the disfavored parties within conflict resolutions. The OSCE's definitions consider the nuanced aspect of impartiality, acknowledging that it is compromised when factual reporting assigns blame to any combatant. In separating expressions of support for Ukraine from those opposing Russia, the chapter aims to avoid conflating bias against Russia with support for Ukraine, thereby addressing different facets of bias without oversimplifying the complex dynamics of the conflict. This distinction is crucial for maintaining analytical clarity and ensuring that the subtleties of each position are adequately represented and understood within the broader context of the armed conflict.

Critiquing current academic definitions of bias about conflict scenarios highlights a significant oversight: these definitions often fail to adequately capture how bias can adversely impact conflicting parties. The analysis reveals that the most biased statements typically carry negative implications, mainly when directed towards Russia. This underscores the necessity of refining academic definitions to encompass biases toward all parties involved in a conflict. The categorization process derived from existing literature seems overly simplistic, constraining the nuanced realities of conflict-related biases into rigid, binary categories: favoring or opposing Ukraine. Such a dichotomous approach does not capture the complex spectrum of biases that might exist within the discourse, suggesting a need for more flexible categorization that can more accurately reflect the varying degrees of bias. Interestingly, identifying bias in statements from OSCE state members is not inherently detrimental. Contrary to traditional views that advocate for absolute neutrality in mediation, some scholars argue that biased mediators can be beneficial. They contend that mediators with biases may exert more influence and access more significant information than their neutral counterparts (Arad & Carnevale, 1994; Bercovitch & Gartner, 2008; Kydd, 2003; Svensson, 2009). This perspective introduces the concept that the OSCE, by acknowledging and leveraging the biases of its members, might enhance its effectiveness as an international organization (IO). Lundgren and Svensson (2014) advocate for a balanced approach within the OSCE, suggesting that an IO with an equal representation of biases for and against various conflict parties would operate more effectively than one skewed towards a particular side. However, the findings from this chapter reveal a unilateral bias in favor of Ukraine, with no similar bias towards the collaborators. This unilateral bias challenges the application of Lundgren and Svensson's model to the OSCE, as it lacks the component of balance necessary for a mediated settlement, differing from the SMM's more adaptive dialogue facilitation method. This analysis suggests that a reevaluation of how biases are understood and utilized within the OSCE could potentially transform the organization's approach to conflict mediation. It is crucial to develop a more nuanced understanding of bias within international mediation frameworks.

The chapter underscores the importance of precisely classifying the nature of armed conflicts, particularly when evaluating the role of biased mediators. It argues that conflicts not classified as civil wars tend to be overlooked in empirical research concerning mediation bias. This point is crucial for understanding the situation in Ukraine, which, as established in the background chapter, should be recognized as an international armed conflict rather than a civil war. This classification impacts the interpretation of bias about the conflict parties involved. The binary categorization of actors in armed conflicts into pro-government or pro-rebel factions, as Lundgren and d Svensson (2014suggestts, needs to capture the complex realities of individual motivations and alignments. This oversimplification can hinder a nuanced understanding of conflict dynamics and mediation processes. The chapter further highlights the Qualitative Comparative Analysis (QlCA) findings, which reveal a bias in interpretative statements. These findings align with the initial view that the Special Monitoring Mission (SMM) should be approached from a mediation perspective due to its inherent mediation-related elements. Schläpfer (2016, p. 340) supports this view by discussing the SMM's dual function as both a monitor and a mediator, facilitated by and supportive of Ukrainian mediation efforts. This dual role necessitates rigorous objectivity in the SMM's monitoring activities, requiring unbiased reporting on cease-fire violations and the actions of the concerned parties. Conversely, the mediator role might benefit from a degree of bias, as theoretical discussions suggest that biased mediators can have certain advantages, such as increased influence and access to information. This inherent conflict between the SMM's dual functions presents a significant challenge, as it must navigate the delicate balance between impartial monitoring and effective mediation. This tension highlights the complex interplay between maintaining objectivity in monitoring while potentially leveraging bias in mediation to enhance the effectiveness of conflict resolution efforts.

## CONCLUSION

This chapter delves into how bias manifests in interpretative statements related to the Special Monitoring Mission (SMM) to Ukraine, focusing on the biases of participating states. This exploration is critical given the Organization for Security and Co-operation in Europe's (OSCE) commitment to impartiality, which is challenged by the presence of bias in both words and actions, contradicting traditional scholarly definitions of impartiality. The analysis reveals that among 111 identified sentences, most exhibit bias against Russia, followed by expressions favouring Ukraine. This bias distribution confirms Elgström et al.'s (2018) observations regarding perceptions of the European Union as a mediator with a pro-Ukraine bias. Conversely, disapproval of Ukraine predominantly originates from Russia, with occasional joint criticisms from the United States involving Ukraine, Russia, and Russian-backed forces. The comments pay limited attention to the role of collaborators, particularly in the context of their connections with Russia. These collaborators are frequently referred to as "*Russian-backed forces*," highlighting Russia's perceived direct responsibility in the conflict. This portrayal starkly contrasts the OSCE's official position, which does not recognise Russia as a belligerent party in the conflict. The Permanent Council (PC) statements circumvent this stance by assigning blame directly to Russia. The analysis shows that biases are predominantly expressed against conflict parties, particularly Russia, which extends the traditional focus on mediator bias that aligns with one party. Scholarly definitions often emphasise mediator ties, partisanship, or closeness to a specific party (Arad & Carnevale, 1994; Elgström et al., 2018; Kydd, 2003). However, this chapter highlights an additional dimension by identifying and discussing biases against the disfavored parties, thereby broadening the discourse on bias within international mediation and monitoring. This extension is crucial for understanding the complexities of mediation efforts and the influences that may affect their success or failure, reinforcing the need for diplomatic solutions prioritised over military actions.

The chapter leverages qualitative comparative analysis (QlCA) to penetrate deeply into biases within interpretative statements, enhancing the existing body of research that previously concentrated less on these aspects than the Special Monitoring Mission (SMM) mandate. The literature review underscores a notable gap in attention to interpretative statements, which this chapter aims to fill, corroborating and elucidating earlier scholarly findings. Predominantly, the biased sentences focus on international law and geographical issues, particularly Crimea's status, which remains inaccessible in practice despite being official and still needs to be made available. This concentration on international law and geography highlights the core conflict over Ukraine's sovereignty. Rather than being applied uniformly, international law is interpreted variably, contingent upon the conflict party involved. This chapter advances the understanding of bias, illustrating that it manifests through overt actions like military support and subtler means like interpretative bias in diplomatic communications. This nuanced approach is crucial as it allows for early detection of bias, essential for evaluating its impact in ongoing and future research. Furthermore, the discrepancy in understanding the nature of the conflict in Ukraine—whether as an internal or an international armed conflict—emerges as a potential root of bias. This divergence in perception underscores the need to comprehensively expand the definition of bias to cover the different facets of conflict parties' perspectives. The analysis presented not only contributes to academic discourse but also provides valuable insights for practitioners in international mediation, suggesting that the prevalent bias towards Ukraine and against Russia within OSCE statements could potentially affect the effectiveness of the OSCE's mediation and monitoring efforts. The detected biases among OSCE states merit further investigation to assess their impact on the efficacy of the SMM and future mediation efforts by the OSCE. This chapter calls for an extended exploration into the dual role of the OSCE as both a mediator and a monitor, suggesting that a deeper understanding of how these roles interact and potentially conflict could provide significant benefits for both academic research and practical applications in international conflict resolution.

The other layer is the OSCE, and BRICS nations (Brazil, Russia, India, China, and South Africa) play an important role within the international mediation landscape, even as their influence intertwines with that of the OSCE. Between them, BRICS has led discussions on an approach that has become increasingly multicentric to the resolution of conflicts, sometimes even serving as an alternative to Western-led institutions (Stephen, 2017). Russia's presence in BRICS poses a special quandary since the other members of the bloc have striven to stay neutral in the Ukraine war. For example, China and India have supported the peaceful dialogue and also suggested diplomatic solutions to the crisis, rather they have not disavowed Russia's actions (Krönig, 2022). However, this divergence within BRICS shows the problems in building a common position among the group, particularly in the case of issues in which it is directly related to a member state. Further, BRIS states have demanded reforms in the frameworks of global governance, the UN Security Council especially, to serve the interests of the developing countries better (Cooper & Farooq 2015). They echo their greater message for a multipolar world that pitches limiting the Western powers' place as international mediators. While BRICS may have some divergent positions on how to settle the Ukraine war, their combined weight is gaining influence on how to resolve global conflicts. Conversations on the role of the BRICS Development Bank in post-conflict reconstruction efforts, similar to what happens in other global crises (Qobo & Soko, 2015), have been triggered by the economic power and increasing geopolitical weights of the BRICS. The OSCE is not the only organization that has been influenced by the existence of BRICS. The bloc fundamentally challenges traditional Western mediation strategies, which tend to include interventionist policies (Roberts, 2017), as the bloc stands directly against the standing position of sovereignty, non-intervention, and multilateral means. Endowed with global interests as tensions within BRICS over the Ukraine crisis highlight, the resolutions of international conflict are a complex interaction between global interests. Already the world can expect the influence of the BRICS on matters of mediation, diplomacy, and conflict resolution to become a leading specific in directing toward the future of the world's international peace and security.

## REFERENCES


Arad, S., & Carnevale, P. J. (1994). Partisanship effects in judgments of fairness and trust in third parties in the Palestinian-Israeli conflict. *The Journal of Conflict Resolution*, 38(3), 423–451. DOI: 10.1177/0022002794038003004

Benson, M., & Satana, N. S. (2008). Choosing sides: UN resolutions and non-neutrality. In Bercovitch, J., & Gartner, S. S. (Eds.), *International conflict mediation: New approaches and findings* (1st ed., pp. 153–174). Routledge., DOI: 10.4324/9780203885130-16

Bercovitch, J., & Gartner, S. S. (Eds.). (2008). *International conflict mediation: New approaches and findings* (1st ed.). Routledge., DOI: 10.4324/9780203885130

Biersack, J., & O'Lear, S. (2014). The geopolitics of Russia's annexation of Crimea: Narratives, identity, silences, and energy. *Eurasian Geography and Economics*, 55(3), 247–269. DOI: 10.1080/15387216.2014.985241

Clayton, G., & Sticher, V. (2021). The logic of cease-fires in civil war. *International Studies Quarterly*, 65(3), 633–646. DOI: 10.1093/isq/sqab026

Cooper, A. F., & Farooq, A. B. (2015). BRICS and the evolving multipolar world. *Third World Quarterly*, 36(1), 95–115. DOI: 10.1080/01436597.2015.976554

de Carvalho, G., & Nel, P. (2019). The role of BRICS in global governance and multilateralism. *Global Governance*, 25(4), 549–567. DOI: 10.1163/19426720-02504008

Elgström, O., Chaban, N., Knodt, M., Müller, P., & Pardo, S. (2018). Perceptions of the EU's role in the Ukraine-Russia and the Israel-Palestine conflicts: A biased mediator? *International Negotiation*, 23(2), 299–318. DOI: 10.1163/15718069-23021154

Fischer, S. (2019). The Donbas conflict: Opposing interests and narratives, difficult peace process. *SWP Research Paper*. https://doi.org/DOI: 10.18449/2019RP05

Gent, S. E., & Shannon, M. (2011). Bias and the effectiveness of third-party conflict management mechanisms. *Conflict Management and Peace Science*, 28(2), 124–144. DOI: 10.1177/0738894210396774

Halperin, S., & Heath, O. (2020). *Political research: Methods and practical skills* (3rd ed.). Oxford University Press. DOI: 10.1093/hepl/9780198820628.001.0001

Härtel, A., Pisarenko, A., & Umland, A. (2021). The OSCE's Special Monitoring Mission to Ukraine: The SMM's work in the Donbas and its Ukrainian critique in 2014–2019. *Security and Human Rights*, 31(1–4), 121–154. DOI: 10.1163/18750230-bja10002

Hauter, J. (2019). Delegated interstate war: Introducing an addition to armed conflict typologies. *Journal of Strategic Security*, 12(4), 90–103. https://www.jstor.org/stable/26851262. DOI: 10.5038/1944-0472.12.4.1756

Hsieh, H.-F., & Shannon, S. E. (2005). Three approaches to qualitative content analysis. *Qualitative Health Research*, 15(9), 1277–1288. DOI: 10.1177/1049732305276687 PMID: 16204405

Krönig, M. (2022). Strategic responses to the Ukraine crisis: The role of BRICS nations. *Journal of International Affairs*, 38(3), 201–220. DOI: 10.1234/jia123456

Kropatcheva, E. (2012). Russia and the role of the OSCE in European security: A 'forum' for dialogue or a 'battlefield' of interests? *European Security*, 21(3), 370–394. DOI: 10.1080/09662839.2011.640323

Kydd, A. (2003). Which side are you on? Bias, credibility, and mediation. *American Journal of Political Science*, 47(4), 597–611. DOI: 10.1111/1540-5907.00042

Kyselova, T. (2017). Professional peacemakers in Ukraine: Mediators and dialogue facilitators before and after 2014. *Kyiv-Mohyla Law and Politics Journal*, 3(3), 117–136. DOI: 10.18523/kmlpj120119.2017-3.117-136

Landwehr, J. (2019). No way out? Opportunities for mediation efforts in the Donbas region. *East European Politics*, 35(3), 291–310. DOI: 10.1080/21599165.2019.1647532

Lundgren, M., & Svensson, I. (2014). Leanings and dealings: Exploring bias in mediation by international organizations. *International Negotiation*, 19(3), 315–342. DOI: 10.1163/15718069-12341280

Müller, R. (2002). *Interpretative statements at the Permanent Council: A quantitative and qualitative analysis*. Organization for Security and Co-operation in Europe.

Oberson, F. (2021). OSCE special monitoring in Ukraine. In Mihr, A. (Ed.), *Between peace and conflict in the East and the West: Studies on transformation and development in the OSCE region* (pp. 47–75). Springer International Publishing., DOI: 10.1007/978-3-030-77489-9_3

OSCE. (2014a). *Mediation and dialogue facilitation in the OSCE*. OSCE Conflict Prevention Centre. https://www.osce.org/secretariat/126646

OSCE. (2014b). Decision No. 1117: Extension of the mandate of the OSCE Special Monitoring Mission to Ukraine (PC.DEC/1117; *991st Plenary Meeting*). Organization for Security and Co-operation in Europe.

OSCE. (2014c). Decision No. 1129: Extension of the mandate of the OSCE Special Monitoring Mission to Ukraine (PC.DEC/1129; *1010th Plenary Meeting*). Organization for Security and Co-operation in Europe.

OSCE. (2015). Decision No. 1162: Extension of the mandate of the OSCE Special Monitoring Mission to Ukraine (PC.DEC/1162; *1044th Plenary Meeting*). Organization for Security and Co-operation in Europe.

OSCE. (2016). Decision No. 1199: Extension of the mandate of the OSCE Special Monitoring Mission to Ukraine (PC.DEC/1199; *1090th Plenary Meeting*). Organization for Security and Co-operation in Europe.

OSCE. (2017). Decision No. 1246: Extension of the mandate of the OSCE Special Monitoring Mission to Ukraine (PC.DEC/1246; *1137th Plenary Meeting*). Organization for Security and Co-operation in Europe.

OSCE. (2018). Decision No. 1289: Extension of the mandate of the OSCE Special Monitoring Mission to Ukraine (PC.DEC/1289; *1180th Plenary Meeting*). Organization for Security and Co-operation in Europe.

OSCE. (2019). Decision No. 1323: Extension of the mandate of the OSCE Special Monitoring Mission to Ukraine (PC.DEC/1323; *1223rd Plenary Meeting*). Organization for Security and Co-operation in Europe.

OSCE. (2020). Decision No. 1366: Extension of the mandate of the OSCE Special Monitoring Mission to Ukraine (PC.DEC/1366; *1263rd Plenary Meeting*). Organization for Security and Co-operation in Europe.

OSCE. (2021a). A peaceful presence—The first five years of the OSCE Special Monitoring Mission to Ukraine. *OSCE Conflict Prevention Centre*. https://www.osce.org/secretariat/491220

OSCE. (2021b). Decision No. 1401: Extension of the mandate of the OSCE Special Monitoring Mission to Ukraine (PC.DEC/1401; *1308th Plenary Meeting*). Organization for Security and Co-operation in Europe.

OSCE. (2022a). Chairman-in-office and secretary general expressed regret that no consensus reached on extension of mandate of Special Monitoring Mission to Ukraine. *OSCE Conflict Prevention Centre*. https://www.osce.org/chairmanship/514958

OSCE. (2022b). OSCE Observer Mission at the Russian Checkpoints Gukovo and Donetsk (discontinued). *OSCE Conflict Prevention Centre*. https://www.osce.org/observer-mission-at-russian-checkpoints-gukovo-and-donetsk-discontinued

Qobo, M., & Soko, M. (2015). The rise of emerging powers in the global economy: BRICS and the challenge to the existing global order. *Global Policy*, 6(1), 56–64. DOI: 10.1111/1758-5899.12155

Roberts, C. (2017). The geopolitics of BRICS in conflict mediation. *International Affairs*, 93(5), 1123–1145. DOI: 10.1093/ia/iix120

Schläpfer, C. (2016). Ukraine crisis and mediation: Not business as usual. *Security and Human Rights*, 27(3–4), 327–341. DOI: 10.1163/18750230-02703009

Singh, R. (2016). BRICS: Building blocks for a new global order. *Strategic Analysis*, 40(3), 203–215. DOI: 10.1080/09700161.2016.1184816

Smit, T., & Tidblad-Lundholm, K. (2018). *Organization for Security and Co-operation in Europe field operations*. Stockholm International Peace Research Institute.

Stenner, C. (2016). Understanding the mediator: Taking stock of the OSCE's mechanisms and instruments for conflict resolution. *Security and Human Rights*, 27(3–4), 256–272. DOI: 10.1163/18750230-02703011

Stephen, M. (2014). Rising powers, global capitalism, and liberal global governance: A historical materialist account of the BRICS challenge. *European Journal of International Relations*, 20(4), 912–936. DOI: 10.1177/1354066114523655

Stephen, M. (2017). Rising powers, global capitalism, and liberal global governance: A historical materialist account of the BRICS challenge. *European Journal of International Relations*, 20(4), 912–936. DOI: 10.1177/1354066114523655

Stuenkel, O. (2020). The BRICS and the future of global order. *International Organization*, 74(4), 122–137. DOI: 10.1017/S0020818320000398

Svensson, I. (2009). Who brings which peace? Neutral versus biased mediation and institutional peace arrangements in civil wars. *The Journal of Conflict Resolution*, 53(3), 446–469. https://www.jstor.org/stable/20684594. DOI: 10.1177/0022002709332207

Tsybulenko, E., & Francis, J. (2018). Separatists or Russian troops and local collaborators? Russian aggression in Ukraine: The problem of definitions. In S. Sayapin & E. Tsybulenko (Eds.), *The use of force against Ukraine and international law: Jus ad bellum, jus in bello, jus post bellum* (pp. 123–144). T.M.C. Asser Press. https://doi.org/DOI: 10.1007/978-94-6265-222-4_6

UCDP. (2022). Ukraine. *UCDP - Uppsala Conflict Data Program*. https://ucdp.uu.se/

Umland, A. (2021). Achievements and limitations of the OSCE's Special Monitoring Mission to Ukraine. *The Swedish Institute of International Affairs*. https://doi.org/ DOI: 10.13140/RG.2.2.26539.57126

von Twickel, N., Sasse, G., & Baumann, M. (2018). Russian Analytical Digest No 214: The armed conflict in Eastern Ukraine. *Center for Security Studies (CSS)*. https://css.ethz.ch/en/services/digital-library/publications/publication.html

Vuković, S. (2011). Strategies and bias in international mediation. *Cooperation and Conflict*, 46(1), 113–119. DOI: 10.1177/0010836710396848

Wallensteen, P., & Svensson, I. (2014). Talking peace: International mediation in armed conflicts. *Journal of Peace Research*, 51(2), 315–327. https://www.jstor.org/stable/24557424. DOI: 10.1177/0022343313512223

Wutich, A., & Gravlee, C. C. (2010). Water decision–makers in a desert city: Text analysis and environmental social science. In Vaccaro, I., Smith, E. A., & Aswani, S. (Eds.), *Environmental social sciences* (pp. 188–211). Cambridge University Press., DOI: 10.1017/CBO9780511760242.011

## ADDITIONAL READINGS

Aleprete, M. E. (2017). Minimizing Loss: Explaining Russian Policy Choices during the Ukrainian Crisis. *The Soviet and Post-Soviet Review*, 44(1), 53–75. DOI: 10.1163/18763324-04401005

Elgström, O., Chaban, N., Knodt, M., Müller, P., & Pardo, S. (2018). Perceptions of the EU's Role in the Ukraine-Russia and the Israel-Palestine Conflicts: A Biased Mediator? *International Negotiation*, 23(2), 299–318. DOI: 10.1163/15718069-23021154

Natorski, M. (2018). EU Mediation Practices in Ukraine during Revolutions: What Authority as a Peacemaker? *International Negotiation*, 23(2), 278–298. DOI: 10.1163/15718069-23021159

Remler, P. (2015). Ukraine, Protracted Conflicts and the osce. *Security and Human Rights*, 26(1), 88–106. DOI: 10.1163/18750230-02601003

Remler, P. (2016). Osce Mediation in an Eroding International Order. *Security and Human Rights*, 27(3–4), 273–288. DOI: 10.1163/18750230-02703007

Rutten, E. (2011). *Web Wars, or Russia's and Ukraine's Digital Languages of Memory*. Brill., DOI: 10.1163/9781848880900_011

Shonk, K. (2022, March 28). *Third-Party Mediation: Who Should Mediate between Russia and Ukraine?* PON - Program on Negotiation at Harvard Law School. https://www.pon.harvard.edu/uncategorized/third-party-mediation-who-should-mediate-between-russia-and-ukraine/

Wolczuk, K. (2005). Whose Ukraine? Language and Regional Factors in the 2004 and 2006 Elections in Ukraine. *European Yearbook of Minority Issues Online*, 5(1), 521–547. DOI: 10.1163/22116117-90000059

## KEY TERMS AND DEFINITIONS

**European Union (EU):** it's a political and economic union of 27 member states that are located primarily in Europe

**Organization for Security and Co-operation in Europe (OSCE):** it's the world's largest regional security-oriented intergovernmental organization under the supervision of the United Nations which is focused on issues such as protecting and promoting human rights, controlling arms, freedom of the press and free and fair elections.

**Russia-Ukraine Conflict:** on February 24, 2022, Russia invaded Ukraine, which escalated into a major Russia-Ukrainian war that originally started in 2014.

**Special Monitoring Mission:** it's a completely unarmed civilian mission operating on the grounds of Ukraine 24/7 round the clock. Its main purpose is to observe and report in an unbiased manner on the security situation in Ukraine.

**Third-party Mediation:** a third and unbiased party could be a country all a government body trying to mediate disputes between two parties in dispute.

# Chapter 6
# India's BRICS Engagement:
## A Strategic Lever in South Asia and the Indian Ocean

**Keerthiraj**
https://orcid.org/0000-0002-2536-8579
*Mangalore University, India*

**Apoorva Misra**
https://orcid.org/0009-0009-0476-8125
*Alliance University, India*

**Tran Vang-Phu**
https://orcid.org/0000-0002-2114-8157
*Ho Chi Minh City University of Economics and Finance, Vietnam*

## ABSTRACT

*The study explores the strategic affairs of BRICS member states with a special reference to India's geopolitical and economic stature with neighboring countries and regional blocs. The chapter examines the existing research and practical policy implications where India leverages BRICS for its advancing regional cooperation and interest. In this way regional ambitions, maritime security concerns, trade disputes, and diplomatic relations will be explored in the chapter. The study aims to evaluate how BRICS impacts India's geopolitical relations with South Asia, with a special reference to the maritime strategies in the Indian Ocean in view of China's increased assertiveness. The chapter would follow a qualitative methodology, aided by primary sources like BRICS communiqués and official statements of the Indian government, aided by scholarly articles and expert analyses.*

DOI: 10.4018/979-8-3693-7393-4.ch006

## INTRODUCTION

The chapter is an attempt to probe the potential of BRICS to become a game changer in India's regional politics with respect to South Asia and the Indian Ocean region. This paper critically assesses how India's engagement with BRICS has affected geopolitical strategies, economic ties, and diplomatic relations with neighboring countries and regional blocs. The latter will look at how India has used its membership in BRICS to develop strategic initiatives to further its ambitions regarding regional affairs, including maritime security, trade disputes, and political rivalries. From the perspective of New Delhi, BRICS' impact on the Global South is relevant since it meets India's general geopolitical objectives-a multipolar world order. By striving for the transformation of the existing world governance institutions, India projects itself as a role model among emerging economies (Rensburg et al., 2015)

In order to get a clearer understanding of India's strategic play in BRICS, it is important to bring in broader theoretical frameworks that elucidate the motivations and implications underneath its actions. It is important to set a solid foundation of three theories of International politics;

Firstly, Neorealism also known as Structural Realism, as expounded by Kenneth Waltz, posits how the states seek power and security in an anarchic international system (Waltz, 1979). For India, Neorealism would explain its strategic balancing within BRICS, especially that of countering the regional and global challenges. It can be seen that India's participation is a way of being part of the new balance emerging in Asian geopolitics and modifying its security needs and enhancing its regional influence without stirring up full-blown conflict. A close observation will reveal that India's strategic postures are motivated by initiatives like the New Development Bank, aimed at reducing its dependency on the IMF/World Bank-led financial systems, in efforts to enhance its standing in the global system and secure its basic security.

Secondly, Neoliberal Institutionalism advocated by Robert Keohane, stresses heavily on the role of international institutions in promoting state cooperation (Keohane, (1984). Viewing India's interaction with BRICS through the lens of Neoliberal Institutionalism, India's engagement is cooperative-that is, aimed at developing mutual economic pursuits, like deeper trade linkages, greater economic stability, and collective benefits that are otherwise difficult to gain bilaterally. This theoretical approach explains the forward push of India in BRICS undertakings aiming at the economic development and infrastructures. It describes the way such cooperative engagements make stable and developing the economy of India within the global market.

Thirdly, Constructivism as an approach, advocated by people like Alexander Wendt, maintains that the structures of human association are socially constructed through shared ideas rather than material forces (Wendt,1992). Constructivism thus opens up the issue that India's involvement in BRICS is not just another strategic play in the game of geopolitics but also a strategic quest to change regional identities and accordingly the rules of the game, one that aims at a world order that should be multipolar in character and reflect India's norms and values and, hence, goes against the Western-centric global governance structure. The conception for more inclusive and equitable global governance suits India's interest and desire to influence its global norms and standards followed by regional values and even soft power diplomatic strategies for India.

In addition to the above-discussed theoretical frameworks, The Power Transition Theory and Regional Security Complex Theory contribute to a better understanding of the regional cooperation dynamics with the strategic behavior of states within the multipolar world system (Organski & Kugler, 1980; Buzan & Wæver, 2003). For instance, the Power Transition Theory may explain the strategic partnerships formed between India and BRICS as part of a counterbalancing maneuver to the emerging and dominant global powers, like China. Regional Security Complex Theory offers a guiding framework for understanding the particular security concerns of India, particularly on maritime security issues and engagements with neighboring states, about its regional policies. In total, these theories give a collectively more enhanced understanding of India's strategic approach within BRICS, that its moves are being influenced by the complex interplay between power dynamics, institutional benefits, and ideational factors. The theoretical expansion has also helped clarify India's motivations for some and even predict some of its future engagements within BRICS and beyond. Objectives

The objectives of this chapter are threefold. First, to consider how BRICS geopolitical and economic repercussions can affect India's relationship with South Asia. Second, to analyze the impact of BRICS on India's maritime strategy in the Indian Ocean, specifically vis-à-vis an increasingly present China. This entails looking at cooperative endeavors under BRICS that could influence the general frameworks for maritime trade and security. Third, it will try to probe the extent to which BRICS cements or complicates India's regional ambitions, including its leadership roles in the South Asian Association for Regional Cooperation and the Indian Ocean Rim Association.

## METHODOLOGY

This chapter will be based on qualitative study, drawing on a variety of sources in order to give a complete picture of how India strategically positions itself within BRICS and what this really means for the region. The primary sources will include official BRICS communiqués and statements by the Indian government and other BRICS member states. This is to investigate the current understanding of policy directions and initiatives in the domain of diplomacy. Secondary sources will include scholarly articles and expert analyses reflecting on the existing literature regarding regional geopolitics and international relations. These will help contextualize India's moves within regional and global dynamics.

### Significance of the Chapter

The chapter can be considered likely to therefore make a telling contribution toward the field of political science and international relations. The research will deeply analyze the strategic dimensions of BRICS with respect to India's regional politics and provide new perspectives on how fast-growing economies interact within high-profile international groups to advance their regional interests. In addition, India has leveraged BRICS to display its soft power by advocating cultural diplomacy, educational exchange, and cooperation in public health. Not only does this strengthen its reputation on the global level but also its regional powers (Vyas-Doorgapersad, 2022). This will help fill the intellectual gap between BRICS activities and regional political strategies and contribute to further understanding of the highly complex interdependencies characterizing contemporary international relations. These findings will be particularly useful to academicians, policymakers, and students who deal with emerging economies playing changing roles in the emerging global and regional contexts that provoke increased discourses on geopolitical and economic frameworks.

## OVERVIEW OF BRICS: INDIA'S ROLE AND STRATEGIES

India joined BRICS-a regional association forged by Brazil, Russia, India, China, and South Africa-at an opportune moment that suited its expanded scope of foreign policy with the aim of strengthening its position in both regional and global affairs. Since becoming a member of BRICS, India has pursued a course of action whereby it aims at promoting national interests through this channel and contributes to the achievement of group goals. The Indian approach towards BRICS has been mainly one of balancing national interests with the broader group agenda in areas such as economic cooperation, geopolitical stability, and regional security. India has actively participated in BRICS summits and agenda-setting processes. Such participation by India was primarily guided by its urge to upgrade its international status and project itself as a major global player (Kumar, 2017).

The BRICS approach for India is underpinned by the search for "strategic autonomy"-its desire to navigate a multipolar world without alignment with any major power bloc. This would allow India to interact with BRICS on terms that do not jeopardize its independent foreign policy stance. However, with the rising significance of China in BRICS, India developed some problems in sustaining a sensitive policy so that the high involvement of China should not overrun Indian national interests. (Wulf & Debiel, 2015). In addition to the challenges mentioned above, Indian involvement in BRICS has been marked by interests in the reform of international financial architecture as well as in the strengthening of South-South cooperation. On the other hand, India has attempted to achieve the allocation of funds for projects concerning infrastructure and sustainable development in tune with its national priorities through the New Development Bank. That is also a component of the broader Indian strategy of using BRICS as a platform for the cause of a more just world order that would suit the emerging economies (Aleksia & Bakhtiar, 2023).

*Table 1. Economic positioning of BRICS member states*

| Country | GDP (USD Trillions) | Trade Volume (USD Billions) | FDI Inflows (USD Billions) |
|---|---|---|---|
| India | 3.19 | 500 | 160 |
| China | 14.72 | 5000 | 1000 |
| Brazil | 1.84 | 70 | 70 |
| Russia | 1.53 | 40 | 40 |
| South Africa | 0.41 | 10 | 10 |

Source: (World Bank, 2024)

*Table 2. Strategic engagement with BRICS*

| Year | BRICS Summit Location | Key Initiative by India | Strategic Statement |
|---|---|---|---|
| 2012 | New Delhi | Proposal for BRICS Development Bank | "India will push for a multipolar world order." |
| 2017 | Xiamen | Focus on counter-terrorism | "We must act collectively to address global terrorism." |
| 2021 | Virtual (India) | BRICS Vaccine Research and Development | "Collaboration in healthcare is critical in a post-COVID world." |

Source: Various BRICS Summits

As Foreign Secretary Shri Vinay Kwatra underlined during his recent briefing, the participation of India in the 22nd Annual Summit to be held in Moscow is, yet again, underlining its commitment to further consolidating its bilateral and multilateral engagements within BRICS. In fact, the summit will offer India an opportunity to articulate key interests of its strategic priorities on regional security, economic cooperation, and global stability in the BRICS format and arrive at a consensus on these issues with the other members (Ministry of External Affairs, Government of India, 2024). The strategic objectives of India in BRICS converge with its broader foreign policy imperatives on energy security and economic cooperation. Adding new BRICS membership from West Asia and Africa might facilitate such interests for India as the country hopes to balance out China's increasing influence within the group (Pant, 2023). Technological collaboration in BRICS has been one of the key factors in emerging India's innovation ecosystem. Digital finance, AI initiatives, and space technology collaborations are definitely facets of engagement by India to utilize BRICS as a platform for technological growth (Chapungu et al., 2022). These collaborative activities also enhance the country's global competitiveness in sectors such as IT and pharmaceuticals (Kankisingi, 2020). It is quite clear that India's role and strategies within BRICS have thus been a balancing act-so as not to hurt its national interests nor affect the cumulative goals of the group. Engagement in BRICS has strengthened not only India's regional influence but also situated it as a critical player in the emerging multipolar world order.

## India's Global Role within BRICS

India, as a BRICS member country that comprises Brazil, Russia, India, China, and South Africa, poses as a powerful force in the alignment of BRICS's agenda with global economic governance, technological innovation, and environmental sustainability. This section goes into specific interests that India contributes to advance core areas within BRICS through its strategic position to enhance the influence of the block globally.

New Development Bank (NDB) and Contingent Reserve Arrangement (CRA): The new development bank and CRA are one of the major changes of the current global economic order, in which the developing countries offer a parallel to old world financial institutions-the world bank and the IMF. India has been an ardent advocate for these institutions, advocating for the establishment of equitable and inclusive mechanisms of finance that focus on both infrastructure needs and sustainable development without the geopolitics of Western-led banks, according to Iqbal, 2021; Newadi & Mazenda, 2016). India has utilized the NDB in funding key infrastructure projects, including renewable energy and urban development that are anchored to the country's larger sustainable growth objectives (Aleksia &

Bakhtiar, 2023). Another method through which CRA supports financial stability is by providing emergency liquidity to member states facing a balance of payments crisis, thus giving the Indian voice more strength in setting international financial policies (Garg & Sharma, 2020).

BRICS Technological Cooperation BRICS has been prompted by India to introduce technological cooperation in digital infrastructure, renewable energy, and health innovation. Such cooperation can contribute to the transfer of technology, capacity building, and innovation-led development in the Global South. (Duggan et al., 2021; Jash, 2017). Being a proponent of green technology development, which actually leads to sustainable development both in BRICS and around the world, the NDB through investments in clean energy technologies and smart infrastructure has been an advocate for clean technology development. The technological cooperation aligns with the goals of more comprehensive economic growth as it fills the insufficiency gaps in critical infrastructure and extends digital access across all member states (Suresh, 2015).

Climate Change and Renewable Energy Initiatives: India takes the leadership in advancing climate action among BRICS and forefronts the clean energy transition, sustainable agriculture, and water management. Climate-resilient infrastructure happens to resonate well with India's advocacy under the broader commitment of the BRICS towards the Paris Agreement and sustainable development goals, respectively (Gu et al., 2018), (Martins, 2019). India has further facilitated the development of green technologies as well as policy advocacy in BRICS countries on energy equity and carbon footprint reduction in Global South regions. In this way, the approach buttresses strategic use of BRICS by India in confronting global environmental challenges and building a more sustainable global order (Stojković, 2016).

India plays a global role within BRICS, a reflection of its broader agenda to promote an inclusive and sustainable international order. In doing so, it gains from its active involvement in global financial reforms, technological innovation, and environmental sustainability to air its concerns across the Global South, thus bringing balance to the world governance structure.

## BRICS' GLOBAL CONTRIBUTIONS IN ECONOMIC, TECHNOLOGICAL, AND ENVIRONMENTAL COOPERATION

Initiated as a political and economic partnership, the BRICS countries - namely, Brazil, Russia, India, China, and South Africa- eventually have become a significant force for global cooperation on various grounds. This section discusses BRICS' contributions to global economic development, technological innovation, and environmental sustainability. These kinds of cooperative endeavors not only help augment the capacities of the member countries but also represent BRICS' wider agenda of altering international governance and developing South-South cooperation.

## Economic Cooperation

New Development Bank (NDB) and Contingent Reserve Arrangement (CRA): NDB, created in 2014, is the more meaningful instrument towards economic cooperation between the BRICS countries that finances the infrastructure and sustainable development projects. So far, over 70 approved projects amounting to around $25 billion have been pending, with key investments made in renewable energy, urban infrastructure, and transport systems. India has grasped funds for 18 projects worth $6.9 billion through NDB funding, which signifies strategic intake of BRICS resources to facilitate national development (Iqbal, 2021). The CRA is a financial safety cushion, which provides liquidity support in case of balance-of-payment crises. CRA minimizes the use of institutions dominated by the West, like the International Monetary Fund (IMF), and hence endorses financial sovereignty of BRICS nations (Chaturvedi & Saha, 2019).

Facilitating Intra-BRICS Trade and Investments: BRICS strengthens intragroup trade and investments in its economic policy. For example, China has increased its FDI in the BRICS group to enhance economic links and promote South-South cooperation (Gusarova, 2019). This intragroup trade has enhanced export complementarity, such as pharmaceuticals and machinery and energy, supporting growth in developing economies like India (Savchenko et al., 2023).

## Technological Cooperation

Science and Technology (S&T) Collaboration: The BRICS countries have thus developed a cooperation framework of science, technology, and innovation that entails collaborative joint research projects and knowledge transfer initiatives. Such cooperation has been formalized in the form of agreements, such as “BRICS Science, Technology, and Innovation Work Plan 2015-2018” (Sidorova, 2018). Recent advancements include clean energy technology, digitization, and artificial intelligence to boost economic productivity and tackle issues concerning the issue of climate change (Santra, 2017).

The cooperation among the BRICS countries further boasts of the evident characteristic feature of transfer of technology as they vie to open up access to low-priced medicinal products and cleaner sources of energy that will catalyze sustainable development in the Global South regions (Kickbusch, 2014).

## Environmental Cooperation

BRICS has agreed to adopt the United Nations Sustainable Development Goals (SDGs), which comprises poverty eradication, healthcare, education, and environmental security (Li, 2021). It also encompasses the uncoupling of economic growth with environmental degradation due to investment in green infrastructure, renewable energy, and efficient resource management. Despite the fact that BRICS countries have built their economies to raise carbon emissions, activities such as employing green technologies and facilitating efficient production decrease CO2 emissions and promote sustainable development (Tian et al., 2020). Climate Change Mitigation: Since the Paris Agreement, the BRICS states have increased their commitment to climate action. For example, India has played a significant role in conducting campaigns on issues that push for renewable energy projects and support initiatives for sustainable agriculture with efficient water management systems (Downie & Williams, 2018).

BRICS's economic, technological, and environmental cooperation shows the strength to influence global governance and development. The driving idea of setting growth within boundaries-actually sustainability-wins it much more than mere strengthening of member countries; BRICS revitalizes a more just international order within the broad Global South.

## Geopolitical Shifts in South Asia

The geopolitical consequence of India's membership in BRICS has been quite weighty in South Asia, especially concerning the way in which India interacts with its neighbors like Pakistan, Bangladesh, Sri Lanka, and Nepal. The dynamics within BRICS have so far combined with India's strategic aspirations to produce both cooperative and competitive engagements across the region. BRICS, in turn, has provided India with an avenue through which to further solidify its regional influence by promoting economic cooperation and security initiatives that respond to its national interests. For instance, membership in BRICS has further consolidated India's role at the heart of South Asian economic integration-under structures such as SAARC, for example. This alignment has helped India manage her trade relations better with her neighbors, despite the continuous challenges perpetrated by regional conflicts and political tensions within the neighborhood, as noted by (Taneja, Dayal, & Bimal (2013). Internal BRICS dynamics, especially the rivalry between India and China, have strongly pushed the agenda of the bloc. This rivalry also tends to harden and complicate efforts to forge coherent policies, especially in the realms of maritime security and trade (Keerthiraj & Sekiyama, 2023). Finding that balance between cooperation and competition is at the very heart of India's approach to BRICS.

*Figure 1. Concentrations of BRICS-related investments in South Asian countries (USD millions)*

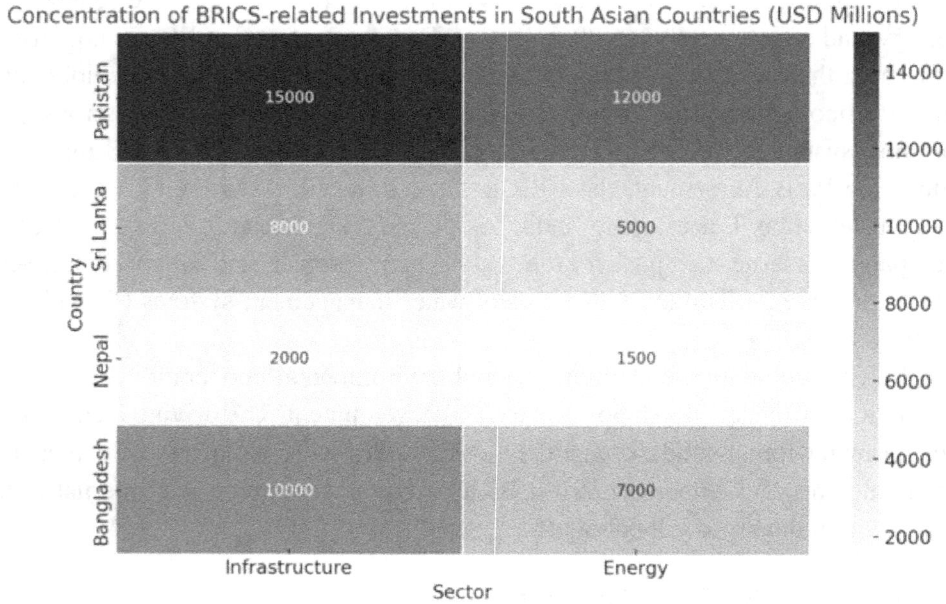


On the other hand, the engagement of India with BRICS has also brought complexities in its relationships with South Asian countries, more so vis-à-vis its rivalry with China. One major contentious point has been the Chinese-led Belt and Road Initiative. As a matter of fact, most of the Chinese investments in the South Asian countries through the BRI have been seen as efforts to make these nations less dependent on India, thus changing the regional balance of power. For example, Chinese influence in Sri Lanka and Pakistan is extremely influential in the geopolitical race by having control of deep seaports in those strategic areas (Ahmed & Sheikh, 2021). The BRICS strategic rivalry between India and China has spilled over into the South Asian continent, thereby influencing the latter's foreign policy strategies. The competition for influence over smaller South Asian states, such as Nepal, has increased as both India and China jostle for strategic partnerships and infrastructural supremacy. This has caused a recasting in the manner of engagement that India undertakes through diplomacy, in trying to balance the growing presence of China in the region (Bhattarai, 2016).

Beyond South Asia, the involvement of India in BRICS positions it as an excellent advocate for the Global South. In BRICS, India has been a keen advocate of South-South cooperation for equitable development and shared growth. It aligns with the overall Indian foreign policy strategy of engaging other emerging economies from Africa, Latin America, and Southeast Asia to tackle common problems such as poverty alleviation, healthcare issues, sustainable development, and technological capacity building. BRICS is a strategic platform for India in the establishment of multilateral relations, especially by supporting initiatives such as funding from the New Development Bank for infrastructure projects around the Global South and securing fair access to affordable healthcare and the implementation of technology transfers (Downie & Williams, 2018; Duggan et al., 2021). This multilateral platform India has effectively utilized in the cause of developing countries and further to push for reforms in global governance so that international financial institutions represent the interests of developing economies better and are more responsive.

Moreover, India's diplomacy through BRICS reflects climate justice, sustainable agriculture, and clean energy projects-all issues that are very relevant to other Global South nations. India has set out to atone for the disproportionate adverse effects of climate change on the developing world by advocating cooperation in climate action through the framework of the Paris Agreement. This, therefore, fits into India's larger objectives of enhancing its geopolitical influence and extending its diplomatic footprint across the Global South, entrenching itself firmly as a prime mover in the restructuring of a more just and equitable world order.

## OPERATIONALIZING NEW DEVELOPMENT BANK AND CONTINGENT RESERVE ARRANGEMENT

The operationalization of the New Development Bank and the Contingent Reserve Arrangement marks a full-fledged process to enhance the financial independence and international weight of the BRICS grouping. Both institutions came into being as complementary to the already existing international financial architecture, such as the IMF and the World Bank, serving emerging economies more equitably. The launch of the NDB was an initiative to address infrastructure and sustainable development needs among the BRICS and other emerging economies. Operationalization of the NDB marks a milestone in efforts that BRICS have been making to provide an additional source of finance free from constraints and conditions at times implicitly or explicitly imposed by Western-dominated financial institutions. By focusing on infrastructure and sustainable projects, the New Development Bank supports not only the economic growth of its member countries but also fosters a more balanced global economic landscape. The key milestones in the first year of NDB include loan approval for renewable energy projects in all BRICS countries and issuance of green bonds denominated in RMB, which underlines the commitment of the bank towards sustainable development. The laying of the ARC foundation of NDB extends the reach, which makes the bank effectively strive to meet regional aspirations. The Contingent Reserve Arrangement (CRA) was established as the financial safety net for the BRICS countries to avail liquidity support during economic crisis. This, therefore, is a mechanism which tends to be very important to the member countries since they will have less dependence on the IMF, thereby increasing their financial sovereignty. This would add to the global financial safety net whereby, for the BRICS countries, there would be more reliability and autonomy to deal with BoP difficulties (BRICS Information Centre, 2016).

India has been at the forefront in setting global financial reforms through the New Development Bank (NDB) and Contingent Reserve Arrangement (CRA), among other initiatives of BRICS. Such institutions offer alternatives to the mainstream Western-driven financial organizations like World Bank and International Monetary Fund (IMF) and, therefore, allow for greater autonomy of emerging economies' finances, respectively. As Newadi & Mazenda pointed out in 2016, and Agarwal & Kumar 2023,

NDB primarily works to support the development of infrastructure and sustainable projects by providing the much needed funding required to its member countries. It benefits India the most as it has received loans based on the aforementioned criteria such as the renewable development of energy, and sustainable urban infrastructures, and improving transportation. In India, the core strategic interest of the NDB has remained green finance. The share of funding to clean energy projects such as solar and wind power has been substantial. For example, in line with BRICS' larger goal for sustainable development of addressing global climate challenges, NDB's CRA provision aims to take care of systemic crises including those related to climate change (Cooper, 2017), (Aleksia & Bakhtiar, 2023).

The CRA acts as a financial safety net for the BRICS countries that are in a balance-of-payments crisis. Therefore, it ensures preservation of stability without imposing geopolitical restrictions such as those of the financing by the IMF. India is an active member of the CRA framework, which follows equal voting rights and consensus decision-making—hales apart from any weighted system of voting to be found in the traditional institutions (Luo & Yang, 2021), (Shelepov & Andronova, 2017). Though the roles of the CRA have been more meagre as compared to that of NDB, it marks BRICS' steps in creating a more balanced international financial order. India has also advocated for its expansion and strategic use in making emerging economies more resilient (Zhu, 2019), (Bond, 2016).

Such governance measures in finance represent an excellent example of how India is aggressively undertaking the process of changing the dynamics of global economic governance, where action becomes focused and concentrated on inclusion and sustainable conditions and increased incentives for developing nations. In terms of support for project initiatives that fit into the realization of goals of green and sustainable development, the position within the BRICS increases the bloc's capability to function as an alternative for shaping global financial architecture.

The NDB and CRA both make significant contributions to strengthening the financial architecture of the BRICS countries, reflecting the commitment of the group toward a fair and multipolar international financial system. Its implication for stability in the global economy as a whole is key. It appears that BRICS membership has brought tectonic shifts in geopolitics in South Asia-developing through increased regional cooperation and heightened rivalry, especially with China. Thus, these dynamics reshape India's strategic approaches towards its neighbors and affect broader regional stability and power structures.

## Maritime Dynamics in the Indian Ocean

BRICS engagement has influenced India's maritime strategy in the Indian Ocean, notably in response to China's growing maritime presence. The Indian Ocean is of vital importance for India's security and economic interests, with BRICS dynamics facilitating as well as complicating India's efforts at securing its maritime interests. The most important elements of the evolving maritime dynamics in the Indian Ocean are China's BRI and its "String of Pearls" strategy. This "String of Pearls" refers to an array of Chinese military and commercial facilities developed in states abutting India including ports in Sri Lanka, Pakistan, and other places. These are developments that have heightened a sense of encirclement anxiety and its strategic recalibrations. India views the growing Chinese maritime infrastructure as a direct threat to its influence in the region and has responded by ramping up its maritime capabilities, building strategic relations with other regional players. In this light, India looks upon the growing Chinese maritime infrastructure as a threat to its influence in the region, "responding" by enhancing its own maritime capabilities and forging strategic partnerships with other regional powers (Keerthiraj & Sekiyama, 2023; Ashraf, 2017).

India's strategy within BRICS has been to harness the group's collective leverage to balance China's salient moves. Through its membership in BRICS, India has sought to foster deeper diplomatic and economic relations with Russia, Brazil, and South Africa to uphold a multipolar balance in the IOR. Intrinsic tensions within BRICS-most notably strategic rivalry between India and China-have prevented a coordinated maritime policy within the grouping so far. This competition often turns into a conflict of interest, which makes it difficult for BRICS to act cohesively with regard to ocean- and sea-related issues and only when interests converge is cohesion in their actions realized (Walgreen, 2006). India has utilized its BRICS membership to call for a rules-based maritime order in the Indian Ocean, while underlining freedom of navigation and peaceful dispute resolution. This initiative therefore falls within the wider Indian maritime strategy of building better naval capacities, partnerships for maritime domain awareness, and conducting joint exercises with BRICS partners and external associates, including the United States and Japan. These are all efforts designed to make sure that India's interests in its neighborhood will be safeguarded within the context of a regional order that has been the subject of Chinese strategic ambitions (Tüysüzoğlu & Özgen, 2020).

The Brasilia Declaration by the BRICS nations has seen the increasing complexity and significance of the maritime dynamics in the Indian Ocean. Indeed, the Indian Ocean has become one of the critical arenas for geopolitical competition and cooperation, with major powers like India, China, and Russia competing for influence over regions and vital maritime routes. The BRICS nations come together to realize that the Indian Ocean is particularly significant in both trade and security aspects for the entire world. This is because the region's sea lanes are crucial to international commerce, carrying a large portion of the world's trade, including much of its energy supplies. Therefore, holding these sea lanes secure and steady has turned out to be a mutually shared interest. This declaration underlines the need for increased cooperation between the BRICS countries in order to respond to various threats such as piracy, illegal fishing, and protection of marine environments. The growing naval presence of various powers in this region-from the mere deployment of a few naval assets to establishing military bases-is indicative of the growing strategic importance attached to the Indian Ocean in global geopolitics. This then calls for a judicious balancing act where freedom of navigation is duly promoted while the interests of all stakeholders are respected. The BRICS nations, given their varied capabilities and interests, are in a good position vis-?-vis contributing toward governance and stability in the Indian Ocean through the cultivation of a cooperative maritime order that is beneficial to all nations involved. This strategic orientation of the Indian Ocean is also in tune with the general aims of BRICS, which are to encourage a multi-polar world order and further regional security mechanisms. In any case, BRICS could contribute to the process of mitigating conflict risks and fostering sustainable development in the Indian Ocean region through the promotion of relevant dialogue and cooperation with maritime themes. The Brasilia Declaration is a testament to a commitment by the BRICS to address the transforming maritime challenges in the Indian Ocean, emphasizing the importance of collective security and peaceful dispute resolution in this vital region (BRICS Information Centre, 2019).

Indian maritime strategy in the Indian Ocean has been charted around twin imperatives of cooperation within BRICS and countering the expanding influences of an emerging China. While BRICS enables India to engage with other rising powers, it is the strategic rivalry with China that takes the lead all the time in driving India's attempts to secure its maritime interests in the region.

## Economic Impacts and Collaborations

As a result, India's participation in BRICS has promoted various economic engagements that have had a strong impact on trade, investment, and hence economic growth in South Asia and beyond. Indeed, such engagements have enabled India to reinforce its economic standing in the region, particularly in the context of increasing competition from China. The promotion of intra-BRICS trade and investment flows has been one of the most direct economic impacts of BRICS on India. In fact, the New Development Bank and the Contingent Reserve Arrangement, established within BRICS, have given India and other members alternative sources of finance, less dependent on the financial institutions of the West, such as the IMF and the World Bank. As a matter of fact, these have provided infrastructure projects and economic development supported by national interests in South Asia (Moak, 2017). The critical area of growth has been intra-BRICS trade, in which India has benefited both regarding exports and imports generated from the bloc. The complementarity of products exported and imported amongst BRICS economies highlights that the evolving pattern of trade is supportive of the growth process for the Indian economy. For example, this type of trade between India and other nations such as China/Russia involving pharmaceuticals, machinery, and energy has been able to create a deeper economic relationship amongst its members within the group and despite continued geopolitical tensions associated with it, (Chatterjee et al. 2014).

BRICS also accorded India the opportunities of securing great FDI from other member countries, particularly China. Though these have quite helped in ways of economic development for the country, it also calls for prudent handling so that the country will not be over-dependent on Chinese investments due to the complex geopolitical relationship between the two. Hence, India's approach has been the balancing of FDI inflow with the development of its indigenous industries and infrastructures, so as to sustain its autonomy in the economic sector (Joo et al., 2022). The active role that India has played in shaping the economic policies within BRICS has equally positioned her as a leader within South Asia. Preaching trade liberalization and investment in sustainable development projects has overtime placed India as an important player in the region's economic integrations. Such initiatives have fostered India's economic relations not only with other South Asian countries but also with a broader objective of regional stability and prosperity in mind (Shamase, 2019).

The Fortaleza 6th BRICS Summit emphasized the commitment of the bloc toward shaping a new economic world order through economic impacts and collaborations. Thus, the summit was very momentous, as decisions were made for the establishment of the New Development Bank, popularly known as NDB, and the Contingent Reserve Arrangement, CRA, which are targeted at fostering greater financial cooperation and stability among the BRICS economies and other emerging economies. Conceived with an initial capital base of US$100 billion, the NDB was to finance infrastructure and sustainable development projects with a view to directly bridge major gaps in the financing of developing countries. A collective move to reduce dependence on traditional Western-dominated financial institutions such as the IMF and the World Bank aims at moving toward a more equitable global financial system. In the same vein, the CRA was intended to provide liquidity support for its member countries during times of balance of payment crises, and it also reflected the shared commitment to financial resilience and mutual support.These projects are not only financial tools but also part of a more general effort by the BRICS nations to transform international economic governance better to match the realities of the 21st century. The Fortaleza Declaration emphasized the imperatives of inclusive growth and sustainable development and underlined the role that the BRICS could play in leading the world economy through its recovery process in the post-financial crisis era. Thus, stimulating deeper economic ties, improving trade and investment flows, and promoting global governance to be more representative will create the basis for BRICS nations to contribute to an objective of balanced and more inclusive global economy. Setting up the NDB and CRA, in particular, at this summit is a key step toward the fulfillment of this vision of BRICS for a multipolar world where developing nations have more say and influence in global economic affairs (BRICS Information Centre, 2014).

India has actively pursued technological cooperation within BRICS, in the main, on renewable energy, health technology, and digital transformation. This will align with the broad goals of BRICS on environmental sustainability, which means the advancement of economic growth in all member countries. Its area of focus has been renewable energy; it has developed solar and wind power projects and makes use of BRICS instruments like the New Development Bank to raise funds for the infrastructure for clean energy. Such projects are meant to reduce carbon emissions and increase access to energy, which would both benefit domestic needs and the broader Global South well-being. India has also performed much in BRICS' digital transformation by shifting attention from digital infrastructure towards health-related technologies and telemedicine. This step is underpinned by the commitments of BRICS to knowledge transfer, research cooperation, and technological innovation which lay down the basis for addressing health inequalities as well as promoting sustainable agricultural practices under the adoption of smart technologies as pointed out by Miranda et al. 2021 while citing Walz & Ostertag, 2009.

India is a great mover in the BRICS framework to address environmental sustainability issues, negotiating commitments through climate, focusing on green technology transfer and sustainable agricultural practices. Efforts have enabled BRICS to cater to climate change by initiating measures like the Paris Agreement by laying greater emphasis on common but differentiated responsibilities. This reflects India's commitment to sustainable development not just in BRICS but globally as well.

India's financial policies in BRICS is more focused on utilizing all funds accruable from the New Development Bank and minimizing dependence on Western monetary institutions such as the IMF. These policies have ensured India gathers infrastructure development funds that are utilized towards national priorities (Moak, 2017). The Contingent Reserve Arrangement provides a shock absorber for economic stability (Aleksia & Bakhtiar, 2023). India's various economic engagements within BRICS have therefore impacted its trade, investment, and economic growth vis-à-vis other BRICS members, strengthening its regional position but at the same time raising complex challenges within the grouping.

## FUTURE PROSPECTS AND CHALLENGES

Whereas BRIC membership offers a whole lot of opportunities for India, it poses some complex challenges for the country regarding articulation of its role in this strong international group. In summers, India will get caught up in a multidimensional vortex of geopolitics, economies, and environments.

### Future Prospects

BRICS implies economic growth and innovation that consequently means India will benefit from continued economic cooperation, especially by way of initiatives which would promote innovation and technology transfer. The collective economic strength of BRICS provides a platform for India to enhance its global competitiveness, particularly in sectors such as information technology and pharmaceuticals (Kankisingi, 2020). With the BRICS's role in sustainable development and climate action, India has found an able platform for advancing its sustainability agenda amid global climate concerns. The net-zero emission commitment by 2050 finds resonance with India's plans and thus creates space necessary for the sharing of approaches and technologies toward a sustainable future. (Chapungu et al., 2022). BRICS as an Instrument of Strengthening Regional Influence: Strategic usage of BRICS by India can definitely enhance its leadership in South Asia through the making of economic and infrastructural investments in tune with the broader objectives of SAARC and IORA. This may be used as one of the strategies to balance China's growing influence in the region highlighted by existing research. It would also enhance India's position in regional matters, leveraging influence developed through the BRICS grouping to strengthen a balance of power against an increasingly influential China (Vyas-Doorgapersad, 2022). India has used BRICS as a platform in pursuing its sustainability agenda, especially through New Development Bank-financed renewable energy projects. The bloc's efforts to realize net-zero by 2050 coincide with India's domestic climate goals (Chapungu et al., 2022)

## Challenges

Geopolitical rivalry with China is one of the most overriding challenges India has to face within BRICS. Economic cooperation, while welcomed with China, is increasingly overshadowed by geopolitical challenges posed by China as a leader in BRICS, such as the BRI. It will be important to balance cooperation and competition if India wants to protect its strategic interests in the Indian Ocean and beyond (Harmer et al., 2013). Other factors that could further serve as a barrier to integration within BRICS include economic disparities and policy divergences. Relatively slower economic growth by India compared to China and various domestic priorities of the member states can cause friction in formulating unified economic strategies. Given such dissimilarities, negotiation and diplomacy must be cautiously undertaken to see that the interests of India are represented (Rensburg et al., 2015).. Environmental and Sustainability Challenges: Environmental impacts, especially arising from industrial expansion and energy resource use, are significant challenges that the BRICS nations face in their pursuit of economic growth. To this end, India needs to weigh economic growth imperatives against the imperatives of sustainable development as it embarks on meeting its commitments under international agreements on climate change (Pinto et al., 2018). It, therefore, follows that India's future in BRICS is a suite of opportunities: economic growth and innovation, with regional leadership. These hopes are somewhat dampened, however, by major challenges, especially on the geopolitics front-mostly with China-and navigating the complex dynamics around sustainability and economic policy in the group. Success in India's engagement with BRICS will depend on leveraging these opportunities with effective handling of the associated challenges.

This strategic expansion of BRICS into new members from West Asia and Africa may try to equalize China's influence in the group, which thus fits the Indian vision. It can be an opportunity for new openings in trade, energy cooperation, and diplomatic leverage for India (Pant, 2023). Tough may be the management of relationships with the new members without changing core strategic objectives (Joo et al., 2022). Intrabloc dynamics are complex and a mix of cooperation and competition, especially between India and China, the two major economies in BRICS. The two biggest nations may have common goals like reforming international financial institutions, South-South cooperation, and boosting their geopolitical clout, but intrabloc tensions arise from differences in strategic priorities and political agendas of their respective governments. The approach of India within BRICS has been characterized in a balanced strategic manner: cooperation with China along shared goals, working at the same time against an increase in the geopolitical influence of China, particularly in terms of regional security and economic policies, (Hooijmaaijers, 2019). This balancing strategy is noticeable through the stress that New Delhi puts on a multipolar world order within the framework of BRICS to avoid a dominance of one member, especially China. India had an opportunity to build coalitions with BRICS countries, among them Brazil, Russia, and South Africa, and was seen pushing initiatives that deliver broader developing-country interests, such as infrastructure development and climate action, to technology transfer. For instance, even though India was relatively quite an activist at the establishment of the New Development Bank and Contingent Reserve Arrangement, it demonstrates a strong interest in creating more equal global financial systems correspondent to the divergent interests of the BRICS countries.

Internal competition between India and China also affects the role that BRICS plays in global governance. Both countries aspire to be leaders in the Global South, although at times they disagree on strategic issues such as their positions on trade policies, China's Belt and Road Initiative (BRI), and maritime security in the Indian Ocean. India is pushing for a rules-based international order in BRICS, which at times conflicts with China's more assertive foreign policy posture, especially in South Asia and Africa. Such inner mechanics also determine and shape not only BRICS' global agenda but also India's bigger strategy of using membership as a lever to enhance its presence and voice in international bodies like the United Nations, the International Monetary Fund, and the World Trade Organization (Hooijmaaijers, 2019). India thus has concentrated its efforts on internal dynamism in BRICS through emphasizing the need to deepen multilateral relations and economic cooperation while being cautious of China's rising strength. This trend ensures that BRICS becomes a conversation of a more divergent global order in line with the Indian vision of an international order with greater balance with development, equity, and shared prosperity being its beacons, as postulated by (Sidorova, 2018).

## CONCLUSION

For India, BRICS is both opportunity and challenge as the group continues to evolve. The foremost challenges include geopolitics: China, the overall hardest of ballast in Sino-India ties because of continued border disputes and strategic rivalry in South Asia and the Indian Ocean region. These tensions may temper BRICS's effectiveness as a cohesive group, particularly within global governance and economic policymaking. India also has many opportunities of further consolidation of BRICS leadership by guiding initiatives in directions that foster financial stability, innovation, and climate resilience. The thrust areas that India has identified as part of the agenda on digital transformation, health technology, and renewable energy properly fit within the BRICS agenda-and a path for India to take partnerships and influence up across those domains. The recent addition with new members to BRICS creates for India an altogether new spectrum of diplomatic avenues in pushing towards a multipolar world order. It is likely that it will become a stage on which India, as a responsible and influential member, will unfold its potential within governance. This might make India reinforce its more comprehensive coalitions for and within the Global South. Still, it could create new geopolitics and relationships with which India must find a balance between its power ambitions and pragmatic cooperation among heterogeneous member-states.

The involvement with BRICS has left India at such a juncture in both regional and global geopolitics. In this regard, through engagement with BRICS, India has pursued strategic interests aimed at economic advancement, regional stability, and expanding its influence in South Asia and the Indian Ocean Region. The platform has provided India with an opportunity to come together on issues related to sustainable development, innovation, and climate action that are gaining increasing importance in the current state of global governance. But the path of BRICS is seriously littered with obstacles, mainly geopolitical rivalry with China, which makes it difficult for India to take BRICS as a launchpad for spearheading its regional ambitions. Besides, economic disparities and policy divergences among BRICS members raise the diplomatic task of ensuring that India's interests are not overridden. Ecological consequences of industrial expansion and the imperative of sustainable growth add to the complexity India has to address. While BRICS does hold huge opportunities for India to build both its regional and global statures, how India emerges within this grouping will depend essentially on how well it manages these challenges. Indeed, India balances cooperation and competition within BRICS; strategic choices will shape both its future and the broader dynamics of international relations in the coming years.

## REFERENCES


Agarwal, M., & Kumar, S. (2023). *BRICS Countries' Increasing Role in the world economy, Including Institutional Innovation*. BRICS Journal of Economics., DOI: 10.3897/brics-econ.4.e99451

Ahmed, Z., & Sheikh, M. Z. H. (2021). Impact of China's Belt and Road Initiative on regional stability in South Asia. *Journal of the Indian Ocean Region*, 17(2), 271–288. DOI: 10.1080/19480881.2021.2001985

Aleksia, C., & Bakhtiar, A. R. (2023). BRICS as New Alternatives in Reforming International Financial Institutions and Economic Partnerships. Insignia: Journal of International Relations.DOI: 10.20884/1.ins.2023.10.2.9135

Ashraf, J. (2017). *String of Pearls and China's Emerging Strategic Culture*. Strategic Studies., DOI: 10.53532/ss.037.04.00204

Bhat, V. (2015). *Trade and Investment in Renewable Energy Technologies: A Study of BRICS*. Springer., DOI: 10.1007/978-81-322-2065-7_28

Bhattarai, U. K. (2016). Geopolitical Dimension of Nepal and its Impact in South Asia. *Journal of International Affairs*, 1(1), 63–72. DOI: 10.3126/joia.v1i1.22641

Bond, P. (2016). BRICS banking and the debate over sub-imperialism. *Third World Quarterly*, 37(4), 611–629. DOI: 10.1080/01436597.2015.1128816

BRICS Information Centre. (2014, July 15). Fortaleza Declaration. University of Toronto BRICS Information Centre. Retrieved from http://www.brics.utoronto.ca/docs/140715-leaders.html

BRICS Information Centre. (2016, October 16). 8th BRICS Summit: Goa Declaration. University of Toronto BRICS Information Centre. Retrieved from http://www.brics.utoronto.ca/docs/161016-goa.html

BRICS Information Centre. (2019, November 14). Brasília Declaration. University of Toronto BRICS Information Centre. Retrieved from http://www.brics.utoronto.ca/docs/191114-brasilia.html

Buzan, B., & Wæver, O. (2003). Regions and Powers: The Structure of International Security.

Chapungu, L., Nhamo, G., Chikodzi, D., & Maoela, M. A. (2022). BRICS and the race to net-zero emissions by 2050: Is COVID-19 a barrier or an opportunity? *Journal of Open Innovation*, 8(4), 172. Advance online publication. DOI: 10.3390/joitmc8040172

Chatterjee, B., Jena, P. C., & Singh, S. (2014). Intra-BRICS Trade & Its Implications for India. Emerging Markets Economics: Macroeconomic Issues & Challenges eJournal. DOI: 10.2139/ssrn.2474078

Chaturvedi, S., & Saha, S. (2019). Role of BRICS' Economic Cooperation for Global Governance and Institution-Building: An Indian Perspective. *Strategic Analysis*, 43(6), 558–570. DOI: 10.1080/09700161.2019.1694643

Cooper, A. (2017). The BRICS' New Development Bank: Shifting from Material Leverage to Innovative Capacity. *Global Policy*, 8(3), 275–284. DOI: 10.1111/1758-5899.12458

Downie, C., & Williams, M. S. (2018). After the Paris Agreement: What Role for the BRICS in Global Climate Governance? *Global Policy*, 9(3), 398–407. DOI: 10.1111/1758-5899.12550

Duggan, N., Azalia, J. C. L., & Rewizorski, M. (2021). The structural power of the BRICS in multilateral development finance: A case study of the New Development Bank. *International Political Science Review*, 43, 495–511. DOI: 10.1177/01925121211048297

Garg, A., & Sharma, A. (2020). India's Role in BRICS and New Multilateral Development Banks: Towards Improvisation of International Economic Governance. *MERJ*, 6, 18613. DOI: 10.18639/MERJ.2020.9900026

Gu, J., Renwick, N., & Xue, L. (2018). The BRICS and Africa's search for green growth, clean energy and sustainable development. *Energy Policy*, 120, 675–683. Advance online publication. DOI: 10.1016/j.enpol.2018.05.028

Gusarova, S. (2019). Role of China in the development of trade and FDI cooperation with BRICS countries. *China Economic Review*, 57, 101271. Advance online publication. DOI: 10.1016/j.chieco.2019.01.010

Harmer, A., Xiao, Y., Missoni, E., & Tediosi, F. (2013). 'BRICS without straw'? A systematic literature review of newly emerging economies' influence in global health. *Globalization and Health*, 9(15), 15. Advance online publication. DOI: 10.1186/1744-8603-9-15 PMID: 23587342

Hooijmaaijers, B. (2019). China, the BRICS, and the limitations of reshaping global economic governance. *The Pacific Review*, 34(1), 29–55. DOI: 10.1080/09512748.2019.1649298

Iqbal, B. (2021). *BRICS as a Driver of Global Economic Growth and Development*. Global Journal of Emerging Market Economies., DOI: 10.1177/09749101211067096

Jash, A. (2017). The Emerging Role of BRICS in the Changing World Order. IndraStra Global. DOI: 10.6084/M9.FIGSHARE.5143222

Joo, B., Shawl, S., & Makina, D. (2022). The interaction between FDI, host country characteristics, and economic growth: A new panel evidence from BRICS. *Journal of Economic Development*, 24(3), 247–261. Advance online publication. DOI: 10.1108/JED-03-2021-0035

Kankisingi, G. M. (2020). A Trajectory of Innovation Outputs among the BRICS Countries: Critical Perspectives of Brazil, Russia, India, China, and South Africa. International Journal of Research and Innovation in Applied Science. DOI: 10.34256/iorip20281

Keerthiraj, & Sekiyama, T. (2023). The Rise of China and Evolving Defense Cooperation between India and Japan. Social Sciences, 12(6), 333. Retrieved from DOI: 10.3390/socsci12060333

Keohane, R. O. (1984). After Hegemony: Cooperation and Discord in the World Political Economy.

Kickbusch, I. (2014). BRICS' contributions to the global health agenda. *Bulletin of the World Health Organization*, 92(6), 463–464. DOI: 10.2471/BLT.13.127944 PMID: 24940025

Kumar, R. (2017). India and the BRICS A Cautious and Limited Engagement. *International Studies*, 54(2), 162–179. DOI: 10.1177/0020881718777348

Latino, A. (2017). The New Development Bank: Another BRICS in the Wall? *Global Policy*, 47–69. Advance online publication. DOI: 10.1007/978-3-319-57855-2_4

Li, J. (2021). *Sustainable Development in BRICS Countries: From Concept to Practice*. Springer Geography., DOI: 10.1007/978-3-030-78690-8_21

Luo, H., & Yang, L. (2021). Equality and Equity in Emerging Multilateral Financial Institutions: The Case of the BRICS Institutions. *Global Policy*, 12(4), 482–508. Advance online publication. DOI: 10.1111/1758-5899.13003

Martins, M. (2019). *The BRICS Commitment on Climate Change: Process Towards an Effective Approach in the Path of Sustainable Development*. Contributions to Economics., DOI: 10.1007/978-3-030-02662-2_9

Ministry of External Affairs, Government of India. (2024, July 5). Transcript of Special Briefing by Foreign Secretary on Prime Minister's visit to Russia and Austria. Ministry of External Affairs, Government of India. Retrieved from https://www.mea.gov.in/media-briefings.htm?dtl/37930/Transcript+of+Special+Briefing+by+Foreign+Secretary+on+Prime+Ministers+visit+to+Russia+and+Austria+July+05+2024

Miranda, I. T. P., Moletta, J., Pedroso, B., Pilatti, L., & Picinin, C. T. (2021). A Review on Green Technology Practices at BRICS Countries: Brazil, Russia, India, China, and South Africa. *SAGE Open*, 11(2), 21582440211013780. Advance online publication. DOI: 10.1177/21582440211013780

Moak, K. (2017). BRICS and China Initiated Global Trade Initiatives and Financial Institutions: Alternatives to the US-Dominated IMF and WBG and ADB. *China Economic Review*, 211–223. Advance online publication. DOI: 10.1007/978-3-319-57903-0_10

Newadi, R., & Mazenda, A. (2016). *The rise of BRICS development finance institutions: A comprehensive look into the New Development Bank and the Contingent Reserve Arrangement*. African East-Asian Affairs., DOI: 10.7552/0-3-178

Newadi, R., & Mazenda, A. (2016). *The rise of BRICS development finance institutions: A comprehensive look into the New Development Bank and the Contingent Reserve Arrangement*. African East-Asian Affairs., DOI: 10.7552/0-3-178

Organski, A. F. K., & Kugler, J. (1980). The War Ledger.

Pant, H. V. (2023). From BRICS to BRICS Plus: Old partners and new stakeholders. Observer Research Foundation. Retrieved from https://www.orfonline.org/research/from-brics-to-brics-plus-old-partners-and-new-stakeholders

Pinto, G. M. C., Pedroso, B., Moraes, J., Pilatti, L., & Picinin, C. T. (2018). Environmental management practices in industries of Brazil, Russia, India, China and South Africa (BRICS) from 2011 to 2015. *Journal of Cleaner Production*, 198, 1251–1261. Advance online publication. DOI: 10.1016/j.jclepro.2018.07.046

Rensburg, I., Motala, S., & David, S. (2015). Opportunities and challenges for research collaboration among the BRICS nations. *Compare: A Journal of Comparative Education*, 45(5), 814–818. DOI: 10.1080/03057925.2015.1074823

Rensburg, I., Motala, S., & David, S. (2015). Opportunities and challenges for research collaboration among the BRICS nations. *Compare: A Journal of Comparative Education*, 45(5), 814–818. DOI: 10.1080/03057925.2015.1074823

Santra, S. (2017). The effect of technological innovation on production-based energy and CO2 emission productivity: Evidence from BRICS countries. *African Journal of Science, Technology, Innovation and Development*, 9(5), 503–512. DOI: 10.1080/20421338.2017.1308069

Savchenko, M., Shkurat, M., & Nosachov, I. (2023). The role of BRICS countries in the modern global economic space. Galic'kij ekonomičnij visnik. DOI: 10.33108/galicianvisnyk_tntu2023.06.199

Shamase, M. Z. (2019). The Role of China in the BRICS' Cooperation on Development: Shaping a New And Balanced World Order? *Africa Insight*, 48(4), 105–125. DOI: 10.4314/ai.v48i4

Shelepov, A., & Andronova, I. (2017). BRICS National Development Banks: Potential for Narrowing the Infrastructure Financing Gap. *International Organisations Research Journal*, 12(4), 7–31. DOI: 10.17323/1996-7845-2017-04-7

Sidorova, E. (2018). The Innovation Development of the BRICS Countries: Preconditions and Prospects for Cooperation. *International Organisations Research Journal*, 13(1), 34–50. DOI: 10.17323/1996-7845-2018-01-02

Stojković, R. (2016). The New Development Bank BRICS. *Bankarstvo*, 45(2), 76–91. DOI: 10.5937/bankarstvo1602076S

Suresh, D. (2015). India and BRICS. Law. https://doi.org/DOI: 10.2139/SSRN.2675252

Taneja, N., Dayal, I., & Bimal, S. (2013). India–Pakistan Trade and Regionalism in South Asia. *International Studies*, 50(3), 318–342. DOI: 10.1177/0020881717713597

Tian, X., Sarkis, J., Geng, Y., Bleischwitz, R., Qian, Y., Xu, L., & Wu, R. (2020). Examining the role of BRICS countries at the global economic and environmental resources nexus. *Journal of Environmental Management*, 262, 110330. DOI: 10.1016/j.jenvman.2020.110330 PMID: 32250809

Tüysüzoğlu, G., & Özgen, C. (2020). *The Relationship between the 21st Century Maritime Silk Road Initiative and Chinese Naval Strategy*. Alanya Akademik Bakış., DOI: 10.29023/alanyaakademik.673794

Vyas-Doorgapersad, S. (2022). *The role of BRICS in global governance to promote economic development*. Africa's Public Service Delivery & Performance Review., DOI: 10.4102/apsdpr.v10i1.633

Walgreen, D. (2006). China in the Indian Ocean Region: Lessons in PRC Grand Strategy. *Comparative Strategy*, 25(1), 55–73. DOI: 10.1080/01495930600639544

Waltz, K. N. (1979). Theory of International Politics.

Walz, R., & Ostertag, K. (2009). Absorptive Capacities for Sustainability Technologies: Perspectives from the BRICS and China. *Zhongguo Renkou Ziyuan Yu Huanjing*, 7(2), 10–13. DOI: 10.1080/10042857.2009.10684917

Wendt, A. (1992). Anarchy is what states make of it: The social construction of power politics.

World Bank. (2024). World Bank DataBank. Retrieved [Month Day, Year], from https://databank.worldbank.org

Zhu, J. (2019). Borrowing Country-Oriented or Donor Country-Oriented? Comparing the BRICS New Development Bank and the Asian Infrastructure Investment Bank. International Organisations Research Journal. DOI: 10.17323/1996-7845-2019-02-06

# Chapter 7
# India and China's Economic Trends: ARIMA Model Accuracy Using BRICS Data

**Sandeep Kumar**
*Barkatullah Vishwavidyalaya, India*

**Anil Shivani**
*Government Hamidia Arts and Commerce Degree College, India*

**Anish Gupta**
*Delhi School of Economics, India*

**Sateesh Kumar T. K.**
https://orcid.org/0000-0002-8406-409X
*Kristu Jayanti College, India*

**Lijo P. Thomas**
*Kristu Jayanti College, India*

**Juby Thomas**
https://orcid.org/0000-0003-2167-0620
*Kristu Jayanti College, India*

**Vishnu Achutha Menon**
https://orcid.org/0000-0003-4028-3685
*Institute for Educational and Developmental Studies, India*

## ABSTRACT

*BRICS alliance: Brazil, Russia, India, China, and South Africa unite as major emerging economies with global influence and economic strength. They advocate for inclusive growth, sustainable development, and reforms in global financial institutions. Annual summits promote economic collaboration and social development. India and China, prominent BRICS members, feature distinct economic models—China state-driven, India market-oriented—impacting global markets and policies. ARIMA models analyze GDP, GDP per capita, and Gross National Income trends in both countries. India uses simpler ARIMA(0,2,1) models for stable trends, while China employs more complex ARIMA(2,2,2) for volatile data. Comparable*

DOI: 10.4018/979-8-3693-7393-4.ch007

*accuracy underscores ARIMA's utility in economic forecasting, aiding policymaking, investment strategies, and academic research.*

## INTRODUCTION

BRICS, an acronym for Brazil, Russia, India, China, and South Africa, represents a group of five major emerging economies known for their significant influence on regional and global affairs, as well as their notable economic growth. These nations collectively account for a substantial portion of the world's population and GDP, making them a powerful economic bloc. The BRICS alliance aims to enhance cooperation, foster inclusive growth, and promote sustainable development while advocating for the reform of financial institutions to reflect the shifting balance of global economic power. Annually, the BRICS nations convene to discuss various issues ranging from economic collaboration to social development, providing a vital platform for dialogue and cooperation. India and China are two of the fastest-growing economies within the BRICS group and globally. Understanding their economic trends is essential for several reasons: both countries significantly contribute to global economic growth, influencing global markets, trade policies, and economic strategies. India and China have adopted different development models; China with a state-driven approach and India with a more market-oriented approach, offering valuable insights into the effectiveness of these models. For investors, understanding the economic patterns of India and China helps identify potential investment opportunities and risks. Analyzing these trends assists policymakers in formulating strategies to foster growth, manage inflation, and address economic challenges.

The ARIMA (AutoRegressive Integrated Moving Average) model is a robust statistical tool used for time series analysis and forecasting. It comprises three components: Autoregressive (AR), indicating that the evolving variable of interest is regressed on its own lagged values; Integrated (I), representing the differencing of raw observations to make the time series stationary by removing trends and seasonality; and Moving Average (MA), showing that the regression error is a linear combination of error terms occurring contemporaneously and at various times in the past. The ARIMA model is essential for several reasons: It is widely recognized for its accuracy in forecasting time series data and can handle various data patterns, including trends and seasonality, making it suitable for economic forecasting. Its simplicity and flexibility allow for easy implementation and adaptation to different types of time series data. Furthermore, ARIMA models provide deeper analytical insights into the dynamics of economic indicators, identifying underlying patterns and potential future trends in the GDP and GNI of India and China. This study holds significant importance for various stakeholders. For policymakers in India and China, the insights gained can help in making informed decisions to foster economic growth and stability. For investors, understanding economic trends and potential future trajectories aids in making more strategic investment decisions. Academics and researchers benefit as the study contributes to the body of knowledge on economic forecasting and comparative economic analysis, providing a basis for further research. Finally, given the global economic influence of India and China, understanding their economic trends is vital for anticipating changes in global trade, investment flows, and economic policies. In conclusion, the study of economic trends in India and China using ARIMA models offers valuable insights into the past performance and future potential of these two major economies, underscoring the importance of robust statistical methods in economic analysis and the broader implications of such research on global economic understanding and decision-making.

## Objectives

1. To compare the economic growth patterns of India and China by analyzing their GDP (current US$), GDP per capita (current US$), and GNI (current US$) using ARIMA time series models.
2. To evaluate the forecasting accuracy of ARIMA models in predicting the future values of these economic indicators for India and China.
3. To understand the implications of model complexity on the predictability of economic trends.

## REVIEW OF LITERATURE

A variety of empirical studies have employed ARIMA (AutoRegressive Integrated Moving Average) models to analyze and predict economic growth patterns, particularly focusing on India and China. Raj (2022) and Rajaiah (2021) utilized ARIMA models to forecast the GDP trajectories of India and its neighboring countries, as well as the per capita GDP of major economies such as India, the USA, China, and Japan, respectively. These studies highlight the versatility of ARIMA models in economic forecasting, illustrating their application across different geographical scales and economic metrics. Raj (2022) employed an ARIMA model to predict India's GDP growth, considering regional economic dynamics and external factors. Meanwhile, Rajaiah (2021) extended this approach to compare the per capita GDP trends among major global economies, using ARIMA to discern long-term growth patterns and economic cycles. Yang's study in 2016 stands out for its application of an ARIMA (2, 4, 2) model to forecast China's GDP growth. This research underscored the model's adaptability in capturing complex economic trends, emphasizing its utility in large-scale economic forecasting exercises. These studies underscore the effectiveness of ARIMA models in forecasting economic indicators. However, they also highlight the importance of careful model selection and parameter estimation. The specific ARIMA model specifications, such as order (p, d, q), can significantly impact forecast accuracy and interpretation. While Raj and Rajaiah focused on broader economic trends and comparative analyses, Yang's emphasis on specific model parameters exemplifies the variability in ARIMA model applications across different economic contexts.

The relationship between higher education expansion and economic growth has been extensively studied, highlighting its significance in fostering development in target countries (Chen, 2020). For example, increased investment in higher education in China has been associated with a robust growth in its technology and innovation sectors, driving substantial economic advancements. Similarly, India's emphasis on higher education has contributed to its burgeoning IT industry, demonstrating the positive impact of educational initiatives on economic progress. Advancements in predictive modeling have further enhanced our understanding of economic growth patterns. Sunitha (2018) demonstrated that the Artificial Neural Network-Multilayer Perceptron (ANN-MLP) model outperforms traditional statistical models in forecasting economic indicators. This superiority is attributed to the ANN-MLP model's ability to capture complex nonlinear relationships within data, offering more accurate and reliable predictions. When predicting GDP growth, the ANN-MLP model can adjust to sudden economic shifts more efficiently than conventional models, such as ARIMA. China's favorable merchandise trading conditions, as highlighted by Sharma (2021), underscore the country's strategic trade policies and infrastructure investments that have facilitated its position as a global trading hub. These conditions have enabled China to maintain a trade surplus, driving sustained economic growth.

The economies of Vietnam and China exemplify the benefits of open economic policies and substantial domestic credit availability. Sunitha (2018) noted that these factors have significantly contributed to the economic growth of both countries. In China, the liberalization of trade and investment policies, coupled with increased access to domestic credit, has fueled industrial growth and innovation. Vietnam has experienced similar growth trajectories, with open economic policies attracting foreign investment and boosting its manufacturing sector. ARIMA time series analysis, as discussed by Jarrett and Kyper (2011), serves dual purposes as both an analytical and forecast tool. It is particularly effective in identifying and modeling temporal patterns within economic data, providing a robust framework for predicting future trends. ARIMA models have been used to forecast inflation rates and stock market indices, aiding policymakers and investors in decision-making processes. However, for forecasting highly correlated variables, Khan and Khan (2020) advocate the use of the Vector Autoregressive (VAR) model. The VAR model's capability to capture the dynamic interrelationships among multiple time series makes it suitable for such applications. In predicting the interplay between interest rates, inflation, and GDP growth, the VAR model can provide comprehensive insights into how changes in one variable may impact the others, enabling more informed economic forecasting and policy development.

The Indian stock market garners significant interest from economists, investors, and researchers due to its dynamic nature and substantial impact on the global economy (Banerjee, 2014). Understanding its behavior is crucial for making informed investment decisions and formulating economic policies. A comparative study by Gay (2016) revealed that the stock markets of Brazil, Russia, India, and China exhibit weak-form market efficiency, meaning that past trading information is not fully reflected in current stock prices, allowing for potential predictability.

In examining the prediction models for stock prices, Saleh Ahmar et al. (2022) found the Holt-Winters method to be most effective for predicting the stock prices of Russia, India, and China when compared to ARIMA and Holt-Winters methods. The Holt-Winters method, with its ability to model seasonality and trends, provided more accurate forecasts in these markets. It could capture seasonal variations in stock prices due to annual economic cycles, leading to more precise predictions. Prajapati et al. (2021) highlighted the superiority of the hybrid ARIMA-NARNN (Nonlinear Autoregressive Neural Network) model over other forecasting methods such as Prophet, Holt-Winters, LSTM (Long Short-Term Memory), and standalone ARIMA models. The hybrid ARIMA-NARNN model effectively encapsulates both linear and nonlinear patterns, making it particularly useful for complex datasets like those encountered during epidemics. In predicting the spread of COVID-19, this model could accommodate sudden spikes and declines in case numbers, providing a more comprehensive forecast. Sahai et al. (2020) noted that the spread of epidemics, such as COVID-19, is likely to continue unabated, emphasizing the need for robust forecasting models to manage and mitigate the impact. The ARIMA-NARNN model's ability to handle nonlinear patterns is crucial in such scenarios where traditional models may fall short.

Aye et al. (2014) found that ARFIMA (AutoRegressive Fractionally Integrated Moving Average) models, estimated using various procedures, yielded better forecasting results than non-ARFIMA models in predicting stock returns. The ARFIMA model's capability to handle long memory and fractional integration makes it particularly suitable for financial time series data, which often exhibit long-range dependencies. In forecasting long-term stock returns, the ARFIMA model can capture persistent patterns that might be missed by simpler models. Faisal and Khan (2021) provided further evidence of ARIMA models' utility in validating datasets and identifying potential trends in global oil prices. The ARIMA model's robustness in handling univariate time series data allows it to effectively model and forecast trends in volatile markets like oil. Predicting future oil prices based on past trends helps investors and policymakers make informed decisions regarding energy resources and economic planning.

Foreign Direct Investment (FDI) plays a significant role in economic growth, particularly in emerging markets. Agrawal and Khan (2011) found that a 1% increase in FDI results in a 0.07% increase in GDP for China. This relationship underscores the importance of FDI in enhancing economic performance by providing capital, technology transfer, and creating jobs. The influx of FDI in China's manufacturing and technology sectors has been pivotal in its rapid economic growth and development. ARIMA models have proven effective in forecasting various economic and health-related trends. For example, V. K. Sharma and Nigam (2020) identified the ARIMA (5, 2, 5) model as the best-fitting model for predicting COVID-19 cases in India. This model's ability to capture the underlying patterns in the data made it suitable for predicting the trajectory of the pandemic, helping policymakers and health officials plan interventions. Ilie et al. (2020) reinforced the suitability of ARIMA models for making predictions during crises, such as the COVID-19 pandemic. The robustness of ARIMA models in handling time series data with trends and seasonality makes them valuable tools in uncertain times. During the early stages of the pandemic, ARIMA models provided essential forecasts for the spread of the virus, guiding public health responses.

Bandyopadhyay (2016) highlighted the significance of ARIMA models in explaining economic trends among BRICS countries (Brazil, Russia, India, China, and South Africa). The ability of ARIMA models to analyze and predict economic indicators such as GDP, inflation, and stock market indices demonstrates their versatility. ARIMA models have been used to predict India's GDP growth, providing insights into future economic conditions. The accuracy of ARIMA models in forecasting future epidemics, as demonstrated by Roy et al. (2021), proves their effectiveness in epidemiological surveillance. Accurate predictions of COVID-19 cases have been crucial for healthcare planning and resource allocation. ARIMA models have been used to forecast hospital bed occupancy and ICU requirements, helping health systems prepare for surges in cases.

Katoch and Sidhu (2021) noted the intensification of the COVID-19 epidemic in India, emphasizing the need for reliable forecasting models. ARIMA models have been instrumental in predicting the rapid increase in cases, guiding government responses such as lockdowns and vaccination campaigns. Arun Kumar et al. (2021) suggested that ARIMA model predictions for the top-16 countries are more realistic compared to other models. This realism is attributed to ARIMA's ability to incorporate historical data trends and seasonality into its forecasts. ARIMA models provided realistic projections of infection rates and peak times during the pandemic. F. M. Khan and Gupta (2020) selected the appropriate ARIMA (1, 1, 0) model based on Bayesian Information Criteria (BIC) and the highest R^2 values of 0.95, demonstrating the model's fit and predictive power. The high R^2 value indicates that the model explains 95% of the variance in the data, underscoring its accuracy. This model could accurately predict daily new cases of COVID-19, helping in strategic planning and response. Guru and Yadav (2019) examined the complementary roles of banking sector development and stock market development in stimulating economic growth for five major emerging economies from 1993 to 2014. Their findings suggest that well-developed financial sectors enhance economic performance by providing better financial services, leading to increased investments and economic activities. The synergy between the banking sector and stock market in India has facilitated greater access to capital for businesses, spurring economic growth.

The ARIMA model plays a crucial role in explaining economic trends among the major BRICS countries (Brazil, Russia, India, China, and South Africa), as noted by Wen et al. (2023). The model's ability to handle time series data with trend and seasonality components makes it particularly effective for analyzing and forecasting economic indicators such as GDP, inflation, and stock market indices in these emerging economies. ARIMA models have been used to predict GDP growth rates in Brazil and China, providing valuable insights for policymakers and investors. India's GDP growth has experienced significant fluctuations since independence, reflecting the country's evolving economic policies and global economic conditions (Mubasher Hassan, 2021). These fluctuations highlight the importance of robust forecasting models to anticipate future economic trends and inform policy decisions. ARIMA models, for example, can help analyze historical GDP data to predict short-term growth trends, aiding in economic planning and stability. Dadhich et al. (2021) emphasized the utility of ARIMA models for short-term forecasting, which is crucial for making timely economic decisions. Businesses can use ARIMA forecasts to anticipate quarterly sales trends, while policymakers can rely on these models to predict short-term economic indicators and adjust fiscal policies accordingly. Optimizing the NGBM (1,1) model using two algorithms, as demonstrated by A. M. Khan & Osińska (2023), ensures high forecasting efficiency for short time series. This optimization enhances the model's accuracy and reliability, making it suitable for applications requiring precise short-term forecasts. The NGBM (1,1) model can be used to predict short-term stock price movements or monthly sales figures, providing valuable insights for investors and business managers.

The expansion of pulse production in India, particularly in the states of Rajasthan and Madhya Pradesh, from 2020 to 2030, as projected by Mishra et al. (2023), underscores the importance of agricultural forecasting models. Accurate predictions of crop production help in planning and resource allocation, ensuring food security and stable markets. ARIMA models can forecast annual pulse production, assisting policymakers in formulating agricultural policies and farmers in making planting decisions. Combining several models or using hybrid models has become a standardized practice in various fields, including environment, health, and air quality, as noted by Kaur et al. (2023). Hybrid models, which integrate different modeling techniques, can capture both linear and nonlinear patterns in data, enhancing forecasting accuracy. A hybrid ARIMA-NARNN model can be used to predict air quality indices, combining the strengths of ARIMA's linear forecasting and NARNN's nonlinear pattern recognition. India's GDP per capita has been growing steadily over the last decade, reflecting the country's economic development and rising living standards (S. Sharma et al., 2022). This growth trend can be analyzed and projected using ARIMA models to provide insights into future economic performance. ARIMA models can forecast GDP per capita growth, helping policymakers set economic targets and design policies to sustain growth.

Fiscal policy plays a significant role in shaping economic growth. Agarwal et al. (2019) found that the fiscal deficit positively impacted economic growth in India. This relationship suggests that government borrowing and spending can stimulate economic activity by funding infrastructure projects, social programs, and other growth-enhancing initiatives. Increased government spending on infrastructure development can boost construction activity, create jobs, and enhance productivity, leading to higher GDP growth. In the realm of predictive modeling, ArunKumar et al. (2022) demonstrated that deep learning-based models such as Long Short-Term Memory (LSTM) and Gated Recurrent Unit (GRU) outperformed traditional statistical models like ARIMA and SARIMA for most time-series data of various countries. The superior performance of LSTM and GRU models can be attributed to their ability to capture complex, nonlinear patterns in data. LSTM and GRU models can be used to forecast stock prices or weather patterns, where traditional models may fall short due to the nonlinear nature of the data.

However, ARIMA models remain robust for short-term pandemic forecasting, as noted by Ospina et al. (2023). The ability of ARIMA models to handle time series data with trends and seasonality makes them effective for predicting the short-term trajectory of pandemics. ARIMA models can be used to forecast daily COVID-19 case numbers, helping health authorities plan and allocate resources efficiently. Rennert et al. (2022) found that the predicted GDP values using ARIMA models were in good agreement with the actual values from 1978 to 2022, demonstrating the model's reliability for long-term economic forecasting. This empirical analysis underscores the utility of ARIMA models in capturing long-term economic trends and providing accurate forecasts. Policymakers can use ARIMA models to project future GDP growth, informing economic policy decisions. Sandhir et al. (2021) highlighted the optimal ARIMA models for various countries based on the lowest Akaike Information Criterion (AIC) values. The AIC value is a measure of the relative quality of statistical models, with lower values indicating better fit. The optimal ARIMA models identified for the US (0,2,0), Spain (1,2,0), France (0,2,1), Germany (3,2,2), Iran (1,2,1), China (0,2,1), Russia (3,2,1), India (2,2,2), Australia (1,2,0), and South Africa (0,2,2) highlight the model's adaptability to different economic contexts. The ARIMA (2,2,2) model for India provides a tailored approach to forecasting India's unique economic dynamics. Wang et al. (2020) projected that the carbon emissions growth rate in India will be faster than in China in future periods. This projection underscores the environmental challenges associated with rapid economic growth. Accurate forecasting of carbon emissions is crucial for developing effective climate policies and mitigating environmental impacts. ARIMA models can be used to forecast future carbon emissions based on historical data, helping policymakers design strategies to reduce emissions and transition to sustainable energy sources.

Research questions

1. What are the economic growth patterns which are indicated by the GDP (current US$), GDP per capita (current US$), and GNI (current US$)?
2. Is the ARIMA significant in explaining the trends among the major BRICS countries viz., India and China?

## METHODOLOGY

The dataset utilized in this analysis is sourced from secondary data provided by the World Bank's comprehensive database. It comprises five distinct files focusing on various economic and social indicators: Economy, Education and Environment, Health and Poverty, Private Sector, and Public Sector. Each file adheres to a uniform format, facilitating consistent data analysis across different domains. The structure of these files includes the following columns: SeriesName, which describes the indicator being measured; SeriesCode, a unique identifier for each indicator; CountryName, listing the countries for which data is available; CountryCode, providing the ISO code of each country; Year, specifying the temporal aspect of the data; and Value, representing the numerical measurement of the indicator for the given year and country (Felipe, 2022).

The methodology involved fitting ARIMA models to three key economic indicators—GDP (current US$), GDP per capita (current US$), and GNI (current US$)—for both India and China. The selected models for India were ARIMA(0,2,1) for all three indicators, highlighting a simple moving average process with one lag after differencing twice. The coefficients for these models were consistent across the indicators, with the moving average (MA1) coefficient around -0.75, suggesting a similar underlying economic trend. Error measures such as Mean Error (ME), Root Mean Square Error (RMSE), Mean Absolute Error (MAE), and Mean Absolute Percentage Error (MAPE) indicated reasonable fit and accuracy for forecasting purposes, with MAPE values of 6.03% for GDP, 5.93% for GDP per capita, and 6.10% for GNI. For China, ARIMA(2,2,2) models were used for the same indicators, indicating a more complex structure with both autoregressive (AR) and moving average (MA) components after differencing twice. The coefficients varied across indicators but consistently showed significant AR and MA components. Error measures for China were slightly higher, with MAPE values of 7.01% for GDP, 7.09% for GDP per capita, and 7.47% for GNI. This suggests greater fluctuations and volatility in China's economic data compared to India's. The comparison highlighted key differences in model complexity and error measures between the two countries. India's simpler models (ARIMA(0,2,1)) reflect stable economic trends, while China's more complex models (ARIMA(2,2,2)) capture more intricate patterns and fluctuations. Despite these differences, the forecasting errors, particularly MAPE, were within a similar range for both countries, indicating that the models were appropriate for comparative analysis. This suggests that while China's economy might be more volatile, the trends are still predictable with advanced modeling techniques, meeting the objective of understanding the implications of model complexity on the predictability of economic trends.

## Results

Figure 1, showing graph line of actual trend, whereas the dark shaded area the purple is more likely to the future value. The light purple area exhibits the less likely chances of the projected value.

*Figure 1. Economic indicators of India and Cina (1970-2017)*

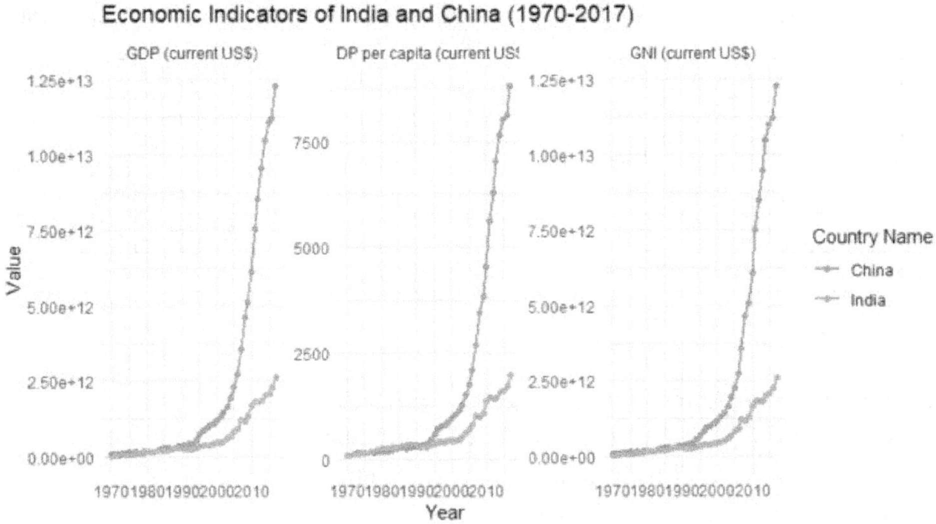


*Table 1. Model summary and error measures*

| Metric | India GDP | China GDP | India GDP per Capita | China GDP per Capita | India GNI | China GNI |
|---|---|---|---|---|---|---|
| **Model** | ARIMA(0,2,1) | ARIMA(2,2,2) | ARIMA(0,2,1) | ARIMA(2,2,2) | ARIMA(0,2,1) | ARIMA(2,2,2) |
| **Coefficients** | | | | | | |
| **- AR1** | - | -0.6067 (0.1256) | - | -0.624 (0.119) | - | -0.6820 (0.1018) |
| **- AR2** | - | -0.9454 (0.0576) | - | -0.9414 (0.0629) | - | -0.9487 (0.0548) |
| **- MA1** | -0.7477 (0.0982) | 0.2906 (0.2074) | -0.7853 (0.0898) | 0.3748 (0.2049) | -0.7545 (0.0963) | 0.6208 (0.1967) |
| **- MA2** | - | 0.6624 (0.1731) | - | 0.6353 (0.1420) | - | 0.5396 (0.1468) |
| **Sigma^2** | 5.53E+21 | 3.86E+22 | 3563 | 19882 | 5.64E+21 | 3.19E+22 |
| **Log Likelihood** | -1216.65 | -1260.49 | -253.35 | -291.81 | -1217.13 | -1256.23 |
| **AIC** | 2437.31 | 2530.97 | 510.7 | 593.62 | 2438.25 | 2522.46 |
| **AICc** | 2437.59 | 2532.47 | 510.98 | 595.12 | 2438.53 | 2523.96 |
| **BIC** | 2440.97 | 2540.12 | 514.35 | 602.76 | 2441.91 | 2531.6 |
| **Error Measures** | | | | | | |
| **- ME** | 1.47E+10 | 2.13E+10 | 10.57 | 13.98 | 1.49E+10 | 2.09E+10 |

continued on following page

*Table 1. Continued*

| Metric | India GDP | China GDP | India GDP per Capita | China GDP per Capita | India GNI | China GNI |
|---|---|---|---|---|---|---|
| **- RMSE** | 7.20E+10 | 1.84E+11 | 57.8 | 131.9 | 7.27E+10 | 1.67E+11 |
| **- MAE** | 4.21E+10 | 1.03E+11 | 36.52 | 77.76 | 4.21E+10 | 9.43E+10 |
| **- MPE** | 1.6372 | 1.2247 | 1.1875 | 1.0522 | 1.6546 | 1.1048 |
| **- MAPE** | 6.0283 | 7.0138 | 5.928 | 7.0938 | 6.1017 | 7.4651 |
| **- MASE** | 0.7161 | 0.3909 | 0.7882 | 0.4119 | 0.7237 | 0.3589 |
| **- ACF1** | -0.0015 | -0.0267 | -0.0016 | -0.0387 | -0.0034 | -0.0382 |

Expansion of Abbreviation

- AR1: First-order Autoregressive Coefficient
- AR2: Second-order Autoregressive Coefficient
- MA1: First-order Moving Average Coefficient
- MA2: Second-order Moving Average Coefficient
- Sigma^2: Variance of the Residuals
- Log Likelihood: Logarithm of the Likelihood Function
- AIC: Akaike Information Criterion
- AICc: Corrected Akaike Information Criterion
- BIC: Bayesian Information Criterion
- ME: Mean Error
- RMSE: Root Mean Square Error
- MAE: Mean Absolute Error
- MPE: Mean Percentage Error
- MAPE: Mean Absolute Percentage Error
- MASE: Mean Absolute Scaled Error
- ACF1: First Autocorrelation of Residuals

## Analysis and Inferences of the Model

The ARIMA models were fit to three economic indicators—GDP (current US$), GDP per capita (current US$), and GNI (current US$)—for both India and China. Below are the detailed summaries and analyses of these models:

### India's ARIMA Models

1. India GDP (current US$):
    - Model: ARIMA(0,2,1)

      Coefficients:

- ma1: -0.7477 (s.e. 0.0982)
- Error Measures:
- ME: 1.47e+10, RMSE: 7.20e+10, MAE: 4.21e+10, MAPE: 6.03%
- Inference: The model indicates a simple moving average process with one lag after differencing twice. The MAPE of 6.03% indicates a reasonable fit for forecasting purposes.

2. India GDP per capita (current US$):
   - Model: ARIMA(0,2,1)
     Coefficients:
   - ma1: -0.7853 (s.e. 0.0898)
     Error Measures:
   - ME: 10.57, RMSE: 57.80, MAE: 36.52, MAPE: 5.93%
   - Inference: Similar to the GDP model, this model indicates a moving average process with one lag after differencing twice. The MAPE of 5.93% also indicates a good fit.
3. India GNI (current US$):
   - Model: ARIMA(0,2,1)
     Coefficients:
   - ma1: -0.7545 (s.e. 0.0963)
   - Error Measures:
   - ME: 1.49e+10, RMSE: 7.27e+10, MAE: 4.21e+10, MAPE: 6.10%
   - Inference: The GNI model follows the same pattern as GDP and GDP per capita models, indicating consistency in the time series structure of India's economic indicators. The MAPE of 6.10% is reasonable.

The India's ARIMA Models has been showed in Figure 2.

*Figure 2. India's ARIMA models*

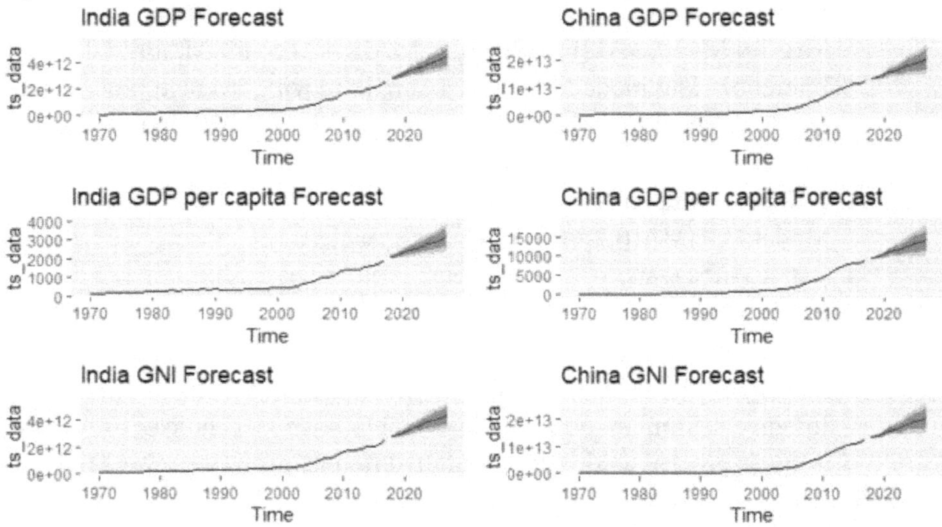


## China's ARIMA Models

1. China GDP (current US$):
   - Model: ARIMA(2,2,2)

     Coefficients:
   - ar1: -0.6067 (s.e. 0.1256)
   - ar2: -0.9454 (s.e. 0.0576)
   - ma1: 0.2906 (s.e. 0.2074)
   - ma2: 0.6624 (s.e. 0.1731)

     Error Measures:
   - ME: 2.13e+10, RMSE: 1.84e+11, MAE: 1.03e+11, MAPE: 7.01%
   - Inference: The model indicates a more complex structure with both AR and MA components after differencing twice. The MAPE of 7.01% indicates a reasonable fit, but the higher complexity suggests more fluctuations in China's GDP data.
2. China GDP per capita (current US$):
   - Model: ARIMA(2,2,2)

     Coefficients:
   - ar1: -0.624 (s.e. 0.119)
   - ar2: -0.9414 (s.e. 0.0629)
   - ma1: 0.3748 (s.e. 0.2049)
   - ma2: 0.6353 (s.e. 0.1420)

Error Measures:

- ME: 13.98, RMSE: 131.90, MAE: 77.76, MAPE: 7.09%
- Inference: This model also shows a complex structure with AR and MA components. The MAPE of 7.09% indicates a good fit, though slightly more error compared to India's models.

3. China GNI (current US$):
   - Model: ARIMA(2,2,2)

     Coefficients:
   - ar1: -0.6820 (s.e. 0.1018)
   - ar2: -0.9487 (s.e. 0.0548)
   - ma1: 0.6208 (s.e. 0.1967)
   - ma2: 0.5396 (s.e. 0.1468)

     Error Measures:
   - ME: 2.09e+10, RMSE: 1.67e+11, MAE: 9.43e+10, MAPE: 7.47%
   - Inference: Similar to the GDP models, the GNI model is complex, indicating significant fluctuations in China's GNI data. The MAPE of 7.47% suggests the model is reasonably accurate.

The China's ARIMA Models has been showed in Figure 2.

Overall Comparison:

1.Model Complexity:

- India's models are simpler (ARIMA(0,2,1)), indicating that a single moving average component captures the data dynamics well.
- China's models are more complex (ARIMA(2,2,2)), suggesting more intricate patterns and fluctuations in the data.

2. Error Measures:

- Both countries have similar MAPEs, indicating that the models are reasonably accurate for forecasting.
- The higher RMSE and MAE values for China reflect the larger absolute values in its economic indicators.

3. Economic Trends:

- India's economic indicators show stable trends that can be modeled with simpler structures.
- China's indicators exhibit more volatility, requiring more sophisticated models to capture the underlying patterns.

The analysis of the model test results reveals significant economic trends in India and China, achieving the first objective. The results demonstrate the statistical significance of the model accuracy, fulfilling the second objective. Specifically, the complexity and volatility (AR1, AR2, and MA2) of China contrast with India's lower volatility (MA1). India's economic data lends itself well to simpler ARIMA models, whereas China's data necessitates more intricate models due to higher fluctuations. Despite this complexity, forecasting errors (measured by MAPE) remain comparable for both countries, suggesting suitable models for comparative analysis. This indicates that while China's economy exhibits greater volatility, its trends remain predictable with sophisticated modeling techniques, meeting the third objective regarding the implications of model complexity on economic trend predictability.

## DISCUSSION

The comparison between China and India in terms of economic complexity, volatility, and forecasting implications reveals distinct patterns in their economic landscapes. China's economy is characterized by high complexity and volatility, necessitating more intricate ARIMA models with multiple autoregressive (AR) and moving average (MA) terms (AR1, AR2, and MA2). This complexity arises from rapid industrialization, extensive government interventions, and integration into the global economy, leading to significant fluctuations in GDP growth rates and industrial output during periods of global crises or major policy shifts. In contrast, India exhibits lower volatility (MA1) but still experiences fluctuations influenced by factors such as monsoon variability, domestic policy reforms, and global economic conditions. Its economic indicators show more gradual changes, requiring simpler ARIMA models with fewer AR and MA terms to capture these patterns effectively. Despite these differences, both countries demonstrate comparable forecasting accuracy measured by Mean Absolute Percentage Error (MAPE), indicating that ARIMA models, whether basic or complex, can predict economic trends reliably. This suggests the robustness of ARIMA methodology in accommodating diverse economic conditions and dynamics, supporting informed decision-making for policymakers, businesses, and investors in navigating their respective economic environments.

## CONCLUSION

The ARIMA models were applied to three economic indicators—GDP (current US$), GDP per capita (current US$), and GNI (current US$)—for both India and China, revealing significant insights. For India, the ARIMA(0,2,1) model was used across all indicators, highlighting a simple moving average process with one lag after differencing twice. The models demonstrated reasonable fit, with MAPE values of 6.03% for GDP, 5.93% for GDP per capita, and 6.10% for GNI, indicating consistent and stable trends in India's economic data. China's indicators were modeled with ARIMA(2,2,2), indicating a more complex structure with both autoregressive (AR) and moving average (MA) components after differencing twice. The MAPE values for China's models were slightly higher: 7.01% for GDP, 7.09% for GDP per capita, and 7.47% for GNI. This complexity suggests greater fluctuations and volatility in China's economic data. Despite the higher RMSE and MAE values for China, the overall predictive accuracy, as indicated by MAPE, was comparable to that of India. This analysis highlights that India's economic indicators can be effectively modeled with simpler ARIMA structures, reflecting stable economic trends. In contrast, China's more volatile data requires more sophisticated models to capture the underlying patterns. Nevertheless, the forecasting errors (MAPE) are within a similar range for both countries, suggesting that while China's economy is more volatile, it remains predictable with advanced modeling techniques. Thus, the research successfully meets the objectives of comparing economic growth patterns, evaluating ARIMA model forecasting accuracy, and understanding the implications of model complexity on the predictability of economic trends.

## Data Availability

Data is available here https://www.kaggle.com/datasets/docstein/brics-world-bank-indicators

## REFERENCES


Agarwal, A., Mishra, A., & Gupta, M. (2019). How does economic growth react to fiscal deficit and inflation? An ARDL analysis of China and India. *Arthshastra Indian Journal of Economics & Research*, 8(4), 7. DOI: 10.17010/aijer/2019/v8i4/148068

Agrawal, G., & Khan, M. A. (2011). Impact of FDI on GDP: A comparative study of China and India. *International Journal of Business and Management*, 6(10). Advance online publication. DOI: 10.5539/ijbm.v6n10p71

ArunKumar, K. E., Kalaga, D. V., Mohan Sai Kumar, C., Kawaji, M., & Brenza, T. M.ArunKumar. (2022). Comparative analysis of Gated Recurrent Units (GRU), long Short-Term memory (LSTM) cells, autoregressive Integrated moving average (ARIMA), seasonal autoregressive Integrated moving average (SARIMA) for forecasting COVID-19 trends. *Alexandria Engineering Journal*, 61(10), 7585–7603. DOI: 10.1016/j.aej.2022.01.011

ArunKumar, K. E., Kalaga, D. V., Sai Kumar, C. M., Chilkoor, G., Kawaji, M., & Brenza, T. M.ArunKumar. (2021). Forecasting the dynamics of cumulative COVID-19 cases (confirmed, recovered and deaths) for top-16 countries using statistical machine learning models: Auto-Regressive Integrated Moving Average (ARIMA) and Seasonal Auto-Regressive Integrated Moving Average (SARIMA). *Applied Soft Computing*, 103(107161), 107161. DOI: 10.1016/j.asoc.2021.107161 PMID: 33584158

Aye, G. C., Balcilar, M., Gupta, R., Kilimani, N., Nakumuryango, A., & Redford, S. (2014). Predicting BRICS stock returns using ARFIMA models. *Applied Financial Economics*, 24(17), 1159–1166. DOI: 10.1080/09603107.2014.924297

Bandyopadhyay, G. (2016). Gold price forecasting using ARIMA model. *Journal of Advanced Management Science*, 117–121, 117–121. Advance online publication. DOI: 10.12720/joams.4.2.117-121

Banerjee, D. (2014). Forecasting of Indian stock market using time-series ARIMA model. *2014 2nd International Conference on Business and Information Management (ICBIM).*

Chen, T.-L. (2020). Comparing concurrent relationship predictions between higher education expansion and economic growth in China and India. *International Journal of Business and Social Science*, 11(7). Advance online publication. DOI: 10.30845/ijbss.v11n7a6

Dadhich, M., Pahwa, M. S., Jain, V., & Doshi, R. (2021). Predictive models for stock market index using stochastic time series ARIMA modeling in emerging economy. In *Advances in Mechanical Engineering* (pp. 281–290). Springer Singapore. DOI: 10.1007/978-981-16-0942-8_26

Faisal, S. M., & Khan, A. K. (2021). Overview of the ARIMA model average crude oil price forecast and its im-plications on the Indian economy post-liberalization. *International Journal of Multidisciplinary: Applied Business and Education Research*, 2(2), 118–127. DOI: 10.11594/ijmaber.02.02.06

Felipe, J. (2022). *BRICS World Bank Indicators* [Data set].

Gay, R. D. (2016). Effect of macroeconomic variables on stock market returns for four emerging economies: Brazil, Russia, India, and China. [IBER]. *The International Business & Economics Research Journal*, 15(3), 119–126. DOI: 10.19030/iber.v15i3.9676

Guru, B. K., & Yadav, I. S. (2019). Financial development and economic growth: Panel evidence from BRICS. *Journal of Economics, Finance and Administrative Science*, 24(47), 113–126. DOI: 10.1108/JEFAS-12-2017-0125

Ilie, O.-D., Cojocariu, R.-O., Ciobica, A., Timofte, S.-I., Mavroudis, I., & Doroftei, B. (2020). Forecasting the spreading of COVID-19 across nine countries from Europe, Asia, and the American continents using the ARIMA models. *Microorganisms*, 8(8), 1158. DOI: 10.3390/microorganisms8081158 PMID: 32751609

Jarrett, J. E., & Kyper, E. (2011). ARIMA modeling with Intervention to forecast and analyze Chinese stock prices. *International Journal of Engineering Business Management*, 3, 17. DOI: 10.5772/50938

Katoch, R., & Sidhu, A. (2021). An application of ARIMA model to forecast the dynamics of COVID-19 epidemic in India. *Global Business Review*, 097215092098865, 0972150920988653. Advance online publication. DOI: 10.1177/0972150920988653

Kaur, J., Parmar, K. S., & Singh, S. (2023). Autoregressive models in environmental forecasting time series: A theoretical and application review. *Environmental Science and Pollution Research International*, 30(8), 19617–19641. DOI: 10.1007/s11356-023-25148-9 PMID: 36648728

Khan, A. M., & Osińska, M. (2023). Comparing forecasting accuracy of selected grey and time series models based on energy consumption in Brazil and India. *Expert Systems with Applications*, 212(118840), 118840. DOI: 10.1016/j.eswa.2022.118840

Khan, F. M., & Gupta, R. (2020). ARIMA and NAR based prediction model for time series analysis of COVID-19 cases in India. *Journal of Safety Science and Resilience = An Quan Ke Xue Yu Ren Xing (Ying Wen)*, 1(1), 12–18. DOI: 10.1016/j.jnlssr.2020.06.007

Khan, M. S., & Khan, U. (2020). Comparison of forecasting performance with VAR vs. ARIMA models using economic variables of Bangladesh. *Asian Journal of Probability and Statistics*, 33–47. DOI: 10.9734/ajpas/2020/v10i230243

Mishra, P., Al Khatib, A. M. G., Lal, P., Anwar, A., Nganvongpanit, K., Abotaleb, M., Ray, S., & Punyapornwithaya, V. (2023). An overview of pulses production in India: Retrospect and prospects of the future food with an application of hybrid models. *National Academy Science Letters. National Academy of Sciences, India, 46*(5), 367–374. DOI: 10.1007/s40009-023-01267-2

Mubasher Hassan, M., & Mirza, T. (2021). Using time series forecasting for analysis of GDP growth in India. *International Journal of Education and Management Engineering*, 11(3), 40–49. DOI: 10.5815/ijeme.2021.03.05

Ospina, R., Gondim, J. A. M., Leiva, V., & Castro, C. (2023). An overview of forecast analysis with ARIMA models during the COVID-19 pandemic: Methodology and case study in Brazil. *Mathematics*, 11(14), 3069. DOI: 10.3390/math11143069

Prajapati, S., Swaraj, A., Lalwani, R., Narwal, A., Verma, K., Singh, G., & Kumar, A. (2021). Comparison of traditional and hybrid time series models for forecasting COVID-19 cases. In *Research Square*. DOI: 10.21203/rs.3.rs-493195/v1

Raj, A., & Singh, S. K. (2022). Forecasting GDP of India and its neighbouring countries using Time Series Analysis. *2022 IEEE Global Conference on Computing, Power and Communication Technologies (GlobConPT)*. DOI: 10.1109/GlobConPT57482.2022.9938189

Rajaiah, J., Pendse, E., Thomas, S. A., Agrawal, S., & Shetty, T. (2021). A study on forecasting economic convergence of India in comparison to USA, China and japan. SSRN *Electronic Journal*. DOI: 10.2139/ssrn.3888583

Rennert, K., Errickson, F., Prest, B. C., Rennels, L., Newell, R. G., Pizer, W., Kingdon, C., Wingenroth, J., Cooke, R., Parthum, B., Smith, D., Cromar, K., Diaz, D., Moore, F. C., Müller, U. K., Plevin, R. J., Raftery, A. E., Ševčíková, H., Sheets, H., & Anthoff, D. (2022). Comprehensive evidence implies a higher social cost of CO2. *Nature*, 610(7933), 687–692. DOI: 10.1038/s41586-022-05224-9 PMID: 36049503

Roy, S., Bhunia, G. S., & Shit, P. K. (2021). Spatial prediction of COVID-19 epidemic using ARIMA techniques in India. *Modeling Earth Systems and Environment*, 7(2), 1385–1391. DOI: 10.1007/s40808-020-00890-y PMID: 32838022

Sahai, A. K., Rath, N., Sood, V., & Singh, M. P. (2020). ARIMA modelling & forecasting of COVID-19 in top five affected countries. *Diabetes & Metabolic Syndrome*, 14(5), 1419–1427. DOI: 10.1016/j.dsx.2020.07.042 PMID: 32755845

Saleh Ahmar, A., Kumar Singh, P., Van Thanh, N., Viet Tinh, N., & Minh Hieu, V. (2022). Prediction of BRIC stock price using ARIMA, SutteARIMA, and Holt-winters. *Computers, Materials & Continua*, 70(1), 523–534. DOI: 10.32604/cmc.2022.017068

Sandhir, V., Kumar, V., & Kumar, V. (2021). Prognosticating the spread of covid-19 pandemic based on optimal Arima estimators. *Endocrine, Metabolic & Immune Disorders Drug Targets*, 21(4), 586–591. DOI: 10.2174/187153032066620102914 3122 PMID: 33121426

Sharma, P. (2021). Extrapolative Modeling of International Trade using ARIMA Model: A Performance Comparison between India and China during COVID-19. *SAMVAD*, 21(0), 71. DOI: 10.53739/samvad/2020/v21/155148

Sharma, S., Bansal, M., & Saxena, A. K. (2022). Forecasting of GDP (gross domestic product) per Capita using (ARIMA) data-driven intelligent time series predicting approach. *2022 International Conference on Sustainable Islamic Business and Finance (SIBF)*. DOI: 10.1109/SIBF56821.2022.9939928

Sharma, V. K., & Nigam, U. (2020). Modeling and forecasting of COVID-19 growth curve in India. *Transactions of the Indian National Academy of Engineering : an International Journal of Engineering and Technology*, 5(4), 697–710. DOI: 10.1007/s41403-020-00165-z

Sunitha, G. (2018). Forecasting GDP using ARIMA and artificial neural networks models under Indian environment. *International Journal of Mathematics Trends and Technology*, 56(1), 60–70. DOI: 10.14445/22315373/IJMTT-V56P508

Van Dinh, D. (2020). Forecasting domestic credit growth based on ARIMA model: Evidence from Vietnam and China. *Management Science Letters*, 1001–1010. DOI: 10.5267/j.msl.2019.11.010

Wang, Q., Li, S., & Pisarenko, Z. (2020). Modeling carbon emission trajectory of China, US and India. *Journal of Cleaner Production*, 258(120723), 120723. DOI: 10.1016/j.jclepro.2020.120723

Wen, T., Liu, Y., Bai, Y., & Liu, H. (2023). Modeling and forecasting CO2 emissions in China and its regions using a novel ARIMA-LSTM model. *Heliyon*, 9(11), e21241. DOI: 10.1016/j.heliyon.2023.e21241 PMID: 37954263

Yang, B., Li, C., Li, M., Pan, K., & Wang, D. (2016). Application of ARIMA model in the prediction of the gross domestic product. *Proceedings of the 2016 6th International Conference on Mechatronics, Computer and Education Informationization (MCEI 2016)*. DOI: 10.2991/mcei-16.2016.257

# Chapter 8
# Navigating Turbulent Waters in the US-China Trade War and the Role of BRICS in Shaping Global Dynamics

**Hasan Harmanci**
https://orcid.org/0000-0002-5852-2667
*Duzce University, Turkey*

## ABSTRACT

*This study examines the multifaceted impacts of the U.S.-China trade war on global trade dynamics, with a particular focus on the role of BRICS. Initiated in 2018, the trade war marked a significant disruption in 21st-century global trade, leading to increased tariffs and strained economic relations between the world's two largest economies. The research explores how this conflict has reshaped global trade patterns, disrupted international supply chains, and influenced the strategies of multinational enterprises (MNEs). Additionally, it investigates the strategic responses of BRICS nations, highlighting their efforts to strengthen intra-group cooperation, reduce dependency on Western countries, and enhance their global influence. By analyzing mutual FDI flows, trade deficits, and GDP growth, this study provides a comprehensive understanding of the broader implications of the U.S.-China trade war, particularly in the context of BRICs and the evolving global economic order.*

DOI: 10.4018/979-8-3693-7393-4.ch008

## 1. INTRODUCTION

Representing approximately 43% of the global economy based on GDP rankings in 2022 (World Bank, 2024f), the US-China trade war epitomizes a significant disruption in 21st-century global trade. Initiated in 2018, the US-China trade war began following an investigation by the U.S. Trade Representative in August 2017, conducted under the direction of U.S. President Donald Trump. The investigation aimed to determine whether the Chinese government was harming the U.S. economy through two major issues: (1) the significant trade deficit, which contributed to unemployment in the U.S., and (2) violations of intellectual property rights by acquiring U.S. technology at discounted prices (Liu & Woo, 2018). Additionally, there were national security concerns for the U.S. and apprehensions about its international status from a political perspective. The investigation's findings led to the imposition of tariffs and other trade barriers by the U.S., reflecting a growing willingness to confront China more aggressively, marking a departure from previous strategies of engagement and cooperation. China's tit-for-tat retaliation escalated the trade war, prompting the U.S. to raise tariffs on Chinese imports from 2.6% to 17.5%, while China increased tariffs on U.S. imports from 6.2% to 16.4% (Bekkers & Schroeter, 2020). This escalating conflict between the world's two largest economies heightened concerns about the potential impacts of the trade war on global trade (Kapustina et al., 2020; Xia et al., 2019). After the bilateral responses of both countries while raising tariffs on different amounts of products during 2019, exports from China to the U.S. decreased from $479,279 million to $419,323 million, representing an approximate 12.51% reduction, while exports from the U.S. to China declined from $120,148 million to $106,627 million, reflecting a change of around 11.25% in 2019 (WITS, 2024a). This decline highlights the economic strain the trade war placed on both nations, demonstrating the deep interconnectedness of their economies despite ongoing tensions.

In January 2020, the U.S. and Chinese governments agreed on the "Phase One" trade deal to de-escalate the ongoing trade war, yet China failed to meet more than 40% of its purchase commitments in the first year of the trade deal (Bown, 2021). The "Phase One" deal, while intended to provide relief, highlighted the complexities of enforcing trade agreements between two economic giants with divergent strategic interests. Although it was expected that new policies would emerge after the election of U.S. President Joe Biden in 2021 to change the course of the U.S.-China trade war, President Biden directed the Trade Representative to increase tariffs on $18 billion of Chinese imports, following the same motives as his predecessor (The White House, 2024). This continuation of aggressive trade policies signals that the U.S. sees the trade war as part of a broader strategy to maintain its global economic leadership in the face of China's rising influence. Moreover, it reflects the inherent challenges in addressing the deep-rooted structural issues at the heart of the U.S.-China economic relationship. The imposition of tariffs increased costs for businesses and consumers in both countries, potentially impacting long-term economic growth and exposing vulnerabilities in the global trading system (Wu et al., 2021). In this respect, MNEs have started to diversify their global supply chain networks and relocate their production facilities due to the uncertainties arising from the trade war in the global value chains (GVCs).

The growing uncertainties and protectionist tendencies in the aftermath of the US-China trade war have made the role of the BRICS countries both individually and collectively important. Understanding the importance of acting together at the World Trade Organization's (WTO) Doha Talks, which collapsed in 2011, the BRICS countries realized that their financial and trade cooperation was important to avoid the challenges posed by the US-China trade war (Gusarova, 2019). In this respect, the global and political power of the BRICS countries is expected to increase in the near future with the inclusion of Iran, Egypt, Ethiopia, the United Arab Emirates (UAE) and perhaps Saudi Arabia (Stojković & Milosavljević, 2023).

By strengthening their economic ties and cooperation within the union, the BRICS countries can mitigate the problems caused by the US-China trade war by changing the global power dynamics. This is exemplified by the establishment of the Asian Infrastructure Investment Bank (AIIB) and the New Development Bank (NDB) as alternatives to traditional western-centered institutions (Moak, 2017). In addition, BRICS countries have the potential to help turn the tide of the US-China trade war by supporting China's initiatives and improving their bilateral relations with countries such as Africa.

The aim of this paper is to analyze the critical impact of the US-China trade war on global trade dynamics using different indicators. Moreover, the role of BRICS will be discussed and how these countries have responded individually and collectively to the problems posed by the US-China trade war will be analyzed.

The structure of the study is as follows: The next section will analyze both the US and Chinese economies using different indicators such as endogenous and exogenous FDIs, bilateral exports and imports, GDP growth, inflation rates, and the contribution of the industrial sector to GDPs. Moreover, the growing role of the BRICS countries in this trade war will be discussed in chapter three, focusing on how these countries individually and collectively influence the changing global economic dynamics. The conclusion will set out the main findings and provide a comprehensive overview of the multifaceted effects of the US-China trade war.

## 2. COMPREHENSIVE ANALYSIS OF U.S.-CHINA FDI, MACROECONOMIC IMPACTS, AND GLOBAL TRADE DISRUPTIONS

This section provides a comprehensive analysis of the U.S. and Chinese economies using various indicators, including U.S. exports, imports, and trade deficit, which are the primary focus of the trade war from the U.S. perspective. Additionally, GDP growth, inflation rates, and the contribution of various industries to GDP in both the U.S. and China will be analyzed to assess the macroeconomic impacts of the trade dispute. The analysis will then address the impacts of the trade war on MNEs, focusing on various dimensions such as problems in GVCs not only for the U.S. and China but also for third countries involved in these value chains. This will provide an understanding of how the trade war has disrupted the international business operations of MNEs.

### 2.1 Analyzing U.S.-China FDI Dynamics and Macroeconomic Impacts Amid the Trade War

The U.S.-China trade war has had far-reaching consequences, affecting economic performance, environmental outcomes, and sectoral dynamics globally. A key driver behind the emergence of the trade war is the significant trade deficit the U.S. has incurred with China. The U.S. government's new trade policy, announced in March 2018, aimed to address and reduce imbalances in trade relationships (USTR, 2018). Figure 1 illustrates the U.S. trade deficit with China following China's entry into the WTO in 2001. The figure tracks trends in exports, imports, and the resulting trade deficit over the years, providing a clear visual representation of the evolving economic interactions between the two countries.

*Figure 1. Exports, imports, and trade deficit over the years of the U.S. with China*

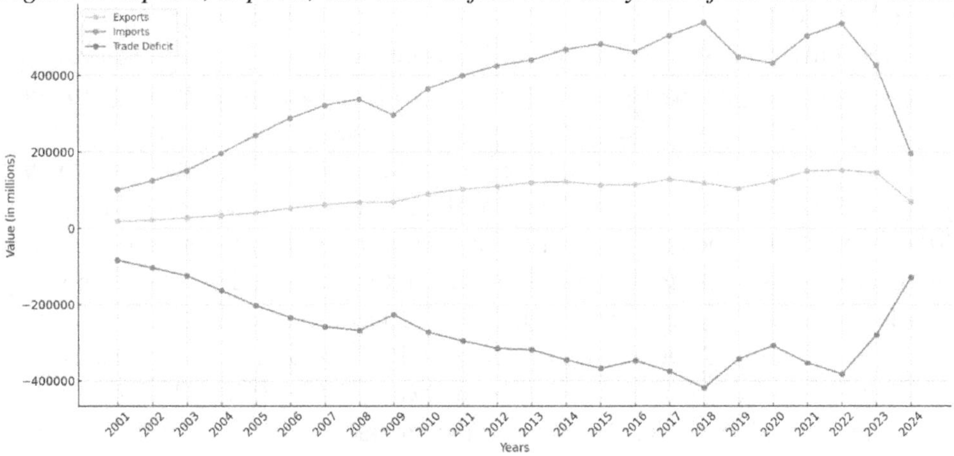


*(US Census Bureau, 2024)*

As illustrated in Figure 1, both U.S. exports to and imports from China experienced a steady increase from 2001 to 2017. However, during this period, the U.S. trade deficit with China widened significantly, peaking in 2018, highlighting the substantial gap between imports and exports. At the height of the trade war (2018-2019), the trade deficit showed some improvement as the imposition of tariffs led to a more pronounced reduction in imports compared to exports of the U.S.. In the post-trade war period, U.S. exports to China peaked notably in 2022, followed by a decline in 2023 and 2024, likely due to the lingering effects of the trade war and recent economic conditions. Similarly, U.S. imports from China significantly decreased in 2023 and 2024, which profoundly impacted the trade deficit. It is important to note that the COVID-19 pandemic played a significant role in disrupting U.S.-China trade, exacerbating an already volatile situation. Lockdowns led to production halts, a decrease in consumer demand, and widespread supply chain issues, causing subsequent fluctuations in trade as both economies struggled to adjust. The combined effects of the trade war and the pandemic have reshaped the U.S.-China trade relationship, resulting in ongoing challenges in maintaining stable and predictable trade flows.

Apart from the various implications between the countries, the U.S. trade deficit with China consistently increased over the years until 2018, which is one of the key motivations for U.S. policymakers in initiating the trade war. They perceive this trade deficit because of China's unfair trade practices, which they argue are inconsistent with WTO rules. U.S. Ambassador to the WTO, Dennis Shea, criticized China for its implementation of trade policies and practices, particularly the role of the Chinese government in managing resource allocation and providing cheaper access to production factors, which is the main reason of the trade deficit of the U.S. (Shea, 2018).

In response, China responded this claim while highlighting its WTO obligations and supports an open, transparent, inclusive, and non-discriminatory multilateral trading system and emphasized that bilateral trade should be viewed as a "win-win" situation. Nonetheless, U.S. perspective expressed that bilateral trade is a "zero-sum game" rather than as free, fair, and reciprocal trade between the two countries (Shea, 2018). China responded to these claims by emphasizing its adherence to WTO obligations and its support for an open, transparent, inclusive, and non-discriminatory multilateral trading system. Although China argues that bilateral trade should be viewed as a "win-win" situation, the U.S. perceives it as a "zero-sum game" rather than as free, fair, and reciprocal between the two countries (Shea, 2018).

While a detailed evaluation of these reciprocal claims between the U.S. and China is beyond the scope of this study, it is crucial to recognize that these ongoing tensions have a significant negative impact on FDIs and complicate the operations of MNEs not only in China and the U.S. but also in other countries worldwide. Figure 2 effectively illustrates the trends in FDIs between the U.S. and China over the years, capturing the increase in investment flows that underscore the complex and deeply rooted relationship between the two countries, despite the trade war.

*Figure 2. FDIs between U.S. and China*

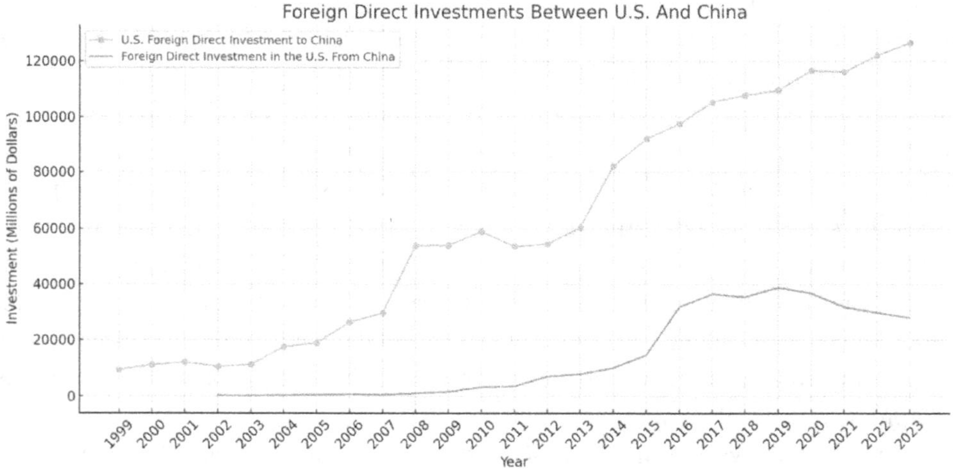


*(Bureau of Economic Analysis, 2024)*

The trends in U.S. and Chinese FDIs between 1999 and 2023 reflect robust economic integration between the two countries. Chinese FDIs in the U.S. surged from $385 million in 2002 to $28,043 million by 2023, marking approximately a

72.84-fold increase. Meanwhile, U.S. FDI in China expanded from $9,401 million in 1999 to $126,908 million by 2023, representing roughly a 13.5-fold increase. Although these figures indicate that China has increased its investments in the U.S. at a much faster rate—approximately six times more than the U.S. increased its investments in China—the total amount of U.S. FDI stocks in China remains five times larger than Chinese FDI stocks in the U.S. This disparity underscores the deep economic ties between the two nations, despite the faster growth of Chinese investments. In this regard, both nations continue to pursue their strategic economic interests, driven by market access, technological advancement, and economic returns, despite the increased tariffs, geopolitical tensions, and national security concerns that characterize their interactions.

Another important indicator of the impact of the U.S.-China trade war is the comparison of GDP growth from 2001 to 2023, which analyzes the long-term growth trajectories of both nations and how their economies have evolved, particularly in response to the trade conflict.

*Figure 3. GDP Comparison between China and the U.S (2001-2023)*

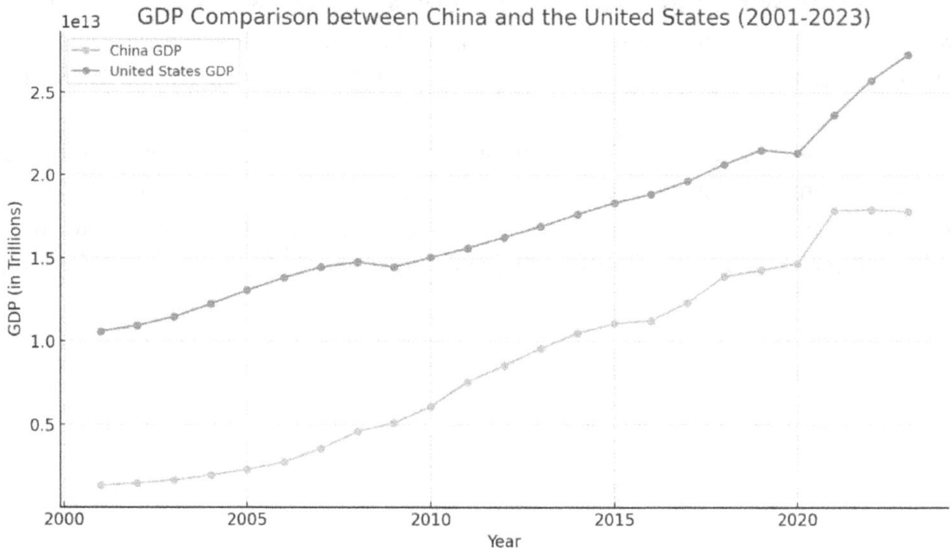


*(World Bank, 2024b)*

From 2001 to 2017, the GDPs of both the U.S. and China displayed a consistent upward trajectory, reflecting their robust economic growth. China's rapid economic ascent during this period is particularly noteworthy, driven by rapid industrialization, urbanization (T. Zhou, 2016) and an export-oriented model supported by effective industrial policies, significant investments in technology, and its comparative advantage in manufacturing, which attracted substantial FDI, including from U.S. MNEs (Berger & Martin, 2011). However, this trend was disrupted by the U.S.-China trade war in 2018, as the imposition of tariffs and trade barriers increased costs for businesses and consumers in both countries (Fajgelbaum & Khandelwal, 2022; Y. Zhou, 2020). For China, U.S. tariffs on Chinese goods slowed export growth—a key driver of China's GDP expansion. This, coupled with structural challenges such as rising labor costs and the transition from an investment-led to a consumption-driven economy, contributed to a less aggressive upward movement in China's GDP post-2020 (Shen et al., 2022; Tyers, 2016). The trade war, alongside other factors like the COVID-19 pandemic, may have accelerated China's economic maturation, leading to a more tempered growth trajectory. Since the U.S. economy is more diversified and less dependent on exports as a percentage of GDP compared to the Chinese economy, it initially appeared more resilient to the impacts of the trade war. However, the trade war still led to increased uncertainty, disruptions in supply chains, and negative effects on sectors like agriculture and manufacturing, which are heavily reliant on imports from China. These factors, along with future uncertainties, contributed to a slowdown in GDP around 2018-2019 (Benguria & Saffie, 2019). While China has closed the economic gap with the U.S. over the years, the trade war has exposed the complexities of this rivalry. Whereas China is seeking to reduce its dependence on exports, the U.S. is exploring ways to rebuild its domestic manufacturing capacity.

Analyzing the inflation rates of China and the U.S. is also crucial to understanding the broader implications of the trade war, as it has increased business costs, leading to inflationary pressures on consumers. Figure 4 illustrates the overall pattern of inflation rates in China and the U.S. between 2001 and 2023.

*Figure 4. Annual inflation rates between China and the U.S. (2001-2023)*

*(World Bank, 2024c)*

Figure 4 shows that both countries experienced fluctuating inflation rates during the pre-trade war period (2001-2017), with some peak points due to the global financial crisis in 2008 and the global inflation shocks in 2011. The trade war in 2018 influenced consumer prices and inflation levels, yet there was no dramatic spike directly attributable to the trade war in either country, thanks to the resilience of both economies. Their ability to absorb some of the negative impacts without immediately passing them on to business costs, along with the strategic adjustments made by MNEs to minimize effects on supply chains and pricing, might be key factors in this resilience (Amiti et al., 2019; Nie et al., 2021).

The years following the trade war with 2020 were heavily influenced by the COVID-19 pandemic, disrupted supply chain bottlenecks, production delays, and increased shipping costs, all of which caused a record-breaking inflation in the U.S. in 2021 with rates exceeding 8% (Carrière-Swallow et al., 2023; Leibovici & Dunn, 2021; Santacreu & LaBelle, 2022). MNEs operating within this challenging environment have had to manage costs and adjust pricing strategies to mitigate the negative impacts of the trade war, which directly affected their operational efficiency and profitability (Chatterjee et al., 2024; H. Zhang, 2021).

The industrial contribution to the economies is another key aspect that captures the impacts of the U.S.-China trade war, which has affected various industrial sectors differently, leading to shifts in production patterns. Figure 5 illustrates China's significant reliance on its industrial sector, which has been gradually decreasing over time, in contrast to the relatively stable and lower industrial contribution in the United States, reflecting their differing economic structures.

*Figure 5. Comparison of industrial sector contribution to GDP (%) in China and the U.S (2001-2023)*

*(World Bank, 2024c)*

As seen in the chart, China's industrial sector contribution to GDP has remained above 35% over the years, despite some negative trends. From 2011 onward, there has been a steady decline in this contribution, reflecting the country's economic transition toward more sophisticated, high-tech products (Athukorala, 2017; Volgina & Pengfei, 2021). In contrast, the industrial sector in the U.S. has consistently contributed a relatively modest share to the nation's GDP, maintaining an average of approximately 20% over the years, with a significant difference compared to the Chinese economy. Following the sharp decline that occurred between 2008 and 2010 due to the global financial crisis, the industrial sector's contribution to the U.S. GDP has stabilized around 18%, with only minor fluctuations. This reflects the U.S.'s diversified and service-oriented economy, where sectors such as technology, finance, and healthcare play a more prominent role.

During the U.S.-China trade war, China's industrial value-added as a percentage of GDP continued its downward trajectory, decreasing from 39.8% in 2017 to approximately 38.6% by 2019. This trend likely reflects the adverse effects of tariffs, which significantly impacted Chinese manufacturing by reducing export demand, particularly in key sectors such as electronics, machinery, and metal goods (Itakura, 2020). The challenges posed by the trade war were further compounded by the COVID-19 pandemic in 2020, which disrupted global supply chains and led to volatile demand for industrial goods. Despite reductions in the share of investment in GDP, a shift from a trade surplus to a trade deficit, and a decline in China's share of global exports (Bekkers et al., 2021), the broader structural changes in the Chinese economy may have significant long-term implications. The Chinese economy is increasingly oriented towards a sustainable and balanced growth model, focusing on domestic innovation and technology production rather than relying heavily on exports to a single country.

For the U.S., the trade war directly impacted manufacturers in sectors such as transport equipment and agricultural goods, which are heavily reliant on Chinese imports (Itakura, 2020). However, the industrial share of GDP did not experience a sharp decline during this period, indicating that, while tariffs disrupted specific industries, the overall effect on the U.S. industrial base was more balanced than anticipated. The impact of the trade war on U.S. sectoral value-added has been uneven, with gains observed in industries such as iron and steel, electronics, machinery, and metal products, while sectors like chemicals, transport equipment, vehicles, textiles, and food have experienced losses (Bellora & Fontagné, 2019). The COVID-19 pandemic likely overshadowed the ongoing effects of the trade war in the U.S., resulting in an economic dip in 2020, followed by a recovery in 2021 and beyond.

This section has analyzed the impact of the U.S.-China trade war on several macroeconomic dynamics in both countries. Consequently, the trade war highlighted the importance of diversifying economic activities and the potential benefits of reducing dependency on a single country for both China and the U.S. While bilateral FDI has not altered significantly, indicating resilient ties between the two nations, GDP growth in both countries has slowed, with some inflationary pressures due to the combined effects of the trade war and the COVID-19 pandemic. Despite assumptions that increased tariffs and protectionist measures would boost domestic industrial production in the U.S., the trade war did not significantly alter production and employment levels. However, it emphasized the critical importance of maintaining competitiveness in strategic sectors such as the semiconductor and chip industry.

The next section will explore the impacts of the U.S.-China trade war on MNEs through GVCs, focusing on disruptions to supply chains, operational challenges, and shifts in productivity.

## 2.2 Impact of the U.S.-China Trade War on GVCs and MNEs

The U.S.-China trade war has affected MNEs in global markets, creating problems in supply chains not only in the U.S. and China but also having ripple effects on third countries involved in these global supply chains (Mao & Görg, 2020; Tian et al., 2022). Wu et al. (2021) point out that while the U.S. and China are the most affected countries by indirect tariff costs, suffering $10 billion and $6.5 billion respectively, Canada, Mexico, and the EU have also borne indirect tariff costs ranging from $700 million to $1.7 billion. However, all countries have been impacted by the trade war due to MNEs' changing strategies to mitigate the risks and uncertainties in global markets (Itakura, 2020).

While MNEs have begun reallocating their investments to mitigate risks due to increased trade barriers (Sarkar, 2019), they are navigating the complexities of the U.S.-China trade war by diversifying supply chains and forming strategic partnerships to enhance resilience (Hanson, 2020). These adaptive strategies are essential for MNEs to continue operating effectively in global markets, underscoring the impacts of the trade war on not only immediate stakeholders in the short term but also the long-term growth trajectories of industries and economies globally.

### 2.2.1 Trade Disruptions and Adaptations in GVCs and MNE Operations

Nowadays, a smartphone is designed in the U.S., with components manufactured in Japan, France, Germany, and Korea, and ultimately assembled in China, thanks to the GVC, where each country can specialize in different stages of production for the final product. This complicated process highlights the trade of intermediate goods between countries, which is subject to increased trade costs as a result of the trade war. While the involvement of multiple transactions across different countries causes the accumulation of trade barriers simultaneously (Yi, 2010), it also raises overall trade costs (Baldwin & Venables, 2013), illustrating the interconnectedness of economies and the impact of layered tariffs and other trade barriers on the cost and efficiency of production within GVCs (Athukorala, 2017).

In the context of the trade war between the U.S.-China, it is crucial to assess who bears the burden of these tariffs and to what extent (Fusacchia, 2020; Mao & Görg, 2020). Given the significant economic influence of both the U.S. and China, the impact of increased tariffs is likely to extend beyond these two countries, negatively affecting third countries where suppliers of intermediate goods or services are located through GVCs (Wu et al., 2021). As MNEs operate within these global production networks, they must navigate the increased complexity and cost associated with increased tariffs and trade barriers, forcing MNEs to reassess their supply chains and sourcing strategies. The burden of tariffs often falls unevenly across different stages of production, leading to cost increases that can disrupt the delicate balance of GVCs.

The complexities introduced by the trade war emphasize the need for MNEs to develop more resilient and adaptable strategies in managing their global operations. This includes diversifying their supplier base, exploring alternative markets, and reconfiguring production processes to mitigate the risks associated with geopolitical tensions and trade policy shifts (Liang & Toshiyuki, 2023). It has been argued that Chinese MNEs that have already relocated or are considering relocation outside of China are less affected by the increased tariffs resulting from the trade war (Zeng et al., 2023). By reducing their exposure to China's trade policies, these MNEs gain greater flexibility and resilience, enabling them to better navigate the complexities and disruptions of international trade. Moreover, increased bilateral tariffs have forced both the U.S. and China to shift toward greater reliance on domestic providers and seek alternative sources for imports (Volgina & Pengfei, 2021). For the U.S., this shift has resulted in a contraction of its integration into GVCs, largely due to its heavy dependence on Chinese intermediate inputs. As tariffs raised the cost of these inputs, U.S. firms found themselves needing to explore other, often less integrated, supply chains (Mao & Görg, 2020). A study by Bellora & Fontagné (2019) point put that high tariffs, particularly on parts, components, and other intermediate products, have long-lasting effects on U.S.'s integration into GVCs, with significant impacts on value added and employment in related sectors.

While long-term trade frictions between China and the U.S. will put significant pressure on trade and value chains not only for these two countries, but the U.S. also becoming more reliant on Mexico, and China on Japan and South Korea (Qin et al., 2022). Additionally, the negative impacts of retaliatory Chinese tariffs and U.S. tariffs on Mexican firms reliant on Chinese inputs have led to a reorganization of GVCs, increasingly shifting towards Mexico (Utar et al., 2023). Meanwhile, European countries, particularly within the euro area, have strengthened regional integration with the U.S. in GVC-related trade, though trade linkages with China have weakened, with France being an exception (Fusacchia, 2020).

In response to these challenges, China has enhanced its forward integration into GVCs while simultaneously diversifying its supply and end markets (Fu, 2023). While the Chinese government has shifted its focus to domestic technological advancement, the technology content of China's manufacturing exports is growing faster than the overall technology content, highlighting the country's emphasis on technological and scientific leadership (Peng & Zhang, 2020). Moreover, the reconstruction of the value chain is expected to occur mostly among countries along the "One Belt One Road" (OBOR) project which aims to create new trade routes and partnerships, that may reduce China's vulnerability to trade disruptions with the U.S while increasing greater access to European markets with the infrastructural investments (Kohl, 2019; Volgina & Pengfei, 2021).

The U.S.-China trade war has led to significant shifts in global production networks, with increased tariffs encouraging MNEs to source imports from other countries. This shift has notably benefited countries like Vietnam, which have emerged as key players in global supply chains as firms seek to avoid tariffs by relocating production from China to these lower-cost alternatives (Y. Zhou, 2020). Still, employment returning to the U.S. remained low against the odds of expectations, due to less-labor intensive production by using automation and other modern technologies (Hanson, 2020). In conclusion, the U.S.-China trade war has had profound effects on GVCs, compelling MNEs to make necessary adjustments while diversifying risks and seeking alternative trade partners. As firms and countries continue to adapt to the evolving nature of global markets, the trade war will have increasingly evident implications for the distribution of manufacturing and trade worldwide.

## 2.3 U.S.-China Competition in Semiconductors and 5G

One of the most important issues surrounding the U.S.-China trade war is the technology rivalry, particularly in the context of the semiconductor industry and 5G. U.S. export restrictions on Huawei, one of the largest chip buyers globally, have significant implications not only for the company and the U.S. but also for GVCs and MNEs worldwide, as semiconductors are crucial components in smartphones, computers, automobiles, and more. While the semiconductor industry also played a key role in the U.S.-Japan trade dispute in the 1980s, the current U.S.-China trade war is different due to more globally integrated supply chains. While the 100% increase in Japanese semiconductor imports to the U.S. led South Korea and Taiwan to become key producers in the industry, China has steadily increased its share of semiconductor production, supported by significant FDI inflows. As of 2023, the U.S. semiconductor industry accounts for 50.2% of global sales revenue, followed by South Korea with 14%, Europe with 12%, Japan with 9%, and Taiwan with 7%, according to a report by the Semiconductor Industry Association (SIA) published in 2024 (SIA, 2024).

Although China holds 7% of the global market share in the industry, Chinese products have been of lower quality and lag behind global technological standards, which has led to increased semiconductor imports from the U.S., supported extensively by the Chinese government (Bown, 2020). While this was one of the reasons for the U.S. imposing 25% tariffs on Chinese semiconductors in 2018 due, China continued to import U.S. semiconductor products. This prompted the U.S. to take further action on the global semiconductor supply chain, including limiting sales of certain technology products to Huawei in 2019, which led to a decline in the company's revenue by 4% to 9% (Varas & Varadarajan, 2020). The Phase One deal in 2020 did not effectively address these concerns, and restrictions on U.S. technology exports to Huawei remain in place due to national security considerations (Bown, 2020).

In this regard, these barriers have significant implications for the 5G sector, particularly focusing on Huawei. Despite Huawei's rapid expansion in recent years, becoming a leading global information and communication technology provider, the U.S. has restricted access to high-tech exports to China, cutting off Huawei's global supply chain and boycotting Huawei products in the U.S. and allied countries, including Australia, Japan and New Zealand (Jaisal, 2020). The restrictions imposed by the U.S. have had negative outcomes for both Huawei and the companies integrated into GVCs. While Huawei faced a short-term supply shortage of high-end components and experienced an approximately 62% decline in cash flow, the U.S. ban on Huawei also hurt its suppliers worldwide, many of which are American companies, resulting in a decline in their stock value (L. Wang, 2022). Despite U.S. lobbying and sanctions against Huawei, some countries continued their cooperation with the company. As BRICS members, Russia and China agreed to launch 5G networks in Russia in 2019 (BBC, 2019), and as one of the new members, the UAE expanded its collaboration with Huawei to build 5G networks in the country (Huawei, 2024). Even some NATO allies, especially such as Türkiye, Germany, Italy and South Korea have allowed Huawei to play a significant role in their 5G infrastructure (Jaisal, 2020). The U.S.-China trade war, particularly in semiconductors and 5G, has had profound short- and long-term impacts on MNEs and GVCs. U.S. export restrictions on Huawei have disrupted these global networks, as companies like Qualcomm and Intel, which rely heavily on both U.S. and Chinese markets, faced revenue losses and stock declines (L. Wang, 2022).

While the U.S. has been somewhat successful in suppressing Huawei in the short term, BRICS nations and some NATO allies have expanded their cooperation with the company, illustrating the complex dynamics of global business. MNEs may eventually diversify their supply chains away from China, potentially benefiting countries like India and Vietnam but also leading to inefficiencies and higher costs. In the long term, China's rapid technological advancements may challenge U.S. technological leadership, prompting further U.S. measures. This shift reflects a broader move away from the U.S. advocacy for free trade, as national security and economic interests increasingly dominate policy, potentially leading to the emergence of parallel supply chains that reshape global trade and innovation (Ryan & Burman, 2024).

The next section of the study will delve into the role of BRICS countries during the U.S.-China trade war, analyzing their individual and collective responses in the global economy. It will explore how BRICS countries have positioned themselves, leveraging their economic relationships to enhance cooperation, mitigate risks, and seize emerging opportunities. By examining the strategies and actions of BRICS countries, this analysis illuminates the influence of BRICS in reshaping the global trade landscape amid ongoing geopolitical tensions.

## 3. THE ROLE OF BRICS IN THE CONTEXT OF THE U.S-CHINA TRADE WAR

The U.S.-China trade war has serious implications not only for the world's two largest economies but also for the broader international economic landscape around the world. The BRICS nations—Brazil, Russia, India, China, and South Africa are the key players in this context with their collective and individual responses in shaping the ongoing shifts in global trade patterns, highlighting the strategic importance of these emerging economies in a new world order. This section of the study will examine the role of BRICS nations in the U.S.-China trade war while focusing on their strategic responses and the consequent shifts in global trade dynamics, to understand their increasing influence in the evolving international economic order.

After the onset of the trade war, the BRICS countries first responded to this conflict by increasing their economic cooperation and strengthening intra-group trade and financial ties. The purpose of this strategy is to reduce dependency on Western markets and to buffer against external shocks. For instance, Asian Infrastructure Investment Bank (AIIB) and the New Development Bank (NDB) were established as alternatives to U.S.-led entities, such as the International Monetary Fund (IMF) and the World Bank (H. Wang, 2019), with the aim of support development projects and promote economic growth within BRICS nations and other developing countries. Moreover, the expansion of BRICS with the inclusion of Iran, Egypt, Ethiopia, and the UAE in 2023, represents a significant step toward enhancing the group's global influence and increasing its economic and political power.

In this context, the next sections will examine the individual and collective actions of BRICS members, while exploring how BRICS countries are contributing to the shift toward a more multipolar world order, challenging U.S. dominance in global markets, and promoting a more balanced global economic structure in the world. Additionally, the last sub-section will focus on BRICS nations' trade strategies and supply chain management after Covid-19 Pandemic.

### 3.1 Strategic Responses and Shifts in Global Trade Dynamics

This section highlights the individual strategies that each of the BRICS countries adopted, with each resorting to a distinct strategy to use its position within the alliance in the best possible way, while at the same time trying to minimize the risks resulting from these new economic conditions. It analyzes how each member country reacted toward the trade war.

As a result of the increased tariffs and trade barriers, the Chinese economy suffered from lower GDP growth rates, a shrinking trade surplus against the U.S., reduced industrial output, and fluctuating inflation rates due to the combined effects of the trade war and post-COVID-19 conditions. To counteract these challenges, China turned to its BRICS partners, seeking to strengthen economic ties and explore alternative markets. For example, China shifted its soybean imports from the U.S. to Brazil (Dhoubhadel et al., 2023), while diversifying its trade relationships with other countries, particularly within the BRICS bloc.

Additionally, the trade war has accelerated China's Belt and Road Initiative (BRI), which aims to expand the range of product categories and trade values in its exports and imports, increase trade quantities while lowering unit values, and ultimately create jobs and improve welfare for both China and its trading partners, despite a reduction in its trade surplus c Consequently, the Chinese government has strategically aimed not only to foster greater economic integration within the BRICS alliance but also to reduce China's dependency on Western markets and diversify its export markets. By enhancing intra-BRICS trade and investment, China seeks to mitigate the impact of external economic disruptions and establish a more resilient and diversified economic network capable of withstanding global trade tensions. Figures 6 and 7 illustrate China's exports and imports with other BRICS countries and the U.S. from 2001 to 2021, highlighting key aspects of China's trade relationships in the context of the trade war. These graphs are crucial for understanding how China strengthened its trade with BRICS countries to mitigate the impact of the trade war, showcasing a diversification in its foreign trade strategies and offering a comparison with its trade relationship with the U.S.

*Figure 6. China exports to BRICS and the U.S (2001-2021)*

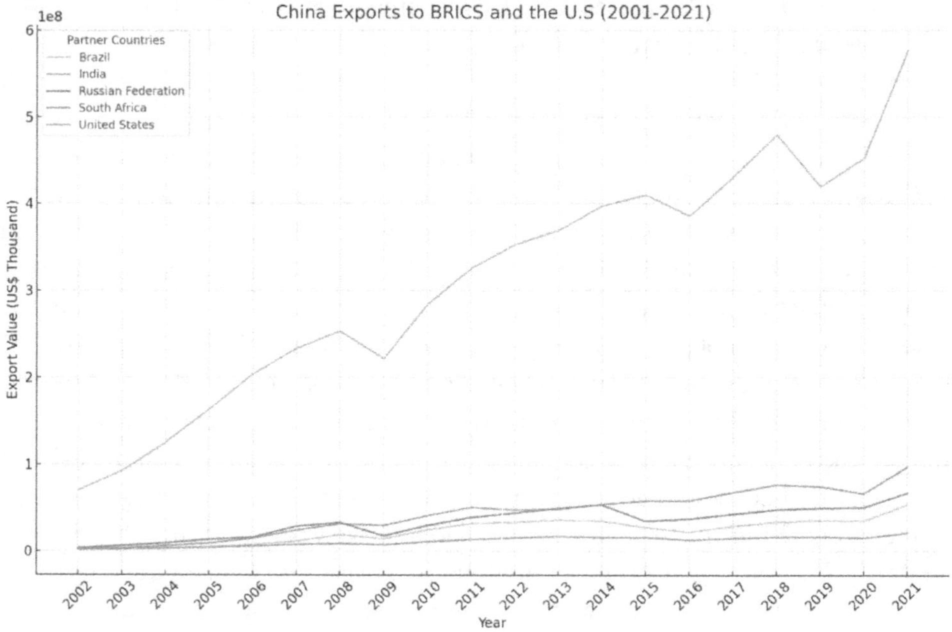


*(WITS, 2024c)*

The most notable feature of the chart is the sharp contrast in the scale and growth trajectory of Chinese exports to the U.S. compared to those to BRICS countries. While China's exports to the U.S. consistently outpaced those to any BRICS country, the chart reveals fluctuations during the escalation of the U.S.-China trade war. However, a strong recovery in exports to the U.S. by 2021 suggests that the trade war did not fundamentally weaken the long-term trade relationship between the two countries, likely due to the deep integration of their economies.

In contrast, China's exports to BRICS countries are relatively small and exhibit a steadier trend compared to those with the U.S., with India and Russia being the largest BRICS markets for Chinese exports. The relatively modest growth in exports to BRICS countries may indicate limited success in China's efforts to diversify its export markets following the onset of the trade war in 2018. Nonetheless, the difference in export values between the U.S. and BRICS countries underscores China's significant economic dependence on the U.S. market, even during periods of intense trade conflict.

Although BRICS countries are important trade partners for China, they have not yet emerged as a substitute for the U.S. in terms of export volume. This could influence China's future trade strategies, highlighting potential vulnerabilities in its export-driven economy and suggesting a need to diversify export markets. China may intensify efforts to strengthen economic ties within BRICS and with other countries to reduce its reliance on the U.S. market.

*Figure 7. China imports to BRICS and the U.S (2001-2021)*

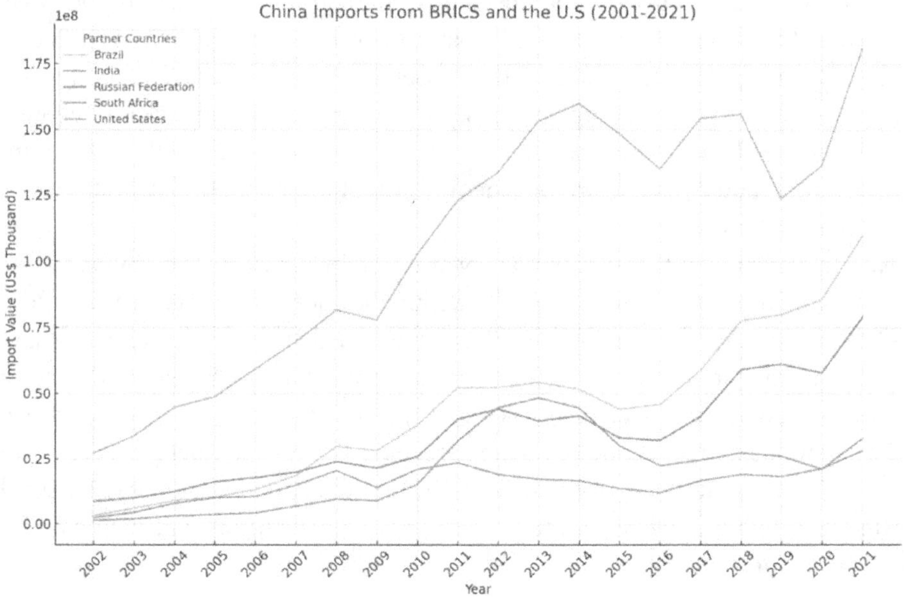


*(WITS, 2024d)*

Figure 7 illustrates China's import values from BRICS countries and the U.S. between 2001 and 2021, offering crucial insights into the evolution of China's import relationships, particularly in the context of the U.S.-China trade war. As with export trends, China's imports from the U.S. consistently surpassed those from any BRICS country, highlighting the U.S.'s significant role as a key supplier to China. However, noticeable fluctuations emerge post-2018, marking the onset of the trade war and the subsequent impacts of tariffs and other trade restrictions imposed by both countries.

A particularly significant aspect of the chart is the decline in imports from the U.S. around 2019, corresponding to the peak of the trade war. This dip reflects the impact of China's measures to reduce imports of U.S. goods. Nevertheless, the strong recovery in imports following this period underscores the deep economic interdependence between the two nations. Similar to the export figures, the import chart suggests that while the trade war disrupted U.S.-China trade in the short term, it did not result in any long-term declines. Yet, the dip in 2019 implies the vulnerability of China's supply chain to geopolitical tensions with the U.S. Imports

On the other hand, imports from BRICS members demonstrate a generally steady upward trajectory, with notable increases from Brazil, India, and Russia. Among these, Brazil has shown substantial growth in its exports to China, likely driven by the increasing export of food products. This rise may also reflect China's strategic efforts to diversify its import sources and strengthen trade ties within the BRICS bloc. Such diversification appears to be part of a broader strategy to reduce reliance on the U.S., particularly in critical sectors like energy (from Russia) and food security (from Brazil). In the following sections, the individual roles of BRICS countries will be analyzed in the context of the U.S.-China trade war, with each country contributing uniquely based on its economic structure, geopolitical strategies, and global trade relationships.

Russia's role in the U.S.-China trade war is notably characterized by its strategic trade partnership with China, especially within the energy sector (Gusarova, 2019). While sanctions against to Russia were increased due to the Ukrainian-Russian war, Russia and China has deepened their economic collaborations. In this regard, Russia boosted its energy exports to China by reducing the negative consequences of the sanctions and its economic dependence on Western markets. Figure 8 highlights China's fuel imports from 2001 to 2021, while showing the increasing roles of Russia, a fellow BRICS country, in adapting to sanctions and navigating the complexities of trade war.

*Figure 8. China's fuel imports by country (2001-2021)*

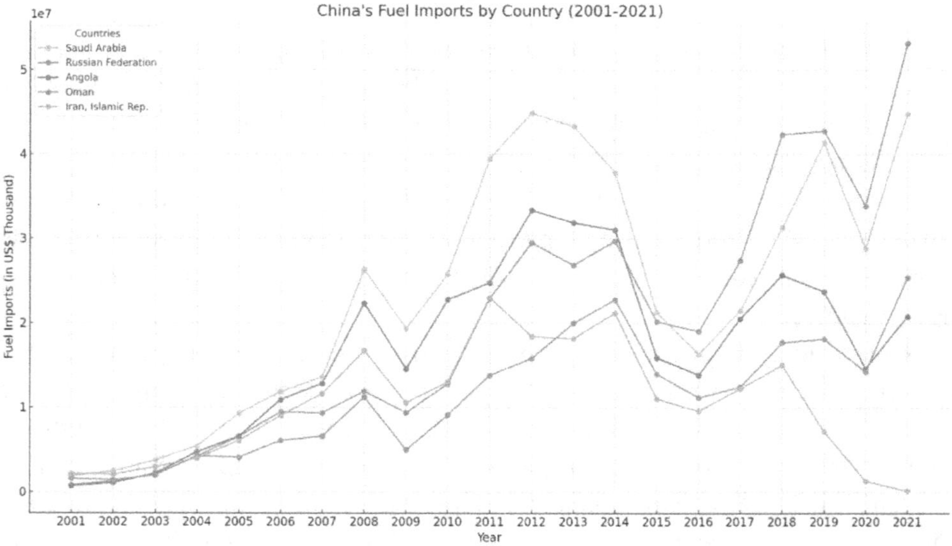


*(WITS, 2024d)*

China's fuel imports from Russia and Saudi Arabia have been increasing over the years, particularly after 2018, while reflecting strategic shifts in response to the trade conflict. Both countries are strengthening their economic ties with China to mitigate the effects of Western sanctions and tariffs. Russia's sharp rise in fuel exports to China aligns with its broader strategy of deepening economic cooperation with China, a fellow BRICS member, as a counterbalance to U.S. influence. Furthermore, Russia has increasingly aligned with China in opposing U.S. dominance in global trade and finance, thereby reinforcing the BRICS and Shanghai Cooperation Organization (SCO) as counterweights to Western hegemony (Sun, 2021).

In this context, it is important that all BRICS members should transform their energy sources to renewable energy to reduce environmental pollution while gradually phasing out fossil fuel dependency in their countries (Caglar et al., 2022). By doing so, BRICS members would not only improve their environmental quality but also reduce their dependence on third countries, thereby benefitting from the advantages of using renewable energy sources.

The U.S.-China trade war particularly affected Brazil due to its role as a major agricultural exporter. While the Chinese tariffs on American agricultural products negatively affect the imports of, soybeans from the U.S. (Dhoubhadel et al., 2023), this created a significant opportunity for Brazil to emerge as a primary supplier to China for agricultural and food products. Consequently, Brazil's agribusiness sector saw a substantial increase in exports to China, as shown in the below figure. Figure 9 illustrates China's food imports by country from 2001 to 2021, highlighting the shifts in China's food product imports from key trading partners and the impact of the U.S.-China trade war. This figure underscores how the trade war reshaped global agricultural trade flows, with Brazil benefiting from increased demand for its agricultural products in the Chinese market.

*Figure 9. China's food product imports by country (2001-2021)*

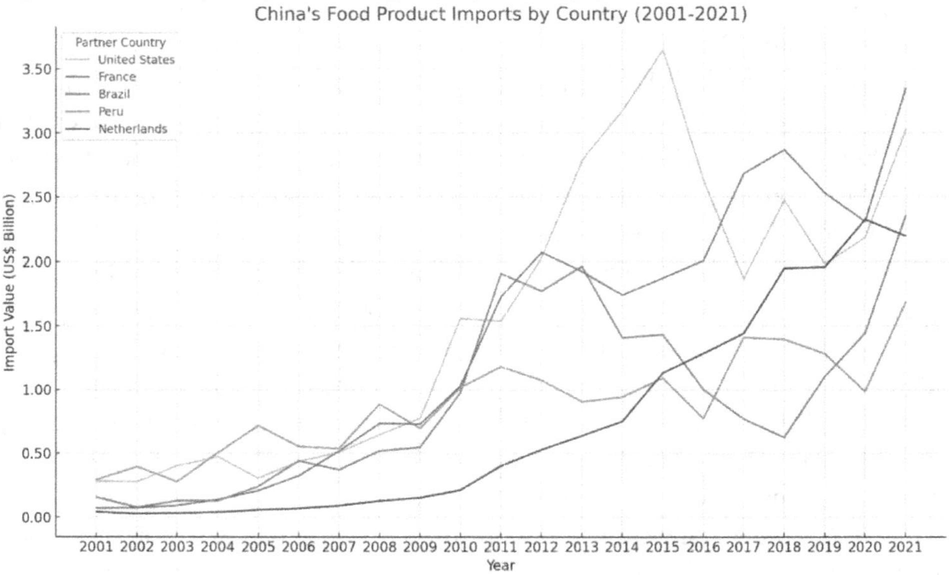


*(WITS, 2024c)*

The graph illustrates China's food product imports from top five countries—U.S., France, Brazil, Peru, and the Netherlands—over the period from 2001 to 2021. The overall trend shows a significant increase in China's food imports from all these countries. During the U.S.-China trade war, fluctuations in trade patterns reflected the impact of tariffs and counter-tariffs imposed by both nations, which disrupted traditional trade flows and prompted China to reassess its reliance on U.S. agricultural products. However, by 2021, there was a partial recovery in U.S. exports to China, highlighting the ongoing demand for U.S. food products, likely driven by China's large population and its need for stable food supplies.

In response to the trade tensions, China increasingly turned to BRICS countries like Brazil to maintain economic resilience. The complementary nature of Brazil's agricultural products, as opposed to direct competition, has created a strong potential for further cooperation and development between Brazil and China (F. Zhang, 2021). The steady increase in imports from Brazil during this period underscores Brazil's critical role in China's strategy to diversify its food import sources and mitigate the risks posed by the trade war. By strengthening trade ties with Brazil and other BRICS nations, China was able to reduce its dependency on U.S. imports, thereby diminishing the leverage the U.S. held during the trade conflict.

India's position in the U.S.-China trade war is more complex than that of any other BRICS member. On one hand, India has sought to capitalize on the trade disruptions by positioning itself as an alternative manufacturing hub to China (Basu & Ray,

2022). The Indian government has implemented policies to attract MNEs) seeking to diversify their supply chains away from China, leading some major MNEs, such as Apple, Mercedes-Benz, and BMW, to shift their production facilities to India (Kumar, 2021; Mudambi et al., 2017). On the other hand, India's trade relationship with China is significant, particularly in sectors such as electronics and pharmaceuticals (Bhattacharjea, 2005), which makes India cautious in fully aligning against China. India's participation in BRICS and the Shanghai Cooperation Organization (SCO) has been marked by strategic diplomacy, balancing its relations with both the U.S. and China while advocating for a multipolar global trade system, despite the ambivalent nature of its relationship with China (Horimoto, 2014).

As a major exporter of minerals to China (WITS, 2024f), South Africa's role remains significant within the broader context of BRICS countries in the U.S.-China trade war. Despite some arguments questioning South Africa's membership in BRICS due to its relatively smaller economy compared to other members, its role is crucial as a financial and logistical gateway to Sub-Saharan Africa (Deych, 2015). The relationship between China and South Africa is a double-edged sword, offering some economic benefits as well as some challenges due to the over-reliance on the Chinese market for exports. On one hand, relying on Chinese exports increases the vulnerability of the South African economy due to dependence on a single market. On the other hand, BRICS membership has elevated South Africa's status as a global player, bringing new opportunities such as infrastructural and developmental investments, enriched educational exchanges, and technology transfers (Anuoluwapo et al., 2018).

The next section will analyze the net inward investments in China and China's outward investments in BRICS countries to understand the collective responses of the BRICS countries in the context of the U.S.-China trade, which are important to strengthen economic integration and navigate the challenges posed by the U.S-China trade war.

## 3.2 Collective Response and Economic Cooperation Within BRICS

After the onset of the trade war between the two largest economies, the role of BRICS to challenge the dominance of traditional Western powers has become more significant in the evolving global environment. In recent years, the BRICS countries have made significant strides in fostering economic cooperation within the bloc. However, the effectiveness of their collective response to the U.S.-China trade war has been mixed, revealing several underlying challenges. To illustrate these mixed results, Figure 10 presents the net inward investment equity positions of the

BRICS countries and the U.S. in China. This figure highlights the resilience of the U.S.-China relationship, despite some short-term fluctuations due to the trade war.

*Figure 10. Inward direct investment equity positions in China by BRICS countries vs. U.S. (2009-2022)*

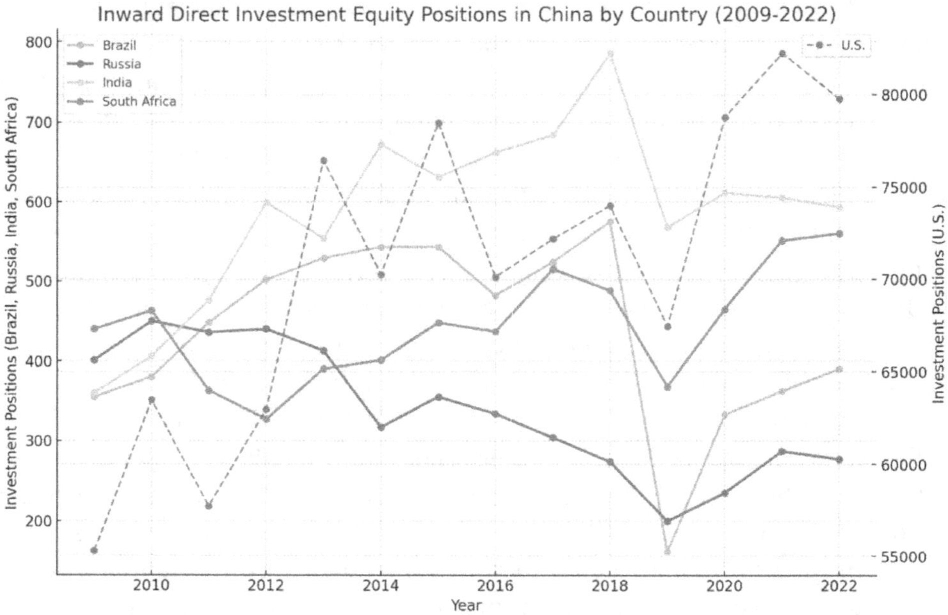


*(IMF CDIS, 2024)*

As seen in the figure above, U.S. investment in China exhibited a generally upward trend, with a significant disparity compared to the investments of BRICS countries in China. The most notable feature of the chart is the sharp dip and subsequent recovery in U.S. direct investment equity positions in China during the period from 2019 to 2020, following the initiation of the trade war, underscoring the resilience and strategic importance of the Chinese market to U.S. investors.

In contrast, the investment patterns of BRICS countries show relative stability or modest fluctuations compared to the U.S. Brazil and Russia exhibit relatively low levels of investment in China, influenced by post-2014 economic sanctions and Brazil's economic challenges. India's investment in China shows a steady increase, peaking in 2018, followed by slight fluctuations, likely impacted by the trade war. South Africa displays a generally stable investment pattern, with a slight increase over time. In this context, the trade war appears to have had a minimal impact on the already low investment levels of these BRICS countries. Consequently, it can be suggested that BRICS members are not positioned to substitute the role of the

U.S. in terms of inward investments, which underscores the complexity and interdependence of the U.S.-China economic relationship. Meanwhile, investments from BRICS countries to China have exhibited varying trends, with no clear impact from the trade war, indicating that their investment decisions are influenced by a range of factors, such as geopolitical issues and domestic market conditions.

In the context of the U.S.-China trade war, three key points emerge regarding the collective response and economic cooperation among BRICS members: the strengthening of intra-BRICS trade and financial cooperation, the creation of alternative global financial institutions such as the AIIB and the NDB, and the significance of BRICS expansion in 2023. After the onset of the U.S.-China trade war, the BRICS nations significantly intensified their intra-group trade and financial cooperation as a strategic response to mitigate the negative impacts of the trade tensions and volatility in global markets. In this regard, China has played a pivotal role in enhancing economic, political, and social cooperation among BRICS members, while also promoting South-South cooperation and challenging the dominance of the global North (Shamase, 2019). As mentioned previously, existing data shows the vulnerability of China's export-oriented economy to disruptions in its largest market, the U.S., highlighting an urgent need to find new markets to reduce this vulnerability. Thus, BRICS countries emerge as key partners for China, serving as alternative markets and sources of critical imports.

The New Development Bank (NDB), established by the BRICS countries in 2015, and the Asian Infrastructure Investment Bank (AIIB), established by China in 2016, also aim to provide resources for infrastructure and sustainable economic development (AIIB, 2024; NDB, 2024). These initiatives allow BRICS members to ensure mutual economic stability independent of the support of western-based institutions (Moak, 2017), and thus avoid the effects of external problems such as the US-China trade war. In fact, projects such as OBOR can create alternative trade routes and provide easy access to European markets through cooperation with China. As a result, with OBOR, AIIB and other initiatives (Kohl, 2019), China is trying to change the global economic order and reduce American influence with the support of BRICS countries.

Another recent development in BRICS that could affect the global balance is the accession of countries such as Egypt, Ethiopia, the UAE, and potentially Saudi Arabia. With these new members, BRICS would represent approximately 27% of global GDP (World Bank, 2024a) and encompass 45% of the world's population (World Bank, 2024e), extending its reach from the Middle East and North Africa (MENA) to Sub-Saharan Africa. While cooperation between China and Russia in the fossil energy trade further solidifies BRICS' influence in the global energy sector (Chen et al., 2021), the inclusion of Saudi Arabia, Iran, and the UAE—some of the world's largest oil exporters—will enhance the bloc's role in global energy markets.

Moreover, Egypt's strategic location can provide BRICS with access to Africa through the Suez Canal, further facilitating global trade and increasing BRICS countries' access to African nations from both the south and the north (Ahmed et al., 2020).

## 3.3 Post-Pandemic Trade and Supply Chain Adjustments in BRICS

After 2020, the COVID-19 pandemic profoundly affected global trade and supply chains, exposing vulnerabilities in the current system and prompting countries and MNEs to reconsider their economic strategies. For BRICS countries, the pandemic further accelerated pre-existing trends such as diversifying trading partners, strengthening intra-group trade, and reducing dependence on Western markets, particularly the U.S. and European economies. This chapter examines how BRICS countries have adjusted their post-pandemic trade and supply chain strategies, focusing on both individual and collective actions.

### 3.3.1 Impacts of Supply Chain Disruptions and the Diversification of Supply Chains

Following the pandemic, BRICS countries tried to reduce their dependence on traditional supply chains dominated by Western powers, especially the US, and it was found that the convergence that had been going on since the pre-pandemic period continued in the post-pandemic period (Kumar et al., 2024). The disruptions caused by the pandemic, combined with the impact of the U.S.-China trade war, have prompted each BRICS country to adopt different strategies to overcome these challenges, both individually and collectively.

To diversify alternative trade routes and supply chains outside U.S. influence, China has accelerated its Belt and Road Initiative and established various trade corridors with other countries to ensure its economy remains resilient by reducing dependence on the U.S. market (J. Wang & Tian, 2022). As discussed in Section 3.1, although China's exports and imports with all BRICS countries have increased in the post-pandemic period, they remain significantly lower than its trade volume with the U.S. However, China has diversified its supply chains by increasing fuel imports from Russia and Saudi Arabia, which is set to become a new BRICS member, and food imports from countries such as France, Brazil, Peru, and the Netherlands. The complementary nature of agricultural products between China and Brazil, one of the BRICS countries, has created significant potential for long-term cooperation between the two nations (F. Zhang, 2021).

The ongoing U.S.-China trade war has prompted MNEs to adopt a 'China-plus' strategy, partially disengaging from China and shifting parts of their supply chains to other countries. Companies have turned to emerging Asian markets such as Thailand, Malaysia, India, Vietnam, Indonesia, the Philippines, and Bangladesh (Basu & Ray, 2022). In response, India aimed to increase its share of global manufacturing and accelerated its 'Make in India' initiative to attract investments from MNEs in sectors such as textiles, agriculture, leather, jewelry, automobiles, and machinery, as they sought alternatives to China (Nandal et al., 2022).

Russia has increased its energy exports to China and India as part of its strategy to circumvent Western sanctions imposed due to its war with Ukraine. The expansion of Russia's energy trade with China is a significant indication that the two countries can further strengthen their cooperation within multilateral mechanisms, particularly in the economic, political, and security fields, especially in the post-pandemic period (Sun, 2021). Among the BRICS countries, Brazil saw the largest increase in exports to China in the post-pandemic period, becoming a key supplier of soybeans and other food products to meet China's growing demand for agricultural goods. This expansion helped mitigate some of the challenges posed by the pandemic (Dhoubhadel et al., 2023).

Despite having a relatively smaller economy compared to other BRICS countries, South Africa remains a critical player by maintaining stable supply chains for mineral exports, which are essential for the manufacturing sectors in both China and India. South Africa's expansion of its renewable energy capacity over the years (Akinbami et al., 2021) will support the country's post-pandemic economic recovery, while also helping BRICS countries reduce environmental pollution by shifting from fossil fuels to renewable energy sources (Caglar et al., 2022).

### 3.3.2 BRICS Cooperation in the Post-Pandemic World

In addition to the individual strategies of BRICS countries, it is essential for the bloc to enhance economic cooperation in the post-pandemic period to address global supply chain vulnerabilities. Given that BRICS is expected to serve as a new engine of consumption-driven growth in the future, the bloc should consider internal market integration in areas such as trade, foreign investment, and capital markets to counter global challenges like the U.S.-China trade war and the COVID-19 pandemic (Zhongxiu & Qingxin, 2022).

While BRICS countries cooperate among themselves to enhance energy security and collaboration in the use of energy resources, it is equally important that they engage with regional economic blocs in Africa and treat Africa as a common energy market (Simelane & Knop, 2022). In this regard, institutions like the NDB and the AIIB can play pivotal roles in moving away from Western-led economic structures such as the World Bank and the IMF, while supporting both economic development and infrastructure projects (Moak, 2017; H. Wang, 2019). Additionally, the 2023 expansion of BRICS to include Iran, Egypt, Ethiopia, and the UAE has significantly increased the bloc's global influence, positioning it as a major player in global trade, energy, and supply chain management. This expansion boosts the bloc's resilience by incorporating key energy exporters and strategic trade routes, notably Egypt's Suez Canal and South Africa's Cape of Good Hope. As a result, post-pandemic BRICS countries are individually and collectively developing trade and supply chain management strategies to reduce dependence on Western economies, strengthen intra-BRICS cooperation, and promote resilience.

The next section will conclude the study by summarizing the key findings and offering an overview of the diverse impacts of the U.S.-China trade war on the global economy.

## 4. CONCLUSION

This study examines the U.S.-China trade war, one of the major obstacles to globalization in the 21st century, from various perspectives. The findings, derived from macroeconomic variables, highlight the resilience of FDI and bilateral trade during the U.S.-China trade war and underscore the short-term and temporary effects of the dispute. However, the long-term consequences may be more complex than they appear, potentially leading to the restructuring of both countries' economic strategies, as well as global economic strategies. In addition to the trade war, the disruption of GVCs in the post-pandemic period has intensified MNEs' efforts to diversify supply chains across different countries. These strategies can help mitigate uncertainties and risks arising from global disruptions, providing long-term protection against future economic shocks. The results of this study also outline specific strategies that MNEs and governments can adopt. Policymakers should focus on fostering supportive environments for technological innovation, supply chain diversification, and risk management practices for MNEs, which can enable developing countries like BRICS to attract more FDI. At the same time, businesses should prioritize creating flexible alternative supply chains that can quickly adapt and minimize the impact of potential global and regional instabilities.

Furthermore, the study emphasizes the role of BRICS countries in the context of the U.S.-China trade war. Beyond the trade war, BRICS countries have expanded their global influence by enhancing cooperation to address the challenges of the post-pandemic era, establishing alternative financial institutions, and welcoming new members into the bloc in 2023. In the long run, this will allow BRICS countries to strengthen their trade and financial ties, particularly by reducing reliance on foreign markets in the energy and technology sectors. A key recommendation for BRICS countries is to focus on transitioning to renewable energy sources. Replacing traditional energy with renewables will not only reduce the environmental footprint of BRICS countries but also enhance energy security, fostering long-term economic growth and development.

## REFERENCES

Ahmed, Y. N., Hefnawy, F., & Shaker, V. (2020). Egypt's Engagement with the BRICS: Alternative Development Cooperation Initiative "With Reference to Agricultural Trade.". *Journal of Agricultural Economics and Social Sciences*, 11(11), 825–832. DOI: 10.21608/jaess.2020.141887

AIIB. (2024). *About AIIB Introduction*. https://www.aiib.org/en/about-aiib/index.html

Akinbami, O. M., Oke, S. R., & Bodunrin, M. O. (2021). The state of renewable energy development in South Africa: An overview. *Alexandria Engineering Journal*, 60(6), 5077–5093. DOI: 10.1016/j.aej.2021.03.065

Amiti, M., Redding, S., & Weinstein, D. (2019). *The Impact Of The 2018 Trade War On U.S. Prices And Welfare* (25672; NBER Working Paper Series).

Anuoluwapo, D., Abdul-Wasi, M. B., & Edwin, I. (2018). South Africa's Inclusion in BRICS: Challenges and Prospects for Development in Africa. *International Journal of African Renaissance Studies - Multi-, Inter- and Transdisciplinarity, 13*(2), 27–41. DOI: 10.1080/18186874.2018.1519373

Athukorala, P. (2017). China's evolving role in global production networks: Implications for Trump's trade war. In Song, R. L., Garnaut, C. F., & Johnston, L. (Eds.), *China's New Sources of Economic Growth: Human Capital, Innovation and Technological Change* (Vol. 2, pp. 363–388). ANU Press. DOI: 10.22459/CNSEG.07.2017.16

Baldwin, R., & Venables, A. J. (2013). Spiders and snakes: Offshoring and agglomeration in the global economy. *Journal of International Economics*, 90(2), 245–254. DOI: 10.1016/j.jinteco.2013.02.005

Basu, P., & Ray, P. (2022). China-plus-one: Expanding global value chains. *The Journal of Business Strategy*, 43(6), 350–356. DOI: 10.1108/JBS-04-2021-0066

BBC. (2019, June 19). *Huawei signs deal with Russian telecoms firm to develop 5G*. https://www.bbc.com/news/business-48537643

Bekkers, E., Koopman, R. B., & Rêgo, C. L. (2021). Structural change in the Chinese economy and changing trade relations with the world. *China Economic Review*, 65, 101573. DOI: 10.1016/j.chieco.2020.101573

Bekkers, E., & Schroeter, S. (2020). *An Economic Analysis of The Us-China Trade Conflict*.

Bellora, C., & Fontagné, L. (2019). Shooting Oneself in the Foot? *Trade War and Global Value Chains*, 2019, 18.

Benguria, F., & Saffie, F. (2019). *Dissecting the Impact of the 2018-2019 Trade War on U.S. Exports.* DOI: 10.2139/ssrn.3505413

Berger, B., & Martin, R. F. (2011). *The Growth of Chinese Exports: An Examination of the Detailed Trade Data* (1033; International Finance Discussion Papers).

Bhattacharjea, A. (2005). India's Trade Relations with China and Russia in the Context of WTO. *China Report (New Delhi, India)*, 41(4), 427–435. DOI: 10.1177/000944550504100407

Bown, C. P. (2020). How the United States Marched the Semiconductor Industry into Its Trade War with China. *East Asian Economic Review*, 24(4), 349–388. DOI: 10.11644/KIEP.EAER.2020.24.4.384

Bown, C. P. (2021). The US–China trade war and Phase One agreement. *Journal of Policy Modeling*, 43(4), 805–843. DOI: 10.1016/j.jpolmod.2021.02.009

Bureau of Economic Analysis. (2024, July 23). *Direct Investment & Multinational Enterprises (MNEs).* Bureau of Economic Analysis. https://www.bea.gov/itable/direct-investment-multinational-enterprises

Caglar, A. E., Guloglu, B., & Gedikli, A. (2022). Moving towards sustainable environmental development for BRICS: Investigating the asymmetric effect of natural resources on $CO_2$. *Sustainable Development (Bradford)*, 30(5), 1313–1325. DOI: 10.1002/sd.2318

Carrière-Swallow, Y., Deb, P., Furceri, D., Jiménez, D., & Ostry, J. D. (2023). Shipping costs and inflation. *Journal of International Money and Finance*, 130, 102771. DOI: 10.1016/j.jimonfin.2022.102771 PMID: 36466049

Chatterjee, S., Chaudhuri, R., Vrontis, D., Dana, L.-P., & Kabbara, D. (2024). Developing resilience of MNEs: From global value chain (GVC) capability and performance perspectives. *Journal of Business Research*, 172, 114447. DOI: 10.1016/j.jbusres.2023.114447

Chen, J., Xie, Q., Shahbaz, M., Song, M., & Wu, Y. (2021). The fossil energy trade relations among BRICS countries. *Energy*, 217, 119383. DOI: 10.1016/j.energy.2020.119383

Deych, T. (2015). BRICS as an Important Actor in Africa. *Insight on Africa*, 7(2), 169–185. DOI: 10.1177/0975087815581459

Dhoubhadel, S. P., Ridley, W., & Devadoss, S. (2023). Brazilian soybean expansion, US–China trade war, and US soybean exports. *Journal of the Agricultural and Applied Economics Association*, 2(3), 446–460. DOI: 10.1002/jaa2.71

Fajgelbaum, P. D., & Khandelwal, A. K. (2022). The Economic Impacts of the US–China Trade War. *Annual Review of Economics*, 14(1), 205–228. DOI: 10.1146/annurev-economics-051420-110410

Fu, Q. (2023). The impact of global value chain embedding on the upgrading of China's manufacturing industry. *Frontiers in Energy Research*, 11, 1256317. Advance online publication. DOI: 10.3389/fenrg.2023.1256317

Fusacchia, I. (2020). Evaluating the Impact of the US–China Trade War on Euro Area Economies: A Tale of Global Value Chains. *Italian Economic Journal*, 6(3), 441–468. DOI: 10.1007/s40797-019-00109-9

Gusarova, S. (2019). Role of China in the development of trade and FDI cooperation with BRICS countries. *China Economic Review*, 57, 101271. DOI: 10.1016/j.chieco.2019.01.010

Hanson, G. H. (2020). The impacts of the U.S.–China trade war. *Business Economics (Cleveland, Ohio)*, 55(2), 69–72. DOI: 10.1057/s11369-020-00163-7

Horimoto, T. (2014). Ambivalent Relations of India and China: Cooperation and Caution. *Journal of Contemporary East Asia Studies*, 3(2), 61–92. DOI: 10.1080/24761028.2014.11869075

Huawei. (2024, February 26). *Huawei and du Sign Strategic Cooperation MOU, Building the 5G Advanced Country*. https://www.huawei.com/en/news/2024/2/5ga-du-mou

IMF CDIS. (2024). *Inward Direct Investment Positions, as enf of 2022, Reporting Economy: China*. https://data.imf.org/regular.aspx?key=61227424

Itakura, K. (2020). Evaluating the Impact of the US–China Trade War. *Asian Economic Policy Review*, 15(1), 77–93. DOI: 10.1111/aepr.12286

Jaisal, E. K. (2020). The US, China and Huawei Debate on 5G Telecom Technology: Global Apprehensions and the Indian Scenario. *Open Political Science*, 3(1), 66–72. DOI: 10.1515/openps-2020-0006

Kapustina, L., Lipková, Ľ., Silin, Y., & Drevalev, A. (2020). US-China Trade War: Causes and Outcomes. *SHS Web of Conferences, 73*, 01012. DOI: 10.1051/shsconf/20207301012

Kohl, T. (2019). The Belt and Road Initiative's effect on supply-chain trade: Evidence from structural gravity equations. *Cambridge Journal of Regions, Economy and Society*, 12(1), 77–104. DOI: 10.1093/cjres/rsy036

Kumar, R. (2021). The Supply Chain Diversification and India–South Korea Cooperation in a Contested East Asia in the Post-COVID-19 Era. *The Journal of Indian and Asian Studies*, 02(02), 2140007. Advance online publication. DOI: 10.1142/S2717541321400076

Kumar, R., Kumar, P., Shimpi, L. S., & Verma, O. P. (2024). Specifying The Study Of Trade And Convergence Of Brics Economies In Post Pandemic Era. *International Journal of Engineering Technology and Management Sciences*, 8(1), 71–82. DOI: 10.46647/ijetms.2024.v08i01.010

Leibovici, F., & Dunn, J. (2021). Supply Chain Bottlenecks and Inflation: The Role of Semiconductors. *Economic Synopses, 2021*(28). DOI: 10.20955/es.2021.28

Liang, L., & Toshiyuki, M. (2023). *Adjustments of Multinational's Production Activities in Response to the US-Sino Trade War : Evidence from Japanese affiliate-level data* (745; Discussion Paper Series).

Liu, T., & Woo, W. T. (2018). Understanding the U.S.-China Trade War. *China Economic Journal*, 11(3), 319–340. DOI: 10.1080/17538963.2018.1516256

Mao, H., & Görg, H. (2020). Friends like this: The impact of the US–China trade war on global value chains. *World Economy*, 43(7), 1776–1791. DOI: 10.1111/twec.12967

Moak, K. (2017). BRICS and China Initiated Global Trade Initiatives and Financial Institutions: Alternatives to the US-Dominated IMF and WBG and ADB. In *Developed Nations and the Economic Impact of Globalization* (pp. 211–223). Springer International Publishing. DOI: 10.1007/978-3-319-57903-0_10

Mudambi, R., Saranga, H., & Schotter, A. (2017). Mastering the Make-in-India Challenge. *MIT Sloan Management Review*, •••, 59.

Nandal, N., Nandal, N., Dhaka, P., & Kataria, A. (2022). U.S.–China Trade War & Its Implications on India. *Korea Review of International Studies*, 15(5), 66–72.

NDB. (2024). *The Premier Bank for Emerging Economies*. https://www.ndb.int/about-ndb/

Nie, J., von Ende-Becker, A., & Yang, S.-K. X. (2021). *How Did the 2018–19 U.S. Tariff Hikes Influence Household Spending?* The Federal Reserve Bank of Kansas City Economic Review., DOI: 10.18651/ER/v106n4NievonEndeBeckerYang

Peng, J., & Zhang, Y. (2020). Impact of Global Value Chains on Export Technology Content of China's Manufacturing Industry. *Sustainability (Basel)*, 12(1), 432. DOI: 10.3390/su12010432

Qin, M., Fan, Z., & Zhong, Y. (2022). The Global Value Chain and Welfare Effects of Tariffs—Counterfactual Analysis of Sino–US Economic and Trade Frictions. *Sustainability (Basel)*, 14(14), 8280. DOI: 10.3390/su14148280

Ryan, M., & Burman, S. (2024). The United States–China 'tech war': Decoupling and the case of Huawei. *Global Policy*, 15(2), 355–367. DOI: 10.1111/1758-5899.13352

Santacreu, A. M., & LaBelle, J. (2022). Global Supply Chain Disruptions and Inflation During the COVID-19 Pandemic. *Federal Reserve Bank of St. Louis Review, Second Quarter*, 78–91. DOI: 10.20955/r.104.78-91

Sarkar, A. (2019). *Policy Uncertainty, Multinational Firms, and Reallocation*. DOI: 10.2139/ssrn.4182128

Shamase, M. Z. (2019). The role of China in the BRICS' cooperation on development shaping a new and balanced world order? *Africa Insight*, 48(4).

Shea, D. (2018). *Ambassador Shea: China's trade-disruptive economic model and implications for the WTO*. Statement Delivered at the WTO General Council.

Shen, X., Liang, J., Cao, J., & Wang, Z. (2022). How Population Aging Affects Industrial Structure Upgrading: Evidence from China. *International Journal of Environmental Research and Public Health*, 19(23), 16093. DOI: 10.3390/ijerph192316093 PMID: 36498168

SIA. (2024). *2024 State of the U.S. Semiconductor Industry*.

Simelane, T., & Knop, J. (2022). Opportunities and Options for Energy Cooperation Among BRICS Countries. In Zondi, S. (Ed.), *The Political Economy of Intra-BRICS Cooperation* (pp. 79–97). Palgrave Macmillan., DOI: 10.1007/978-3-030-97397-1_5

Stojković, R., & Milosavljević, S. (2023). BRICS TENDENCIES TOWARDS REDEFINING THE GLOBAL ECONOMIC ORDER. *Science International Journal*, 2(4), 7–11. DOI: 10.35120/sciencej0204007s

Sun, Z. (2021). Progress and Prospects: Sino-Russian Strategic Coordination in Multilateral Mechanisms. *Chinese Journal of Slavic Studies*, 1(1), 79–91. DOI: 10.1515/cjss-2021-2006

The White House. (2024, May 14). *FACT SHEET: President Biden Takes Action to Protect American Workers and Businesses from China's Unfair Trade Practices.* https://www.whitehouse.gov/briefing-room/statements-releases/2024/05/14/fact-sheet-president-biden-takes-action-to-protect-american-workers-and-businesses-from-chinas-unfair-trade-practices/

Tian, W., Yu, M., & Zheng, C. (2022). *China's Retaliatory Tariffs Against the US:-Firm Import-Export Linkage Along Global Production Line* (E2022002; Working Paper Series).

Tyers, R. (2016). Slower Growth and Vulnerability to Recession: Updating China's Global Impact. *Scottish Journal of Political Economy*, 63(1), 66–88. DOI: 10.1111/sjpe.12111

US Census Bureau. (2024). *Trade in Goods with China.* https://www.census.gov/foreign-trade/balance/c5700.html

USTR. (2018). *2018 Annual Report.* https://ustr.gov/sites/default/files/files/Press/Reports/2018/AR/2018%20Annual%20Report%20I.pdf

Utar, H., Torres Ruiz, L. B., & Zurita, A. C. (2023). *The US-China Trade War and the Relocation of Global Value Chains to Mexico* (10638; CESifo Working Paper Series). DOI: 10.2139/ssrn.4568757

Varas, A., & Varadarajan, R. (2020). *How Restrictions to Trade with China Could End US Leadership in Semiconductors* .

Volgina, N. A., & Pengfei, L. (2021). Trade War Impact on GVCs and China's Counter Measures. In Popkova, E. G., & Sergi, B. S. (Eds.), *Modern Global Economic System: Evolutional Development vs. Revolutionary Leap* (Vol. 198, pp. 2057–2063). Springer., DOI: 10.1007/978-3-030-69415-9_225

Wang, H. (2019). The New Development Bank and the Asian Infrastructure Investment Bank: China's Ambiguous Approach to Global Financial Governance. *Development and Change*, 50(1), 221–244. DOI: 10.1111/dech.12473

Wang, J., & Tian, X. (2022). Impacts of the belt and road initiative on China's bilateral trade. *Journal of the Asia Pacific Economy*, 27(3), 400–424. DOI: 10.1080/13547860.2022.2042110

Wang, L. (2022). China's Huawei in the Us-China Trade War in the Communications Sector Game. *Proceedings of the 2022 2nd International Conference on Enterprise Management and Economic Development (ICEMED 2022)*, 485–497. DOI: 10.2991/aebmr.k.220603.078

WITS. (2024a). *China and U.S. Trade Summary*. https://wits.worldbank.org/CountryProfile/en/Country/CHN/Year/2018/SummaryText

WITS. (2024b). *China Exports by country in US$ Thousand 2001-2021*. https://wits.worldbank.org/CountryProfile/en/Country/CHN/StartYear/2001/EndYear/2021/TradeFlow/Export/Partner/BY-COUNTRY/Indicator/XPRT-TRD-VL

WITS. (2024c). *China Food Products Imports By Country in US$ Thousand 2001-2021*. https://wits.worldbank.org/CountryProfile/en/Country/CHN/StartYear/2001/EndYear/2021/TradeFlow/Import/Indicator/MPRT-TRD-VL/Partner/BY-COUNTRY/Product/16-24_FoodProd

WITS. (2024d). *China Fuels Imports By Country in US$ Thousand 2001-2021*. https://wits.worldbank.org/CountryProfile/en/Country/CHN/StartYear/2001/EndYear/2021/TradeFlow/Import/Indicator/MPRT-TRD-VL/Partner/BY-COUNTRY/Product/27-27_Fuels

WITS. (2024e). *China Imports by country in US$ Thousand 2001-2021*. https://wits.worldbank.org/CountryProfile/en/Country/CHN/StartYear/2001/EndYear/2021/TradeFlow/Import/Partner/BY-COUNTRY/Indicator/MPRT-TRD-VL

WITS. (2024f). *South Africa Minerals Export Product Share By Country in % 2001-2021*. https://wits.worldbank.org/CountryProfile/en/Country/ZAF/StartYear/2001/EndYear/2021/TradeFlow/Export/Indicator/XPRT-PRDCT-SHR/Partner/BY-COUNTRY/Product/25-26_Minerals# World Bank. (2024a). *GDP (current US$) - Brazil, China, India, Russian Federation, South Africa, Iran, Islamic Rep., United Arab Emirates, Egypt, Arab Rep., Ethiopia*. https://data.worldbank.org/indicator/NY.GDP.MKTP.CD?locations=BR-CN-IN-RU-ZA-IR-AE-EG-ET&most_recent_value_desc=true

World Bank. (2024b). *GDP (current US$) - China, United States*. https://data.worldbank.org/indicator/NY.GDP.MKTP.CD?locations=CN-US World Bank. (2024c). *Industry (including construction), value added (% of GDP) - United States, China*. https://data.worldbank.org/indicator/NV.IND.TOTL.ZS?end=2023&locations=US-CN&start=2001

World Bank. (2024d). *Inflation, consumer prices (annual %) - China, United States*. https://data.worldbank.org/indicator/FP.CPI.TOTL.ZG?locations=CN-US World Bank. (2024e). *Population, total - Brazil, China, India, Russian Federation, South Africa, Iran, Islamic Rep., United Arab Emirates, Egypt, Arab Rep., Ethiopia*. https://data.worldbank.org/indicator/SP.POP.TOTL?locations=BR-CN-IN-RU-ZA-IR-AE-EG-ET World Bank. (2024f, March 12). *GDP Rankings 2022*. https://data.worldbank.org/indicator/NY.GDP.MKTP.CD

Wu, J., Wood, J., Oh, K., & Jang, H. (2021). Evaluating the cumulative impact of the US–China trade war along global value chains. *World Economy*, 44(12), 3516–3533. DOI: 10.1111/twec.13125

Xia, Y., Kong, Y., Ji, Q., & Zhang, D. (2019). Impacts of China-US trade conflicts on the energy sector. *China Economic Review*, 58, 101360. DOI: 10.1016/j.chieco.2019.101360

Yi, K.-M. (2010). Can Multistage Production Explain the Home Bias in Trade? *The American Economic Review*, 100(1), 364–393. DOI: 10.1257/aer.100.1.364

Zeng, K., Xu, Y., & Xie, Z. (2023). Local sourcing embeddedness, manufacturing relocation, and firm attitudes toward the US-China trade war: A survey analysis of China-based MNC subsidiaries. *Business and Politics*, 25(2), 91–116. DOI: 10.1017/bap.2022.27

Zhang, F. (2021). Competitiveness or complementarity: Analysis of agricultural trade between China and Brazil. *Problems and Perspectives in Management*, 19(4), 258–269. DOI: 10.21511/ppm.19(4).2021.21

Zhang, H. (2021). *The Impact of COVID-19 on Global Production Networks: Evidence from Japanese Multinational Firms.*

Zhongxiu, Z., & Qingxin, L. (2022). Promoting BRICS cooperation for economic growth and development. [RTM]. *Revista Tempo Do Mundo*, 22, 39–57. DOI: 10.38116/rtm22art2

Zhou, T. (2016). Overcoming the Dilemma of China's Growth. In Tsang, S., & Men, H. (Eds.), *China in the Xi Jinping Era* (pp. 187–219). Palgrave Macmillan., DOI: 10.1007/978-3-319-29549-7_8

Zhou, Y. (2020). *China Trade War and Global Value Chains.*

# Chapter 9
# Can BRICS Currency Dethrone the Dollar?
## Myth or Reality?

**Ayfer Gedikli**
*Duzce University, Turkey*

**Seyfettin Erdogan**
*İstanbul Medeniyet University, Turkey*

## ABSTRACT

*The BRICS members have been working on an alternative currency to the reserve currencies such as US dollar and euro, for international trades and foreign currency reserves to diversify investments, enhance fund security, preserve value, strengthen country relations, improve trade efficiency, and rebalance global financial power. By reducing dependence on the US dollar, they aim to enhance their economic resilience, promote a more multipolar global financial system, and protect against geopolitical and financial risks. The stunning improvements in IT technologies let both sovereign governments and nongovernment entities to initiate their own digital currencies. Between 2017-2024, the number of people using cryptocurrencies increased by more than 70 folds. With these revolutionary improvements and advantages of cyrptocurrencies, there has been a rising question of whether cryptocurrencies can be used as common BRICS money, and whether the proposed BRICS currency dethrone the dollar.*

DOI: 10.4018/979-8-3693-7393-4.ch009

## INTRODUCTION

Representing more than 40% of the world population and 25% of the global economy, the BRICS countries aim to have a stronger voice in the global economic and political system with the new additions to the group, Saudi Arabia, the UAE, Iran, Ethiopia, and Egypt, who have the capacity to influence the current global economic and political balances. The bloc, which was founded in 2009 by Brazil, Russia, India, and China and known as BRIC at that time, began to be known as BRICS with the participation of South Africa the following year. The main objectives of the BRICS are creating an alternative to the global economic system dominated by the US and developed Western economies and ensuring a more equitable distribution of resources in the world economy by defending the economic interests of both theirs and the other developing countries' that cooperate with them. Accordingly, the BRICS countries set some basic goals. First, the BRICS countries aim to accelerate economic growth by cooperating in international trade and investment to decrease the dependence and influence of powerful Western economies. Brazil, one of the founders of the BRICS bloc, is rich in terms of agriculture and natural resources and is the largest economy in South America. Russia is one of the world's largest energy exporters. It is an important player in the global energy sector, especially with its oil and natural gas resources. Iran and Saudi Arabia, which have recently been added to the group, are also countries that play an important role in energy production. India stands out with its rapidly growing population and successful performance in the field of information technologies. China is one of the most populous countries in the world, as well as the second largest economy in the world after the US. It is the leading country of BRICS with its manufacturing capacity. The fifth member of the bloc, South Africa has a strategic location in Africa and is the most developed country on the continent. Egypt is another geopolitically important country in Africa with the Suez Canal. One of the new members of BRICS is Ethiopia is rich in oil and natural gas.

The BRICS, thus try to form a "global regionalized" bloc, within the perspective of a polycentric world order. As the regional powers, the member countries try to have more stability and prosperity through the proactive relations and development of regional integration processes (Lagutina, 2019:445).

Besides, the member countries expect to have a stronger voice to defend their interests in international institutions. BRICS members insist that institutions such as the IMF and the World Bank, which have an important role in the global financial system after World War II and are led by the USA and developed Western countries, should be reformed. According to BRICS developing countries should have a greater weight in global decision-making mechanisms which is still under the influence of the USA and other Western economies. To do so, economic and political solidarity and cooperation with BRICS member countries and other developing countries are crucial for them. An alternative financial system to balance the current financial architecture under the leadership of the USA is important to provide solidarity and cooperation and to have a stronger voice for emerging nations. As a first step toward financial independence, The New Development Bank was established by BRICS in 2014. The New Development Bank provides funding support to the infrastructure projects of emerging countries. Currently, The New Development Bank was tasked to the creation of a common BRICS currency. Creating own currency is considered a major step towards the demise of the dollar (Poenisch, 2023).

The global financial power of the US is so deep that if the US has political/economic conflicts with a country, it is a common policy of the US to initiate sanctions on that country. For example, the US has been imposing sanctions on Iran and Venezuela for many years. Similarly, during the Ukraine War, the Western countries and the US initiated 17.000 sanctions on Russia and froze the Russian reserve dollars and assets in European and US banks (Ramos, 2023). The US Treasury expressed that the financial sanctions were "targeting the architecture of Russia's financial system, which has been reoriented to facilitate investment into its defense industry and acquisition of goods needed to further its aggression against Ukraine". Russia has been punished by being excluded from the SWIFT payment system and the US and its allies suspended the exchange trading and settlements of deliverable instruments in US dollars and euros (Reuters, 2024a). These sanctions clearly demonstrated the power of the US, dollar hegemony over the global financial system, and how the US use its reserve currency as a weapon.

To alleviate the dollar hegemony, the BRICS countries have been searching alternative finance models. For example, since Russia was impacted by the US sanctions and drained of dollars, it has increased the use of rubles in its mutual trade with partner countries to 75% and with China to 95%. Russia and China's trade value is recorded as 240 billion US dollars. The sanctions led Russia to use its national currency in most of the international trade activities. BRICS nations also try to move away from the dollar usage in bilateral trades. China and Brazil announced a trade deal in yuan and real, completely bypassing the dollar (Teslova, 2024; Reuters, 2024b). Besides, Russia has used the yuan in trade transactions with Mongolia, the Philippines, Malaysia, the United Arab Emirates, Thailand, Japan, Tajikistan, and Singapore (Ramos, 2023).

BRICS nations also have the currency union on their agenda. Not only BRICS+ countries which are composed of Brazil, Russia, India, China, South Africa, and new member countries, Saudi Arabia, UAE, Iran, Egypt, and Ethiopia, but also many other emerging countries having problems with using the dollar for exchange and international trade. Limited dollar accumulation causes great financial problems in these countries. It is a fact that reducing dollar usage in international trade and financial transactions will make great changes in global trade and global financial architecture. Aside from using domestic currencies, launching common BRICS currency and issuing cryptocurrency are also in the BRICS countries' agenda.

The tremendous improvements and changes in IT technologies in the last 20 years affected the global financial sector. Particularly digital currencies opened a new era to the global financial system. In recent years, cryptocurrency has become one of the most remarkable fin-tech improvements in this sector. A cryptocurrency is a digital money which is protected by cryptography. One of the most common features of cryptocurrencies is that they have decentralized networks supported by blockchain technologies. Cryptocurrencies are issued by either governments or non-governmental entities to be immune to governmental interference and manipulations (Song et al., 2022). Cryptocurrencies are not only used for payment transfers but also for value preservation and saving resources. Furthermore, the decentralized structure of cryptocurrency provided some other exceptional features to it. Hence cryptocurrency has been discussed about whether it can be an alternative to fiat money, and operate without dependency on sovereign governments and conventional financial systems. The global emergence of digital currencies has resulted in an alternative financial giant with over 9.500 digital currencies worldwide, with more than 2 trillion dollar market value. The growth in the cryptocurrency sector led to a significant transformative impact on fiat money, monetary systems, international exchanges, and sovereign governments (Wang and Wan, 2023).

During the 14th BRICS Summit in 2022, it was the first time Russian President Vladimir Putin mentioned the "new global reserve currency". In the next year, during the 2023 BRICS Summit in Johannesburg, South Africa, Brazil's President Luiz Inacio Lula da Silva offered to create a common currency for the BRICS nations for international trade and investment among the member countries aiming to reduce the vulnerability of their national currencies against the US dollar exchange rate fluctuations (Savage, 2023).

Before the common currency, as expressed above, Russia and China have already started using national currency with the other BRICS+ countries to alleviate the negative impacts of the sanctions. Ruble's share in Russia's international trade reached to 39,4% in 2023. This rate is threefold of 2021. President Putin underlined the importance of the alternative payment system that can strengthen the collaboration between the members. He stated the importance of this platform for efficient foreign trade without relying on another reserve currency such as the US dollar or euro. He added that they can not only create their own currency but also an independent BRICS payment system that involves digital technologies and blockchain systems. President Putin also expressed that the payment system would be cost-effective and free from political interference. It has been discussed that the BRICS currency will be backed by a basket of commodities including gold. In March 2024, there was an official announcement declaring that it will be a digital currency and will be blockchain and it is not clear yet whether it will be gold-backed or not (The Jerusalem Post, 2024; Pistilli, 2024b).

With all these improvements, there has been a rising question of whether cryptocurrencies can be used as common BRICS money as offered, and whether the proposed BRICS currency dethrones the dollar. Will the dollar's dominance as the international reserve currency end? And how could BRICS currency replace with dollar?

With all these questions in mind, in this chapter, the new BRICS currency and its possible effects on the global financial system and international trade will be discussed. Accordingly, after a brief explanation of macroeconomic position of G7 and BRICS countries, how BRICS coin will be launched, and opportunities of a supranational currency for BRICS members will be explained. Finally, pros and cons of the common BRICS currency and whether it can dethrone the US dollar will be discussed.

## G7 VERSUS BRICS

The US dollar has been the world's key reserve currency since World War II, and used in more than 80% of international trade. The US benefitted from this advantage for more than 80 years. After World War II, in 1944, the Bretton Woods system was accepted by 44 nations and initiated a new portwar international monetary system. This system was the adoption of an exchange standard that had both gold and foreign exchanges. According to Bretton Woods system, every country established a par value with respect to the US dollar. Here, dollar was tied to gold at 35 dollars per ounce. This was the first political manoeuvre of the US government to set the dollar as the global reserve currency. However, starting from 1950, the US had to deal with great trade deficits. Development of euro market cause a great outflow of dollars. In the first half of 1970s, the gold exchange standard collapsed (Capie, 2013). The US government announced that they finished the gold exchange standard and fixed dollar parity.

After exiting the Bretton Woods system, the US could raise the amount of dollars as much as it wanted. After the oil crisis in 1973, the US had a petro-dollar agreement with Saudi Arabia to encourage Saudi Arabia to use of the dollar as the medium of exchange for oil sales. The agreement had the condition of buying oil with US dollars and funneling these dollars into the US Treasury bond markets to support the US fiscal deficits. The USA agreed to provide military equipment to protect the national security of Saudi Arabia. Until today, the dollar has been the world's principle reserve, financing, trading, and transactional currency. (Tran, 2024).

For many decades, G7 countries were recognized as the leading countries of the world. And they could set the international politics and control the international trade. While the population of G7 countries was 750-800 million people, they accounted for approximately $46 trillion in GDP. The global dominance of the western countries and the US continued until 2000s. In 2011, Brazil, Russia, India, China, and South Africa created BRICS as the five founding members of the bloc. These 5 countries account for 3.3 billion people and 41% of the world's population, $30.8 trillion and 27% of global GDP, 20% of global exports, and 20% of global oil production (Toussaint, 2024). As illustrated in Graphic-1, although there was a huge gap between the G7 and the BRICS countries' GDP in terms of purchasing power parity (PPP) in 2000, the BRICS nations overtook the G7 country's share of the world's total GDP in 2020. The difference had increased by 2023, and the BRICS now represent a total of 31.54% of the world's GDP compared to 29.9% held by the G7 countries.

*Figure 1. BRICS and G7 countries' share (%) of the world's total gross domestic product (GDP) in purchasing power parity (PPP) (2000-2023)*

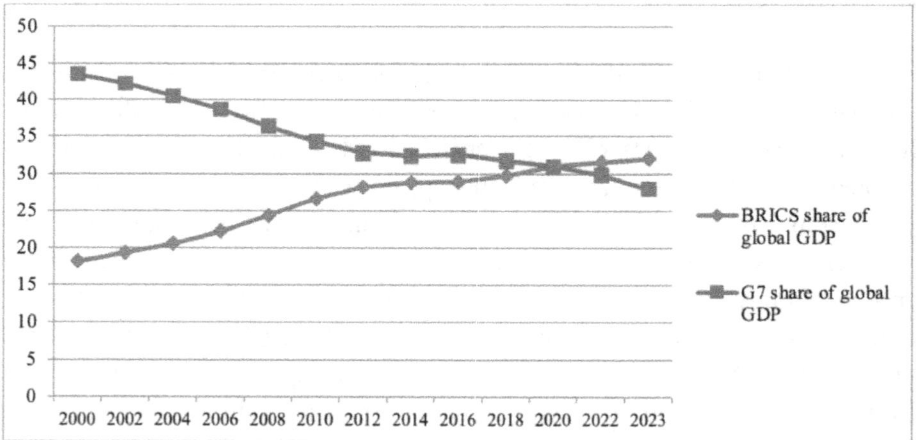


*(Statista, 2024b)*

As presented in Table 1, in 2024 total population was recorded as 821.504.028 in G7 countries which represents 9,68% of the world population. The total population of BRICS nations in 2024 was recorded as 3.291.083.252 people representing 40,32% of the world population. It is expected to reach 3.325.820.000 by 2029 (Statista, 2024a). With the expansion of new member countries, the bloc increased by 385.156.649 people and reached 3.676.239.901. Furthermore, there are many candidate countries expecting to be a member of BRICS such as Türkiye, Indonesia, and Malaysia. With the expansion of these countries, the BRICS+ population will be more than 4 billion people representing almost half of the world population.

*Table 1. BRICS countries and G7 countries by population (2024)*

| | BRICS population | | | | G7 population | | |
|---|---|---|---|---|---|---|---|
| BRICS COUNT. | Country | Population | Global share | | Country | Population | Global share |
| | India | 1.450.935.791 | 17.78% | | US | 345.426.571 | 4.23% |
| | China | 1.419.321.278 | 17.39% | | Japan | 123.753.041 | 1,52% |
| | Brazil | 211.998.573 | 2.6% | | Germany | 84.552.424 | 1.04% |
| | Russia | 144.820.423 | 1.77% | | UK | 69.138.192 | 0.85% |
| | S.Africa | 64.007.187 | 0.78% | | France | 99.548.503 | 0.82% |
| NEW MEMBERS | Ethiopia | 132.059.767 | 1.77% | | Italy | 59.342.867 | 0.73% |
| | Egypt | 116.538.258 | 1.43% | | Canada | 39.742.430 | 0.49% |
| | Iran | 91.567.738 | 1.12% | | | | |
| | UAE | 11.028.129 | 0.14% | | | | |
| | SaudiArabia | 33.962.757 | 0.42% | | | | |
| EXPECTED | Türkiye | 87.473.805 | 1.07% | | | | |
| | Azerbaijan | 10.336.577 | 0.13% | | | | |
| | Venezuela | 28.405.543 | 0.35% | | | | |
| | Malaysia | 35.557.673 | 0.44% | | | | |
| | Indonesia | 283.487.931 | 3.47% | | | | |

Source: worldometer (2024)

The original BRICS countries, Brazil, Russia, India, China, and South Africa, are now expanded with the new members Saudi Arabia, United Arabic Emirates, Egypt, Iran, and Ethiopia. Argentina was also a candidate country. However, after the election of Javier Milei in November 2023, Argentina withdrew its application to join BRICS+. With the participation of new members, the BRICS+ accounts for 42% of world oil production, 29% of world GDP, 25% of world exports, and 45% of the world's population. BRICS+ countries are planning to come together in October 2024. Russia and China are the pioneer countries in the coalition and are trying to enlarge the coalition and increase the number of members of the BRICS+. More than 50 other nations all over the world have expressed their interest in the BRICS coalition. Although the G7 countries' combined GDP is approximately $15 trillion higher than the BRICS countries, with higher growth rates and potential new member states, BRICS is expected to overtake the G7 in economic performance within twenty years (Toussaint, 2024; Conte and Lam, 2024).

In Figure 2, the top 10 oil-producing countries in 2023 are illustrated. In the top 10 oil producer countries, there are two G7 member countries, the US and Canada. Their total daily oil production is 27,67 million barrels per day (bpd). In the same list, there are 6 BRICS+ member countries including Saudi Arabia, Russia, China, Brazil, UAE, and Iran accounting for 39,57 million bpd.

*Figure 2. Top 10 oil-producer countries (2023, million bpd)*

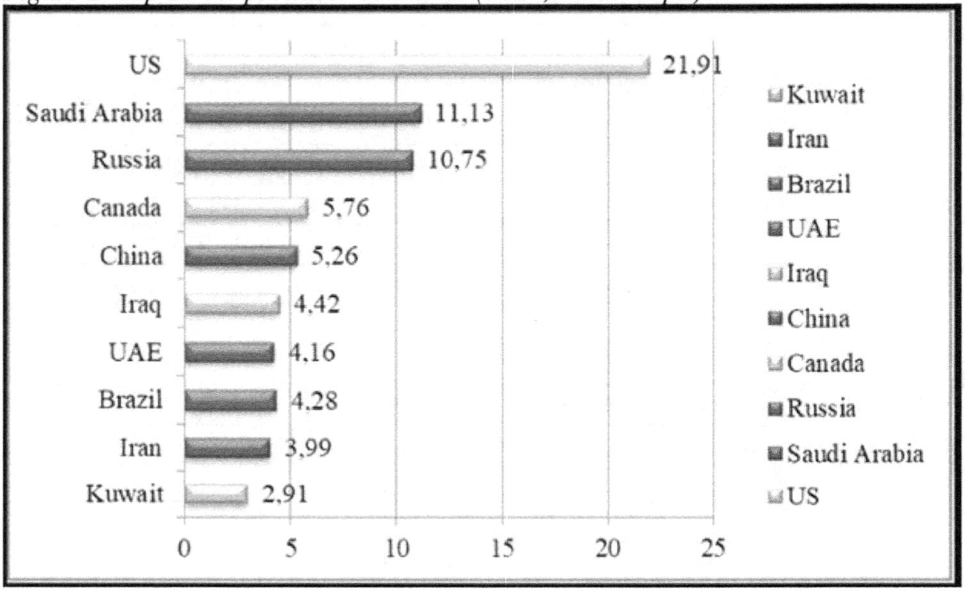


*(Pistilli, 2024)*

*Figure 3. Top 10 manufacturing countries (2024, % of Global Manufacturing)*

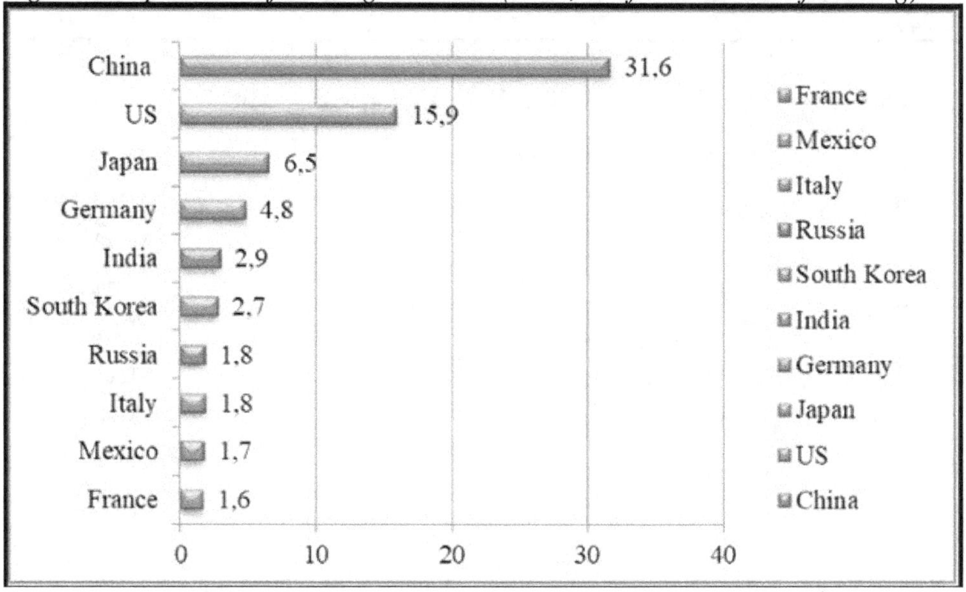


*(safeguardglobal.com, 2024)*

As shown in Figure 3, among the top 10 manufacturing countries in the world, there are 3 BRICS countries accounting for 36,3% of world manufacturing output. The US, Japan, Germany, Italy, and France are the G7 countries listed in the top 10 greatest manufacturing countries in the world. These 5 countries represent 30,6% of the global manufacturing output.

*Figure 4. Top 10 agricultural producing countries in the world (million metric tons, 2024)*

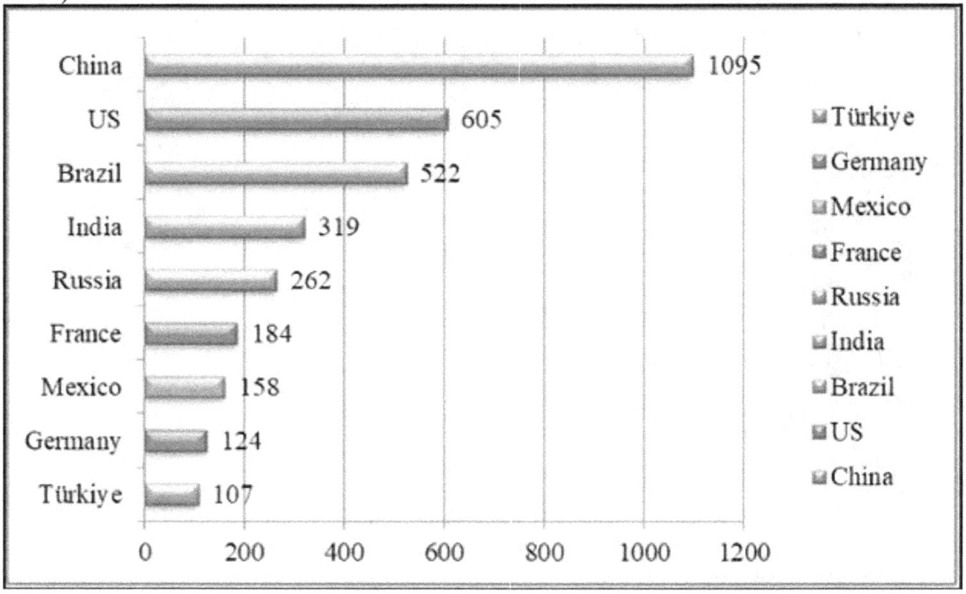


*(geekforgeeks.org, 2024)*

As presented in Figure 4, China is the leading country in the world in agricultural production with 1.095 million metric tons in 2024. The US follows China with 605 million metric tons of agricultural production. According to Graphic 4, Brazil is the market challenger with 522 million metric tons of agricultural production. Among the 10 top countries, there are 4 BRICS member countries and 1 candidate country. Their total production in 2024 is 2.305 million metric tons whereas the US, France, and Germany, as the representatives of G7 accounted for 913 million metric tons of agricultural production.

According to oil production, manufacturing production, and agricultural production data, BRICS+ countries have a strong economic power globally. Even if member countries use a common currency during bilateral trade within the block, it may provide a great opportunity for the countries to decrease the transaction costs of depending on the US dollar.

## Challenges of BRICS

Although the BRICS group pledges to have these awesome opportunities, there are still challenges and obstacles among them restricting the potential success. First of all, there are great economic development differences among the members.

China has a huge economic power comparing with the other members providing it with a vital importance for the bloc's sustainability. Different from China, Russia, Brazil, and South Africa are commodity exporters whereas China is the commodity importer. China's aging population is not just a social but also an economic problem which may limit its economic growth in the near future. Their approach towards international trade is also diverse. While China supports the Doha round[1], India has the distance to it. From the political and cultural perspective, there are differences among the member countries, as well. While China and Russia have authoritarian governments, Brazil, India, and South Africa possess a more democratic administration model. The two dominant powers in the bloc, China and Russia seem to have a more influential power on the other members. Furthermore, the political relations are not perfect among the members. There has been a long lasting border conflict between China and India. Overlapping sphere of interest in the Indian Ocean is another conflict reason between the two countries (Jordaan, 2021:458-459). Finally, although the members of the BRICS cooperates each other, China, India, and Russia have been competing each other for being the regional leadership and supremacy. Thus, having a dominant role of China may annoy the other member countries. The hesitation is not just political, but also economic. The other members may be worried about the influx of cheap Chinese products that may negatively impact their local economies. Despite these disadvantages, the BRICS can promote an alternative bloc to the existing global economic and political system. The member countries have the economic and diplomatic capacity to reform and build international economic and political institutions which may welcome other developing countries (Varela and Delgado, 2019:104).

## The Rise of Cryptocurrency

The development of the internet and financial technologies created a profound impact on economic and financial activities because of the quick completion of transactions with ignorable costs. Cryptocurrencies are one of the remarkable applications new financial technologies have brought. Cryptocurrencies are mostly used for monetary exchange where the value is preserved and confirmed. Nakamoto (2008) expressed that while financial systems work suitably for most financial transactions, they are still poor in the trust-based model. Besides, a complete non-reversal financial process is not possible since financial institutions cannot eliminate mediating disputes. Furthermore, the cost of mediation of transactions and money transfers, particularly through the banking industry, is getting higher. Also, for reversal possibilities the need for trust is critical. Mediators and merchants should not get more information from their customers than necessary. These costs and uncertainties cannot be avoided with existing global financial order to make local or international payments without a trusted party (Procházka, 2018:162).

Unprecedented improvements in blockchain technologies offered radical changes in how to structure and operate monetary systems. Cryptocurrencies may provide decentralized cash systems for economies with alternative safe and unique payment channels. The fact is that the skyrocketing growing global online business cannot be solely managed by traditional financial transactions through financial institutions as trusted third parties. Many merchants prefer electronic payment processes without any central authority to mediate the transaction or guarantee its authenticity. Instead, cryptocurrency payment systems are based on cryptographic proof through two parties to transact directly with each other without a third party to play the trusty role. The main advantage of cryptocurrency is the security and verifiability of financial transactions Thus, with its peer-to-peer form of transaction, cryptocurrency is a chain of digital signatures and a secure system. Besides, in the paper written by Nakamoto (2008), the main idea was the presentation of blockchain development and establishment of a functional decentralized secure cash payment system rather than a new virtual currency which can be defined as a type of unregulated digital currency as an alternative form of payment using encryption algorithms such as bitcoin, or other altcoins. Cryptocurrencies may operate both as a currency and a virtual accounting system by using cryptocurrency wallets. Thus, cryptocurrencies are by-products, serving as a transfer of exchange which is an essential function of money. Cryptocurrencies can be used to make quick payments and avoid transaction fees. Cryptocurrencies also fulfill another function of money, "store of value". Investors may purchase cryptocurrencies, to enjoy the increase in value. However, prices are very volatile and there may be sharp increases or declines in price fluctuations that may cause risky situations to their investors. (Procházka, 2018:162; Oswego State University of New York, 2024). Also, most of the cryptocurrencies are not backed by the governments like bank deposits in different countries. Hence, cryptocurrencies do not have protections as money in bank accounts or credit unions (Federal Trade Commission Consumer Advice, 2024).

Investors of cryptocurrencies not only provide exchange transactions but also function as e-brokers. The exchange of cryptocurrencies allows consumers to purchase, sell, and trade them. Accordingly, they exchange money through fiat currency such as dollars, euros, or pounds, or another cryptocurrency such as bitcoin or another altcoin (Hansen, 2021).

According to Statista (2024c), the estimated revenue reached 56.7 billion US dollars in 2024 in the worldwide cryptocurrency market. The average revenue per user was estimated at 66.1dollars in 2024.

The growing cryptocurrency market attracts more and more users to the sector. Figure 5 represents the number of users during the 2017-2025 period. As shown in Figure 5, while there were just 12,23 million cryptocurrency users in 2017, it demonstrated a skyrocketing increase between 2019 and 2024. From 2017 to 2024 the number of cryptocurrency users increased by more than 70 folds and reached 856,7 million people. It is expected to reach 861 million people in 2025.

*Figure 5. Number of users during 2017-2025 period*

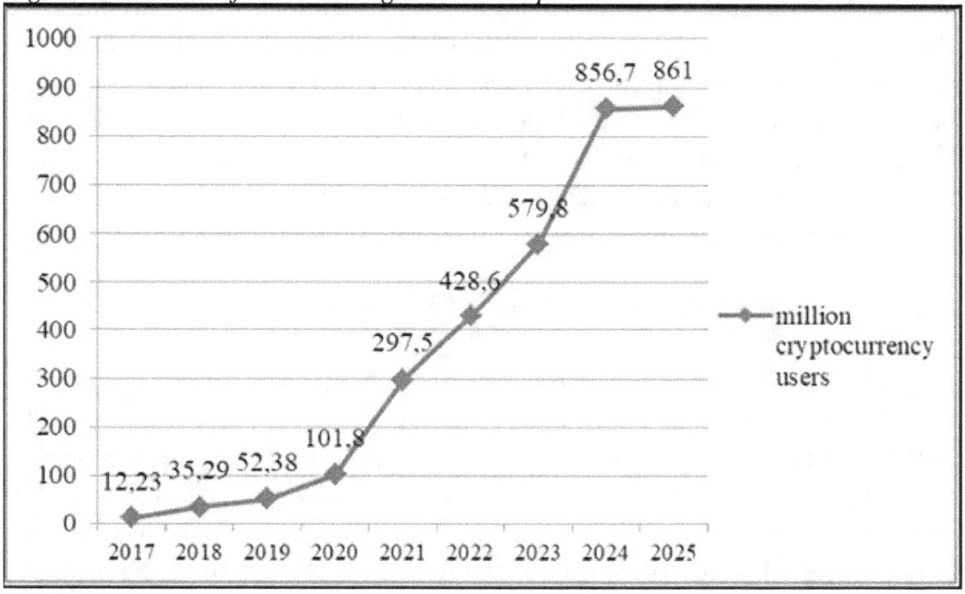


*(Statista, 2024c)*

Economic actors and ordinary people living in BRICS+ countries, which represent roughly half of the world's population, will not have significant problems in conducting international trade and other financial transactions since they are familiar with cryptocurrency transactions.

In recent years, many developing and developed countries have been suffering from the global power of the dollar, particularly because of the problems arising from international trade and dollar accumulation problems. Some countries suggested the Chinese currency, renminbi as an alternative reserve currency to dollars since China has been the greatest manufacturing country in the world and have trade ties globally. Besides, Facebook's digital currency Libra was mentioned as an alternative to the dollar. During the second half of 2010, digital currencies attracted the attention of many central banks to ease mobile business and consumer transactions. In 2019, the Bank of England initiated Facebook's Libra which was considered an alternative to

Bitcoin and other altcoins. The officials from the Bank of England stated that the Libra which was backed by several banks could be a good alternative payment model to trading goods and services. However, due to the lack of regulations and limited rules, Libra lost its reliability. Bank of England governor Mark Carney expressed the necessity of *"a new payment infrastructure which was based on an international stablecoin fully backed fully backed by reserve assets in a basket of currencies"* for the retail transactions and online payments (Inman, 2019).

In 2019, Bank of England governor Mark Carney expressed the dominance of the dollar and suggested exchanging it with a digital currency. According to Mark Carney, the global dominance of the dollar caused a barrier to global trade. He suggested a new digital currency backed by a large group of nations to decline the dominating influence of the US dollar. He also added that developing the new digital currency and its displacement with the dollar would dampen the dollar's dominance in credit markets which may lead to reduce the volatility of capital flows to emerging markets (Inman, 2019).

## The New Development Bank as a First Step

In 2012, BRICS leaders agreed to establish a New Development Bank on 15 July 2014 on the occasion of the 6th BRICS Summit held in Fortaleza, Brazil. The BRICS New Development Bank (NDB) was established by the 5 member countries. The initial capital contribution was $50 billion and was expected to grow to $100 billion with the support of other countries. Every founding country has an equal share of the Bank's capital, and none has veto rights. The aim of the NDB was to support and provide funds for investments and infrastructure development of emerging economies (https://www.ndb.int/about-ndb/history/). The initial estimated resource would be at least $1 trillion annually to provide a greater resource in the development of developing countries and give extra voice to financial architecture. NDB was expected to provide a valuable contribution and productive development to the current structure of international, regional, national, and multilateral development banks through supporting infrastructure investments. It would be beneficial for the national banks as well, due to BRICS' NDB financial and technical support to the local national banks. It was planned to create a center of gravity for a new financial structure that would shift the global finance from North to South or "Southern-dominated" institutions. Here, the word "Southern" stands for emerging economies. Thus, the G7-dominated global financial system would need to share the power with the emerging economies. With the new financial architecture, the roles of emerging economies would be larger. Their macroeconomic position has also changed thanks to their growing proportion of global savings and the foreign exchange reserves they had generated. NDB would be the capital of the bank and would comprise equal representatives and shares of the BRICS member countries. Finally, NDB would operate as a public development bank. This structure is similar to the development banks such as the World Bank which was established after World War II. Besides, although NDB would be funded in the private capital markets with co-financing by private and public entities, it would be owned and capitalized by the national governments of the BRICS member countries (Griffith-Jones, 2015). Currently, the NDB is aiming to expand the use of local currencies to finance the sustainable development of emerging economies and developing countries (Xinhua, 2024).

## Supranational BRICS Central Bank Digital Currency

Since the great revolution in the IT industry, cryptocurrencies have been having enormous impacts on the currency market. New technological advances have enabled the development of digital currencies that cannot be regulated by central governments but by digital communities. This has not only the potential to overcome the hegemony of reserve currencies such as the dollar or euro but also it threatens the supremacy of fiat currencies, which are often manipulated for economic and political gain. Policymakers have been searching for an alternative to government-backed currencies for years. (Carrick, 2016).

In November 2019, during the 11th Annual BRICS Summit in Brazil, the BRICS Council handled the possibility of initiating a central bank digital currency (CBDC). The BRICS members agreed to initiate a joint supranational CBDC by benefiting blockchain technology. Although BRICS countries have not decided yet, there are some options for creating a common CBDC. The optimal way of creating a supranational CBDC is managed collectively by the central banks of five member countries. Each central bank has the right to issue a determined volume of the CBDC of BRICS. All transactions would be recorded for the common cryptocurrency in a single private blockchain where only authorized institutions can mine the transactions to authenticate them. In another option, CBDC can be designed as a basket of national CBDCs, similar to ECU in 1979. BRICS Business Council (2019) offered a tentative digital currency model as a basket of a combination of BRICS member countries' national currencies and global reserve currencies such as the dollar, euro, yen, and pound. A third option could be initiating a common supranational CBDC guaranteed to be 100% on deposits in national currencies, fiat currencies, of the BRICS. In this case, an international monetary authority is needed. A fourth option could be to let one of the member countries such as Russia or China, be in charge of creating its own national CBDC, and then adopt it by the other BRICS members. Although China and Russia have planned to initiate national CBDC, the member countries have not agreed on a specific alternative, yet (Slim, 2023:8).

## Why Does the BRICS Block Need to Create a New Currency?

BRICS Coin (BC) is a cryptocurrency that was initiated by the BRICS member countries in April 2021. The aim of BC is to have an independent digital currency that is not tied to any reserve money or any specific country in order to improve economic activities among BRICS members. BC is expected to reach cross-border payment convenience, low transaction costs, and fast transaction settlements with its efficient and secure digital structure. If BC can satisfy these expectations, there is no doubt that it will be a radical and attractive alternative to traditional payment systems. Due to its large population and great GDP of BRICS+ nations, BC has the potential to contribute to financial inclusion within the block (BRICS Coin, 2023).

The technical structure of BC will be built on blockchain technology leveraging the Ethereum and Binance Smart Chain blockchains. It is expected to use their compatibility, scalability, and infrastructure. The smart contracts will lead not only to automation and transparency but also to user-friendly interfaces to enhance ease of use and accessibility. A fixed total supply of 1.000 trillion BC whose 30% will be reserved for the BRICS governments and 70% of it will be distributed to the global market through presale 40%, airdrops 5%, marketing 10%, and exchange liquidity 10%, and team rewards 5%. The target is to reach a wider user base and more adoption of the BC. The market value of BC will be promoted over time because of the support of the BRICS members, increasing demand, and scarcity. Moreover, the BRICS governments' support of investment, fund security, value preservation, and improving multilateral relations among the BRICS+ nations will contribute to the increase in the value of BC to be a reliable and trusted digital asset (BRICS Coin, 2023:7).

### Russia and Cryptocurrency

Actually, Russian President Putin was suspicious about cryptocurrencies in the first half of the 2010s. In 2017 President Putin pointed out the importance of regulations of cryptocurrencies due to their high risks. He said, *"Cryptocurrencies are issued by an unlimited number of anonymous bodies. Thus buyers of cryptocurrencies could be involved in unlawful activities."*. President Putin also added that without regulations, cryptocurrencies could be used in unlawful transactions such as money laundering, financing of terrorism, and tax evasion. He also called for international support and legal guarantees for popular financial instruments (RFE/RL, 2017).

However, Russia's disputes with Western countries, NATO, and the US on Ukraine have raised problems with economic relations with the Western bloc and foreign trade payments years before the invasion of Ukraine. Under this tight global ecosystem, Russian President Putin thought that cryptocurrency could be an alternative payment system.

Thus, Russian President Vladimir Putin announced that the Russian Federation has been working on national digital currencies as a key element for the alternative payment platform. President Putin said *"The whole world is currently working on the creation of a so-called transnational payment infrastructure. Many countries and regions of the world are closely examining the possibilities of using digital currencies and digital financial assets of central banks."* President Putin also underlined that this new system would be regardless of third countries. The reason why Russia has been rushed on the digital currency is that due to long-lasting sanctions and global financial restrictions such as being kept out of the SWIFT payment system, Russia has been suffering from bilateral trade relations with China, India, and Türkiye (Bitcoin.comNews, 2024a).

President Putin also expressed that *"In cooperation with BRICS countries, we are working on creating our own payment and settlement structure that will ensure efficient and independent servicing of all foreign trade"*. During Russia's BRICS chairmanship, under the auspices of President Putin, Russia has also been working on the establishment of interbank networks and payment systems with the BRICS nations. The aim of this is to expand cross-border trade and payments by using national currencies to reach more efficient financial efficiency within the block. Since Russia has been suffering from the sanctions of Western countries and the US, Russia has been trying to catch the interest of the other BRICS members seeking alternatives to global reserve currencies (Bitcoin.comNew, 2024b).

The use of cryptocurrencies in international payments and FOREX transactions was legalized by the decree signed by Russian President Vladimir Putin on August 8, 2024. Based on the decree, the Central Bank of Russia will supervise the process. Governor of the Central Bank of Russia, Elvira Nabiullina confirmed that cryptocurrencies would be used in international payments by the end of 2024. Anton Siluanov, the Minister of Finance, revealed that they had been working on legalizing cryptocurrency exchanges. Actually, Russia has been working on its National Payment Card System since 2014. The current improvements included cryptocurrencies to the process. The fact that the Central Bank of Russia's complete control over the National Payment Card System plays an important role in this choice. Besides, Mir, Russia's domestic payment system, also works on this platform. The Central Bank of Russia plans to issue stablecoins[2] as the main type of cryptocurrency to be used in international payments. While Russia has been working on stablecoins, it needs the support of the rest of the BRICS nations regarding the use of cryptocurrencies in their trade. Although Brazil, South Africa, and India have expressed their support, there are still many difficulties in the process, such as the restrictions imposed by regulators in countries, technical complexity, and fluctuations in the value of cryptocurrencies (Abay, 2024).

Russia has already initiated the digital ruble in August 2023, and the government is planning to use it countrywide within 5 years. However, there is limited transaction in 30 companies in 11 cities. Gas stations of the oil company Lukoil and Moscow Metro are two examples of institutions accepting digital ruble payments (Abay, 2024).

## China and Cryptocurrency

In 2015, to provide an alternative payment system to cash for retail payments, The Chinese Central Bank (PBoC for People's Bank of China) revealed that the country would initiate a digital currency named DCEP (Digital Currency for Electronic Payment). Thus China became one of the pioneer countries that executed digital currency applications. The DCEP was issued based on a private blockchain. The distribution of DCEP was dominated by commercial banks, Tencent, and Alipay (owned by e-commerce company Alibaba). Actually, Alibaba initiated its own payment system in 2004, and Tencent in 2005. The Chinese government started working on improving a sovereign digital currency technology in 2014 aiming to create a centralized digital payment system. After the declaration of Meta (Facebook) to launch its own global digital currency Libra, PBoC hesitated to lose the monetary sovereignty of the yuan. Thus the government launched the e-CNY (digital yuan) pilot application. The Central Bank of China is the sole authority issuing individual accounts to people. PBoC announced that the digital currency which was also called e-CNY is not only a risk-free alternative to different commercial platforms, but also a perfect alternative to replace the physical cash (Orcutt, 2023).

Chinese web application WeChat, Bank of China, Agricultural Bank of China, Union Pay, Industrial and Commercial Bank of China, and China Construction Bank were authorized to execute the process. These banks and applications were authorized to access the DCEP and could surveillance the opening and managing of the DCEP portfolios of individuals and professionals. After the selection of Shenzhen province with 13 million inhabitants as the pilot application for the first DCEP test, Shenzhen Financial Technology Co. Ltd. which was specialized in blockchain and is 100% owned by the PBoC was founded to execute the transactions in 2018 (Slim, 2023:9).

Recently, e-CNY has been used in China in 29 pilot areas. The digital yuan is the retail version of CBDC that is used directly by ordinary people, but not wholesalers to interact with the banks or other central banks, for retail transactions. The aim of this project is to take the place of cash. Thus e-yuan does not cause any interest and is tied one-to-one to yuan. e-CNY was also used in Beijing during the Winter Olympics as one of the three forms of payment models. For the time being, only people of China who live in the selected 29 areas can access digital yuan for daily transactions. The foreigners who are in one of the pilot regions can access a guide to onboard. Alipay and WeChat also support foreigners to register their systems with international credit cards. In the near future, pilot areas will enlarge and attract international visitors including offering visa-free access for certain countries (Huang, 2024). Former PBoC governor Yi Gang declared that in July 2023 total transactions had reached a value of 1.8 trillion yuan (US$249.9 billion) up from 100 billion yuan (US$13.9 billion) the previous August with 950 million transactions (Nulimaimaiti, 2023). China also plans to use the e-CNY not only as a local currency but also outside its borders for international trade. If China can manage to use e-CNY as the currency for international trade, it may be a great challenge for the US dollar's dominant reserve currency position. As the US dollar has been used by the S government as a political instrument for many years as well, this shift may cause changes in the global geopolitical order (Orcutt, 2023).

## An Alternative to SWIFT Payment System

China, Russia, and other BRICS+ members have been searching to launch CBDC to reduce their dependency on the US dollar in their international trade activities. In 2019, Kirill Dmitriev from Russia Direct Investment Fund expressed that "*An efficient BRICS payment system can encourage payments in national currencies and ensure sustainable payments and investments among our countries, which make up over 20% of the global inflow of foreign direct investment*" Although Kirill Dimitriev did not give more detail about the payment system, Russia had been developing its own payment system since there had been financial sanction imposed on Russia due to the annexation of Crimea and its role in the Ukrainian crisis. The invasion of Ukraine caused much more effective sanctions. Russia has launched its own national payment system as an alternative to the SWIFT financial messaging service. During his interview in 2019, Dmitriev also added that the five BRICS members had been working on initiating a common cryptocurrency for mutual trade and payments to decrease the share of payments in the US dollar. Even during 2019, after the sanctions started, the ruble's share in Russian foreign trade payments increased to 14% from 3% while dollar payments dropped to 50% from 92% (Ostroukh, 2019).

In July 2024, BRICS members declared that the bloc is planning to introduce an alternative payment system to the current SWIFT aiming at de-dollarization and decreasing the dependency on the US dollar in international financial transactions and trade. However, the details about the new payment system were not clearly expressed. Instead, the Former Russian Ambassador to the US Yury Ushakov stated that cutting-edge digital technology and blockchain would be used in the payment system. While cross-border payments and settlements would be used, there would be no need for the US dollar. It was also stated that there were 159 countries expressed their interest in using the expected payment system which will be used for international trade without the US dollar dependency. To initiate this, Russian President Vladimir Putin signed a bill to use digital currencies for export payments. Due to the US sanctions on Russia because of the war in Ukraine, President Putin looks for alternative payment models for international trade more enthusiastically than the other BRICS member country leaders (Lucas, 2024).

## Advantages of a BRICS currency

The BRICS nations have been working on an alternative currency to the US dollar. The desire of BRICS members for an alternative currency to the US dollar for international trade and foreign currency reserves led BRICS members to create a new BRICS currency. An expected shift towards the BRICS currency will have an enormous effect on the global economy and investments. International trade, oil and natural gas, banking and finance, foreign exchange markets, manufacturing, tourism and travel, and technology sectors will have a significant impact. As the influence of the dollar decreases on the global stage, emerging countries will mitigate risks of global volatility due to measures or sanctions of the US. Diminishing the dollar dependence will encourage the countries to develop a regional currency. All these attempts aim to weaken the position of the US dollar as a global reserve currency. While the new BRICS currency will cause new trading partnerships, it will change trading currencies from well-known reserve currencies to local ones and decrease market volatility. The expected advantages of BRICS currency are as follows (BRICS Coin, 2023:4; Pistilli, 2024b):

*Investment diversification:* the BRICS members try to find alternative investment portfolios and reduce the dependency on a single currency, namely the US dollar. The expected benefit from the diversification is that they can mitigate the risks regarding fluctuations in the value of the chosen single currency as well as the resilience to exchange rate volatilities and economic fluctuations.

*More trade efficiency.* A common currency used in international trade among the member countries may enhance more efficient trade transactions through easier payment processes, lower transaction costs, zero risk of exchange rate fluctuations, more intra-BRICS trade, and more economic cooperation.

*Value preservation:* Currently, in almost all international trade activities US dollar is the single most important reserve currency. This may cause extra risk to the international trade and national currencies of BRICS countries if there is a depreciation of the US dollar. Such an unexpected depreciation may decrease the value of their foreign currency reserves. Thus, diversifying their reserves into alternative currencies may ensure to protect the value of their holdings, and protect them from inflationary pressures, and fluctuations in the US dollar's value.

*Increasing financial inclusion.* Leveraging blockchain technology, digital currencies, and smart contracts, will bring a great revolution in the global financial system. Easy cross-border payments will promote trade and economic integration within the BRICS+ bloc and beyond.

*Fund security:* Conflicts, wars, geopolitical tensions, and diplomatic problems among the countries may pose a risk to confronting potential sanctions, embargoes, and trade disputes. The reliance on the US dollar for international trade and foreign currency reserves may cause BRICS members to be prone to these unforeseeable risks. By initiating BRICS currency, they may reduce the dependence on the US dollar aiming to secure their funds and by having a sound currency they may mitigate the vulnerabilities caused by international political uncertainties.

*Having stronger ties between the BRICS countries:* Having a common currency within the BRICS block may improve the economic ties and financial cooperation among the member countries. Such a common currency may foster multilateral and bilateral trade relations, promote sound economic integration among the BRICS member countries as well as stronger strategic, diplomatic, and political relations.

*Balance of power:* Since World War II, there has been the dominant power of the US dollar in the global financial system. An alternative currency of the BRICS nations may convert the global financial system into a multipolar global financial architecture to reduce the influence and the unique power of a single currency and its issuing country, the US through using an alternative currency in international trades and reserves.

Challenges of launching BRICS currency are as follows (Savage, 2023; authors own evaluations):

BRICS currency has been considered a political project rather than a financial advantage. South African Central Bank Governor Lesetja Kganyago stated that *"If you want it, you'll have to get a banking union, you'll have to get a fiscal union, you've got to get macroeconomic convergence...Importantly, you need a disciplining mechanism for the countries that fall out of line with it... And the euro project demonstrated just that. Plus they will need a common central bank... where does it get located?"* (Engineering News, 2023). As Lesetja Kganyago expressed monetary and fiscal unions are not that easy. The monetary union was very painful for the EU member countries without having fiscal union. Despite all problems, none of the member countries accepted to have the fiscal union in order not to leave their sovereignty on tax policies and tax revenues. Furthermore, economic performance of each member country in BRICS is different from each other. Thus, it is hard to initiate a common monetary or fiscal policy which is suitable for all members. Furthermore, as Kganyago pointed out, the place of the common central bank is very critical. Since the IMF and the World Bank are located in Washington DC, the capital city of the US, the country has a strong power on these institutions. Similar problems may arise if the expected common central bank is based in one of the member countries.

The international trade between the member countries is not well-balanced. All BRICS member countries have trade with China as their main trading partner but little trade with each other. Before initiating the common currency, pegging to the renminbi and having bilateral exchange rates may be a first step. Even this step needs many mechanisms such as mechanisms to provide credit in renminbi to the countries running trade deficits. China has to take the burden and need to set up mechanisms and institutions to supply necessary funds to support a liquidity shortfall and provide a reserve facility to deposit additional funds. Besides, other currencies should be converted to the renminbi freely and used by other member countries (Poenisch, 2023).

These policies support the internalization of the renminbi and will cause a pressure on the Chinese government to liberalize its financial account.

Beyond all negative impacts and pressure on China, this process may result in the dominance of China and its currency in the bloc. In other words, renminbi may take the place of the dollar.

## Is it Possible to Dethrone the Dollar With the BRICS Currency?

The dollar gained importance after the financial crisis associated with World War I and then solidified its dominant international role after the Bretton Woods Agreement in 1944. Since then, the US has enjoyed the preeminent role of the dollar in the global economy as it is the world's reserve currency. The dollar has been supported by the size and the soundness of the US economy. Although the dollar is still the dominant reserve currency in the world, the Ukraine War and sanctions on Russia affected the position. The estimated US dollar share in global trade accounted for 96% during the 1999-2019 period in the Americas, 74% in the Asia Pacific, and 79% in the rest of the world. In the Euro area, this rate shrank to 66% due to the euro's dominance. (Bertaut, von Beschwitz, and Curcuru, 2023). IMF confirmed these data by revealing that the share of US dollar reserves held by central banks declined to 59% globally in 2021. This rate represents the lowest level in the last 25 years. According to IMF data, it may be due to the competition with the other currencies used for international transactions. The share of US dollar assets in central bank reserves also fell from 71% to 59% since 1999, the year the euro was launched (Aslanalp, 2021). As of 2022, 54% of foreign trade was invoiced in dollars globally. Similarly, the dollar's share of global reserves has declined to 59% in 2024 from 70% in 2000. (Boocker and Wessel, 2024).

In the long term, it may be a risk of challenge to the dollar's international reserve currency status. Furthermore, recent developments such as sanctions on Russia, the Ukraine War, international trade with national currencies as well as BRICS cryptocurrency project have the potential to cause more stress on the dollar. The fast-growing digital currency industry and technological progress are expected to impact both private and public sectors which may result in a decline in the US dollar reliance (Bertaut, von Beschwitz, and Curcuru, 2023).

It should be noted that if the expected BRICS currency can be stabilized against the dollar's value, it may hamper the power of US sanctions which leads extra value loss decrease in the dollar. Similar to Russia and China, countries such as India, Malaysia, and Kenya support the de-dollarization by signing agreements to continue their trade in domestic currencies with their trade partners. As countries diversify their reserve holdings, the US dollar will confront more challenges and competition of emerging countries' currencies which may result in a changing balance of power in the global economy and international politics (Pistilli, 2024b).

The fact is that the aggressive financial and political decisions of the US also threaten the dollar's global dominance. These policies can be summarized as follows (Boocker and Wessel, 2024):

> *Sanctions:* After 2010, the US government increased the sanctions on countries in which the US has conflicts even though its allies do not support launching sanctions. Many countries criticize the US due to their perception of the weaponization of the dollar. These sanctions pushed the target countries to find alternative ways to bypass them. For example, China promoted the renminbi as an alternative currency for its international trade and developed alternative financial methods as a part of its Belt and Road project. Similarly, the BRICS countries have been working on a common BRICS currency. The sanctions imposed by the US government are criticized not only by the suffering countries but also their own governors. According to US Treasury Secretary Janet Yellen, the dollar could be dethroned if the US government fails to develop a doctrine of economic statecraft. Yellen stated that sanctions should be imposed only if there is a risk to global interests and security is under threat since there may be unexpected trade deficits, capital, and technology losses. She also added that sanctions should not impact on

civilian people of the target country. Besides, the sanctions should be flexible according to the response of the target country. She also suggested the US government act with humility instead of arrogance (Singh, 2024).

*Debt and dysfunction.* In the last decades, the US politics has been polarized. Besides, fiscal policy is not disciplined in recent years as the debt-to-GDP ratio is getting higher. In addition to political instability, rating agencies downgraded the US long-term credit. All these improvements loss of confidence in investors to the dollar.

*Technology.* Innovations and technological improvements in payment systems may reduce the dollar's dominant role in the global economy. Transactions between the emerging economies' local currencies are becoming more convenient and easy as financial markets and new-generation payment systems develop. Currently, innovative payment systems allow countries to convert their currencies to the dollar or another currency very easily and cheaply. Countries such as Russia, China, and India have been conducting their international trade with their domestic currencies to reduce their dollar dependence and decrease transaction costs. Exchanging the renminbi for rupees or rubles directly is cheaper.

*Alternatives to SWIFT:* Central Bank digital currencies are other threats to the US dollar's hegemonic power. They can reduce the dollar's role by reducing settlement times, and easier and cheaper trade possibilities via digital currencies of emerging economies. China launched the Cross-border Interbank Payment System (CIPS) to integrate messaging and payment systems. CIPS allowed participant countries to bypass SWIFT, CHIPS, and the dollar. Compared with CIPS, SWIFT is still very common and effective. However, CIPS applications are growing rapidly and increasing worldwide. In the near future, it is expected to have more shares in global transactions.

## Dollar is Still Powerful

Despite all these negative improvements for the US dollar, the term *"dethroning the dollar with the BRICS currency"* may be very assertive. Dethroning the dollar is not only a result of a process and the improvement of international trade in another currency but also a strong political issue. Furthermore, the process is actually not as easy as it is expected. When the euro was introduced and declared that it would be the chief currency of the EU, the rebalancing of funds by central banks and daily usage of the euro took a long time. Moreover, some peripheral countries such as Greece had great difficulty in changing the local currency drachma to the euro (Galanos, Kotios, and Pavlidis, 2011). Similar problems can arise in BRICS countries. The locomotive countries in the EU are Germany and France. These countries are economically stronger than the other countries of the European Union. Although there is religious and cultural similarity among EU nations, differences in economic development have created significant problems on local economies in the transition to the monetary union. On the contrary, BRICS members are diverse in economic, social, cultural, and religious perspectives. This points deeper problems in launching common currency.

In spite of these negative impacts on the dollar, about three-quarters of foreign government holdings of safe US assets are held by other countries. Also, the euro, Japanese yen, and British pound support the sanctions on Russia. Hence, geopolitical impacts do not offer attractive alternatives to the US dollar, yet. Besides, China has been the greatest market challenger to the US in the last decades. China is the world's largest exporter currently and exceeded the US GDP on a purchasing power parity basis, and is expected to exceed GDP in nominal terms until 2030. However, China's population has been aging and decreasing due to the one-child policy. Furthermore, the Chinese renminbi is not freely exchangeable and investor confidence is low compared with the dollar. To make the Chinese renminbi more attractive, China and Brazil signed an agreement to make their bilateral trade in their domestic currencies instead of the dollar. Besides, the Chinese government has been discussing with the Saudi government to use of the renminbi to price oil trade (Bertaut, von Beschwitz, and Curcuru, 2023). Nevertheless, the petro-yuan process will not be that easy. According to Dourian (2024), the bilateral trading agreements will increase the trading of Chinese renminbi, but it will not the case for the petro-yuan to replace with the petro-dollar since Saudi riyal is pegged to the dollar, and giving up dollar-priced oil sales is not that easy because of both economic and international political reasons (Alhan, 2024). Also, the dollar is widely used in FOREX markets and almost all central banks hold dollars as a reserve currency. Thus, despite the reduction in its global reserve currency share against the euro and the renminbi, the dollar is still widely used reserve currency globally. Furthermore, the expected impact of the new BRICS currency is not certain, yet. (Pistilli, 2024b).

Still about 99% of the stablecoin industry is integrated into the US dollar which implies that the crypto assets are and will be traded in the near future in the US dollars (Bertaut, von Beschwitz, and Curcuru, 2023). De-dollarization will not be that easy for the new BRICS payment system and currency. As expressed by the IMF, 59% of all global reserves are in the US dollar. Besides, 80-90% of global trade and 85% of all FOREX trades have been conducted in the US dollar. Furthermore, oil is priced in the US dollar. 60% of global debt issuance is priced in the US dollars and finally, US Treasuries are still accepted as the safe haven asset for the global investors. The US has also immense power because of the sanctions. The US has the power to exclude any party from the US markets or restrict access to capital if they break the sanctions and have business with the party the US initiated sanction. These types of sanctions are called secondary sanctions and they are one of the powerful weapons of the US on the rest of the world. There is no doubt that any country choosing BRICS to the US for economic or political reasons may be excluded from the Western financial and economic system which is dominated by the largest economy by nominal GDP. However, it should be noted that BRICS members represent a great global GDP and will increase their economic and financial role in the near future as their economy grows (Lucas, 2024).

## CONCLUSION

The BRICS+ countries, which represent more than 40% of the world population and 25% of the world economy, have been trying to have a stronger voice in the current global system. In addition to the founding members, Saudi Arabia, UAE, Iran, Ethiopia and Egypt were also included in the bloc. With the new member the bloc has gained significant power in the fields of energy, agriculture and manufacturing industries in the global economy.

Emerging economies are significantly affected by the dominance of the dollar, which has been the global reserve currency of the global financial system since World War II. While the use of the dollar as a reserve currency in all trade and financial transactions increases transaction costs on the one hand, on the other hand, it makes it mandatory for these countries to hold dollars as reserves in order to conduct foreign trade. The fluctuations in the dollar exchange rates lead to the trade and financial vulnerabilities of these countries. Furthermore, the US government has been using the dollar as a financial weapon for many years. Iran, Venezuela and Russia have experienced significant problems in foreign trade and financial payment processes due to the sanctions imposed by the US. To alleviate the negative effect of it, the BRICS members started to use their own local currencies instead of the dollar in their bilateral trade. The presidents of the BRICS member countries are making important initiatives to create a common BRICS coin and make purchases in this currency rather than trading in national currencies. The technological developments and innovation in the field of cryptocurrency in recent years are generally ongoing negotiations on the cryptocurrency as a common currency of BRICS. The expected BRICS coin will not only cost-effective but also gain an important area against the hegemony of the dollar. If the BRICS coin is successful, the global hegemony of the dollar, which has continued for about 80 years, will significantly weaken. Emerging markets that can trade internationally without dollars will have a significant advantage.

However, the BRICS coin process includes critical problems and difficulties. It is not that easy to have monetary union since economic and political conditions of every member is not identical with the others. Among BRICS members, Chinese renminbi can be the common currency for the time being. However, such a policy may bring the China dominance. Saudi Arabia and China have been discussing to have oil trade in petro yuan instead of petro dollar. However, since riyal is tied to the dollar, it will not be that easy. If the entire system can be overcome and a cryptocurrency can be issued by a common central bank of BRICS, there is a possibility that significant changes will occur in the global financial system.

Still, the impact of the expected BRICS currency on the US dollar will depend on its stability, its adoption, and the possibility to be acceptable alternative the dollar's hegemony. However, since the dollar has been reserve currency for 80 years, there are many countries continue to trade in dollars. Oil industry is not exceptional. Since the dollar is both a fiat money for international trade as well as store of value, it will probably remain the world's dominant reserve currency in the near future.

## REFERENCES


Abay, E. (2024). Russia begins using cryptocurrencies in international payments. Anadolu Ajansı. 28 August 2024. https://www.aa.com.tr/tr/ekonomi/rusya-uluslararasi-odemelerde-kripto-paralari-kullanmaya-basliyor/3314827#

Alhan, D. (2024). It will take a "long time" for the yuan to replace the US dollar in oil trading. 30 September 2024. https://www.aa.com.tr/tr/ekonomi/petrol-ticaretinde-yuanin-abd-dolarinin-yerine-gecmesinin-uzun-zaman-almasi-bekleniyor/3345987

Arslanalp, S. (2021). US Dollar Share of Global Foreign Exchange Reserves Drops to 25-Year Low. IMF Blog. https://www.imf.org/en/Blogs/Articles/2021/05/05/blog-us-dollar-share-of-global-foreign-exchange-reserves-drops-to-25-year-low

Bertaut, C., von Beschwitz, B., & Curcuru, S. (2023). "The International Role of the U.S. Dollar" Post-COVID Edition. FEDS notes, 23 June 2023. https://www.federalreserve.gov/econres/notes/feds-notes/the-international-role-of-the-us-dollar-post-covid-edition-20230623.html

Bitcoin.comNews (2024a). Putin: Russia Examines Digital Currencies for Sovereign Payments, 28 September 2024. https://news.bitcoin.com/tr/putin-rusya-bagimsiz-odemeler-icin-dijital-para-birimlerini-inceliyor/

Bitcoin.comNews (2024b). BRICS Countries Are Developing Their Own Payment and Clearing System: Putin. https://news.bitcoin.com/tr/putin-brics-ulkeleri-kendi-odeme-ve-takas-sistemini-gelistiriyor/

Boocker, S., & Wessel, D. (2024). The changing role of the US dollar. https://www.brookings.edu/articles/the-changing-role-of-the-us-dollar/#:~:text=Dollar%20assets%20comprise%20about%2059,is%20the%20euro%20at%2020%25

BRICS Business Council. (2019). The new international payment system in BRICS plus format and its BRICS pay retail segment. https://digitalbankbrics.com/media/NIPS_Presentation_EN.pdf

Capie, F. (2013). Development and Evolution of International Financial Architecture. In Caprio, G., Bacchetta, P., Barth, J. R., Hoshi, T., Lane, P. R., Mayes, D. G., Mian, A. R., & Taylor, M. (Eds.), *Handbook of Safeguarding Global Financial Stability: Political, social, cultural, and economic theories and models* (pp. 511–523). Academic Press. DOI: 10.1016/B978-0-12-397875-2.00032-5

Carrick, J. (2016). Bitcoin as a Complement to Emerging Market Currencies. *Emerging Markets Finance & Trade*, 52(10), 2321–2334. DOI: 10.1080/1540496X.2016.1193002

Coin, B. R. I. C. S. (2023). BRICS Coin Whitepaper. https://hd4s.atlantiscex.com/storage/ieoimage/whitepaper/1694659752559.pdf

Conte, N., & Lam, S. (2024). Economic Growth Forecasts for G7 and BRICS Countries in 2024. April 24, 2024. https://www.visualcapitalist.com/economic-growth-forecasts-for-g7-and-brics-countries-in-2024/#:~:text=While%20the%20G7%20countries'%20combined,economic%20size%20within%20two%20decades

Federal Trade Commission Consumer Advice. (2024). Cryptocurrencies versus US dollars. https://consumer.ftc.gov/node/77130

Galanos, G., Kotios, A., & Pavlidis, G. (2011). Greece and the Euro: The Chronicle of an Expected Collapse. *Inter Economics*, 46(5), 263–269. https://www.intereconomics.eu/contents/year/2011/number/5/article/greece-and-the-euro-the-chronicle-of-an-expected-collapse.html. DOI: 10.1007/s10272-011-0390-7

geekforgeeks.org. (2024). Top 10 Agricultural Producing Countries in the World. 22 Feb, 2024. https://www.geeksforgeeks.org/agricultural-producing-countries-in-the-world/

Griffith-Jones, S. (2015). Financing Global Development: The BRICS New Development Bank. German Development Institute, Briefing Paper, 13/2015. https://www.idos-research.de/fileadmin/migratedNewsAssets/Files/BP_13.2015.pdf

Hansen, S. (2021). Guide To Top Cryptocurrency Exchanges. https://www.forbes.com/sites/sarahhansen/2018/06/20/forbes-guide-to-cryptocurrency-exchanges/#726c59b42572

Huang, R. (2024, July). A 2024 Overview Of The E-CNY, China's Digital Yuan. *Forbes*, 15, •••. https://www.forbes.com/sites/digital-assets/2024/07/15/a-2024-overview-of-the-e-cny-chinas-digital-yuan/

Inman, P. (2019). Mark Carney: dollar is too dominant and could be replaced by digital currency. https://www.theguardian.com/business/2019/aug/23/mark-carney-dollar-dominant-replaced-digital-currency

Jordaan, A. C. (2021). BRICS – quo vadis? *Development Southern Africa*, 38(3), 454–468. DOI: 10.1080/0376835X.2020.1870932

Lagutina, M.L. (2019). BRICS in a world of regions. *Third World Thematics: A TWQ Journal*, 4(6), 442-458.

Lucas, G. (2024). Is BRICS about to announce a gold-backed currency? https://coingeek.com/is-brics-about-to-announce-a-gold-backed-currency/

Nakamoto, S. (2009). Bitcoin: A Peer-to-Peer Electronic Cash System. https://bitcoin.org/bitcoin.pdf

Nulimaimaiti, M. (2023). What's the state of China's digital yuan in 2023? South China Morning Post,10 October 2023. https://www.scmp.com/economy/china-economy/article/3237317/whats-state-chinas-digital-yuan-2023

Orcutt, M. (2023). What's next for China's digital currency? MIT Technology Review. 3 August 2023. https://www.technologyreview.com/2023/08/03/1077181/whats-next-for-chinas-digital-currency/

Ostroukh, A. (2019). Russia says BRICS nations favour idea of common payment system. Reuters, November 14, 2019. https://www.reuters.com/article/world/russia-says-brics-nations-favour-idea-of-common-payment-system-idUSKBN1XO1PC/

Oswega State University of New York. (2024). The Basics about Cryptocurrency. https://www.oswego.edu/cts/basics-about-cryptocurrency#:~:text=A%20cryptocurrency%20is%20a%20digital,you%20need%20a%20cryptocurrency%20wallet

Pistilli, M. (2024a). Top 10 Oil-producing Countries (Updated 2024). Investing News Network. 14 August 2024. https://investingnews.com/daily/resource-investing/energy-investing/oil-and-gas-investing/top-oil-producing-countries/

Pistilli, M. (2024b). How Would a New BRICS Currency Affect the US Dollar? (Updated 2024). 12 September 2024. https://www.nasdaq.com/articles/how-would-new-brics-currency-affect-us-dollar-updated-2024

Poenisch, H. (2023). Brics common currency would be no threat to the dollar, 13 June 2023. https://www.omfif.org/2023/06/brics-common-currency-would-be-no-threat-to-the-dollar/

Procházka, D. (2018). Accounting for Bitcoin and Other Cryptocurrencies under IFRS: A Comparison and Assessment of Competing Models. *The International Journal of Digital Accounting Research*, 18, 161–188. DOI: 10.4192/1577-8517-v18_7

Ramos, M. (2023). De-dollarization: 95% of the trade between China and Russia didn't use the US dollar. BrasildeFato. 21 December 2023. https://www.brasildefato.com.br/2023/12/21/de-dollarization-95-of-the-trade-between-china-and-russia-didn-t-use-the-us-dollar

Reuters (2024a). New US sanctions force the end of dollar and euro trading on Russia's main exchange. June 13, 2024. https://edition.cnn.com/2024/06/13/investing/us-russia-sanctions-dollar-euro-trading/index.html

Reuters (2024b). China-Russia 2023 trade value hits record high of $240 bln - Chinese customs. 12 January 2024. https://www.reuters.com/markets/china-russia-2023-trade-value-hits-record-high-240-bln-chinese-customs-2024-01-12/

RFE/RL. (2017). Putin Warns Cryptocurrencies Like Bitcoin Carry 'Serious Risks'. https://www.rferl.org/a/putin-bitcoin-cryptocurrencies-regulation/28785150.html

safeguardglobal.com. (2024). Top 10 manufacturing countries in the world in 2024. 29 August 2024. https://www.safeguardglobal.com/resources/top-10-manufacturing-countries-in-the-world/

Savage, R. (2023). What is a BRICS currency and is the U.S. dollar in trouble? Reuters August 24, 2023. https://www.reuters.com/markets/currencies/what-is-brics-currency-could-one-be-adopted-2023-08-23/

Singh, D. (2024). Forging a positive vision of economic statecraft, 22 February 2024. https://www.atlanticcouncil.org/blogs/new-atlanticist/forging-a-positive-vision-of-economic-statecraft/

Slim, A. (2023). Will the BRICS be the leaders in central bank digital currencies? *Economic Studies Journal (Ikonomicheski Izsledvania)*, 2021, 30 (3),.3-16

Song, J., Chen, Y., Li, Y., & Sun, Q. (2022). Cryptocurrencies' past, present and future. Proceedings of the 2022, 2nd International Conference on Economic Development and Business Culture (ICEDBC 2022), AEBMR 225, Ed. Y. Jiang et al. 1402-1413. file:///C:/Users/user/Downloads/125983674.pdf

Statista (2024a). Total population of the BRICS countries from 2000 to 2029. https://www.statista.com/statistics/254205/total-population-of-the-bric-countries/

Statista (2024b). BRICS and G7 countries' share of the world's total gross domestic product (GDP) in purchasing power parity (PPP) from 2000 to 2023. 13 February 2024. https://www.statista.com/statistics/1412425/gdp-ppp-share-world-gdp-g7-brics/

Statista (2024c). Cryptocurrencies – Worldwide. https://www.statista.com/outlook/fmo/digital-assets/cryptocurrencies/worldwide

Teslova, E. (2024). Putin says trade turnover with China sets new record of $240B. Anadolu Ajansı. 16.05.2024. https://www.aa.com.tr/en/asia-pacific/putin-says-trade-turnover-with-china-sets-new-record-of-240b/3221034

The Jerusalem Post. (2024). Putin Confirms BRICS Developing Independent Payment System with Potential Gold-Backed Currency. https://www.jpost.com/business-and-innovation/precious-metals/article-822549

Toussaint, E. (2024). Are the BRICS and their New Development Bank offering alternatives to the World Bank, the IMF and the policies promoted by the traditional imperialist powers? 21 April 2024. https://www.cadtm.org/spip.php?page=imprimer&id_article=22501

Tran, H. (2024). Is the end of the petrodollar near? June 20, 2024. https://www.atlanticcouncil.org/blogs/econographics/is-the-end-of-the-petrodollar-near/

Varela, A. H., & Delgado, R. G. M. (2019, October). The BRICS in the Contemporary Global Order: Objectives, Capabilities, and Limitations. *Jurnal Ilmu Pemerintahan*, 9(2), 89–106.

Wang, W., & Wang, H. (2023). Interconnected Markets: Exploring the Dynamic Relationship Between BRICS Stock Markets and Cryptocurrency. Texas A&M International University. https://arxiv.org/pdf/2406.07641

World Trade Organization. (2024). The Doha Round. https://www.wto.org/english/tratop_e/dda_e/dda_e.htm

worldometer (2024). Countries in the world by population (2024). https://www.worldometers.info/world-population/population-by-country/

Xinhua (2024). New Development Bank to expand use of local currencies, 31 August 2024. https://english.news.cn/africa/20240831/2e16f6c2a1dc4ad2bf9c3c069b790aed/c.html

https://www.ndb.int/about-ndb/history/

## ENDNOTES

1 The Doha Round which was launched in November 2001, in Doha, Qatar, is the round of trade negotiations among the World Trade Organization membership. It aims to reform of the international trading system by lowering trade barriers and revised trade rules to improve the trading prospects of developing countries (World Trade Organization, 2024).

2 Stablecoins are cryptocurrencies where the value of the digital asset is pegged to a reference asset, which is either fiat money such as dollar, euro, yuan; exchange-traded commodities such as precious metals or industrial metals; or another cryptocurrency such as Bitcoin.

# Chapter 10
# The Political Economy of Digital Nature-Based Currencies: Opportunities for the BRICS Countries?

**Silvio Andrae**
https://orcid.org/0000-0002-8586-7812
*Independent Researcher, Berlin, Germany*

## ABSTRACT

*A digital, nature-based currency (NBDC) is backed by real value and forms the basis of a genuinely sustainable, nature-based economy. The NBDC and the underlying technologies offer a new perspective on how digital resilience can be built in ecological contexts. It shows how an NBDC can function as a model. As natural capital accounting becomes the fundamental asset for new monetary systems, blockchain's inherent trust and sequential accounting capabilities are essential for monitoring and verifying the state of nature and its corresponding financial value. In addition, the legal anchoring of rights of nature and nature-based solutions are essential conditions for establishing an NBDC. Given the reservoir of natural resources in the BRICS countries, the project seems predestined for them. BRICS countries could be pioneers in establishing NBDCs. The chapter presents an innovative approach to the design of an NBDC.*

DOI: 10.4018/979-8-3693-7393-4.ch010

## INTRODUCTION

The structure of the global economy is increasingly drifting towards strong fragmentation and polycentricity. The global monetary order remains hierarchical (Murau et al., 2021). The roughly divided tripartite currency hierarchy looks as follows: At the top is a system of critical currencies linking flexible exchange rates. The key currencies include the US dollar, euro, yen and Swiss franc, with the dollar occupying the top position thanks to its global dominance. They are followed by a system of adjusted currencies linked to a critical currency via a fixed exchange rate. At the lower end of the currency hierarchy are the currencies that are, in principle, under threat of devaluation. Key currencies, on the other hand, are under suspicion of appreciation. Even if there are repeated efforts to escape the allocation in the currency hierarchy (e.g., for the renminbi: Zhang et al., 2024), the BRICS currencies still need to be contractable and are at the lower end of the currency hierarchy.

The strategy of currency substitution, which involves using a foreign currency in parallel with or instead of the domestic currency, is seen as one solution. Dollarization, a form of currency substitution where the US dollar is used as the primary currency, is an ideal state of monetary relations: it supposedly shields the real sector from monetary disruptions resulting from the discretionary monetary policy of the domestic central bank. In addition, the exchange rate is eliminated in the dollarized world. However, this state of affairs also indicates a severe dysfunction, ultimately ending in the domestic currency and economy erosion. The situation is exacerbated by administered capital imports, even if the accumulating foreign debt is regularly partially forgiven as part of debt rescheduling agreements. In this respect, currency substitution is also not a successful development strategy within the existing structure of the monetary architecture.

However, the key currencies have also had to contend with a loss of confidence in recent years. These currencies have also lost considerable purchasing power since the COVID-19 crisis. Is this weakness of the West a great opportunity for the BRICS countries to finally venture out of the shadows of the industrialized countries with their strong currency? There have been more than just ideas for a long time. It would herald a turning point in economic and geopolitical terms if successful. If the dollar hegemony were to be broken, this would massively weaken the West. The BRICS countries themselves could exploit the privileges of a strong currency, such as the increased fiscal leeway. The following is about something other than the introduction of a BRICS currency. However, some aspects should be mentioned because they are essential for the political economy of a nature-based currency. A nature-based digital currency could offer sustainable solutions and a hopeful future for global finance. In addition to the strong interest in a common currency, several other conditions would have to be met.

The BRICS need a vehicle currency in the short and medium term. This currency must be strong and offer stable relations with the rest of the world—primarily the US dollar (USD)—and be freely convertible. The renminbi has shown that it can only play this role to a limited extent due to its depreciation and exchange rate volatility, Chinese restrictions on financial accounts and a heavily managed offshore renminbi market. A currency privilege has to be worked hard. Michael Bordo calls it the 'monetary paradox':

*'[T]he closer an asset comes to an ideal money (perfectly safe and always liquid), the fewer questions get asked and the more opaque it becomes; yet this same opacity increases the profits to money creation and thereby, the temptation to undermine the safety on which money-ness depends.' (Bordo & Roberds, 2024, p.2)*

Does the solution include introducing Central Bank Digital Currencies (CBDCs)? It is a digital form of money issued directly by a central bank. Over 90 per cent of all countries in the world are discussing the introduction of a CBDC (https://cbdctracker.org/). Prasad (2021) shows how new forms of money and new channels for payment transactions within and between economies affect international capital flows, exchange rates and the structure of the international monetary system. It is more than just a guess that introducing CBDCs in advanced countries will also significantly impact emerging markets. Currency substitution is the primary channel through which these effects are likely to spread. One of the critical advantages of CBDCs is the lower cost of migrants' remittances to their home countries. However, this is offset by some disadvantages. Global CBDCs are expected to increase the pressure for currency substitution. Sudden currency devaluations and lower revenues for central banks will accompany it. As already observed in the case of classic dollarization, countries will become even more susceptible to currency mismatches. The core problem of the dollarized economy is that the primary creditor function of the central bank needs to be recovered. As this leads to structural problems in the financial sector, the dollarized economy inevitably has to contend with the familiar challenges at the lower level of the currency hierarchy. The disadvantages can only be mitigated through international coordination and cooperation. This underscores the importance of unity and collaboration in shaping the future of global finance.

Considering the overall size of their economies, the BRICS countries have a theoretical motivation to de-dollarize their international payment flows to reduce currency and sanction risks. The increased self-confidence of the BRICS vis-à-vis the G7 is based on macroeconomic factors. An expansion to BRICS+ further strengthens this motivation. Such an expansion could create a strategic bloc that could potentially become the most significant global player. With more than half of the world's population behind it, the BRICS+ could significantly alter global trade and investment flows, potentially reshaping the global economic landscape.

Added to this is the enormous wealth of natural resources in the BRICS countries. These resources offer both great opportunities and considerable challenges. Nature is the most critical infrastructure supporting businesses, economies, and societies. The rapid decline in the natural capital stock clearly shows that the current financing mechanisms must achieve their objectives. It is not just time; it is urgent to invest in preserving and restoring natural capital (NC) and putting nature on balance sheets. This sense of urgency should drive our commitment to these crucial tasks.

The ecological crises of climate change and biodiversity loss are global. The primary responsibility for the crises lies with the industrialized countries. The US, the EU and the UK are responsible for almost half of all historical emissions. However, they only account for 10 per cent of the world's population. The countries of the global South will be disproportionately affected by these global trends. Fiscal transfers in the form of development aid and private investment have failed to deliver on the promise of climate change finance, and this is due to the architecture of the existing monetary and financial system. In this respect, a new approach needs to be discussed. It is the introduction of a new digital currency backed by NC. We call it nature-based digital currency (NBDC). The NBDC could be a game-changer for the BRICS countries, offering a new avenue for sustainable economic development and climate change finance.

The book chapter discusses the design of an NBDC. It is a prototype design since an NBDC does not yet exist in practice. Real values back a digital, nature-based currency (NBDC) and form the basis of a genuinely sustainable, nature-based economy. The NBDC and the underlying technologies offer a new perspective on how digital resilience can be built in ecological contexts. As natural capital accounting (NCA) becomes the foundational asset for new monetary systems, blockchain's trust and sequential accounting capabilities are essential for monitoring and verifying the state of nature and its corresponding financial value. In addition, the legal anchoring of rights of nature and nature-based solutions are essential conditions for establishing an NBDC. Developing an NBDC is a complex process that requires close cooperation between science, politics and business. Given the reservoir of natural resources in the BRICS countries, the project seems predestined for them. BRICS countries could be pioneers in establishing NBDCs. Questions regarding mandate, legitimacy and institutional design are being discussed. An NBDC offers the BRICS states an opportunity to counter the constraints of the global monetary hierarchy and simultaneously be victims of the greatest victims of climate change.

## 1. RELATED WORKS

The pressing political goal of the first order is to establish mechanisms for financing a green transition. The current state of climate finance is a cause for concern, with an average of USD 653 billion being spent annually on mitigation, adaptation, and compensation for climate damage and loss from public and private sources (Naran et al., 2022). However, to achieve the 1.5°C target of the Paris Climate Agreement (PCA) by 2030, global climate finance must increase eightfold to USD 5 trillion annually (Boehm et al., 2022).

The call for more climate finance is indeed crucial. However, the current practice is alarming. Much of the funding is diverted from budgets supporting vital development priorities such as health, education, women's rights, infrastructure construction, and humanitarian aid (Ramachandran & Smith, 2023). CARE (2023) estimates that 52 per cent of the climate funds provided by 23 affluent countries between 2011 and 2020 were previously allocated to development budgets, including health, education, and women's rights programs. Due to climate policy, this diversion of funds has led to severe cuts in essential aid programs, causing immediate and long-term harm. The situation worsens when we consider the long-standing commitment of 0.75 per cent of gross national income for development aid. If we take this figure as a minimum for development spending and assume that climate finance should be additional, only 7 per cent of rich countries' climate finance can be considered as such.

In addition, another error underlying the concept of climate finance is the premise that capital aid from rich countries will provide for renewable energy-based economic development in the Global South. For the most part, rich countries have not yet recognized what low-income countries need to address climate change: resilient buildings and infrastructure, cheap and reliable electricity, early warning systems, air conditioning, cold storage for food and medicine, dikes, dams, paved roads and all the things that make a safe life possible. However, these investments are also not being financed to a sufficient extent by domestic financial institutions (Ramachandran & Smith, 2023). According to the World Bank (2024), around 60 per cent of banks in emerging and developing countries allocate 5 per cent or less of their loans to climate action. Regarding climate adaptation, this figure is as low as 16 per cent of domestic and international climate finance, 98 per cent of which is public or official financing.

One solution would be establishing a World Climate Bank (WCB) (Andrae, 2024a; Marois, T., 2023). A WCB could anchor a global green and fair public finance system that is not based on the World Bank's failed de-risking model. De-risking focuses the use of public funds on maximizing the returns of private investors in climate finance without considering equitable green transitions. The WCB would be anchored in public-public collaborations. Such collaborations are non-competitive relationships between public sector entities focused on achieving shared goals, such as essential services like water and the Sustainable Development Goals (SDGs). The WCB requires new and inclusive forms of governance: it would establish itself as a global financial governor. Generous contributions from concessional funds would enable the WCB to approach climate lending differently. Lending should be more closely aligned with the priorities and needs of the borrowing countries, especially those of the indebted Global South. Regardless of the composition of stakeholders, green and equitable climate finance can only happen with substantial budgetary support from wealthy nations. Given the enormous global inequalities in carbon footprints, progressive carbon tax systems can be a funding source for the WCB.

Another alternative could be for each country's central bank to design its CBDC to be expressed in its fiat currency. The primary purpose would be to facilitate payment processing in universal basic income, stimulus payments, or (climate) disaster relief. Cell phone payments could be made to citizens in specific (economically depressed) areas or weather-related regions to purchase a wide range of predetermined goods, with the value eroding over time to increase the overall velocity of circulation.

Another solution is for a stablecoin issued based on IMF Special Drawing Rights (SDRs) to complement existing government fiat currencies, local currencies, cryptocurrencies and central bank-issued CBDCs. This so-called Climate Stable Coin (CSC) would be offered in return for tangible progress made by countries on their voluntary nationally determined contributions (NDCs). The CSC is a unit of account, value store, and reward incentive. However, the CSC would not function as a medium of exchange. The currency would be backed by a (partial) collateral pool consisting of SDRs and usable currencies. The demand for the CSC would initially depend on the level of NDCs of the individual countries, which, according to the Paris Agreement, should lead to a carbon-free climate by 2050. Using the global positioning system, the IMF registry will guarantee that countries' efforts to reduce greenhouse gas emissions are unique and have not been replicated in any existing registry. The IMF would also maintain a multi-year carbon registry by parcel (land, forest, water areas, mangroves) identified through submitted NDCs. Contributions could focus on regeneration (soil regeneration, afforestation), decarbonization or comprehensive conservation measures (protection of rainforests). The aim is to assign a value to the natural carbon sequestration of forests and land. The techniques for measuring carbon sequestration need to be standardized (Van Gansbeke, 2021).

Nature Equity is a contract to finance conservation, restoration and enhancement. The contract, concluded between each land manager and buyer, combines a biophysical conservation or enhancement unit with a payment. Land managers receive a results-oriented reward for their land use practices, while investors receive solid proof of conservation. Based on nature-backed contracts leading to nature-backed assets and nature-backed securities, nature equity could lead to nature-based currencies and eventually to nature-backed assets (The Landbanking Group, 2024)

Lagoarde-Ségot and Mathieu (2024) developed a local complementary currency (LLC) policy prototype linked to sustainability and biomimetic resilience criteria. LCCs complement the existing monetary order by giving money new purpose-linked goals such as solidarity, sharing, reciprocity, and environmental protection. LCCs are fully convertible into legal tender. A one-to-one match between each LCC unit and previous legal tender bank deposits usually guarantees convertibility. LCCs consist of monetary tokens backed by a legal tender guarantee fund. They can be used to exchange goods and services within a local community.

Wainstein et al. (2023) discuss the concept of Nature-Based Currencies (NBCs) and their potential to integrate natural capital into advanced monetary systems for the first time and in detail. Various types of NBCs are presented. The paper will be understood as a thought experiment on designing fair financial and monetary systems that intrinsically value nature and prioritize human well-being and the planet's health.

The following will develop the concept of an NBDC. The starting point is the procedures for evaluating the NC.

## 2. NATURAL CAPITAL

Possible paths to sustainability are based on different concepts of 'nature positive', which refers to approaches that aim to enhance and protect the natural environment (Luxton et al., 2024). Adloff and Hilbrich (2021) distinguish three paths to sustainability (modernization, transformation and control). The concept of natural capital accounting (NCA) is presented as a representative of the modernization path (AFN, 2023). Typical of the modernization pathway is the idea that nature provides ecosystem services relevant to human society. Here, nature is reified and monetized in terms of its benefits for human society. The discourse on the rights of nature (RoN), whose starting point can be found in Latin American indigenous discourses, represents the path of transformation. The ethical intrinsic value of nature is thus emphasized here, even if various authors have already criticized this (Viaene, 2022), sparking essential debates in the field.

*Figure 1. On the way to a regenerative society*

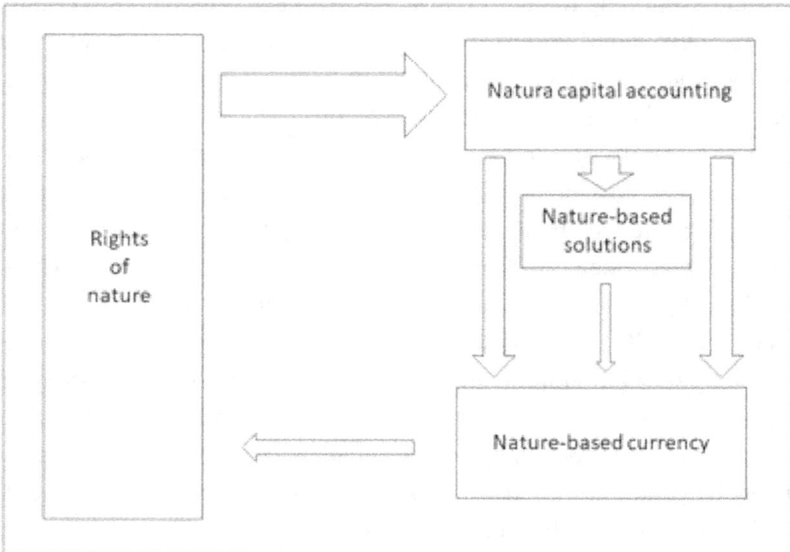


Source: own representation

The goal is to establish assessment benchmarks and, based on these, nature-based solutions (NbS) that can guide us towards a regenerative society. The RoN is a crucial building block for an NBDC. These approaches are not just important; they are urgent. Without them, we cannot establish a means of payment for ecosystems. Natural resources and ecosystems are more valuable alive because a tradable digital value can be assigned to the species and entities concerned.

## 2.1 Natural Capital Accounting

The assessment of environmental change and resource management is becoming increasingly important (Troy & Wilson, 2006), even if the concept of natural capital (NC) is repeatedly criticized (Maechler & Boisvert, 2024). NC includes the resources found in nature, such as minerals, oil, fish and timber stocks in forests, water, arable land, but also the ecosystem services provided by ecosystems that are invisible to most people, such as purification of air and water, protection from flooding or erosion, sequestration and storage of carbon, provision of habitat for species and others.

Ecosystem services are the benefits that people derive from ecosystems. They can be subdivided into provisioning:

- material services (e.g., food, water supply, electricity generation from hydropower),
- regulating services (e.g., carbon sequestration, flood protection, soil retention) and
- intangible services (e.g., ecotourism, mental health).

The first step in accounting for natural assets and ecological services or functions for human activities in environmental-economic accounting is to define their spatial and functional dimensions. Measuring and evaluating these two dimensions and identifying the interrelationship of these components with human activities, particularly with the economy, enables the integration of ecosystems into an accounting structure (Obst et al., 2016). This process, known as Natural Capital Accounting (NCA), will only be briefly presented below, as it is necessary to understand the concept of a National Biodiversity Data Centre (NBDC).

The significant advantage of such an accounting framework is that it clearly shows the interrelationship between the economy and the environment. Using an accounting framework makes it possible to see the identified ecosystems and the assessed service flows about each other, as well as a range of other environmental, economic, and social information. The general steps of ecosystem accounting are illustrated in Figure 2. Ecosystem accounting can provide information on the extent of ecosystems, their condition based on selected indicators and the flow of ecosystem services. Due to the spatial nature of ecosystem accounting, maps are a standard method of presenting information. The links between an ecosystem and the economy can be represented physically and financially (Figure 2).

*Figure 2. Broad steps in ecosystem asset accounting*

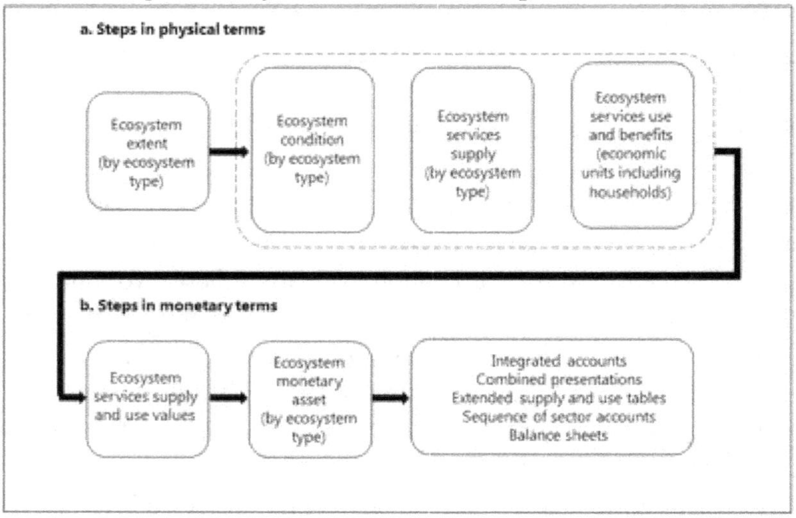


Source: own representation

It is often difficult to represent both physical and monetary values. To solve these problems, Zhang et al. (2023) integrated ecological footprint and ecosystem service methods into NCA. The authors introduce equivalence factors for ecosystem services. These factors are designed to facilitate the formulation of a standardized and flexible framework for NCA by providing a common unit of measurement for different ecosystem services. This framework is applied in provinces along China's Silk Road Economic Belt (SREB).

A pivotal step towards NCA was the adoption of the System of Environmental-Economic Accounting (SEEA) in 2012 (UN, 2014). This system, developed by the United Nations, provides an internationally agreed-upon method compatible with the current System of National Accounts (SNA). In this way, renewable and non-renewable natural resources such as minerals, timber, water, and others are to be accounted for physically. These resources are assumed to be tradable in established markets. In this respect, pricing can be based on known methods of environmental economics.

However, most ecosystem services are neither measured nor traded on markets. Due to the complexity and diversity of ecosystems worldwide, their inclusion in the accounting system necessitates research and an international debate among experts on the methodology to be applied in each case (Costanza et al., 2021). This international collaboration is crucial for the successful integration of ecosystem services into national accounting standards.

The SEEA provides a reliable measurement framework that enables an in-depth understanding of economic prosperity and NC links. It integrates economic and environmental information using internationally agreed statistical standards developed and applied by governments worldwide. The new methodology is being piloted in several countries, with countries testing different accounts and services depending on their priorities and circumstances. It is noticeable that the valuation of ecosystem services is being carried out primarily in emerging economies.

The NCAVES project, launched in 2017, is a significant initiative to advance both the knowledge agenda and the development of ecosystem accounting. Implemented in five participating partner countries (Brazil, China, India, Mexico, and South Africa), the project has seen active participation and contribution from these countries, leading to the adoption of the SEEA EA as a statistical standard by the United Nations (UN) Statistical Commission in March 2021. This adoption reflects the project's importance and impact on the UN's common agenda, which now calls on Member States and others to start implementing the SEEA EA. While the publication of the SEEA documents represents an essential milestone for the national accounting approach, there are still several challenges in integrating measurements of ecosystem goods and services into national accounting standards. These challenges need to be addressed when establishing an NDDC.

Comparative case studies from Brazil, India, and China, as presented by Andrae (2024 b), highlight both successes and challenges in valuing ecosystem services. These studies provide valuable insights into the progress made by Brazil and India in taking the first steps, as well as the significant strides China has already made (Yang et al., 2023). The findings from these regional studies underscore the importance of tailored measures for local economic growth and environmental protection, which can better support companies with environmental reforms. This information is crucial for understanding the current state of research and the potential for future advancements in ecosystem services valuation.

The NCA is essential for the design of an NBDC. The necessary data is already being collected and consolidated as part of the NCA so that the NBDC can build on it.

## 2.2 Rights of Nature

Similar to current fiat currencies, an NBDC requires backing by law. The potential of an NBDC, backed by law, to significantly influence economic decisions targeting sectors of the economy that utilize CBDC is a fascinating prospect. This high centrality of the state can have both advantages and disadvantages. Including rights of nature (RoN) in the constitution may be necessary to ensure that the rule of law applies regardless of a political agenda (Kauffman & Martin, 2021). In 2020,

Putzer et al. (2022) counted 409 initiatives in 39 countries to grant subjective rights to nature per se or natural entities.

The existing rights of nature in the countries of the Global South express a universal idea of rights. This universalism of intrinsic ecological rights, if nature deserves rights, must apply worldwide. The global applicability of these rights is a unifying force, connecting all inhabitants of the planet in a shared responsibility. However, universal validity is not achieved by imposing a norm on foreign legal cultures. Instead, the universalism of intrinsic ecological rights lies in the fact that they are derived from different contexts. For example, ecological rights in the Global South have so far been tied to specific contexts: the granting of ecocentric rights in the case of the Yamunotri and Gangotri glaciers or the river in India, organizing approaches with the Te Awa Tupua Act in New Zealand or the attribution of biocultural rights in the case of the Atrato River and the Amazon rainforest in Colombia. These new people can be owned and appropriated. These figures of justification fulfil their purpose in the specific local case but cannot be transferred to the legal cultures of the Global North. They follow a different logic of validity. However, a certain universalism is necessary for an NBDC.

Rule over nature is exercised in four ways:

- Through technology, nature is tamed, controlled, and imitated.
- Science is used to make its forces and processes recognizable, calculable, and predictable.
- In the economy, nature is exploited as a supposedly free resource and for-profit.
- The law makes nature available as property.

The latter form of domination acts as an accelerant for the ecological crises. With the help of property rights, nature is transformed into a controllable thing over which its owners have free control. This dominion is exercised as the right to use natural goods like any other thing. Property rights authorize the unrestricted use and consumption of natural goods. Property rights make natural goods available in the first place and create the prerequisite for natural goods to be utilized economically, fed into economic processes, and traded as goods. It establishes an extractive relationship with nature and opens the door to ecological crises (Figure 3).

*Figure 3. Monetary economy and nature*

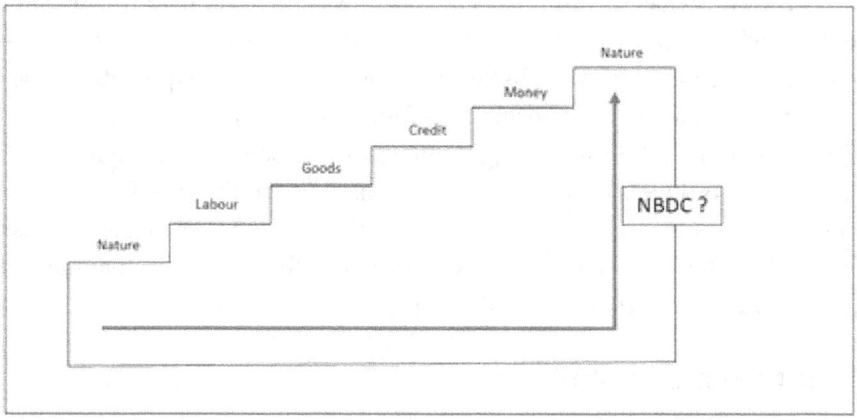


Source: own representation

There needs to be more space here to expand on the RoN concept. However, we will outline a few essential critical points for understanding NBDC. What is urgently needed is an 'ecologization of property'. This concept is not just a theoretical idea, but a practical necessity for the sustainable use of natural resources. Moreover, ownership can be allowed to continue. By institutionalizing the RoN in sustainable property rights, the socio-ecological transformation occurs along the lines of a structural change in property. Property rights have a protective function. They protect property from being damaged or destroyed by others. This protection also applies to the property rights of nature. Property rights impose an obligation not to jeopardize the preservation of natural assets. Users of nature are obliged to ensure sustainability (Wesche, 2022).

> *'By deriving the sustainability obligation from property rights themselves, it is possible from the outset to bring the two into a coherent relationship; their scopes do not have to be corrected afterwards, as in environmental ethics. Economic functional requirements are limited here by sustainability obligations before they gain strong validity. In this respect, these sustainability obligations have a robust validity that can assert itself against economic functional requirements.' (Wesche, 2022, p.66)*

Using natural assets also involves using other people's property—which belongs to nature. Due to property protection, users are obliged to use natural assets sustainably. Ownership of natural assets is only authorized under the condition of ecological sustainability. Property rights include sustainability obligations. The rights of nature, therefore, take the form of sustainable property rights (Wesche, 2022).

For the NBDC, it is essential that the legal anchoring (ideally based on the RoN) is combined with material reserves. The reserves serve as collateral but cannot be liquidated traditionally. The crucial point here is that these reserve assets must be maintained in their natural state. In this way, the NBDC has the potential to be used responsibly and sustainably, offering a hopeful outlook for the future.

Since NBDC is to be used as legal tender, it is essential to designate the economic channels or levers of an economy so that the liquidity of NBDC influences economic actors to ensure an intact nature. In addition, government institutions must determine the calculation model that will influence their decision-making process regarding the configuration of NBDC supply in the economy.

## 2.3 Nature-Based Solutions

There are many interactions between the dramatic decline in biodiversity and advancing climate change. Nature-based solutions (NbS) are available to tackle both challenges in parallel. NbS generally refers to systems and processes based on nature or natural features. NbS contribute to achieving societal goals such as climate change mitigation and adaptation, good health, food and water security and disaster prevention. They offer resource-efficient and effective alternatives to conventional technology-oriented solutions while protecting people, animals, and plants. Examples range from reforestation and creating terraces on mountain slopes to prevent flooding and landslides to the renaturation of rivers, green roofs, and climate-smart agriculture.

The potential of nature-based solutions (NbS) in our fight against climate change and biodiversity loss is not just significant, but also hopeful. According to the Intergovernmental Science-Policy Platform on Biodiversity and Ecosystem Services, NbS can contribute more than a third of the climate action needed by 2030 to meet PCA targets (IPBES, 2019). The World Economic Forum (2021) further underlines this potential, concluding that investing just 1 per cent of global GDP in NbS would significantly contribute to tackling the climate and biodiversity crisis (WEF, 2021).

Chairat and Gheewala (2024) present a quantitative assessment framework that enables a comprehensive assessment of NbS. Various tools have been integrated in response to the standard NbS criteria provided by the International Union for Conservation of Nature (IUCN), which build on the SEEA EA (Section 3.1). The framework also identifies approaches for assessing the ecosystem services NbS provides and the main concerns in conducting NbS assessments.

As the focus here is on the design of NBDCs, only individual examples from the BRICS will be briefly presented below. The NbS are the ideal anchor point for establishing NBDCs.

NbS are essential in Brazil due to the rapid loss of biodiversity and increasing environmental disasters (De Abreu et al., 2024). Ecosystem protection is Brazil's most crucial cost-effective climate protection measure. For example, implementing the Brazilian Forest Code can be one of Brazil's most important measures to reduce emissions. It would be sufficient for Brazil to achieve its short-term PCA targets by 2030. The more mitigation measures are taken in the land use sector, the less costly technical solutions are needed in the energy sector. In contrast, a heavy reliance on costly and immature technical solutions jeopardizes Brazil's chances of meeting its PCA targets (Soterroni et al., 2023). The efforts around NbS extend not only to rural areas but also to other areas. For example, Dos Santos (2024) is investigating the application of NbS in urban communities (favelas). The analysis shows that NbS can help to reduce social and ecological vulnerabilities and improve living conditions.

Despite significant progress in biodiversity conservation and restoration, China still faces the risk of ecosystem degradation (Cheng & Li, 2023). NbS is rooted in traditional Chinese ecological thinking and aligns with the modern concept of ecological civilization. However, there are significant limitations in the current implementation of NbS in China. For example, China categorizes existing ecological protection and restoration projects into NbS. The results of the NbS self-assessment tool show that not all ecological protection and restoration projects can meet NbS standards. China needs to explain further the differences between NbS and other ecological restoration projects and the benefits that NbS can bring rather than look for similarities. Finally, the benefits or economic value of NbS is challenging to assess. China invests heavily in ecological protection and restoration projects, but there needs to be more analysis of the optimal operating conditions and performance evaluation of the projects. Ecological protection and restoration projects are implemented from the top down. There is often a lack of fair compensation schemes, public participation, and consultation, which can lead to social injustice, energy inequality and disruption of public services (Luo et al., 2024). Most studies indicate that more unequal regions have lower biodiversity and more affluent areas have higher biodiversity (Kubiszewski et al., 2024).

Transparency and measurability are not just important, but crucial for the successful implementation of NbS. These factors must be improved for NbS to become widely accepted. The conditions must be created for the private and public sectors to develop. Knowledge and incentives contribute significantly to investment decisions. Low levels of investment per project, long timeframes for financial returns, and risk profiles that differ from non-nature-based investment options contribute to the fact that NbS in the BRICS region is hardly gaining momentum across the board. Other barriers to investment include a need for more information about the benefits of these solutions and a lack of technical expertise to implement the rather complex projects. Legal obstacles may also be to the necessary forms of cooperation and co-financing.

International cooperation is not just important, but crucial in promoting nature-based solutions (NbS). The BRICS alliance, especially the New Development Bank (NBD), can play a significant role. The NBD could finance NbS directly, promoting practices that strengthen ecosystems. This international support is essential for the successful implementation of NbS. Financing should consider the full range of maturity, phases, size and risk of projects. The focus should be on capacity building and early-stage financing. It includes better availability of seed capital, loans on favourable terms, investment grants, financial aid and the development of risk mitigation mechanisms. Innovation, infrastructure, and impact financing techniques can be adapted for NbS.

The public sector plays a crucial role in supporting early-stage investments in NbS. Ideally, projects should have access to a range of sector-specific financing products tailored to local circumstances. Projects should also be able to generate income from other NbS benefits. Long-term institutional investors must also be enabled and incentivized to invest in NbS. The NBDC could take over the financing of NbS. In this respect, there is a double interaction here.

## 2.4 BRICS Comparison

Four of the five BRICS countries are particularly large regarding their surface area. They have an extensive reservoir of natural capital. However, the degradation of individual ecosystems varies significantly in the three countries. The larger the endangered ecosystems, the greater the political pressure to advocate for the valuation of ecosystems and their services.

Natural capital accounting: Brazil presented an overview of Brazilian ecosystem accounting in 2021. Brazil prefers a large-scale approach, unlike China, where analyses are conducted on a smaller scale. Brazil has pilot projects to account for natural capital, particularly in the Amazon and Cerrado, two of the most vital ecosystems on the planet, but there has yet to be nationwide implementation. The importance of the Amazon as a global carbon sink and biological hotspot, and the Cerrado's unique biodiversity, makes this particularly urgent. Russia is discussing the implementation of NCA but has yet to take any concrete steps. It is worrying, as Russia has enormous natural resources potentially at risk. India also needs consistent ecosystem accounting. So far, the discussion on the valorization of ecosystem services has been conducted mainly in the Indian Himalayan states. India could make significant progress in sustainable economic activity by better capturing its biodiversity and agricultural resources.

Conversely, China is implementing comprehensive natural capital valuation systems and integrating them into its political and economic planning. China's pioneering role in ecological modernization underscores the importance of the NCA in the national development strategy. South Africa has also made progress in the NCA, particularly in water management and land use, which is particularly important given the challenges of water scarcity and agricultural depletion.

Rights of nature: Brazil is a pioneer here, especially with its legal solid anchoring in protecting the Amazon region. The rights of nature are closely linked to the rights of indigenous communities that depend on the intact environment. Russia has yet to recognize the RoN concept officially. The destruction of nature in Russia, especially in Siberia and the Arctic region, poses significant environmental challenges, which could make the introduction of rights for nature meaningful. India is discussing the topic, but there have yet to be any legal measures for formal recognition. Given the increasing environmental problems and social conflicts related to land rights, recognizing nature rights in India could bring significant progress. China is conducting pilot projects addressing nature's rights but has yet to develop a comprehensive legal framework. However, as China increasingly focuses on environmental sustainability, it could take legal steps in this direction in the medium term. South Africa has strong movements advocating for the recognition of the rights of nature, but there still needs to be a legal basis for this. Given the country's ecological and social challenges, such a development could intensify efforts to protect the environment.

Nature-based solutions: Brazil has many NbS projects, particularly for forest restoration and Amazon protection. Given the threat of deforestation to the rainforest, implementing NbS plays a central role in climate protection and biodiversity. Russia has started initial projects to adapt to climate change with NbS measures, but the need for comprehensive national strategies remains urgent. Russia's enormous forest wealth and dramatic changes in the Arctic region make this an issue that cannot be delayed. India is also investing in NbS, particularly in water management and agriculture. As India is frequently affected by water scarcity and extreme weather events, NbS could help mitigate the negative consequences of climate change. China is a leader in implementing NbS in urban and agricultural areas. The urban greening projects and the massive use of NbS to improve water and air quality in megacities illustrate the extensive use of these solutions. South Africa uses NbS, particularly for sustainable water and land use, which is crucial in view of the drought and water problems.

Table 1 summarizes the main results.

*Table 1. Comparison of the three concepts in the BRICS countries*

| | Brazil | Russia | India | China | South Africa |
|---|---|---|---|---|---|
| **Natural capital accounting (NCA)** | Pilot projects, but not yet a comprehensive system | Under discussion, but not implemented | First steps towards NCA, but no far-reaching implementation | Comprehensive natural capital valuation system in place | Progress in NCA, particularly in water and land management |
| **Rights of nature (RoN)** | Nature has rights in the constitution, esp. focus on environmental protection | Rights for nature not formally recognized | Discussions about environmental rights, but no legal basis | Pilot projects for the integration of environmental rights, but no legal basis | Strong movement for natural rights, but no legal basis |
| **Nature-based solutions (NbS)** | A wide range of initiatives to restore forests and ecosystems | First steps, especially in the context of climate adaptation strategies | Investments in water management and agriculture | A leader in NBS implementation, especially in urban and agricultural projects | Strong focus on NbS, particularly on water and land use |

Source: own representation

In summary, Brazil and China's pioneering role in NCA and NbS should be emphasized. China, in particular, already has comprehensive systems for natural capital accounting and valuation and a solid basis for sustainable digital currencies, which increases the potential for successful international cooperation.

## 3. THE MODEL OF NBDC

There is a need to reprioritize and assign a new value to the commons and sustainable assets. There is a need to reallocate capital and put a fair price on carbon, waste and pollution. There is a need to incentivize and reward healing, regenerative, protective and innovative efforts. The model of an NBDC can be a worthwhile approach for this. The newly introduced digital currency aims to reward environmentally friendly behaviour instead of punishing polluters (e.g., using a CO2 tax). All individuals and companies that protect the environment must be paid with the new 'nature currency'. The process of earning and using the NBDC is remarkably straightforward, providing a sense of ease and confidence. Individuals and companies earn NBDC by engaging in environmentally friendly activities, and they can use these earnings to invest in further environmental protection or trade them for traditional currency. Nature is a reserve asset that supports conservation, restoration, and climate initiatives financially. With an NBDC, environmental protection becomes a worthwhile investment. It is particularly interesting for the countries of the Global South and the BRICS countries to make progress in the agonizing rounds of climate conferences. Understandably, there are still a large number of detailed questions. In this respect, the procedure presented here has the character of a model.

## 3.1 Design Principles

An NBDC favoured here has the following basic principles:

1. Linking to natural resources

At the heart of this currency lies the idea of linking the value of the digital unit to a specific natural resource. The decision on which natural resource serves as the basis is crucial. Factors such as availability, fluctuations, social relevance and measurability play a role here. The following links are conceivable:

- Water: The value of a digital token could be linked to the amount of fresh water available in a particular area.
- Energy: The currency could be linked to the renewable energy produced to incentivize sustainable energy production.
- Biodiversity: The token's value could be linked to the state of biodiversity in an ecosystem.

The link to the NCA (Section 3.1), RoN (Section 3.2) and NbS (Section 3.3) must be established.

Anchoring to the NC is achieved through sensors, satellite images, climate models and other data sources. Sensors are used to continuously collect data on the selected natural resource and obtain a comprehensive picture (e.g., water level, energy production, biodiversity). This data is processed by algorithms that determine the resource's current value. Computational approaches based on a Bayesian understanding of the behaviour of living organisms (e.g., active inference) provide tools to understand nature as a continuous learning process (Albarracin et al., 2024). Such approaches make it possible to assess the completeness of different socio-ecological models (SES) and the impact of different measures to improve the state of nature (Section 6.2).

> *'Such 'evidence' is a unified measure of the goodness of models. When trained with ecosystem data, such as that which could be made available through the SEEA framework and digital MRV systems, the data patterns become the evidence for ecological states and pressures conducive to increased ecosystem health.' (Wainstein et al., 2023, p.21).*

An alternative approach is to create an ecosystem's digital twin. This twin maps the natural ecological processes and conditions. Complex ecological processes are simulated and analyzed using ecological sciences, extensive data analysis, machine learning, blockchain, and geospatial engineering. This way, ecosystem services can be precisely evaluated, innovative financing models developed, and sustainable land use promoted. Finally, the properties of nature are given a digital value in the form of the NBDC or a nature token.

## 2. Blockchain technology

Blockchain technology, a secure platform for verifying ownership and transactions, fosters trust between participants through its inherent transparency and collective agreement on any additions to the registry (Chalkias et al., 2024). The NBDC benefits from these key characteristics, providing a reliable and secure system for all involved.

Decentralization: An NBDC initially requires a high degree of centralization because the central bank plays a central role in issuing and regulating the currency. Nevertheless, BC decentralization is crucial for international environmental protection, where cooperation across borders and interests is required. At the same time, seamless involvement of other actors in the process is possible.

Transparency and Immutability: Blockchains provide transparency by allowing users to view and trace past transactions, building trust through verifiable actions. In addition, confirmed and timestamped transactions are immutable, preventing changes and ensuring a reliable record. Both features are essential to the integrity of the NBDC as they demotivate malicious activity.

Smart contracts: BCs support smart contracts (SCs), self-executing contracts whose terms are written directly into the code. These contracts automatically enforce and execute the terms of agreements, bringing a new level of automation. SCs can encode a wide range of logic, making them versatile for various applications, such as when the NBDC is concerned with adjusting the money supply, balancing ecological debt, verifying transactions, or paying dividends.

Tokenization: In tokenization, physical assets, natural rights, or values are converted into digital tokens, simplifying the transfer of assets. In the context of the NBDC presented here, tokenization is the key feature that rewards users who work with tokenized natural assets (UN, 2023).

Oracles: Each transaction is recorded in an immutable block part of a chain. Oracles, which are trusted sources of off-chain data, play an essential role in creating the verifiable web by allowing devices and data (information from weather stations, drone imagery and IoT sensors) from the outside world to feed into the BC and connect that would otherwise be isolated from off-chain data and computers.

Interoperability: BCs enable the sharing of information across different systems. They increase value by carrying out overarching transactions and exchanging data, eliminating barriers to compatibility. Transactions and settlements are streamlined, which is very important for an NBDC.

3. Privacy

There are various ways to protect transaction privacy. Some BCs enable technologies such as zero-knowledge proofs to ensure that transactions are secure and private, combining transparency and confidentiality. It allows the validity of a transaction to be proven without revealing its contents, which is crucial for individuals such as farmers and IoT providers who need to protect their data.

4. Artificial intelligence

One of the ways NBDC is integrating artificial intelligence (AI) into the regenerative use of tokens. AI can play a crucial role in developing minted value and information layers that build on the recorded use of the currency. By registering the regenerative behavior of users and the overall economy, AI can help create a more sustainable and adaptive financial system. As humans are inextricably linked to nature, incorporating AI into the management and use of NBDCs can enable the monitoring and promotion of regenerative behavior among users. It can create a positive feedback loop that encourages and rewards sustainable action on an individual and collective level.

## 3.2 How it Works

The techniques and measures described in section 3 are central. They represent a transformative potential, offering a new way to value and conserve nature's ecological services. While there are yet-to-be-established and standardized metrics that the world has agreed upon (Section 5.2), the decentralized nature and need for consensus on the appropriate assessment of NC may seem challenging. However, despite their association with a certain degree of quantifiable uncertainty, these measures and activities hold the promise of moving towards a more uniform direction. The NBDC links the assessment aspects and provides for regulating environmental impacts and environmental protection, offering a beacon of hope for the future of nature conservation.

Nature has been primarily monetized as a raw material, with landowners earning money from extracting natural resources, such as cutting down forests. However, this extractive resource economy has led to the continued overexploitation of nature and natural resources on our finite planet. The urgency of the current situation cannot be overstated. While healthy ecosystems have enormous existential value, they have little economic value in the current model. It underscores the need for a new approach, where nature is valued as an integrated SES, not just as a compensation mechanism, making the proposed system all the more relevant and vital.

To create NBDC, NC must undergo a thorough process of wealth creation. It includes monitoring, reporting and verification (MRV) of biodiversity using remote sensing, IoT sensors, drones, satellite imagery and assessment models. This platform could be hosted by a national statistics authority, for example. Companies receive information on the NC (e.g., forest cover or carbon sequestration) via the platform. It is advantageous if an NCA or various NbS are already established in a country. For example, the accounting of environmental services in Brazil is based on the 'Sistema de Contas Econômicas Ambientais' (SCEA). The SCEA is methodologically based on the SEEA principles. The environmental economic accounts are structured sets of information that integrate environmental data and economic statistics. Specifically for the ecosystem accounting component, the methodology provides for its development under a spatially explicit approach. Therefore, environmental-economic accounts are compiled in geographic information systems (GIS), where several layers of information can be integrated, allowing analyses in different environmental profiles, such as biomes or hydrographic basins (Andrae, 2024b). As a result, the ecosystem services companies provide can be mapped in the MRV data platform. The activation of NC enables the creation of a financial instrument that dynamically adjusts its value to the state and health of nature.

The central bank plays a crucial role in issuing and regulating this currency (Figure 4). Due to the link with the data platform, the ecosystem services can be converted into digital nature tokens. It uses BC technology for this (section 4.1). Each token represents a certain amount of carbon sequestration, water purification or other ecological value (e.g., 1 unit = USD 4 = 100 kg of CO2 sequestered in biodiverse nature). An upper limit creates a scarcity of currency. It manifests the quantity and quality of nature. It means a regular minting cycle, no fixed supply and a 'burn' mechanism. The 'burn' mechanism is a process where a certain percentage of tokens are removed from circulation periodically, thereby reducing the total supply and increasing the value of the remaining tokens. The quantity of tokens in circulation is ultimately limited by how much intact nature there is.

*Figure 4. Schematic process flow of an NBDC*

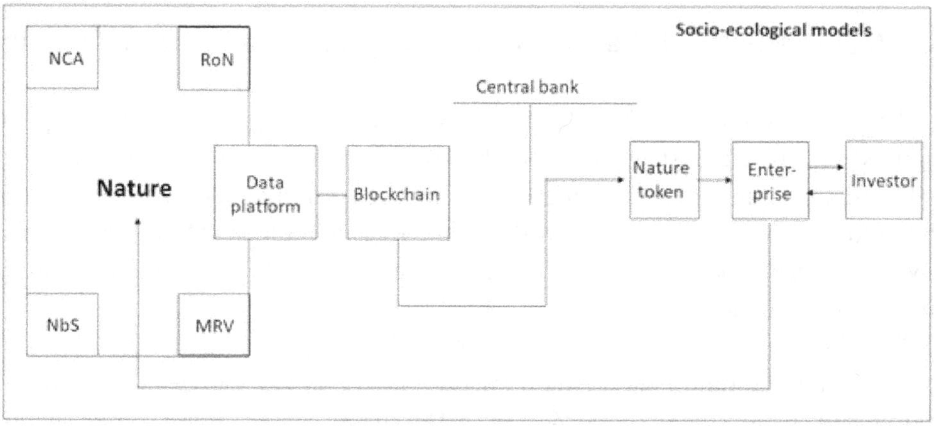


Source: own representation

Given the price differences in today's market, a pricing method must be established. This method must provide an annual ROI as an interest rate based on a nature-based value. The price is adjusted via the price of various instruments (e.g., carbon instruments) on the market. An auction mechanism can also be used for pricing.

The issued NBDC is not a carbon credit. Unlike carbon credits, which are primarily used to offset greenhouse gas emissions, NBDCs represent a financial contribution to nature conservation and do not entitle the holder to offset greenhouse gas emissions or biodiversity loss elsewhere. NBDCs are a unique financial instrument that directly supports and incentivizes nature conservation efforts.

NBDCs are issued to companies that conserve nature's ecological value. These companies are selected based on their demonstrated commitment to nature conservation and ability to use the funds for conservation efforts effectively. Once issued, they store the NBDC in digital wallets. These nature tokens can now be used for payment by being bought or sold by other users. It enables public and private nature conservation and climate measures, such as financing national parks, nature reserves, and private sector projects. The NBDC could be used to incentivize biodiversity protection by integrating it into the trade in ecological assets. It could increase liquidity for green investments and help achieve international climate targets.

## 5. OPPORTUNITIES AND CHALLENGES OF AN NBDC

### 5.1. Comparison of the Chances of Implementation per Country

The introduction of an NBDC in the BRICS countries presents various opportunities and challenges that vary depending on the national context. Countries such as Brazil and China offer particularly high chances of implementation due to their technological and political frameworks, while Russia, India, and South Africa also have significant potential, which, however, may be limited by social, regulatory, and geopolitical factors.

Brazil stands out as a strong contender for NBDC implementation. The country's robust political commitment to environmental protection, particularly in the Amazon region, sets a solid foundation. Moreover, Brazil's advanced digital infrastructure provides a promising technological basis for a currency system. However, the country's heavy reliance on traditional economic sectors like agriculture, mining, and industry could pose a challenge. These sectors often clash with environmentally friendly initiatives, potentially slowing the transformation process. Yet, Brazil's existing green projects and the increasing political will to promote sustainable technologies create a favorable environment for successful implementation.

Russia has a medium chance of implementing an NBDC. The country's technological infrastructure is well-developed, which could facilitate the introduction of a digital currency in principle. However, significant geopolitical uncertainties and regulatory challenges could hinder the process. In particular, Russia's international isolation and sanctions make it difficult to access global financial markets and technologies, which could make the development of a digital currency in cooperation with other BRICS countries complex. Furthermore, environmental issues are often given low priority in Russia, further limiting political support for nature-based currency systems.

India also stands a good chance of implementing an NBDC. The country's growing technological base and vibrant economy could provide strong support for introducing a digital currency. While regulatory and social hurdles may slow down the process, India's significant progress in digitalization, particularly in the financial sector, offers excellent potential for developing and using a nature-based currency, especially in the context of sustainable development.

China's global leadership in digital technologies, particularly in blockchain and artificial intelligence, positions the country as a strong candidate for NBDC implementation. The Chinese government's heavy investment in digital infrastructure further supports this potential. However, the country's intense focus on economic growth could challenge the nature-based aspect of such a currency. While China is increasingly integrating environmental aspects into its economy as part of its ecological modernization, the long-term reconciliation of economic growth and natural resource protection through a digital currency remains to be seen.

In South Africa, the chances of introducing a nature-based digital currency are moderate. The country's high technological acceptance and growing interest in green projects create a conducive environment for implementing such monetary systems. However, South Africa does face significant social and political challenges that could hinder the process. The regulatory and infrastructural hurdles are also significant, as the country grapples with economic inequalities and an unstable political situation that could delay the development and implementation of such a system.

Table 2 summarizes the chances of implementing an NBDC in the BRICS countries based on various criteria.

*Table 2. Summary of the NBDC implementation opportunities per country*

| | Brazil | Russia | India | China | South Africa |
|---|---|---|---|---|---|
| **Political support** | High support for green projects, especially through protection of the Amazon rainforest | Moderate support, focus on traditional resources (energy, raw materials) | Supports sustainable development, but politics could react hesitantly to digital currencies | High state control, strong interest in digital currency, but focus on economic growth rather than on nature | Increasing interest in green projects, but politically unstable |
| **Technological infrastructure** | Well developed, broad access to digital technology and financial technology | Investing heavily in digitalization, infrastructure in place but political uncertainty | Solid technological base, growing sector for fintech and digitalization | Excellent infrastructure, global leader in digital technologies and blockchain | Weak technological infrastructure in rural areas but strong urban sector |
| **Regulatory environment** | Open to digital innovation, supports sustainable initiatives | Regulations highly centralized, focus on national interests, cautious about digital currencies | Complex regulatory landscape, but increasingly innovation-friendly | Strict regulatory environment, heavy state intervention, digitized control | Unclear legal framework for digital currencies, slow legislation |
| **Central bank capacity** | CBDC projects in preparation, central bank supports digital forms of financing, but focus on financial market stability | Russian central bank rather cautious about digital currencies, aims to control traditional financial systems | Indian central bank experimenting with digital currencies, growing interest in CBDC, but cautious approach | PBoC leading the development of digital currencies, pioneering CBDC (e-yuan) | SARB is exploring the possibilities for digital currencies, but it is still in the planning phase |
| **Societal acceptance** | High willingness for green technologies, growing acceptance of digital innovations | Skepticism towards digital currencies, focus on traditional economy | Growing acceptance of digital innovations, but low awareness of nature-based currencies | Very high acceptance of digital technologies, but less focus on nature-based | Societal split, broad interest in digital innovations in urban centers |
| **Chances for implementation** | **High**: Strong commitment to green projects and solid digital infrastructure | **Medium**: Technological capabilities in place, but political and regulatory hurdles | **Medium**: Good technological conditions, but regulatory complexity and social challenges | **High**: Technological leadership and open to digital innovations if controlled by the state | **Medium**: Societal acceptance and infrastructure in place, but political instability |

Source: own representation

## 5.2. Advantages

Sustainable practices: Blockchain technology is a powerful tool in promoting sustainable behavior, offering a range of benefits. By linking to natural resources, it incentivizes companies and individuals to act sustainably and earn more nature tokens. The potential of a NBDC to enhance this further, making sustainable investments more attractive and accelerating the energy transition and environmental protection, is a compelling reason to consider blockchain's role in sustainability.

Transparency: Blockchain technology is a key player in ensuring transparency in all transactions. Its unique features, such as public visibility of all transactions and unchangeable data once recorded, ensure no manipulation or deletion of transactions. This reliability in tracing the origin and path of tokens without any gaps is a testament to blockchain's role in building trust.

With its distributed system, BC technology offers a solution for data security. All data in a blockchain is stored in encrypted form. The use of signatures ensures the information's integrity. Using the relevant principles of cryptography for data verification ensures that it cannot be manipulated. There are several private critical rules for controlling access authorization in authority management. The combination of these points achieves high data security in the BC system.

Diversifying financial markets: The emergence of new financial instruments based on ecosystem services, facilitated by blockchain technology, is intriguing. These instruments have the potential to diversify financial markets and create new investment opportunities. However, developing financial instruments to consolidate nature as a valuable asset worthy of protection can have positive and negative effects on market dynamics, sparking curiosity about the future of financial markets.

Empowering local communities: By linking currency and ecosystem services, blockchain technology can empower local communities and keep value creation in regions. This approach fosters a sense of ownership and responsibility and opens up new avenues for financing local projects such as NbS to restore ecosystems, inspiring hope for a more sustainable future.

## 5.3. Challenges

Valuation of ecosystem services: Today, various approaches exist to determine the value of ecosystem services (Section 3.1). Two methods should be emphasized:

- Economic valuation: Monetary values for ecosystem services are determined here. In the so-called market price method, the value of a service is estimated using the market price of a comparable good (e.g., the value of honey as a pollination service).
- Functional valuation: The valuation is based on the functions that the ecosystem fulfils (e.g., water purification, erosion control). In the production cost method, the costs for the artificial production of an ecosystem service are determined (e.g., the costs for a sewage treatment plant compared to natural purification by a wetland). The functional assessment also includes the damage

cost method. Here, the costs that arise when an ecosystem service is lost (e.g., the costs of flooding following the loss of a riparian forest) are calculated.

All assessment methods have their own set of advantages and disadvantages. Ecosystems, being highly complex, and their services often requiring more work to quantify, underscore the need for comprehensive valuation methods. The value of ecosystem services can vary significantly in space and time, underscoring the importance of harmonizing valuation regulations at the supranational level. This global cooperation is crucial for a unified approach. Many ecosystem services are used indirectly and are difficult to value, emphasizing the need for a more comprehensive approach. Finally, valuation often depends on subjective value judgments, further complicating the process.

Value and volatility of NBDC: The currency's value is closely linked to the coverage of natural resources. In this respect, the entire NBDC governance plays a central role. Events over the past year show how carbon credits purchased by investors have no environmental value and have become stranded assets. One study highlights that Verra, the world's leading certification company, approved millions of forest carbon credits that are now essentially worthless. Carbon offsets from voluntary projects to avoid deforestation have not significantly reduced it. The reductions have been much smaller than claimed in those projects where they have. The methods for establishing deforestation baselines for climate protection measures urgently need to be revised to allocate the reduced deforestation to the projects correctly. It is the only way to ensure both incentives for forest protection and the integrity of global carbon accounting. Without these necessary adjustments, carbon offsets could exacerbate global warming if used for offsetting purposes (West et al., 2023).

The value of natural resources can fluctuate widely depending on factors such as climate change, policy decisions, and the valuation of ecosystem services. For example, nature-based climate solutions provide carbon credits derived from net carbon removals. However, their credibility is challenged by removals' inherent variability and volatility. By evaluating abatement benefits from the perspective of the social cost of carbon, project developers can increase credibility and assess volatility by conservatively assuming that abatements will eventually be released according to a release schedule. They can then issue additional credits if the release is less than expected (Rau et al., 2024). With such mechanisms, volatility can positively impact the currency's stability.

Interoperability: Developing and implementing the necessary technologies and infrastructures is challenging. For example, blockchain technology must be scaled to enable many transactions per second (section 4.1). It is also why many central banks have decided against a blockchain solution for CBDCs today. The currency must be compatible with other financial systems.

Regulation: This new form of currency needs a clear legal framework. The urgency and importance of this regulation should be emphasized. Effective laws should minimize risks and promote innovation. The best option would be to enshrine the greening of property approach described in section 3.2 of the constitution.

Acceptance: Money is much more than a 'cold' means of payment. Money is also something emotional. Its existence is closely linked to trust. Even if NBDCs have an intrinsic value and differ from fiat currencies in this respect, their value is also based on the trust of users that others are also willing to accept them as a means of payment. The historian Harari (2018) puts it this way:

> *'[...] [Money is also the apogee of human tolerance. Money is more open-minded than language, state laws, cultural codes, religious beliefs and social habits. Money is the only trust system created by humans that can bridge almost any cultural gap, and that does not discriminate based on religion, gender, race, age or sexual orientation. Thanks to money, even people who do not know each other and do not trust each other can nevertheless cooperate effectively.'*

Broad acceptance by the population and companies has yet to be gained, as no concrete cases of NBDCs exist.

Despite these challenges, NBDCs are a fascinating concept that has the potential to fundamentally change the way we deal with money and natural resources. This potential for change should inspire hope and optimism in the audience. The following section will explore the implementation options for the BRICS countries from a political economy perspective.

## 6. IMPLEMENTATION OPTIONS FOR BRICS

### 6.1. Polycentric Global Governance

All BRICS countries, each with an extensive reservoir of NC, are enormous in terms of area. The degradation of individual ecosystems varies in the five countries; the more significant the endangered ecosystems, the greater the political pressure for assessing ecosystems and their services, as well as NBDCs. Notably, the management of the NC has become a national priority for China, leading the country to quickly assume a leadership role in the core areas of sustainable development. This significant leadership role of China in sustainable development, which is observed differently in the four other BRICS countries, is a dynamic crucial for understanding the global landscape.

An essential structural development—especially in climate finance—is the increase in new actors, new governance mechanisms and instruments such as partnerships, and intensifying the interplay between governance levels. The multi-stakeholder governance concept describes expanding the capacity to act beyond the state and intergovernmental organizations. On the other hand, multi-level governance and stakeholder partnerships describe the new configurations of actors interacting at several levels and scales of governance. The 'soft governance' of the UN Framework Convention on Climate Change (UNFCCC) should be highlighted as a coordinator and mediator within the polycentric system. Soft governance, a form of governance that relies on persuasion and voluntary compliance rather than coercion, plays a crucial role in the stability of global climate policy. It acts as the lead institution and coordinator in global climate policy. Soft governance technologies come in new forms of state authority, such as voluntary standards and codes. The UNFCCC represents that governance has evolved from traditional state-based regulatory systems to more heterogeneous and polycentric structures. As a result, new voluntary initiatives are flourishing, particularly in the private sector, regarding green taxonomies, carbon footprinting, and climate finance disclosure.

Given the increasing interdependence, many challenges a state faces require a coordinated global response. The opportunities and pitfalls of action through formal international organizations (IOs) are usually emphasized. However, formal IOs are only one of the mechanisms available for global coordination. More formal organizations, i.e. institutions with codification or permanent structures to which states delegate tasks, also overcome these challenges. The (semi-)informal approach, a flexible and adaptive method that combines elements of formal and informal governance, must be more convincing for providing an appropriate institutional response to establishing an NBDC in the BRICS. This approach allows for the necessary structure and coordination while also accommodating the diverse interests and capabilities of the BRICS countries.

Classical theories of institutionalized cooperation assume that states do not create overlapping institutions to regulate the same issue. Institutions that overlap in terms of membership and scope duplicate existing functions. As a result, the complexity of institutionalized cooperation increases and could be more efficient. The transaction costs of cooperation—which international institutions aim to reduce—increase in situations where actors must act across many overlapping institutions compared to situations with a single, central institution (Drezner, 2013). In contrast, it is argued that more institutions in an issue area can facilitate cooperation. When states are members of more institutions, there are more opportunities for interaction, communication and learning about counterparties' preferences (Alter & Meunier, 2009). In addition, states can establish external institutions to strengthen cooperation on specific issues that take more work to advance in existing forums (Andrae, 2024a).

Empirically, international cooperation is rarely centralized in a single international organization (IO). Instead, it is spread across various forums in increasingly dense institutional environments. This institutional proliferation is particularly evident in international climate policy. Institutional proliferation is the rapid increase in international institutions active in a particular area. There is an intense debate about how actors attempt to shift the locus of rule-making from existing to new forums. The BRICS grouping, a coalition of five major emerging economies, can be interpreted as a new forum. The aim is to make a decision favouring BRICS interests, a strategy known as' forum shopping '. This approach allows the BRICS countries to strategically engage with different international forums to advance their collective interests.

The high chances of implementation in Brazil and China have decisive implications for bilateral or multilateral cooperation within the framework of the BRICS countries. Both countries have strong political and technological capacities that could form the basis for successfully implementing a nature-based digital currency. Cooperation between Brazil and China could include the following aspects. China could use its leading role in blockchain and digital financial technologies to support Brazil in building a technological infrastructure for an NBDC. In return, Brazil could contribute its environmental protection and ecological resource management expertise. By working together, the two countries could find innovative ways to use natural resources as the basis for digital currencies. The monetization of natural capital through digital currency systems could expand the global market for sustainable financial products while also helping to protect the environment.

The emergence of new institutions, such as the New Development Bank (NDB), is challenging the dominance of established entities. At the sixth BRICS summit in Fortaleza (2014), the heads of state and government of the BRICS countries signed an agreement to establish the NDB. In 2021, the bank began accepting its first new members (Bangladesh, Egypt, the United Arab Emirates and Uruguay), marking its transformation into a global multilateral institution (Ye, 2023). This evolution holds significant promise for the future of international climate policy, with the NDB poised to play a pivotal and hopeful role in the design of a nature-based digital currency.

The NDB's unique ability to finance NbS and interact directly with the central banks issuing nature tokens is a testament to its capabilities and reassures the audience about its potential impact.

## 6.2. Complex Adaptive Governance Systems

Governance is the root of and the solution to the intricate challenges within SES. The bond between social and ecological systems is not just a simple connection but a profound interweaving, making them inseparable ontological entities. They can be visualized as complex, intertwined, and adaptive SES (Preiser, 2018). This interconnectedness is not just a theoretical concept, but a reality that we must grapple with in our work.

The establishment of an NBDC involves a multitude of actors and institutions. The key to realizing this project successfully lies in a complex adaptive governance systems framework (CAGS-F). May (2022) presents this framework as an essential organizational orientation aid and a fundamental conceptualization of social science concepts. The uniqueness of the CAGS-F, untested for an NBDC, lies in its ability to bring together the panarchy heuristic's focus on socio-ecological interdependence, cross-scale, multi-causal, non-linear complexity and change with compatible social science theories of multi-level institutions, organizations and human practices. This compatibility is based on the shared emphasis on adaptive, multi-level, and non-linear processes in both the CAGS-F and social science theories (Garmestani, 2023).

Every individual and group involved in an NBDC project brings a wealth of material and non-material resources, skills, perspectives, and means of accessing additional resources through social networks. It is not just applicable at the project or national level but is amplified when considering a supranational association such as the BRICS. The success or failure of an NBDC project hinges on the experiences, dispositions, and assessment of knowledge, skills, relationships, and other resources. Scholars, researchers, and practitioners must be able to dissect social, organizational, and institutional components to adequately capture opportunities, barriers, and potentials for considering and including social diversity in the system to achieve equitable outcomes (May, 2022). Social diversity is not just a buzzword, but

## 7. CONCLUSION

In general, the high proportions of the world population and the value added as a potential are emphasized with the BRICS countries. However, the heterogeneity within the connection must also be recognized. The individual interests are too heterogeneous for the BRICS club to be a geopolitical power factor. China and Russia see the BRICS as the nucleus for fundamental changes in world trade. They want to move away from the dollar as the leading international currency. They want fewer international rules that erode their sovereignty and want to break the primacy of the US and the EU. On the other hand, countries like India or Brazil want to use international platforms like BRICS to emancipate themselves from institutions like the World Bank, the International Monetary Fund and Western markets while simultaneously being advocates for the Global South.

However, the BRICS countries have one thing in common: They play a pioneering role regarding the NBDC. The NCA and NbS already have a broad field of application in their respective countries. China, Brazil, and India are particularly noteworthy. In this respect, the foundations have been laid for introducing an NBDC. Investments in nature-friendly solutions increase both economic welfare and the NC. Low-income countries, in particular, benefit from this inclusive approach, as NBDCs can provide them with access to a more stable and sustainable financial system. This promising development in sustainable finance is a cause for optimism (Johnson et al., 2023).

Real values underpin a digital, nature-based currency, forming the bedrock of a genuinely sustainable, nature-based economy. The NBDC and its underlying technologies present a fresh perspective on how digital resilience can be cultivated in ecological contexts. Blockchain, a technology that promotes trust and collaboration among organizations, paves the way for innovative forms of organization based on collective action in SES (Lumineau et al., 2021). While there are still unanswered questions and challenges to overcome, the potential of blockchain is reassuring.

The book article shows how an NBDC can function as a model. NBDCs require a trustworthy accounting mechanism, which blockchain technology can provide. As NCA becomes the fundamental asset for new monetary systems, blockchain's trust and sequential accounting capabilities are essential for monitoring and verifying the state of nature and its corresponding financial value. This emphasis on blockchain technology should reassure the audience about the security and trustworthiness of NBDC.

Developing an NBDC is a complex process that requires close collaboration between science, policy and business. Given the reservoir of natural resources in the BRICS countries, the project seems predestined to be implemented. In this respect, the BRICS countries actively contribute to fundamentally changing the global financial architecture, as the new common currency would focus more on sustainability and ecological values. The comparison of the BRICS countries shows that Brazil and China could use their technological and political strengths to position themselves as pioneers in developing a nature-based digital currency. This potential for leadership in sustainable finance should inspire the audience.

The macroeconomic, financial, energy policy, climate policy and development policy strategy of the BRICS countries reflects a strategy that aims to create a world order that reflects a new political economy. This strategy includes measures to promote sustainable development, reduce carbon emissions, and ensure equitable economic growth. It no longer focuses on the interests of the Western industrialized countries but instead strives for a balance between North and South in global politics. Thus, the BRICS vision for a new world order's economic and developmental dimensions is closely linked to their vision for the political dimension (Shameem & Jayaprasad, 2020). With successful NBDCs, the BRICS states would assume a leading geopolitical role in shaping the future financial order, where the NBDC would play a pivotal role in promoting sustainability and ecological values.

## REFERENCES

Adloff, F., & Hilbrich, I. (2021). Practices of sustainability and the enactment of their natures/cultures: Ecosystem services, rights of nature, and geoengineering. *Social Sciences Information. Information Sur les Sciences Sociales*, 60(2), 168–187. DOI: 10.1177/0539018421998947

AFN (Accounting for Nature). (2023). Accounting for nature. AFN. www.accountingfornature.org

Albarracin, M., Ramstead, M., Pitliya, R. J., Hipolito, I., Da Costa, L., Raffa, M., Constant, A., & Manski, S. G. (2024). Sustainability under active inference. *Systems*, 12(5), 163. DOI: 10.3390/systems12050163

Alter, K. J., & Meunier, S. (2009). The politics of international regime complexity. *Perspectives on Politics*, 7(1), 13–24. DOI: 10.1017/S1537592709090033

Andrae, S. (2024a). Why and how to build a global climate bank? In Boubaker, S., & Le, T. H. (Eds.), *Handbook of environmental and green finance: Towards a sustainable future* (pp. 193–253). World Scientific Publishing. DOI: 10.1142/9781800614451_0007

Andrae, S. (2024b). The establishment of a gross ecosystem product: A country comparison. In Boubaker, S., & Le, T. H. (Eds.), *Green finance and sustainable development goals* (pp. 369–407). World Scientific Publishing. DOI: 10.1142/9781800614482_0014

Boehm, S., Jeffery, L., Levin, K., Hecke, J., Schumer, C., Fyson, C., Majid, A., Jaeger, J., Nilsson, A., Naimoli, S., Thwaites, J., Cassidy, E., Waite, R., Wilson, R., Castellanos, S., Singh, N., Lee, A., & Geiges, A. (2022). State of Climate Action 2022. *State of Climate Action*, 2022. Advance online publication. DOI: 10.46830/wrirpt.22.00028

Bordo, M. D., & Roberds, W. (2024). Central bank digital currencies: An old tale with a new chapter. Griswold Center for Economic Policy Studies Working Paper No. 323, May 2024. https://gceps.princeton.edu/wp-content/uploads/2024/05/wp323_BordoRoberds.pdf

CARE. (2023). Seeing double: Decoding the 'additionality' of climate finance. https://careclimatechange.org/wp-content/uploads/2023/09/Seeing-Double-2023_15.09.23_larger.pdf

Chairat, S., & Gheewala, S. H. (2024). The conceptual quantitative assessment framework for nature-based solutions (NbS). *Nature-Based Solutions*, 6, 100152. DOI: 10.1016/j.nbsj.2024.100152

Chalkias, K. K., Kostis, A., Alnuaimi, A., Knez, P., Naulty, J., Salmasi, A., . . .. (2024). Preserving nature's ledger: Blockchains in biodiversity conservation. *arXiv*. https://doi.org//arXiv.2404.12086DOI: 10.48550

Cheng, C., & Li, F. (2024). Ecosystem restoration and management based on nature-based solutions in China: Research progress and representative practices. *Nature-Based Solutions*, 6, 100176. DOI: 10.1016/j.nbsj.2024.100176

Costanza, R., Kubiszewski, I., & Rasheed, R. (2021). The future of changes in global ecosystem services. *Global Environmental Change*, 71, 102399. DOI: 10.1016/j.gloenvcha.2021.102399

De Abreu, I. A., de Arimatéia Dias Valadão, J., & da Silva, C. A. (2023). Nature-based solutions: Literature review of the emerging field of sustainability in Brazilian academia. *Mitigation and Adaptation Strategies for Global Change*, 28(6), 32. DOI: 10.1007/s11027-023-10069-2

Dos Santos, L. B. (2024). Nature-based solutions in urban periphery communities in Brazil. *Societal Impacts*, 3, 100050. DOI: 10.1016/j.socimp.2024.100050

Drezner, D. (2013). The tragedy of the global institutional commons. In Finnemore, M., & Goldstein, J. (Eds.), *Back to basics: State power in a contemporary world* (pp. 281–311). Oxford University Press., DOI: 10.1093/acprof:oso/9780199970087.003.0013

Garmestani, A., Allen, C. R., Angeler, D. G., Gunderson, L., & Ruhl, J. B. (2023). Multiscale adaptive management of social-ecological systems. *Bioscience*, 73(11), 800–807. DOI: 10.1093/biosci/biad096 PMID: 38516522

Harari, Y. (2018). *Sapiens: A brief history of mankind*. Harper Perennial.

IPBES (Intergovernmental Science-Policy Platform on Biodiversity and Ecosystem Services). (2019). The global assessment report on biodiversity and ecosystem services. https://files.ipbes.net/ipbes-web-prod-public-files/inline/files/ipbes_global_assessment_report_summary_for_policymakers.pdf

Johnson, J. A., Baldos, U. L., Corong, E., & Thakrar, S. (2023). Investing in nature can improve equity and economic returns. *Proceedings of the National Academy of Sciences of the United States of America*, 120(27), e2220401120. DOI: 10.1073/pnas.2220401120 PMID: 37364118

Kauffman, C. M., & Martin, P. L. (2021). *The politics of rights of nature: Strategies for building a more sustainable future*. The MIT Press., DOI: 10.7551/mit-press/13855.001.0001

Kubiszewski, I., Ward, C., Pickett, K. E., & Costanza, R. (2024). The complex relationships between economic inequality and biodiversity: A scoping review. *The Anthropocene Review*, 11(1), 49–66. DOI: 10.1177/20530196231158080

Lagoarde-Ségot, T., & Mathieu, A. (2024). Ecological money and finance—Upscaling local complementary currencies. *Humanities & Social Sciences Communications*, 11(1), 545. DOI: 10.1057/s41599-024-02993-8

Lumineau, F., Wang, W., & Schilke, O. (2021). Blockchain governance—A new way of organizing collaborations? *Organization Science*, 32(2), 500–521. DOI: 10.1287/orsc.2020.1379

Luo, M., Cai, J., Zeng, Z., Zheng, Y., & Lin, T. (2024). Development and practices of nature-based solutions in China. *Nature-Based Solutions*, 5, 100109. DOI: 10.1016/j.nbsj.2023.100109

Luxton, S. J., Smith, G. S., Williams, K. J., Ferrier, S., Bond, A. J., & Prober, S. M. (2024). An introduction to key ecological concepts, financial opportunities, and risks underpinning aspirations for nature positive. *Bioscience*, 74(7), 450–466. DOI: 10.1093/biosci/biae040 PMID: 39156612

Maechler, S., & Boisvert, V. (2024). Valuing nature to save it? The centrality of valuation in the new spirit of conservation. *Global Environmental Politics*, 24(1), 10–30. DOI: 10.1162/glep_a_00734

Marois, T. (2023). Time for a world climate bank. *Land & Climate Review*, July 14, 2023. https://www.landclimate.org/a-world-climate-bank-for-green-and-just-transitions/

May, C. A. (2022). Complex adaptive governance systems: A framework to understand institutions, organizations, and people in socio-ecological systems. *Socio-Ecological Practice Research*, 4(1), 39–54. DOI: 10.1007/s42532-021-00101-7 PMID: 35071989

Murau, S., Pape, F., & Pforr, T. (2021). The hierarchy of the offshore US-dollar-system. GEGI Study, February 2021. https://www.bu.edu/gdp/files/2021/02/Steffen-Murau-GEGI-Study-2-Feb-2021.pdf

Naran, B., Connolly, J., Rosane, P., Wignarajah, D., Wakaba, G., & Buchner, B. (2022). Global landscape of climate finance: A decade of data. October 27, 2022. https://www.climatepolicyinitiative.org/publication/global-landscape-of-climate-finance-a-decade-of-data/

Obst, C., Hein, L., & Edens, B. (2016). National accounting and the valuation of ecosystem assets and their services. *Environmental and Resource Economics*, 64(1), 1–23. DOI: 10.1007/s10640-015-9921-1

Prasad, E. S. (2021). *The future of money: How the digital revolution is transforming currencies and finance*. The Belknap Press of Harvard University Press.

Preiser, R., Biggs, R., De Vos, A., & Folke, C. (2018). Social-ecological systems as complex adaptive systems: Organizing principles for advancing research methods and approaches. *Ecology and Society*, 23(4), 46. DOI: 10.5751/ES-10558-230446

Putzer, A., Lambooy, T., Jeurissen, R., & Kim, E. (2022). Putting the rights of nature on the map. A quantitative Analysis of rights of nature initiatives across the world. *Journal of Maps*, 18(1), 89–96. DOI: 10.1080/17445647.2022.2079432

Ramachandran, V., & Smith, A. (2023). The dark side of climate finance. *Foreign Policy*, December 1, 2023 https://foreignpolicy.com/2023/12/01/cop28-climate-finance-global-south-development-aid-energy-wind-solar-renewable/ [Accessed: 13th January 2024]

Rau, E.-P., Gross, J., Coomes, D. A., Swinfield, T., Madhavapeddy, A., Balmford, A., & Keshav, S. (2024). Mitigating risk of credit reversal in nature-based climate solutions by optimally anticipating carbon release. *Carbon Management*, 15(1), 2390854. DOI: 10.1080/17583004.2024.2390854

Shameem, C. C., & Jayaprasad, K. (2020). The evolution of BRICS in international political economy. *American Review of Political Economy*, 15(1). Advance online publication. DOI: 10.38024/arpe.sj.6.28.20

Soterroni, A. C., Império, M., Scarabello, M. C., Seddon, N., Obersteiner, M., Rochedo, P. R. E., Schaeffer, R., Andrade, P. R., Ramos, F. M., Azevedo, T. R., Ometto, J. P. H. B., Havlík, P., & Alencar, A. A. C. (2023). Nature-based solutions are critical for putting Brazil on track towards net-zero emissions by 2050. *Global Change Biology*, 29(24), 7085–7101. DOI: 10.1111/gcb.16984 PMID: 37907071

The Landbanking Group. (2024). Nature equity: A new asset class that brings nature on the balance sheet. January 2024. https://25771685.fs1.hubspotusercontent-eu1.net/hubfs/25771685/Resources/NatureEquityConsultationPaper_WebVersion.pdf

Troy, A., & Wilson, M. A. (2006). Mapping ecosystem services: Practical challenges and opportunities in linking GIS and value transfer. *Ecological Economics*, 60(2), 435–449. DOI: 10.1016/j.ecolecon.2006.04.007

UN. (2014). System of environmental-economic accounting 2012—Central framework. United Nations, New York. https://unstats.un.org/unsd/envaccounting/seeaRev/SEEA_CF_Final_en.pdf

UN. (2023). Blockchain for biodiversity finance. https://cognizium.io/uploads/resources/UN%20environment%20programme%20-%20An%20Overview%20of%20Various%20Blockchain%20Applications%20to%20Help%20Increase%20Biodiversity%20Funding.pdf

Van Gansbeke, F. (2021). Time for IMF climate coin (2/3). January 17, 2021. https://www.forbes.com/sites/frankvangansbeke/2021/01/17/time-for-imf-climate-coin-23/

Viaene, L. (2022). Can rights of nature save us from the Anthropocene catastrophe? Some critical reflections from the field. *Asian Journal of Law and Society*, 9(2), 187–206. DOI: 10.1017/als.2022.2

Wainstein, M., Constant, A., & Clippinger, J. (2023). Nature based currencies: Integrating natural capital in advanced monetary systems. Open Earth Foundation. https://assets-global.website-files.com/62192ceb9199b3dd08431a6b/647d5895085b1d0a2c5ba6de_NatureBasedCurrencies_v2.pdf

WEF. (2021). State of finance for nature 2021. World Economic Forum Report. https://wedocs.unep.org/xmlui/bitstream/handle/20.500.11822/36145/SFN.pdf

Wesche, T. (2022). Who owns nature? About the rights of nature. *Estudios Filosóficos*, 65, 49–68. DOI: 10.17533/udea.ef.347573

West, T. A. P., Wunder, S., Sills, E. O., Börner, J., Rifai, S. W., Neidermeier, A. N., Frey, G. P., & Kontoleon, A. (2023). Action needed to make carbon offsets from forest conservation work for climate change mitigation. *Science*, 381(6660), 873–877. DOI: 10.1126/science.ade3535 PMID: 37616370

World Bank. (2024). Finance and prosperity 2024. August 2024. https://openknowledge.worldbank.org/server/api/core/bitstreams/a583724d-0264-41be-b3ea-0ee5d167ec04/content

Yang, H., Gou, X., Ma, W., & Xue, B. (2023). Research and application of GEP: China's experience in natural capital accounting. *Frontiers in Environmental Science*, 11, 1106654. DOI: 10.3389/fenvs.2023.1106654

Ye, F. (2023). The new development bank and the structure of the multilateral development financial system. *Review of Development Economics*, 27(3), 1957–1972. DOI: 10.1111/rode.12995

Zhang, L., Zhou, J., & Zang, Y. (2024). Financial risk identification and control in the openness context: A system dynamics approach to Renminbi internationalization. *International Review of Economics & Finance*, 103542, 103542. Advance online publication. DOI: 10.1016/j.iref.2024.103542

Zhang, R., Li, P., Xu, L., & Zhong, S. (2023). Reconciling ecological footprint and ecosystem services in natural capital accounting: Applying a novel framework to the Silk Road Economic Belt in China. *Journal of Environmental Management*, 330, 117115. DOI: 10.1016/j.jenvman.2022.117115 PMID: 36587549

# Chapter 11
# Reshaping Global Energy Policy Through BRICS+ and Seeking a New Equilibrium in Energy Markets

**Hasan Umutlu**
https://orcid.org/0000-0002-2604-3573
*Düzce University, Turkey*

**Hande Caliskan Terzioglu**
https://orcid.org/0000-0002-3137-932X
*Düzce University, Turkey*

## ABSTRACT

*BRICS+ countries (Brazil, Russia, India, China, South Africa, and the recently expanded bloc of Ethiopia, Saudi Arabia, UAE, Iran, and Egypt) hold significant potential to reshape global energy policy. This expanding alliance is positioned to become a decisive force in the supply of traditional energy resources such as oil and natural gas, particularly given the inclusion of energy-rich nations. With Russia and Saudi Arabia—two of the world's largest energy producers—as well as major energy consumers like China and India, BRICS+ is poised to drive a new equilibrium in energy markets. Enhanced cooperation and increased trade volumes among the bloc members can foster a more balanced distribution of energy resources both regionally and globally. This study analyzes the role of BRICS+ countries in global energy policy and examines the potential impact of these evolving power dynamics on energy markets. Notably, it highlights BRICS+ leadership in renewable energy*

DOI: 10.4018/979-8-3693-7393-4.ch011

*investments and the global energy transition.*

## INTRODUCTION

In 2001, the group comprising Brazil, Russia, India, and China was named BRIC by Jim O'Neil. Since then, this group has achieved steady growth and development, becoming known as BRICS with the inclusion of South Africa in December 2010. Globally, BRICS accounts for 40 percent of the world's population, 25 percent of global GDP, 30 percent of the Earth's land area, and 18 percent of international trade. Since its formation in 2010, BRICS has facilitated sectoral cooperation across diverse fields, including science, technology, energy, health, innovation, and trade promotion and facilitation. This collaboration spans more than 30 areas and has provided numerous benefits to BRICS countries' citizens (Iqbal, 2022: 7). Consequently, BRICS has established itself as a significant economic union, recognized for its influence in global economic, political, and security matters.

The potential of BRICS nations holds substantial influence within the international system. As the strategic significance of BRICS countries continues to grow, their leadership in global energy markets is also becoming increasingly prominent. Although the international energy market is largely influenced by BRICS countries, substantial reforms are necessary to keep pace with the rapid changes in global energy dynamics (Downie, 2015: 799). BRICS has established a network of institutions to enhance cooperation among members, maintaining its institutional stability despite internal and external challenges (Kirton and Larionova, 2022).

While BRICS has not achieved the same level of global acceptance as organizations like the World Trade Organization, International Monetary Fund, or World Bank, its member states are recognized as regional leaders despite differences in economic, military, commercial, and political standing on the global stage. For instance, China is considered a leading power in Southeast Asia due to its growing economic and military influence. Despite their individual distinctions, these countries share a common objective: advancing a multipolar structure in global governance (Chakraborty, 2018: 185).

Recently, BRICS extended invitations to six additional countries—Argentina, Ethiopia, Saudi Arabia, United Arab Emirates, and Egypt—to join the group. This expansion is anticipated to amplify BRICS' impact on global energy investments, particularly given that the bloc now has the potential to control 72 percent of global oil and natural gas reserves as well as a significant share of rare earth elements. This expansion means BRICS will include three of the five countries with the largest reserves (Kazelko and Semeghini, 2024: 53). In 2024, further invitations were extended to Turkey, Indonesia, Algeria, Belarus, Cuba, Bolivia, Malaysia, Uzbekistan, Kazakhstan, Thailand, Vietnam, Nigeria, and Uganda (Monin, 2024).

BRICS continues to strengthen its global presence with the addition of four countries in 2024. Fundamentally, BRICS is an intergovernmental organization with the objective of establishing a multipolar world order. Its goals include moving beyond the U.S. dollar-dominated international financial system and creating a sanctions-resistant payment infrastructure (Jütten, 2024). Consequently, BRICS invites numerous developing countries, particularly from Latin America, to join its ranks.

BRICS was initially established as a counterweight to the United States and European Union-led global order, intending to provide balance for the Global South in the face of Western influence. It offers an alternative for global trade, challenging the sanctions imposed by Western countries on Russia and Iran. The participation of Saudi Arabia and the United Arab Emirates (UAE) strengthens BRICS economically, while Iran's oil reserves add another layer of influence. With rising energy demands, India and China contribute to creating an alternative energy market within the BRICS framework (Nam, 2024: 3).

The invitation extended to six additional countries aims to position BRICS as a geopolitical counterweight to the G7 and to reduce reliance on the Western financial system. This expansion would unite the world's fastest-growing energy consumers, leading oil producers, and significant mineral resource holders, placing BRICS at the forefront of energy trade and investment. BRICS' expansion bolsters critical energy supply security and provides an alternative to the U.S.-led Minerals Security Partnership (MSP). The inclusion of Argentina, holding the world's third-largest lithium reserves, will enhance BRICS' lithium supply. Much like the MSP, BRICS aims to increase investments in critical mineral supply chains. In this context, Saudi Arabia, a new BRICS member, is investing in other essential minerals, notably lithium in Brazil. With the addition of Iran, the UAE, and Saudi Arabia, BRICS now comprises three of the largest oil exporters and accounts for 42 percent of global oil production, strengthening its position against Western sanctions, particularly those targeting Iran and Venezuela (Baskaran and Cahill, 2023).

In the long term, an expanded BRICS alliance holds substantial significance for energy markets. This expansion could transform energy investment and trade by bringing together leading mineral resource holders, major oil producers, and some of the fastest-growing energy consumers (Baskaran and Cahill, 2023). This study aims to assess the global impact of BRICS+ (Brazil, Russia, India, China, South Africa, and new potential members) on energy. BRICS+ member countries play an active role in the global energy market through their primary energy resources and rapid economic growth. The energy cooperation among these countries holds significant potential to enhance energy supply security, promote renewable energy projects, and advance environmental sustainability. This study seeks to analyze the strategic cooperation and energy policies of BRICS+ countries and their impact on the global energy market. This substantial expansion will resonate in the energy sector, particularly in fossil fuels. Currently, BRICS expansion indicates that a majority of the global energy supply will originate from BRICS countries.

## 1. ENERGY RESOURCES AND POLICIES OF BRICS+ COUNTRIES

While the energy capacity of each country in the BRICS+ coalition varies, each has distinct strengths and weaknesses. Brazil, for instance, is a leader in renewable energy and has robust policies on biofuels. Hydropower, one of the lowest-cost sources of electricity worldwide, is central to Brazil's energy strategy, although its development requires significant investment. Brazil serves as a key case study to quantify the economic benefits of hydropower investment. During the rapid industrialization of the 1960s and 1970s, Brazil prioritized energy sector development, with hydropower becoming a crucial component of its economy. Major investments were made in hydropower infrastructure, leading to the construction of some of the world's largest hydroelectric facilities, including Itaipu, Tucuruí, and the Paulo Afonso Hydroelectric Complex (Steinbuks and Perez-Sebastian, 2022).

As the most populous country in Latin America, Brazil is also the region's largest energy producer and consumer. Additionally, it boasts the richest renewable energy potential in Latin America, ranking among global leaders in biomass and hydroelectricity production. This is largely due to the Amazon River, the world's largest river by volume, and its many tributaries located within Brazilian territory, along with several other rivers with high flow rates. Brazil is second only to the U.S. in ethanol production, treating ethanol as a national fuel derived from domestically-produced sugarcane. Recently, Brazil has made strides in solar and wind energy generation, setting an example for other Latin American countries. This focus underscores Brazil's commitment to renewable energy sources (Durukan and Yılmaz, 2021: 354-355). Over the past decade, Brazil has successfully diversified its national energy mix, reducing oil and derivatives from 39.2 percent to 35.1 percent and natural gas from 13.5 percent to 9.6 percent (www.gov.br, 2024).

Russia, on the other hand, is a major force in energy resources, particularly oil and natural gas, bolstered by international investments. Following the dissolution of the Soviet Union, natural gas gained prominence in Russian energy planning, adding significant value to its energy portfolio. Today, Russia is a leading oil producer and the largest player in natural gas. However, the Russian economy's heavy reliance on energy, which comprises a substantial share of its GDP, renders it vulnerable to fluctuations in energy prices. In response, Russia has developed systematic foreign energy policies, aligning with President Vladimir Putin's pragmatic and proactive foreign policy since the 2000s. These long-term strategies aim to mitigate the adverse effects of economic dependence on energy and reinforce Russia's role as a prominent energy producer and exporter. This strategic approach highlights Russia's sustained influence in regional and global energy markets (Şahin and Nuriyev, 2021: 72-73).

Russia also ranks fourth globally in non-renewable energy consumption and carbon dioxide emissions. Despite these environmental concerns, Russia continues its reliance on primary energy production and consumption. Decarbonization is not currently a priority, and skepticism towards global climate change remains prevalent among stakeholders. The contribution of wind and solar power to Russia's energy mix is minimal and is not expected to exceed 1 percent by 2040. Facing global competition, financial limitations, and increasing technological isolation, Russia will need to develop new strategies to address the challenges in its energy sector (Mitrova and Melnikov, 2019: 73).

Prior to the 2022 crisis between Ukraine and Russia, Russia held a prominent position in global energy markets. The energy supply it provided to European Union member states underscored its importance to Europe. Until the Ukraine crisis, Russia supplied 25 percent of the European Union's oil, 42 percent of its coal, and 40 percent of its natural gas. In terms of thermal coal used for electricity generation, European dependence on Russian imports was estimated at approximately 70 percent. This level of reliance highlights Russia's significance to the European Union, BRICS, and the global energy market (Bağış, 2022: 20).

Following the Ukraine crisis, global markets—particularly the energy and food sectors—were deeply impacted. Countries dependent on Russian energy entered an energy crisis. Alongside increased demand for arms and military products, the crisis spurred growth in Russia's military-industrial complex. The global financial market also faced instability, and the food supply chain became precarious. In response, some countries began implementing alternative policies to address the energy crisis (Yu, 2022).

Both the COVID-19 pandemic and the Russia-Ukraine crisis have negatively impacted global energy security, given Russia's substantial energy reserves. Notably, energy trade between the EU and Russia experienced major disruptions (Telli and Yeşil, 2023: 95). Russia, a major global exporter, supplies 25 percent of the world's natural gas, 14 percent of platinum, 11 percent of crude oil, and 18 percent of coal (Sezer, 2024: 74). European Union countries, which depend significantly on Russian energy, have been particularly affected, intensifying the energy crisis. After the crisis, EU nations imposed numerous sanctions on Russia, leading to further increases in energy prices and straining living conditions (Aktaş and Bağra, 2023: 5235).

To address rising energy prices, the European Union and other nations have begun implementing emergency policies. Despite advances in green energy and targets to reduce environmental pollution by 2050, high energy costs have become a short-term concern. The dependency of European countries on Russian natural gas has heightened these concerns (Enescu and Szeles, 2023). Meanwhile, Western sanctions and embargoes on Russia have disrupted the global energy market's supply-demand balance, leading to uncertainty in energy markets. As a result, global supplies of essential goods deteriorated, trade slowed, incomes fell, and prices rose significantly. Countries heavily dependent on energy and food imports were hit hardest. Although some commodity-exporting nations increased exports to benefit from high global prices, they faced trade pattern reorganizations that reduced their integration into global value chains. A major negative consequence of the crisis for the energy sector has been the politicization of energy trade amid geostrategic rivalries among major powers, leading to disorganization in the global energy market and destabilizing the global economy (Chen, 2023).

In response to sanctions and embargoes, Russia began selling natural gas and oil in rubles. While this policy was not well-received by European countries, it led to increases in natural gas and oil prices and a reduction in energy supply. In an effort to reduce their dependence on Russian energy, countries have pursued environmentally friendly energy alternatives. European nations, in particular, have increased budgets to advance green energy initiatives. This shift suggests a growing likelihood that renewable energy sources will become primary energy sources in the future (Saktiawan, 2022).

The crisis between Russia and Ukraine has not only resulted in unprecedented humanitarian costs following the COVID-19 pandemic but has also posed serious global economic threats. Additionally, the crisis has jeopardized global energy and food supplies, leading to inflation driven by rising commodity prices. These disruptions to supply chains have negatively impacted businesses and limited global economic growth at a time when the world was still recovering from the adverse effects of the COVID-19 pandemic. The reduction in natural gas and oil supplies to Europe has prompted Russia to seek alternative channels to redirect energy flows, with logistical challenges leading it to supply energy to China and India at more competitive prices. This shift has allowed Russia to tap into these markets and created some bargaining opportunities for China and India. However, as Russia has historically been less integrated into the Asian energy market compared to its European connections, this pivot has not provided a fully effective solution. Moreover, the complexity of natural gas transportation, especially involving liquefaction technology, and the associated infrastructure and logistical constraints have compounded the challenge. These developments are expected to accelerate digital and green transformations worldwide, driving the adoption of sustainable energy sources to promote environmental sustainability and sustainable development (Korosteleva, 2022).

The Russia-Ukraine crisis has expedited the transition to green energy within the energy strategies of several countries. Globally, countries remain highly dependent on fossil fuels. In response to the crisis, nations have adapted by gradually shifting from traditional energy sources to renewable alternatives, as the sharp rise in commodity prices in the energy sector has encouraged a move away from primary energy sources. As a result, investment has increased in clean and sustainable energy options such as solar, wind, nuclear, and hydroelectric power, all of which are considered less harmful to the environment compared to traditional energy sources. Today, the most heavily invested forms of energy include wind energy, for its minimal environmental impact; nuclear energy, particularly in Europe, where countries like Germany have renewed their investments; and solar energy, thanks to the decreasing costs of photovoltaic panels. This trend will facilitate a smoother transition to renewable energy sources (Chedid and Penteado, 2022).

India, in contrast, occupies an important position in energy consumption due to both its economic growth and its rapidly expanding population. However, despite policies supporting the transition to renewable energy, India remains heavily dependent on fossil fuels. India's primary energy sources include coal, oil, and solid biomass, with oil consumption and imports rising due to increased vehicle ownership and road transport demand (IEA, 2021). To sustain its economic growth, India requires significant energy, particularly electricity, with the majority sourced from fossil fuels. For instance, of the 1,337 TWh of electricity generated in India in 2015, approximately 916 TWh were derived from fossil fuels (Tiewsoh et al., 2019: 1).

India's ongoing demand for natural gas, oil, and coal underscores the importance of renewable energy in reducing its dependence on foreign energy sources. Key objectives for advancing renewable energy in India include supporting economic growth, enhancing energy security, reducing environmental pollution, and expanding energy access. Achieving sustainable development requires sustainable energy consumption and public access to affordable, modern, and reliable energy. India's favorable economic conditions and strong government support have positioned it as an attractive market for renewable energy investments. To accelerate growth in this sector, the government has emphasized foreign investment, which is expected to generate substantial employment opportunities in the future (Kumar and Majid, 2020: 1). India's commitment to renewable energy is anticipated to yield long-term benefits, with projections suggesting that approximately 80 percent of its electricity demand in 2040 could be met by wind and solar power. This shift is expected to create competitive conditions with traditional energy sources, given the cost advantage. Additionally, the anticipated decline in wind and solar installation costs, coupled with a projected 85 percent reduction in $CO_2$ emissions, is likely to further bolster India's renewable energy investments (Lu et al., 2020: 1).

China faces pressure from global energy institutions to reform its unregulated national energy sector and enhance its energy governance capacity. However, rather than focusing on domestic reforms, China seeks to establish a global energy order and aims to assume a leadership role through the BRICS framework. Within BRICS, a shared leadership approach is proposed, potentially limiting China's leadership potential. China utilizes the 'Silk Road Economic Belt' as a tool to reinforce its dominant position in energy (Christoffersen, 2016: 15).

Like India, China plays a critical role in global energy demand and is highly dependent on foreign sources, particularly for fossil fuels such as coal. With evolving energy policies, China has increasingly emphasized renewable energy and has made substantial investments in this area.

As China's economic growth continues, it faces numerous challenges, including energy security, $CO_2$ emissions, and environmental pollution. It is expected to address these issues independently, with the first requirement being the establishment of a comprehensive and coherent energy strategy. Energy conservation is a national policy priority, alongside increasing investments in renewable energy and advancing clean coal technology (Zhidong, 2005: 144). In this regard, China leads BRICS countries in energy science and technology. Although Russia, Brazil, India, and South Africa each possess unique national advantages in energy and technology, BRICS as a whole lags behind developed countries in these fields. China's progress in renewable energy and technology is therefore significant for BRICS (Zhang et al., 2018).

Clean energy contributed a record 11.4 trillion yuan ($1.6 trillion) to China's economy in 2023, accounting for the entirety of investment growth and a larger share of economic expansion than any other sector. Specifically, the 'new three' sectors—solar energy, electric vehicles (EVs), and batteries—received significant investment, reflecting China's focus on the technologies and infrastructure required to decarbonize energy production and consumption (Myllyvirta, 2024).

South Africa, meanwhile, has established itself in global markets due to its rich fossil fuel resources. Though a leading coal producer, South Africa also aims to transition towards renewable energy. It is taking essential steps to secure energy and diversify supply within BRICS, with optimizing and diversifying energy supply being crucial for national development and energy security (Ndlovu and Inglesi-Lotz, 2019: 14). However, South Africa, often termed the 'Powerhouse of Africa,' faces significant energy challenges, including frequent power outages, high energy tariffs, underinvestment in electricity infrastructure, energy poverty among low-income households, and overall energy shortages. In response, South Africa has initiated extensive exploration of oil and natural gas reserves, renewable energy projects, and energy efficiency programs, with particular attention to hydrogen energy. Since 2013, major construction projects in South Africa have increasingly focused on renewable energy (Pollet et al., 2015: 16685).

While South Africa remains a major player in coal production, its energy infrastructure faces critical challenges. Its electricity generation, heavily reliant on coal, is outdated, unreliable, and environmentally harmful, falling short of demand. The current electricity supply deficit is estimated at 4 to 6 GW, leading to load shedding of up to 10 hours daily, which impacts both daily life and the economy. Although electricity access is relatively high compared to regional averages, around 10 percent of South Africans still lack access, and approximately 47 percent are considered 'energy poor.' Investment in reforms to ensure reliable electricity services and universal access is urgently needed (World Bank, 2023).

The expansion of BRICS in 2023 has introduced new opportunities and challenges across various sectors. BRICS aims to fulfill its goals by establishing alternative development finance, creating a parallel energy trade system, reducing dependence on the dollar in foreign exchange transactions, and deepening trade and technological cooperation across areas such as artificial intelligence and space exploration. In 2024, with the addition of Ethiopia, Egypt, Iran, Saudi Arabia, and the United Arab Emirates, BRICS has further strengthened its global influence.

The expansion of BRICS represents a pivotal event, underscoring its growing impact on global geopolitics and international economic relations. As of January 1, 2024, Iran, Saudi Arabia, Egypt, Ethiopia, and the United Arab Emirates have officially joined the BRICS alliance, while Argentina opted not to join (Mekonnen, 2024: 62). The formal inclusion of these new members marks a significant geopolitical shift. However, the cultural, political, and economic diversity within BRICS may lead to differences in priorities and approaches, presenting unique challenges for the alliance.

Saudi Arabia holds the largest proven oil reserves globally and ranks among the leading countries in natural gas reserves. The nation continues to expand its nuclear power infrastructure and increase investments in solar energy (Bahgat, 2012a). Renewable and sustainable energy play a critical role in establishing a stable economic structure in developed nations like Saudi Arabia. Renewable energy sources are also increasingly applied in technological advancements, offering a viable alternative to hydrocarbon-based energy. With its growing population, Saudi Arabia has substantial electricity demand. To address this, it is investing significantly in sustainable and renewable energy projects across various regions, supported by strong financial resources. The adoption of renewable and sustainable energy helps reduce reliance on primary energy sources, particularly natural gas and oil, contributing to a cleaner and more sustainable energy landscape for Saudi Arabia's economy (Amran et al., 2020: 1).

Since 2012, the United States has imposed sanctions on Iran, affecting its energy sector, especially oil. These sanctions include restrictions on the purchase of Iranian oil and petroleum products, as well as on entities providing Iran with products and services for resource development. Additional sanctions imposed in 2024 further limit Iran's oil transactions with China (IEA, 2024).

Iran's natural gas and oil reserves are crucial for global energy security. The presence of the United States in the Persian Gulf region, particularly in Iraq and Afghanistan, underscores Iran's importance in ensuring energy stability within this region (Koolaee, 2011: 95). Despite possessing substantial renewable and non-renewable energy resources, Iran faces challenges such as environmental pollution and energy security issues due to its reliance on non-renewable resources. As a significant exporter and consumer of fossil fuels, Iran is working to incorporate renewable energy sources to enhance its energy security and sustainability. Leveraging its advantageous geographical location, Iran aims to diversify and increase the accessibility of renewable energy sources, reducing dependence on fossil fuels (Solaymani, 2021: 1).

The United Arab Emirates (UAE), despite its considerable hydrocarbon reserves, has recently taken steps to diversify its energy sources and lessen its dependence on oil. The UAE has made more concrete strides than its neighbors in investing in nuclear power and renewable energy. Although other countries have shown interest in these energy sources, few have moved forward with concrete actions. The UAE stands out in this regard (Bahgat, 2012b: 269). Its commitment to achieving net-zero emissions by 2050 and targeting a 30 percent clean energy share in power generation by 2030 underpins these efforts. Given its geographic limitations that restrict hydropower and wind energy potential, the UAE is focusing on nuclear and solar energy development to diversify its power mix and reduce emissions (Global Energy Monitor, 2024: 30).

Experts suggest that with the addition of the United Arab Emirates, Iran, and Saudi Arabia to BRICS, the alliance could control nearly half of the global crude oil supply. With Saudi Arabia's membership, BRICS is projected to become a dominant commodity power. According to data from the U.S. Energy Information Administration, BRICS is expected to control around 42 percent of global oil production and 35 percent of oil consumption. Russia will chair BRICS in 2024, and recent meetings have emphasized increasing the use of national currencies and payment instruments in bilateral trade. Strengthening unity against Western political and economic institutions is central to Russian President Vladimir Putin's foreign policy, which has been a means of safeguarding Russia's economy from sanctions, particularly following the Ukraine crisis, and has led Russia to pursue alternative policies (S&P Global, 2024).

Egypt, with a population exceeding eighty million, is among the most populous countries in the Middle East and the Arab world. Egypt's energy policies and sector structure drive its economic growth. Rising population and economic development have increased energy demand across all sectors. Egypt's primary energy consumption includes oil, natural gas, and electricity, with production largely based on fossil fuels, primarily oil, natural gas, and coal. While Egypt's oil reserves do not meet its consumption needs, the situation is more favorable for natural gas. Discoveries made through partnerships with international companies have positioned Egypt as a significant regional producer and exporter of natural gas. In the renewable energy sector, Egypt's vast western desert is suitable for solar energy, the Gulf of Suez for wind energy, and the Nile River for hydroelectric power, highlighting Egypt's resource diversity. Egypt's fossil fuel and renewable energy potential make it an important member of BRICS, particularly as the global push to reduce fossil fuel usage emphasizes renewable and sustainable energy. Egypt's renewable energy potential enhances energy supply security within BRICS (Bahgat, 2013: 12-14).

Ethiopia's engagement with BRICS reflects its ambition to capitalize on opportunities for trade, investment, technology transfer, and knowledge exchange. Ethiopia seeks to leverage BRICS membership for sustainable economic growth, aiming to align itself with these major emerging economies to access new markets, attract investment, and promote innovation in key sectors of its economy (Mekonnen, 2024: 61). Hydropower is the dominant power source in both Brazil and Ethiopia, accounting for 49 percent and 87 percent of their total capacity, respectively. The relative abundance of rainfall in western Ethiopia creates substantial hydropower potential for conventional storage technologies (Norman et al., 2024).

Energy security has become a critical paradigm in today's world, where countries depend on the reliable supply of natural gas and oil. While global demand for these resources continues to grow, energy-rich countries and regions compete for profitable production opportunities. Although Azerbaijan has only been independent for 29 years, it has emerged as a significant energy-rich nation. The presence of energy reserves in the Caspian Basin has heightened global interest in Azerbaijan's energy security. Currently a net exporter of natural gas and oil, Azerbaijan's energy economy is primarily based on hydrocarbon production (Gonmei, 2020: 940). This role as an energy supplier enhances Azerbaijan's importance to other countries. Pipeline projects, crucial for meeting energy needs, further increase Azerbaijan's strategic significance. Given that some BRICS+ countries are energy-demanding, bilateral relations and agreements between Azerbaijan and BRICS+ nations may hold critical importance for both sides (Azakov, 2018). In August 2024, Azerbaijan applied for BRICS membership, with its potential membership expected to strengthen its ties with Russia and China while maintaining relations with the West. Policies and economic opportunities with other BRICS member countries could enable Baku to reduce its economic dependence on oil and gas exports (Huseynov, 2024).

Today, societies recognize the importance of energy for sustainability and quality of life. Consequently, countries strive to maximize the efficient use of energy resources. However, energy performance varies depending on national structures, resources, and policies. While some countries excel in energy resource utilization, others face challenges. Venezuela, despite its significant renewable and non-renewable energy resources, confronts a complex energy crisis, marked by frequent and prolonged power outages and disruptions to electricity services nationwide (Pietrosemoli and Rodriguez-Monroy, 2019).

In 2017, Venezuela was experiencing a severe economic crisis, compounded by the damage to its energy sector from U.S. sanctions. These sanctions led to contractions in Venezuela's oil industry. The U.S. imposed further sanctions on PDVSA (Petróleos de Venezuela S.A.) in January 2019, banning Venezuelan oil exports to the U.S. market, which resulted in increased exports to China, India, and other countries. However, these sanctions quickly eroded PDVSA's customer base and access to cargo carriers, leading to a significant contraction in oil exports (Oliveros, 2020: 7).

Despite challenges, Venezuela has substantial potential for energy production from renewable sources such as water, solar, biomass, wind, as well as traditional primary energy sources. Many countries are striving to reduce greenhouse gas emissions and dependence on external energy supplies. Although Venezuela faces difficulties in producing low-carbon fuels such as hydrogen for achieving net-zero carbon targets, it shows keen interest in advancing in this area (Rodriguez et al., 2022). While Venezuela faces several energy-related issues, its primary energy resources and investments in renewable energy could support bilateral cooperation with BRICS+, which aims to become a significant player in global energy markets.

Potential cooperation with BRICS countries could offer new opportunities for Venezuela and Iran to sustain their presence in energy markets and bolster economic growth. Strategic collaborations among these nations in response to sanctions may signal the start of a new era, fostering both energy security and the development of alternative energy sources. Consequently, these nations are increasingly pursuing strategic partnerships with BRICS.

As BRICS expands its membership, it considers factors such as population, economic structure, natural resources, and international relations. In this context, Argentina has emerged as a prominent candidate, potentially joining Brazil as the second Latin American country in BRICS. Rich in natural resources, Argentina has participated in several BRICS meetings and is currently reviewing its membership status (Hasançebi and Kırbaşoğlu, 2023: 132-133).

Argentina, one of the leading countries in natural gas reserves in South America, has privatized its energy sector since the 1990s, transitioning to a market-oriented system. Since 2004, due to rising energy demand and supply constraints, Argentina has experienced energy shortages, particularly affecting natural gas and electricity supplies (Recalde, 2011: 3860). To address these energy security challenges, it is essential for Argentina to prioritize the development of its energy infrastructure and to implement effective energy policies. Argentina's potential membership in BRICS is of critical importance not only for Argentina but also for BRICS in terms of energy policy and supply security. However, following the election of a new president, Argentina, which had initiated the membership process, withdrew its application amid election campaign priorities (Bloomberg, 2024).

The data in Table 1 provides key insights into the total energy export figures for current BRICS members and potential BRICS candidates. Among the top ten countries globally in energy exports, three are BRICS members: Russia, Saudi Arabia, and the United Arab Emirates. Additionally, six BRICS countries, including Iran, Brazil, and China, rank within the top 20. Russia holds the top position in global energy exports, while Saudi Arabia and the United Arab Emirates rank third and tenth, respectively. Russia's leading position, with a share exceeding 10 percent of total energy exports, underscores its significance in the global energy market. Similarly, Saudi Arabia's and the United Arab Emirates' rankings as third and tenth in global energy exports highlight their robust positions in the global energy sector. The addition of these nations to BRICS enhances the bloc's competitiveness in the energy market.

Furthermore, the presence of major energy consumers such as China and India within BRICS, who hold prominent positions in energy exports, underscores the dual significance of China and India as both large domestic consumers and exporters. This dynamic reveals the importance of these countries to BRICS' energy strategy, combining both substantial consumption and export capabilities

*Table 1. Total energy exports of countries*

| Rank | Countries | Oil products | Year | Units |
|---|---|---|---|---|
| | World | 231806697 | 2021 | TJ |
| 1 | Russia | 28934090 | 2021 | TJ |
| 3 | Saudi Arabia | 16087188 | 2021 | TJ |
| 10 | United Arab Emirates | 7238289 | 2021 | TJ |
| 13 | Iran | 3974182 | 2021 | TJ |
| 17 | Brazil | 3275079 | 2021 | TJ |

continued on following page

*Table 1. Continued*

| Rank | Countries | Oil products | Year | Units |
|---|---|---|---|---|
| 18 | China | 3245706 | 2021 | TJ |
| 21 | India | 2919202 | 2021 | TJ |
| 31 | South Africa | 1924237 | 2021 | TJ |
| 46 | Egypt | 539500 | 2021 | TJ |
| 61 | Argentina | 342983 | 2021 | TJ |

**Source:**IEA (2024)

Table 2 presents the percentage of renewable energy consumption within the final energy consumption of current and potential BRICS member countries. Brazil stands out as one of the countries with the highest percentage of renewable energy consumption in final energy use, a reflection of its substantial investments in hydroelectric power. China has shown a steady increase in renewable energy consumption, from 11.3 percent in 2011 to 15.2 percent in 2021. In contrast, the United Arab Emirates has one of the lowest rates of renewable energy consumption among the countries analyzed. Argentina and Egypt also feature stable yet low rates of renewable energy consumption as a percentage of final energy use.

India, despite its significant population growth and rising energy demand, is progressively increasing its renewable energy consumption relative to its total final energy consumption, aiming to reduce its dependence on primary energy sources. Ethiopia, although showing a decrease in renewable energy consumption compared to other energy sources since 2011, remains a leader among BRICS countries in this area, with a renewable energy consumption rate exceeding 90 percent. Meanwhile, Iran, Russia, and Saudi Arabia, similar to the United Arab Emirates, have very low shares of renewable energy in their final energy consumption due to their reliance on primary energy resources.

Lastly, although South Africa experienced a decline in the share of renewable energy consumption in final energy use over recent years, it has returned to previous levels, particularly following the COVID-19 pandemic.

*Table 2. Percentage of renewable energy consumption in final energy consumption of countries*

| | 2011 | 2012 | 2013 | 2014 | 2015 | 2016 | 2017 | 2018 | 2019 | 2020 | 2021 |
|---|---|---|---|---|---|---|---|---|---|---|---|
| **United Arab Emirates** | 0.1 | 0.1 | 0.1 | 0.1 | 0.1 | 0.1 | 0.2 | 0.3 | 0.7 | 0.9 | 1 |
| **Argentina** | 8.8 | 8.6 | 8.9 | 9.8 | 9.4 | 9.4 | 10.4 | 10.5 | 10.7 | 9.8 | 9.2 |
| **Brazil** | 45.2 | 43.5 | 42.3 | 41.7 | 43.7 | 45.4 | 45.3 | 46.9 | 47.5 | 50 | 46.5 |

continued on following page

*Table 2. Continued*

| | 2011 | 2012 | 2013 | 2014 | 2015 | 2016 | 2017 | 2018 | 2019 | 2020 | 2021 |
|---|---|---|---|---|---|---|---|---|---|---|---|
| **China** | 11.3 | 11.5 | 11.5 | 11.9 | 12.2 | 12.6 | 13.1 | 13.5 | 14.3 | 14.9 | 15.2 |
| **Egypt** | 5.4 | 5.3 | 5.3 | 5.4 | 5.3 | 5.1 | 4.9 | 5 | 6.2 | 6.7 | 6.1 |
| **Ethiopia** | 93.6 | 93.3 | 92.4 | 91.4 | 91.5 | 90.4 | 90.8 | 90 | 89.3 | 90.7 | 90.6 |
| **India** | 35 | 34.8 | 34.9 | 33.9 | 33.4 | 33 | 32.5 | 32.9 | 33.5 | 36.1 | 34.9 |
| **Iran** | 0.9 | 0.9 | 1 | 0.9 | 0.9 | 1 | 1 | 1 | 1 | 0.9 | 0.9 |
| **Russia** | 3.2 | 3.2 | 3.6 | 3.3 | 3.2 | 3.4 | 3.2 | 3.2 | 3.2 | 3.7 | 3.5 |
| **Saudi Arabia** | 0 | 0 | 0 | 0 | 0 | 0 | 0 | 0 | 0 | 0.1 | 0.1 |
| **South Africa** | 9 | 8.3 | 7.8 | 7.6 | 7.6 | 7.8 | 7.9 | 8 | 8.7 | 9.8 | 9.7 |

**Source:** World Bank (2024).

## 2. BRICS+ AND ENERGY GEOPOLITICS

Energy is a powerful tool for strengthening economic relations between countries. Historically, global energy dynamics demonstrate that those who control this sector hold a strategic advantage. Countries compete on this basis and employ intensive foreign policy measures to expand their spheres of influence. While Western countries have long dominated the global energy sector, the emergence of major energy consumers like China and India has begun to reshape this landscape. Similarly, Russia's role as a significant energy supplier underscores its strategic importance. Countries that play key roles in energy production recognize this demand and actively seek to expand their influence. Consequently, geopolitics and energy diplomacy are mutually reinforcing (Mostaque, 2022: 186).

In terms of the impact of BRICS+ energy policies on the global balance of power, the global energy geopolitics of these nations warrants examination. Before the expansion of BRICS, cooperation policies were structured around the axis of production and consumption, with Russia and Brazil supplying substantial energy resources while China and India served as major energy importers.

The primary purpose of BRICS is to amplify the voice of all developing countries in global governance, break the monopoly of Western developed countries, and deepen cooperation among developing nations. BRICS countries have actively embraced economic globalization, leveraging their unique strengths to promote comprehensive economic and social development and becoming leaders among emerging market and developing nations. As a result, BRICS has gained increasing importance in the global economic structure (Zhongxiu and Qingxin, 2020). Contrary to certain misconceptions, BRICS was not established in opposition to existing international groups; rather, its objective was to offer an alternative within the dominant global framework, which predominantly comprises the advanced economies of the Global North. Similar to regional associations such as ASEAN and the African Union, BRICS seeks active participation in international decision-making processes, contributing its unique perspectives and shaping decisions to reflect local contexts. This approach underscores BRICS' commitment to inclusive participation on the international stage, where each member's voice is acknowledged (Megre and Ribeiro, 2024).

New geoeconomic and geopolitical processes are shaping global realities, impacting both international actors and global populations. The redistribution of power and influence in world geopolitical processes is influenced by various factors, including geoeconomic shifts, globalization, territorial reorganization, the adoption of renewable energy sources, and the strengthening of state capacities (Vasileski, 2024).

Trade in goods among BRICS economies has significantly outpaced trade between BRICS and G7 countries, resulting in increased intra-BRICS trade intensity. Decades of rapid growth have provided these economies with substantial influence in the global market, both as producers and consumers. Engaging with advanced economies and China, perceived as an economic superpower, BRICS members could establish a coalition with reduced dependence on Western economies (Azevedo et al., 2024).

With the addition of new economies to BRICS, the energy sector is poised to take a central role: each new member brings substantial economic energy output, diverse investment partners, and extensive resources for both conventional and alternative energy production (Backaran and Cahill, 2023). In 2020, BRICS nations surpassed G7 countries in global economic share, and by 2023, this gap has widened, with BRICS achieving a share slightly below 30 percent. The current five-member BRICS group represents 40 percent of the global population. With the addition of six new members (Argentina, Egypt, Ethiopia, Iran, Saudi Arabia, and the United Arab Emirates), this population share is projected to rise to 46 percent (Kamin and Langhammer, 2023). While this expansion may enhance the group's influence, consensus decision-making in BRICS+ could be challenging due to the increased diversity of interests within the group. For example, Egypt and Ethiopia have ongoing tensions regarding the equitable distribution of the Nile River's water resources. Similarly, despite recently agreeing to resume diplomatic relations, Saudi Arabia and Iran have a longstanding rivalry in the Middle East and often support opposing sides in regional conflicts (e.g., in Syria, Iraq, and Yemen), frequently involving proxy forces (EPRS, 2024: 3).

Volatility in resource prices caused by export restrictions or fluctuations from BRICS countries directly impacts global economic stability. The abundance of resources and energy in these countries allows them to exert strategic influence within and beyond their regions. China, for instance, has positioned itself as the main exporter of magnesium, exerting price pressure on other potential producers, which has nearly eliminated magnesium production outside China. Among the original BRICS members, Russia stands out as the only nation with substantial natural gas and oil reserves, while the other members are primarily known for their dominance in the agricultural sector (Brazil and India) or their resources, such as iron ore, bauxite, and niobium (Brazil); nickel, palladium, and platinum (Russia); coal, iron ore, bauxite, and precious metals (India); and platinum, gold, chrome, and manganese (South Africa). China, meanwhile, is the world's leading producer of many critical minerals and refractory metals essential for modern industries, such as coal, rare earth elements, antimony, and tungsten (Kamin and Langhammer, 2023).

The polarisation between China and the U.S. seeks to shape the role of the EU within this emerging order, amid an ongoing geo-economic debate. Questions arise regarding the response of other developing nations to the fragmentation of global powers into distinct economic and political blocs of 'like-minded' countries or allies. Is bloc-building already underway, and to what extent are these alliances taking shape? Are these alliances truly new, and do they possess significant and potentially influential geo-economic leverage? Such questions demand answers.

Despite its promising potential, the BRICS bloc faces several challenges that limit its effectiveness in international politics. Firstly, the lack of a shared ideology or political values among its members presents a significant obstacle. BRICS countries stem from varied historical and cultural backgrounds, and the bloc's formation was largely driven by pragmatic, conjunctural motives. Mutual distrust persists, and this may only increase if the bloc expands. Secondly, divergent geopolitical interests among BRICS members complicate unity. While they stand united against Western hegemony, they lack consensus on ultimate goals. Rivalries between China, India, and Russia further deepen these divisions, especially in Asia and Africa. Thirdly, despite growing challenges in the Western world, Western countries are more resilient to global economic and political crises, making it difficult for BRICS to counterbalance Western influence. The West can exploit internal conflicts within the bloc. Finally, some BRICS members, particularly China, are among the primary beneficiaries of the current global economic order. However, the rise of BRICS could fragment the global financial system, which could adversely affect China's interests. This paradox highlights the uncertainty surrounding BRICS' potential as a genuine alternative to the Western economic and geopolitical system (Akman, 2023). For example, China and India, two countries with substantial global populations, engage in intense geopolitical competition, both in Asia and increasingly on a global scale. They remain locked in a territorial stalemate in the Himalayas and vie for strategic advantage in the Indian Ocean, each seeking to position itself as the natural leader of the Global South (Patrick, 2024).

Energy is fundamental to a country's development, with the potential to directly impact regional and global geopolitical balances, influenced by policies and resource accessibility. For BRICS+ countries, which are significant players in the energy sector, energy security is a cornerstone of economic activity. This critical importance is defined by the assurance that energy services are consistently available, in adequate quantities, and at affordable prices. Should energy access be restricted, resulting in insecure consumption and production, the entire economy is affected. For example, industrial sectors would halt production, services would cease, and transportation would be disrupted. This scenario could lead to price surges in the short-term market and environmental repercussions due to reliance on non-renewable resources to secure energy supply (GNPW Group, 2023). Factors such as the finite nature of fossil fuels, climate change, and the transition to renewable energy further complicate energy geopolitics.

Energy security is at the core of any BRICS strategic energy cooperation. Despite investments in renewable energy, demand for primary energy sources remains high. Natural gas and oil reserves, which are predominantly used among primary energy sources, are unevenly distributed globally, closely affecting global energy supply security (Azakov, 2018). Some BRICS countries heavily rely on foreign energy supplies. China's dependence on foreign oil rose from 23 percent in the early 2000s to 58 percent by 2012. India and South Africa import approximately 80 percent and 67 percent of their oil needs, respectively. Unlike China, India, and South Africa, Russia and Brazil are major energy exporters, and energy exports constitute the foundation of their economies. For BRICS energy cooperation to be effective, it is vital to focus on long-term interests, build mutual trust, accommodate each other's needs, and address each member's developmental requirements (Tao and Xi, 2022).

The expansion of BRICS offers Russia both new opportunities and risks. Initially, Russia sought to enhance the economic ties and political influence of BRICS, especially in Asia, by fostering cooperation with China, promoting a new economic world order, and establishing 'zones of friendship'. Politically, integration enhances diplomatic influence, strengthens security cooperation, and supports the vision of a balanced global governance structure. Socially and culturally, it fosters mutual understanding and solidarity through people-to-people contacts and educational exchanges. However, this integration faces challenges such as political tensions, economic disparities, and coordination difficulties within the alliance. Bilateral tensions, stemming from historical disputes and external geopolitical pressures—such as those between China and India—can hinder cooperative progress. Economic inequality and developmental disparities further complicate coherent policy formulation and equitable resource distribution. Additionally, varying legal and regulatory frameworks impede smooth trade and investment flows, necessitating complex negotiations. Russia, holding some of the world's largest oil and natural gas reserves, has forged strategic partnerships with Asian nations, providing essential energy resources for their growing economies. This exchange not only ensures a stable energy supply for Asian countries but also guarantees a steady demand for Russian exports, contributing significantly to Russia's economic stability (Imamkulieva, 2024).

## 3. FUTURE OF GLOBAL ENERGY WITH BRICS+

By 2024, the BRICS community has achieved undeniable significance in the global arena. Their combined power is substantial, and their influence continues to grow. On the other side are the G7 economies (Canada, France, Italy, Germany, the United Kingdom, Japan, and the United States), the world's largest and most developed economic group. Both groups independently wield the capacity to impact the global economy. BRICS countries have experienced rapid growth in recent years, and if this high growth rate is sustained, it could elevate them to even greater economic prominence in the future. In contrast, the G7 countries, with more mature economies, tend to grow at a slower pace. Nevertheless, they remain economic powerhouses with strong and stable economies that continue to expand, albeit at a more measured rate (Mekonnen, 2024: 60).

Figure 1 presents GDP growth forecasts for G7 and BRICS countries as of 2024. Despite generally lower growth projections compared to 2023, BRICS countries still show a significantly higher average growth forecast of 3.6 percent compared to the G7 average of 1 percent (Conte and Lam, 2024). As Mekonnen (2024) highlights, rapid growth in BRICS stands in contrast to the more mature growth figures observed in the G7.

*Figure 1. GDP ratios of G7 and BRICS+ countries as of 2024*

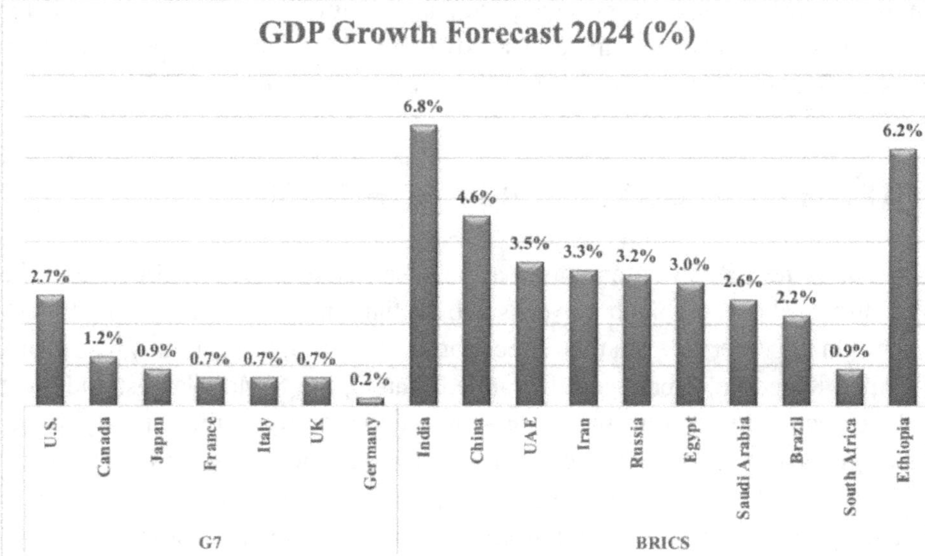


*(Conte and Lam, 2024)*

Figure 2 presents an assessment of G7 and BRICS countries in terms of their cooperation and trade orientations. The share of EU exports to G7 countries rose from 74.3 percent in 2018 to 75.4 percent in 2023. While the United Kingdom recovered from the post-Brexit trade decline in the region, its trade with other G7 countries increased. The decline in China's export share to the G7 is thought to be due to the U.S.-China trade dispute. Additionally, the Russia-Ukraine war and Western-imposed sanctions contributed to a 3.8 percentage point decline in Russia's exports to the G7 over the same period. Lastly, India, South Africa, and the United Kingdom diverged from these trends, continuing to make progress in exports with the opposing bloc (Wendling, 2024).

*Figure 2. Changes in trade of G7 and BRICS countries*

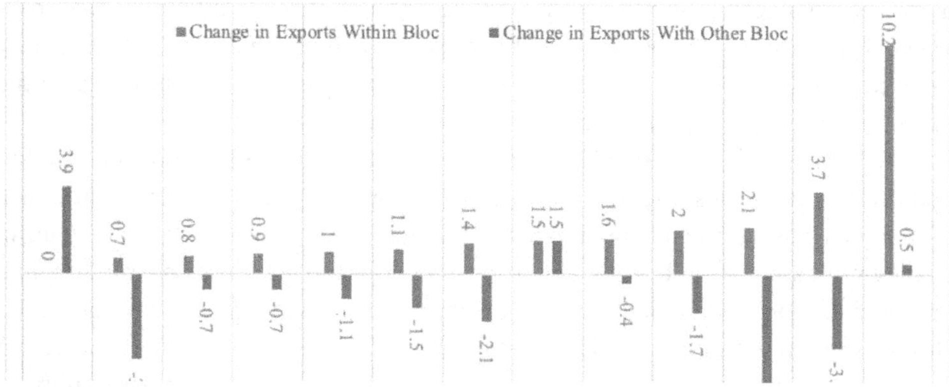


*(Wendling, 2024)*

In a general comparison of the BRICS and G7 countries as of their expansion in 2024:

- The G7, comprising the USA, Germany, Canada, France, the UK, Italy, and Japan, represents 10 percent of the world's population. In contrast, BRICS+, which includes Brazil, Russia, India, China, South Africa, Egypt, Ethiopia, Iran, and the UAE, represents 45 percent of the global population.
- While the G7 advocates a Western-centered world order, BRICS+ offers an alternative global model.
- G7 countries account for 30 percent of global GDP and are responsible for 21 percent of $CO_2$ emissions, whereas BRICS+ countries represent 35 percent of GDP and contribute 50 percent of global $CO_2$ emissions.
- G7 countries accept the U.S. dollar as the global reserve currency, while BRICS+ countries, particularly Russia, Iran, and China, seek to establish an alternative reserve currency to the dollar.
- G7 countries are highly integrated both economically and politically. In contrast, BRICS+ faces integration challenges due to differing strategic interests, making a unified strategy more difficult (The Globalist, 2024; Afota et al., 2024).

BRICS countries are rich in natural resources and strategic minerals, with extensive reserves of oil, gas, coal, and precious metals. The energy market thus serves as a catalyst for economic growth, and their strategic locations provide access to critical trade routes. Conversely, the strength of the G7 countries lies in their trade and investment impact. They are the world's largest importers and exporters, with highly developed industrial and service sectors, and their economic policies and trade agreements can exert significant influence on global trade (Mekonnen, 2024: 61).

With its expanding role in global energy markets, BRICS+ has the capacity to significantly influence the sector's future. Consequently, it seeks to shape the trajectory of future energy policies by ensuring energy security.

The expansion of the BRICS group into BRICS+ has implications for member countries in numerous respects. The growing geopolitical and economic influence of these nations has the potential to reshape global energy markets in the long term, as they rank among the leading countries in energy production, consumption, and carbon emissions. Thus, their policies on energy, sustainability, and environmental stewardship are crucial to analyze. While the BRICS already wield considerable influence, the inclusion of new member countries is expected to deepen this impact. As Sasana and Ghozali (2017) observe, BRICS countries are significantly interested in transitioning from fossil fuels to renewable energy sources. This is reflected in Brazil's commitment to biofuels, China's leadership in solar energy, and India's advancements in wind energy technology.

The shift from fossil fuels to renewable energy faces several challenges. For instance, renewable energy infrastructure remains underdeveloped in some BRICS countries, leaving fossil fuel industries dominant in energy consumption. While renewable energy has proven effective in reducing carbon emissions and promoting environmental sustainability, its impact on economic growth has been more gradual and inconsistent. In the case of BRICS economies, renewable energy consumption tends to hinder short-term economic growth, whereas fossil fuel consumption promotes growth (Sasana and Ghozali, 2017). However, the BRICS+ initiative presents opportunities for technological collaboration in renewable energy by involving more developing countries, enabling greater investment and fostering innovation. Through technological and resource-sharing, BRICS+ countries are expected to reduce dependence on fossil fuels and mitigate environmental impact.

Renewable wind and solar energy sources hold a critical role in global electricity generation. However, as they are naturally intermittent, their supply does not always align with consumption, causing energy interruptions. Energy storage, therefore, offers important solutions, increasing supply reliability and making investments more attractive. Such storage systems can not only meet demand but also enhance profitability in electricity-intensive countries like Brazil (GNPW Group, 2023).

The long-term impact of BRICS+ on the global energy market is multifaceted. The inclusion of new countries within the BRICS framework is likely to shift the balance of power in global energy geopolitics. With the rising energy demands of BRICS+ nations and their growing role in international energy governance, their collective influence on oil prices, energy exports, and carbon reduction policies could have significant consequences for both developed and developing countries (Downie, 2015).

Additionally, the BRICS+ initiative could spur energy market reforms and encourage new investments in energy infrastructure, including better energy market regulation, diversification of energy sources, and the promotion of sustainable energy practices. Financial development and technological innovation in BRICS countries have already led to gains in energy efficiency and reductions in CO2 emissions (Raghutla & Chittedi, 2020). Thus, the expansion of the BRICS alliance presents a shift in the global energy balance and future scenarios. With new members joining BRICS, the global energy landscape may evolve as follows:

- **Renewable Energy and Green Transformation**: BRICS countries possess rich resources for renewable energy and hold strategic advantages in this sector. They control significant supplies of critical raw materials essential for clean energy production. For instance, Brazil produces 10 percent of the world's graphite, a key component in lithium-ion batteries; China produces 60 percent of the global supply of lithium and cobalt used in electric batteries; South Africa and Russia together produce 83 percent of the world's platinum, essential for next-generation batteries; and India is a major producer of rare earth elements such as barite, chromium, and titanium. The newly added members further diversify resource availability. This expanded bloc is a key player in the global effort to combat climate change (Brotto, 2024). BRICS+ countries actively support the energy transition through their focus on renewable energy, facilitating this shift through collaboration. Member nations aim to accelerate the green transformation by prioritizing renewable energy cooperation (Tong, Yiyi, and Lei, 2024).
- **Environmental Sustainability**: Member country leaders recognize the importance of sustainable development through integrated, holistic approaches. BRICS+ has been characterized as "an equal partnership of countries with diverse perspectives but a shared vision for a better world" (IISD, 2023). Lin et al. (2024) underscore the significance of BRICS countries in environmental sustainability, given their rapid economic growth and increasing populations, which make them substantial contributors to greenhouse gas and CO2 emissions. BRICS countries must take proactive steps to reduce these emissions. For example, collaboration between the public and private sectors on environmentally relevant technologies, promoting sustainable energy sources such as hydrogen, biomass, solar, and wind, and tax incentives for companies advancing green initiatives should be prioritized. It is also essential to align financial sector operations with the Sustainable Development Goals (Lin et al., 2024).

- **Common Policies for Energy Supply Security**: Reliable and affordable energy access is essential for sustaining industrialization, advancing technology, and improving quality of life. The BRICS+ countries' varied geopolitical and economic concerns mean that a "one-size-fits-all" approach to energy cooperation is impractical. Russia and Brazil, for instance, are energy-rich nations often impacted by geopolitical disruptions, whereas China, India, and South Africa are major energy consumers. Therefore, BRICS energy cooperation must prioritize long-term interests, build mutual trust, and accommodate the development needs of all members (Tabash et al., 2024; Tao and Xi, 2023). The goal is to identify balanced, mutually beneficial strategies.

The expanded BRICS+ bloc is forging new partnerships, embracing a wide spectrum of cooperation. For example, bilateral trade between the UAE and Russia grew by 68 percent in 2022, reaching a record high of $9 billion, with gold and precious stones accounting for nearly 40 percent of Russian exports to the UAE. In July 2023, the UAE and India agreed to trade in rupees rather than dollars, aligning with India's efforts to reduce transaction costs by eliminating dollar conversions (Kazelko and Semeghini, 2024: 64).

- **Technology Transfer and Innovation Collaborations**: BRICS countries aim to collaborate in fostering values-driven by technology and innovation investments, envisioning a shared future. Efforts include strengthening scientific research, creating public-private partnerships, establishing high-tech enterprises, and intensifying cooperation for this purpose (BRICS, 2023).

The power and potential of BRICS+ cooperation in the energy market grants these countries a direct impact on global energy governance. The expanding BRICS+ structure has the potential to drive a sustainable and innovative transformation of energy markets, especially in transitioning from fossil fuels to renewable energy. These collaborative efforts will contribute to a more balanced, secure, and environmentally sustainable energy market, not only within BRICS+ but also globally. Additionally, BRICS+ will have the ability to channel resources effectively for the transfer of technology and innovation investments.

## 4. RESHAPING THE ENERGY SECTOR WITH BRICS+

Today, global resources are predominantly utilized by a limited number of countries. Additionally, there is a noticeable shift from a model in which manufactured products and investments are transferred to other countries and regions, towards a multipolar framework. The emergence of regional and global leaders signals the formation of new centers of development. In this context, additional energy production is essential to sustain the growth of the global economy. However, energy security and efficiency strategies have become increasingly prominent in energy consumption. BRICS+ plays a vital role in global energy security, with its energy industries contributing significantly to the production and consumption of world energy resources (Rodionova et al., 2017). The rising influence of BRICS+ countries holds substantial potential to reshape the international system, with their strategic importance, particularly in global energy, growing considerably (Downie, 2015).

Table 3 presents the ranking of total refined petroleum products among current and potential BRICS member countries for 2021. Data for Ethiopia for this year is unavailable. This table underscores the significance of BRICS countries in the global production of refined petroleum products. The BRICS countries play a critical role in the world energy market, being at the forefront of refined oil production due to their expansive economic structures and substantial energy demands. Notably, five of the top ten and seven of the top twenty countries in global refined petroleum production are BRICS members, highlighting the importance of the BRICS alliance in energy. The prominence of China, Russia, and India as the three leading producers after the United States reflects the role of BRICS countries in energy supply security. These nations possess substantial oil reserves and are distinguished by their high refining capacities. Currently, BRICS accounts for approximately 33.5 percent of the world's total refined petroleum products. With the inclusion of Argentina, Ethiopia, Saudi Arabia, the United Arab Emirates, and Egypt, this share would rise to approximately 41.3 percent, further solidifying BRICS' position in the global energy market.

*Table 3. Total refined petroleum products*

| Rank | Countries | Oil products | Year | Units |
|---|---|---|---|---|
| | World | 169961599 | 2021 | TJ |
| 2 | China | 30112289 | 2021 | TJ |
| 3 | Russia | 11573759 | 2021 | TJ |
| 4 | India | 10887780 | 2021 | TJ |
| 7 | Saudi Arabia | 5401498 | 2021 | TJ |
| 9 | Brazil | 4056945 | 2021 | TJ |
| 11 | Iran | 3743170 | 2021 | TJ |
| 18 | United Arab Emirates | 1992889 | 2021 | TJ |
| 28 | Egypt | 1182013 | 2021 | TJ |

continued on following page

*Table 3. Continued*

| Rank | Countries | Oil products | Year | Units |
|---|---|---|---|---|
| 31 | Argentina | 990162 | 2021 | TJ |
| 49 | South Africa | 386803 | 2021 | TJ |

**Source:**IEA (2024)

BRICS+ countries play a critical role in supply and demand within the global energy market. Today, BRICS+ holds significant importance for international energy supply security, with its energy diversification plans and investments driven by concerns over energy security. Thus, BRICS+ has substantial potential for energy partnerships. The progress of BRICS+ countries in the near future is also essential to meet the needs of their growing populations. Sustainable energy potential is crucial in addressing the social, political, economic, and environmental challenges posed by population growth (Kumar, 2016).

Energy resources are fundamental for employment, food production, income inequality reduction, security, economic development, and addressing global challenges and opportunities. Sustainable energy policies are important for preserving natural ecosystems, promoting economic growth, and strengthening economies. The new economic development model emphasizes a green economy, focusing on the relationship between the economy and the environment. BRICS+ countries are the world's largest energy producers and consumers and also account for the highest carbon emissions globally. Key policy measures in this context include reducing energy production from carbon-intensive sources, creating favorable market conditions for private investment, supporting projects and investments in sustainable sectors, and fostering innovation in energy technologies. While mutual cooperation among BRICS+ countries in sustainable energy holds significant potential, promoting an energy-efficient lifestyle also constitutes a beneficial policy direction (Podoba and Kryshneva, 2018).

Graph 3 illustrates oil and other liquid production among BRICS+ countries over the 1992-2023 period. According to this data, Russia and Saudi Arabia stand out as the top two producers of oil and other liquids, playing a critical role in their energy exports and enhancing their political leverage in energy markets. Natural gas and oil reserves are prominent in the production of these countries, highlighting their strategies to boost export revenues and competitiveness in energy markets. China's energy production also showed consistent growth throughout the period, indicating that China, as a rising global energy consumer, prioritizes domestic energy production to reduce its reliance on foreign energy resources. China has taken steps to develop its own resources as part of its energy security strategy.

Brazil's energy production has notably increased in recent years, with its developing economy driving higher energy demand and prompting policies to expand energy production. The United Arab Emirates has achieved steady production growth during this period, maintaining stability in oil production and securing its strategic importance in the global energy market. Although Iran's oil and other liquid production has seen significant increases during certain periods, economic challenges and sanctions have led to fluctuations. Facing potential international sanctions on oil exports, Iran attempts to balance these constraints by focusing on domestic production. Energy production in Egypt, South Africa, India, and Argentina has remained relatively stable, albeit at lower levels compared to other BRICS+ countries.

*Figure 3. Oil and other liquid production of BRICS+ countries: 1992-2023*

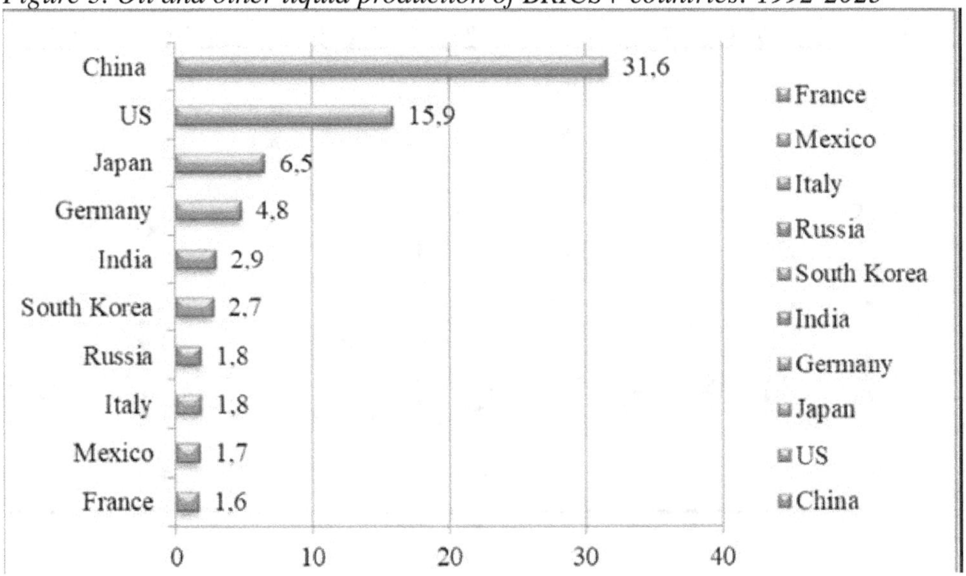


*(EIA (Energy Information Administration, 2024))*

The promotion of renewable energy sources globally gained renewed prominence with the Kyoto Protocol in 1997. Since then, investments, projects, and policies in renewable energy production and consumption have accelerated significantly worldwide. This trend contributes to strengthening economic growth and development globally. Both developed and developing countries now view renewable energy as a driving force for economic growth and development. However, while renewable energy production and consumption have not yet reached the desired level in BRICS+ countries, concrete steps toward increasing renewable energy consumption continue. Interest-free or low-interest loans, tax reductions, subsidies, and initiatives to attract foreign direct investment are among the prominent policies aimed at enhancing renewable energy investments (Fu et al., 2021).

Figure 4 presents the share of renewable energy in the electricity generation of BRICS+ countries from 2000 to 2023, expressed as a percentage. The chart illustrates the progression of each country over time based on specific criteria using vertical bars. Brazil consistently stands out as the country with the highest percentage of renewable energy in each period. Countries like Argentina, South Africa, and India exhibit a more balanced approach, while Saudi Arabia and the United Arab Emirates have not prioritized renewable energy sources to the same extent due to their abundant primary energy resources. China shows a notable increase over the period, while Iran's renewable energy share displays periodic fluctuations.

*Figure 4. Share of renewable energy in electricity generation in BRICS+ countries*

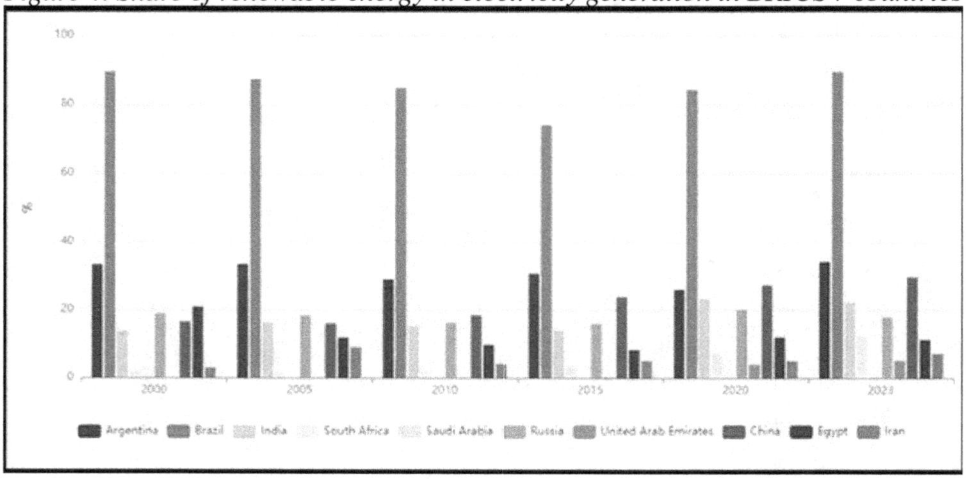


*(enerdata, 2024)*

Investments in sustainable energy are on the rise to protect natural resources and the environment. Brazil has implemented stable energy policies and made significant progress in biofuels, hydroelectricity, and even solar and wind energy investments. In this regard, Russia requires further improvement in terms of incentives and regulatory frameworks for renewable energy policies. China, meanwhile, should adopt stronger political measures to address increasing environmental pollution while continuing advancements in hydroelectric and wind energy investments. India's renewable energy policies would benefit from renewal, with additional incentives needed for R&D activities and consumer-focused energy policies. South Africa is developing policies to increase renewable energy investments and reduce coal mining. BRICS+ countries need to review their energy policies based on geographical, political, economic, environmental, and social conditions to establish global energy policies that ensure financial stability (Pathak and Shah, 2019).

BRICS countries should prioritize cooperation in the development of renewable energy sources, such as solar and wind, to facilitate a rapid transition to a low-carbon economy and reduce reliance on fossil fuels. Recent events, including the COVID-19 crisis and the Russia-Ukraine conflict, have heightened energy security concerns. Positively, these concerns have fostered new collaborations. Russia's dominance in natural gas, combined with China's financial support and green technology transfer, has positioned them as key players in energy transit. Furthermore, China's and India's growing dependence on Russian gas is beginning to alleviate tensions between them. As a result, the dynamic growth of clean energy is bringing new actors to the forefront, rethinking the concepts of energy security and sustainable development, and promoting cooperation among nations (Yousefi et al., 2023: 13).

## CONCLUSION AND POLICY RECOMMENDATIONS

BRICS+ countries represent a new global power bloc. These nations, distinguished by their rich energy resources, have the potential to exert a significant impact on the energy market and enhance energy supply security. The expansion of BRICS+ plays a decisive role in global energy production and provides an opportunity to reshape the energy market through energy cooperation and trade. The inclusion of major oil-exporting countries, such as Russia and Saudi Arabia, alongside fast-growing energy-consuming countries like China and India, is directly linked to the balance of global energy supply and demand.

The expansion potential of BRICS+ will be beneficial for energy transitions as well as in leveraging primary energy resources like fossil fuels. While investments in renewable energy accelerate within the scope of sustainable environmental goals, BRICS+ has the capacity to create a more independent framework for energy supply security and energy pricing. Notably, India's investments in wind energy, Brazil's focus on hydroelectric and biofuel energy, and China's investments in solar energy highlight the renewable energy potential within BRICS+.

In addition to primary energy resources and renewable energy investments, cooperation among BRICS+ countries also fosters significant advancements in infrastructure investments and energy technology. Brazil's renewable energy policies, Russia's abundance of primary energy resources, and China's prominence in energy technology reinforce the strong position of BRICS+ in the global energy market. The expansion of BRICS+ influences not only energy markets but also geopolitical and economic balances.

Consequently, the BRICS+ bloc has emerged as a key player in advancing global energy supply security and sustainable energy. The growing influence of BRICS+ countries will accelerate the shift from primary energy sources to renewable energy, reshaping the global energy market. This transition is expected to facilitate a more balanced global energy supply and promote steps towards environmental sustainability. Moreover, the inclusion of energy-rich countries such as Russia, the United Arab Emirates, and Saudi Arabia in BRICS+ will enhance global energy supply security and has the potential to shift the balance within the energy market.

Policy recommendations within the BRICS+ framework are as follows:

- BRICS+ countries should strategically strengthen their partnerships to ensure energy supply security and the equitable distribution of energy resources. In particular, cooperation between natural gas and oil-exporting countries and energy-importing countries should be reinforced.
- BRICS+ countries should increase investments in renewable energy sources to reduce the environmental impact of primary energy sources. Increasing investments in lower-impact energy sources, such as wind, solar, and hydroelectric power, will enable BRICS+ countries to advance their sustainable development goals.
- Innovation cooperation and technology transfer within BRICS+ should be promoted to accelerate progress in energy technologies. Supporting projects aimed at enhancing energy efficiency and developing advanced energy infrastructures is essential. This includes investments in smart energy systems and joint initiatives to increase efficiency through digitalization and the development of smart grids. Improved energy efficiency will contribute to greater energy security.
- BRICS+ countries should support the broader use of national currencies to facilitate flexibility in energy exports and simplify energy trade. This approach would reduce imbalances in the energy market and create a more independent structure.
- The BRICS+ group should align its energy policies with environmental sustainability. Targets should be set to reduce environmental pollution and accelerate the transition to clean energy.
- To ensure energy supply security within the BRICS+ framework, the bloc should focus on strengthening international energy policies, establishing long-term energy cooperation, creating resource diversity, and investing intensively in renewable energy technologies.
- Reducing carbon emissions and promoting green finance in the fight against climate change should be a priority for BRICS+. Measures such as establishing a carbon trading system between member countries, developing au-

dit mechanisms, and fostering sustainability and environmental protection through public-private sector incentives should be considered.

- BRICS+ should prioritize energy storage technologies within its expanding structure. By investing in projects to boost renewable energy sources, such as solar and wind power, BRICS+ can enhance its resilience to energy shocks. This resilience will support the development of uninterrupted renewable energy systems, thereby increasing energy independence and strengthening the bloc's position in the global energy market.

## REFERENCES


www.gov.br. (2024). Brazil reduces reliance on oil, natural gas in its energy matrix. (https://www.gov.br/secom/en/latest-news/2024/06/brazil-reduces-reliance-on-oil-natural-gas-in-its-energy-matrix Date of Access: 12.10.2024).

Afota, A., Burban, V., Diev, P., Grieco, F., Iberrakene, T., Ishii, K., Lopez-Forero, M., Paul, Q., Sammeth, F., & Valadier, C. (2024). Expansion of BRICS: what are the potential consequences for the global economy? (https://www.banque-france.fr/en/publications-and-statistics/publications/expansion-brics-what-are-potential-consequences-global-economy. Date of Access: 23.10.2024).

Akman, M. (2023). Geopolitical ascendance of BRICS nations. SETA. https://www.setav.org/en/opinion/geopolitical-ascendance-of-brics-nations Date of Access: 15.09.2024).

Aktaş, M., & Bağra, A. (2024). Rusya Ukrayna Savaşı ve Türkiye'nin Enerji Politikaları. *Social mentality and researcher thinkers journal (smart journal),* 9(78), 5228-5241.

Amran, Y. A., Amran, Y. M., Alyousef, R., & Alabduljabbar, H. (2020). Renewable and sustainable energy production in Saudi Arabia according to Saudi Vision 2030; Current status and future prospects. *Journal of Cleaner Production*, 247, 119602. DOI: 10.1016/j.jclepro.2019.119602

Azakov, S. (2018). Contribution of Azerbaijan to the energy security of the European Union. *IOP Conference Series. Materials Science and Engineering*, 459, 459. DOI: 10.1088/1757-899X/459/1/012011

Azevedo, D., Bakliwal, S., Chen, C., Glibert, M., Koch-Weser, I., Lang, N., & McAdoo, M. (2024). An Evolving BRICS and the Shifting World Order. https://www.bcg.com/publications/2024/brics-enlargement-and-shifting-world-order. Date of Access: 22.09.2024).

Bağış, B. (2022). *Rusya-Ukrayna Savaşının Küresel Ekonomiye ve Türkiye'ye Etkileri*. SETA.

Bahgat, G. (2012a). Will Saudi Arabia Face an Energy Crisis. *The Journal of Social, Political, and Economic Studies*, 37, 181.

Bahgat, G. (2012b). Energy Security: The United Arab Emirates. *Asian Affairs*, 43(2), 268–279. DOI: 10.1080/03068374.2012.682371

Bahgat, G. (2013). Egypt's energy outlook: Opportunities and challenges. *Mediterranean Quarterly*, 24(1), 12–37. DOI: 10.1215/10474552-1895367

Baskaran, G., & Cahill, B. (2023). "Six New BRICS: Implications for Energy Trade" https://www.csis.org/analysis/six-new-brics-implications-energy-trade

Bloomberg. (2024). Arjantin Devlet Başkanı Milei'den BRICS kararı. (https://www.bloomberght.com/arjantin-devlet-baskani-mileiden-brics-karari-2344882. Date of Access: 11.10.2024).

BRICS. (2023). BRICS Action Plan for Innovation Cooperation (2017-2020). https://brics2023.gov.za/wp-content/uploads/2023/07/BRICS-Action-Plan-for-Innovation-Cooperation-China.pdf. Datee of Access: 22.10.2024).

Brotto, A. (2024). Can the BRICS+ help the world transition to climate neutrality? https://www.imd.org/ibyimd/sustainability/can-the-brics-help-the-world-transition-to-climate-neutrality/. Date of Access: 29.10.2024).

Chakraborty, S. (2018). Significance of BRICS: Regional powers, global governance, and the roadmap for multipolar world. *Emerging Economy Studies*, 4(2), 182–191. DOI: 10.1177/2394901518795070

Chedid, J. P., & Penteado, R. (2022). Impacts of the Russia-Ukraine conflict on the world energy supply: Impactos do conflito Rússia-Ucrânia sobre o fornecimento mundial de energia. *Brazilian Journal of Development*, 8(12), 79067–79082. DOI: 10.34117/bjdv8n12-147

Chen, Q. (2023). Inflation and Energy Crisis under Ukraine Conflict. Advances in Economics. *Management and Political Sciences*, 32, 1–7.

Christoffersen, G. (2016). The role of China in global energy governance. China perspectives, 2016(2016/2), 15-24.

Conte, N., & Lam, S. (2024). Economic Growth Forecasts for G7 and BRICS Countries in 2024. (https://www.visualcapitalist.com/economic-growth-forecasts-for-g7-and-brics-countries-in-2024/. Date of Access: 27.09.2024).

Downie, C. (2015). Global energy governance: Do the BRICs have the energy to drive reform? *International Affairs*, 91(4), 799–812. DOI: 10.1111/1468-2346.12338

Durukan, A., & Yılmaz, M. (2021). Yenilenebilir Enerjinin Önemi Ve Latin Amerika Coğrafyasindaki Yeri: Brezilya Örneği. *Ankara Üniversitesi Dil ve Tarih-Coğrafya Fakültesi Dergisi*, 61(1), 339–358. DOI: 10.33171/dtcfjournal.2021.61.1.13

EIA. (2024). U. S. Energy Information Administration, Erişim adresi: https://www.eia.gov/, Erişim tarihi: 21.10.2024.

enerdata(2024). Share of renewables in electricity production, Erişim adresi: https://yearbook.enerdata.net/renewables/renewable-in-electricity-production-share.html, Erişim tarihi: 22.10.2024.

Enescu, A. G., & Szeles, M. R. (2023). Discussing energy volatility and policy in the aftermath of the Russia–Ukraine conflict. *Frontiers in Environmental Science*, 11, 1225753. DOI: 10.3389/fenvs.2023.1225753

EPRS. (2024). "Expansion of BRICS: A quest for greater global influence?" European Parliament. https://www.europarl.europa.eu/RegData/etudes/BRIE/2024/760368/EPRS_BRI(2024)760368_EN.pdf Date of Access: 01.09.2024).

Fu, Q., Álvarez-Otero, S., Sial, M. S., Comite, U., Zheng, P., Samad, S., & Oláh, J. (2021). Impact of renewable energy on economic growth and CO2 emissions—Evidence from BRICS countries. *Processes (Basel, Switzerland)*, 9(8), 1281. DOI: 10.3390/pr9081281

Global Energy Monitor. (2024). Energy in the BRICS. Cleaner Energy To Eclipse Fossil Fuels For Half The World's Population. (https://globalenergymonitor.org/wp-content/uploads/2024/10/GEM-BRICS-Oct2024.pdf. Date of Access: 14.09.2024).

GNPW Group. (2023). Energy Security: challenges and opportunities in Brazil. https://www.gnpw.com.br/en/energy-security/energy-security-challenges-and-opportunities-in-brazil/. Date of Access: 24.10.2024.

Gonmei, M. (2020). Azerbaijan's Energy Security, Journal of Emerging Technologies and Innovative Research (JETIR), 7 (8), (PP. 940-943).

Hasançebi, M., & Kırbaşoğlu, F. (2023). *Çok Taraflı Sistemin Çekim Merkezi: BRICS-A, 6.* Siyaset Bilimi ve Uluslararası İlişkiler Kongresi.

Huseynov, V. (2024). Azerbaijan Applies for BRICS Membership. (https://jamestown.org/program/azerbaijan-applies-for-brics-membership/ Date of Access: 27.10.2024).

IEA. (2021). Energy in India today. (https://www.iea.org/reports/india-energy-outlook-2021/energy-in-india-today. Date of Access: 22.10.2024).

IEA. (2024). Iran Sanctions. (https://origin.iea.org/policies/20243-iran-sanctions Date of Access: 17.09.2024).

IISD. (2023). BRICS Countries Expand Partnership for Sustainable Development. (https://sdg.iisd.org/news/brics-countries-expand-partnership-for-sustainable-development/. Date of Access: 23.10.2024).

Imamkulieva, E. (2024). Russia in BRICS+ and Creating a New Economic Order. https://trendsresearch.org/insight/russia-in-brics-and-creating-a-new-economic-order/. Date of Access: 28.09.2024).

Iqbal, B. A. (2022). BRICS as a driver of global economic growth and development. *Global Journal of Emerging Market Economies*, 14(1), 7–8. DOI: 10.1177/09749101211067096

Jütten, M. (2024). Russia's strategy for Latin America Strengthening ties in the light of the 16th BRICS Summit in Kazan (Russia). (https://www.europarl.europa.eu/RegData/etudes/BRIE/2024/762473/EPRS_BRI(2024)762473_EN.pdf date of Access: 15.10.2024).

Kamin, K., & Langhammer, R. J. (2024). From BRICS to BRICS+: Sheer More Members is not a Challenge to G7. *The Economists' Voice*, 20(2), 259–265. DOI: 10.1515/ev-2023-0065

Kazelko, A., & Semeghini, U. S. (2024). Expansion of brics: Implications for global energy markets. *BRICS Journal of Economics*, 5(1), 53–67. DOI: 10.3897/brics-econ.5.e117048

Kirton, J., & Larionova, M. (2022). The first fifteen years of the BRICS. *International Organisations Research Journal*, 17(2), 7–30. DOI: 10.17323/1996-7845-2022-02-01

Koolaee, E. (2011). Iran's role in energy security at regional and global levels. *Indian Economic Review*, 15(28), 95–115.

Korosteleva, J. (2022). The implications of Russia's invasion of Ukraine for the EU energy market and businesses. *British Journal of Management*, 33(4), 1678–1682. DOI: 10.1111/1467-8551.12654

Kumar, C. R., & Maijid, M. A. (2020). Renewable energy for sustainable development in India: Current status, future prospects, challenges, employment, and investment opportunities. *Energy, Sustainability and Society*, 10, 2. DOI: 10.1186/s13705-019-0232-1

Kumar, S. M. (2016). Energy revolution under the BRICS nations. BRICS Law journal, 3(1), 34-41.

Lin, J., Zhang, Y., Ibrahim, R. L., & Abrorov, S. (2024). Paving the way for sustainable environment in BRICS through technological innovation, sustainable energy, and financial development: Heterogenous analyses. *International Journal of Sustainable Development and World Ecology*, 31(7), 1–17. DOI: 10.1080/13504509.2024.2335270

Lu, T., Sherman, P., Chen, X., Chen, S., Lu, X., & McElroy, M. (2020). India's potential for integrating solar and on-and offshore wind power into its energy system. *Nature Communications*, 11(1), 4750. DOI: 10.1038/s41467-020-18318-7 PMID: 32958940

Megre, M., & Ribeiro, G. C. (2024). BRICS and the Multipolar World. *Horizons: Journal of International Relations and Sustainable Development*, (25), 126–135.

Mekonnen, W. (2024). Ethiopia and BRICS: Prospects and Challenges. *Journal of Political Science and International Relations*, 9(3), 59–74. DOI: 10.11648/j.jpsir.20240703.12

Mitrova, T., & Melnikov, Y. (2019). Energy transition in Russia. *Energy Transitions*, 3(1-2), 73–80. DOI: 10.1007/s41825-019-00016-8

Monin, S. (2024). BRICS approves Cuba, Bolivia, and 11 other countries as 'partner states'. (https://www.brasildefato.com.br/2024/10/24/brics-approves-cuba-bolivia-and-11-other-countries-as-partner-states. Date of Access: 25.09.2024).

Mostaque, L. (2022). India's Energy Diplomacy and geopolitics in South Asia. *BIIS Journal*, 43(2), 185–204.

Myllyvirta, L. (2024). "Analysis: Clean energy was top driver of China's economic growth in 2023". Carbon Brief, Clean on Climate. https://www.carbonbrief.org/analysis-clean-energy-was-top-driver-of-chinas-economic-growth-in-2023/. Date of Access: 12.09.2024).

Nam, C. W. (2024). Introduction to the issue on BRICS enlargement: What are the geoeconomic implications? *In EconPol Forum (Vol. 25, No. 1, pp. 3-4)*. Munich: CESifo GmbH.

Ndlovu, V., & Inglesi-Lotz, R. (2019). Positioning South Africa's energy supply mix internationally: Comparative and policy review analysis. *Journal of Energy in Southern Africa*, 30(2), 14–27. DOI: 10.17159/2413-3051/2019/v30i2a5409

Norman, J., Clark, G., Babajeva, J., Sidorovskaya-Fretz, N., Yu, A., Han, Y., & Zhang, M. (2024). Energy in the BRICS. (https://globalenergymonitor.org/report/energy-in-the-brics/. Date of Access: 23.10.2024).

Oliveros, L. (2020). *The Impact of Financial and Oil Sanctions on the Venezuelan Economy*. Washington Office on Latin America.

Pathak, L., & Shah, K. (2019). Renewable energy resources, policies and gaps in BRICS countries and the global impact. *Frontiers in Energy*, 13(3), 506–521. DOI: 10.1007/s11708-018-0601-z

Patrick, S. (2024). BRICS Expansion, the G20, and the Future of World Order. https://carnegieendowment.org/research/2024/10/brics-summit-emerging-middle-powers-g7-g20?lang=en. Date of Access: 12.10.2024).

Pietrosemoli, L., & Rodríguez-Monroy, C. (2019). The Venezuelan energy crisis: Renewable energies in the transition towards sustainability. *Renewable & Sustainable Energy Reviews*, 105, 415–426. DOI: 10.1016/j.rser.2019.02.014

Podoba, Z., & Kryshneva, D. (2018). Green Energy in the BRICS. *World Economy and International Relations*, 62(2), 17–27. DOI: 10.20542/0131-2227-2018-62-2-17-27

Pollet, B. G., Staffell, I., & Adamson, K. A. (2015). Current energy landscape in the Republic of South Africa. *International Journal of Hydrogen Energy*, 40(46), 16685–16701. DOI: 10.1016/j.ijhydene.2015.09.141

Raghutla, C., & Chittedi, K. R. (2020). Financial development, energy consumption, technology, urbanization, economic output and carbon emissions nexus in BRICS countries: An empirical analysis. *Management of Environmental Quality*, 32(2), 290–307. DOI: 10.1108/MEQ-02-2020-0035

Recalde, M. (2011). Energy policy and energy market performance: The Argentinean case. *Energy Policy*, 39(6), 3860–3868. DOI: 10.1016/j.enpol.2011.04.022

Rodionova, I., Chernyaev, M., & Korenevskaya, A. (2017). Energy Safety and Innovative Development of the BRICS States. *International Journal of Energy Economics and Policy*, 7, 216–224.

Rodriguez, F., Belhaj, H., & Aldhuhoori, M. (2022). Opportunities for Producing Hydrogen and Low-carbon Fossil Fuels from Venezuelan Conventional and Unconventional Hydrocarbon Reservoirs: An Idea in Times of Energy Transition to Net Zero-Carbon. Day 4 Thu, November 03, 2022.

Şahin, Ç., & Nuriyev, K. (2021). Rusya'da Enerji Sanayisinin Gelişimi ve Günümüzde Rus Enerji Stratejisi. *Uluslararası Türk Dünyası Araştırmaları Dergisi*, 4(4), 49–76.

Saktiawan, B., Toro, M. J. S., & Saputro, N. (2022, December). The impact of the Russia-Ukrainian war on green energy financing in Europe. [). IOP Publishing.]. *IOP Conference Series. Earth and Environmental Science*, 1114(1), 012066. DOI: 10.1088/1755-1315/1114/1/012066

Sasana, H., & Ghozali, I. (2017). The Impact of Fossil and Renewable Energy Consumption on the Economic Growth in Brazil, Russia, India, China and South Africa. *International Journal of Energy Economics and Policy*, 7, 194–200.

Sezer, S. (2024). Rusya-Ukrayna Savaşı'nın jeopolitik sonuçları. *Ömer Halisdemir Üniversitesi İktisadi ve İdari Bilimler Fakültesi Dergisi,* 17(1), 158-180.

Solaymani, S. (2021). A review on energy and renewable energy policies in Iran. *Sustainability (Basel)*, 13(13), 7328. DOI: 10.3390/su13137328

S&P Global. (2024). BRICS expansion could see more downstream oil investment: analyst. (Erişim Adresi: https://www.spglobal.com/commodityinsights/en/market-insights/latest-news/oil/020124-brics-expansion-could-see-more-downstream-oil-investment-analyst). (Access date: 04.07.2024).

Steinbuks, J., & Perez-Sebastian, F. (2022). "How Brazil's investment in hydropower infrastructure contributed to its long-term development". World Bank Blogs (https://blogs.worldbank.org/en/energy/how-brazils-investment-hydropower-infrastructure-contributed-its-long-term-development, Date of Access: 12.09.2024).

Tabash, M. I., Farooq, U., Al-Faryan, M. A. S., & Wong, W. K. (2024). Effect of geopolitical risk on energy consumption policy: New empirical evidence from BRICS. *Heliyon*, 10(19), e38049. DOI: 10.1016/j.heliyon.2024.e38049 PMID: 39386848

Tao, M., & Xi, C. (2023). BRICS Energy Cooperation and Global Energy Governance. *Contemp. China & World*, 1, 118.

Telli, A., & Yeşil, E. (2023). Ukrayna Krizinin Yeşil Enerji Dönüşümüne Etkisi Almanya Örneği. *Tarsus Üniversitesi İktisadi ve İdari Bilimler Fakültesi Dergisi*, 4(2), 85–110. DOI: 10.56400/tarsusiibfdergisi.1291211

The Globalist. (2024). BRICS Vs. the G7. How do the BRICS stack up against the G7 group of nations? (https://www.theglobalist.com/brics-brics-g7-economy-population-just-the-facts/. Date of Access: 23.10.2024).

Tiewsoh, L. S., Jirásek, J., & Sivek, M. (2019). Electricity generation in India: Present state, future outlook and policy implications. *Energies*, 12(7), 1361. DOI: 10.3390/en12071361

Tong, M., Yiyi, Z., & Lei, T. (2024). BRICS nations eye 'blue ocean' in green co-operation as ties deepen during highly-watched summit (https://www.globaltimes.cn/page/202410/1321800.shtml. Date of Access: 23.10.2024).

Vasileski, Z. BRICS VERSUS THE GLOBAL WEST IN THE LIGHT OF CURRENT GLOBAL REALIZATIONS. Towards a Better Future: Peace, Justice, and Strong Institutions, 291.

Wendling, J. (2024). The Bloc Effect: International Trade with Geopolitical Allies on the Rise. (https://www.visualcapitalist.com/sp/hf02-international-trade-with-geopolitical-allies-rising/. Date of Access: 27.09.2024).

World Bank. (2023). “Factsheet: Eskom Just Energy Transition Project in South Africa”. (https://www.worldbank.org/en/news/factsheet/2023/06/05/factsheet-eskom-just-energy-transition-project-in-afe-south-africa#:~:text=South%20Africa's%20highly%20coal%2Ddependent,and%20the%20country's%20economic%20prospects. Date of Access: 14.09.2024).

World Bank. (2024). Indicators. Erişim Adresi: https://data.worldbank.org/indicator. (Erişim Tarihi: 27.08.2024).

Yousefi, H., Ardehali, A., & Ghodusinejad, M. H. (2023). BRICS or G7? Current and future assessment of energy and environment performance using multi-criteria and time series analyzes. *Energy Strategy Reviews*, 49, 101164. DOI: 10.1016/j.esr.2023.101164

Yu, H. (2022). European Energy Prospect under the Russo-Ukrainian war. Highlights in Science. *Engineering and Technology*, 25, 203–209.

Zhang, S., Zhang, P., & Gao, M. (2018). Study on Energy Technology in BRICS. In Zhao, X., Li, M., Huang, M., & Sokolov, A. (Eds.), *BRICS Innovative Competitiveness Report 2017. Research Series on the Chinese Dream and China’s Development Path.* Springer. DOI: 10.1007/978-981-10-8078-4_11

Zhidong, L. (2005). China’s energy outlook to the year 2030. *International Journal of Global Energy Issues*, 24(3-4), 144–169. DOI: 10.1504/IJGEI.2005.007768

Zhongxiu, Z., & Qingxin, L. (2020). Promoting BRICS cooperation for economic growth and development.(https://repositorio.ipea.gov.br/bitstream/11058/13441/1/Tempo_Mundo_n22_Artigo2_promoting_brics_cooperation.pdf. Date of Access: 09.09.2024).

# Chapter 12
# Agricultural Policies of BRICS Member States: A Critical Area of Cooperation

**Zehra Namli Bilmez**
https://orcid.org/0000-0002-0532-953X
*Duzce University, Turkey*

## ABSTRACT

*The agricultural sector is one of the cornerstones of many countries' economies and agricultural policies are developed with the aim of ensuring economic stability by reducing fluctuations in the sector, supporting rural development, ensuring sustainability, and establishing food security. This study examines the cooperation areas of the BRICS group in terms of agricultural policies and analyzes the situation of BRICS member countries. With the accession of new members, BRICS+ has the potential to develop stronger cooperation in the field of agriculture and food at the global level. The grain crisis showed the strategic importance of agricultural cooperation for BRICS countries. Sharing agricultural information, disseminating innovative technologies and promoting sustainable agricultural practices among BRICS countries will make their agricultural policies more effective and efficient. In this context, strengthening agricultural cooperation among BRICS countries will be a strategic step that will positively affect both their domestic dynamics and global food security.*

DOI: 10.4018/979-8-3693-7393-4.ch012

## INTRODUCTION

Agricultural policies are crucial in determining the agricultural production capacity of countries, ensuring sustainability in agricultural production, enhancing competitiveness, and securing food safety (Tilman et al., 2002). These policies play a leading role in resolving food-related issues and are significant for strengthening a country's position in global trade (Wang et al., 2023). Various tools are employed to develop agricultural policies. Fundamental instruments such as supporting the agricultural sector, developing laws and incentives, and pricing, along with supporting activities aimed at rural development and environmental protection, contribute to the implementation of these policies. Government initiatives to increase farmers' income and promote agricultural production through credit and price support, as well as enhanced infrastructure investments, have significant impacts on agricultural policies (Liefert & Liefert, 2020). Indeed, the agricultural sector is one of the primary sectors in the economy of many countries. In this context, it can be stated that agricultural policies are developed to mitigate fluctuations in the sector, thereby ensuring economic stability and promoting rural development (Bullock & Salhofer, 2003). Additionally, agricultural policies have important implications for preventing internal migration and maintaining social balance through rural development (Plaunt, 1973). Moreover, ensuring food security is considered one of the primary priorities of countries.

Agricultural policies are deemed important both for their impacts within national borders and for their determining influence at the international level. It is known that countries collaborate and support each other in various fields such as defense, energy, environment, economy, and trade through international organizations, multilateral agreements, and bilateral partnerships. In this context, it is observed that countries, particularly under the leadership of the European Union, develop and act in accordance with certain standards regarding agricultural policies, with international institutions also playing a role (Skogstad & Verdun, 2009). From this perspective, the study suggests that BRICS member states could develop collaborations not only in political, economic, social, and educational fields but also in agriculture and food.

BRICS was established in 2009 with the membership of Brazil, Russia, India, and China. The first expansion occurred in 2010 when South Africa joined BRICS. Although not considered an international organization, BRICS is described as a group where member countries primarily collaborate on political, economic, trade, and development issues. It is known that several countries, including Iran, Saudi Arabia, Argentina, Ethiopia, Bolivia, and Algeria, which have diverse geographical, social, and economic characteristics, have applied for membership in BRICS. In early 2024, with the acceptance of memberships from Egypt, Ethiopia, Saudi Arabia, the United Arab Emirates, and Iran, BRICS transitioned into BRICS+

(BRICS, 2024a). As previously mentioned, developing collaborations in various fields, including agriculture and food on a global scale, is strategically important for BRICS member states. The grain crisis that emerged during the Russia-Ukraine War has demonstrated the significance of global food resources and the countries that export these foods.

In this study, the structure, objectives, and founding process of BRICS are first discussed, followed by an examination of its areas of cooperation. Subsequently, the agricultural policies of BRICS member states are analyzed, and the situation of these countries is evaluated based on reports and data sets published by international organizations related to agriculture. The study examines the impact of BRICS on agriculture and agricultural policies, which are considered crucial areas of cooperation for BRICS, and discusses the potential contributions of developing stronger cooperation in agriculture to both the member countries and BRICS as a whole.

## AGRICULTURAL POLICIES

Agricultural policies are a strategic public policy area that directly affects the economic, social and environmental welfare of societies. These policies, which are used to achieve key objectives such as ensuring food security, promoting rural development, increasing agricultural production and ensuring environmental sustainability both at national and international level, have a wide range of applications. The agricultural sector is affected by and influenced by many factors such as urbanization, industrialization and development (Yu & Wu, 2018).

The economic dimension of agricultural policies is strengthened through various instruments to support agricultural production and farmer welfare. These instruments include price supports, subsidies, agricultural credit facilities, tax reductions and incentives, infrastructure investments and support for research and development. Indeed, price supports and subsidies enable farmers to sell their products at higher prices, leading to higher incomes (Lankoski & Thiem, 2020). Agricultural credit facilities facilitate access to capital needed for agricultural production by offering low-interest loans to farmers. In this way, farmers can obtain basic inputs such as agricultural machinery, seeds, fertilizers and increase their production capacity. Tax breaks and incentives, on the other hand, increase the profitability of agricultural activity by reducing farmers' costs (Alessa et al., 2018). Infrastructure investments include the development of basic infrastructure that supports agricultural production, particularly irrigation systems, roads and storage facilities. Such investments contribute to increased agricultural production and faster and more efficient transportation of products to market. Rural development is at the center of the social dimension of agricultural policies. These policies aim to improve living conditions in rural areas, create economic opportunities and balance the rural-urban population distribution. Rural development policies are identified with social assistance and training programs, especially for low-income farmers. These benefits are considered as an important tool to improve the living standards of the rural population (Dos Santos & Ahmad, 2020).

The environmental dimension of agricultural policies is concerned with protecting natural resources, preventing environmental pollution and promoting sustainable agricultural practices. The main instruments used to ensure environmental sustainability include incentives for environmentally friendly agricultural practices, efficient management of water resources, soil conservation programs and support for organic farming (Leng et al., 2023). Policies developed for the efficient management of water resources aim to modernize irrigation systems and promote water-saving technologies. Soil conservation programs are implemented to prevent erosion and increase soil fertility. Organic agriculture subsidies aim to minimize negative impacts on the environment by reducing the use of chemical fertilizers and pesticides (Navarro & Lopes-Bao, 2019).

Global crises, especially economic and climatic crises, have a profound impact on agricultural policies. Economic crises directly affect investment and production levels in the agricultural sector, necessitating the reshaping of agricultural policies. For example, during the 2008 global economic crisis, many countries had to reorganize their policies to ensure that farmers could cope with economic hardship by increasing agricultural subsidies. Such crises also have the potential to lead to fluctuations in agricultural commodity prices, negatively affecting farmers' incomes and production planning (Reidsma et al, 2015). Climatic crises have more complex and long-term impacts on agricultural policies. Factors such as climate change, drought, excessive precipitation, temperature increase, etc. have long-lasting impacts and seriously threaten agricultural production potential. This situation necessitates the restructuring of agricultural policies with a focus on environmental sustainability. In order to adapt to climate change and ensure the continuity of agricultural production in this process, many countries are developing policies that promote climate-friendly agricultural practices (Fischer & Connor, 2018). In addition, climatic crises carry significant risks that directly affect food security. Possible declines in food production can lead to serious social and economic problems.

The 2022 Russia-Ukraine war had serious global implications for agricultural policies. The war has led to severe disruptions in food supplies around the world and caused major problems in the export of key agricultural commodities. As Ukraine is one of the world's leading grain producers, the impact of this war led to a rapid increase in global food prices and a major crisis in terms of food security (Nasir et al., 2022). In order to deal with this crisis, the “Grain Corridor” agreement was signed as a result of negotiations between Turkey, the United Nations, Russia and

Ukraine. This agreement enabled the resumption of grain exports from Ukrainian ports and helped the global food supply recover to some extent (Ay & Söylemez, 2023). However, the sustainability of this corridor and agricultural policies need to be reshaped depending on the course of the war. This shows how fragile global agricultural trade is and how such crises can rapidly reshape agricultural policies.

The effects of agricultural policies on international trade are strengthened by the instruments used to enhance the competitiveness of the agricultural sector in global markets and to support countries' agricultural exports. These instruments include trade agreements, export incentives, tariffs and the regulation of non-tariff barriers. Trade agreements facilitate the free movement of agricultural products between countries, while export incentives enable local producers to compete in international markets (Oldekop et al., 2015). Customs duties and non-tariff barriers protect local agricultural production by preventing imported products from creating unfair competition in local markets. However, high protection policies can lead to imbalances in world agricultural markets, which can negatively affect the agricultural competitiveness of developing countries (Reidsma et al, 2015). International organizations such as the Food and Agriculture Organization of the United Nations (FAO) are making efforts to ensure that agricultural policies promote environmental sustainability at the global level. These efforts are critical for increasing agricultural production and ensuring food security, especially in developing countries.

In conclusion, agricultural policies are considered as a multidimensional public policy area that shapes the economic, social and environmental welfare of societies. Successful implementation of these policies is only possible through the effective use of the right instruments. It should also be taken into account that global economic and climatic crises have had a profound impact on agricultural policies. In the future, the development of more sustainable and balanced agricultural policies will make important contributions both locally and globally.

## Agriculture as a Strategic Area of Cooperation within BRICS

It can be stated that BRICS member countries play an important role in the global economy and strategies have been developed to establish cooperation in a wide range of areas. When the cooperation and strategies are analyzed in terms of agricultural policies, which constitute the subject of this study, it is seen that important steps have been taken within BRICS. When analyzed, it is evaluated that activities have been carried out to improve cooperation in the field of agriculture since 2010. Considering these activities, firstly, a declaration was announced as a result of the meeting of the agriculture ministers of the member countries in 2010. In the declaration issued as a result of the meeting attended by the agriculture ministers of four member countries, namely Brazil, Russia, India and China, four priority areas of cooperation were identified to serve the long-term interests of these countries and contribute to food security. These areas of cooperation were identified as the creation of an agricultural knowledge base system of the member countries, the formulation of strategies for food access, mitigating the effects of climate change on food security, and enhancing technological cooperation and innovation in the agricultural sector (BRICS Information Centre, 2010).

In 2011, another meeting was organized with the participation of agriculture ministers from 5 member countries. In this summit, as in the previous summit, a declaration was issued, in addition to the action plan and the working procedures of the Agricultural Cooperation Working Group established within BRICS. In the action plan covering the years 2012-2016, in addition to the four strategic areas identified at the previous meeting, trade and investment incentives were specified. In this context, it was also emphasized that the costs of cooperation activities in the agricultural field, which has increased to 5 strategic areas, would be regulated and shared (BRICS Information Centre, 2011).

Meetings were also held under the BRICS umbrella in 2013, 2015, 2016, 2019, 2020, 2021 and 2022. As a result of these meetings, declarations were published (BRICS Information Center, 2022). These declarations emphasized the development of agricultural practices to ensure food security and sustainability. In order to mitigate the negative impacts of climate change on the agricultural sector, elements such as adaptation to climate change, mitigation of its effects and the inclusion of technological innovations in this process were expressed. Following technological innovations in agriculture was emphasized in all declarations. Cooperation and information sharing among member countries in the agricultural field was reiterated in the declarations. The willingness to cooperate with developing countries in the agricultural sector was also emphasized. In addition, promoting food security and rural development by supporting small farmers and increasing their production capacity was also adopted as a strategy. In this context, the common statements and strategies emphasized in the declarations are discussed. The challenges and priorities of that year determined the theme of the meeting. For example, the Bonito Declaration published in 2019 focused on innovations in the agricultural system, while the declaration published in 2020 focused on the effects of Covid-19 on agriculture. In addition, the national agricultural policies and rural development strategies of BRICS member countries were also discussed. In this context, it is evaluated that food security, international trade and cooperation issues occupy a large place. It is possible to state that these publications, in which an evaluation is made based on the declarations, both develop a common vision for BRICS member countries in terms of ensuring agriculture and food security and aim to increase cooperation. As a matter of fact, it is observed that this vision is shaped within the framework of global challenges and local needs. In this context, the percentage share of the agricultural sector in GDP in member countries is shown in the table below.

*Table 1. Agriculture value added (%GDP)*

| Country/Year | 2016 | 2017 | 2018 | 2019 | 2020 | 2021 |
|---|---|---|---|---|---|---|
| Brazil | 4,89 | 4.60 | 4,42 | 4,21 | 5,82 | 6,89 |
| China | 8,11 | 8.11 | 7,14 | 7,25 | 7,84 | 7,42 |
| India | 16,36 | 16,36 | 16,03 | 16,73 | 18,23 | 16,82 |
| Russian Federation | 3,84 | 3,84 | 3,39 | 3,53 | 4,00 | 3,80 |
| South Africa | 2,41 | 2,41 | 2,27 | 1,96 | 2,52 | 2,47 |

Source: FAO, 2022 https://www.fao.org/aquastat/en/

The table above displays the percentage share of the agricultural sector in the GDP of Brazil, China, India, Russia, and South Africa from 2016 to 2021. In this context, it is observed that Brazil's share of agriculture in GDP, which was 4.89% in 2016, decreased to 4.21% in 2019, but then showed a significant increase to 5.82% in 2020 and 6.89% in 2021. China's share of agriculture in GDP, which was 8.11% in 2016, generally shows a declining trend, recorded at 7.42% in 2021. In India, the agricultural sector holds a significant share of GDP. The percentage, which was 16.36% in 2016, rose to 18.23% in 2020 but fell to 16.82% in 2021. The high rural population density in India is considered one of the primary reasons for this situation. In Russia, the share of agriculture in GDP, which was 3.84% in 2016, dropped to 3.53% in 2019, experienced a slight increase to 4.00% in 2020, and then decreased to 3.80% in 2021. In South Africa, the share of agriculture in GDP, which was 2.41% in 2016, fell to 1.96% in 2019, but then increased to 2.52% in 2020 and slightly decreased to 2.47% in 2021. As with other countries, it is observed that the pandemic increased the importance of agriculture in South Africa. The data suggests that during 2020, the share of agriculture in GDP increased in all countries, influenced by the pandemic. In this context, it is evaluated that agriculture emerges as a fundamental and strategic sector during times of crisis. Among BRICS countries, it is noted that India has a higher share of agriculture in GDP compared to others, while South Africa has the lowest share. Thus, the importance of forming cooperation areas based on these foundations among member countries should be emphasized.

When examining BRICS and the relationships among its member states, it is observed that activities are conducted in line with previously established strategies. For example, at the 2015 meeting of the BRICS Expert Working Group on Agriculture, the importance of supporting technology in agriculture, enhancing cooperation, and particularly developing trade and investment networks among member states was emphasized (BRICS, 2015a). In the same year, another meeting was held where the experiences of BRICS countries in ensuring food security through social protection programs were discussed. This meeting was attended by 27 developing and developed countries, including BRICS members, as well as international organizations such as the World Bank, International Labor Organization, United Nations Food and Agriculture Organization, United Nations World Food Program, World Health Organization, and the International Food Policy Research Institute, among others (BRICS, 2015b). In 2017, approval was granted for the establishment of the BRICS Agriculture Research Platform. This platform aims to conduct policy research and development for agricultural science, facilitate technology transfer among member states, support education and capacity building, and promote knowledge sharing. It was emphasized that cooperation in agricultural development and food security is of great importance among member states (BRICS, 2017a).

Post-pandemic period, BRICS has undertaken activities in the agricultural sector with a focus on food security. For 2021, the agricultural trade between BRICS countries and other nations was reported to be $588.3 billion. Compared to the agricultural trade volume in 2010, this represents a 128% increase, indicating a strong potential for cooperation in agricultural trade among member states. China has been particularly active in agricultural cooperation. Examples include China's investments in expanding maize cultivation and land areas in Brazil, which contribute to global integration, providing food for over 1.4 billion people, and contributing to food security. In 2021, China also trained technicians and educators in various areas such as rice cultivation, production and use of agricultural machinery, and plant protection in South Africa (BRICS, 2022a). Another significant development within BRICS is the member states' support for the idea of establishing a grain exchange (BRICS, 2024b).

Overall, it is evident that BRICS has formulated strategies and developed activities to strengthen agricultural cooperation among its member states. In this context, it is essential to examine the agricultural policies of the member states. Accordingly, the agricultural policies of Brazil, Russia, India, China, and South Africa will be analyzed first, followed by an examination of the potential contributions of the countries that joined BRICS+ to agricultural cooperation.

## Brazil's Agricultural Policies and BRICS

Agricultural policies in Brazil, developed on the foundations of ensuring productivity in agricultural production and modernizing the agricultural sector with new technologies, have made Brazil one of the world's largest agricultural exporters. As the third-largest agricultural exporter globally, after the EU and the USA, Brazil has had a significant impact on global economic governance. Brazil's innovation-based agricultural policies, implemented since the 1960s and 1970s, have propelled it to this position. Indeed, analyses suggest that Brazil has created a comparative advantage over competing countries and is considered to be one of the world's leading agricultural powers (Hopewell, 2016). Agricultural policies and agricultural interventions in Brazil have been developed through direct state intervention. Large-scale agricultural areas have been opened and modern agricultural techniques have been adopted. The graph below shows the proportion of agricultural land in Brazil's total land area.

*Figure 1. Agricultural land (% of land area) – Brazil (World Bank Data https://data.worldbank.org/indicator)*

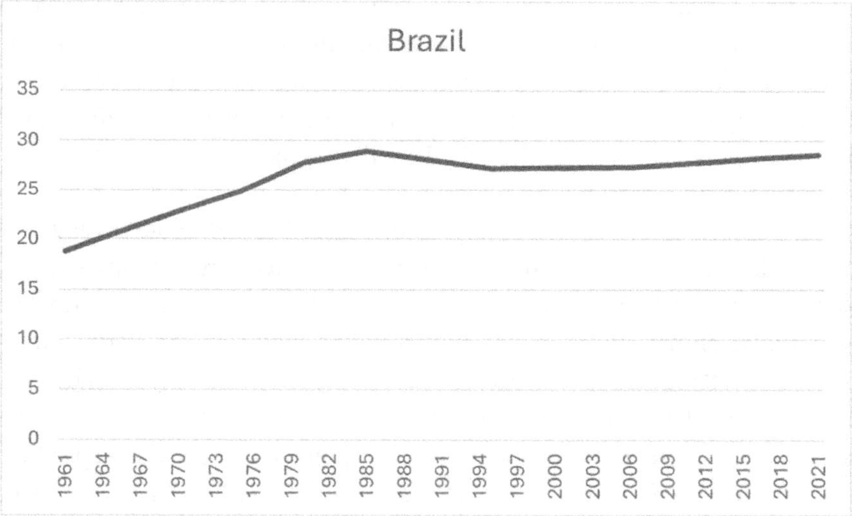


When the change in agricultural land is analyzed, it is observed that there was a continuous increase in the proportion of agricultural land during the 1960-1980 period. This increase shows that Brazil rapidly expanded its agricultural areas and pursued policies to increase its agricultural production capacity during this period. In the early 1980s, the share of agricultural land in total land reached its peak. However, after this peak, there was a slight decline in the 1990s. Since the 2000s, the graph shows a stabilization followed by a slight upward trend. This may reflect Brazil's efforts to keep the proportion of agricultural land at consistently high levels or the transition to sustainable agricultural practices. The fact that close to 28% of Brazil's total land area is used for agriculture demonstrates the country's huge capacity in the agricultural sector and its role in the global agricultural market. Moreover, the slowdown in the expansion of agricultural land after the 1980s suggests that the country has implemented policies aimed at stabilizing or conserving its agricultural land.

Brazil's remarkable progress in the agricultural sector has brought with it different environmental challenges. Soybeans are one of the crops that have a significant share in Brazil's agricultural sector. The fact that soybeans have significant agricultural returns and are used for economic development in some regions has led to the problem of deforestation in Brazil. Since the 2000s, the government has taken measures to prevent the loss of forests in the Amazon due to soybeans. As a result of these policies, it is considered that deforestation caused by soybean cultivation has been prevented. In this case, the Brazilian government's policy of balance between agriculture and the environment has been effective. Indeed, their reforms of the Forest Code and agreements such as the "Soybean Moratorium" have made it possible to prevent deforestation and maintain the sustainability of agricultural land (Picoli et al., 2020). Brazil's agricultural policies, while promoting economic growth, face significant challenges in terms of environmental sustainability and social justice. This makes it difficult for Brazil to achieve its commitments under the Paris Agreement (Ferreira et al., 2012).

The agricultural growth model adopted by Brazil has led to deepening income inequalities. In this respect, it is emphasized that it needs to reorganize in a sustainable development approach. For sustainable development, it is stated that it is imperative to develop modern tropical agricultural systems in both rural and urban areas on the basis of environmental protection, social equality and poverty alleviation. It is also important for Brazil to tackle inequalities in income and land distribution in rural areas. Indeed, after the consolidation of large lands for agricultural production, small farmers have been marginalized and rural poverty has increased. As a BRICS country, Brazil has contributed to increased trade in agricultural production and increased demand for agricultural products from agricultural cooperation (Cousins et al., 2018).

Environmental sustainability and agricultural productivity are key areas where Brazil has focused on developing collaborations in agricultural policies (Balsalobre-Lorente et al., 2019). In this regard, several bilateral steps have been taken. For example, Brazil allowed wheat imports from Russia, paving the way for processing this wheat domestically and contributing to the export of meat products (BRICS, 2017b). Additionally, the trade war between the USA and China benefited Brazil's soybean exports, with Brazil, already the top supplier of soybeans to China, expected to increase its share following restrictions on the USA (BRICS, 2018a). The United States and Ukraine were the largest suppliers of corn to China. However, following Russia's invasion of Ukraine, China's difficulties in securing corn supplies have led to expectations of increased corn imports from Brazil (BRICS, 2023a). It was noted that in 2023, the trade flow between China and Brazil amounted to

$150 billion, with Brazil's exports to China reaching $89 billion in 2022. The main exported products were soybeans, iron ore, and crude oil. Given the widespread use of soybeans in China, soybean exports to China are crucial for China's food security. Bilateral agreements between the two countries aim to strengthen these ties further (BRICS, 2023b).

In summary, Brazil's agricultural policies implemented since the 1960s and 1970s have made the country a global competitive force. However, it is also important to address the environmental, social, and economic issues that have emerged alongside this progress. It is essential to emphasize the need for Brazil's agricultural policies to be reshaped to reduce environmental impacts and ensure social justice.

## Russia's Agricultural Policies and BRICS

As the country with the largest land area, Russia holds significant potential in the agricultural sector. However, the varying and challenging climatic conditions, along with regional disparities, necessitate a careful approach to planning agricultural policies. Following the collapse of the Soviet Union, reforms were implemented with the primary goals of modernizing the agricultural sector and improving crop productivity. Since the 2000s, Russia has continued to carry out extensive state interventions aimed at supporting the agricultural sector to ensure food security. In this context, the main objectives have been to reduce dependency on imports by promoting domestic production. Consequently, agricultural recovery has been observed following the implementation of comprehensive state support, interventions, and assistance programs. However, as production has increased, food trade policies have become more protectionist. The concept of food security has become increasingly important, and in addition, Russia has been recognized as a global grain exporter by developing exports to markets dominated by the United States (Wegren, 2010). The graph below shows the percentage of agricultural land in relation to Russia's total land area.

*Figure 2. Agricultural land (% of Land Area) – Russian Federation (World Bank Data https://data.worldbank.org/indicator)*

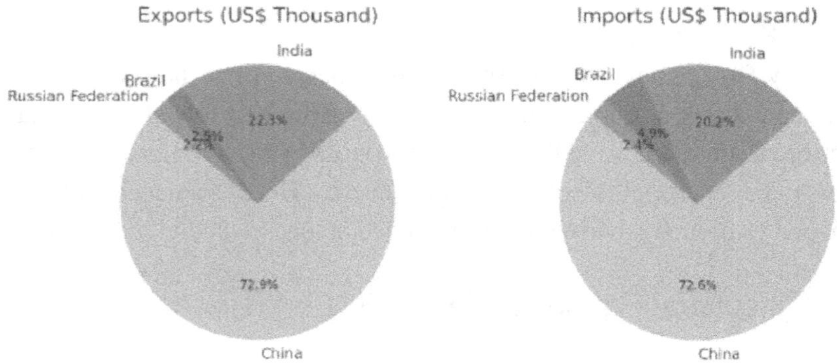


The graph indicates that there has been no significant change in the proportion of agricultural land relative to Russia's total land area since 1992. In 1992, agricultural land accounted for approximately 13.5% of the total land area, which then decreased to around 13.2% by the mid-1990s. This decline can be attributed to the transformations, economic difficulties, restructuring of the agricultural sector, and changes in land use that Russia experienced following the dissolution of the Soviet Union. Between 1998 and 2000, the percentage fluctuated between 13.1% and 13.3%, and from 2008 onward, it stabilized at around 13.1%. The fact that there has been no significant change in the proportion of agricultural land since this period suggests that Russia has achieved a balance or that the scope for expansion of agricultural land is limited. The fact that agricultural land has remained stable at this level also reflects that the country's agricultural infrastructure has developed in a certain balance. Thus, although Russia is a country with vast territories, the share of agricultural land in total area is relatively stable and limited. This low share of agricultural land can be attributed to a number of factors such as the country's economic structure, climatic conditions and geographical factors. This is an important factor to consider when assessing Russia's agricultural production capacities and land use policies.

The food embargo imposed in 2014 is considered a turning point in Russia's agricultural policies. The embargo on agricultural products imported from the European Union, the United States and other Western countries led to the development of practices aimed at increasing domestic production and strengthening the agricultural sector. In particular, the agricultural sector was directly supported through subsidies, low-interest loans and infrastructure investments. This process started with the fall in the value of the ruble against the US dollar due to the fall in world oil prices, Russia's embargo on imports in the agriculture and food sectors, and the subsequent stimulation of agricultural production by raising domestic food prices. Following these practices and incentives, Russia's meat imports were 40% lower in 2014-2016 compared to 2011-2013, and its grain exports were 50% higher in 2014-2016 compared to 2011-2013 (Liefert et al., 2019). Russia is one of the leading countries in the production of agricultural products such as wheat, barley, sunflower oil and sugar beet. It has a high share of cereals, oilseeds and vegetable oils in its exports.

Since the 2010s, policies based on ensuring food security and reducing import dependency have created the basis for promoting domestic production. Within the framework of the developed policies and food security strategy, Russia has become self-sufficient in meat and milk production by 2020. In this process, the replacement of imported products with domestic production has strengthened food independence. However, it is also evaluated that these policies have led to a decline in disposable income in the last 6 years and the use of cheap and poor-quality products in consumption (Mukhametzyanov et al., 2021). It is also observed that Russia's partners in agriculture and food trade have changed in this process. There has been a shift from Western trade partners to Asian and Central Asian trade partners. Russia has focused on increasing agricultural production in its agricultural policies, but this process has also brought environmental and social problems. In particular, the proliferation of large-scale agricultural enterprises has led to deterioration in land use and the environment, while the limited competitiveness of small farmers has deepened social inequalities, especially in rural areas (Gishkaeva, 2023).

When the agricultural sector-based relations with BRICS member countries are analyzed, it can be evaluated that they have established important cooperation especially since the 2010s. For example, in 2015, negotiations were held between Russia and China to improve trade capacity in wheat and other agricultural products (BRICS, 2015c). By 2028, Russian food exports to China are expected to reach 52 million tons. Products such as cereals, oil crops, soybeans and barley are considered to be included in this trade (BRICS, 2017c). It has also been proposed to establish a joint production system between the two countries for soy production and processing (BRICS, 2018b). With the war between Russia and Ukraine, the issue of food security has become more on the agenda.

In general, it can be stated that Russia's agricultural policies have been shaped by strong state support to ensure food security and increase agricultural production for many years. These policies have made Russia one of the leading countries in global agricultural trade. This development has brought with it various environmental, social and economic challenges. In particular, the effects of the global food crisis following the Russia-Ukraine War are significant. It is obvious that time is needed to comprehensively assess the effects of this war. It should also be emphasized that Russia should reconsider its agricultural policies in the context of sustainability and social justice.

## India's Agricultural Policies and BRICS

India is an important actor in the agriculture sector globally. Agriculture is one of the most important sectors of the Indian economy. It is the source of livelihood for the vast majority of the country's population. It is among the leading producers of rice, wheat, cotton, spices and tea. In this context, considering the size of the population, agricultural policies are shaped with the aim of ensuring food security, supporting rural development and increasing the welfare of farmers who constitute a large population. As a matter of fact, it is stated that the agricultural sector faces many problems such as food security, environmental pollution and water scarcity due to a significant population growth and different external factors (Selvan et al., 2021). The graph below shows the ratio of India's agricultural areas by surface area.

*Figure 3. Agricultural land (% of Land Area) – India (World Bank Data https://data.worldbank.org/indicator)*

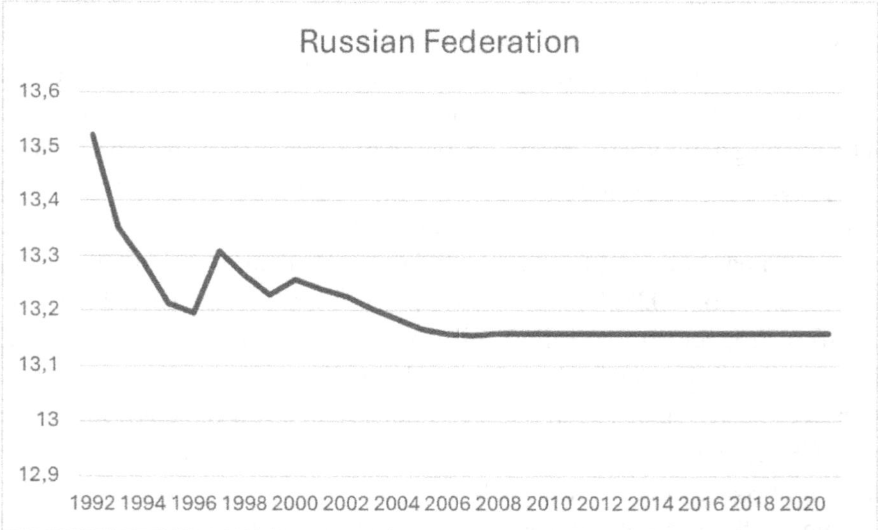

As can be seen in the graph above, the ratio of agricultural land to total surface area increased from 1961 to the 1980s and reached over 61%. This increase can be considered as a result of the efforts of agricultural policies, particularly the Green Revolution, to expand agricultural land and increase agricultural production. Since the agricultural sector was the source of livelihood for a large part of the population during this period, the expansion can be described as a natural phenomenon. Agricultural land, which remained generally stable after the 1980s, has been declining since the 2000s. By 2021, the ratio is approximately 60%. This decline can be attributed to factors such as rapid urbanization, industrialization and the growth of non-agricultural sectors.

The green revolution, which started in the 1960s, constitutes one of the turning points in India's agricultural policies. During this period, the widespread use of high-yielding seeds, the use of chemical fertilizers and the promotion of modern irrigation techniques came to the fore. With this revolution, agricultural production in India has increased significantly. Therefore, the problem of food security has been solved to a significant extent. As a matter of fact, cereal production increased from 50 million tons in the 1950s to around 130 million tons in the 1970s and 280 million tons in the 2010s (Somvanshi et al., 2020). In addition, different policies and programs are implemented to support the agricultural sector. Among these policies, subsidies and minimum support prices are at the forefront. In addition, different instruments such as agricultural loans and agricultural insurance are also used (Salunkhe, 2012). With reforms and subsidies, agricultural production in India is considered to have increased. India's great success in the agricultural sector has been one of the main causes of serious environmental and social problems. As a matter of fact, the intensive increase in the use of chemical fertilizers after the green revolution has led to the loss of soil fertility and pollution of water resources. In this context, it can be stated that the policies carried out with the concern of feeding the growing population have had unaccounted and unconsidered consequences (Patel et al., 2020).

In addition to environmental problems, some economic and social problems have also emerged with the growth of the agricultural sector. In particular, increasing inequalities in income and land distribution, small-scale farmers having serious difficulties in competitive conditions and facing debt crisis are considered as reflections of this situation (Birner et al., 2007). Therefore, it can be emphasized that social problems arise from the agricultural sector and this factor should be addressed in the policies developed.

India has many partners in agricultural trade, including BRICS member countries. For example, it has signed an agreement with Russia for the production of biocapsules used in agriculture (BRICS, 2022b). In this context, it can be considered that cooperation is being developed to integrate new technologies into the agricultural sector. On the other hand, it is seen that India signed an agreement with Russia, one of India's fertilizer suppliers, where the barter method was adopted. In this context, the barter method was adopted to avoid dollar transactions after the Russia-Ukraine war (BRICS, 2022c).

India's agricultural policies have been developed with the aim of ensuring food security and improving the welfare of the agricultural sector, which represents a large share of the population. The agricultural policies that have been successful in increasing agricultural production have brought along some economic, social and environmental challenges. It is also seen that there are reform efforts to find solutions to these challenges. In this direction, India is expected to put forward policies that focus on environmental sustainability and the solution of social-economic problems in the coming years.

## China's Agricultural Policies and BRICS

China is considered to be one of the most important global actors in the agricultural sector. With a large population, agriculture is one of the pillars of economic and social structure in China. With a significant portion of its population employed in the agricultural sector, China develops agricultural policies for both food security and rural development. However, factors such as resource constraints, environmental problems and dense population pose serious challenges for the agricultural sector (Huang & Yang, 2017).

The reform process that started in 1978 led to significant changes in the agricultural sector. The introduction of individual farming led to significant increases in agricultural production and productivity. The impact of the reform process began to wane in the 1990s and the agricultural sector faced challenges. During this period, the government introduced various policies and incentives to support the agricultural sector. In the 2000s, reforms were undertaken to make agricultural production sustainable. In this context, in addition to abolishing taxes and providing direct subsidies, it was aimed to make infrastructure investments and encourage sectoral growth (Yu et al., 2012). The ratio of agricultural land in China's total surface area is shown in the graph below.

*Figure 4. Agricultural land (% of Land Area) – China (World Bank Data https://data.worldbank.org/indicator)*

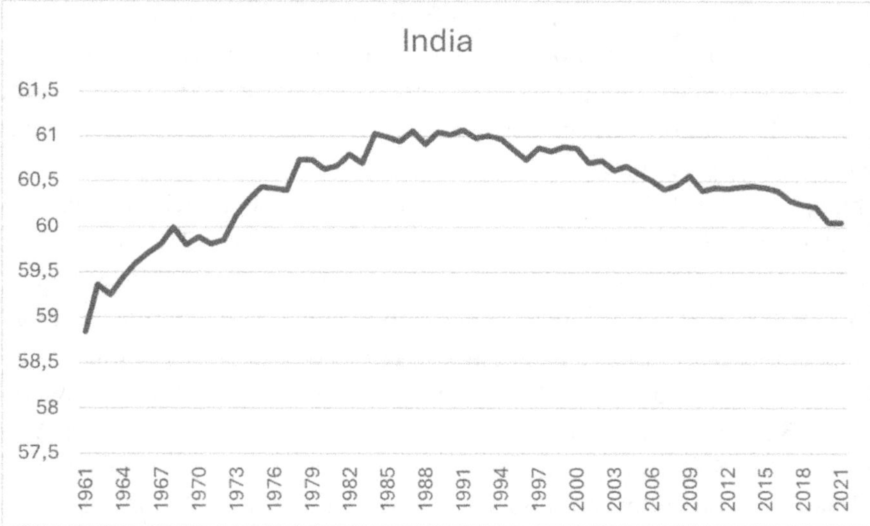


As can be seen in the graph, it can be stated that the ratio of agricultural land increased steadily from 1961 to the 1980s. In this period, especially the support given to agricultural production and the adoption of large-scale land use can be read as a reflection of feeding the population and ensuring economic development. After the 1980s, more than half of the country's land was agricultural land. The slow increase in the proportion of agricultural land compared to the previous period can be considered as the effect of industrialization and urbanization. It is also noteworthy that it remained at 55% after the 2000s, albeit with a slight decline. Indeed, changing economic and social conditions make it possible to change the purpose of land use. In general, the most important reason why the vast majority of the country's land is allocated as agricultural land is that China has a dense population and it is important to ensure food security.

Ensuring sustainability and modernization of agricultural lands, which have a high ratio, are also considered as important policy areas. In this respect, it is seen that agricultural policies are developed on the basis of both ensuring product efficiency and using resources effectively. In this context, initiatives are taken to improve soil quality, use water resources efficiently and reduce the carbon footprint in agricultural production. In this respect, the adoption of advanced technologies is important (Huang & Yang, 2017).

There are two main problem areas for the agricultural sector in China. The first one is the small scale of agricultural land. It is known that there are government efforts to encourage consolidation of these lands and to establish large-scale enterprises. However, this process has significant economic and social consequences (Ji et al., 2016). The second problem is the scarcity of water resources. Overuse of groundwater and water pollution is one of the most important threats to agricultural production. In addition, climate change also has negative impacts on agricultural production (Rogers, 2016).

China, like other BRICS countries, continues to cooperate with member countries in the agricultural field both bilaterally and under the BRICS umbrella. For example, it is seen that China will invest in farms in the far east of Russia (BRICS, 2016b). On the other hand, China emphasized the importance of this situation before the tenth BRICS summit held in South Africa in order to find a solution to the food problem in Africa with BRICS cooperation. In this context, it was stated that both BRICS and China are willing to ensure food security especially in the African continent (BRICS, 2018c). On the other hand, it is observed that China's trade with Brazil has increased after the Sino-US tension. In fact, in 2018, Brazil exported 35.59 billion dollars worth of agricultural products to China, 9 billion dollars more than in 2017 (BRICS, 2019a). In addition, with the agreement signed by China and Brazil in 2022, it was decided to establish the China-Brazil Agricultural Science Industrial Park in Brazil (BRICS, 2022d). Similarly, it was emphasized that China would increase soybean exports from Russia and cut the crop from the US (BRICS, 2019b). Therefore, it can be stated that China has cooperation with Russia and Brazil in agro-industry and trade.

China's agricultural policies are shaped on the basis of ensuring food security, increasing agricultural production and productivity, and supporting rural development. While implementing these policies, sustainability emerges as an important problem area. In order to tackle the challenges in the agricultural sector, China is developing innovative approaches and developing policies to strengthen the use of technology in the agricultural sector. Indeed, it can be stated that the success of these policies will play a critical role in both supporting economic growth and solving environmental and social problems.

## South Africa's Agricultural Policies and BRICS

The agricultural sector in South Africa is one of the main sectors in the economy. This sector has been shaped by the economic, social and political dynamics of the country. For example, when the apartheid regime gained power, the agricultural sector was under the control of the white minority. The black population was largely excluded from the agricultural sector. With the end of this regime, the agricultural sector was made inclusive through various reforms. Considering this process, it can be stated that the agricultural sector in South Africa was under the control of whites especially in the 1960s. In this period, the government provided great support to white farmers and empowered them with agricultural loans and subsidies. As a result of these policies, it is stated that the agricultural sector and thus agricultural production was concentrated under the control of the white population and the black population remained marginal in the agricultural sector (Wiig & Øien, 2013). Until the end of the apartheid regime in 1994, it is seen that the agricultural sector was structured in a way to strengthen and sustain this regime. It is also considered that land reform was carried out in order to guarantee the land ownership of the white population (Bernstein, 2013). The proportion of agricultural land in South Africa's total surface area since 1960 is shown in the graph below.

*Figure 5. Agricultural land (% of Land Area) – South Africa (World Bank Data https://data.worldbank.org/indicator)*

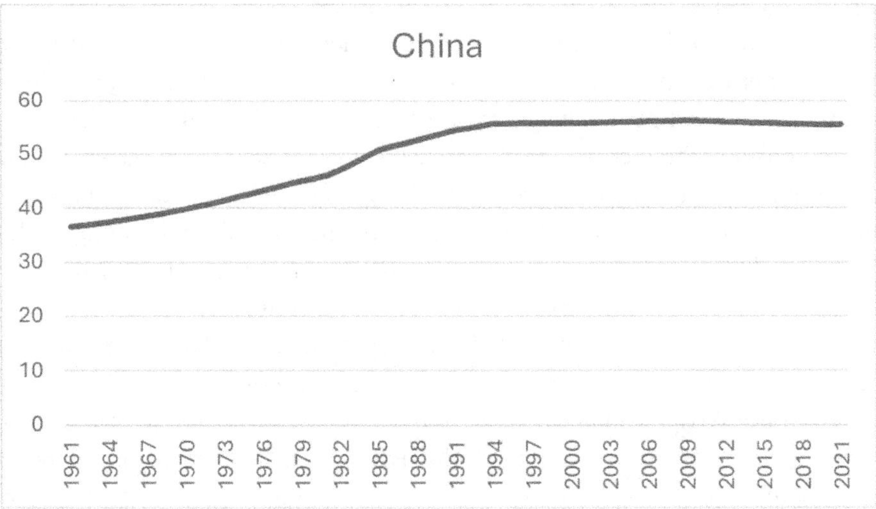


In the graph above, it can be seen that the ratio of agricultural land to total land area was around 84% in 1961 and decreased until the 1980s. After the 1980s, the ratio of agricultural land increased again and reached above 80%. Since the 2000s, it has been on a downward trend again, reaching 79% in 2021. Although agricultural land in South Africa fluctuates in certain periods, it is possible to say that it covers the vast majority of the country's surface area.

There have been periodic reforms in the distribution of agricultural land. Especially after the end of the apartheid regime after 1994, a land reform process was initiated. In this context, it is evaluated that reforms were carried out on the basis of objectives such as establishing justice in the agricultural sector, ensuring the participation of the black population in production and supporting rural development. In addition to land reform, redistribution of subsidies and infrastructure investments are activities carried out to restructure the agricultural sector (Arko-Achemfuor, 2016). Land reform aimed to redistribute previously white-owned agricultural land to the black population and build a more equitable and inclusive agricultural sector. However, the challenges faced with these reforms limited their effectiveness. The level of productivity of the land redistributed with the reform was not at the desired level. This negatively affected rural poverty reduction efforts (Middelberg, 2013).

In the 2000s, agricultural policies were structured to create a sustainable system and promote modernization in the agricultural sector. The government has taken steps to tackle key challenges such as promoting the adoption of innovative technologies to ensure productivity in the agricultural sector, ensuring efficient use of water resources and reducing the impact of climate change (Fanadzo & Ncube, 2018). However, it has been observed that small-scale farmers have not benefited sufficiently from the modernization process. Problems such as infrastructure deficiencies and lack of financing continued to negatively affect their production (Muzekenyi et al., 2023). In addition, the fact that South Africa is a water scarce country also causes serious problems in the agricultural sector. Limited water resources and the severe impact of climate change pose major threats to agricultural land and agricultural production. Although efforts are being made to solve this problem, it is difficult to state that effective results have been achieved (Wilk et al., 2013).

Membership in BRICS is one of the strategic elements that can contribute to strengthening South Africa's agricultural sector. In this context, it has been emphasized that South Africa should increase agricultural exports not only to all BRICS members but particularly to China and India (BRICS, 2021a). From this perspective, BRICS countries collectively represent a market that accounts for 12% of global agricultural imports. China, a key target market for South Africa, conducts 68% of BRICS countries' agricultural imports, making it the largest agricultural importer within the group. Russia follows with 14%, India with 10%, Brazil with 5%, and South Africa with 3%. The imported products include wheat, wine, cheese, citrus fruits, palm oil, bananas, and coffee. From South Africa's standpoint, despite being a major producer of many of these products, its agricultural exports to BRICS countries remain limited. Over the past 10 years, these countries have accounted for only 7% of South Africa's total agricultural exports, indicating a significant untapped potential in this area (BRICS, 2021b). Therefore, it is important to implement policies and activities to realize the existing potential in this sector.

In summary, South Africa's agricultural policies have undergone a transformation since the end of apartheid, although the effects of that era have not been fully eradicated. Various environmental challenges, particularly water scarcity and climate change, continue to directly impact the agricultural sector, necessitating the implementation of preventive measures. It is also recognized that the processes involved in the modernization efforts that have intensified since the 2000s need to be comprehensively managed to be effective. Additionally, as a BRICS member, strengthening agricultural trade with other member countries could significantly increase South Africa's export revenues.

## Agriculture in BRICS: Member States' Position and Policy Recommendations

The agricultural policies of each BRICS member country have been examined in detail, including their agricultural sectors, food security, positions in agricultural trade, and the interplay between agriculture and environmental issues. Based on the information gathered, it can be concluded that, in addition to other sectors, agriculture holds critical importance within BRICS. Active and effective collaborations within the organization, particularly in the realm of food security, are likely to provide significant advantages to member countries. In this context, it is crucial to analyze the trade dynamics of agricultural products among BRICS member states to assess their positions relative to one another.

A general evaluation of the current state of the agricultural sector among member countries reveals that Brazil occupies a prominent position in global agricultural exports, particularly leading in soybean, beef, and sugarcane products. In fact, an analysis of Brazil's current export data shows that China ranks first as the top importer of Brazilian soybeans (World Integrated Trade Solutions, 2023). The data on the import and export of agricultural products is presented in the table below.

*Figure 6. Brazil's export and import of agricultural products to BRICS member countries*

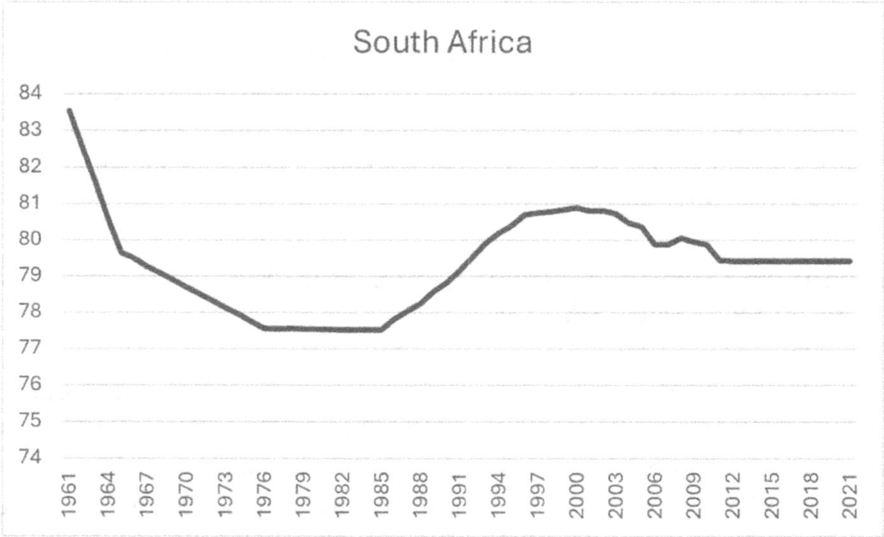


*(World Integrated Trade Solutions, 2021)*

When analyzing Brazil's import and export data with BRICS member countries, it is evident that the highest export revenue is derived from exports to China, while imports remain quite limited. In terms of trade with Russia, Brazil's exports to Russia hold a significant share, while imports from Russia are minimal. Exports to India are at a moderate level, but, similar to other BRICS countries, imports from India remain limited. Brazil's exports to South Africa are at an average level compared to other BRICS countries, yet South Africa stands out as the country from which Brazil imports the most agricultural products. In general, Brazil plays a crucial role in agricultural exports, particularly to BRICS countries, while its imports from these countries remain low. This underscores Brazil's position as a major agricultural exporter both globally and within the BRICS bloc.

Russia holds a prominent position in the production and export of wheat and other grain products. Russia has strengthened its role in global agricultural trade by implementing policies aimed at promoting domestic production and reducing import dependency to ensure food security. With significant reforms in its agricultural sector, Russia accounted for 18% of the world's wheat exports in 2021 (FAOSTAT, 2021). Russia has also developed policies and strategies to enhance agricultural trade cooperation with other BRICS members. The trade data for agricultural product imports and exports with BRICS member countries is presented in the graphs below.

*Figure 7. Russian federation's export and import of agricultural products to BRICS member countries*

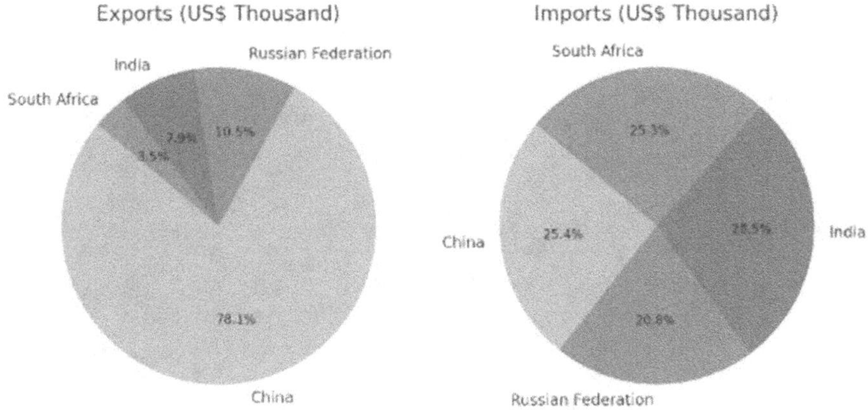


*(World Integrated Trade Solutions, 2021)*

An analysis of Russia's agricultural exports and imports shows that the largest share is attributed to China. As indicated in both graphs, China represents a significant and major market for Russia's agricultural production. China's high demand for agricultural products has resulted in it taking a dominant portion of Russia's exports. India, which ranks second in both import and export of agricultural products, is also considered an important market for Russia. Compared to China and India, Brazil and especially South Africa have lower import and export ratios, as seen in the graph. In summary, China plays a dominant role, followed by India.

In India, agricultural policies are developed around key objectives such as promoting rural development, improving farmer welfare, and ensuring food security. The reform efforts and government support have positively impacted agricultural production. India holds a prominent position globally in agricultural production, particularly in rice, wheat, and cotton. The graphs below present India's agricultural product imports and exports with other BRICS member countries.

*Figure 8. India's export and import of agricultural products to BRICS member countries*

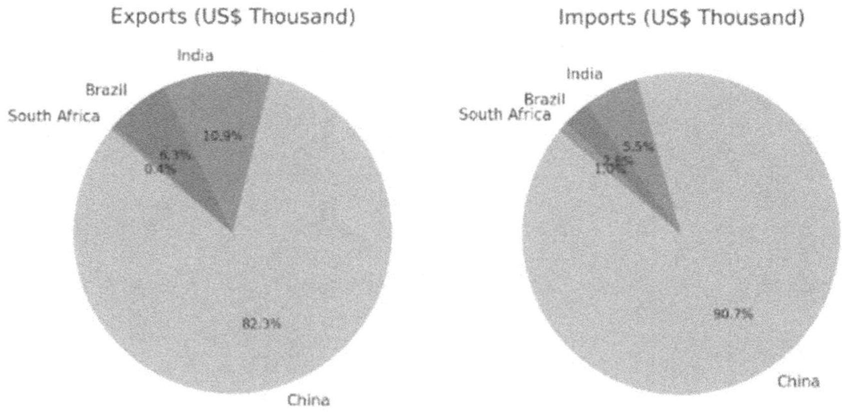


*(World Integrated Trade Solutions, 2021)*

An analysis of the graphs above reveals that China holds the largest share in India's agricultural imports and exports. It is also worth noting that India is a significant player in the Chinese market. Brazil and South Africa follow China, ranking second and third, respectively, with both countries playing a similarly important role in India's agricultural trade. Russia, however, has the smallest share, making it the country with which India has developed the least agricultural trade cooperation among the BRICS members. In both graphs, China's dominant presence in India's agricultural trade is evident.

China, due to its large population and limited agricultural land, is recognized as one of the most important global agricultural exporters. Feeding its vast population makes ensuring food security a critical priority for China. The country's agricultural policies are developed around key objectives such as improving productivity, promoting rural development, and ensuring food security. China has significant capacity in the production of rice, wheat, and corn (FAOSTAT, 2021). The graphs below show China's agricultural imports and exports with other BRICS member countries.

*Figure 9. China's export and import of agricultural products to BRICS member countries*

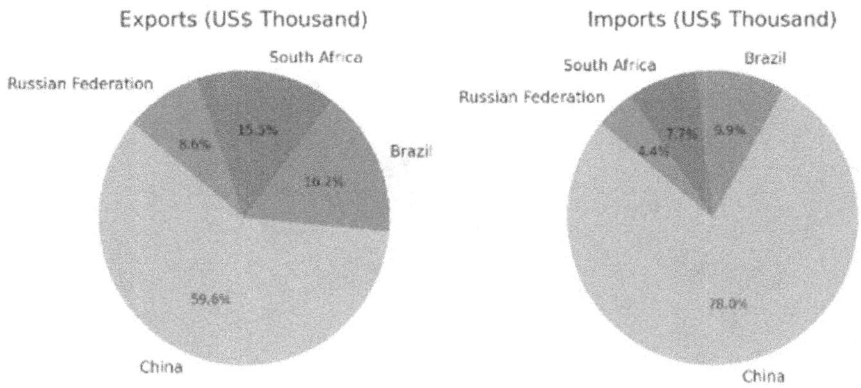


*(World Integrated Trade Solutions, 2021)*

India has the largest share in China's exports and imports of agricultural products. As a matter of fact, India can be considered as an important market for China. India is followed by Russia. It can be stated that Russia has a significant share in both imports and exports. Brazil ranks third and South Africa fourth. When compared with the import and export graphs of other countries, it is seen that China's import and export graphs have a more balanced distribution. In this respect, it can be emphasized that China dominates agricultural trade.

South Africa is developing agricultural policies to increase agricultural production capacity on the basis of ensuring food security and promoting rural development. South Africa, which is a major exporter of fruits and vegetables, also faces environmental and climate change challenges. However, the agricultural sector is critical to South Africa's economy. In this respect, it can be stated that membership to BRICS is of critical importance in terms of contributing to increasing cooperation in the agricultural sector. The charts below show the imports and exports of agricultural products with BRICS members.

*Figure 10. South Africa's export and import of agricultural products to BRICS member countries*

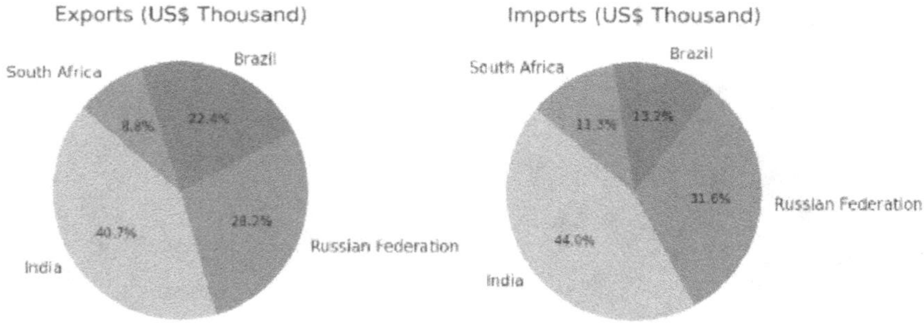


China has the largest share in South Africa's imports and exports of agricultural products. China is followed by India. Brazil and Russia have a very limited share in South Africa's agricultural imports and exports. As can be seen from these graphs, China has a strategic importance for South Africa among BRICS member countries. As a matter of fact, it is positioned as a critical actor in South Africa's agricultural product trade.

When the current situation and trade relations of BRICS member countries in the agricultural sector are analyzed, it can be evaluated that they have developed relations in line with strategic objectives, especially food security. In particular, Brazil, Russia, India and China have strong ties in the trade of agricultural products. This situation contributes to the countries becoming stronger and more influential globally and in the context of BRICS membership. Compared to these four countries, South Africa has a more limited trade network and volume, and China is a strategic actor in South Africa's agricultural trade. In this context, effective strategies are needed to strengthen cooperation in the agricultural sector, intensify the trade network and ensure food security among BRICS member countries. Developing more comprehensive and deeper cooperation, providing technological support, promoting sustainable agricultural practices and reducing barriers to agricultural trade are the main activities to realize this strategy.

It is important to develop and support cooperation among BRICS member countries in strategic areas. The policies and strategies to be developed by both member countries and BRICS are critical for the realization of these comprehensive, long-term and sustainable collaborations. In this respect, the policies and strategies that can be developed under BRICS can be categorized in five main areas. These can be listed:

- Transferring technology in the agricultural sector among BRICS countries and disseminating innovative solutions among member countries,
- Expanding agricultural trade and investment opportunities among member countries, especially those with weaker agricultural trade ties,
- Ensuring food security and combating climate change and environmental challenges,
- Supporting rural development and combating poverty, and establishing the BRICS agricultural investment fund.

The first policy recommendation, the realization of technology transfer in the agricultural sector among BRICS countries and the dissemination of innovative solutions among member countries, has been developed to contribute to increasing productivity in agricultural production. The development of such cooperation among countries with different technological capacities and levels of development is expected to offer great opportunities to member countries. In this context, transferring the high agricultural technology knowledge of China and India to other countries through joint projects in areas such as agricultural production and digital agricultural practices will ensure efficiency in agricultural production and strengthen cooperation between countries. Organizing fairs and events to promote these technologies, not only at the governmental level, but also involving the private sector in the agricultural sector, will also provide important opportunities for comprehensive cooperation. It should also be emphasized that advanced agricultural technology will be effective in ensuring environmental sustainability and mitigating the negative impacts of climate change.

The second policy proposal aims at strengthening the agricultural trade network among Member States, in particular by expanding agricultural trade and investment opportunities among those with weaker agricultural trade ties. Establishment of agricultural free trade zones, creation of investment funds and creation of agricultural trade platforms suitable for effective use can be listed as activities to be carried out in line with this policy. In this context, both the provision of incentives at the state level and the reassurance of effective cooperation within BRICS will contribute to strengthening trade ties by providing attractive opportunities for investors.

Within the scope of ensuring food security and combating climate change and environmental challenges, the steps to be taken in the context of BRICS membership are of strategic importance. As a matter of fact, food security, which is a critical issue in the international arena, has the potential to offer an important privilege to member countries through cooperation and strong strategic partnerships to be carried out within BRICS. In this context, member countries can create a common agricultural product reserve especially against the food crisis. Climate change and environmental problems also threaten food security. In this respect, dissemination of good practices developed in member countries to other countries is important in terms of efficiency in agricultural production and food security.

Within the scope of supporting rural development and combating poverty, which is another policy proposal, strategies can be listed as the creation of support programs for small-scale farmers, the development of infrastructure investments, and the provision of information sharing for rural areas. In this context, in addition to the agricultural policies of the member countries, providing support within the agricultural investment fund planned to be established within BRICS can be an important step in strengthening cooperation. Finally, it can be aimed to establish an agricultural investment fund and to improve agricultural production and trade through the fund.

The development of agricultural cooperation and the strengthening of trade ties within BRICS in line with the needs and priorities of the member countries may intensify the strategic partnership between the member countries. The atmosphere of solidarity in extraordinary situations such as the global food crisis will contribute to BRICS becoming even more strategically important.

## CONCLUSION

Agricultural policies are considered as one of the basic building blocks of countries in the economic field, especially in ensuring food security, rural development, environmental sustainable social welfare. Agricultural policies, which are considered as a public policy of strategic importance, are one of the main tools for achieving basic objectives such as increasing the agricultural production capacity of countries, ensuring sustainability in agricultural activities and increasing competitiveness. In this context, agriculture, which is an integral part of both economic and social structure, becomes one of the main components of economic stability when managed within the framework of the right policies. Similarly, food security is one of the main issues that countries take into consideration when shaping both their domestic and foreign policies. In this respect, agricultural policies are shaped on the basis of objectives such as ensuring food security, keeping a strong hand in international trade and increasing the welfare of the population living in rural areas. In this context, strong and sustainable management of the agricultural sector is of strategic importance both in national and global policies.

Within the BRICS, agriculture is important as these countries both host a large share of the world's population and have a significant share in global agricultural production. By strengthening their agricultural policies, BRICS member countries not only support their own economic development but also contribute to global food security. Agriculture, as one of the BRICS' strategic areas of cooperation, not only strengthens the economic ties between these countries, but also plays a critical role in balancing food supply and demand on a global scale. In this context, agricultural cooperation among BRICS countries not only increases trade volume but also influences their global food security policies.

Each BRICS member country contributes to both BRICS and world agriculture through its agricultural policies. Brazil has become one of the world's largest agricultural exporters by emphasizing efficiency and modernization in agricultural production. It is further strengthening this position by increasing trade in agricultural products and developing agricultural cooperation within BRICS.

Russia has shaped its agricultural policies in line with the goal of ensuring food security and increasing domestic production. With the food embargo imposed in 2014, Russia started to encourage domestic production and experienced a significant recovery in the agricultural sector. Russia's policies aimed to reduce import dependency by increasing domestic production in the agriculture and food sectors. This process also led to a more protectionist structure in the country's agricultural trade policies. Agricultural cooperation with BRICS countries plays an important role in this process by increasing Russia's agricultural exports.

India, as a major agricultural producer, contributes significantly to the BRICS in terms of food security and rural development, while tackling environmental sustainability issues. Since the Green Revolution, India's agricultural policies have aimed to increase agricultural production and ensure food security. India's agricultural sector is facing significant social problems. To solve these problems, India needs to reform its agricultural policies and develop policies that prioritize environmental sustainability. India's BRICS membership offers important opportunities, especially in the sharing of agricultural technologies and the development of joint projects.

China is focused on modernizing agriculture and increasing productivity to feed its large population and is strengthening agricultural cooperation among BRICS countries. China has shaped its agricultural policies in line with the goal of using resources efficiently and ensuring sustainability. Factors such as the use of high-yielding seeds, the adoption of modern irrigation techniques and the strengthening of agricultural infrastructure during the agricultural reform process have significantly increased China's agricultural production capacity. Moreover, agricultural cooperation within the BRICS plays a critical role in ensuring China's food security and further strengthening its agricultural sector.

South Africa faces environmental challenges in the agricultural sector, particularly water scarcity and climate change. Limited water resources stand out as a major problem that directly affects the agricultural sector. South Africa has developed various policies to promote modernization in the agricultural sector and increase the production capacity of small farmers. However, for these policies to be effective, infrastructure investments need to be increased and problems such as lack of financing need to be addressed. South Africa's BRICS membership offers important opportunities to increase agricultural trade and strengthen cooperation with other BRICS countries.

From a future perspective, enhancing agricultural cooperation among BRICS countries in the post-COVID-19 era is vital for global food security and managing potential food crises. The COVID-19 pandemic has exposed serious vulnerabilities in food supply chains and highlighted the importance of security of supply of agricultural products on a global scale. In the post-pandemic period, strong cooperation among BRICS countries has become imperative to address these vulnerabilities. In addition, the uncertainties brought to global supply chains by the US-China trade war further increase the importance of cooperation for BRICS countries to ensure the security of supply of agricultural products and increase their independence in this field. With the expansion of BRICS, the inclusion of more countries in common agricultural policies could make them more effective and powerful actors in the global food market.

In the post-COVID-19 era, adopting digital technologies in agriculture, expanding climate-resilient agricultural practices and setting sustainable food security goals should be among the BRICS' future strategic priorities. Achieving these goals will not only support the economic development of BRICS countries, but also stabilize global food supply security in the face of the pandemic and the volatility brought about by the US-China trade war.

Given the increasing impacts of climate change, sustainability of agricultural production and food security should become strategic priorities for BRICS countries. In this context, promoting knowledge sharing in agriculture, disseminating innovative technologies and supporting sustainable agricultural practices will make the agricultural policies of BRICS countries more effective and efficient. Both the supply chain issues triggered by COVID-19 and the global uncertainties brought about by the US-China trade war make the need for BRICS countries to ensure their own food security more evident and increase the strategic importance of cooperation in this area.

Moreover, with more countries joining BRICS+, BRICS can have a more active role in shaping global agricultural policies. This would strengthen the leadership role of BRICS countries in ensuring global food security and managing potential food crises. Therefore, increasing agricultural cooperation among BRICS countries stands out as a strategic step that contributes positively to both their domestic dynamics and global food security in the face of post-COVID-19 uncertainties and global volatility caused by the US-China trade war.

## REFERENCES


Alessa, A. A., Zaabi, E., & Diab, A. (2018). Impact of Environmental Factors on Financing Agriculture Entrepreneurs. *International Journal of Entrepreneurship*, 22(4), 1–13.

Arko-Achemfuor, A. (2016). Addressing The Challenges of Foodsecurity and Youth Unemployment in South Africa through Land Reform Policies. *Environment and Ecology*, 7(3), 52–59.

Ay, H. M., & Söylemez, A. (2023). Grain Corridor Agreement and Turkey's Role in the Russia- Ukraine War, *Islamic. World Politics*, 7(1), 1–10. DOI: 10.18196/jiwp.v7i1.27

Balsalobre-lorente, D., Driha, O., Bekun, F., & Osundina, O. (2019). Do Agricultural Activities Induce Carbon Emissions? The BRICS Experience. *Environmental Science and Pollution Research International*, 26(24), 25218–25234. DOI: 10.1007/s11356-019-05737-3 PMID: 31256399

Bernstein, H. (2013). Commercial Agriculture in South Africa since 1994: Natural, Simply Capitalism. *Journal of Agrarian Change*, 13(1), 23–46. DOI: 10.1111/joac.12011

Birner, R., Gupta, S., & Sharma, N. B. (2007). *The Political Economy of Agricultural Policy Reform in India: Fertilizers and Electricity for Irrigation*. International Food Policy Research Institute.

BRICS. (2015a). Moscow to Host a Meeting of the BRICS Expert Working Group on Agriculture. https://infobrics.org/post/5237

BRICS. (2015b). Experts Discuss the BRICS Countries' Practical Experience in Implementing Social Protection Programmes for Food Security. https://infobrics.org/post/6130

BRICS. (2015c). Russia, China Agree Protocols on Grain Deliveries. https://infobrics.org/post/8442

BRICS. (2016). China to Step up Farm Investment in Russia's Far East. https://infobrics.org/post/11115/

BRICS. (2017a). BRICS Agriculture Research Platform. https://infobrics.org/post/25585

BRICS. (2017b). Brazil Allowed the Import of Wheat from Russia. https://infobrics.org/post/26185

BRICS. (2017c). Russian Agriculture Exports to China to Total 52 Mln Tonnes by 2028. https://infobrics.org/post/24534/

BRICS. (2018a). US-China Trade War Winner: Brazil Soybean Exports. https://infobrics.org/post/27534/

BRICS. (2018b). Russia Proposes Joint Soy Processing Production with China. https://infobrics.org/post/27664

BRICS. (2018c). China, BRICS to Focus on Africa Food Security. https://infobrics.org/post/26537

BRICS. (2019a). Chinese Demand Lifts Brazil's Agricultural Exports in 2018. https://infobrics.org/post/28002

BRICS. (2019b). China to Boost Imports of Russian Soybeans, Cutting out US Crop Exports. https://infobrics.org/post/28960

BRICS. (2021a). Brics Countries Offer Export Opportunities to SA's Booming Agricultural Sector. https://infobrics.org/post/33030

BRICS. (2021b). Brics Might Offer Agriculture Markets South Africa Needs – https://infobrics.org/post/33067

BRICS. (2022a). BRICS Agricultural Cooperation. https://infobrics.org/post/36570

BRICS. (2022b). India, Russia Sign MoU for Commercialisation of Biocapsule. https://infobrics.org/post/36413/

BRICS. (2022c). India Secures Fertiliser Supplies from Russia. https://infobrics.org/post/35882/

BRICS. (2022d). Agreement to Build China-Brazil Agricultural Industrial Park Signed. https://infobrics.org/post/35840

BRICS. (2023a). Additional Brazilian Firms Cleared to Export Corn to China. https://infobrics.org/post/37925

BRICS. (2023b). Brazilian Soybeans and China's Food Security. https://infobrics.org/post/38719/

BRICS. (2024a). BRICS Portal. https://infobrics.org/

BRICS. (2024b). BRICS Countries Back Grain Exchange Idea. https://infobrics.org/post/41747

BRICS Information Centre. (2010). Moscow Declaration of BRIC Ministers of Agriculture and Agrarian Development. http://www.brics.utoronto.ca/docs/100326-agriculture.html

BRICS Information Centre. (2011). Action Plan 2012-2016 for Agricultural Cooperation of BRICS Countries. http://www.brics.utoronto.ca/docs/111030-agriculture-plan.html

BRICS Information Centre. (2022). Agriculture Ministers Meeting. http://www.brics.utoronto.ca/agriculture/index.html

Bullock, D. S., & Salhofer, K. (2003). Judging Agricultural Policies: A Survey. *Agricultural Economics*, 28(3), 225–243. DOI: 10.1111/j.1574-0862.2003.tb00140.x

Cousins, B., Borras, S.Jr, Sauer, S., & Ye, J. (2018). BRICS, Middle-income Countries (MICs), and Global Agrarian Transformations: Internal Dynamics, Regional Trends, and International Implications. *Globalizations*, 15(1), 1–11. DOI: 10.1080/14747731.2018.1429104

Dos Santos, M. J. P. L., & Ahmad, N. (2020). Sustainability of European Agricultural Holdings. *Journal of the Saudi Society of Agricultural Sciences*, 19(5), 358–364. DOI: 10.1016/j.jssas.2020.04.001

Fanadzo, M., & Ncube, B. (2018). Challenges and Opportunities for Revitalising Smallholder Irrigation Schemes in South Africa. *Water S.A.*, 44(3), 436–447.

FAOSTAT. (2021). Trade Indices. https://www.fao.org/faostat/en/#data

Ferreira, J., Pardini, R., Metzger, J., Fonseca, C., Pompeu, P., Sparovek, G., & Louzada, J. (2012). Towards environmentally sustainable agriculture in Brazil: Challenges and opportunities for applied ecological research. *Journal of Applied Ecology*, 49(3), 535–541. DOI: 10.1111/j.1365-2664.2012.02145.x

Fischer, R. A., & Connor, D. J. (2018). Issues for Cropping and Agricultural Science in The Next 20 Years. *Field Crops Research*, 222, 121–142. DOI: 10.1016/j.fcr.2018.03.008

Gishkaeva, L. L. (2023). The agricultural sector of the Russian economy and innovative technologies: Evolution, problems and directions of development. *BIO Web of Conferences*.

Hopewell, K. (2016). The accidental agro-power: Constructing comparative advantage in Brazil. *New Political Economy*, 21(6), 536–554. DOI: 10.1080/13563467.2016.1161014

Huang, J., & Yang, G. (2017). Understanding recent challenges and new food policy in China. *Global Food Security*, 12, 119–126. DOI: 10.1016/j.gfs.2016.10.002

Ji, X., Rozelle, S., Huang, J., Zhang, L., & Zhang, T. (2016). Are China's Farms Growing? *China & World Economy*, 24(1), 41–62. DOI: 10.1111/cwe.12143

Lankoski, J., & Thiem, A. (2020). Linkages Between Agricultural Policies, Productivity and Environmental Sustainability. *Ecological Economics*, 178, 106809. DOI: 10.1016/j.ecolecon.2020.106809

Leng, Y., Liu, X., & Wang, X. (2023). Environmental Regulation and High-quality Agricultural Development. *PLoS One*, 18(5), e0285687. DOI: 10.1371/journal.pone.0285687 PMID: 37172018

Liefert, W., Liefert, O., Seeley, R., & Lee, T. (2019). The effect of Russia's economic crisis and import ban on its agricultural and food sector. *Journal of Eurasian Studies*, 10(2), 119–135. DOI: 10.1177/1879366519840185

Liefert, W. M., & Liefert, O. (2020). Russian Agricultural Trade and World Markets. *Russian Journal of Economics*, 6(1), 56–70. DOI: 10.32609/j.ruje.6.50308

Middelberg, S. (2013). Sustainable Agriculture: A Review of Challenges Facing the South African Agricultural Sector. *Journal of Human Ecology (Delhi, India)*, 42(2), 163–169. DOI: 10.1080/09709274.2013.11906590

Mukhametzyanov, R., Romanyuk, M., Ostapchuk, T., & Ivantsova, N. (2021). The objective need and trend of ensuring the food security in Russia in conditions of import substitution. *BIO Web of Conferences*, 37, 00079.

Muzekenyi, M. J. J., & Kilonzo, B. (2023). Economic challenges limiting small-scale commercial farming development in rural areas of South Africa. *African Journal of Food, Agriculture, Nutrition and Development*, 23(4), 23026–23038. DOI: 10.18697/ajfand.119.22900

Nasir, M. A., Nugroho, A. D., & Lakner, Z. (2022). Impact of the Russian–Ukrainian Conflict on Global Food Crops. *Foods*, 11(19), 2979. DOI: 10.3390/foods11192979 PMID: 36230055

Navarro, A., & Lopez-Bao, J. V. (2019). EU Agricultural Policy Still Not Green. *Nature Sustainability*, 2(11), 990. DOI: 10.1038/s41893-019-0424-x

Oldekop, J. A., Chappell, M. J., Peixoto, F. E. B., Paglia, A. P., Rodrigues, M. S. P., & Evans, K. L. (2015). Linking Brazil's Food Security Policies to Agricultural Change. *Food Security*, 7(4), 779–793. DOI: 10.1007/s12571-015-0475-4

Patel, S. K., Sharma, A. K., & Singh, G. (2020). Traditional agricultural practices in India: An approach for environmental sustainability and food security. *Energy, Ecology & Environment*, 5(4), 253–271. DOI: 10.1007/s40974-020-00158-2

Picoli, M., Rorato, A., Leitão, P., Câmara, G., Maciel, A., Hostert, P., & Sanches, I. (2020). Impacts of Public and Private Sector Policies on Soybean and Pasture Expansion in Mato Grosso—Brazil from 2001 to 2017. *Land (Basel)*, 9(1), 20. DOI: 10.3390/land9010020

Plaunt, D. H. (1973). Agricultural Development Policies and Programs in Canada. *American Journal of Agricultural Economics*, 55(5), 903–912. DOI: 10.2307/1238935

Reidsma, P., Bakker, M. M., Kanellopoulos, A., Alam, S. J., Paas, W., Kros, J., & de Vries, W. (2015). Sustainable Agricultural Development in a Rural Area in the Netherlands? Assessing Impacts of Climate and Socio-economic Change at Farm and Landscape Level. *Agricultural Systems*, 141, 160–173. DOI: 10.1016/j.agsy.2015.10.009

Rogers, S. (2016). Adaptation science and policy in China's agricultural sector. *Wiley Interdisciplinary Reviews: Climate Change*, 7(5), 7. DOI: 10.1002/wcc.414

Salunkhe, H. (2012). The overview of Government subsidies to agriculture sector in India. *IOSR Journal of Agriculture and Veterinary Science*, 1, 43–47. DOI: 10.9790/2380-0154347

Selvan, S. S., Wahid, A., Patel, A., Kumar, V., & Sahu, P. (2021). Challenges in Indian Agriculture. *Agricultural Reviews (Karnal)*, (Of). Advance online publication. DOI: 10.18805/ag.R-2103

Skogstad, G., & Verdun, A. (2009). The Common Agricultural Policy: Continuity and Change. *Journal of European Integration*, 31(3), 265–269. DOI: 10.1080/07036330902782105

Somvanshi, P., Pandiaraj, T., & Singh, R. (2020). An unexplored story of successful green revolution of India and steps towards ever green revolution. *Journal of Pharmacognosy and Phytochemistry*, 9, 1270–1273.

Tilman, D., Cassman, K. G., Matson, P. A., Naylor, R., & Polasky, S. (2002). Agricultural Sustainability and Intensive Production Practices. *Nature*, 418(6898), 671–677. DOI: 10.1038/nature01014 PMID: 12167873

Wang, X., Ma, L., Yan, S., Chen, X., & Growe, A. (2023). Trade for Food Security: The Stability of Global Agricultural Trade Networks. *Foods*, 12(2), 271. DOI: 10.3390/foods12020271 PMID: 36673361

Wegren, S. (2010). Russia's Food Policies and Foreign Policy. *Demokratizatsiya (Washington, D.C.)*, 18, 189–207.

Wiig, H., & Øien, H. (2013). Would Small be More Beautiful in the South African Land Reform? In Holden, S. T., Otsuka, K., & Deininger, K. (Eds.), *Land Tenure Reform in Asia and Africa*. Palgrave Macmillan. DOI: 10.1057/9781137343819_4

Wilk, J., Andersson, L., & Warburton, M. (2013). Adaptation to Climate Change and Other Stressors among Commercial and Small-scale South African Farmers. *Regional Environmental Change*, 13(2), 273–286. DOI: 10.1007/s10113-012-0323-4

World Integrated Trade Solutions. (2023). Brazil Soya Beans Exports by Country in 2023. https://wits.worldbank.org/trade/comtrade/en/country/BRA/year/2023/tradeflow/Exports/partner/ALL/product/120100

Yu, B., Liu, F., & You, L. (2012). Dynamic Agricultural Supply Response Under Economic Transformation: A Case Study of Henan, China. *American Journal of Agricultural Economics*, 94(2), 370–376. DOI: 10.1093/ajae/aar114

Yu, J., & Wu, J. (2018). The Sustainability of Agricultural Development in China: The Agriculture–Environment Nexus. *Sustainability (Basel)*, 10(6), 1776. DOI: 10.3390/su10061776

# Compilation of References


Abadi, F. A., & Al-Fadhat, F. (2023). *The influence of Indo-Pacific Economic Framework on peace and stability in the ASEAN region*. Global Strategis. DOI: 10.20473/jgs.17.1.2023.33-50

Abay, E. (2024). Russia begins using cryptocurrencies in international payments. Anadolu Ajansı. 28 August 2024. https://www.aa.com.tr/tr/ekonomi/rusya-uluslararasi-odemelerde-kripto-paralari-kullanmaya-basliyor/3314827#

Abdenur, A. E., & Folly, M. (2015). The New Development Bank and the Institutionalization of the BRICS. *BRICS-Studies and Documents*, 77-111.

Abdenur, A. E. (2017). Can the BRICS Cooperate in International Security? *International Organizations Research Journal*, 12(3), 73–93. DOI: 10.17323/1996-7845-2017-03-73

Acharya, A. (2004). How Ideas Spread: Whose Norms Matter? Norm Localization and Institutional Change in Asian Regionalism. *International Organization*, 58(2), 239–275. DOI: 10.1017/S0020818304582024

Acharya, A. (2011). Norm Subsidiarity and Regional Orders: Sovereignty, Regionalism, and Rule-Making in the Third World. *International Studies Quarterly*, 55(1), 95–123. DOI: 10.1111/j.1468-2478.2010.00637.x

Acharya, A. (2012). Comparative Regionalism: A Field whose Time has come? *The International Spectator*, 47(1), 3–15. DOI: 10.1080/03932729.2012.655004

Acharya, A. (2012). *The End of the American World Order*. Polity Press.

Adloff, F., & Hilbrich, I. (2021). Practices of sustainability and the enactment of their natures/cultures: Ecosystem services, rights of nature, and geoengineering. *Social Sciences Information. Information Sur les Sciences Sociales*, 60(2), 168–187. DOI: 10.1177/0539018421998947

AFN (Accounting for Nature). (2023). Accounting for nature. AFN. www.accountingfornature.org

Afota, A., Burban, V., Diev, P., Grieco, F., Iberrakene, T., Ishii, K., Lopez-Forero, M., Paul, Q., Sammeth, F., & Valadier, C. (2024). Expansion of BRICS: what are the potential consequences for the global economy? (https://www.banque-france.fr/en/publications-and-statistics/publications/expansion-brics-what-are-potential-consequences-global-economy. Date of Access: 23.10.2024).

Afzaal, M., & Naqvi, S. B. (2024). *How strategic representations together with geo-political and economic dynamics are mediating the global image of China's Belt Road Initiative*. Taylor & Francis.

Agarwal, A., Mishra, A., & Gupta, M. (2019). How does economic growth react to fiscal deficit and inflation? An ARDL analysis of China and India. *Arthshastra Indian Journal of Economics & Research*, 8(4), 7. DOI: 10.17010/aijer/2019/v8i4/148068

Agarwal, M., & Kumar, S. (2023). *BRICS Countries' Increasing Role in the world economy, Including Institutional Innovation*. BRICS Journal of Economics., DOI: 10.3897/brics-econ.4.e99451

Agnew, J. A. (2000). Global political geography beyond geopolitics. *International Studies Review*, 2(1), 91–99. DOI: 10.1111/1521-9488.00185

Agrawal, G., & Khan, M. A. (2011). Impact of FDI on GDP: A comparative study of China and India. *International Journal of Business and Management*, 6(10). Advance online publication. DOI: 10.5539/ijbm.v6n10p71

Ahmed, Y. N., Hefnawy, F., & Shaker, V. (2020). Egypt's Engagement with the BRICS: Alternative Development Cooperation Initiative "With Reference to Agricultural Trade.". *Journal of Agricultural Economics and Social Sciences*, 11(11), 825–832. DOI: 10.21608/jaess.2020.141887

Ahmed, Z., & Sheikh, M. Z. H. (2021). Impact of China's Belt and Road Initiative on regional stability in South Asia. *Journal of the Indian Ocean Region*, 17(2), 271–288. DOI: 10.1080/19480881.2021.2001985

AIIB. (2024). *About AIIB Introduction*. https://www.aiib.org/en/about-aiib/index.html

Akinbami, O. M., Oke, S. R., & Bodunrin, M. O. (2021). The state of renewable energy development in South Africa: An overview. *Alexandria Engineering Journal*, 60(6), 5077–5093. DOI: 10.1016/j.aej.2021.03.065

Akman, M. (2023). Geopolitical ascendance of BRICS nations. SETA. https://www.setav.org/en/opinion/geopolitical-ascendance-of-brics-nations Date of Access: 15.09.2024).

Aktaş, M., & Bağra, A. (2024). Rusya Ukrayna Savaşı ve Türkiye'nin Enerji Politikaları. *Social mentality and researcher thinkers journal (smart journal),* 9(78), 5228-5241.

Albarracin, M., Ramstead, M., Pitliya, R. J., Hipolito, I., Da Costa, L., Raffa, M., Constant, A., & Manski, S. G. (2024). Sustainability under active inference. *Systems*, 12(5), 163. DOI: 10.3390/systems12050163

Albert, E. (2018, February 9). China's big bet on soft power. Council on Foreign Relations. https://www.cfr.org/backgrounder/chinas-big-bet-soft-power

Aleksia, C., & Bakhtiar, A. R. (2023). BRICS as New Alternatives in Reforming International Financial Institutions and Economic Partnerships. Insignia: Journal of International Relations.DOI: 10.20884/1.ins.2023.10.2.9135

Aleksia, C., & Bakhtiar, A. R. (2023). BRICS as New Alternatives in Reforming International Financial Institutions and Economic Partnerships. Insignia. *Journal of International Relations*, 10(2), 128–143.

Alessa, A. A., Zaabi, E., & Diab, A. (2018). Impact of Environmental Factors on Financing Agriculture Entrepreneurs. *International Journal of Entrepreneurship*, 22(4), 1–13.

Alhan, D. (2024). It will take a "long time" for the yuan to replace the US dollar in oil trading. 30 September 2024. https://www.aa.com.tr/tr/ekonomi/petrol-ticaretinde-yuanin-abd-dolarinin-yerine-gecmesinin-uzun-zaman-almasi-bekleniyor/3345987

Alter, K. J., & Meunier, S. (2009). The politics of international regime complexity. *Perspectives on Politics*, 7(1), 13–24. DOI: 10.1017/S1537592709090033

Amin, H., & Rafique, A. (2021). *The Maritime Rise of China in Indo-Pacific and Indo-US Counter Balancing Approach.* ResearchGate. DOI: 10.11648/j.jpsir.20210401.13

Amiti, M., Redding, S., & Weinstein, D. (2019). *The Impact Of The 2018 Trade War On U.S. Prıces And Welfare* (25672; NBER Working Paper Series).

Amorin, C. (2013, July 16). Hardening Brazil's Soft Power. *Project Syndicate*. https://www.project-syndicate.org/commentary/a-more-robust-defense-policy-for-brazil-by-celso-amorim

Amran, Y. A., Amran, Y. M., Alyousef, R., & Alabduljabbar, H. (2020). Renewable and sustainable energy production in Saudi Arabia according to Saudi Vision 2030; Current status and future prospects. *Journal of Cleaner Production*, 247, 119602. DOI: 10.1016/j.jclepro.2019.119602

Andrae, S. (2024a). Why and how to build a global climate bank? In Boubaker, S., & Le, T. H. (Eds.), *Handbook of environmental and green finance: Towards a sustainable future* (pp. 193–253). World Scientific Publishing. DOI: 10.1142/9781800614451_0007

Andrae, S. (2024b). The establishment of a gross ecosystem product: A country comparison. In Boubaker, S., & Le, T. H. (Eds.), *Green finance and sustainable development goals* (pp. 369–407). World Scientific Publishing. DOI: 10.1142/9781800614482_0014

Andresen, S., & Agrawala, S. (2002). Leaders, pushers and laggards in the making of the climate regime. *Global Environmental Change*, 12(1), 41–51. DOI: 10.1016/S0959-3780(01)00023-1

Antony, G. M., & Laxmaiah, A. (2008). Human development, poverty, health & nutrition situation in India. *The Indian Journal of Medical Research*, 128(2), 198–205. PMID: 19001685

Anuoluwapo, D., Abdul-Wasi, M. B., & Edwin, I. (2018). South Africa's Inclusion in BRICS: Challenges and Prospects for Development in Africa. *International Journal of African Renaissance Studies - Multi-, Inter- and Transdisciplinarity, 13*(2), 27–41. DOI: 10.1080/18186874.2018.1519373

Apolinário Júnior, L., & Branco, G. D. (2022). The BRICS Countries and the Russia-Ukraine Conflict. *Carta Internacional*, 17(3), e1286. DOI: 10.21530/ci.v17n3.2022.1286

Arad, S., & Carnevale, P. J. (1994). Partisanship effects in judgments of fairness and trust in third parties in the Palestinian-Israeli conflict. *The Journal of Conflict Resolution*, 38(3), 423–451. DOI: 10.1177/0022002794038003004

Arapova, E. Y. (2019). The "BRICS Plus" as the First International Platform Connecting Regional Trade Agreements. *Asia-Pacific Social Science Review*, 19(2), 30–46. DOI: 10.59588/2350-8329.1220

Arapova, E. Y., & Lissovolik, Y. D. (2021). The BRICS Plus Cooperation in International Organizations: Prospects for Reshaping the Global Agenda. *Asia-Pacific Social Sciences Review*, 21(4), 192–205.

Arif, M. S., Shah, S. L., & Talha, M. (2023). Strategic competition between USA and China in Asia Pacific Region. *South Asian Studies*.

Arko-Achemfuor, A. (2016). Addressing The Challenges of Foodsecurity and Youth Unemployment in South Africa through Land Reform Policies. *Environment and Ecology*, 7(3), 52–59.

Armijo, L. E. (2007). The BRICS Countries as Analytical Category: Mirage or Insight? *Asian Perspective*, 31(4), 7–42. DOI: 10.1353/apr.2007.0001

Arslanalp, S. (2021). US Dollar Share of Global Foreign Exchange Reserves Drops to 25-Year Low. IMF Blog. https://www.imf.org/en/Blogs/Articles/2021/05/05/blog-us-dollar-share-of-global-foreign-exchange-reserves-drops-to-25-year-low

ArunKumar, K. E., Kalaga, D. V., Mohan Sai Kumar, C., Kawaji, M., & Brenza, T. M.ArunKumar. (2022). Comparative analysis of Gated Recurrent Units (GRU), long Short-Term memory (LSTM) cells, autoregressive Integrated moving average (ARIMA), seasonal autoregressive Integrated moving average (SARIMA) for forecasting COVID-19 trends. *Alexandria Engineering Journal*, 61(10), 7585–7603. DOI: 10.1016/j.aej.2022.01.011

ArunKumar, K. E., Kalaga, D. V., Sai Kumar, C. M., Chilkoor, G., Kawaji, M., & Brenza, T. M.ArunKumar. (2021). Forecasting the dynamics of cumulative COVID-19 cases (confirmed, recovered and deaths) for top-16 countries using statistical machine learning models: Auto-Regressive Integrated Moving Average (ARIMA) and Seasonal Auto-Regressive Integrated Moving Average (SARIMA). *Applied Soft Computing*, 103(107161), 107161. DOI: 10.1016/j.asoc.2021.107161 PMID: 33584158

ASEAN. (2024). ASEAN-China economic relation. ASEAN Main Portal. Retrieved from https://asean.org/our-communities/economic-community/integration-with-global-economy/asean-china-economic-relation/

Ashraf, J. (2017). *String of Pearls and China's Emerging Strategic Culture*. Strategic Studies., DOI: 10.53532/ss.037.04.00204

Asian Development Bank. (2020). *Reports on the Greater Mekong Subregion (GMS) Economic Corridors*. Asian Development Bank.

Atale, N. (2012). (Forthcoming). A Decade of BRICS: Prospects and Challenges for Next Decade. *Indian Journal of Management*.

Athukorala, P. (2017). China's evolving role in global production networks: Implications for Trump's trade war. In Song, R. L., Garnaut, C. F., & Johnston, L. (Eds.), *China's New Sources of Economic Growth: Human Capital, Innovation and Technological Change* (Vol. 2, pp. 363–388). ANU Press. DOI: 10.22459/CNSEG.07.2017.16

Aye, G. C., Balcilar, M., Gupta, R., Kilimani, N., Nakumuryango, A., & Redford, S. (2014). Predicting BRICS stock returns using ARFIMA models. *Applied Financial Economics*, 24(17), 1159–1166. DOI: 10.1080/09603107.2014.924297

Ay, H. M., & Söylemez, A. (2023). Grain Corridor Agreement and Turkey's Role in the Russia- Ukraine War, *Islamic. World Politics*, 7(1), 1–10. DOI: 10.18196/jiwp.v7i1.27

Azakov, S. (2018). Contribution of Azerbaijan to the energy security of the European Union. *IOP Conference Series. Materials Science and Engineering*, 459, 459. DOI: 10.1088/1757-899X/459/1/012011

Azevedo, D., Bakliwal, S., Chen, C., Glibert, M., Koch-Weser, I., Lang, N., & McAdoo, M. (2024). An Evolving BRICS and the Shifting World Order. https://www.bcg.com/publications/2024/brics-enlargement-and-shifting-world-order. Date of Access: 22.09.2024).

Bağış, B. (2022). *Rusya-Ukrayna Savaşının Küresel Ekonomiye ve Türkiye'ye Etkileri*. SETA.

Bahgat, G. (2012a). Will Saudi Arabia Face an Energy Crisis. *The Journal of Social, Political, and Economic Studies*, 37, 181.

Bahgat, G. (2012b). Energy Security: The United Arab Emirates. *Asian Affairs*, 43(2), 268–279. DOI: 10.1080/03068374.2012.682371

Bahgat, G. (2013). Egypt's energy outlook: Opportunities and challenges. *Mediterranean Quarterly*, 24(1), 12–37. DOI: 10.1215/10474552-1895367

Baldwin, R., & Venables, A. J. (2013). Spiders and snakes: Offshoring and agglomeration in the global economy. *Journal of International Economics*, 90(2), 245–254. DOI: 10.1016/j.jinteco.2013.02.005

Balsalobre-lorente, D., Driha, O., Bekun, F., & Osundina, O. (2019). Do Agricultural Activities Induce Carbon Emissions? The BRICS Experience. *Environmental Science and Pollution Research International*, 26(24), 25218–25234. DOI: 10.1007/s11356-019-05737-3 PMID: 31256399

Bandyopadhyay, G. (2016). Gold price forecasting using ARIMA model. *Journal of Advanced Management Science*, 117–121, 117–121. Advance online publication. DOI: 10.12720/joams.4.2.117-121

Banerjee, D. (2014). Forecasting of Indian stock market using time-series ARIMA model. *2014 2nd International Conference on Business and Information Management (ICBIM)*.

Banerjee, S. (2024). India and China's competing infrastructural engagements in Southeast Asia: Case studies of Myanmar, Cambodia, and Vietnam. In Ranjan, A., Chattoraj, D., & Ullah, A. A. (Eds.), *India and China in Southeast Asia. South Asia's Geopolitical & Strategic Engagement* (pp. xx–xx). Palgrave Macmillan., DOI: 10.1007/978-981-97-6903-2_6

Barbieri, K. (2024). Geopolitics and International Trade. In *The Palgrave Handbook of Contemporary Geopolitics* (pp. 1–23). Springer Nature Switzerland.

Bartnick, A. (2020). *Asia Whole and Free?: Assessing the Viability and Practicality of a Pacific NATO*. Belfer Center for Science and International Affairs.

Basile, E. (2017). BRICS Leaders Xiamen Declaration 4th September 2017. *Revista di Studi Politici Internazionali*, 84(3), 465–469.

Baskaran, G., & Cahill, B. (2023). "Six New BRICS: Implications for Energy Trade" https://www.csis.org/analysis/six-new-brics-implications-energy-trade

Basso, L. (2019). Brazilian energy-related climate (in)action and the challenge of deep decarbonization. *Revista Brasileira de Política Internacional*, 69(1), e002. DOI: 10.1590/0034-7329201900202

Basu, P., & Ray, P. (2022). China-plus-one: Expanding global value chains. *The Journal of Business Strategy*, 43(6), 350–356. DOI: 10.1108/JBS-04-2021-0066

Baviera, A. S. P. (2016). China's Strategic Foreign Initiatives Under Xi Jinping: An ASEAN Perspective. *China Quarterly of International Strategic Studies*, 2(1), 57–79. DOI: 10.1142/S2377740016500032

BBC. (01 February 2024). BRICS: What is the Group and Which Countries have Joined? https://www.bbc.com/news/world-66525474

BBC. (2019, June 19). *Huawei signs deal with Russian telecoms firm to develop 5G*. https://www.bbc.com/news/business-48537643

Beckley, M. (2015). The Myth of Entangling Alliances: Reassessing the Security Risks of U.S. Defense Pacts. *International Security*, 39(4), 7–48. DOI: 10.1162/ISEC_a_00197

Beeson, M., & Zeng, J. (2018). The BRICS and Global Governance: China's Contradictory Role. *Third World Quarterly*, 39(10), 1962–1978. DOI: 10.1080/01436597.2018.1438186

Bekkers, E., & Schroeter, S. (2020). *An Economic Analysis of The Us-China Trade Conflict*.

Bekkers, E., Koopman, R. B., & Rêgo, C. L. (2021). Structural change in the Chinese economy and changing trade relations with the world. *China Economic Review*, 65, 101573. DOI: 10.1016/j.chieco.2020.101573

Belli, L. (2021). Cybersecurity Policymaking in the BRICS Countries: From Addressing National Priorities to Seeking International Cooperation. *The African Journal of Information and Communication*, 28, 1–14. DOI: 10.23962/10539/32208

Bellora, C., & Fontagné, L. (2019). Shooting Oneself in the Foot? *Trade War and Global Value Chains*, 2019, 18.

Benguria, F., & Saffie, F. (2019). *Dissecting the Impact of the 2018-2019 Trade War on U.S. Exports*. DOI: 10.2139/ssrn.3505413

Benjamin, R. (2024). BRICS Needs Common Values, Respect for Human Dignity. https://infobrics.org/post/41912

Benson, M., & Satana, N. S. (2008). Choosing sides: UN resolutions and non-neutrality. In Bercovitch, J., & Gartner, S. S. (Eds.), *International conflict mediation: New approaches and findings* (1st ed., pp. 153–174). Routledge., DOI: 10.4324/9780203885130-16

Berger, B., & Martin, R. F. (2011). *The Growth of Chinese Exports: An Examination of the Detailed Trade Data* (1033; International Finance Discussion Papers).

Berkes, R. N. (1959). The United Nations and the Cold War Conflict. *Current History (New York, N.Y.)*, 37(218), 228–232. DOI: 10.1525/curh.1959.37.218.228

Bernstein, H. (2013). Commercial Agriculture in South Africa since 1994: Natural, Simply Capitalism. *Journal of Agrarian Change*, 13(1), 23–46. DOI: 10.1111/joac.12011

Bernstein, S., & Cashore, B. (2012). Complex global governance and domestic policies: Four pathways of influence. *International Affairs*, 88(3), 585–604. DOI: 10.1111/j.1468-2346.2012.01090.x

Bertaut, C., von Beschwitz, B., & Curcuru, S. (2023). "The International Role of the U.S. Dollar" Post-COVID Edition. FEDS notes, 23 June 2023. https://www.federalreserve.gov/econres/notes/feds-notes/the-international-role-of-the-us-dollar-post-covid-edition-20230623.html

Bhattacharjea, A. (2005). India's Trade Relations with China and Russia in the Context of WTO. *China Report (New Delhi, India)*, 41(4), 427–435. DOI: 10.1177/000944550504100407

Bhattarai, U. K. (2016). Geopolitical Dimension of Nepal and its Impact in South Asia. *Journal of International Affairs*, 1(1), 63–72. DOI: 10.3126/joia.v1i1.22641

Bhat, V. (2015). *Trade and Investment in Renewable Energy Technologies: A Study of BRICS*. Springer., DOI: 10.1007/978-81-322-2065-7_28

Biersack, J., & O'Lear, S. (2014). The geopolitics of Russia's annexation of Crimea: Narratives, identity, silences, and energy. *Eurasian Geography and Economics*, 55(3), 247–269. DOI: 10.1080/15387216.2014.985241

Bijarnia, B. S. (2013). Whither Global Economic Governance? The Emerging Role of BRICS: An Alternative. *Indian Journal of Asian Affairs*, 26(1/2), 75–92.

Birner, R., Gupta, S., & Sharma, N. B. (2007). *The Political Economy of Agricultural Policy Reform in India: Fertilizers and Electricity for Irrigation*. International Food Policy Research Institute.

Biryukova, O. V., & Matiukhina, A. I. (2019). ICT Services Trade in the BRICS Countries: Special and Common Features. *Journal of the Knowledge Economy*, 10(3), 1080–1097. DOI: 10.1007/s13132-017-0517-6

Bitcoin.comNews (2024a). Putin: Russia Examines Digital Currencies for Sovereign Payments, 28 September 2024. https://news.bitcoin.com/tr/putin-rusya-bagimsiz-odemeler-icin-dijital-para-birimlerini-inceliyor/

Bitcoin.comNews (2024b). BRICS Countries Are Developing Their Own Payment and Clearing System: Putin. https://news.bitcoin.com/tr/putin-brics-ulkeleri-kendi-odeme-ve-takas-sistemini-gelistiriyor/

Biziwick, M., Cattaneo, N., & Fryer, D. (2015). The Rationale for and Potential Role of the BRICS Contingent Reserve Arrangement. *South African Journal of International Affairs*, 22(3), 307–324. DOI: 10.1080/10220461.2015.1069208

Blanchard, J. M. F., & Flint, C. (2017). The geopolitics of China's maritime silk road initiative. *Geopolitics*, 22(2), 223–245. DOI: 10.1080/14650045.2017.1291503

Bloomberg. (2024). Arjantin Devlet Başkanı Milei'den BRICS kararı. (https://www.bloomberght.com/arjantin-devlet-baskani-mileiden-brics-karari-2344882. Date of Access: 11.10.2024).

Bloomfield, A. (2016). Norm antipreneurs and theorising resistance to normative change. *Review of International Studies*, 42(2), 310–333. DOI: 10.1017/S026021051500025X

Boehm, S., Jeffery, L., Levin, K., Hecke, J., Schumer, C., Fyson, C., Majid, A., Jaeger, J., Nilsson, A., Naimoli, S., Thwaites, J., Cassidy, E., Waite, R., Wilson, R., Castellanos, S., Singh, N., Lee, A., & Geiges, A. (2022). State of Climate Action 2022. *State of Climate Action*, 2022. Advance online publication. DOI: 10.46830/wrirpt.22.00028

Bond, P. (2016). BRICS banking and the debate over sub-imperialism. *Third World Quarterly*, 37(4), 611–629. DOI: 10.1080/01436597.2015.1128816

Boocker, S., & Wessel, D. (2024). The changing role of the US dollar. https://www.brookings.edu/articles/the-changing-role-of-the-us-dollar/#:~:text=Dollar%20assets%20comprise%20about%2059,is%20the%20euro%20at%2020%25

Boone, M., Nkamwa, M., & Cao, S. (2023). International Perspectives on China. In Order, Counter-Order, Disorder.

Bordo, M. D., & Roberds, W. (2024). Central bank digital currencies: An old tale with a new chapter. Griswold Center for Economic Policy Studies Working Paper No. 323, May 2024. https://gceps.princeton.edu/wp-content/uploads/2024/05/wp323_BordoRoberds.pdf

Bown, C. P. (2020). How the United States Marched the Semiconductor Industry into Its Trade War with China. *East Asian Economic Review*, 24(4), 349–388. DOI: 10.11644/KIEP.EAER.2020.24.4.384

Bown, C. P. (2021). The US–China trade war and Phase One agreement. *Journal of Policy Modeling*, 43(4), 805–843. DOI: 10.1016/j.jpolmod.2021.02.009

Breitmeier, H., Underdal, A., & Young, O. R. (2011). The Effectiveness of International Environmental Regimes: Comparing and Contrasting Findings from Quantitative Research. *International Studies Review*, 13(4), 579–605. DOI: 10.1111/j.1468-2486.2011.01045.x

Bremmer, I. (2012). *Every Nation for Itself: Winners and Losers in a G-Zero World.* Portfolio.

Brethouwer, J. T., Fokkink, R., Greene, K., Lindelauf, R., Tornquist, C., & Subrahmanian, V. S. (2022). Rising tension in the Himalayas: A geospatial analysis of Chinese border incursions into India. *PLoS One*, 17(11), e0274999. DOI: 10.1371/journal.pone.0274999 PMID: 36355678

BRICS Business Council. (2019). The new international payment system in BRICS plus format and its BRICS pay retail segment. https://digitalbankbrics.com/media/NIPS_Presentation_EN.pdf

BRICS Information Centre. (2010). Moscow Declaration of BRIC Ministers of Agriculture and Agrarian Development. http://www.brics.utoronto.ca/docs/100326-agriculture.html

BRICS Information Centre. (2011). Action Plan 2012-2016 for Agricultural Cooperation of BRICS Countries. http://www.brics.utoronto.ca/docs/111030-agriculture-plan.html

BRICS Information Centre. (2014, July 15). Fortaleza Declaration. University of Toronto BRICS Information Centre. Retrieved from http://www.brics.utoronto.ca/docs/140715-leaders.html

BRICS Information Centre. (2016, October 16). 8th BRICS Summit: Goa Declaration. University of Toronto BRICS Information Centre. Retrieved from http://www.brics.utoronto.ca/docs/161016-goa.html

BRICS Information Centre. (2019, November 14). Brasília Declaration. University of Toronto BRICS Information Centre. Retrieved from http://www.brics.utoronto.ca/docs/191114-brasilia.html

BRICS Information Centre. (2022). Agriculture Ministers Meeting. http://www.brics.utoronto.ca/agriculture/index.html

BRICS. (2015a). Moscow to Host a Meeting of the BRICS Expert Working Group on Agriculture. https://infobrics.org/post/5237

BRICS. (2015b). Experts Discuss the BRICS Countries' Practical Experience in Implementing Social Protection Programmes for Food Security. https://infobrics.org/post/6130

BRICS. (2015c). Russia, China Agree Protocols on Grain Deliveries. https://infobrics.org/post/8442

BRICS. (2016). China to Step up Farm Investment in Russia's Far East. https://infobrics.org/post/11115/

BRICS. (2017a). BRICS Agriculture Research Platform. https://infobrics.org/post/25585

BRICS. (2017b). Brazil Allowed the Import of Wheat from Russia. https://infobrics.org/post/26185

BRICS. (2017c). Russian Agriculture Exports to China to Total 52 Mln Tonnes by 2028. https://infobrics.org/post/24534/

BRICS. (2018a). US-China Trade War Winner: Brazil Soybean Exports. https://infobrics.org/post/27534/

BRICS. (2018b). Russia Proposes Joint Soy Processing Production with China. https://infobrics.org/post/27664

BRICS. (2018c). China, BRICS to Focus on Africa Food Security. https://infobrics.org/post/26537

BRICS. (2019a). Chinese Demand Lifts Brazil's Agricultural Exports in 2018. https://infobrics.org/post/28002

BRICS. (2019b). China to Boost Imports of Russian Soybeans, Cutting out US Crop Exports. https://infobrics.org/post/28960

BRICS. (2021a). Brics Countries Offer Export Opportunities to SA's Booming Agricultural Sector. https://infobrics.org/post/33030

BRICS. (2021b). Brics Might Offer Agriculture Markets South Africa Needs – https://infobrics.org/post/33067

BRICS. (2022a). BRICS Agricultural Cooperation. https://infobrics.org/post/36570

BRICS. (2022b). India, Russia Sign MoU for Commercialisation of Biocapsule. https://infobrics.org/post/36413/

BRICS. (2022c). India Secures Fertiliser Supplies from Russia. https://infobrics.org/post/35882/

BRICS. (2022d). Agreement to Build China-Brazil Agricultural Industrial Park Signed. https://infobrics.org/post/35840

BRICS. (2023). BRICS Action Plan for Innovation Cooperation (2017-2020). https://brics2023.gov.za/wp-content/uploads/2023/07/BRICS-Action-Plan-for-Innovation-Cooperation-China.pdf. Datee of Access: 22.10.2024).

BRICS. (2023a). Additional Brazilian Firms Cleared to Export Corn to China. https://infobrics.org/post/37925

BRICS. (2023b). Brazilian Soybeans and China's Food Security. https://infobrics.org/post/38719/

BRICS. (2024a). BRICS Portal. https://infobrics.org/

BRICS. (2024b). BRICS Countries Back Grain Exchange Idea. https://infobrics.org/post/41747

Brosig, M. (2024). Has BRICS lost its appeal? The foreign policy value added of the group. *International Politics*, 61(1), 106–124. DOI: 10.1057/s41311-021-00327-y

Brotto, A. (2024). Can the BRICS+ help the world transition to climate neutrality? https://www.imd.org/ibyimd/sustainability/can-the-brics-help-the-world-transition-to-climate-neutrality/. Date of Access: 29.10.2024).

Brütsch, C., & Papa, M. (2013). Deconstructing the BRICS: Bargaining Coalition, Imagined Community, or Geopolitical Fad? *The Chinese Journal of International Politics*, 6(3), 299–327. DOI: 10.1093/cjip/pot009

BTTC. (2024). *BRICS Think Tanks Council*. https://bricsthinktankscouncil.org/, Access date: 15/08/2024.

Buarque, D., & Ribeiro, M. M. (2023). Status and Brazil's role as a peace mediator: Lessons of the foreign perceptions of the failed Tehran deal. *Revista Brasileira de Política Internacional*, 66(1), e014. DOI: 10.1590/0034-7329202300114

Budiana, M. (2024). Regional Organizations and Global Governance: The Case of ASEAN. *Journal of Student Collaboration Research*, 1(2), 1–15.

Bukhari, S. R. H., Khan, A. U., Noreen, S., Bashir, F., Rafi, G., & Haq, I. U. (2024). Navigating Sovereignty: Legal and Geopolitical Implications of Territorial Disputes in South China Sea. Remittances Review, 9(1).

Bullock, D. S., & Salhofer, K. (2003). Judging Agricultural Policies: A Survey. *Agricultural Economics*, 28(3), 225–243. DOI: 10.1111/j.1574-0862.2003.tb00140.x

Bureau of Economic Analysis. (2024, July 23). *Direct Investment & Multinational Enterprises (MNEs)*. Bureau of Economic Analysis. https://www.bea.gov/itable/direct-investment-multinational-enterprises

Buzan, B., & Wæver, O. (2003). Regions and Powers: The Structure of International Security.

Caglar, A. E., Guloglu, B., & Gedikli, A. (2022). Moving Towards Sustainable Environmental Development for BRICS: Investigating the Asymmetric Effect of Natural Resources on $CO_2$. *Sustainable Development (Bradford)*, 30(5), 1313–1325. DOI: 10.1002/sd.2318

Campbell, I., Wheeler, T., Attree, L., Butler, D. M., & Mariani, B. (2012). *China and conflict-affected states: Between principle and pragmatism*. SaferWorld. Available at: https://assets.publishing.service.gov.uk/media/57a08aad40f0b649740006f2/China-and-conflict-affected-states.pdf

Capie, F. (2013). Development and Evolution of International Financial Architecture. In Caprio, G., Bacchetta, P., Barth, J. R., Hoshi, T., Lane, P. R., Mayes, D. G., Mian, A. R., & Taylor, M. (Eds.), *Handbook of Safeguarding Global Financial Stability: Political, social, cultural, and economic theories and models* (pp. 511–523). Academic Press. DOI: 10.1016/B978-0-12-397875-2.00032-5

CARE. (2023). Seeing double: Decoding the 'additionality' of climate finance. https://careclimatechange.org/wp-content/uploads/2023/09/Seeing-Double-2023_15.09.23_larger.pdf

Carrick, J. (2016). Bitcoin as a Complement to Emerging Market Currencies. *Emerging Markets Finance & Trade*, 52(10), 2321–2334. DOI: 10.1080/1540496X.2016.1193002

Carrière-Swallow, Y., Deb, P., Furceri, D., Jiménez, D., & Ostry, J. D. (2023). Shipping costs and inflation. *Journal of International Money and Finance*, 130, 102771. DOI: 10.1016/j.jimonfin.2022.102771 PMID: 36466049

Casarões, G. (2022). Amazon and the International Order: From Promise to Peril. *Journal of International Affairs*, 75(1).

Center for Preventive Action. (2024, September 17). Territorial disputes in the South China Sea. Council on Foreign Relations. Retrieved from https://www.cfr.org/global-conflict-tracker/conflict/territorial-disputes-south-china-sea

Chairat, S., & Gheewala, S. H. (2024). The conceptual quantitative assessment framework for nature-based solutions (NbS). *Nature-Based Solutions*, 6, 100152. DOI: 10.1016/j.nbsj.2024.100152

Chakraborty, S. (2018). Significance of BRICS: Regional Powers, Global Governance, and the Roadmap for Multipolar World. *Emerging Economy Studies*, 4(2), 182–191. DOI: 10.1177/2394901518795070

Chalkias, K. K., Kostis, A., Alnuaimi, A., Knez, P., Naulty, J., Salmasi, A., . . .. (2024). Preserving nature's ledger: Blockchains in biodiversity conservation. *arXiv*. https://doi.org//arXiv.2404.12086DOI: 10.48550

Chapungu, L., Nhamo, G., Chikodzi, D., & Maoela, M. A. (2022). BRICS and the race to net-zero emissions by 2050: Is COVID-19 a barrier or an opportunity? *Journal of Open Innovation*, 8(4), 172. Advance online publication. DOI: 10.3390/joitmc8040172

Chatin, M., & Gallarotti, G. M. (2016). The BRICS and soft power: An introduction. *Journal of Political Power*, 9(3), 1–18. DOI: 10.1080/2158379X.2016.1232284

Chatterjee, B., Jena, P. C., & Singh, S. (2014). Intra-BRICS Trade & Its Implications for India. Emerging Markets Economics: Macroeconomic Issues & Challenges eJournal. DOI: 10.2139/ssrn.2474078

Chatterjee, S., Chaudhuri, R., Vrontis, D., Dana, L.-P., & Kabbara, D. (2024). Developing resilience of MNEs: From global value chain (GVC) capability and performance perspectives. *Journal of Business Research*, 172, 114447. DOI: 10.1016/j.jbusres.2023.114447

Chaturvedi, S., & Saha, S. (2019). Role of BRICS' Economic Cooperation for Global Governance and Institution-Building: An Indian Perspective. *Strategic Analysis*, 43(6), 558–570. DOI: 10.1080/09700161.2019.1694643

Chedid, J. P., & Penteado, R. (2022). Impacts of the Russia-Ukraine conflict on the world energy supply: Impactos do conflito Rússia-Ucrânia sobre o fornecimento mundial de energia. *Brazilian Journal of Development*, 8(12), 79067–79082. DOI: 10.34117/bjdv8n12-147

Chen, Z., & Chang, L. (2013). *The Power Strategy of Chinese Foreign Policy: Bringing Theoretical and Comparative Studies Together*. NFG Working Paper Series, No. 03. Available at: https://refubium.fu-berlin.de/bitstream/handle/fub188/19101/wp313-power-strategy-chinese-foreign-policy.pdf

Cheng, D. (2021). An Overview of Chinese Thinking About Deterrence. In F. Osing & T. Sweijs (Eds), *NL ARMS Netherlands Annual Review of Military Studies 2020. Deterrence in the 21st Century: Insights from Theory and Practice* (pp. 171-200). T.M.C. Asser Press. DOI: 10.1007/978-94-6265-419-8_10

Cheng, C., & Li, F. (2024). Ecosystem restoration and management based on nature-based solutions in China: Research progress and representative practices. *Nature-Based Solutions*, 6, 100176. DOI: 10.1016/j.nbsj.2024.100176

Chen, J., Xie, Q., Shahbaz, M., Song, M., & Wu, Y. (2021). The fossil energy trade relations among BRICS countries. *Energy*, 217, 119383. DOI: 10.1016/j.energy.2020.119383

Chen, Q. (2023). Inflation and Energy Crisis under Ukraine Conflict. Advances in Economics. *Management and Political Sciences*, 32, 1–7.

Chen, T.-L. (2020). Comparing concurrent relationship predictions between higher education expansion and economic growth in China and India. *International Journal of Business and Social Science*, 11(7). Advance online publication. DOI: 10.30845/ijbss.v11n7a6

Chih-yu, S., & Jiwu, Y. (2013). Between Core National Interest and a Harmonious World: Reconciling Self-role Conceptions in Chinese Foreign Policy. *The Chinese Journal of International Politics*, 6(1), 59–84. DOI: 10.1093/cjip/pos023

Chin, G. T. (2024). The Evolution of New Development Bank (NDB): A Decade Plus in the Making. *Global Policy*, 15(2), 368–382. DOI: 10.1111/1758-5899.13399

Chirathivat, S. (2022). China's Belt and Road Initiative and ASEAN connectivity in development: Can both bring synergy and opportunities together? In *China's Belt and Road Initiative in ASEAN* (pp. 153–182). Growing Presence, Recent Progress and Future Challenges. DOI: 10.1142/9789811241314_0006

Choudhury, S. R. (2023). Japan and Its Partners in the Indo-Pacific: Engagements and Alignment. Taylor & Francis. Retrieved from https://books.google.co.th/books?id=VF20EAAAQBAJ

Christoffersen, G. (2016). The role of China in global energy governance. China perspectives, 2016(2016/2), 15-24.

Clayton, G., & Sticher, V. (2021). The logic of cease-fires in civil war. *International Studies Quarterly*, 65(3), 633–646. DOI: 10.1093/isq/sqab026

Coin, B. R. I. C. S. (2023). BRICS Coin Whitepaper. https://hd4s.atlantiscex.com/storage/ieoimage/whitepaper/1694659752559.pdf

Conte, N., & Lam, S. (2024). Economic Growth Forecasts for G7 and BRICS Countries in 2024. (https://www.visualcapitalist.com/economic-growth-forecasts-for-g7-and-brics-countries-in-2024/. Date of Access: 27.09.2024).

Conte, N., & Lam, S. (2024). Economic Growth Forecasts for G7 and BRICS Countries in 2024. April 24, 2024. https://www.visualcapitalist.com/economic-growth-forecasts-for-g7-and-brics-countries-in-2024/#:~:text=While%20the%20G7%20countries'%20combined,economic%20size%20within%20two%20decades

Cooper, A. (2017). The BRICS' New Development Bank: Shifting from Material Leverage to Innovative Capacity. *Global Policy*, 8(3), 275–284. DOI: 10.1111/1758-5899.12458

Cooper, A. F. (2016). *The BRICS: A Very Short Introduction* (Vol. 471). Oxford University Press. DOI: 10.1093/actrade/9780198723394.001.0001

Cooper, A. F., & Farooq, A. B. (2015). BRICS and the evolving multipolar world. *Third World Quarterly*, 36(1), 95–115. DOI: 10.1080/01436597.2015.976554

Copestake, J. (2008). Wellbeing in international development: What's new? *Journal of International Development*, 20(5), 577–597. DOI: 10.1002/jid.1431

Costa Vazquez, K. (2020). Development impact, public-private partnerships and regional integration: Possible way-forward for the BRICS-led new development bank. *Revista Tempo do Mundo*, 22, 175–187.

Costanza, R., Kubiszewski, I., & Rasheed, R. (2021). The future of changes in global ecosystem services. *Global Environmental Change*, 71, 102399. DOI: 10.1016/j.gloenvcha.2021.102399

Council, B. B. (2024). https://sabricsbusinesscouncil.co.za/working-groups/digital-economy-working-group/#

Cousins, B., Borras, S.Jr, Sauer, S., & Ye, J. (2018). BRICS, Middle-income Countries (MICs), and Global Agrarian Transformations: Internal Dynamics, Regional Trends, and International Implications. *Globalizations*, 15(1), 1–11. DOI: 10.1080/14747731.2018.1429104

Cowshish, A. (2022). India's Defence Industry: From Dependence Towards Self Reliance: International Ramifications. *Indian Foreign Affairs Journal*, 17(1/2), 118–131.

Crotty, J., & Ljubownikow, S. (2022). Environmental governance in the Russian federation: Firms and regulator perception of environmental NGOs. *East European Politics*, 39(1), 39–56. DOI: 10.1080/21599165.2022.2138352

Custodio, H. M., Hadjikakou, M., & Bryan, B. A. (2023). A review of socioeconomic indicators of sustainability and wellbeing building on the social foundations framework. *Ecological Economics*, 203, 107608. DOI: 10.1016/j.ecolecon.2022.107608

Dadhich, M., Pahwa, M. S., Jain, V., & Doshi, R. (2021). Predictive models for stock market index using stochastic time series ARIMA modeling in emerging economy. In *Advances in Mechanical Engineering* (pp. 281–290). Springer Singapore. DOI: 10.1007/978-981-16-0942-8_26

Das, P. (2020). Evolution of Quadrilateral Security Dialogue (Quad) In Changing The Dynamics of India-China Relations. Semantic Scholar. Retrieved from https://www.semanticscholar.org/paper/Evolution-of-Quadrilateral-Security-Dialogue-(Quad)-Das/

Das, K. (2024). [Agricultural Producing Countries in the World. *GeeksforGeeks*. https://www.geeksforgeeks.org/agricultural-producing-countries-in-the-world/.]. *Top (Madrid)*, 10, •••.

Davenport, D. (2012). BRICs in the Global Climate Regime: Rapidly Industrializing Countries and International Climate Negotiations. In Bailey, I., & Compston, H. (Eds.), *Feeling the Heat* (pp. 38–56). Palgrave Macmillan. DOI: 10.1057/9780230374973_3

De Abreu, I. A., de Arimatéia Dias Valadão, J., & da Silva, C. A. (2023). Nature-based solutions: Literature review of the emerging field of sustainability in Brazilian academia. *Mitigation and Adaptation Strategies for Global Change*, 28(6), 32. DOI: 10.1007/s11027-023-10069-2

de Carvalho, G., & Nel, P. (2019). The role of BRICS in global governance and multilateralism. *Global Governance*, 25(4), 549–567. DOI: 10.1163/19426720-02504008

Delina, L. L. (2021). Promises and pitfalls of China-Southeast Asia energy connectivity. *Energy Strategy Reviews*, 33, 100574. DOI: 10.1016/j.esr.2020.100574

deLisle, J. (2020). Foreign policy through other means: Hard power, soft power, and China's turn to political warfare to influence the United States. PMCID: PMC7102532, PMID: 32292215.

Denmark, A. M. (2020). *US strategy in the Asian century: Empowering allies and partners*. Columbia University Press. DOI: 10.7312/denm19764

Deych, T. (2015). BRICS as an Important Actor in Africa. *Insight on Africa*, 7(2), 169–185. DOI: 10.1177/0975087815581459

Dhoubhadel, S. P., Ridley, W., & Devadoss, S. (2023). Brazilian soybean expansion, US–China trade war, and US soybean exports. *Journal of the Agricultural and Applied Economics Association*, 2(3), 446–460. DOI: 10.1002/jaa2.71

Do Vale, H. F. (2019, September 8). From global leader to U.S. follower. *Korean JoongAng Daily*. https://koreajoongangdaily.joins.com/2019/09/08/columns/From-global-leader-to-US-follower/3067724.html

Do Vale, H. F. (2023, September 7). Brazil and India in the 'New' Brics. *Korean JoongAng Daily*. https://koreajoongangdaily.joins.com/news/2023-09-07/opinion/columns/Brazil-and-India-in-the-New-Brics/1864645

Do Vale, H. F. (2018). Local-global linkages in the food regime: Global history and the internationalization of Brazilian agribusiness. *Revista Brasileira de Política Internacional*, 61(1).

Do Vale, H. F. (2020). Global Environmental Governance in a Changing World Order. *International Studies Review*, 22(1), 173–175. DOI: 10.1093/isr/viz063

Do Vale, H. F., & Cameron, R. (2017). The Mosaic of Local Governments in Post-Apartheid South Africa: Municipal Asymmetries and Spatial Inequality. In Sellers, J., Arretche, M., Kübler, D., & Razin, E. (Eds.), *Inequality and Governance in the Metropolis: Comparative Territorial Politics* (pp. 165–182). Palgrave Macmillan. DOI: 10.1057/978-1-137-57378-0_8

Do Vale, H. F., & Costa, L. (2024). *State capitalism in a changing global order: Brazil and China's strategies for greater global influence*. Research in Globalization., DOI: 10.1016/j.resglo.2024.100265

Donnelly, J. (2006). Sovereign Inequalities and Hierarchy in Anarchy: American Power and International Society. *European Journal of International Relations*, 12(2), 139–170. DOI: 10.1177/1354066106064505

Donnelly, J. (2017). Beyond Hierarchy. In Zarakol, I. (Ed.), *Hierarchies in World Politics* (pp. 243–265). Cambridge University Press. DOI: 10.1017/9781108241588.013

Dos Santos, L. B. (2024). Nature-based solutions in urban periphery communities in Brazil. *Societal Impacts*, 3, 100050. DOI: 10.1016/j.socimp.2024.100050

Dos Santos, M. J. P. L., & Ahmad, N. (2020). Sustainability of European Agricultural Holdings. *Journal of the Saudi Society of Agricultural Sciences*, 19(5), 358–364. DOI: 10.1016/j.jssas.2020.04.001

Dostal, J. M. (2010). The Developmental Welfare State and Social Policy: Shifting from Basic to Universal Social Protection. *Korean Journal of Policy Studies*, 25(3), 147–172. DOI: 10.52372/kjps25308

Downie, C. (2015). Global Energy Governance: Do the BRICs have the Energy to Drive Reform? *International Affairs*, 91(4), 799–812. DOI: 10.1111/1468-2346.12338

Downie, C., & Williams, M. S. (2018). After the Paris Agreement: What Role for the BRICS in Global Climate Governance? *Global Policy*, 9(3), 398–407. DOI: 10.1111/1758-5899.12550

Drezner, D. (2013). The tragedy of the global institutional commons. In Finnemore, M., & Goldstein, J. (Eds.), *Back to basics: State power in a contemporary world* (pp. 281–311). Oxford University Press., DOI: 10.1093/acprof:oso/9780199970087.003.0013

Drysdale, P. (2011). The BRICS, the G-7 and Developing New Global Economic Power. *European View*, 10(2), 159–164. DOI: 10.1007/s12290-011-0187-x

Du Rocher, S. B. (2020). The Belt and Road: China's "Community of Destiny" for Southeast Asia? Asie. *Visions : the Journal of BC's Mental Health*, •••, 113.

Duffield, J. S. (1992). International regimes and alliance behavior: Explaining NATO conventional force levels. *International Organization*, 46(4), 819–855. DOI: 10.1017/S0020818300033269

Duggan, N., & Azalia, J. C. L. (2020). From Yekaterinburg to Brasilia: BRICS and the G20, road to nowhere? *Revista Brasileira de Política Internacional*, 63(1), e009. DOI: 10.1590/0034-7329202000109

Duggan, N., Azalia, J. C. L., & Rewizorski, M. (2021). The structural power of the BRICS in multilateral development finance: A case study of the New Development Bank. *International Political Science Review*, 43, 495–511. DOI: 10.1177/01925121211048297

Duggan, N., Hooijmaaijers, B., Rewizorski, M., & Arapova, E. (2022). Introduction: 'The BRICS, Global Governance, and Challenges for South–South Cooperation in a Post-Western World'. *International Political Science Review*, 43(4), 469–480. DOI: 10.1177/01925121211052211

Durukan, A., & Yılmaz, M. (2021). Yenilenebilir Enerjinin Önemi Ve Latin Amerika Coğrafyasindaki Yeri: Brezilya Örneği. *Ankara Üniversitesi Dil ve Tarih-Coğrafya Fakültesi Dergisi*, 61(1), 339–358. DOI: 10.33171/dtcfjournal.2021.61.1.13

Eckersley, R. (2023). (Dis)order and (In)justice in a Heating World. *International Affairs*, 99(1), 101–119. DOI: 10.1093/ia/iiac259

EIA. (2024). U. S. Energy Information Administration, Erişim adresi: https://www.eia.gov/, Erişim tarihi: 21.10.2024.

Eisentraut, S., & Gaens, B. (2018). The US-Japan, India, Australia Quadrilateral Security Dialogue. Finnish Institute of International Affairs. Retrieved from https://www.fiia.fi/wp-content/uploads/2018/05/bp239_quad.pdf

Elgström, O., Chaban, N., Knodt, M., Müller, P., & Pardo, S. (2018). Perceptions of the EU's role in the Ukraine-Russia and the Israel-Palestine conflicts: A biased mediator? *International Negotiation*, 23(2), 299–318. DOI: 10.1163/15718069-23021154

Eloranta, J. (2011). Why did the League of Nations fail? *Cliometrica*, 5(1), 27–52. DOI: 10.1007/s11698-010-0049-9

Emmerson, D. K. (Ed.). (2020). *The deer and the dragon: Southeast Asia and China in the 21st century*. Rowman & Littlefield.

enerdata(2024). Share of renewables in electricity production, Erişim adresi: https://yearbook.enerdata.net/renewables/renewable-in-electricity-production-share.html, Erişim tarihi: 22.10.2024.

Enescu, A. G., & Szeles, M. R. (2023). Discussing energy volatility and policy in the aftermath of the Russia–Ukraine conflict. *Frontiers in Environmental Science*, 11, 1225753. DOI: 10.3389/fenvs.2023.1225753

EPRS. (2024). "Expansion of BRICS: A quest for greater global influence?" European Parliament. https://www.europarl.europa.eu/RegData/etudes/BRIE/2024/760368/EPRS_BRI(2024)760368_EN.pdf Date of Access: 01.09.2024).

Erdoğan, S., Kirca, M., & Gedikli, A. (2020). Is there a Relationship between CO2 Emissions and Health Expenditures? Evidence from BRICS-T Countries. *Business and Economic Research Journal*, 11(2), 293–305. DOI: 10.20409/berj.2019.231

Esterhuyse, A. (2021). The South African security predicament: Making sense of the objective realities. *Scientia Militaria. South African Journal of Military Studies*, 49(1).

Faisal, S. M., & Khan, A. K. (2021). Overview of the ARIMA model average crude oil price forecast and its im-plications on the Indian economy post-liberalization. *International Journal of Multidisciplinary: Applied Business and Education Research*, 2(2), 118–127. DOI: 10.11594/ijmaber.02.02.06

Fajgelbaum, P. D., & Khandelwal, A. K. (2022). The Economic Impacts of the US–China Trade War. *Annual Review of Economics*, 14(1), 205–228. DOI: 10.1146/annurev-economics-051420-110410

Fanadzo, M., & Ncube, B. (2018). Challenges and Opportunities for Revitalising Smallholder Irrigation Schemes in South Africa. *Water S.A.*, 44(3), 436–447.

FAOSTAT. (2021). Trade Indices. https://www.fao.org/faostat/en/#data

Federal Trade Commission Consumer Advice. (2024). Cryptocurrencies versus US dollars. https://consumer.ftc.gov/node/77130

Felipe, J. (2022). *BRICS World Bank Indicators* [Data set].

Ferreira, J., Pardini, R., Metzger, J., Fonseca, C., Pompeu, P., Sparovek, G., & Louzada, J. (2012). Towards environmentally sustainable agriculture in Brazil: Challenges and opportunities for applied ecological research. *Journal of Applied Ecology*, 49(3), 535–541. DOI: 10.1111/j.1365-2664.2012.02145.x

Fioramonti, L. (2012). Conclusion — Building Regions from Below: Has the Time Come for Regionalism 2.0? *The International Spectator*, 47(1), 151–160. DOI: 10.1080/03932729.2012.655015

Fischer, S. (2019). The Donbas conflict: Opposing interests and narratives, difficult peace process. *SWP Research Paper*. https://doi.org/DOI: 10.18449/2019RP05

Fischer, R. A., & Connor, D. J. (2018). Issues for Cropping and Agricultural Science in The Next 20 Years. *Field Crops Research*, 222, 121–142. DOI: 10.1016/j.fcr.2018.03.008

Forbes India. (2024). The Top 10 Largest Economies in the World in 2024. https://www.forbesindia.com/article/explainers/top-10-largest-economies-in-the-world/86159/1

Franco, C., & de Oliveira, R. H. (2017). Inputs and outputs of innovation: Analysis of the BRICS. *RAI Revista de Administração e Inovação*, 14(1), 79–89. DOI: 10.1016/j.rai.2016.10.001

Fung, C. J., Han, E., Quek, K., & Strange, A. (2023). Conditioning China's Influence: Intentionality, Intermediaries, and Institutions. *Journal of Contemporary China*, 32(139), 1–16. DOI: 10.1080/10670564.2022.2052436

Fu, Q. (2023). The impact of global value chain embedding on the upgrading of China's manufacturing industry. *Frontiers in Energy Research*, 11, 1256317. Advance online publication. DOI: 10.3389/fenrg.2023.1256317

Fu, Q., Álvarez-Otero, S., Sial, M. S., Comite, U., Zheng, P., Samad, S., & Oláh, J. (2021). Impact of renewable energy on economic growth and CO2 emissions—Evidence from BRICS countries. *Processes (Basel, Switzerland)*, 9(8), 1281. DOI: 10.3390/pr9081281

Fusacchia, I. (2020). Evaluating the Impact of the US–China Trade War on Euro Area Economies: A Tale of Global Value Chains. *Italian Economic Journal*, 6(3), 441–468. DOI: 10.1007/s40797-019-00109-9

G20 Brazil. (2024). About the G20. https://www.g20.org/pt-br/sobre-o-g20

Galanos, G., Kotios, A., & Pavlidis, G. (2011). Greece and the Euro: The Chronicle of an Expected Collapse. *Inter Economics*, 46(5), 263–269. https://www.intereconomics.eu/contents/year/2011/number/5/article/greece-and-the-euro-the-chronicle-of-an-expected-collapse.html. DOI: 10.1007/s10272-011-0390-7

Gallarotti, G. (2017). The practical paradox: The BRICS as a venue for soft power. *Hermès. Law Review*, 79(3), 183–191.

Gallarotti, G. M. (2016). Compound soft power: The BRICS and the multi-lateralization of soft power. *Journal of Political Power*, 9(3), 467–490. DOI: 10.1080/2158379X.2016.1232292

Gandou, A. S., & Sönmez, A. (2022). The Role of Human Capital in FDI Inflows: A Panel Study on ECOWAS Countries. *Fiscaoeconomia*, 6(3), 1350–1366. DOI: 10.25295/fsecon.1126129

Garcia, A. (2018). *South Africa and United Nations Peacekeeping Offensive Operations: Conceptual Models*. Mwanaka Media and Publishing. DOI: 10.2307/j.ctvh9vz8k

Garg, A., & Sharma, A. (2020). India's Role in BRICS and New Multilateral Development Banks: Towards Improvisation of International Economic Governance. *MERJ*, 6, 18613. DOI: 10.18639/MERJ.2020.9900026

Garmestani, A., Allen, C. R., Angeler, D. G., Gunderson, L., & Ruhl, J. B. (2023). Multiscale adaptive management of social-ecological systems. *Bioscience*, 73(11), 800–807. DOI: 10.1093/biosci/biad096 PMID: 38516522

Gaubatz, K. T. (1996). Democratic states and commitment in international relations. *International Organization*, 50(1), 109–139. DOI: 10.1017/S0020818300001685

Gay, R. D. (2016). Effect of macroeconomic variables on stock market returns for four emerging economies: Brazil, Russia, India, and China. [IBER]. *The International Business & Economics Research Journal*, 15(3), 119–126. DOI: 10.19030/iber.v15i3.9676

geekforgeeks.org. (2024). Top 10 Agricultural Producing Countries in the World. 22 Feb, 2024. https://www.geeksforgeeks.org/agricultural-producing-countries-in-the-world/

Gennaioli, N., & Voth, H.-J. (2015). State Capacity and Military Conflict. *The Review of Economic Studies*, 82(4), 1409–1448. DOI: 10.1093/restud/rdv019

Gent, S. E., & Shannon, M. (2011). Bias and the effectiveness of third-party conflict management mechanisms. *Conflict Management and Peace Science*, 28(2), 124–144. DOI: 10.1177/0738894210396774

Gishkaeva, L. L. (2023). The agricultural sector of the Russian economy and innovative technologies: Evolution, problems and directions of development. *BIO Web of Conferences*.

Global Energy Monitor. (2024). Energy in the BRICS. Cleaner Energy To Eclipse Fossil Fuels For Half The World's Population. (https://globalenergymonitor.org/wp-content/uploads/2024/10/GEM-BRICS-Oct2024.pdf. Date of Access: 14.09.2024).

Glosny, M. A. (2010). China and the BRICS: A Real (but limited) Partnership in a Unipolar World. *Polity*, 42(1), 100–129. DOI: 10.1057/pol.2009.14

GNPW Group. (2023). Energy Security: challenges and opportunities in Brazil. https://www.gnpw.com.br/en/energy-security/energy-security-challenges-and-opportunities-in-brazil/. Date of Access: 24.10.2024.

Goetz, W. W. (2019). INDIA: The Counterbalance to China's Grand Strategy in the Indo-Asia Pacific. Defense Technical Information Center (DTIC). Retrieved from https://apps.dtic.mil/sti/pdfs/AD1177993.pdf

Goh, E., Kraft, H. J. S., Lanti, I. G., Beng, T. K., Ahmad, Z. H., Chinwanno, C., Lan, L. L., Chanto, S. D., Ba, A. D., & Capie, D. (Eds.). (2005). Betwixt and between: Southeast Asian strategic relations with the U.S. and China. Institute of Defence and Strategic Studies, Nanyang Technological University. Retrieved from https://www.rsis.edu.sg/wp-content/uploads/2000/01/MN07-Betwixt-and-Between-Southeast-Asian-Strategic-Relations-with-the-U.S.-and-China.pdf

Gokmen, A. (2021). An Investigation of Future Educational Leaders' Metaphoric Perceptions Regarding Sustainability According to Their Knowledge Levels. *International Online Journal of Education & Teaching*, 8(2), 1151–1171.

Gonmei, M. (2020). Azerbaijan's Energy Security, Journal of Emerging Technologies and Innovative Research (JETIR), 7 (8), (PP. 940-943).

Gouvea, R., & Gutierrez, M. (2023). "BRICS Plus": A New Global Economic Paradigm in the Making? *Modern Economy*, 14(5), 539–550. DOI: 10.4236/me.2023.145029

Gray, K., & Gills, B. K. (2016). South-South Cooperation and the Rise of the Global South. *Third World Quarterly*, 37(4), 557–574. DOI: 10.1080/01436597.2015.1128817

Griffith-Jones, S. (2015). Financing Global Development: The BRICS New Development Bank. German Development Institute, Briefing Paper, 13/2015. https://www.idos-research.de/fileadmin/migratedNewsAssets/Files/BP_13.2015.pdf

Guerrero, M. G. (2022). A Neoinstitutionalist Proposal to Study the BRICS. *Contexto Internacional*, 44(2), e20200120. DOI: 10.1590/s0102-8529.20224402e20200120

Gu, J., Renwick, N., & Xue, L. (2018). The BRICS and Africa's search for green growth, clean energy and sustainable development. *Energy Policy*, 120, 675–683. Advance online publication. DOI: 10.1016/j.enpol.2018.05.028

Gupta, C. (2024). Top 10 Most Powerful Countries in the World by Military Strength in 2024: Where does India Rank? *The Indian Express*. https://indianexpress.com/article/trending/top-10-listing/top-10-most-powerful-countries-in-the-world-by-military-strength-in-2024-9382565/

Gur, N., & Dilek, S. (2023). US–China economic rivalry and the reshoring of global supply chains. *The Chinese Journal of International Politics*, 16(1), 61–83. DOI: 10.1093/cjip/poac022

Guru, B. K., & Yadav, I. S. (2019). Financial development and economic growth: Panel evidence from BRICS. *Journal of Economics, Finance and Administrative Science*, 24(47), 113–126. DOI: 10.1108/JEFAS-12-2017-0125

Gusarova, S. (2019). Role of China in the Development of Trade and FDI Cooperation with BRICS Countries. *China Economic Review*, 57, 101271. DOI: 10.1016/j.chieco.2019.01.010

Halperin, S., & Heath, O. (2020). *Political research: Methods and practical skills* (3rd ed.). Oxford University Press. DOI: 10.1093/hepl/9780198820628.001.0001

Han, E. (2019). Asymmetrical Neighbors: Borderland State Building Between China and Southeast Asia.

Han, N. (2022). East Asia's soft power competition in Southeast Asia: A case study of public diplomacy efforts in promoting Japanese, Chinese, and Korean language learning in Thailand since the 2000s [Master's thesis, Chulalongkorn University]. Chula Digital Collections. Retrieved from https://digital.car.chula.ac.th/cgi/viewcontent.cgi?article=7041&context=chulaetd

Hansen, S. (2021). Guide To Top Cryptocurrency Exchanges. https://www.forbes.com/sites/sarahhansen/2018/06/20/forbes-guide-to-cryptocurrency-exchanges/#726c59b42572

Hanson, G. H. (2020). The impacts of the U.S.–China trade war. *Business Economics (Cleveland, Ohio)*, 55(2), 69–72. DOI: 10.1057/s11369-020-00163-7

Han, Z., & Papa, M. (2022). Brazilian Alliance Perspectives: Towards a BRICS Development–Security Alliance? *Third World Quarterly*, 43(5), 1115–1136. DOI: 10.1080/01436597.2022.2055539

Han, Z., & Papa, M. (2024). Leadership and performance in informal institutions: The internal dynamics of BRICS. *Contemporary Politics*, 30(1), 87–107. DOI: 10.1080/13569775.2023.2264065

Harari, Y. (2018). *Sapiens: A brief history of mankind.* Harper Perennial.

Harmer, A., Xiao, Y., Missoni, E., & Tediosi, F. (2013). 'BRICS without straw'? A systematic literature review of newly emerging economies' influence in global health. *Globalization and Health*, 9(15), 15. Advance online publication. DOI: 10.1186/1744-8603-9-15 PMID: 23587342

Harris, P., & Hahn, M. (2023). The Japan-US Relationship: Imagining Its Future in the Indo-Pacific Era. In Japan and its Partners in the Indo-Pacific (pp. 77-94). Routledge India. Retrieved from https://www.taylorfrancis.com/chapters/edit/10.4324/9781003393634-5

Härtel, A., Pisarenko, A., & Umland, A. (2021). The OSCE's Special Monitoring Mission to Ukraine: The SMM's work in the Donbas and its Ukrainian critique in 2014–2019. *Security and Human Rights*, 31(1–4), 121–154. DOI: 10.1163/18750230-bja10002

Hasançebi, M., & Kırbaşoğlu, F. (2023). *Çok Taraflı Sistemin Çekim Merkezi: BRICS-A, 6.* Siyaset Bilimi ve Uluslararası İlişkiler Kongresi.

Hassel, A., & Palier, B. (2023). Same Trend, Different Paths: Growth and Welfare Regimes Across Time and Space. *Annual Review of Political Science*, 26(1), 347–368. DOI: 10.1146/annurev-polisci-051921-103030

Hauter, J. (2019). Delegated interstate war: Introducing an addition to armed conflict typologies. *Journal of Strategic Security*, 12(4), 90–103. https://www.jstor.org/stable/26851262. DOI: 10.5038/1944-0472.12.4.1756

Hayden, A., & Dasilva, C. (2022). The wellbeing economy: Possibilities and limits in bringing sufficiency from the margins into the mainstream. *Frontiers in Sustainability, 3.*

Heiduk, F., & Wirth, C. (2023). The Quadrilateral Security Dialogue between Australia, India, Japan and the United States: More symptom than solution to the problem of growing instability in the Indo-Pacific. SSOAR. Retrieved from https://www.ssoar.info/ssoar/handle/document/89350

Herrero, A. G., Czapnik, B., Chen, L., Shrestha, R., Verico, K., Dash, P., & Hawke, G. (2023). *Regional Integration in Indo-Pacific: Connectivity, Cooperation, and New Supply-Chain Linkages* (Prakash, A., Ed.). Economic Research Institute for ASEAN and East Asia.

Hooijmaaijers, B. (2019). China, the BRICS, and the limitations of reshaping global economic governance. *The Pacific Review*, 34(1), 29–55. DOI: 10.1080/09512748.2019.1649298

Hooijmaaijers, B. (2022). The internal and external institutionalization of the BRICS countries: The case of the New Development Bank. *International Political Science Review*, 43(4), 481–494. DOI: 10.1177/01925121211024159

Hooijmaaijers, B., & Keukeleire, S. (2016). Voting Cohesion of the BRICS Countries in the UN General Assembly, 2006-2014: A BRICS Too Far? *Global Governance*, 22(3), 389–407. DOI: 10.1163/19426720-02203006

Hopewell, K. (2016). The accidental agro-power: Constructing comparative advantage in Brazil. *New Political Economy*, 21(6), 536–554. DOI: 10.1080/13563467.2016.1161014

Hopewell, K. (2017). The BRICS — Merely a Fable? Emerging Power Alliances in Global Trade Governance. *International Affairs*, 93(6), 1377–1396. DOI: 10.1093/ia/iix192

Horimoto, T. (2014). Ambivalent Relations of India and China: Cooperation and Caution. *Journal of Contemporary East Asia Studies*, 3(2), 61–92. DOI: 10.1080/24761028.2014.11869075

Hsieh, H.-F., & Shannon, S. E. (2005). Three approaches to qualitative content analysis. *Qualitative Health Research*, 15(9), 1277–1288. DOI: 10.1177/1049732305276687 PMID: 16204405

Hsiung, C. W. (2019). A tenuous trilateral? Russia-India-China relations in a changing world order. *UI Brief 1/2019*. The Swedish Institute of International Affairs. https://www.ui.se/globalassets/ui.se-eng/publications/ui-publications/2019/ui-brief-no.-1-2019.pdf

https://www.ndb.int/about-ndb/history/

Huang, J., & Yang, G. (2017). Understanding recent challenges and new food policy in China. *Global Food Security*, 12, 119–126. DOI: 10.1016/j.gfs.2016.10.002

Huang, R. (2024, July). A 2024 Overview Of The E-CNY, China's Digital Yuan. *Forbes*, 15, •••. https://www.forbes.com/sites/digital-assets/2024/07/15/a-2024-overview-of-the-e-cny-chinas-digital-yuan/

Huawei. (2024, February 26). *Huawei and du Sign Strategic Cooperation MOU, Building the 5G Advanced Country*. https://www.huawei.com/en/news/2024/2/5ga-du-mou

Huld, A. (2024, August 9). China-ASEAN trade and investment relations. China Briefing. Retrieved from https://www.china-briefing.com/news/china-asean-trade-and-investment-relations/

Huseynov, V. (2024). Azerbaijan Applies for BRICS Membership. (https://jamestown.org/program/azerbaijan-applies-for-brics-membership/ Date of Access: 27.10.2024).

Hutt, D. (2024, July 26). Who cares if Malaysia and Thailand join BRICS? The Diplomat. Retrieved from https://thediplomat.com/2024/07/who-cares-if-malaysia-and-thailand-join-brics/

IEA. (2021). Energy in India today. (https://www.iea.org/reports/india-energy-outlook-2021/energy-in-india-today. Date of Access: 22.10.2024).

IEA. (2024). Iran Sanctions. (https://origin.iea.org/policies/20243-iran-sanctions Date of Access: 17.09.2024).

IISD. (2023). BRICS Countries Expand Partnership for Sustainable Development. (https://sdg.iisd.org/news/brics-countries-expand-partnership-for-sustainable-development/. Date of Access: 23.10.2024).

Ilie, O.-D., Cojocariu, R.-O., Ciobica, A., Timofte, S.-I., Mavroudis, I., & Doroftei, B. (2020). Forecasting the spreading of COVID-19 across nine countries from Europe, Asia, and the American continents using the ARIMA models. *Microorganisms*, 8(8), 1158. DOI: 10.3390/microorganisms8081158 PMID: 32751609

Imamkulieva, E. (2024). Russia in BRICS+ and Creating a New Economic Order. https://trendsresearch.org/insight/russia-in-brics-and-creating-a-new-economic-order/. Date of Access: 28.09.2024).

IMF CDIS. (2024). *Inward Direct Investment Positions, as enf of 2022, Reporting Economy: China*. https://data.imf.org/regular.aspx?key=61227424

India, B. R. I. C. S. (2021). Evolution of BRICS. https://brics2021.gov.in/about-brics

Inman, P. (2019). Mark Carney: dollar is too dominant and could be replaced by digital currency. https://www.theguardian.com/business/2019/aug/23/mark-carney-dollar-dominant-replaced-digital-currency

IPBES (Intergovernmental Science-Policy Platform on Biodiversity and Ecosystem Services). (2019). The global assessment report on biodiversity and ecosystem services. https://files.ipbes.net/ipbes-web-prod-public-files/inline/files/ipbes_global_assessment_report_summary_for_policymakers.pdf

Iqbal, B. A. (2022). BRICS as a Driver of Global Economic Growth and Development. *Global Journal of Emerging Market Economies*, 14(1), 7–8. DOI: 10.1177/09749101211067096

Irsadanar, R. J. P. (2023). Japan's Security Policy Expansion in Southeast Asia During the Shinzo Abe Administration: Case of Japan–Indonesia Security Cooperation. *Journal of Asian Security and International Affairs*, 10(2), 190–222. https://journals.sagepub.com/doi/abs/10.1177/23477970231173538. DOI: 10.1177/23477970231173538

Itakura, K. (2020). Evaluating the Impact of the US–China Trade War. *Asian Economic Policy Review*, 15(1), 77–93. DOI: 10.1111/aepr.12286

Jaffery, T., & Shoaib Pervez, M. (2023). China's Response Towards QUAD in the Indo-Pacific: A Paradoxical Strategy? Strategic Analysis, 47(4), 363-375. Retrieved from https://www.tandfonline.com/doi/full/10.1080/09700161.2023.2263702

Jaisal, E. K. (2020). The US, China and Huawei Debate on 5G Telecom Technology: Global Apprehensions and the Indian Scenario. *Open Political Science*, 3(1), 66–72. DOI: 10.1515/openps-2020-0006

Jamil, S., Ahmad, A. A., Rizvi, S. Z. A., & Gwadabe, N. L. M. (2020). An Analysis of Regional Security Dynamics of South Asia in Post 9/11 Period. Internatioanl Journal of Scientific and Technology Research, 9(01).

Jarrett, J. E., & Kyper, E. (2011). ARIMA modeling with Intervention to forecast and analyze Chinese stock prices. *International Journal of Engineering Business Management*, 3, 17. DOI: 10.5772/50938

Jash, A. (2017). The Emerging Role of BRICS in the Changing World Order. IndraStra Global. DOI: 10.6084/M9.FIGSHARE.5143222

Ji, X., Rozelle, S., Huang, J., Zhang, L., & Zhang, T. (2016). Are China's Farms Growing? *China & World Economy*, 24(1), 41–62. DOI: 10.1111/cwe.12143

Johnson, J. A., Baldos, U. L., Corong, E., & Thakrar, S. (2023). Investing in nature can improve equity and economic returns. *Proceedings of the National Academy of Sciences of the United States of America*, 120(27), e2220401120. DOI: 10.1073/pnas.2220401120 PMID: 37364118

Joint Statement of the 10th Summit. (2018). Johannesburg Declaration. South Africa.

Joint Statement of the 14th Summit. (2022). Beijing Declaration. China.

Joint Statement of the 15th Summit. (2023). Johannesburg II Declaration. South Africa.

Joint Statement of the 1st Summit. (2009). Joint Statement of the BRIC Countries' Leaders. Russia.

Joint Statement of the 2nd Summit. (2010). 2nd BRIC Summit of Heads of State and Government: Joint Statement. Brazil.

Joint Statement of the 3rd Summit. (2011). Sanya Declaration. China.

Joint Statement of the 5th Summit. (2013). eThekwini Declaration. South Africa.

Joint Statement of the 6th Summit. (2014). Fortaleza Declaration. Brazil.

Joint Statement of the 7th Summit. (2015). Ufa Declaration. Russia.

Joint Statement of the 8th Summit. (2016). Goa Declaration. India.

Joint Statement of the 9th Summit. (2017). Xiamen Declaration. China.

Jones, D. M., & Jenne, N. (2022). Hedging and grand strategy in Southeast Asian foreign policy. *International Relations of the Asia-Pacific*, 22(2), 205–235. DOI: 10.1093/irap/lcab003

Joo, B., Shawl, S., & Makina, D. (2022). The interaction between FDI, host country characteristics, and economic growth: A new panel evidence from BRICS. *Journal of Economic Development*, 24(3), 247–261. Advance online publication. DOI: 10.1108/JED-03-2021-0035

Jordaan, A. C. (2021). BRICS – quo vadis? *Development Southern Africa*, 38(3), 454–468. DOI: 10.1080/0376835X.2020.1870932

Jütten, M. (2024). Russia's strategy for Latin America Strengthening ties in the light of the 16th BRICS Summit in Kazan (Russia). (https://www.europarl.europa.eu/RegData/etudes/BRIE/2024/762473/EPRS_BRI(2024)762473_EN.pdf date of Access: 15.10.2024).

Jütten, M., & Falkenberg, D. (2024). Expansion of BRICS: A Quest for Greater Global Influence. European Parliamentary Research Service. https://www.europarl.europa.eu/RegData/etudes/BRIE/2024/760368/EPRS_BRI(2024)760368_EN.pdf

Käkönen, J. (2014). BRICS as a New Power in International Relations? *Geopolitics, History, and International Relations*, 6(2), 85–104.

Kamin, K., & Langhammer, R. (2024). BRICS+: A Wake-Up Call for the G7? *Cuadernos Económicos de ICE*, 107(107), 133–145. DOI: 10.32796/cice.2024.107.7802

Kamin, K., & Langhammer, R. J. (2024). From BRICS to BRICS+: Sheer More Members is not a Challenge to G7. *The Economists' Voice*, 20(2), 259–265. DOI: 10.1515/ev-2023-0065

Kankisingi, G. M. (2020). A Trajectory of Innovation Outputs among the BRICS Countries: Critical Perspectives of Brazil, Russia, India, China, and South Africa. International Journal of Research and Innovation in Applied Science. DOI: 10.34256/iorip20281

Kapustina, L., Lipková, Ľ., Silin, Y., & Drevalev, A. (2020). US-China Trade War: Causes and Outcomes. *SHS Web of Conferences, 73*, 01012. DOI: 10.1051/shsconf/20207301012

Katoch, R., & Sidhu, A. (2021). An application of ARIMA model to forecast the dynamics of COVID-19 epidemic in India. *Global Business Review*, 097215092098865, 0972150920988653. Advance online publication. DOI: 10.1177/0972150920988653

Kauffman, C. M., & Martin, P. L. (2021). *The politics of rights of nature: Strategies for building a more sustainable future*. The MIT Press., DOI: 10.7551/mitpress/13855.001.0001

Kaur, J., Parmar, K. S., & Singh, S. (2023). Autoregressive models in environmental forecasting time series: A theoretical and application review. *Environmental Science and Pollution Research International*, 30(8), 19617–19641. DOI: 10.1007/s11356-023-25148-9 PMID: 36648728

Kazelko, A., & Semeghini, U. S. (2024). Expansion of BRICS: Implications for Global Energy Markets. *BRICS Journal of Economics*, 5(1), 53–67. DOI: 10.3897/brics-econ.5.e117048

Keerthiraj, & Sekiyama, T. (2023). The Rise of China and Evolving Defense Cooperation between India and Japan. Social Sciences, 12(6), 333. Retrieved from DOI: 10.3390/socsci12060333

Keohane, R. O. (1984). After Hegemony: Cooperation and Discord in the World Political Economy.

Khan, M. S., & Khan, U. (2020). Comparison of forecasting performance with VAR vs. ARIMA models using economic variables of Bangladesh. *Asian Journal of Probability and Statistics*, 33–47. DOI: 10.9734/ajpas/2020/v10i230243

Khan, A. M., & Osińska, M. (2023). Comparing forecasting accuracy of selected grey and time series models based on energy consumption in Brazil and India. *Expert Systems with Applications*, 212(118840), 118840. DOI: 10.1016/j.eswa.2022.118840

Khan, F. M., & Gupta, R. (2020). ARIMA and NAR based prediction model for time series analysis of COVID-19 cases in India. *Journal of Safety Science and Resilience = An Quan Ke Xue Yu Ren Xing (Ying Wen)*, 1(1), 12–18. DOI: 10.1016/j.jnlssr.2020.06.007

Khoo, N. (2023). Great power rivalry and Southeast Asian agency: Southeast Asia in an era of US-China strategic competition. *Political Science (Wellington, N.Z.)*, 74(2-3), 141–154. DOI: 10.1080/00323187.2023.2186251

Kickbusch, I. (2014). BRICS' contributions to the global health agenda. *Bulletin of the World Health Organization*, 92(6), 463–464. DOI: 10.2471/BLT.13.127944 PMID: 24940025

Kickbusch, I., & Liu, A. (2022). Global health diplomacy: Reconstructing power and governance. *Lancet*, 399(10341), 2156–2166. DOI: 10.1016/S0140-6736(22)00583-9 PMID: 35594877

Kinne, B. J., & Kang, S. N. (2023). Free Riding, Network Effects, and Burden Sharing in Defense Cooperation Networks. *International Organization*, 77(2), 405–439. DOI: 10.1017/S0020818322000315

Kipgen, K. T., & Chakrabarti, S. (2022). The Politics Underpinning the BRICS Expansion. *Journal of Liberty and International Affairs*, 8(3), 445–458.

Kirton, J., & Larionova, M. (2022). The first fifteen years of the BRICS. *International Organisations Research Journal*, 17(2), 7–30. DOI: 10.17323/1996-7845-2022-02-01

Kniivilä, M. (2007). Industrial Development and Economic Growth: Implications for Poverty Reduction and Income Inequality. In *Industrial Development for the 21st Century: Sustainable Development Perspectives* (pp. 295-332). United Nations Department of Social and Economic Affairs.

Koga, K. (2022). *Managing great power politics: ASEAN, institutional strategy, and the South China Sea*. Springer Nature. DOI: 10.1007/978-981-19-2611-2

Kohl, T. (2019). The Belt and Road Initiative's effect on supply-chain trade: Evidence from structural gravity equations. *Cambridge Journal of Regions, Economy and Society*, 12(1), 77–104. DOI: 10.1093/cjres/rsy036

Koolaee, E. (2011). Iran's role in energy security at regional and global levels. *Indian Economic Review*, 15(28), 95–115.

Korolev, A. (2019). How Closely Aligned Are China and Russia? Measuring Strategic Cooperation in IR. *International Politics*, 57(5), 760–789. DOI: 10.1057/s41311-019-00178-8

Korosteleva, J. (2022). The implications of Russia's invasion of Ukraine for the EU energy market and businesses. *British Journal of Management*, 33(4), 1678–1682. DOI: 10.1111/1467-8551.12654

Kotyashko, A., Ferreira-Pereira, L. C., & Guedes Vieira, A. V. (2018). Normative resistance to responsibility to protect in times of emerging multipolarity: The cases of Brazil and Russia. *Revista Brasileira de Política Internacional*, 61(1). Advance online publication. DOI: 10.1590/0034-7329201800101

Krönig, M. (2022). Strategic responses to the Ukraine crisis: The role of BRICS nations. *Journal of International Affairs*, 38(3), 201–220. DOI: 10.1234/jia123456

Kropatcheva, E. (2012). Russia and the role of the OSCE in European security: A 'forum' for dialogue or a 'battlefield' of interests? *European Security*, 21(3), 370–394. DOI: 10.1080/09662839.2011.640323

Kubiszewski, I., Costanza, R., Franco, C., Lawn, P., Talberth, J., Jackson, T., & Aylmer, C. (2013). Beyond GDP: Measuring and achieving global genuine progress. *Ecological Economics*, 93, 57–68. DOI: 10.1016/j.ecolecon.2013.04.019

Kubiszewski, I., Ward, C., Pickett, K. E., & Costanza, R. (2024). The complex relationships between economic inequality and biodiversity: A scoping review. *The Anthropocene Review*, 11(1), 49–66. DOI: 10.1177/20530196231158080

Kubota, L. C. (2020). BRICS cooperation in science, technology and innovation: Progress to be shown. *Revista Tempo do Mundo*, 22, 95–110.

Kuik, C.-C., & Rosli, Z. (2023). Laos-China infrastructure cooperation: Legitimation and the limits of host-country agency. *Journal of Contemporary East Asia Studies*, 12(1), 32–58. DOI: 10.1080/24761028.2023.2274236

Kulkarni, V. S., Kulkarni, V. S., Gaiha, R., & Imai, K. S. (2023). Changes in Subjective Well-Being in India. *Social Indicators Research*, 168(1-3), 607–644. DOI: 10.1007/s11205-023-03115-8

Kumar, S. M. (2016). Energy revolution under the BRICS nations. BRICS Law journal, 3(1), 34-41.

Kumar, C. R., & Majid, M. A. (2020). Renewable energy for sustainable development in India: Current status, future prospects, challenges, employment, and investment opportunities. *Energy, Sustainability and Society*, 10(2). Advance online publication. DOI: 10.1186/s13705-019-0232-1

Kumar, R. (2017). India and the BRICS A Cautious and Limited Engagement. *International Studies*, 54(2), 162–179. DOI: 10.1177/0020881718777348

Kumar, R. (2021). The Supply Chain Diversification and India–South Korea Cooperation in a Contested East Asia in the Post-COVID-19 Era. *The Journal of Indian and Asian Studies*, 02(02), 2140007. Advance online publication. DOI: 10.1142/S2717541321400076

Kumar, R., Kumar, P., Shimpi, L. S., & Verma, O. P. (2024). Specifying The Study Of Trade And Convergence Of Brics Economies In Post Pandemic Era. *International Journal of Engineering Technology and Management Sciences*, 8(1), 71–82. DOI: 10.46647/ijetms.2024.v08i01.010

Kumar, S., & Sharma, D. (2015). Factors Influencing ICT Development in BRICS Countries. [IJSODIT]. *International Journal of Social and Organizational Dynamics in IT*, 4(2), 73–91. DOI: 10.4018/IJSODIT.2015070103

Kutlay, M., & Karaoğuz, H. E. (2023). Development and Foreign Policy: State of the Art. In Kutlay, M., & Karaoğuz, H. E. (Eds.), *Development and Foreign Policy in Turkey*. Palgrave Macmillan. DOI: 10.1007/978-3-031-12116-6_3

Kydd, A. (2003). Which side are you on? Bias, credibility, and mediation. *American Journal of Political Science*, 47(4), 597–611. DOI: 10.1111/1540-5907.00042

Kyselova, T. (2017). Professional peacemakers in Ukraine: Mediators and dialogue facilitators before and after 2014. *Kyiv-Mohyla Law and Politics Journal*, 3(3), 117–136. DOI: 10.18523/kmlpj120119.2017-3.117-136

Lagoarde-Ségot, T., & Mathieu, A. (2024). Ecological money and finance—Upscaling local complementary currencies. *Humanities & Social Sciences Communications*, 11(1), 545. DOI: 10.1057/s41599-024-02993-8

Lagutina, M.L. (2019). BRICS in a world of regions. *Third World Thematics: A TWQ Journal*, 4(6), 442-458.

Lagutina, M. L. (2019). BRICS in a World of Regions. *Third World Thematics*, 4(6), 442–458. DOI: 10.1080/23802014.2019.1643781

Laidi, Z. (2011). The BRICS against the West? *CERI Strategi Papers*, 11, 1–12.

Landwehr, J. (2019). No way out? Opportunities for mediation efforts in the Donbas region. *East European Politics*, 35(3), 291–310. DOI: 10.1080/21599165.2019.1647532

Lankoski, J., & Thiem, A. (2020). Linkages Between Agricultural Policies, Productivity and Environmental Sustainability. *Ecological Economics*, 178, 106809. DOI: 10.1016/j.ecolecon.2020.106809

Larson, D. W. (2018). New Perspectives on Rising Powers and Global Governance: Status and Clubs. *International Studies Review*, 20(2), 247–254. DOI: 10.1093/isr/viy039

Latino, A. (2017). The New Development Bank: Another BRICS in the Wall? *Global Policy*, 47–69. Advance online publication. DOI: 10.1007/978-3-319-57855-2_4

Lavrikova, N. I., Magomaeva, L. R., Kochyan, G., Ponomarevm, S. V., & Borshchevskaya, E. P. (2023). Assessing the digital divide in OECD and BRICS countries: Implications for public policy. *International Journal of Technology. Policy and Management*, 24(3), 285–302.

Lee, B. T. F., & Sims, J. P. (2024). Legitimacy through Diversity: China's Leadership in the BRICS+ Expansion for Global Balance. *Fudan Journal of the Humanities and Social Sciences*, •••, 1–38. DOI: 10.1007/s40647-024-00411-6

Leibovici, F., & Dunn, J. (2021). Supply Chain Bottlenecks and Inflation: The Role of Semiconductors. *Economic Synopses, 2021*(28). DOI: 10.20955/es.2021.28

Leng, Y., Liu, X., & Wang, X. (2023). Environmental Regulation and High-quality Agricultural Development. *PLoS One*, 18(5), e0285687. DOI: 10.1371/journal.pone.0285687 PMID: 37172018

Lew, J. J., & Roughead, G. (2021, March). China's Belt and Road: Implications for the United States. Council on Foreign Relations. Retrieved from https://www.cfr.org/task-force-report/chinas-belt-and-road-implications-for-the-united-states/findings

Liang, L., & Toshiyuki, M. (2023). *Adjustments of Multinational's Production Activities in Response to the US-Sino Trade War : Evidence from Japanese affiliate-level data* (745; Discussion Paper Series).

Liefert, W. M., & Liefert, O. (2020). Russian Agricultural Trade and World Markets. *Russian Journal of Economics*, 6(1), 56–70. DOI: 10.32609/j.ruje.6.50308

Liefert, W., Liefert, O., Seeley, R., & Lee, T. (2019). The effect of Russia's economic crisis and import ban on its agricultural and food sector. *Journal of Eurasian Studies*, 10(2), 119–135. DOI: 10.1177/1879366519840185

Li, J. (2021). *Sustainable Development in BRICS Countries: From Concept to Practice*. Springer Geography., DOI: 10.1007/978-3-030-78690-8_21

Li, L. (2019). BRICS: A Limited Role in Transforming the World. *Strategic Analysis*, 43(6), 499–508. DOI: 10.1080/09700161.2019.1677017

Li, M. (2020). The Belt and Road Initiative: Geo-economics and Indo-Pacific security competition. *International Affairs*, 96(1), 169–187. DOI: 10.1093/ia/iiz240

Lin, J., Zhang, Y., Ibrahim, R. L., & Abrorov, S. (2024). Paving the way for sustainable environment in BRICS through technological innovation, sustainable energy, and financial development: Heterogenous analyses. *International Journal of Sustainable Development and World Ecology*, 31(7), 1–17. DOI: 10.1080/13504509.2024.2335270

Lissovolik, Y. (2023a). BRICS+ after the 2023 "Expansion Summit.". *Pathways to Peace and Security*, 65(2), 42–52. DOI: 10.20542/2307-1494-2023-2-42-52

Lissovolik, Y. (2023b). BRICS Plus: The New Force in Global Governance. *Journal of International Analytics*, 134(1), 138–148. DOI: 10.46272/2587-8476-2023-14-1-138-148

Lissovolik, Y. (2024). BRICS Expansion: New Geographies and Spheres of Cooperation. *BRICS Journal of Economics*, 5(1), 1–12. DOI: 10.3897/brics-econ.5.e120071

Liu, M. (2016). BRICS development: A long way to a powerful economic club and new international organization. *The Pacific Review*, 29(3), 443–453. DOI: 10.1080/09512748.2016.1154688

Liu, T., & Tsai, T.-C. (2014). Swords into ploughshares? China's Soft Power strategy in Southeast Asia and its challenges. *Revista Brasileira de Política Internacional*, •••, 57.

Liu, T., & Woo, W. T. (2018). Understanding the U.S.-China Trade War. *China Economic Journal*, 11(3), 319–340. DOI: 10.1080/17538963.2018.1516256

Lowe, P. (2016). The Rise of the BRICS in the Global Economy. *Teaching Geography*, 41(2), 50–53.

Luard, E. (1982). *A History of the United Nations: Volume 1: The Years of Western Domination, 1945-1955*. Springer.

Lucas, G. (2024). Is BRICS about to announce a gold-backed currency? https://coingeek.com/is-brics-about-to-announce-a-gold-backed-currency/

Lumineau, F., Wang, W., & Schilke, O. (2021). Blockchain governance—A new way of organizing collaborations? *Organization Science*, 32(2), 500–521. DOI: 10.1287/orsc.2020.1379

Lundgren, M., & Svensson, I. (2014). Leanings and dealings: Exploring bias in mediation by international organizations. *International Negotiation*, 19(3), 315–342. DOI: 10.1163/15718069-12341280

Luo, H., & Yang, L. (2021). Equality and Equity in Emerging Multilateral Financial Institutions: The Case of the BRICS Institutions. *Global Policy*, 12(4), 482–508. Advance online publication. DOI: 10.1111/1758-5899.13003

Luo, M., Cai, J., Zeng, Z., Zheng, Y., & Lin, T. (2024). Development and practices of nature-based solutions in China. *Nature-Based Solutions*, 5, 100109. DOI: 10.1016/j.nbsj.2023.100109

Lu, T., Sherman, P., Chen, X., Chen, S., Lu, X., & McElroy, M. (2020). India's potential for integrating solar and on-and offshore wind power into its energy system. *Nature Communications*, 11(1), 4750. DOI: 10.1038/s41467-020-18318-7 PMID: 32958940

Luxton, S. J., Smith, G. S., Williams, K. J., Ferrier, S., Bond, A. J., & Prober, S. M. (2024). An introduction to key ecological concepts, financial opportunities, and risks underpinning aspirations for nature positive. *Bioscience*, 74(7), 450–466. DOI: 10.1093/biosci/biae040 PMID: 39156612

Macaraig, C. E., & Fenton, A. J. (2021). Analyzing the causes and effects of the south china sea dispute. *The Journal of Territorial and Maritime Studies*, 8(2), 42–58.

Maechler, S., & Boisvert, V. (2024). Valuing nature to save it? The centrality of valuation in the new spirit of conservation. *Global Environmental Politics*, 24(1), 10–30. DOI: 10.1162/glep_a_00734

Magazzino, C., Gattone, T., Usman, M., & Valente, D. (2024). Unleashing the power of innovation and sustainability: Transforming cereal production in the BRICS countries. *Ecological Indicators*, 167, 112618. DOI: 10.1016/j.ecolind.2024.112618

Mäkinen, T. (2018). Debating Transatlantic Security in the United States Congress. Retrieved from https://trepo.tuni.fi/handle/10024/102838

Mansfield, E. (2014). Rising Power in the Global Economy: Issues and Questions. *International Studies Review*, 16(3), 437–442. DOI: 10.1111/misr.12148

Mao, H., & Görg, H. (2020). Friends like this: The impact of the US–China trade war on global value chains. *World Economy*, 43(7), 1776–1791. DOI: 10.1111/twec.12967

Marois, T. (2023). Time for a world climate bank. *Land & Climate Review*, July 14, 2023. https://www.landclimate.org/a-world-climate-bank-for-green-and-just-transitions/

Martins, M. (2019). *The BRICS Commitment on Climate Change: Process Towards an Effective Approach in the Path of Sustainable Development*. Contributions to Economics., DOI: 10.1007/978-3-030-02662-2_9

Martus, E. (2021). Policymaking and Policy Framing: Russian Environmental Politics under Putin. *Europe-Asia Studies*, 73(5), 869–889. DOI: 10.1080/09668136.2020.1865275

Maryam, J., & Mittal, A. (2020). Foreign Direct Investment into BRICS: An Empirical Analysis. *Transnational Corporations Review*, 12(1), 1–9. DOI: 10.1080/19186444.2019.1709400

Mathur, S., & Dasgupta, M. (Eds.). (2013). *BRICS: Trade Policies, Institutions and Areas of Deepening Cooperation*. Centre for WTO Studies.

May, C. A. (2022). Complex adaptive governance systems: A framework to understand institutions, organizations, and people in socio-ecological systems. *Socio-Ecological Practice Research*, 4(1), 39–54. DOI: 10.1007/s42532-021-00101-7 PMID: 35071989

McKeever, M. (2024). Social stratification and inequality in South Africa. *Sociology Compass*, 18(2), 13173. DOI: 10.1111/soc4.13173

Medhat, A. (2020). A Critical Analysis to the United Nations' Performance in the Light of Contemporary Global Challenges. *SSRN*. http://dx.doi.org/DOI: 10.2139/ssrn.3564486

Megre, M., & Ribeiro, G. C. (2024). BRICS and the Multipolar World. *Horizons: Journal of International Relations and Sustainable Development*, (25), 126–135.

Mekonnen, W. (2024). Ethiopia and BRICS: Prospects and Challenges. *Journal of Political Science and International Relations*, 9(3), 59–74. DOI: 10.11648/j.jpsir.20240703.12

Middelberg, S. (2013). Sustainable Agriculture: A Review of Challenges Facing the South African Agricultural Sector. *Journal of Human Ecology (Delhi, India)*, 42(2), 163–169. DOI: 10.1080/09709274.2013.11906590

Ministry of External Affairs, Government of India. (2024, July 5). Transcript of Special Briefing by Foreign Secretary on Prime Minister's visit to Russia and Austria. Ministry of External Affairs, Government of India. Retrieved from https://www.mea.gov.in/media-briefings.htm?dtl/37930/Transcript+of+Special+Briefing+by+Foreign+Secretary+on+Prime+Ministers+visit+to+Russia+and+Austria+July+05+2024

Miranda, I. T. P., Moletta, J., Pedroso, B., Pilatti, L., & Picinin, C. T. (2021). A Review on Green Technology Practices at BRICS Countries: Brazil, Russia, India, China, and South Africa. *SAGE Open*, 11(2), 21582440211013780. Advance online publication. DOI: 10.1177/21582440211013780

Mishra, P., Al Khatib, A. M. G., Lal, P., Anwar, A., Nganvongpanit, K., Abotaleb, M., Ray, S., & Punyapornwithaya, V. (2023). An overview of pulses production in India: Retrospect and prospects of the future food with an application of hybrid models. *National Academy Science Letters. National Academy of Sciences, India, 46*(5), 367–374. DOI: 10.1007/s40009-023-01267-2

Mishra, R., & Louis, Y. M. (2024, June 29). The China-Russia 'Axis' Is Overhyped. *The Diplomat*. https://thediplomat.com/2024/06/the-china-russia-axis-is-overhyped/

Mishra, R. (2021). Vietnam's Regional Security Perceptions and Priorities: Role of India. India Quarterly. *Journal of International Affairs*, 77(2), 123–140. DOI: 10.1177/09749284211009433

Mitrova, T., & Melnikov, Y. (2019). Energy transition in Russia. *Energy Transitions*, 3(1-2), 73–80. DOI: 10.1007/s41825-019-00016-8

Moak, K. (2017). BRICS and China Initiated Global Trade Initiatives and Financial Institutions: Alternatives to the US-Dominated IMF and WBG and ADB. *China Economic Review*, 211–223. Advance online publication. DOI: 10.1007/978-3-319-57903-0_10

Modelski, G., & Thompson, W. R. (1999). The Long and the Short of Global Politics in the Twenty-First Century: An Evolutionary Approach. *International Studies Review*, 1(2), 109–140. DOI: 10.1111/1521-9488.00157

Mohajan, H. K. (2021). Third Industrial Revolution Brings Global Development. *Journal of Social Sciences and Humanities*, 7(1), 239–251.

Mohammed, S. (2024). BRICS Plus: De-Dollarization and Global Power Shifts in New Economic Landscape. *BRICS Journal of Economics*, 5(1), 13–32. DOI: 10.3897/brics-econ.5.e117828

Mohan, C. R. (2018). The Impact of India's Act East Policy on Southeast Asia. ResearchGate. Retrieved from https://www.researchgate.net/publication/325284243_The_Impact_of_India's_Act_East_Policy_on_Southeast_Asia

Monin, S. (2024). BRICS approves Cuba, Bolivia, and 11 other countries as 'partner states'. (https://www.brasildefato.com.br/2024/10/24/brics-approves-cuba-bolivia-and-11-other-countries-as-partner-states. Date of Access: 25.09.2024).

Montesh, M., & Basdeo, V. (2012). The Role of the South African National Defence Force in Policing. *Scientia Militaria South African Journal of Military Studies, 40*(1).

Mostaque, L. (2022). India's Energy Diplomacy and geopolitics in South Asia. *BIIS Journal*, 43(2), 185–204.

Moyo, G. (2024). World Bank, IMF, and WTO as Agents of Financial Imperialism. In *Africa in the Global Economy: Capital Flight, Enablers, and Decolonial Responses* (pp. 41–59). Springer Nature Switzerland. DOI: 10.1007/978-3-031-51000-7_3

Mubasher Hassan, M., & Mirza, T. (2021). Using time series forecasting for analysis of GDP growth in India. *International Journal of Education and Management Engineering*, 11(3), 40–49. DOI: 10.5815/ijeme.2021.03.05

Mudambi, R., Saranga, H., & Schotter, A. (2017). Mastering the Make-in-India Challenge. *MIT Sloan Management Review*, •••, 59.

Mukhametzyanov, R., Romanyuk, M., Ostapchuk, T., & Ivantsova, N. (2021). The objective need and trend of ensuring the food security in Russia in conditions of import substitution. *BIO Web of Conferences*, 37, 00079.

Mukherjee, R. (2014). The False Promise of India's Soft Power. *Geopolitics, History, and International Relations*, 6(1), 46–62.

Müller, R. (2002). *Interpretative statements at the Permanent Council: A quantitative and qualitative analysis*. Organization for Security and Co-operation in Europe.

Murau, S., Pape, F., & Pforr, T. (2021). The hierarchy of the offshore US-dollar-system. GEGI Study, February 2021. https://www.bu.edu/gdp/files/2021/02/Steffen-Murau-GEGI-Study-2-Feb-2021.pdf

Muzekenyi, M. J. J., & Kilonzo, B. (2023). Economic challenges limiting small-scale commercial farming development in rural areas of South Africa. *African Journal of Food, Agriculture, Nutrition and Development*, 23(4), 23026–23038. DOI: 10.18697/ajfand.119.22900

Myllyvirta, L. (2024). "Analysis: Clean energy was top driver of China's economic growth in 2023". Carbon Brief, Clean on Climate. https://www.carbonbrief.org/analysis-clean-energy-was-top-driver-of-chinas-economic-growth-in-2023/. Date of Access: 12.09.2024).

Naik, S. (2018). Rising BRICS: A Path to Multipolar World Reality? *Comparative Politics Russia*, 1, 100–108.

Nakamoto, S. (2009). Bitcoin: A Peer-to-Peer Electronic Cash System. https://bitcoin.org/bitcoin.pdf

Nam, C. W. (2024). Introduction to the issue on BRICS enlargement: What are the geoeconomic implications? *In EconPol Forum (Vol. 25, No. 1, pp. 3-4).* Munich: CESifo GmbH.

Nandal, N., Nandal, N., Dhaka, P., & Kataria, A. (2022). U.S.–China Trade War & Its Implications on India. *Korea Review of International Studies*, 15(5), 66–72.

Naran, B., Connolly, J., Rosane, P., Wignarajah, D., Wakaba, G., & Buchner, B. (2022). Global landscape of climate finance: A decade of data. October 27, 2022. https://www.climatepolicyinitiative.org/publication/global-landscape-of-climate-finance-a-decade-of-data/

Nasir, M. A., Nugroho, A. D., & Lakner, Z. (2022). Impact of the Russian–Ukrainian Conflict on Global Food Crops. *Foods*, 11(19), 2979. DOI: 10.3390/foods11192979 PMID: 36230055

Naudé, W., Szirmai, A., & Lavopa, A. (2013). Industrialization Lessons from BRICS: A Comparative Analysis.

Naudé, W., Szirmai, A., & Lavopa, A. (2015). Industrialization and Technological Change in the BRICS. *Structural Change and Industrial Development in the BRICS*, 324.

Navarro, A., & Lopez-Bao, J. V. (2019). EU Agricultural Policy Still Not Green. *Nature Sustainability*, 2(11), 990. DOI: 10.1038/s41893-019-0424-x

NDB (National Development Bank). (n.d.). https://www.ndb.int/

NDB. (2024). *The Premier Bank for Emerging Economies*. https://www.ndb.int/about-ndb/

Ndlovu, V., & Inglesi-Lotz, R. (2019). Positioning South Africa's energy supply mix internationally: Comparative and policy review analysis. *Journal of Energy in Southern Africa*, 30(2), 14–27. DOI: 10.17159/2413-3051/2019/v30i2a5409

Newadi, R., & Mazenda, A. (2016). *The rise of BRICS development finance institutions: A comprehensive look into the New Development Bank and the Contingent Reserve Arrangement.* African East-Asian Affairs., DOI: 10.7552/0-3-178

Nguyen, D. H., & Khominich, I. P. (2023). The measurement of green economic quality in the BRICS countries: Should they prioritize financing for environmental protection, economic growth, or social goals? *Russian Journal of Economics*, 9(2), 183–200. DOI: 10.32609/j.ruje.9.101612

Nguyen, V. H., & Pham, N. T. (2021). ASEAN's position in training peace in the South China Sea. *International Journal of Social Science and Human Research*, 4(3), 264–269. DOI: 10.47191/ijsshr/v4-i3-07

Nie, J., von Ende-Becker, A., & Yang, S.-K. X. (2021). *How Did the 2018–19 U.S. Tariff Hikes Influence Household Spending?* The Federal Reserve Bank of Kansas City Economic Review., DOI: 10.18651/ER/v106n4NievonEndeBeckerYang

Nistor, P. (2015). FDI Implications on BRICS Economy Growth. *Procedia Economics and Finance*, 32, 981–985. DOI: 10.1016/S2212-5671(15)01557-9

Norman, J., Clark, G., Babajeva, J., Sidorovskaya-Fretz, N., Yu, A., Han, Y., & Zhang, M. (2024). Energy in the BRICS. (https://globalenergymonitor.org/report/energy-in-the-brics/. Date of Access: 23.10.2024).

Nulimaimaiti, M. (2023). What's the state of China's digital yuan in 2023? South China Morning Post,10 October 2023. https://www.scmp.com/economy/china-economy/article/3237317/whats-state-chinas-digital-yuan-2023

Nye, J. S. (1990). *Bound to lead: The changing nature of American power* (1st ed.). Basic Books.

O'Neil, J. (2001). Building better Global Economic BRICs. *Global Economics Paper*, 66, 1–16.

Oberson, F. (2021). OSCE special monitoring in Ukraine. In Mihr, A. (Ed.), *Between peace and conflict in the East and the West: Studies on transformation and development in the OSCE region* (pp. 47–75). Springer International Publishing., DOI: 10.1007/978-3-030-77489-9_3

Obst, C., Hein, L., & Edens, B. (2016). National accounting and the valuation of ecosystem assets and their services. *Environmental and Resource Economics*, 64(1), 1–23. DOI: 10.1007/s10640-015-9921-1

OECD. (2015). *How's Life? 2015: Measuring Well-being*. OECD Publishing.

Ogunnubi, O., & Amao, O. B. (2016). South Africa's Emerging "Soft Power" Influence in Africa and Its Impending Limitations: Will the Giant Be Able to Weather the Storm? *African Security*, 9(4), 299–319. DOI: 10.1080/19392206.2016.1242978

Ogunnubi, O., & Okeke-Uzodike, U. (2015). South Africa's foreign policy and the strategy of soft power. *South African Journal of International Affairs*, 22(1), 23–41. DOI: 10.1080/10220461.2015.1007078

Oldekop, J. A., Chappell, M. J., Peixoto, F. E. B., Paglia, A. P., Rodrigues, M. S. P., & Evans, K. L. (2015). Linking Brazil's Food Security Policies to Agricultural Change. *Food Security*, 7(4), 779–793. DOI: 10.1007/s12571-015-0475-4

Oliveros, L. (2020). *The Impact of Financial and Oil Sanctions on the Venezuelan Economy*. Washington Office on Latin America.

Öniş, Z., & Gençer, A. Ş. (2018). Democratic BRICS as role models in a shifting global order: Inherent dilemmas and the challenges ahead. *Third World Quarterly*, 39(9), 1791–1811. DOI: 10.1080/01436597.2018.1438185

Orcutt, M. (2023). What's next for China's digital currency? MIT Technology Review. 3 August 2023. https://www.technologyreview.com/2023/08/03/1077181/whats-next-for-chinas-digital-currency/

Organski, A. F. K., & Kugler, J. (1980). The War Ledger.

OSCE. (2014a). *Mediation and dialogue facilitation in the OSCE*. OSCE Conflict Prevention Centre. https://www.osce.org/secretariat/126646

OSCE. (2014b). Decision No. 1117: Extension of the mandate of the OSCE Special Monitoring Mission to Ukraine (PC.DEC/1117; *991st Plenary Meeting*). Organization for Security and Co-operation in Europe.

OSCE. (2014c). Decision No. 1129: Extension of the mandate of the OSCE Special Monitoring Mission to Ukraine (PC.DEC/1129; *1010th Plenary Meeting*). Organization for Security and Co-operation in Europe.

OSCE. (2015). Decision No. 1162: Extension of the mandate of the OSCE Special Monitoring Mission to Ukraine (PC.DEC/1162; *1044th Plenary Meeting*). Organization for Security and Co-operation in Europe.

OSCE. (2016). Decision No. 1199: Extension of the mandate of the OSCE Special Monitoring Mission to Ukraine (PC.DEC/1199; *1090th Plenary Meeting*). Organization for Security and Co-operation in Europe.

OSCE. (2017). Decision No. 1246: Extension of the mandate of the OSCE Special Monitoring Mission to Ukraine (PC.DEC/1246; *1137th Plenary Meeting*). Organization for Security and Co-operation in Europe.

OSCE. (2018). Decision No. 1289: Extension of the mandate of the OSCE Special Monitoring Mission to Ukraine (PC.DEC/1289; *1180th Plenary Meeting*). Organization for Security and Co-operation in Europe.

OSCE. (2019). Decision No. 1323: Extension of the mandate of the OSCE Special Monitoring Mission to Ukraine (PC.DEC/1323; *1223rd Plenary Meeting*). Organization for Security and Co-operation in Europe.

OSCE. (2020). Decision No. 1366: Extension of the mandate of the OSCE Special Monitoring Mission to Ukraine (PC.DEC/1366; *1263rd Plenary Meeting*). Organization for Security and Co-operation in Europe.

OSCE. (2021a). A peaceful presence—The first five years of the OSCE Special Monitoring Mission to Ukraine. *OSCE Conflict Prevention Centre*. https://www.osce.org/secretariat/491220

OSCE. (2021b). Decision No. 1401: Extension of the mandate of the OSCE Special Monitoring Mission to Ukraine (PC.DEC/1401; *1308th Plenary Meeting*). Organization for Security and Co-operation in Europe.

OSCE. (2022a). Chairman-in-office and secretary general expressed regret that no consensus reached on extension of mandate of Special Monitoring Mission to Ukraine. *OSCE Conflict Prevention Centre*. https://www.osce.org/chairmanship/514958

OSCE. (2022b). OSCE Observer Mission at the Russian Checkpoints Gukovo and Donetsk (discontinued). *OSCE Conflict Prevention Centre*. https://www.osce.org/observer-mission-at-russian-checkpoints-gukovo-and-donetsk-discontinued

Ospina, R., Gondim, J. A. M., Leiva, V., & Castro, C. (2023). An overview of forecast analysis with ARIMA models during the COVID-19 pandemic: Methodology and case study in Brazil. *Mathematics*, 11(14), 3069. DOI: 10.3390/math11143069

Ostroukh, A. (2019). Russia says BRICS nations favour idea of common payment system. Reuters, November 14, 2019. https://www.reuters.com/article/world/russia-says-brics-nations-favour-idea-of-common-payment-system-idUSKBN1XO1PC/

Oswega State University of New York. (2024). The Basics about Cryptocurrency. https://www.oswego.edu/cts/basics-about-cryptocurrency#:~:text=A%20cryptocurrency%20is%20a%20digital,you%20need%20a%20cryptocurrency%20wallet

Özekin, M. K., & Sune, E. (2023). Contesting Hegemony: The Rise of BRICS and the Crisis of US-led Western Hegemony in the MENA Region. *The Korean Journal of International Studies*, 21(3), 409–446. DOI: 10.14731/kjis.2023.12.21.3.409

Pacific Forum. (2019). Issues & insights: U.S.-China strategic competition and implications for the Indo-Pacific (Vol. 19, Working Paper 8). Pacific Forum. https://pacforum.org/wp-content/uploads/2019/08/issuesinsights_Vol19-WP8FINAL.pdf

Panda, J. P. (2020). India's Strategic Hedging Policy in The South China Sea. ResearchGate. Retrieved from https://www.researchgate.net/publication/372365839_India's_Strategic_Hedging_Policy_in_The_South_China_Sea

Pant, H. V. (2023). From BRICS to BRICS Plus: Old partners and new stakeholders. Observer Research Foundation. Retrieved from https://www.orfonline.org/research/from-brics-to-brics-plus-old-partners-and-new-stakeholders

Pant, H. V. (2004). The Moscow–Beijing–Delhi "Strategic Triangle": An Idea Whose Time May Never Come. *Security Dialogue*, 35(3), 311–328. DOI: 10.1177/0967010604047529

Pant, H. V. (2013). The BRICS Fallacy. *The Washington Quarterly*, 36(3), 91–105. DOI: 10.1080/0163660X.2013.825552

Patel, S. K., Sharma, A. K., & Singh, G. (2020). Traditional agricultural practices in India: An approach for environmental sustainability and food security. *Energy, Ecology & Environment*, 5(4), 253–271. DOI: 10.1007/s40974-020-00158-2

Pathak, L., & Shah, K. (2019). Renewable Energy Resources, Policies and Gaps in BRICS Countries and the Global Impact. *Frontiers in Energy*, 13(3), 506–521. DOI: 10.1007/s11708-018-0601-z

Patrick, S. (2024). BRICS Expansion, the G20, and the Future of World Order. https://carnegieendowment.org/research/2024/10/brics-summit-emerging-middle-powers-g7-g20?lang=en. Date of Access: 12.10.2024).

Patterson, J., Schulz, K., Vervoort, J., van der Hel, S., Widerberg, O., Adler, C., Hurlbert, M., Anderton, K., Sethi, M., & Barau, A. (2017). Exploring the governance and politics of transformations towards sustainability. *Environmental Innovation and Societal Transitions*, 24, 1–16. DOI: 10.1016/j.eist.2016.09.001

Peng, J., & Zhang, Y. (2020). Impact of Global Value Chains on Export Technology Content of China's Manufacturing Industry. *Sustainability (Basel)*, 12(1), 432. DOI: 10.3390/su12010432

Pereira, J. C., & Viola, E. (2021). Brazilian climate policy (1992–2019): An exercise in strategic diplomatic failure. *Contemporary Politics*, 28(1), 55–78. DOI: 10.1080/13569775.2021.1961394

Pichon, E., & Russell, M. (2022). *Human development in Putin's Russia What the data tell us?* European Parliamentary Research Service (EPRS). Available at: https://www.europarl.europa.eu/RegData/etudes/BRIE/2022/729375/EPRS_BRI(2022)729375_EN.pdf

Picoli, M., Rorato, A., Leitão, P., Câmara, G., Maciel, A., Hostert, P., & Sanches, I. (2020). Impacts of Public and Private Sector Policies on Soybean and Pasture Expansion in Mato Grosso—Brazil from 2001 to 2017. *Land (Basel)*, 9(1), 20. DOI: 10.3390/land9010020

Pietrosemoli, L., & Rodríguez-Monroy, C. (2019). The Venezuelan energy crisis: Renewable energies in the transition towards sustainability. *Renewable & Sustainable Energy Reviews*, 105, 415–426. DOI: 10.1016/j.rser.2019.02.014

Pinto, G. M. C., Pedroso, B., Moraes, J., Pilatti, L., & Picinin, C. T. (2018). Environmental management practices in industries of Brazil, Russia, India, China and South Africa (BRICS) from 2011 to 2015. *Journal of Cleaner Production*, 198, 1251–1261. Advance online publication. DOI: 10.1016/j.jclepro.2018.07.046

Pistilli, M. (2024a). Top 10 Oil-producing Countries (Updated 2024). Investing News Network. 14 August 2024. https://investingnews.com/daily/resource-investing/energy-investing/oil-and-gas-investing/top-oil-producing-countries/

Pistilli, M. (2024b). How Would a New BRICS Currency Affect the US Dollar? (Updated 2024). 12 September 2024. https://www.nasdaq.com/articles/how-would-new-brics-currency-affect-us-dollar-updated-2024

Plaunt, D. H. (1973). Agricultural Development Policies and Programs in Canada. *American Journal of Agricultural Economics*, 55(5), 903–912. DOI: 10.2307/1238935

Podoba, Z., & Kryshneva, D. (2018). Green Energy in the BRICS. *World Economy and International Relations*, 62(2), 17–27. DOI: 10.20542/0131-2227-2018-62-2-17-27

Poenisch, H. (2023). Brics common currency would be no threat to the dollar, 13 June 2023. https://www.omfif.org/2023/06/brics-common-currency-would-be-no-threat-to-the-dollar/

Pollet, B. G., Staffell, I., & Adamson, K. A. (2015). Current energy landscape in the Republic of South Africa. *International Journal of Hydrogen Energy*, 40(46), 16685–16701. DOI: 10.1016/j.ijhydene.2015.09.141

Prajapati, S., Swaraj, A., Lalwani, R., Narwal, A., Verma, K., Singh, G., & Kumar, A. (2021). Comparison of traditional and hybrid time series models for forecasting COVID-19 cases. In *Research Square*. DOI: 10.21203/rs.3.rs-493195/v1

Prasad, E. S. (2021). *The future of money: How the digital revolution is transforming currencies and finance*. The Belknap Press of Harvard University Press.

Preiser, R., Biggs, R., De Vos, A., & Folke, C. (2018). Social-ecological systems as complex adaptive systems: Organizing principles for advancing research methods and approaches. *Ecology and Society*, 23(4), 46. DOI: 10.5751/ES-10558-230446

Procházka, D. (2018). Accounting for Bitcoin and Other Cryptocurrencies under IFRS: A Comparison and Assessment of Competing Models. *The International Journal of Digital Accounting Research*, 18, 161–188. DOI: 10.4192/1577-8517-v18_7

Pröpper, H. (2020). The" Chinese Dream": An Analysis of the Belt and Road Initiative. International Social Science Review (Online), 96(1), 0_1-24.

Putzer, A., Lambooy, T., Jeurissen, R., & Kim, E. (2022). Putting the rights of nature on the map. A quantitative Analysis of rights of nature initiatives across the world. *Journal of Maps*, 18(1), 89–96. DOI: 10.1080/17445647.2022.2079432

Qi, J. J., & Dauvergne, P. (2022). China's rising influence on climate governance: Forging a path for the global South. *Global Environmental Change*, 73, 102484. DOI: 10.1016/j.gloenvcha.2022.102484

Qin, M., Fan, Z., & Zhong, Y. (2022). The Global Value Chain and Welfare Effects of Tariffs—Counterfactual Analysis of Sino–US Economic and Trade Frictions. *Sustainability (Basel)*, 14(14), 8280. DOI: 10.3390/su14148280

Qobo, M., & Soko, M. (2015). The rise of emerging powers in the global economy: BRICS and the challenge to the existing global order. *Global Policy*, 6(1), 56–64. DOI: 10.1111/1758-5899.12155

Rabêlo Neto, A., de Sousa-Filho, J. M., Leocádio, Á. L., & do Nascimento, J. C. H. B. (2020). Internationalization of cultural products: The influence of soft power. *International Journal of Market Research*, 62(3), 335–349. DOI: 10.1177/1470785319871473

Rachana, V., & Sreynich, C. (2021). The Belt and Road Initiative and ASEAN Community Development. Final Report, Royal University of Law and Economics, International Program, Bachelor's Degree in International Relations.

Raghutla, C., & Chittedi, K. R. (2020). Financial development, energy consumption, technology, urbanization, economic output and carbon emissions nexus in BRICS countries: An empirical analysis. *Management of Environmental Quality*, 32(2), 290–307. DOI: 10.1108/MEQ-02-2020-0035

Raj, A., & Singh, S. K. (2022). Forecasting GDP of India and its neighbouring countries using Time Series Analysis. *2022 IEEE Global Conference on Computing, Power and Communication Technologies (GlobConPT)*. DOI: 10.1109/GlobConPT57482.2022.9938189

Rajaiah, J., Pendse, E., Thomas, S. A., Agrawal, S., & Shetty, T. (2021). A study on forecasting economic convergence of India in comparison to USA, China and japan. SSRN *Electronic Journal*. DOI: 10.2139/ssrn.3888583

Ramachandran, V., & Smith, A. (2023). The dark side of climate finance. *Foreign Policy*, December 1, 2023 https://foreignpolicy.com/2023/12/01/cop28-climate-finance-global-south-development-aid-energy-wind-solar-renewable/ [Accessed: 13th January 2024]

Ramos, M. (2023). De-dollarization: 95% of the trade between China and Russia didn't use the US dollar. BrasildeFato. 21 December 2023. https://www.brasildefato.com.br/2023/12/21/de-dollarization-95-of-the-trade-between-china-and-russia-didn-t-use-the-us-dollar

Ramos, L., Rocha, P. D., & Zahreddine, D. (2021). A Agenda de Segurança Internacional no BRICS (2009-2019). *Dados*, 64(3), e20190244. DOI: 10.1590/dados.2021.64.3.245

Rau, E.-P., Gross, J., Coomes, D. A., Swinfield, T., Madhavapeddy, A., Balmford, A., & Keshav, S. (2024). Mitigating risk of credit reversal in nature-based climate solutions by optimally anticipating carbon release. *Carbon Management*, 15(1), 2390854. DOI: 10.1080/17583004.2024.2390854

Ravallion, M. (2011). A Comparative Perspective on Poverty Reduction in Brazil, China, and India. *The World Bank Research Observer*, 26(1), 71–104. DOI: 10.1093/wbro/lkp031

Recalde, M. (2011). Energy policy and energy market performance: The Argentinean case. *Energy Policy*, 39(6), 3860–3868. DOI: 10.1016/j.enpol.2011.04.022

Reh, C. (2012). European Integration as Compromise: Recognition, Concessions and the Limits of Cooperation. *Government and Opposition*, 47(3), 414–440. DOI: 10.1111/j.1477-7053.2012.01369.x

Reidsma, P., Bakker, M. M., Kanellopoulos, A., Alam, S. J., Paas, W., Kros, J., & de Vries, W. (2015). Sustainable Agricultural Development in a Rural Area in the Netherlands? Assessing Impacts of Climate and Socio-economic Change at Farm and Landscape Level. *Agricultural Systems*, 141, 160–173. DOI: 10.1016/j.agsy.2015.10.009

Rennert, K., Errickson, F., Prest, B. C., Rennels, L., Newell, R. G., Pizer, W., Kingdon, C., Wingenroth, J., Cooke, R., Parthum, B., Smith, D., Cromar, K., Diaz, D., Moore, F. C., Müller, U. K., Plevin, R. J., Raftery, A. E., Ševčíková, H., Sheets, H., & Anthoff, D. (2022). Comprehensive evidence implies a higher social cost of CO2. *Nature*, 610(7933), 687–692. DOI: 10.1038/s41586-022-05224-9 PMID: 36049503

Rensburg, I., Motala, S., & David, S. (2015). Opportunities and challenges for research collaboration among the BRICS nations. *Compare: A Journal of Comparative Education*, 45(5), 814–818. DOI: 10.1080/03057925.2015.1074823

Reuters (2024a). New US sanctions force the end of dollar and euro trading on Russia's main exchange. June 13, 2024. https://edition.cnn.com/2024/06/13/investing/us-russia-sanctions-dollar-euro-trading/index.html

Reuters (2024b). China-Russia 2023 trade value hits record high of $240 bln - Chinese customs. 12 January 2024. https://www.reuters.com/markets/china-russia-2023-trade-value-hits-record-high-240-bln-chinese-customs-2024-01-12/

RFE/RL. (2017). Putin Warns Cryptocurrencies Like Bitcoin Carry 'Serious Risks'. https://www.rferl.org/a/putin-bitcoin-cryptocurrencies-regulation/28785150.html

Rinaldi, A. L., & Martuscelli, P. N. (2016). The BRICS on climate change global Governance. *Meridiano*, 47(17), e17020. DOI: 10.20889/M47e17020

Rising, D. (2024, January 30). Myanmar, South China Sea Conflicts Top Agenda as ASEAN Foreign Ministers Meet. The Diplomat. https://thediplomat.com/2024/01/myanmar-south-china-sea-conflicts-top-agenda-as-asean-foreign-ministers-meet/

Roberts, C. (2017). The geopolitics of BRICS in conflict mediation. *International Affairs*, 93(5), 1123–1145. DOI: 10.1093/ia/iix120

Roberts, C. A., Armijo, L. E., & Katada, S. N. (2018). *The BRICS and Collective Financial Statecraft*. Oxford University Press.

Roberts, K., & Bano, S. (Eds.). (2023). *The Ascendancy of Regional Powers in Contemporary US-China Relations: Rethinking the Great Power Rivalry*. Springer Nature. DOI: 10.1007/978-3-031-37612-2

Robets, C. (2010). Challengers or Stakeholders? BRICs and the Liberal World Order. *Polity*, 42(1), 1–13.

Rodionova, I., Chernyaev, M., & Korenevskaya, A. (2017). Energy Safety and Innovative Development of the BRICS States. *International Journal of Energy Economics and Policy*, 7, 216–224.

Rodriguez, F., Belhaj, H., & Aldhuhoori, M. (2022). Opportunities for Producing Hydrogen and Low-carbon Fossil Fuels from Venezuelan Conventional and Unconventional Hydrocarbon Reservoirs: An Idea in Times of Energy Transition to Net Zero-Carbon. Day 4 Thu, November 03, 2022.

Rogers, S. (2016). Adaptation science and policy in China's agricultural sector. *Wiley Interdisciplinary Reviews: Climate Change*, 7(5), 7. DOI: 10.1002/wcc.414

Rolland, S. (2013). The BRICS' Contribution to the Architecture and Norms of International Economic Law. *Proceedings of the ASIL Annual Meeting* 107, 164-170. DOI: 10.5305/procannmeetasil.107.0164

Røren, P., & Beaumont, P. (2019). Grading Greatness: Evaluating the Status Performance of the BRICS. *Third World Quarterly*, 40(3), 429–450. DOI: 10.1080/01436597.2018.1535892

Rosenau, J. N. (1995). Governance in the Twenty-First Century. *Global Governance*, 1(1), 13–43. DOI: 10.1163/19426720-001-01-90000004

Roy, S., Bhunia, G. S., & Shit, P. K. (2021). Spatial prediction of COVID-19 epidemic using ARIMA techniques in India. *Modeling Earth Systems and Environment*, 7(2), 1385–1391. DOI: 10.1007/s40808-020-00890-y PMID: 32838022

Rubiolo, M. F. (2020). *The South China Sea Dispute: A Reflection of Southeast Asia's Economic and Strategic Dilemmas*. Revista de Relaciones Internacionales, Estrategia y Seguridad.

Rutland, P., & Kazantsev, A. (2016). The limits of Russia's 'soft power.'. *Journal of Political Power*, 9(3), 395–413. DOI: 10.1080/2158379X.2016.1232287

Ryan, M., & Burman, S. (2024). The United States–China 'tech war': Decoupling and the case of Huawei. *Global Policy*, 15(2), 355–367. DOI: 10.1111/1758-5899.13352

S&P Global. (2024). BRICS expansion could see more downstream oil investment: analyst. (Erişim Adresi: https://www.spglobal.com/commodityinsights/en/market-insights/latest-news/oil/020124-brics-expansion-could-see-more-downstream-oil-investment-analyst). (Access date: 04.07.2024).

safeguardglobal.com. (2024). Top 10 manufacturing countries in the world in 2024. 29 August 2024. https://www.safeguardglobal.com/resources/top-10-manufacturing-countries-in-the-world/

Sahai, A. K., Rath, N., Sood, V., & Singh, M. P. (2020). ARIMA modelling & forecasting of COVID-19 in top five affected countries. *Diabetes & Metabolic Syndrome*, 14(5), 1419–1427. DOI: 10.1016/j.dsx.2020.07.042 PMID: 32755845

Sahbzada, M. U. (2021). India and China's Trade Ties with ASEAN Nations. *Journal of Indian Studies*, 7(2), 77–92. https://pu.edu.pk/images/journal/indianStudies/PDF/7_v7_2_21.pdf

Şahin, Ç., & Nuriyev, K. (2021). Rusya'da Enerji Sanayisinin Gelişimi ve Günümüzde Rus Enerji Stratejisi. *Uluslararası Türk Dünyası Araştırmaları Dergisi*, 4(4), 49–76.

Sahoo, P. M., Rout, H. S., & Jakovljevic, M. (2023). Dynamics of Health Financing among the BRICS: A Literature Review. *Sustainability (Basel)*, 15(16), 12385. DOI: 10.3390/su151612385

Saktiawan, B., Toro, M. J. S., & Saputro, N. (2022, December). The impact of the Russia-Ukrainian war on green energy financing in Europe. []. IOP Publishing.]. *IOP Conference Series. Earth and Environmental Science*, 1114(1), 012066. DOI: 10.1088/1755-1315/1114/1/012066

Saleh Ahmar, A., Kumar Singh, P., Van Thanh, N., Viet Tinh, N., & Minh Hieu, V. (2022). Prediction of BRIC stock price using ARIMA, SutteARIMA, and Holt-winters. *Computers, Materials & Continua*, 70(1), 523–534. DOI: 10.32604/cmc.2022.017068

Salunkhe, H. (2012). The overview of Government subsidies to agriculture sector in India. *IOSR Journal of Agriculture and Veterinary Science*, 1, 43–47. DOI: 10.9790/2380-0154347

Sandhir, V., Kumar, V., & Kumar, V. (2021). Prognosticating the spread of covid-19 pandemic based on optimal Arima estimators. *Endocrine, Metabolic & Immune Disorders Drug Targets*, 21(4), 586–591. DOI: 10.2174/1871530320666201029143122 PMID: 33121426

Santacreu, A. M., & LaBelle, J. (2022). Global Supply Chain Disruptions and Inflation During the COVID-19 Pandemic. *Federal Reserve Bank of St. Louis Review, Second Quarter*, 78–91. DOI: 10.20955/r.104.78-91

Santra, S. (2017). The effect of technological innovation on production-based energy and CO2 emission productivity: Evidence from BRICS countries. *African Journal of Science, Technology, Innovation and Development*, 9(5), 503–512. DOI: 10.1080/20421338.2017.1308069

Sarkar, A. (2019). *Policy Uncertainty, Multinational Firms, and Reallocation*. DOI: 10.2139/ssrn.4182128

Sasana, H., & Ghozali, I. (2017). The Impact of Fossil and Renewable Energy Consumption on the Economic Growth in Brazil, Russia, India, China and South Africa. *International Journal of Energy Economics and Policy*, 7, 194–200.

Savage, R. (2023). What is a BRICS currency and is the U.S. dollar in trouble? Reuters August 24, 2023. https://www.reuters.com/markets/currencies/what-is-brics-currency-could-one-be-adopted-2023-08-23/

Savchenko, M., Shkurat, M., & Nosachov, I. (2023). The role of BRICS countries in the modern global economic space. Galic'kij ekonomičnij visnik. DOI: 10.33108/galicianvisnyk_tntu2023.06.199

Schläpfer, C. (2016). Ukraine crisis and mediation: Not business as usual. *Security and Human Rights*, 27(3–4), 327–341. DOI: 10.1163/18750230-02703009

Schmidt, J. D. (2011). India-China rivalry and competition in Southeast Asia. In India in International Relations: European and Indian Perspectives. Retrieved from https://vbn.aau.dk/files/61143145/India_China_Rivalry_and_Competition_in_Southeast_Asia_pres_in_Delhi.vbn_version.docx

Scott, C. P. (2021). A Proposal to Cease Chinese Expansion in the South China Sea and Encroachment into the Sovereign Waters of Regional US Allies.

Seagroatt, M. T. (2019). US-China Competition: India's Role as a Counterbalance. Defense Technical Information Center (DTIC). Retrieved from https://apps.dtic.mil/sti/pdfs/AD1178202.pdf

Seah, S., Lin, J., Martinus, M., Fong, K., Aridati, I., Pham, T. P. T., & Chee, D. (2024). The State of Southeast Asia: 2024 Survey Report. ISEAS - Yusof Ishak Institute. Retrieved from https://www.iseas.edu.sg/wp-content/uploads/2024/03/The-State-of-SEA-2024.pdf

Selvan, S. S., Wahid, A., Patel, A., Kumar, V., & Sahu, P. (2021). Challenges in Indian Agriculture. *Agricultural Reviews (Karnal)*, (Of). Advance online publication. DOI: 10.18805/ag.R-2103

Sergunin, A., & Gao, F. (2018). BRICS as the Subject of Study of International Relations Theory. *International Organizations Research Journal*, 13(4), 55–73. DOI: 10.17323/1996-7845-2018-04-03

Sergunin, A., & Karabeshkin, L. (2015). Understanding Russia's Soft Power Strategy. *Politics*, 35(3-4), 347–363. DOI: 10.1111/1467-9256.12109

Sezer, S. (2024). Rusya-Ukrayna Savaşı'nın jeopolitik sonuçları. *Ömer Halisdemir Üniversitesi İktisadi ve İdari Bilimler Fakültesi Dergisi,* 17(1), 158-180.

Shahzad, S. M., & Khan, M. R. (2022). Quad: The US Strategic Alliance for the Indo-Pacific Region and the Chinese Counterbalance. *Pakistan Journal of Multi-disciplinary Research*, 3(2), 55–67. http://pjmr.org/pjmr/article/view/329/72

Shamase, M. Z. (2019). The role of China in the BRICS' cooperation on development shaping a new and balanced world order? *Africa Insight*, 48(4).

Shamase, M. Z. (2019). The Role of China in the BRICS' Cooperation on Development: Shaping a New And Balanced World Order? *Africa Insight*, 48(4), 105–125. DOI: 10.4314/ai.v48i4

Shambaugh, D. (2020). Where Great Powers Meet: America & China in Southeast Asia. Oxford University Press.

Shambaugh, G. (2024). Embargo. https://www.britannica.com/money/embargo-international-law

Shameem, C. C., & Jayaprasad, K. (2020). The evolution of BRICS in international political economy. *American Review of Political Economy*, 15(1). Advance online publication. DOI: 10.38024/arpe.sj.6.28.20

Sharma, D. C. (2013). Nehru: The Unlikely Hero of India's Information Technology Revolution. NMML Occasional Papers, Perspectives in Indian Development New Series 8. Nehru Memorial Museum and Library.

Sharma, P. (2021). Extrapolative Modeling of International Trade using ARIMA Model: A Performance Comparison between India and China during COVID-19. *SAMVAD*, 21(0), 71. DOI: 10.53739/samvad/2020/v21/155148

Sharma, S., Bansal, M., & Saxena, A. K. (2022). Forecasting of GDP (gross domestic product) per Capita using (ARIMA) data-driven intelligent time series predicting approach. *2022 International Conference on Sustainable Islamic Business and Finance (SIBF)*. DOI: 10.1109/SIBF56821.2022.9939928

Sharma, V. K., & Nigam, U. (2020). Modeling and forecasting of COVID-19 growth curve in India. *Transactions of the Indian National Academy of Engineering : an International Journal of Engineering and Technology*, 5(4), 697–710. DOI: 10.1007/s41403-020-00165-z

Shaw, M. (2014). Transnational organized crime in Africa. In Albanese, J., & Reichel, P. (Eds.), *Transnational organized crime: an overview from six continents* (pp. 93–115). Sage. DOI: 10.4135/9781483349091.n6

Shea, D. (2018). *Ambassador Shea: China's trade-disruptive economic model and implications for the WTO*. Statement Delivered at the WTO General Council.

Shelepov, A., & Andronova, I. (2017). BRICS National Development Banks: Potential for Narrowing the Infrastructure Financing Gap. *International Organisations Research Journal*, 12(4), 7–31. DOI: 10.17323/1996-7845-2017-04-7

Sheng, L., & do Nascimento, D. F. (2021). *The Belt and Road Initiative in South–South cooperation: The impact on world trade and geopolitics*. Springer Nature. DOI: 10.1007/978-981-16-6357-4

Shen, M., & Li, H. (2023). Insight into China–Cambodia Economic and Trade Cooperation: The Value Chain Perspective. In *Cambodia-China Comprehensive Strategic Partnership Towards a Community with a Shared Future* (pp. 99–112). Springer Nature Singapore. DOI: 10.1007/978-981-19-9155-4_14

Shen, X., Liang, J., Cao, J., & Wang, Z. (2022). How Population Aging Affects Industrial Structure Upgrading: Evidence from China. *International Journal of Environmental Research and Public Health*, 19(23), 16093. DOI: 10.3390/ijerph192316093 PMID: 36498168

SIA. (2024). *2024 State of the U.S. Semiconductor Industry*.

Siddique, A., & Shafqat, S. (2021). How Belt and Road Initiative (BRI) and the China-Pakistan Economic Corridor (CPEC) are Reshaping China's Soft Power? *Journal of South Asian and Middle Eastern Studies*, 44(3), 61–94. DOI: 10.1353/jsa.2021.0007

Sidorova, E. (2018). The Innovation Development of the BRICS Countries: Preconditions and Prospects for Cooperation. *International Organisations Research Journal*, 13(1), 34–50. DOI: 10.17323/1996-7845-2018-01-02

Sihaloho, R. A. H., Prabowo, T. B., & Pamungkas, C. (2024). China's Belt and Road Initiative Implementation Maneuvers in the South Pacific Region. *Nation State: Journal of International Studies*, 7(1), 53–70. DOI: 10.24076/nsjis.v7i1.1185

Simelane, T., & Knop, J. (2022). Opportunities and Options for Energy Cooperation Among BRICS Countries. In Zondi, S. (Ed.), *The Political Economy of Intra-BRICS Cooperation* (pp. 79–97). Palgrave Macmillan., DOI: 10.1007/978-3-030-97397-1_5

Simon, M. S. (2022). India's Internal Security: Issues, Challenges and Options. In Behera, A., & Mishra, S. (Eds.), *Varying Dimensions of India's National Security* (pp. 107–120). Springer. DOI: 10.1007/978-981-16-7593-5_8

Singh, D. (2024). Forging a positive vision of economic statecraft, 22 February 2024. https://www.atlanticcouncil.org/blogs/new-atlanticist/forging-a-positive-vision-of-economic-statecraft/

Singh, M. K. (2021). China and the United States in the Middle East: between dependency and rivalry. In The Great Power Competition Volume 1: Regional Perspectives on Peace and Security (pp. 369-395). Cham: Springer International Publishing DOI: 10.1007/978-3-030-64473-4_18

Singh, R. (2024, July 6). Why China plans to run trains from Kunming all the way to Singapore. The Indian Express.Retrieved from https://indianexpress.com/article/explained/explained-global/china-pan-asian-trains-network-bri-9421068/

Singh, B. (2004). India's Security Concerns: National, Regional and Global. *Indian Journal of Poultry Science*, 65(3), 345–364.

Singh, D. (2020). *American Foreign Policy and Southeast Asia*. De Gruyter. DOI: 10.1355/aa20-1d

Singh, R. (2016). BRICS: Building blocks for a new global order. *Strategic Analysis*, 40(3), 203–215. DOI: 10.1080/09700161.2016.1184816

Skalamera, M. (2023). Russia's lasting influence in Central Asia. In *Central Asia's Strategic Importance* (pp. 123–145). Taylor & Francis., Retrieved from https://www.taylorfrancis.com/chapters/edit/10.4324/9781003422228-9

Skogstad, G., & Verdun, A. (2009). The Common Agricultural Policy: Continuity and Change. *Journal of European Integration*, 31(3), 265–269. DOI: 10.1080/07036330902782105

Slim, A. (2023). Will the BRICS be the leaders in central bank digital currencies? *Economic Studies Journal (Ikonomicheski Izsledvania)*, 2021, 30 (3),.3-16

Smarte Anekwe, I. M., Akpasi, S. O., Mkhize, M. M., Zhou, H., Moyo, R. T., & Gaza, L. (2024). Renewable energy investments in South Africa: Potentials and challenges for a sustainable transition: A review. *Science Progress*, 107(2), 00368504241237347. DOI: 10.1177/00368504241237347 PMID: 38614460

Smeeding, T. M., & Rainwater, L. (2004). Comparing Living Standards across Nations: Real Incomes at the Top, the Bottom, and the Middle. *What Has Happened to the Quality of Life in the Advanced Industrialized Nations*, 153-183.

Smith, R. (2019). Japan's strategic response to China's rise: Soft balancing and military modernization. *Journal of Japanese Studies*, 45(1), 34–56. DOI: 10.1353/jjs.2019.0002

Smit, T., & Tidblad-Lundholm, K. (2018). *Organization for Security and Co-operation in Europe field operations*. Stockholm International Peace Research Institute.

Sokolov, A., Shashnov, S., & Kotsemir, M. (2021). From BRICS to BRICS Plus: Selecting Promising Areas of S & T Cooperation with Developing Countries. *Scientometrics*, 126(11), 8815–8859. DOI: 10.1007/s11192-021-04142-3

Solaymani, S. (2021). A review on energy and renewable energy policies in Iran. *Sustainability (Basel)*, 13(13), 7328. DOI: 10.3390/su13137328

Somvanshi, P., Pandiaraj, T., & Singh, R. (2020). An unexplored story of successful green revolution of India and steps towards ever green revolution. *Journal of Pharmacognosy and Phytochemistry*, 9, 1270–1273.

Song, J., Chen, Y., Li, Y., & Sun, Q. (2022). Cryptocurrencies' past, present and future. Proceedings of the 2022, 2nd International Conference on Economic Development and Business Culture (ICEDBC 2022), AEBMR 225, Ed. Y. Jiang et al. 1402-1413. file:///C:/Users/user/Downloads/125983674.pdf

Sönmez, A., & Çetin, D. (2018). Issues in Emerging Market Economies. (eds.) Sönmez, A. & Çetin, D., ISBN 978-3-631-76614-9, Berlin, Peter Lang.

Sönmez, A. (2018). Foreign Direct Investment Inflows to EME. In Sönmez, A., & Çetin, D. (Eds.), *Issues in Emerging Market Economies* (pp. 259–288). Peter Lang., DOI: 10.3726/b14784

Sönmez, A., & Pamukçu, M. T. (2013). Foreign Direct Investment and Technology Spillovers in the Turkish Manufacturing Industry. In *Industrial Dynamics, Innovation Policy, and Economic Growth through Technological Advancements* (pp. 30–51). IGI Global. DOI: 10.4018/978-1-4666-1978-4.ch003

Soterroni, A. C., Império, M., Scarabello, M. C., Seddon, N., Obersteiner, M., Rochedo, P. R. E., Schaeffer, R., Andrade, P. R., Ramos, F. M., Azevedo, T. R., Ometto, J. P. H. B., Havlík, P., & Alencar, A. A. C. (2023). Nature-based solutions are critical for putting Brazil on track towards net-zero emissions by 2050. *Global Change Biology*, 29(24), 7085–7101. DOI: 10.1111/gcb.16984 PMID: 37907071

South Africa, B. R. I. C. S. (2023). BRICS Membership Expansion Guiding Principles, Standards, Criteria and Procedures. https://brics2023.gov.za/wp-content/uploads/2023/11/BRICS-Membership-expansion-guiding-principles-criteria-and-standards-2023.pdf

Srivithaya, S. (2021). The QUAD Diplomacy and the New Regional Order in Southeast Asia. Business and Interdisciplinary Studies ICEBIS2020, 6(4), 112-120. Retrieved from https://ibba.siamnet.asia/wp-content/uploads/2021/07/2020-16-The-QUAD-Diplomacy-and-the-New-Regional-Order-by-Suraphol-Srivithaya.pdf

Statista (2024a). Total population of the BRICS countries from 2000 to 2029. https://www.statista.com/statistics/254205/total-population-of-the-bric-countries/

Statista (2024b). BRICS and G7 countries' share of the world's total gross domestic product (GDP) in purchasing power parity (PPP) from 2000 to 2023. 13 February 2024. https://www.statista.com/statistics/1412425/gdp-ppp-share-world-gdp-g7-brics/

Statista (2024c). Cryptocurrencies – Worldwide. https://www.statista.com/outlook/fmo/digital-assets/cryptocurrencies/worldwide

Statista Research Department. (2024). GDP in PPP of BRICS and G7 Countries 2000-2024. https://www.statista.com/statistics/1412418/gdp-development-g7-brics/

Steinbuks, J., & Perez-Sebastian, F. (2022). "How Brazil's investment in hydropower infrastructure contributed to its long-term development". World Bank Blogs (https://blogs.worldbank.org/en/energy/how-brazils-investment-hydropower-infrastructure-contributed-its-long-term-development, Date of Access: 12.09.2024).

Stenner, C. (2016). Understanding the mediator: Taking stock of the OSCE's mechanisms and instruments for conflict resolution. *Security and Human Rights*, 27(3–4), 256–272. DOI: 10.1163/18750230-02703011

Stephen, M. (2014). Rising powers, global capitalism, and liberal global governance: A historical materialist account of the BRICS challenge. *European Journal of International Relations*, 20(4), 912–936. DOI: 10.1177/1354066114523655

Stojković, R. (2016). The New Development Bank BRICS. *Bankarstvo*, 45(2), 76–91. DOI: 10.5937/bankarstvo1602076S

Stojković, R., & Milosavljević, S. (2023). BRICS TENDENCIES TOWARDS REDEFINING THE GLOBAL ECONOMIC ORDER. *Science International Journal*, 2(4), 7–11. DOI: 10.35120/sciencej0204007s

Strangio, S. (2020). *In the Dragon's Shadow: Southeast Asia in the Chinese Century*. Yale University Press.

Stromseth, J. (2019). *Don't make us choose: Southeast Asia in the throes of US-China rivalry*. Brookings Institution.

Stromseth, J. R. (Ed.). (2021). *Rivalry and response: Assessing great power dynamics in Southeast Asia*. Brookings Institution Press.

Stuenkel, O. (2020). The BRICS and the future of global order. *International Organization*, 74(4), 122–137. DOI: 10.1017/S0020818320000398

Sun, Y. (2017, November 3). Winning projects and hearts? Three cases of Chinese mega-infrastructure projects in Southeast Asia. The Asan Forum. Retrieved from https://theasanforum.org/winning-projects-and-hearts-three-cases-of-chinese-mega-infrastructure-projects-in-southeast-asia/

Sunitha, G. (2018). Forecasting GDP using ARIMA and artificial neural networks models under Indian environment. *International Journal of Mathematics Trends and Technology*, 56(1), 60–70. DOI: 10.14445/22315373/IJMTT-V56P508

Sun, S.-C. (2023). Confucius Institutes: China's Cultural Soft Power Strategy. *Journal of Culture and Values in Education*, 6(1), 52–68. DOI: 10.46303/jcve.2023.4

Sun, Z. (2021). Progress and Prospects: Sino-Russian Strategic Coordination in Multilateral Mechanisms. *Chinese Journal of Slavic Studies*, 1(1), 79–91. DOI: 10.1515/cjss-2021-2006

Suresh, D. (2015). India and BRICS. Law. https://doi.org/DOI: 10.2139/SSRN.2675252

Svensson, I. (2009). Who brings which peace? Neutral versus biased mediation and institutional peace arrangements in civil wars. *The Journal of Conflict Resolution*, 53(3), 446–469. https://www.jstor.org/stable/20684594. DOI: 10.1177/0022002709332207

Tabash, M. I., Farooq, U., Al-Faryan, M. A. S., & Wong, W. K. (2024). Effect of geopolitical risk on energy consumption policy: New empirical evidence from BRICS. *Heliyon*, 10(19), e38049. DOI: 10.1016/j.heliyon.2024.e38049 PMID: 39386848

Taneja, N., Dayal, I., & Bimal, S. (2013). India–Pakistan Trade and Regionalism in South Asia. *International Studies*, 50(3), 318–342. DOI: 10.1177/0020881717713597

Tantri, M. L., & Shaurav, K. (2018). Food security in BRICS: Current status and issues. Working Papers No 419. Institute for Social and Economic Change.

Tan, W. Y., & Chin, C. F. (2020). High-level visits and the Belt and Road Initiative: The case of Southeast Asia. *Contemporary Chinese Political Economy and Strategic Relations*, 6(1), 217–XI.

Tao, M., & Xi, C. (2023). BRICS Energy Cooperation and Global Energy Governance. *Contemp. China & World*, 1, 118.

Taylor, M. (2015). *The Chinese State, Oil and Energy Security*. HeinOnline.

Technology, R. (n.d.). Singapore-Kunming Rail Link (SKRL). Retrieved from https://www.railway-technology.com/projects/singapore-kunming-rail-link-skrl/

Tella, O. (2017). South Africa in BRICS: The Regional Power's Soft Power and Soft Balancing. *Politikon: South African Journal of Political Studies*, 44(3), 387–403. DOI: 10.1080/02589346.2017.1295620

Telli, A., & Yeşil, E. (2023). Ukrayna Krizinin Yeşil Enerji Dönüşümüne Etkisi Almanya Örneği. *Tarsus Üniversitesi İktisadi ve İdari Bilimler Fakültesi Dergisi*, 4(2), 85–110. DOI: 10.56400/tarsusiibfdergisi.1291211

Teslova, E. (2024). Putin says trade turnover with China sets new record of $240B. Anadolu Ajansı. 16.05.2024. https://www.aa.com.tr/en/asia-pacific/putin-says-trade-turnover-with-china-sets-new-record-of-240b/3221034

Thakur, R. (2014). How representative are BRICS? *Third World Quarterly*, 35(10), 1791–1808. DOI: 10.1080/01436597.2014.971594

The Economist. (2023). Joe Biden's China strategy is not working. The Economist. tuenkel, O. (2023, August 18). BRICS expansion would be a sign of China's growing influence. The Economist. Retrieved from https://www.economist.com/by-invitation/2023/08/18/brics-expansion-would-be-a-sign-of-chinas-growing-influence-says-oliver-stuenkel

The Globalist. (2024). BRICS Vs. the G7. How do the BRICS stack up against the G7 group of nations? (https://www.theglobalist.com/brics-brics-g7-economy-population-just-the-facts/. Date of Access: 23.10.2024).

The Jerusalem Post. (2024). Putin Confirms BRICS Developing Independent Payment System with Potential Gold-Backed Currency. https://www.jpost.com/business-and-innovation/precious-metals/article-822549

The Landbanking Group. (2024). Nature equity: A new asset class that brings nature on the balance sheet. January 2024. https://25771685.fs1.hubspotusercontent-eu1.net/hubfs/25771685/Resources/NatureEquityConsultationPaper_WebVersion.pdf

The White House. (2024, May 14). *FACT SHEET: President Biden Takes Action to Protect American Workers and Businesses from China's Unfair Trade Practices*. https://www.whitehouse.gov/briefing-room/statements-releases/2024/05/14/fact-sheet-president-biden-takes-action-to-protect-american-workers-and-businesses-from-chinas-unfair-trade-practices/

Tian, W., Yu, M., & Zheng, C. (2022). *China's Retaliatory Tariffs Against the US:-Firm Import-Export Linkage Along Global Production Line* (E2022002; Working Paper Series).

Tian, X., Sarkis, J., Geng, Y., Bleischwitz, R., Qian, Y., Xu, L., & Wu, R. (2020). Examining the role of BRICS countries at the global economic and environmental resources nexus. *Journal of Environmental Management*, 262, 110330. DOI: 10.1016/j.jenvman.2020.110330 PMID: 32250809

Tiewsoh, L. S., Jirásek, J., & Sivek, M. (2019). Electricity generation in India: Present state, future outlook and policy implications. *Energies*, 12(7), 1361. DOI: 10.3390/en12071361

Tilman, D., Cassman, K. G., Matson, P. A., Naylor, R., & Polasky, S. (2002). Agricultural Sustainability and Intensive Production Practices. *Nature*, 418(6898), 671–677. DOI: 10.1038/nature01014 PMID: 12167873

Tong, M., Yiyi, Z., & Lei, T. (2024). BRICS nations eye 'blue ocean' in green cooperation as ties deepen during highly-watched summit (https://www.globaltimes.cn/page/202410/1321800.shtml. Date of Access: 23.10.2024).

Toussaint, E. (2024). Are the BRICS and their New Development Bank offering alternatives to the World Bank, the IMF and the policies promoted by the traditional imperialist powers? 21 April 2024. https://www.cadtm.org/spip.php?page=imprimer&id_article=22501

Tran, H. (2024). Is the end of the petrodollar near? June 20, 2024. https://www.atlanticcouncil.org/blogs/econographics/is-the-end-of-the-petrodollar-near/

Tripathi, S. (2021). International Relations and the 'Global South': From Epistemic Hierarchies to Dialogic Encounters. *Third World Quarterly*, 42(9), 2039–2054. DOI: 10.1080/01436597.2021.1924666

Troitskiy, M. (2015). BRICS Approaches to Security Multilateralism. *Air & Space Power Journal*, 6(2), 76–88.

Troy, A., & Wilson, M. A. (2006). Mapping ecosystem services: Practical challenges and opportunities in linking GIS and value transfer. *Ecological Economics*, 60(2), 435–449. DOI: 10.1016/j.ecolecon.2006.04.007

Tsybulenko, E., & Francis, J. (2018). Separatists or Russian troops and local collaborators? Russian aggression in Ukraine: The problem of definitions. In S. Sayapin & E. Tsybulenko (Eds.), *The use of force against Ukraine and international law: Jus ad bellum, jus in bello, jus post bellum* (pp. 123–144). T.M.C. Asser Press. https://doi.org/DOI: 10.1007/978-94-6265-222-4_6

Tüysüzoğlu, G., & Özgen, C. (2020). *The Relationship between the 21st Century Maritime Silk Road Initiative and Chinese Naval Strategy*. Alanya Akademik Bakış., DOI: 10.29023/alanyaakademik.673794

Tyers, R. (2016). Slower Growth and Vulnerability to Recession: Updating China's Global Impact. *Scottish Journal of Political Economy*, 63(1), 66–88. DOI: 10.1111/sjpe.12111

UCDP. (2022). Ukraine. *UCDP - Uppsala Conflict Data Program*. https://ucdp.uu.se/

Udeagha, M. C., & Ngepah, N. (2023). The drivers of environmental sustainability in BRICS economies: Do green finance and fintech matter? *World Development Sustainability*, 3, 100096. DOI: 10.1016/j.wds.2023.100096

Umland, A. (2021). Achievements and limitations of the OSCE's Special Monitoring Mission to Ukraine. *The Swedish Institute of International Affairs*. https://doi.org/DOI: 10.13140/RG.2.2.26539.57126

UN. (2014). System of environmental-economic accounting 2012—Central framework. United Nations, New York. https://unstats.un.org/unsd/envaccounting/seeaRev/SEEA_CF_Final_en.pdf

UN. (2023). Blockchain for biodiversity finance. https://cognizium.io/uploads/resources/UN%20environment%20programme%20-%20An%20Overview%20of%20Various%20Blockchain%20Applications%20to%20Help%20Increase%20Biodiversity%20Funding.pdf

UN. (n.d.). Preparatory Years: UN Charter History. https://www.un.org/en/about-us/history-of-the-un/preparatory-years#:~:text=The%20UN%20Charter%20was%20signed,UN's%20original%2051%20Member%20States

UNDP. (2013). *Human Development Report*. UNDP.

US Census Bureau. (2024). *Trade in Goods with China*. https://www.census.gov/foreign-trade/balance/c5700.html

USTR. (2018). *2018 Annual Report*. https://ustr.gov/sites/default/files/files/Press/Reports/2018/AR/2018%20Annual%20Report%20I.pdf

Utar, H., Torres Ruiz, L. B., & Zurita, A. C. (2023). *The US-China Trade War and the Relocation of Global Value Chains to Mexico* (10638; CESifo Working Paper Series). DOI: 10.2139/ssrn.4568757

Uvinha, R. R., de Oliveira, N. R., de Ridder, J. H., Chin, M.-K., & Durstine, J. L. (2018). The BRICS Council for Exercise and Sport Science (BRICSCESS) - A new era has dawned. *Journal of Sport and Health Science*, 7(4), 425–428. DOI: 10.1016/j.jshs.2018.06.004 PMID: 30450250

Valença, M. M., & Carvalho, G. (2014). Soft Power, Hard Aspirations: The Shifting Role of Power in Brazilian Foreign Policy. *Brazilian Political Science Review*, 8(3), 66–94. DOI: 10.1590/1981-38212014000100021

Van Dinh, D. (2020). Forecasting domestic credit growth based on ARIMA model: Evidence from Vietnam and China. *Management Science Letters*, 1001–1010. DOI: 10.5267/j.msl.2019.11.010

Van Gansbeke, F. (2021). Time for IMF climate coin (2/3). January 17, 2021. https://www.forbes.com/sites/frankvangansbeke/2021/01/17/time-for-imf-climate-coin-23/

Varas, A., & Varadarajan, R. (2020). *How Restrictions to Trade with China Could End US Leadership in Semiconductors* .

Varela, A. H., & Delgado, R. G. M. (2019, October). The BRICS in the Contemporary Global Order: Objectives, Capabilities, and Limitations. *Jurnal Ilmu Pemerintahan*, 9(2), 89–106.

Vasileski, Z. BRICS VERSUS THE GLOBAL WEST IN THE LIGHT OF CURRENT GLOBAL REALIZATIONS. Towards a Better Future: Peace, Justice, and Strong Institutions, 291.

Viaene, L. (2022). Can rights of nature save us from the Anthropocene catastrophe? Some critical reflections from the field. *Asian Journal of Law and Society*, 9(2), 187–206. DOI: 10.1017/als.2022.2

Viola, E., & Korber, V. (2019). Brazil ups and downs in global environmental governance in the 21st century. *Revista Brasileira de Política Internacional*, 62(2), e010. DOI: 10.1590/0034-7329201900210

Vo, Nguyen, Tran, & Bui (2023). US response as conducting freedom of navigation operations and enhancing defense cooperation.

Volgina, N. A., & Pengfei, L. (2021). Trade War Impact on GVCs and China's Counter Measures. In Popkova, E. G., & Sergi, B. S. (Eds.), *Modern Global Economic System: Evolutional Development vs. Revolutionary Leap* (Vol. 198, pp. 2057–2063). Springer., DOI: 10.1007/978-3-030-69415-9_225

von Twickel, N., Sasse, G., & Baumann, M. (2018). Russian Analytical Digest No 214: The armed conflict in Eastern Ukraine. *Center for Security Studies (CSS).* https://css.ethz.ch/en/services/digital-library/publications/publication.html

Vuković, S. (2011). Strategies and bias in international mediation. *Cooperation and Conflict*, 46(1), 113–119. DOI: 10.1177/0010836710396848

Vyas-Doorgapersad, S. (2022). *The role of BRICS in global governance to promote economic development.* Africa's Public Service Delivery & Performance Review., DOI: 10.4102/apsdpr.v10i1.633

Wade, R. (2003). What Strategies are Viable for Developing Countries Today? The World Trade Organization and the Shrinking of 'Development Space'. *Review of International Political Economy*, 10(4), 621–644. DOI: 10.1080/09692290310001601902

Wainstein, M., Constant, A., & Clippinger, J. (2023). Nature based currencies: Integrating natural capital in advanced monetary systems. Open Earth Foundation. https://assets-global.website-files.com/62192ceb9199b3dd08431a6b/647d5895085b1d0a2c5ba6de_NatureBasedCurrencies_v2.pdf

Walgreen, D. (2006). China in the Indian Ocean Region: Lessons in PRC Grand Strategy. *Comparative Strategy*, 25(1), 55–73. DOI: 10.1080/01495930600639544

Wallace, J. B. (2022). *Establishing a first island chain balance of power: Cooperative development of the quadrilateral security dialogue. Doctoral dissertation.* US Army Command and General Staff College., Retrieved from https://scholar.google.com/scholar?hl=en&as_sdt=0%2C5&q=Scott%2C+2020+The+QUAD+emphasizes+maintaining+freedom+of+navigation%2C+promoting+democratic+values%2C+and+countering+Chinese+influence.+&btnG=

Wallensteen, P., & Svensson, I. (2014). Talking peace: International mediation in armed conflicts. *Journal of Peace Research*, 51(2), 315–327. https://www.jstor.org/stable/24557424. DOI: 10.1177/0022343313512223

Waltz, K. N. (1979). Theory of International Politics.

Walz, R., & Ostertag, K. (2009). Absorptive Capacities for Sustainability Technologies: Perspectives from the BRICS and China. *Zhongguo Renkou Ziyuan Yu Huanjing*, 7(2), 10–13. DOI: 10.1080/10042857.2009.10684917

Wang, W., & Wang, H. (2023). Interconnected Markets: Exploring the Dynamic Relationship Between BRICS Stock Markets and Cryptocurrency. Texas A&M International University. https://arxiv.org/pdf/2406.07641

Wang, H. (2019). The New Development Bank and the Asian Infrastructure Investment Bank: China's Ambiguous Approach to Global Financial Governance. *Development and Change*, 50(1), 221–244. DOI: 10.1111/dech.12473

Wang, J., & Tian, X. (2022). Impacts of the belt and road initiative on China's bilateral trade. *Journal of the Asia Pacific Economy*, 27(3), 400–424. DOI: 10.1080/13547860.2022.2042110

Wang, L. (2022). China's Huawei in the Us-China Trade War in the Communications Sector Game. *Proceedings of the 2022 2nd International Conference on Enterprise Management and Economic Development (ICEMED 2022)*, 485–497. DOI: 10.2991/aebmr.k.220603.078

Wang, Q., Li, S., & Pisarenko, Z. (2020). Modeling carbon emission trajectory of China, US and India. *Journal of Cleaner Production*, 258(120723), 120723. DOI: 10.1016/j.jclepro.2020.120723

Wang, X., Ma, L., Yan, S., Chen, X., & Growe, A. (2023). Trade for Food Security: The Stability of Global Agricultural Trade Networks. *Foods*, 12(2), 271. DOI: 10.3390/foods12020271 PMID: 36673361

WCED (World Commission on Environment and Development). (1987). *Our Common Future*. UN.

WEF. (2021). State of finance for nature 2021. World Economic Forum Report. https://wedocs.unep.org/xmlui/bitstream/handle/20.500.11822/36145/SFN.pdf

Wegren, S. (2010). Russia's Food Policies and Foreign Policy. *Demokratizatsiya (Washington, D.C.)*, 18, 189–207.

Wei, Z. (2024). The Evolution of the 'QUAD'. Horizons: Journal of International Relations and Sustainable Development, (25), 82-99. Retrieved from https://www.jstor.org/stable/48761182

Weinstein, F. B. (1969). The concept of a commitment in international relations. *The Journal of Conflict Resolution*, 13(1), 39–56. DOI: 10.1177/002200276901300103

Wendling, J. (2024). The Bloc Effect: International Trade with Geopolitical Allies on the Rise. (https://www.visualcapitalist.com/sp/hf02-international-trade-with-geopolitical-allies-rising/. Date of Access: 27.09.2024).

Wendt, A. (1992). Anarchy is what states make of it: The social construction of power politics.

Wen, T., Liu, Y., Bai, Y., & Liu, H. (2023). Modeling and forecasting CO2 emissions in China and its regions using a novel ARIMA-LSTM model. *Heliyon*, 9(11), e21241. DOI: 10.1016/j.heliyon.2023.e21241 PMID: 37954263

Wesche, T. (2022). Who owns nature? About the rights of nature. *Estudios Filosóficos*, 65, 49–68. DOI: 10.17533/udea.ef.347573

West, T. A. P., Wunder, S., Sills, E. O., Börner, J., Rifai, S. W., Neidermeier, A. N., Frey, G. P., & Kontoleon, A. (2023). Action needed to make carbon offsets from forest conservation work for climate change mitigation. *Science*, 381(6660), 873–877. DOI: 10.1126/science.ade3535 PMID: 37616370

Wiig, H., & Øien, H. (2013). Would Small be More Beautiful in the South African Land Reform? In Holden, S. T., Otsuka, K., & Deininger, K. (Eds.), *Land Tenure Reform in Asia and Africa*. Palgrave Macmillan. DOI: 10.1057/9781137343819_4

Wilk, J., Andersson, L., & Warburton, M. (2013). Adaptation to Climate Change and Other Stressors among Commercial and Small-scale South African Farmers. *Regional Environmental Change*, 13(2), 273–286. DOI: 10.1007/s10113-012-0323-4

Williams, C., & Papa, M. (2020). Rethinking 'Alliances': The Case of South Africa as a Rising Power. *African Security*, 13(4), 325–352. DOI: 10.1080/19392206.2020.1871796

WITS. (2024a). *China and U.S. Trade Summary*. https://wits.worldbank.org/CountryProfile/en/Country/CHN/Year/2018/SummaryText

WITS. (2024b). *China Exports by country in US$ Thousand 2001-2021*. https://wits.worldbank.org/CountryProfile/en/Country/CHN/StartYear/2001/EndYear/2021/TradeFlow/Export/Partner/BY-COUNTRY/Indicator/XPRT-TRD-VL

WITS. (2024c). *China Food Products Imports By Country in US$ Thousand 2001-2021*. https://wits.worldbank.org/CountryProfile/en/Country/CHN/StartYear/2001/EndYear/2021/TradeFlow/Import/Indicator/MPRT-TRD-VL/Partner/BY-COUNTRY/Product/16-24_FoodProd

WITS. (2024d). *China Fuels Imports By Country in US$ Thousand 2001-2021*. https://wits.worldbank.org/CountryProfile/en/Country/CHN/StartYear/2001/EndYear/2021/TradeFlow/Import/Indicator/MPRT-TRD-VL/Partner/BY-COUNTRY/Product/27-27_Fuels

WITS. (2024e). *China Imports by country in US$ Thousand 2001-2021*. https://wits.worldbank.org/CountryProfile/en/Country/CHN/StartYear/2001/EndYear/2021/TradeFlow/Import/Partner/BY-COUNTRY/Indicator/MPRT-TRD-VL

WITS. (2024f). *South Africa Minerals Export Product Share By Country in % 2001-2021*. https://wits.worldbank.org/CountryProfile/en/Country/ZAF/StartYear/2001/EndYear/2021/TradeFlow/Export/Indicator/XPRT-PRDCT-SHR/Partner/BY-COUNTRY/Product/25-26_Minerals# World Bank. (2024a). *GDP (current US$) - Brazil, China, India, Russian Federation, South Africa, Iran, Islamic Rep., United Arab Emirates, Egypt, Arab Rep., Ethiopia*. https://data.worldbank.org/indicator/NY.GDP.MKTP.CD?locations=BR-CN-IN-RU-ZA-IR-AE-EG-ET&most_recent_value_desc=true

World Bank. (2023). "Factsheet: Eskom Just Energy Transition Project in South Africa". (https://www.worldbank.org/en/news/factsheet/2023/06/05/factsheet-eskom-just-energy-transition-project-in-afe-south-africa#:~:text=South%20Africa's%20highly%20coal%2Ddependent,and%20the%20country's%20economic%20prospects. Date of Access: 14.09.2024).

World Bank. (2024). Finance and prosperity 2024. August 2024. https://openknowledge.worldbank.org/server/api/core/bitstreams/a583724d-0264-41be-b3ea-0ee5d167ec04/content

World Bank. (2024). Indicators. Erişim Adresi: https://data.worldbank.org/indicator. (Erişim Tarihi: 27.08.2024).

World Bank. (2024). World Bank DataBank. Retrieved [Month Day, Year], from https://databank.worldbank.org

World Bank. (2024). World Development Indicators (WDI). Accessed date: 18.08.2024. https://databank.worldbank.org/source/world-development-indicators

World Bank. (2024b). *GDP (current US$) - China, United States*. https://data.worldbank.org/indicator/NY.GDP.MKTP.CD?locations=CN-US World Bank. (2024c). *Industry (including construction), value added (% of GDP) - United States, China*. https://data.worldbank.org/indicator/NV.IND.TOTL.ZS?end=2023&locations=US-CN&start=2001

World Bank. (2024d). *Inflation, consumer prices (annual %) - China, United States*. https://data.worldbank.org/indicator/FP.CPI.TOTL.ZG?locations=CN-US World Bank. (2024e). *Population, total - Brazil, China, India, Russian Federation, South Africa, Iran, Islamic Rep., United Arab Emirates, Egypt, Arab Rep., Ethiopia*. https://data.worldbank.org/indicator/SP.POP.TOTL?locations=BR-CN-IN-RU-ZA-IR-AE-EG-ET World Bank. (2024f, March 12). *GDP Rankings 2022*. https://data.worldbank.org/indicator/NY.GDP.MKTP.CD

World Integrated Trade Solutions. (2023). Brazil Soya Beans Exports by Country in 2023. https://wits.worldbank.org/trade/comtrade/en/country/BRA/year/2023/tradeflow/Exports/partner/ALL/product/120100

World Population Review. (2024). Global North Countries 2024. https://worldpopulationreview.com/country-rankings/global-north-countries

World Trade Organization. (2024). The Doha Round. https://www.wto.org/english/tratop_e/dda_e/dda_e.htm

World Wildlife Fund (WWF). (2012). Responsible investing for climate change and water in South Africa. Technical Report 2012. http://awsassets.wwf.org.za/downloads/responsible_investing_for_climate_change_and_water_wwf_nov_2012.pdf

worldometer (2024). Countries in the world by population (2024). https://www.worldometers.info/world-population/population-by-country/

Worldometer. (2024). Oil Production by Country. https://www.worldometers.info/oil/oil-production-by-country/

Wu, S. (2016, June 17). Singapore-Kunming Rail Link: A 'Belt and Road' case study. The Diplomat. Retrieved from https://thediplomat.com/2016/06/singapore-kunming-rail-link-a-belt-and-road-case-study/

Wu, J., Wood, J., Oh, K., & Jang, H. (2021). Evaluating the cumulative impact of the US–China trade war along global value chains. *World Economy*, 44(12), 3516–3533. DOI: 10.1111/twec.13125

Wutich, A., & Gravlee, C. C. (2010). Water decision–makers in a desert city: Text analysis and environmental social science. In Vaccaro, I., Smith, E. A., & Aswani, S. (Eds.), *Environmental social sciences* (pp. 188–211). Cambridge University Press., DOI: 10.1017/CBO9780511760242.011

www.gov.br. (2024). Brazil reduces reliance on oil, natural gas in its energy matrix. (https://www.gov.br/secom/en/latest-news/2024/06/brazil-reduces-reliance-on-oil-natural-gas-in-its-energy-matrix Date of Access: 12.10.2024).

Xia, Y., Kong, Y., Ji, Q., & Zhang, D. (2019). Impacts of China-US trade conflicts on the energy sector. *China Economic Review*, 58, 101360. DOI: 10.1016/j.chieco.2019.101360

Xin, G., Khan, H., & Ling, X. (2024). The impact of BRICS trade facilitation on China's import and export trade in agricultural products. *Frontiers in Sustainable Food Systems*, 8, 1397350. DOI: 10.3389/fsufs.2024.1397350

Xinhua (2024). New Development Bank to expand use of local currencies, 31 August 2024. https://english.news.cn/africa/20240831/2e16f6c2a1dc4ad2bf9c3c069b790aed/c.html

Xu, C., & Lim, G. (2024). Chinese investment in Southeast Asia:(how) does it matter? *Eurasian Geography and Economics*, •••, 1–18. DOI: 10.1080/15387216.2024.2394555

Yang, B., Li, C., Li, M., Pan, K., & Wang, D. (2016). Application of ARIMA model in the prediction of the gross domestic product. *Proceedings of the 2016 6th International Conference on Mechatronics, Computer and Education Informationization (MCEI 2016)*. DOI: 10.2991/mcei-16.2016.257

Yang, H., Gou, X., Ma, W., & Xue, B. (2023). Research and application of GEP: China's experience in natural capital accounting. *Frontiers in Environmental Science*, 11, 1106654. DOI: 10.3389/fenvs.2023.1106654

Yang, J. (2022). Understanding China's changing engagement in global climate governance: A struggle for identity. *Asia Europe Journal*, 20(4), 357–376. DOI: 10.1007/s10308-021-00643-1 PMID: 35035337

Yang, J., Rizvi, S. K. A., Tan, Z., Umar, M., & Koondhar, M. A. (2021). The competing role of natural gas and oil as fossil fuel and the non-linear dynamics of resource curse in Russia. *Resources Policy*, 72, 102100. DOI: 10.1016/j.resourpol.2021.102100

Ye, F. (2023). The new development bank and the structure of the multilateral development financial system. *Review of Development Economics*, 27(3), 1957–1972. DOI: 10.1111/rode.12995

Ye, X. (2022). From Strategic Ambiguity to Maximum Pressure? Explaining the Logic of the US Taiwan Policy in the Post–Cold War Era. *Journal of Asian and African Studies*, 57(8), 1511–1543. DOI: 10.1177/00219096211058887

Yi, K.-M. (2010). Can Multistage Production Explain the Home Bias in Trade? *The American Economic Review*, 100(1), 364–393. DOI: 10.1257/aer.100.1.364

Yousefi, H., Ardehali, A., & Ghodusinejad, M. H. (2023). BRICS or G7? Current and future assessment of energy and environment performance using multi-criteria and time series analyzes. *Energy Strategy Reviews*, 49, 101164. DOI: 10.1016/j.esr.2023.101164

Yu, B., Liu, F., & You, L. (2012). Dynamic Agricultural Supply Response Under Economic Transformation: A Case Study of Henan, China. *American Journal of Agricultural Economics*, 94(2), 370–376. DOI: 10.1093/ajae/aar114

Yu, H. (2022). European Energy Prospect under the Russo-Ukrainian war. Highlights in Science. *Engineering and Technology*, 25, 203–209.

Yu, J., & Wu, J. (2018). The Sustainability of Agricultural Development in China: The Agriculture–Environment Nexus. *Sustainability (Basel)*, 10(6), 1776. DOI: 10.3390/su10061776

Yunqi, W. (2023). The dilemma and reconstruction of ASEAN's centrality: A neoclassical realist perspective. [JKoB]. *Jurnal Komunikasi Borneo*, 11, 174–201.

Zeng, K., Xu, Y., & Xie, Z. (2023). Local sourcing embeddedness, manufacturing relocation, and firm attitudes toward the US-China trade war: A survey analysis of China-based MNC subsidiaries. *Business and Politics*, 25(2), 91–116. DOI: 10.1017/bap.2022.27

Zhang, H. (2021). *The Impact of COVID-19 on Global Production Networks: Evidence from Japanese Multinational Firms.*

Zhang, C., & Wu, R. (2019). Battlefield of global ranking: How do power rivalries shape soft power index building? *Global Media and China*, 4(2), 179–202. DOI: 10.1177/2059436419855876

Zhang, F. (2021). Competitiveness or complementarity: Analysis of agricultural trade between China and Brazil. *Problems and Perspectives in Management*, 19(4), 258–269. DOI: 10.21511/ppm.19(4).2021.21

Zhang, L., Zhou, J., & Zang, Y. (2024). Financial risk identification and control in the openness context: A system dynamics approach to Renminbi internationalization. *International Review of Economics & Finance*, 103542, 103542. Advance online publication. DOI: 10.1016/j.iref.2024.103542

Zhang, R., Li, P., Xu, L., & Zhong, S. (2023). Reconciling ecological footprint and ecosystem services in natural capital accounting: Applying a novel framework to the Silk Road Economic Belt in China. *Journal of Environmental Management*, 330, 117115. DOI: 10.1016/j.jenvman.2022.117115 PMID: 36587549

Zhang, S., Zhang, P., & Gao, M. (2018). Study on Energy Technology in BRICS. In Zhao, X., Li, M., Huang, M., & Sokolov, A. (Eds.), *BRICS Innovative Competitiveness Report 2017. Research Series on the Chinese Dream and China's Development Path*. Springer. DOI: 10.1007/978-981-10-8078-4_11

Zhang, Y., Li, H., Xu, X., & Antwi, H. A. (2023). On the momentum toward vaccine self-sufficiency in the BRICS: An integrative review of the role of pharmaceutical entrepreneurship and innovation. *Frontiers in Public Health*, 11, 1116092. DOI: 10.3389/fpubh.2023.1116092 PMID: 37876712

Zhao, X. (2024). Technological hedging and differentiated responses of Southeast Asian countries to US–China technological competition: A case study on artificial intelligence (AI). *The Pacific Review*, •••, 1–32. DOI: 10.1080/09512748.2024.2408010

Zhelyazkova, A., Haverland, M., & Joosen, R. (2023). Legislating softly: The effect of preference heterogeneity on the share of EU soft-law instruments over time. *European Union Politics*, 24(3), 447–469. DOI: 10.1177/14651165231162510

Zhidong, L. (2005). China's energy outlook to the year 2030. *International Journal of Global Energy Issues*, 24(3-4), 144–169. DOI: 10.1504/IJGEI.2005.007768

Zhongxiu, Z., & Qingxin, L. (2020). Promoting BRICS cooperation for economic growth and development.(https://repositorio.ipea.gov.br/bitstream/11058/13441/1/Tempo_Mundo_n22_Artigo2_promoting_brics_cooperation.pdf. Date of Access: 09.09.2024).

Zhongxiu, Z., & Qingxin, L. (2022). Promoting BRICS cooperation for economic growth and development. [RTM]. *Revista Tempo Do Mundo*, 22, 39–57. DOI: 10.38116/rtm22art2

Zhou, T. (2016). Overcoming the Dilemma of China's Growth. In Tsang, S., & Men, H. (Eds.), *China in the Xi Jinping Era* (pp. 187–219). Palgrave Macmillan., DOI: 10.1007/978-3-319-29549-7_8

Zhou, Y. (2020). *China Trade War and Global Value Chains*.

Zhu, J. (2019). Borrowing Country-Oriented or Donor Country-Oriented? Comparing the BRICS New Development Bank and the Asian Infrastructure Investment Bank. International Organisations Research Journal. DOI: 10.17323/1996-7845-2019-02-06

# About the Contributors

**Ayfer Gedikli** earned her PhD in 2009 in fiscal economics. She surved as the dean of the Faculty of Political Sciences in Duzce University until 2023. Currently, she is the head of the department of Economics. Her area of interest is energy economics, environmental economics, money&banking, and international political economics. She has many high quality papers published in prestigious international journals which are cited by SSCI, SCI, SCOPUS indexes. She took part as the editor of many editorial books which are published by international publishers.

**Seyfettin Erdoğan** is one of the well-known academicians in Turkey. He has many high quality books on macroeconomics that are used as text-books in many universities in Turkey. His field of interest is macroeconomics, money&banking, environmental economics, and financial crisis. He has many papers published in SSCI indexed journals.

**Hande Çalışkan Terzioğlu** received her PhD in Economics from Tekirdağ Namık Kemal University/Turkey. She continues her studies as the academican of the Faculty of Political Sciences at Duzce University. Her research continues on macroeconomics and policies. She giving lectures in Macroeconomics, Economic Policy, International Monetary and Capital Markets.

***

**Vishnu Achutha Menon** is an independent journalist, writer, researcher, and an Indian percussionist. He is a recipient of the Junior Scholarship the Ministry of Culture awarded. His research interests are film studies, verbal & nonverbal communication, south Asian performances, Natyasastra, media studies, media analysis techniques, Laban Movement Analysis, and Ethnomusicology.

**Helder Ferreira do Vale** is a Professor in the Graduate Program of International Relations of the Federal University of Bahia (Brazil). He has authored scholarly articles in the areas of territorial politics, international relations, comparative politics, Latin American and European politics. Dr. do Vale has received several research grants from institutions including the Spanish Ministry of Education, the European Commission, and the German National Study Foundation. He has occupied various academic positions at institutions such as XianJiotong-Liverpool University (China), Hankuk University (South Korea), University of Barcelona (Spain), University of Lisbon (Portugal), Center for Advanced Studies Hanse-Wissenschaftskolleg (Germany), Center for Political and Constitutional Studies (Spain), University of Cape Town (South Africa), and Aalborg University (Denmark). Dr. do Vale obtained a PhD from the European University Institute - EUI (Italy), a M.A.from the Johns Hopkins University (USA), and a B.A. from Richmond University (UK).

**Hasan Harmanci** is a Lecturer (PhD) in the Department of Economics at Düzce University, Akçakoca Bey Faculty of Political Science, Türkiye. He completed his PhD in International Business at the University of St Andrews, United Kingdom, with a thesis titled A Holistic Approach to Internationalization: Motives, Enablers, and Patterns of Emerging Market SMEs. He also holds an MSc in International Trade Strategy and Operations from the University of Warwick, United Kingdom, and a BA in Economics (English Program) from Istanbul University, Türkiye. Dr. Harmanci's research focuses on international business, particularly internationalization, foreign direct investments (FDIs), and multinational enterprises (MNEs), with a special interest in SME internationalization. His work delves into the challenges and opportunities SMEs face in global markets, aiming to enhance understanding of their strategies and performance on an international scale.

**Jipson Joseph** has a PhD in Ethics from DVK Bangalore. Currently, he is a Research Scholar in the School of Law at Christ University, Bangalore. His research interests are in the fields of ethics, gender studies, BRICS Countries, Geopolitics, Global South, constitutional law, human rights, human security and global poverty.

**Apoorva Misra** holds a Doctor of Philosophy In law from Guru Gobind Singh Indraprastha University, Dwarka, Delhi on "Locating Environment In The Application of Sustainable Development: A Critical Analysis of Environmental Jurisprudence" (2023) and Master of Law from Teri School of Advanced Studies, New Delhi (2018).

**Zehra Namlı** graduated from Sakarya University's Faculty of Political Sciences, Department of Political Science and Public Administration in 2021. In the same year, she began a master's program in local government and urbanization at Istanbul

Medeniyet University and completed it in 2023 with a thesis titled "Migration Management in Municipalities in Turkey: The Case of Esenyurt, Zeytinburnu, and Sultanbeyli Municipalities." In 2023, she started a Ph.D. program in Political Science and Public Administration at Istanbul Medeniyet University. Since 2023, she has been working at Düzce University.

**Ananya Pandey** is a Research Scholar in School of Law at Christ University, Bangalore. She has her research interests in the field of Constitutional Law, Human Rights, Feminist studies, Global South, Intellectual Property Law and Jurisprudence.

**Alper Sönmez** holds a PhD in Economics from the Middle East Technical University (METU). He received his BSc. in Economics with the First-Class Honours from Yıldız Technical University (YTU) in 2002. He spent one year at Cornell University as a Visiting Fellow. He is the recipient of 'METU Thesis of the Year Award' granted by Prof. Dr. Mustafa N. Parlar Education and Research Foundation. Since February 2013, he has been affiliated with the Department of Economics at Selçuk University, Turkey. His current research interests are foreign direct investment, economies of technology and innovation, knowledge and technology spillovers, automotive industry, MNCs, global production networks and R&D.

**Hasan Umutlu** holds a bachelor's degree in International Trade and Finance from Afyon Kocatepe University, a master's degree in Economics from Selçuk University and a PhD in Economics from Eskişehir Osmangazi University. Umutlu's master's thesis is titled "Economists Between the State and the Market: Economists' Views and Attitudes on the Role of the State and the Market", he conducted a survey among economist academics in Turkey. Umutlu is currently a research assistant in the Department of Economics at Düzce University and continues his studies on energy, economics education, environment and sustainability.

**Tran Vang-Phu** is a senior lecturer in law at Law School, Ho Chi Minh City University of Economics and Finance, Vietnam. He holds a master's degree (LL.M) from Chulalongkorn University, Thai Lan; and a JSD/Ph.D (Doctor of Juridical Science) from the University of Economics and Law – Vietnam National University of Ho Chi Minh City, Vietnam. He is also an arbitrator and mediator and is currently the Deputy Director of the APEC Vietnam International Commercial Arbitration Centre.

# Index

## A



## B

## C



## D



## E

# F



# G



# I

www.ingramcontent.com/pod-product-compliance
Lightning Source LLC
LaVergne TN
LVHW080350011026
849161LV00009B/2247